FAMOUS SPEECHES

BY

EMINENT AMERICAN STATESMEN

COLLECTED AND EDITED BY

FREDERICK C. HICKS, LL. B., LITT. D.

PROFESSOR OF LAW AND LAW LIBRARIAN
YALE LAW SCHOOL

ST. PAUL
WEST PUBLISHING COMPANY
1929

Hicks' Sp.A.S.

PREFACE

THE spoken word is more important to-day than it ever has been. Twenty years ago, the voice of the public speaker could reach at most only three or four thousand auditors. Now by means of amplifiers it may be heard by an assemblage of a hundred thousand; while, through radio transmission, millions may sit in their own homes and hear the same speech. To reinforce the effect, if the speaker, the subject and the occasion are of national importance, thousands of newspapers print the speech in full and many more comment upon it. A public address, as never before in the world's history, is a means of influencing and appealing to public opinion.

There are already indications of renewed interest in public speaking as a result of the new conditions. Listeners have acquired a higher standard of criticism, in consequence of which speakers cannot afford to be inaccurate in statements of fact or slipshod in methods of presentation. They know that the effects produced will be widespread and immediate.

It is a common lament that oratory as an art is dead. The truth of this statement may, however, be doubted. The style of oratory, or more accurately of public speaking, has indeed changed; but this fact only goes to prove that the art has survived. It would have been dead long ago if it had not taken account of modern ideas of appropriateness. The art of the speaker, now as of old, consists in the power to inform and to persuade. To-day, this can best be done by directness and simplicity of diction. The speeches of the past which are still admired had that characteristic qualifying them to live. In this volume are such speeches by Seward, Benjamin and Lincoln—speeches almost devoid of the florid and oratorical, made on great occasions, when the speakers were in deadly earnest and anxious only to be understood.

Most of the speeches contained in this volume are of the simple, direct type. Arranged in chronological order, they recall in sequence some of the questions which have agitated the American mind in the last seventy-five years. This, however, is merely an incidental consequence of the arrangement, for the speeches were chosen for their quality as public addresses rather than as historical documents. It is not contended that there is shown a progressive development from the less good to the better or best of to-day, or that a retrogression appears. All that is asserted is that they illustrate art adapting public speech to special purposes in the temper of their respective times, and that each has some quality which drew particular attention to it.

In the judgment of the editor, all of the speeches chosen are by persons having a claim to be described as statesmen. By statesmen are meant not merely officeholders or "dead politicians," but any one of either sex who deals with public questions in a statesmanlike manner. The speeches are not only by Presidents, Governors, Cabinet Members, Ambassadors, and legislators, but by statesmen in business, education, the Church, social reform, law, judicial administration, and journalism. They deal with such subjects as slavery, state's rights, woman suffrage, the Irish question, labor, single tax, the negro question, free silver, imperialism, the Philippines, oleomargarine, the Panama Canal, the recall of judges and of judicial decisions, boss rule, free speech, the League of Nations, chemistry in war, national defense, peace, the United States Supreme Court, prohibition, religion and politics, law enforcement, reduction of naval armaments, and the four American wars which occurred during the period covered by the book. There are memorial speeches, debates in Congress, speeches in political conventions, in constitutional conventions, in international conferences, before bar associations, in patriotic societies, oral Presidential messages to Congress, presentation speeches, nominating speeches, and campaign speeches.

They are offered, not with any conviction that invariably the best have been chosen from the great output of American public speech since 1850, but that, with the generous help of persons too numerous to name, a representative selection has been made.

FREDERICK C. HICKS.

YALE LAW SCHOOL.

TABLE OF CONTENTS

†

FAMOUS SPEECHES

BY

EMINENT AMERICAN
STATESMEN

WILLIAM H. SEWARD

THE HIGHER LAW

SPEECH IN THE UNITED STATES SENATE, MARCH 11, 1850,
ON THE ADMISSION OF CALIFORNIA TO THE UNION

[William Henry Seward was born in Florida, Orange county, New York, on May 16, 1801. He was graduated from Union College, Schenectady, New York, in 1820; studied law in the office of John Anthon in New York City, and with John Duer and Ogden Hoffman, in Goshen, New York; and began the practice of law in Auburn, New York. He was a member of the state Senate from 1830 to 1834, and Governor of New York, 1838 to 1842. From 1849 to 1861, he was a United States Senator. In 1860, he lost the Republican nomination for President of the United States through the opposition of Horace Greeley. He served as Secretary of State in the cabinets of Lincoln and Johnson, 1861 to 1869. He was severely wounded on the same night that Lincoln was assassinated. While Secretary of State, he concluded a treaty with Russia providing for the purchase of Alaska by the United States, and a convention with Great Britain for the settlement of the Alabama claims. He died in Auburn, New York, on October 16, 1872.

Seward's speech, printed below, was part of the great debate on the Compromise of 1850. He was the spokesman of President Taylor, in opposition to Clay, Webster, and Calhoun, in urging the admission of California as a "free" or nonslavery state, without any compromises favorable to the "slave" states. Although his view did not prevail—all of the compromise measures being passed in September, 1850—his speech marked an epoch in the discussions of slavery in the Senate. It was said that it showed "more breadth of view, more vigor of thought, and a more profound and masterly treatment of the subject than was displayed by either Clay or Webster." For the first time it gave adequate representation to the large party in

HICKS' SP.A.S.—1 [1]

the North that believed that the moral question involved in slavery transcended all others in importance.

The phrase "there is a Higher Law than the Constitution," used by Seward in this speech, stirred the whole country. His enemies accused him of maintaining that there was a law antagonistically superior to the Constitution. A repudiation of this interpretation was made in 1853, probably with Seward's approval, in a memoir by George E. Baker, editor of his speeches. Read the words in their context, said Mr. Baker, and it will be perceived "that, while Governor Seward devoutly recognizes the law of God, and its paramount claims both on individuals and nations, he was far from asserting a contradiction between that law and the American Constitution. * * * On the contrary, he declares that they agree in demanding freedom and justice for the new domain."]

Mr. President: Four years ago, California, a Mexican Province, scarcely inhabited and quite unexplored, was unknown even to our usually immoderate desires, except by a harbor, capacious and tranquil, which only statesmen then foresaw would be useful in the oriental commerce of a far distant, if not merely chimerical, future.

A year ago, California was a mere military dependency of our own, and we were celebrating with unanimity and enthusiasm its acquisition, with its newly-discovered but yet untold and untouched mineral wealth, as the most auspicious of many and unparalleled achievements.

To-day, California is a State, more populous than the least and richer than several of the greatest of our thirty States. This same California, thus rich and populous, is here asking admission into the Union, and finds us debating the dissolution of the Union itself.

No wonder if we are perplexed with ever-changing embarrassments! No wonder if we are appalled by ever-increasing responsibilities! No wonder if we are bewildered by the ever-augmenting magnitude and rapidity of national vicissitudes!

Shall California be received? For myself, upon my individual judgment and conscience, I answer, Yes. For myself, as an instructed representative of one of the States, of that one even of the States which is soonest and longest to be pressed in commercial and political rivalry by the new Commonwealth, I answer, Yes. Let California come in. Every new State, whether she come from the East or from the West, every new

State, coming from whatever part of the continent she may, is always welcome. But California, that comes from the clime where the West dies away into the rising East; California, that bounds at once the empire and the continent; California, the youthful queen of the Pacific, in her robes of freedom, gorgeously inlaid with gold—is doubly welcome.

And now I inquire, first, *Why should California be rejected*? All the objections are founded only in the circumstances of her coming, and in the organic law which she presents for our confirmation.

1st. California comes *unceremoniously,* without a *preliminary* consent of Congress, and therefore by usurpation. This allegation, I think, is not quite true; at least not quite true in spirit. California is here not of her own pure volition. We tore California violently from her place in the Confederation of Mexican States, and stipulated, by the treaty of Guadalupe Hidalgo, that the territory should be admitted by States into the American Union as speedily as possible.

But the letter of the objection still holds. California does come without having obtained a preliminary consent of Congress to form a Constitution. But Michigan and other States presented themselves in the same unauthorized way, and Congress *waived the irregularity,* and sanctioned the usurpation. California pleads these precedents. Is not the plea sufficient?

But it has been said by the honorable Senator from South Carolina [Mr. Calhoun] that the Ordinance of 1787 secured to Michigan the right to become a State, when she should have sixty thousand inhabitants, and that, owing to some neglect, Congress delayed taking the census. This is said in palliation of the irregularity of Michigan. But California, as has been seen, had a treaty, and Congress, instead of giving previous consent, and instead of giving her the customary Territorial Government, as they did to Michigan, failed to do either, and thus practically refused both, and so abandoned the new community, under most unpropitious circumstances, to anarchy. California then made a Constitution for herself, but not unnecessarily and presumptuously, as Michigan did. She made a Constitution for herself, and she comes here under the law, the paramount law, of self-preservation.

In that she stands justified. Indeed, California is more than justified. She was a *colony,* a *military* colony. All colonies, especially military colonies, are incongruous with our political system, and they are equally open to corruption and exposed to oppression. They are, therefore, not more unfortunate in their own proper condition than fruitful of dangers to the parent Democracy. California, then, acted wisely and well in establishing self-government. She deserves not rebuke, but praise and approbation. Nor does this objection come with a good grace from those who offer it. If California were now content to receive only a Territorial charter, we could not agree to grant it without an inhibition of slavery, which, in that case, being a Federal act, would render the attitude of California, as a Territory, even more offensive to those who now repel her than she is as a State, with the same inhibition in the Constitution of her own voluntary choice.

A second objection is, that *California has assigned her own boundaries without the previous authority of Congress.* But she was left to organize herself without any boundaries fixed by previous law or by prescription. She was obliged, therefore, to assume boundaries, since without boundaries she must have remained unorganized.

A third objection is, that *California is too large.*

I answer, first, there is no common standard of States. California, although greater than many, is less than one of the States.

Secondly. California, if too large, may be divided with her own consent, and a similar provision is all the security we have for reducing the magnitude and averting the preponderance of Texas.

Thirdly. The boundaries of California seem not at all *unnatural.* The territory circumscribed is altogether contiguous and compact.

Fourthly. The boundaries are *convenient.* They embrace only inhabited portions of the country, commercially connected with the port of San Francisco. No one has pretended to offer boundaries more in harmony with the physical outlines of the region concerned, or more convenient for civil administration.

But to draw closer to the question, What shall be the boundaries of a new State? concerns—

First. The State herself; and California of course is content.

Secondly. Adjacent communities; Oregon does not complain of encroachment, and there is no other adjacent community to complain.

Thirdly. The other States of the Union; the larger the Pacific States, the smaller will be their relative power in the Senate. All the States now here are either Atlantic States or inland States, and surely they may well indulge California in the largest liberty of boundaries.

The fourth objection to the admission of California is, that *no census had been taken, and no laws prescribing the qualifications of suffrage and the apportionment of Representatives in Convention, existed before her Convention was held.*

I answer, California was left to act *ab initio.* She must begin somewhere, without a census, and without such laws. The Pilgrim Fathers began in the same way on board the Mayflower; and, since it has been objected that some of the electors in California may have been aliens, I add, that all of the Pilgrim Fathers were aliens and strangers to the Commonwealth of Plymouth.

Again, the objection may well be *waived,* if the Constitution of California is satisfactory, first to herself, secondly to the United States.

Not a murmur of discontent has followed California to this place.

As to ourselves, we confine our inquiries about the Constitution of a new State to four things—

1st. The *boundaries* assumed; and I have considered that point in this case already.

2d. That the domain within the State is secured to us; and it is admitted that this has been properly done.

3d. That the Constitution shall be republican, and not aristocratic and monarchical. In this case the only objection is, that the Constitution, inasmuch as it inhibits slavery, is altogether too republican.

4th. That the representation claimed shall be just and equal. No one denies that the population of California is sufficient to demand two Representatives on the Federal basis; and, secondly, a new census is at hand, and the error, if there is one, will be immediately corrected.

The fifth objection is, *California comes under Executive influence.*

1st. In her coming as a free State.

2d. In her coming at all.

The first charge rests on suspicion only, is peremptorily denied, and the denial is not controverted by proofs. I dismiss it altogether.

The second is true, to the extent that the President advised the people of California, that, having been left without any civil government, under the military supervision of the Executive, without any authority of law whatever, their adoption of a Constitution, subject to the approval of Congress, would be regarded favorably by the President. Only a year ago, it was complained that the exercise of the military power to maintain law and order in California, was a fearful innovation. But now the wind has changed, and blows even stronger from the opposite quarter.

May this Republic never have a President commit a more serious or more dangerous usurpation of power than the act of the present eminent Chief Magistrate, in endeavoring to induce legislative authority to relieve him from the exercise of military power, by establishing civil institutions regulated by law in distant provinces! Rome would have been standing this day, if she had had only such generals and such tribunes.

But the objection, whether true in part, or even in the whole, is immaterial. The question is, not what moved California to impress any particular feature on her Constitution, nor even what induced her to adopt a Constitution at all; but it is whether, since she has adopted a Constitution, she shall be admitted into the Union.

I have now reviewed all the objections raised against the admission of California. It is seen that they have no foundation in the law of nature and of nations. Nor are they founded in the Constitution, for the Constitution prescribes no form or manner of proceeding in the admission of new States, but leaves the whole to the discretion of Congress. "Congress may admit new States." The objections are all merely formal and technical. They rest on precedents which have not always, nor even generally, been observed. But it is said that we ought now to establish a safe precedent for the future.

I answer, 1st: It is too late to seize this occasion for that purpose. The irregularities complained of being unavoidable, the caution should have been exercised when, 1st, Texas was annexed; 2d, when we waged war against Mexico; or, 3d, when we ratified the treaty of Guadalupe Hidalgo.

I answer, 2d: We may establish precedents at pleasure. Our successors will exercise *their* pleasure about following them, just as we have done in such cases.

I answer, 3d: States, nations, and empires, are apt to be peculiarly capricious, not only as to the *time,* but even as to the *manner,* of their being born, and as to their subsequent political changes. They are not accustomed to conform to precedents. California sprang from the head of the nation, not only complete in proportions and full armed, but ripe for affiliation with its members.

I proceed now to state my reasons for the opinion that *California ought to be admitted.* The population of the United States consists of natives of Caucasian origin, and exotics of the same derivation. The native mass rapidly assimilates to itself and absorbs the exotic, and thus these constitute one homogeneous people. The African race, bond and free, and the aborigines, savage and civilized, being incapable of such assimilation and absorption, remain distinct, and, owing to their peculiar condition, they constitute inferior masses, and may be regarded as accidental if not disturbing political forces. The ruling homogeneous family planted at first on the Atlantic shore, and following an obvious law, is seen continually and rapidly spreading itself westward year by year, subduing the wilderness and the prairie, and thus extending this great political community, which, as fast as it advances, breaks into distinct States for municipal purposes only, while the whole constitutes one entire contiguous and compact nation.

Well-established calculations in political arithmetic enable us to say

That the aggregate population of the nation now is......	22,000,000
That 10 years hence it will be.........................	30,000,000
That 20 years hence it will be.........................	38,000,000
That 30 years hence it will be.........................	50,000,000
That 40 years hence it will be.........................	64,000,000
That 50 years hence it will be.........................	80,000,000
That 100 years hence, that is, in the year 1950, it will be..	200,000,000

equal nearly to one-fourth of the present aggregate population of the globe, and double the population of Europe at the time of the discovery of America. But the advance of population on the Pacific will far exceed what has heretofore occurred on the Atlantic coast, while emigration even here is outstripping the calculations on which the estimates are based. There are silver and gold in the mountains and ravines of California. The granite of New England and New York is barren.

Allowing due consideration to the increasing density of our population, we are safe in assuming, that long before this mass shall have attained the maximum of numbers indicated, the entire width of our possessions from the Atlantic to the Pacific ocean will be covered by it, and be brought into social maturity and complete political organization.

The question now arises, Shall this one great people, having a common origin, a common language, a common religion, common sentiments, interests, sympathies, and hopes, remain one political State, one Nation, one Republic, or shall it be broken into two conflicting and probably hostile Nations or Republics? There cannot ultimately be more than two; for the habit of association is already formed, as the interests of mutual intercourse are being formed. It is already ascertained where the centre of political power must rest. It must rest in the agricultural interests and masses, who will occupy the interior of the continent. These masses, if they cannot all command access to both oceans, will not be obstructed in their approaches to that one, which offers the greatest facilities to their commerce.

Shall the American people, then, be divided? Before deciding on this question, let us consider our position, our power, and capabilities.

The world contains no seat of empire so magnificent as this; which, while it embraces all the varying climates of the temperate zone, and is traversed by wide expanding lakes and long-branching rivers, offers supplies on the Atlantic shores to the over-crowded nations of Europe, while on the Pacific coast it intercepts the commerce of the Indies. The nation thus situated, and enjoying forest, mineral, and agricultural resources unequalled, if endowed also with moral energies adequate to the achievement of great enterprises, and favored with a Government adapted to their character and condition, must command the empire of the seas, which alone is real empire.

We think that we may claim to have inherited physical and intellectual vigor, courage, invention, and enterprise; and the systems of education prevailing among us open to all the stores of human science and art.

The old world and the past were allotted by Providence to the pupilage of mankind, under the hard discipline of arbitrary power, quelling the violence of human passions. The new world and the future seem to have been appointed for the maturity of mankind, with the development of self-government operating in obedience to reason and judgment.

We have thoroughly tried our novel system of Democratic Federal Government, with its complex, yet harmonious and effective combination of distinct local elective agencies, for the conduct of domestic affairs, and its common central elective agencies, for the regulation of internal interests and of intercourse with foreign nations; and we know that it is a system equally cohesive in its parts, and capable of all desirable expansion; and that it is a system, moreover, perfectly adapted to secure domestic tranquillity, while it brings into activity all the elements of national aggrandizement. The Atlantic States, through their commercial, social, and political affinities and sympathies, are steadily renovating the Governments and the social constitutions of Europe and of Africa. The Pacific States must necessarily perform the same sublime and beneficent functions in Asia. If, then, the American people shall remain an undivided nation, the ripening civilization of the West, after a separation growing wider and wider for four thousand years, will, in its circuit of the world, meet again and mingle with the declining civilization of the East on our own free soil, and a new and more perfect civilization will arise to bless the earth, under the sway of our own cherished and beneficent democratic institutions.

We may then reasonably hope for greatness, felicity, and renown, excelling any hitherto attained by any nation, if, standing firmly on the continent, we loose not our grasp on the shore of either ocean. Whether a destiny so magnificent would be only partially defeated, or whether it would be altogether lost, by a relaxation of that grasp, surpasses our wisdom to determine, and happily it is not important to be determined. It is enough, if we agree that expectations so grand, yet so reasonable and so just, ought not to be in any degree disappointed. And now it seems to me that the perpetual unity of the Empire hangs on the decision of this day and of this hour.

California is already a State, a complete and fully appointed State. She never again can be less than that. She can never again be a province or a colony; nor can she be made to shrink and shrivel into the proportions of a federal dependent Territory. California, then, henceforth and forever, must be, what she is now, a State.

The question whether she shall be one of the United States of America *has* depended on her and on us. Her election has been made. Our consent alone remains suspended; and that consent must be pronounced now or never. I say *now* or *never*. Nothing prevents it now, but want of agreement among ourselves. Our harmony cannot increase while this question remains open. We shall never agree to admit California, unless we agree now. Nor will California abide delay. I do not say that she contemplates independence; but, if she does not, it is because she does not anticipate rejection. Do you say that she can have no motive? Consider, then, her attitude, if rejected. She needs a Constitution, a Legislature, and Magistrates; she needs titles to that golden domain of yours within her borders; good titles, too; and you must give them on your own terms, or she must take them without your leave. She needs a mint, a custom-house, wharves, hospitals, and institutions of learning; she needs fortifications, and roads, and railroads; she needs the protection of an army and a navy; either your stars and stripes must wave over her ports and her fleets, or she must raise aloft a standard for herself; she needs, at least, to know whether you are friends or enemies; and, finally, she needs, what no American community can live without, sovereignty and independence —either a just and equal share of yours, or sovereignty and independence of her own.

Will you say that California could not aggrandize herself by separation? Would it, then, be a mean ambition to set up within fifty years, on the Pacific coast, monuments like those which we think two hundred years have been well spent in establishing on the Atlantic coast?

Will you say that California has no ability to become independent? She has the same moral ability for enterprise that inheres in us, and that ability implies command of all physical means. She has advantages of position. She is practically further removed from us than England. We cannot reach her by railroad, nor by unbroken steam navigation. We can send no armies over the prairie, the mountain, and the desert, nor across the remote and narrow Isthmus within a foreign jurisdiction, nor around the Cape of Storms. We may send a navy there, but she has only to open her mines, and she can seduce our navies and appropriate our floating bulwarks to her own defence. Let her only seize our domain within her borders, and our commerce in her ports, and she will have at once revenues and credit adequate to all her necessities. Besides, are we so moderate, and has the world become so just, that we have no rivals and no enemies to lend their sympathies and aid to compass the dismemberment of our empire?

Try not the temper and fidelity of California—at least not now, not yet. Cherish her and indulge her until you have extended your settlements to her borders, and bound her fast by railroads, and canals, and telegraphs, to your interests—until her affinities of intercourse are established, and her habits of loyalty are fixed—and then she can never be disengaged.

California would not go alone. Oregon, so intimately allied to her, and as yet so loosely attached to us, would go also; and then at least the entire Pacific coast, with the western declivity of the Sierra Nevada, would be lost. It would not depend at all upon us, nor even on the mere forbearance of California, how far eastward the long line across the temperate zone should be drawn, which should separate the Republic of the Pacific from the Republic of the Atlantic. Terminus has passed away, with all the deities of the ancient Pantheon, but his sceptre remains. Commerce is the God of boundaries, and no man now living can foretell his ultimate decree.

But it is insisted that the admission of California shall be attended by a *compromise* of questions which have arisen out of *slavery!*

I am opposed to any such compromise, in any and all the forms in which it has been proposed; because, while admitting the purity and the patriotism of all from whom it is my misfortune to differ, I think all legislative compromises, not absolutely necessary, radically wrong and essentially vicious. They involve the surrender of the exercise of judgment and conscience on distinct and separate questions, at distinct and separate times, with the indispensable advantages it affords for ascertaining truth. They involve a relinquishment of the right to reconsider in future the decisions of the present, on questions prematurely anticipated. And they are acts of usurpation as to future questions of the province of future legislators.

Sir, it seems to me as if slavery had laid its paralyzing hand upon myself, and the blood were coursing less freely than its wont through my veins, when I endeavor to suppose that such a compromise has been effected, and that my utterance forever is arrested upon all the great questions—social, moral, and political—arising out of a subject so important, and as yet so incomprehensible.

What am I to receive in this compromise? Freedom in California. It is well; it is a noble acquisition; it is worth a sacrifice. But what am I to give as an equivalent? A recognition of the claim to perpetuate slavery in the District of Columbia; forbearance towards more stringent laws concerning the arrest of persons suspected of being slaves found in the free States; forbearance from the *Proviso* of Freedom in the charters of new Territories. None of the plans of compromise offered demand less than two, and most of them insist on all of these conditions. The equivalent, then, is, some portion of liberty, some portion of human rights in one region for liberty in another region. But California brings gold and commerce as well as freedom. I am, then, to surrender some portion of human freedom in the District of Columbia, and in East California and New Mexico, for the mixed consideration of liberty, gold, and power, on the Pacific coast.

This view of legislative compromises is not *new*. It has widely prevailed, and many of the State Constitutions interdict the introduction of more than one subject into one bill submitted for legislative action.

It was of such compromises that Burke said, in one of the loftiest bursts of even his majestic parliamentary eloquence:

"Far, far from the Commons of Great Britain be all manner of real vice; but ten thousand times farther from them, as far as from pole to pole, be the whole tribe of spurious, affected, counterfeit, and hypocritical virtues! These are the things which are ten thousand times more at war with real virtue, these are the things which are ten thousand times more at war with real duty, than any vice known by its name and distinguished by its proper character.

"Far, far from us be that false and affected candor that is eternally in treaty with crime—that half virtue, which, like the ambiguous animal that flies about in the twilight of a compromise between day and night, is, to a just man's eye, an odious and disgusting thing. There is no middle point, my Lords, in which the Commons of Great Britain can meet tyranny and oppression."

But, sir, if I could overcome my repugnance to compromises in general, I should object to this one, on the ground of the *inequality* and *incongruity* of the interests to be compromised. Why, sir, according to the views I have submitted, California ought to come in, and must come in, whether slavery stand or fall in the District of Columbia; whether slavery stand or fall in New Mexico and Eastern California; and even whether slavery stand or fall in the slave States. California ought to come in, being a free State; and, under the circumstances of her conquest, her compact, her abandonment, her justifiable and necessary establishment of a Constitution, and the inevitable dismemberment of the empire consequent upon her rejection, I should have voted for her admission even if she had come as a slave State. California ought to come in, and must come in at all events. It is, then, an independent, a paramount question. What, then, are these questions arising out of slavery, thus interposed, but collateral questions? They are unnecessary and incongruous, and therefore false issues, not introduced designedly, indeed, to defeat that great policy, yet unavoidably tending to that end.

Mr. Foote. Will the honorable Senator allow me to ask him, if the Senate is to understand him as saying that he would vote for the admission of California if she came here seeking admission as a slave State?

Mr. Seward. I reply, as I said before, that even if California had come as a slave State, yet coming under the extraordinary circumstances I have described, and in view of the consequences of a dismemberment of the empire, consequent upon her rejection, I should have voted for her admission, even though she had come as a slave State. But I should not have voted for her admission otherwise.

I remark in the next place, that consent on my part would be disingenuous and fraudulent, because the compromise would be unavailing.

It is now avowed by the honorable Senator from South Carolina [Mr. Calhoun] that nothing will satisfy the slave States but a compromise that will convince them that they can remain in the Union consistently with their honor and their safety. And what are the concessions which will have that effect. Here they are, in the words of that Senator:

"The North must do justice by conceding to the South an equal right in the acquired territory, and do her duty by causing the stipulations relative to fugitive slaves to be faithfully fulfilled—cease the agitation of the slave question, and provide for the insertion of a provision in the Constitution, by an amendment, which will restore to the South in substance the power she possessed, of protecting herself, before the equilibrium between the sections was destroyed by the action of this Government."

These terms amount to this: That the free States having already, or although they may hereafter have, majorities of population, and majorities in both Houses of Congress, shall concede to the slave States, being in a minority in both, the unequal advantage of an equality. That is, that we shall alter the Constitution so as to convert the Government from a national democracy, operating by a constitutional majority of voices, into a Federal alliance, in which the minority shall have a veto against the majority. And this is nothing less than to return to the original Articles of Confederation.

I will not stop to protest against the injustice or the inexpediency of an innovation which, if it was practicable, would be so entirely subversive of the principle of democratic institutions. It is enough to say that it is totally impracticable. The free States, Northern and Western, have acquiesced in the long and nearly unbroken ascendency of the slave States under the Constitution, because the result happened under the Constitution. But they have honor and interests to preserve, and there is nothing in the nature of mankind or in the character of that people to induce an expectation that they, loyal as they are, are insensible to the duty of defending them. But the scheme would still be impracticable, even if this difficulty were overcome. What is proposed is a *political* equilibrium. Every political equilibrium requires a *physical* equilibrium to rest upon, and is valueless without it. To constitute a physical equilibrium between the slave States and the free States, requires, first, an equality of territory, or some near approximation. And this is already lost. But it requires much more than this. It requires an equality or a proximate equality in the number of slaves and freemen. And this must be perpetual.

But the census of 1840 gives a slave basis of only 2,500,000, and a free basis of 14,500,000. And the population on the slave basis increases in the ratio of 25 per cent. for ten years, while that on the free basis advances at the rate of 38 per cent. The accelerating movement of the free population, now complained of, will occupy the new Territories with pioneers, and every day increases the difficulty of forcing or insinuating slavery into regions which freemen have pre-occupied. And if this were possible, the African slave trade is prohibited, and the domestic increase is not sufficient to supply the new slave States which are expected to maintain the equilibrium. The theory of a new political equilibrium claims that it once existed, and has been lost.

When lost, and how? It began to be lost in 1787, when preliminary arrangements were made to admit five new free States in the Northwest Territory, two years before the Constitution was finally adopted; that is, it began to be lost two years before it began to exist!

Sir, the equilibrium, if restored, would be lost again, and lost more rapidly than it was before. The progress of the free population is to be accelerated by increased emigration, and by new tides from South America and from Europe and Asia, while that of the slaves is to be checked and retarded by inevitable partial emancipation. "Nothing," says Montesquieu, "reduces a man so low as always to see freemen, and yet not be free. Persons in that condition are natural enemies of the State, and their numbers would be dangerous if increased too high." Sir, the fugitive slave colonies and the emancipated slave colonies in the free States, in Canada, and in Liberia, are the best guaranties South Carolina has for the perpetuity of slavery.

Nor would success attend any of the details of the compromise. And, first, I advert to the proposed alteration of the law concerning fugitives from service or labor. I shall speak on this as on all subjects, with due respect, but yet frankly and without reservation. The Constitution contains only a compact, which rests for its execution on the States. Not content with this, the slave States induced legislation by Congress; and the Supreme Court of the United States have virtually decided that the whole subject is within the province of Congress, and exclusive of State authority. Nay, they have decided that slaves are to be regarded not merely as persons to be claimed, but as property and chattels, to be seized without any legal authority or claim whatever. The compact is thus subverted by the procurement of the slave States. With what reason, then, can they expect the States *ex gratia* to reassume the obligations from which they caused those States to be discharged? I say, then, to the slave States, you are entitled to no more stringent laws; and that such laws would be useless. The cause of the inefficiency of the present statute is not at all the leniency of its provisions. It is a law that deprives the alleged refugee from a legal obligation not assumed by him, but imposed upon him by laws enacted before he was born, of the writ of *habeas corpus,*

and of any certain judicial process of examination of the claim
set up by his pursuer, and finally degrades him into a chattel
which may be seized and carried away peaceably wherever
found, even although exercising the rights and responsibilities
of a free citizen of the Commonwealth in which he resides, and
of the United States—a law which denies to the citizen all the
safeguards of personal liberty, to render less frequent the escape of the bondman. And since complaints are so freely made
against the one side, I shall not hesitate to declare that there
have been even greater faults on the other side. Relying on the
perversion of the Constitution which makes slaves mere chattels, the slave States have applied to them the principles of the
criminal law, and have held that he who aided the escape of his
fellow-man from bondage was guilty of a larceny in stealing
him. I speak of what I know. Two instances came within my
own knowledge, in which Governors of slave States, under the
provision of the Constitution relating to fugitives from justice,
demanded from the Governor of a free State the surrender of
persons as thieves whose alleged offences consisted in constructive larceny of the rags that covered the persons of female
slaves, whose attempt at escape they permitted or assisted.

We deem the principle of the law for the recapture of fugitives, as thus expounded, therefore, unjust, unconstitutional,
and immoral; and thus, while patriotism withholds its approbation, the consciences of our people condemn it.

You will say that these convictions of ours are disloyal.
Grant it for the sake of argument. They are, nevertheless, honest; and the law is to be executed among us, not among you;
not by us, but by the Federal authority. Has any Government
ever succeeded in changing the moral convictions of its subjects
by force? But these convictions imply no disloyalty. We reverence the Constitution, although we perceive this defect, just as
we acknowledge the splendor and the power of the sun, although
its surface is tarnished with here and there an opaque spot.

Your Constitution and laws convert hospitality to the refugee
from the most degrading oppression on earth into a crime, but
all mankind except you esteem that hospitality a virtue. The
right of extradition of a fugitive from justice is not admitted by

HICKS' SP.A.S.—2

the law of nature and of nations, but rests in voluntary compacts. I know of only two compacts found in diplomatic history that admitted extradition of slaves. Here is one of them. It is found in a treaty of peace made between Alexander, Comnenus, and Leontine, Greek Emperors at Constantinople, and Oleg, King of Russia, in the year 902, and is in these words:

"If a Russian slave take flight, or even if he is carried away by any one under pretence of having been bought, his master shall have the right and power to pursue him, and hunt for and capture him wherever he shall be found; and any person who shall oppose the master in the execution of this right shall be deemed guilty of violating this treaty, and be punished accordingly."

This was in the year of Grace 902, in the period called the "Dark Ages," and the contracting Powers were despotisms. And here is the other:

"No person held to service or labor in one State, under the laws thereof, escaping into another, shall, in consequence of any law or regulation therein, be discharged from such service or labor, but shall be delivered up, on claim of the party to whom such service or labor is due."

This is from the Constitution of the United States in 1787, and the parties were the republican States of this Union. The law of nations disavows such compacts; the law of nature, written on the hearts and consciences of freemen, repudiates them. Armed power could not enforce them, because there is no public conscience to sustain them. I know that there are laws of various sorts which regulate the conduct of men. There are constitutions and statutes, codes mercantile and codes civil; but when we are legislating for States, especially when we are founding States, all these laws must be brought to the standard of the laws of God, and must be tried by that standard, and must stand or fall by it. This principle was happily explained by one of the most distinguished political philosophers of England in these emphatic words:

"There is but one law for all, namely, that law which governs all law, the law of our Creator, the law of humanity, justice, equity, the law of nature and of nations. So far as any laws fortify this primeval law, and give it more precision, more energy, more effect, by their declarations, such laws enter into the sanctuary and participate in the sacredness of its character; but the man who quotes as precedents the abuses of tyrants and robbers, pollutes the very fountains of justice, destroys the foundations of all law, and therefore removes the only safeguard against evil men, whether governors or governed; the guard which prevents governors from becoming tyrants, and the governed from becoming rebels."

There was deep philosophy in the confession of an eminent English judge. When he had condemned a young woman to death, under the late sanguinary code of his country, for her first petty theft, she fell down dead at his feet: "I seem to myself," said he, "to have been pronouncing sentence, not against the prisoner, but against the law itself."

To conclude on this point. We are not slaveholders. We cannot, in our judgment, be either true Christians or real freemen, if we impose on another a chain that we defy all human power to fasten on ourselves. You believe and think otherwise, and doubtless with equal sincerity. We judge you not, and He alone who ordained the conscience of man and its laws of action can judge us. Do we, then, in this conflict of opinion, demand of you an unreasonable thing in asking that, since you will have property that can and will exercise human powers to effect its escape, you shall be your own police, and in acting among us as such you shall conform to principles indispensable to the security of admitted rights of freemen? If you will have this law executed, you must alleviate, not increase, its rigors.

Another feature in most of these plans of compromise is a bill of peace for slavery in the District of Columbia; and this bill of peace we cannot grant. We of the free States are, equally with you of the slave States, responsible for the existence of slavery in this District, the field exclusively of our common legislation. I regret that, as yet, I see little reason to hope that a majority in favor of emancipation exists here. The Legislature of New York, from whom, with great deference, I dissent, seems willing to accept now the extinction of the slave trade, and waive emancipation. But we shall assume the whole responsibility if we stipulate not to exercise the power hereafter when a majority shall be obtained. Nor will the plea with which you would furnish us be of any avail. If I could understand so mysterious a paradox myself, I never should be able to explain to the apprehension of the people whom I represent how it was that an absolute and express power to legislate in all cases over the District of Columbia was embarrassed and defeated by an implied condition not to legislate for the abolition of slavery in this District. Sir, I shall vote for that measure, and am willing to appropriate any means necessary to carry it into execution. And, if I shall be asked what I did to embellish the capital of my country, I will point to her freedmen, and say, these are the monuments of my munificence!

If I was willing to advance a cause that I deem sacred by disingenuous means, I would advise you to adopt those means of compromise which I have thus examined. The echo is not quicker in its response than would be that loud and universal cry of repeal, that would not die away until the *habeas corpus* was secured to the alleged fugitive from bondage, and the symmetry of the free institutions of the capital was perfected.

I apply the same observations to the proposition for a waiver of the Proviso of ·Freedom in Territorial charters. Thus far you have only direct popular action in favor of that Ordinance, and there seems even to be a partial disposition to await the action of the people of the new Territories, as we have compulsorily waited for it in California. But I must tell you, nevertheless, in candor and in plainness, that the spirit of the people of the free States is set upon a spring that rises with the pressure put upon it. That spring, if pressed too hard, will give a recoil that will not leave here one servant who knew his master's will, and did it not.

You will say that this implies violence. Not at all. It implies only peaceful, lawful, constitutional, customary action. I cannot too strongly express my surprise that those who insist that the people of the slave States cannot be held back from remedies outside of the Constitution, should so far misunderstand us of the free States as to suppose we would not exercise our constitutional rights to sustain the policy which we deem just and beneficent.

I come now to notice the suggested *compromise of the boundary between Texas and New Mexico.* This is a judicial question in its nature, or at least a question of legal right and title. If it is to be compromised at all, it is due to the two parties, and to national dignity as well as to justice, that it be kept separate from compromises proceeding on the ground of expediency, and be settled by itself alone.

I take this occasion to say, that while I do not intend to discuss the questions alluded to in this connection by the honorable and distinguished Senator from Massachusetts, I am not able to agree with him in regard to the alleged obligation of Congress to admit four new slave States, to be formed in the State of Texas. There are several questions arising out of that subject, upon which I am not prepared to decide now, and which I desire to reserve for future consideration. One of these is, whether the Article of Annexation does really deprive Congress of the right to exercise its choice in regard to the subdivision of Texas into four additional States. It seems to me by no means so plain a question as the Senator from Massachusetts assumed, and that it must be left to remain an open question, as it is a great question, whether Congress is not a party whose future consent is necessary to the formation of new States out of Texas.

Mr. Webster. Supposing Congress to have the authority to fix the number, and time of election, and apportionment of Representatives, etc., the question is, whether, if new States are formed out of Texas, to come into this Union, there is not a solemn pledge by law that they have a right to come in as slave States?

Mr. Seward. When the States are once formed, they have the right to come in as free or slave States, according to their own choice; but what I insist is, that they cannot be formed at all without the consent of Congress, to be hereafter given, which consent Congress is not obliged to give. But I pass that question for the present, and proceed to say that I am not prepared to admit that the Article of the Annexation of Texas is itself constitutional. I find no authority in the Constitution of the United States for the annexation of foreign countries by a resolution of Congress, and no power adequate to that purpose but the treaty-making power of the President and the Senate. Entertaining this view, I must insist that the constitutionality of the annexation of Texas itself shall be cleared up before I can agree to the admission of any new States to be formed within Texas.

Mr. Foote. Did not I hear the Senator observe that he would admit California, whether slavery was or was not precluded from these Territories?

Mr. Seward. I said I would have voted for the admission of California even as a slave State, under the extraordinary circumstances which I have before distinctly described. I say that now; but I say also, that before I would agree to admit any more States from Texas, the circumstances which render such act necessary must be shown, and must be such as to determine my obligation to do so; and that is precisely what I insist cannot be settled now. It must be left for those to whom the responsibility will belong.

Mr. President, I understand, and I am happy in understanding, that I agree with the honorable Senator from Massachusetts, that there is no obligation upon Congress to admit four new slave States out of Texas, but that Congress has reserved her right to say whether those States shall be formed and admitted or not. I shall rely on that reservation. I shall vote to admit no more slave States, unless under circumstances absolutely compulsory—and no such case is now foreseen.

Mr. Webster. What I said was, that if the States hereafter to be made out of Texas choose to come in as slave States, they have a right so to do.

Mr. Seward. My position is, that they have not a right to come in at all, if Congress rejects their institutions. The subdivision of Texas is a matter optional with both parties, Texas and the United States.

Mr. Webster. Does the honorable Senator mean to say that Congress can hereafter decide whether they shall be slave or free States?

Mr. Seward. I mean to say that Congress can hereafter decide whether any States, slave or free, can be framed out of Texas. If they should never be framed out of Texas, they never could be admitted.

Another objection arises out of the principle on which the demand for compromise rests. That principle assumes a classification of the States as Northern and Southern States, as it is expressed by the honorable Senator from South Carolina [Mr. Calhoun], but into slave States and free States, as more directly expressed by the honorable Senator from Georgia [Mr. Berrien]. The argument is, that the States are severally equal, and that these two classes were equal at the first, and that the Constitution was founded on that equilibrium; that the States being equal, and the classes of the States being equal in rights, they are to be regarded as constituting an association in which each State, and each of these classes of States, respectively, contribute in due proportions; that the new Territories are a common acquisition, and the people of these several States and classes of States have an equal right to participate in them, respectively; that the right of the people of the slave States to emigrate to the Territories with their slaves as property is necessary to afford such a participation on their part, inasmuch as the people of the free States emigrate into the same Territories with their property. And the argument deduces from this right the principle that, if Congress exclude slavery from any part of this new domain, it would be only just to set off a portion of the domain—some say south of 36° 30', others south of 34°—which should be regarded at least as free to slavery, and to be organized into slave States.

Argument ingenious and subtle, declamation earnest and bold, and persuasion gentle and winning as the voice of the turtle dove when it is heard in the land, all alike and altogether have failed to convince me of the soundness of this principle of the proposed compromise or of any one of the propositions on which it is attempted to be established.

How is the original equality of the States proved? It rests on a syllogism of Vattel, as follows: All men are equal by the law of nature and of nations. But States are only lawful aggregations of individual men, who severally are equal. Therefore, States are equal in natural rights. All this is just and sound. But assuming the same premises, to wit, that all men are equal by the law of nature and of nations, the right of property in slaves falls to the ground; for one who is equal to another cannot be the owner or property of that other. But you answer, that the Constitution recognises property in slaves. It would be sufficient, then, to reply, that this constitutional recognition must be void, because it is repugnant to the law of nature and of nations. But I deny that the Constitution recognises property in man. I submit, on the other hand, most respectfully, that the Constitution not merely does not affirm that principle, but, on the contrary, altogether excludes it.

The Constitution does not *expressly* affirm anything on the subject; all that it contains is two incidental allusions to slaves. These are, first, in the provision establishing a ratio of representation and taxation; and, secondly, in the provision relating to fugitives from labor. In both cases, the Constitution designedly mentions slaves, not as slaves, much less as chattels, but as *persons*. That this recognition of them as persons was designed is historically known, and I think was never denied. I give only two of the manifold proofs. First, John Jay, in the *Federalist*, says:

"Let the case of the slaves be considered, as it is in truth, a peculiar one. Let the compromising expedient of the Constitution be mutually adopted which regards them as *inhabitants*, but as debased below the equal level of free inhabitants, which regards the slave as divested of two-fifths of the man."

Yes, sir, of two-fifths, but of only two-fifths; leaving still three-fifths; leaving the slave still an *inhabitant*, a person, a living, breathing, moving, reasoning, immortal man.

The other proof is from the Debates in the Convention. It is brief, and I think instructive:

"August 28, 1787.

"Mr. Butler and Mr. Pinckney moved to require fugitive slaves and servants to be delivered up like convicts.

"Mr. Wilson. This would oblige the Executive of the State to do it at public expense.

"Mr. Sherman saw no more propriety in the public seizing and surrendering a slave or a servant than a horse.

"Mr. Butler withdrew his proposition, in order that some particular provision might be made, apart from this article."

"August 29, 1787.

"Mr. Butler moved to insert after article 15: 'If any person bound to service or labor in any of the United States shall escape into another State, he or she shall not be discharged from such service or labor in consequence of any regulation subsisting in the State to which they escape, but shall be delivered up to the person justly claiming their service or labor.' "

"After the engrossment, September 15, page 550, article 4, section 2, the third paragraph, the term 'legally' was struck out, and the words 'under the laws thereof' inserted after the word 'State,' in compliance with the wishes of some who thought the term 'legal' equivocal, and favoring the idea that slavery was legal in a *moral view.*"—Madison Debates, pp. 487, 492.

I deem it established, then, that the Constitution does not recognise property in man, but leaves that question, as between the States, to the law of nature and of nations. That law, as expounded by Vattel, is founded on the reason of things. When God had created the earth, with its wonderful adaptations, He gave dominion over it to Man, absolute human dominion. The title of that dominion, thus bestowed, would have been incomplete, if the Lord of all terrestrial things could himself have been the property of his fellow-man.

The right to *have* a slave implies the right in some one to *make* the slave; that right must be equal and mutual, and this would resolve society into a state of perpetual war. But if we grant the original equality of the States, and grant also the constitutional recognition of slaves as property, still the argument we are considering fails. Because the States are not parties to the Constitution as States; it is the Constitution of the People of the United States.

But even if the States continue as States, they surrendered their equality as States, and submitted themselves to the sway of the numerical majority, with qualifications or checks; first, of the representation of three-fifths of slaves in the ratio of representation and taxation; and, secondly, of the equal representation of States in the Senate.

The proposition of an established classification of States as *slave States* and *free States,* as insisted on by some, and into *Northern* and *Southern,* as maintained by others, seems to me purely imaginary, and of course the supposed equilibrium of those classes a mere conceit. This must be so, because, when the Constitution was adopted, twelve of the thirteen States were slave States, and so there was no equilibrium. And so as to the classification of States as Northern States and Southern States. It is the maintenance of slavery by law in a State, not parallels of latitude, that makes it a Southern State; and the absence of this, that makes it a Northern State. And so all the States, save one, were Southern States, and there was no equilibrium. But the Constitution was made not only for Southern and Northern States, but for States neither Northern nor Southern—the Western States, their coming in being foreseen and provided for.

It needs little argument to show that the idea of a joint stock association, or a copartnership, as applicable even by its analogies to the United States, is erroneous, with all the consequences fancifully deduced from it. The United States are a political state, or organized society, whose end is government, for the security, welfare, and happiness of all who live under its protection. The theory I am combating reduces the objects of government to the mere spoils of conquest. Contrary to a theory so debasing, the preamble of the Constitution not only asserts the sovereignty to be, not in the States, but in the People, but also promulgates the objects of the Constitution:

"We, the people of the United States, in order to form a *more perfect union,* establish *justice,* insure *domestic tranquillity,* provide for the *common defence,* promote the *general welfare,* and secure the *blessings of liberty,* do ordain and establish this Constitution."

Objects sublime and benevolent! They exclude the very idea of conquests, to be either divided among States or even enjoyed by them, for the purpose of securing, not the blessings of liberty, but the evils of slavery. There is a novelty in the principle of the compromise which condemns it. Simultaneously with the establishment of the Constitution, Virginia ceded to the United States her domain, which then extended to the Mississippi, and was even claimed to extend to the Pacific Ocean. Congress accepted it, and unanimously devoted the domain to Freedom, in the language from which the Ordinance now so severely condemned was borrowed. Five States have already been organized on this domain, from all of which, in pursuance of that Ordinance, slavery is excluded. How did it happen that this theory of the equality of States, of the classification of States, of the equilibrium of States, of the title of the States to common enjoyment of the domain, or to an equitable and just partition between them, was never promulgated, nor even dreamed of, by the slave States, when they unanimously consented to that Ordinance?

There is another aspect of the principle of compromise which deserves consideration. It assumes that slavery, if not the only institution in a slave State, is at least a ruling institution, and that this characteristic is recognised by the Constitution. But *slavery* is only *one* of many institutions there. Freedom is equally an institution there. Slavery is only a temporary, accidental, partial and incongruous one. Freedom, on the contrary, is a perpetual, organic, universal one, in harmony with the Constitution of the United States. The slaveholder himself stands under the protection of the latter, in common with all the free citizens of the State. But it is, moreover, an indispensable institution. You may separate slavery from South Carolina, and the State will still remain; but if you subvert Freedom there, the State will cease to exist. But the principle of this compromise gives complete ascendency in the slave States, and in the Constitution of the United States, to the subordinate, accidental, and incongruous, institution over its paramount antagonist. To reduce this claim for slavery to an absurdity, it is only necessary to add that there are only two States in which slaves are a majority, and not one in which the slaveholders are not a very disproportionate minority.

But there is yet another aspect in which this principle must be examined. It regards the domain only as a possession, to be enjoyed either in common or by partition by the citizens of the old States. It is true, indeed, that the national domain is ours. It is true it was acquired by the valor and with the wealth of the whole nation. But we hold, nevertheless, no arbitrary power over it. We hold no arbitrary authority over anything, whether acquired lawfully or seized by usurpation. The Constitution regulates our stewardship; the Constitution devotes the domain to union, to justice, to defence, to welfare, and to liberty.

But there is a higher law than the Constitution, which regulates our authority over the domain, and devotes it to the same
noble purposes. The territory is a part, no inconsiderable part,
of the common heritage of mankind, bestowed upon them by
the Creator of the Universe. We are his stewards, and must
so discharge our trust as to secure in the highest attainable
degree their happiness. How momentous that trust is, we may
learn from the instructions of the founder of modern philosophy:

"No man," says Bacon, "can by care-taking, as the Scripture
saith, add a cubit to his stature in this little model of a man's
body; but, in the great frame of kingdoms and commonwealths,
it is in the power of princes or estates to add amplitude and greatness to their kingdoms. For, by introducing such ordinances,
constitutions, and customs, as are wise, they may sow greatness
to their posterity and successors. But these things are commonly not observed, but left to take their chance."

This is a State, and we are deliberating for it, just as our
fathers deliberated in establishing the institutions we enjoy.
Whatever superiority there is in our condition and hopes over
those of any other "kingdom" or "estate" is due to the fortunate circumstance that our ancestors did not leave things to
"take their chance," but that they "added amplitude and greatness" to our commonwealth "by introducing such ordinances,
constitutions, and customs, as were wise." We in our turn
have succeeded to the same responsibilities, and we cannot approach the duty before us wisely or justly, except we raise ourselves to the great consideration of how we can most certainly
"sow greatness to our posterity and successors."

And now the simple, bold, and even awful question which presents itself to us is this: Shall we, who are founding institutions, social and political, for countless millions; shall we, who
know by experience the wise and the just, and are free to choose
them, and to reject the erroneous and unjust; shall we establish human bondage, or permit it by our sufferance to be established? Sir, our forefathers would not have hesitated an hour.
They found slavery existing here, and they left it only because
they could not remove it. There is not only no free State which
would now establish it, but there is no slave State, which, if it

had had the free alternative as we now have, would have founded slavery. Indeed, our revolutionary predecessors had precisely the same question before them in establishing an organic law under which the States of Ohio, Indiana, Michigan, Illinois, and Wisconsin, have since come into the Union, and they solemnly repudiated and excluded slavery from those States forever. I confess that the most alarming evidence of our degeneracy which has yet been given is found in the fact that we even debate such a question.

Sir, there is no Christian nation, thus free to choose as we are, which would establish slavery. I speak on due consideration, because Britain, France, and Mexico, have abolished slavery, and all other European States are preparing to abolish it as speedily as they can. We cannot establish slavery, because there are certain elements of the security, welfare, and greatness of nations, which we all admit or ought to admit, and recognise as essential; and these are the security of natural rights, the diffusion of knowledge, and the freedom of industry. Slavery is incompatible with all of these, and just in proportion to the extent that it prevails and controls in any republican State, just to that extent it subverts the principle of democracy, and converts the State into an aristocracy or a despotism. I will not offend sensibilities by drawing my proofs from the slave States existing among ourselves. But I will draw them from the greatest of the European slave States.

The population of Russia in Europe, in 1844, was......... 54,251,000
Of these were serfs.................................... 53,500,000
The residue nobles, clergy, and merchants, etc........... 751,000

The Imperial Government abandons the control over the fifty-three and a half millions to their owners; and these owners, included in the 751,000, are thus a privileged class, or aristocracy. If ever the Government interferes at all with the serfs, who are the only laboring population, it is by edicts designed to abridge their opportunities of education, and thus continue their debasement. What was the origin of this system? Conquest, in which the captivity of the conquered was made perpetual and hereditary. This, it seems to me, is identical with American slavery, only at one and the same time exaggerated by the greater disproportion between the privileged classes and the slaves in their respective numbers, and yet relieved of the unhappiest feature of American slavery, the distinction of castes. What but this renders Russia at once the most arbitrary despotism and the most barbarous State in Europe? And what is its effect, but industry comparatively profitless, and sedition, not occasional and partial, but chronic and pervading the Empire. I speak of slavery not in the language of fancy, but in the language of philosophy. Montesquieu remarked upon the proposition to introduce slavery into France, that the demand for slavery was the demand of luxury and corruption, and not the demand of patriotism. Of all slavery, African slavery is the worst, for it combines practically the features of what is distinguished as real slavery or serfdom with the personal slavery known in the oriental world. Its domestic features lead to vice, while its political features render it injurious and dangerous to the State.

I cannot stop to debate long with those who maintain that slavery is itself practically economical and humane. I might be content with saying that there are some axioms in political science that a statesman or a founder of States may adopt, especially in the Congress of the United States, and that among those axioms are these: That all men are created equal, and have inalienable rights of life, liberty, and the choice of pursuits of happiness; that knowledge promotes virtue, and righteousness exalteth a nation; that freedom is preferable to slavery, and that democratic Governments, where they can be maintained by acquiescence, without force, are preferable to institutions exercising arbitrary and irresponsible power.

It remains only to remark that our own experience has proved the dangerous influence and tendency of slavery. All our apprehensions of dangers, present and future, begin and end with slavery. If slavery, limited as it yet is, now threatens to subvert the Constitution, how can we, as wise and prudent statesmen, enlarge its boundaries and increase its influence, and thus increase already impending dangers? Whether, then, I regard merely the welfare of the future inhabitants of the new Territories, or the security and welfare of the whole people of the United States, or the welfare of the whole family of mankind, I cannot consent to introduce slavery into any part of this con-

tinent which is now exempt from what seems to me so great
an evil. These are my reasons for declining to compromise the
question relating to slavery as a condition of the admission of
California.

*In acting upon an occasion so grave as this, a respectful con-
sideration is due to the arguments, founded on extraneous considerations, of Senators who commend a course different from
that which I have preferred.* The first of these arguments is,
that Congress has no power to legislate on the subject of slavery
within the Territories.

Sir, Congress *may* admit new States; and since Congress
may admit, it follows that Congress may *reject* new States.
The discretion of Congress in admitting is absolute, except that,
when admitted, the State must be a republican State, and must
be a *State;* that is, it shall have the constitutional form and
powers of a State. But the greater includes the less, and therefore Congress may impose *conditions* of admission not inconsistent with those fundamental powers and forms. Boundaries
are such. The reservation of the public domain is such. The
right to divide is such. The Ordinance excluding slavery is
such a condition. The organization of a Territory is ancillary
or preliminary; it is the inchoate, the *initiative* act of admission,
and is performed under the clause granting the powers necessary to execute the express powers of the Constitution.

This power comes from the treaty-making power also, and I
think it well traced to the power to make needful rules and regulations concerning the public domain. But this question is
not a material one now; the power is here to be exercised. The
question now is, How is it to be exercised? not whether we
shall exercise it at all, however derived. And the right to regulate property, to administer justice in regard to *property, is assumed* in every Territorial charter. If we have the power to
legislate concerning property, we have the power to legislate
concerning personal rights. Freedom is a *personal* right; and
Congress, being the supreme legislature, has the same right in
regard to property and personal rights in Territories that the
States would have if organized.

The next of this class of arguments is, that the inhibition of
slavery in the new Territories is *unnecessary;* and when I come

to this question, I encounter the loss of many who lead in favor
of admitting California. I had hoped, some time ago, that upon
the vastly important question of inhibiting slavery in the new
Territories, we should have had the aid especially of the distinguished Senator from Missouri [Mr. Benton] ; and when he
announced his opposition to that measure I was induced to exclaim—

> Cur in theatrum, Cato severe, venisti?
> An ideo, tantum, veneras ut exires?

But, sir, I have no right to complain. The Senator is crowning a life of eminent public service by a heroic and magnanimous
act in bringing California into the Union. Grateful to him for
this, I leave it to himself to determine how far considerations
of human freedom shall govern the course which he thinks proper to pursue.

The argument is, that the *Proviso is unnecessary*. I answer,
there, then, can be no error in insisting upon it. But why is it
unnecessary? It is said, *first,* by reason of *climate.* I answer,
if this be so, why do not the representatives of the slave States
concede the Proviso? They deny that the climate prevents the
introduction of slavery. Then I will leave nothing to a contin-
gency. But, in truth, I think the weight of argument is against
the proposition. Is there any climate where slavery has not existed? It has prevailed all over Europe, from sunny Italy to
bleak England, and is existing now, stronger than in any other
land, in ice-bound Russia. But it will be replied, that this is not
African slavery. I rejoin, that only makes the case the stronger.
If this vigorous Saxon race of ours was reduced to slavery
while it retained the courage of semi-barbarism in its own high
northern latitude, what security does climate afford against the
transplantation of the more gentle, more docile, and already enslaved and debased African to the genial climate of New Mexico and Eastern California?

Sir, there is no climate uncongenial to slavery. It is true it
is less productive than free labor in many northern countries.
But so it is less productive than free white labor in even tropical
climates. Labor is in quick demand in all new countries. Slave
labor is cheaper than free labor, and it would go first into new
regions; and wherever it goes it brings labor into dishonor, and

therefore free white labor avoids competition with it. Sir, I might rely on climate if I had not been born in a land where slavery existed—and this land was all of it north of the fortieth parallel of latitude; and if I did not know the struggle it has cost, and which is yet going on, to get complete relief from the institution and its baleful consequences. I desire to propound this question to those who are now in favor of dispensing with the Wilmot Proviso: Was the Ordinance of 1787 necessary or not? Necessary, we all agree. It has received too many elaborate eulogiums to be now decried as an idle and superfluous thing. And yet that Ordinance extended the inhibition of slavery from the thirty-seventh to the fortieth parallel of north latitude. And now we are told that the inhibition named is unnecessary anywhere north of 36° 30′! We are told that we may rely upon the laws of God, which prohibit slave labor north of that line, and that it is absurd to re-enact the laws of God. Sir, there is no human enactment which is just that is not a re-enactment of the law of God. The Constitution of the United States and the Constitutions of all the States are full of such re-enactments. Wherever I find a law of God or a law of nature disregarded, or in danger of being disregarded, there I shall vote to reaffirm it, with all the sanction of the civil authority. But I find no authority for the position that climate prevents slavery anywhere. It is the indolence of mankind in any climate, and not any natural necessity, that introduces slavery in any climate.

I shall dwell only very briefly on the argument derived from the Mexican laws. The proposition, that those laws must remain in force until altered by laws of our own, is satisfactory; and so is the proposition that those Mexican laws abolished and continue to prohibit slavery. And still I deem an enactment by ourselves wise, and even necessary. Both of the propositions I have stated are denied with just as much confidence by Southern statesmen and jurists as they are affirmed by those of the free States. The population of the new Territories is rapidly becoming an American one, to whom the Mexican code will seem a foreign one, entitled to little deference or obedience.

Slavery has never obtained anywhere by express legislative

authority, but always by trampling down laws higher than any mere municipal laws—the laws of nature and of nations. There can be no oppression in superadding the sanction of Congress to the authority which is so weak and so vehemently questioned. And there is some possibility, if not probability, that the institution might obtain a foothold surreptitiously, if it should not be absolutely forbidden by our own authority.

What is insisted upon, therefore, is not a mere abstraction or a mere sentiment, as is contended by those who waive the Proviso. And what is conclusive on the subject is, that it is conceded on all hands that the effect of insisting on it is to prevent the intrusion of slavery into the region to which it is proposed to apply it.

It is insisted that the diffusion of slavery will not increase its evils. The argument seems to me merely specious, and quite unsound. I desire to propose one or two questions in reply to it. Is slavery stronger or weaker in these United States, from its diffusion into Missouri? Is slavery weaker or stronger in these United States, from the exclusion of it from the Northwest Territory! The answers to these questions will settle the whole controversy.

And this brings me to the great and all-absorbing argument that the Union is in danger of being dissolved, and that it can only be saved by compromise. I do not know what I would not do to save the Union; and therefore I shall bestow upon this subject a very deliberate consideration.

I do not overlook the fact that the entire delegation from the slave States, although they differ in regard to the details of compromise proposed, and perhaps in regard to the exact circumstances of the crisis, seem to concur in this momentous warning. Nor do I doubt at all the patriotic devotion to the Union which is expressed by those from whom this warning proceeds. And yet, sir, although such warnings have been uttered with impassioned solemnity in my hearing every day for near three months, my confidence in the Union remains unshaken. I think they are to be received with no inconsiderable distrust, because they are uttered under the influence of a controlling interest to be secured, a paramount object to be gained; and that is an equilibrium of power in the Republic. I think they are to be

received with even more distrust, because, with the most profound respect, they are uttered under an obviously high excitement. Nor is that excitement an unnatural one. It is a law
of our nature that the passions disturb the reason and judgment
just in proportion to the importance of the occasion, and the
consequent necessity for calmness and candor. I think they
are to be distrusted, because there is a diversity of opinion in
regard to the nature and operation of this excitement. The
Senators from some States say that it has brought all parties
in their own region into unanimity. The honorable Senator
from Kentucky [Mr. Clay] says that the danger lies in the violence of party spirit, and refers us for proof to the difficulties
which attended the organization of the House of Representatives.

Sir, in my humble judgment, it is not the fierce conflict of
parties that we are seeing and hearing; but, on the contrary, it
is the agony of distracted parties—a convulsion resulting from
the too narrow foundations of both the great parties, and of all
parties—foundations laid in compromises of natural justice and
of human liberty. A question, a moral question, transcending
the too narrow creeds of parties, has arisen; the public conscience expands with it, and the green withes of party associations give way and break, and fall off from it. No, sir; it is
not the State that is dying of the fever of party spirit. It is
merely a paralysis of parties, premonitory however of their restoration, with new elements of health and vigor to be imbibed
from that spirit of the age which is so justly called Progress.

Nor is the evil that of unlicensed, irregular, and turbulent
faction. We are told that twenty Legislatures are in session,
burning like furnaces, heating and inflaming the popular passions. But these twenty Legislatures are constitutional furnaces. They are performing their customary functions, imparting
healthful heat and vitality while within their constitutional jurisdiction. If they rage beyond its limits, the popular passions
of this country are not at all, I think, in danger of being inflamed to excess. No, sir; let none of these fires be extinguished. Forever let them burn and blaze. They are neither
ominous meteors nor baleful comets, but planets; and bright
and intense as their heat may be, it is their native temperature,

and they must still obey the law which, by attraction toward this solar centre, holds them in their spheres.

I see nothing of that conflict between the Southern and Northern States, or between their representative bodies, which seems to be on all sides of me assumed. Not a word of menace, not a word of anger, not an intemperate word, has been uttered in the Northern Legislatures. They firmly but calmly assert their convictions; but at the same time they assert their unqualified consent to submit to the common arbiter, and for weal or woe abide the fortunes of the Union.

What if there be less of moderation in the Legislatures of the South? It only indicates on which side the balance is inclining, and that the decision of the momentous question is near at hand. I agree with those who say that there can be no peaceful dissolution—no dissolution of the Union by the secession of States; but that disunion, dissolution, happen when it may, will and must be revolution. I discover no omens of revolution. The predictions of the political astrologers do not agree as to the time or manner in which it is to occur. According to the authority of the honorable Senator from Alabama [Mr. Clemens], the event has already happened, and the Union is now in ruins. According to the honorable and distinguished Senator from South Carolina [Mr. Calhoun], it is not to be immediate, but to be developed by time.

What are the omens to which our attention is directed? I see nothing but a broad difference of opinion here, and the excitement consequent upon it.

I have observed that revolutions which begin in the palace seldom go beyond the palace walls, and they affect only the dynasty which reigns there. This revolution, if I understand it, began in this Senate chamber a year ago, when the representatives from the Southern States assembled here and addressed their constituents on what were called the aggressions of the Northern States. No revolution was designed at that time, and all that has happened since is the return to Congress of legislative resolutions, which seem to me to be only conventional responses to the address which emanated from the Capitol.

Sir, in any condition of society there can be no revolution without a cause, an adequate cause. What cause exists here?

We are admitting a new State; but there is nothing new in that. We have already admitted seventeen before. But it is said that the slave States are in danger of losing political power by the admission of the new State. Well, sir, is there anything new in that? The slave States have always been losing political power, and they always will be while they have any to lose. At first, twelve of the thirteen States were slave States; now only fifteen out of the thirty are slave States. Moreover, the change is constitutionally made, and the Government was constructed so as to permit changes of the balance of power, in obedience to changes of the forces of the body politic. Danton used to say, "It's all well while the people cry Danton and Robespierre; but wo for me if ever the people learn to say, Robespierre and Danton!" That is all of it, sir. The people have been accustomed to say, "the South and the North;" they are only beginning now to say, "the North and the South."

Sir, those who would alarm us with the terrors of revolution have not well considered the structure of this Government, and the organization of its forces. It is a Democracy of property and persons, with a fair approximation towards universal education, and operating by means of universal suffrage. The constituent members of this Democracy are the only persons who could subvert it; and they are not the citizens of a metropolis like Paris, or of a region subjected to the influences of a metropolis like France; but they are husbandmen, dispersed over this broad land, on the mountain and on the plain, and on the prairie, from the Ocean to the Rocky Mountains, and from the Great Lakes to the Gulf; and this people are now, while we are discussing their imaginary danger, at peace and in their happy homes, as unconcerned and uninformed of their peril as they are of events occurring in the moon. Nor have the alarmists made due allowance in their calculations for the influence of conservative reaction, strong in any Government, and irresistible in a rural Republic, operating by universal suffrage. That principle of reaction is due to the force of the habits of acquiescence and loyalty among the people. No man better understood this principle than Machiavelli, who has told us, in regard to factions, that "no safe reliance can be placed in the force of nature and the bravery of words, except it be corroborate

by custom." Do the alarmists remember that this Government
has stood sixty years already without exacting one drop of
blood?—that this Government has stood sixty years, and treason
is an obsolete crime? That day, I trust, is far off when the
fountains of popular contentment shall be broken up; but,
whenever it shall come, it will bring forth a higher illustration
than has ever yet been given of the excellence of the Democratic
system; for then it will be seen how calmly, how firmly, how nobly, a great people can act in preserving their Constitution;
whom "love of country moveth, example teacheth, company
comforteth, emulation quickeneth, and glory exalteth."

When the founders of the new Republic of the South come to
draw over the face of this empire, along or between its parallels
of latitude or longitude, their ominous lines of dismemberment,
soon to be broadly and deeply shaded with fraternal blood, they
may come to the discovery then, if not before, that the natural
and even the political connections of the region embraced forbid
such a partition; that its possible divisions are not Northern
and Southern at all, but Eastern and Western, Atlantic and Pacific; and that Nature and Commerce have allied indissolubly
for weal and woe the seceders and those from whom they are to
be separated; that while they would rush into a civil war to restore an imaginary equilibrium between the Northern States
and the Southern States, a new equilibrium has taken its place,
in which all those States are on the one side, and the boundless
West is on the other.

Sir, when the founders of the Republic of the South come to
draw those fearful lines, they will indicate what portions of the
continent are to be broken off from their connection with the
Atlantic, through the St. Lawrence, the Hudson, the Delaware,
the Potomac, and the Mississippi; what portion of this people
are to be denied the use of the lakes, the railroads, and the canals, now constituting common and customary avenues of travel, trade, and social intercourse; what families and kindred are
to be separated, and converted into enemies; and what States
are to be the scenes of perpetual border warfare, aggravated by
interminable horrors of servile insurrection. When those por-
tentous lines shall be drawn, they will disclose what portion of
this people is to retain the army and the navy, and the flag of

so many victories; and on the other hand, what portion of the people is to be subjected to new and onerous imposts, direct taxes, and forced loans, and conscriptions, to maintain an opposing army, an opposing navy, and the new and hateful banner of sedition. Then the projectors of the new Republic of the South will meet the question—and they may well prepare now to answer it—What is all this for? What intolerable wrong, what unfraternal injustice, have rendered these calamities unavoidable? What gain will this unnatural revolution bring to us? The answer will be: All this is done to secure the institution of African slavery.

And then, if not before, the question will be discussed, What is this institution of slavery, that it should cause these unparalleled sacrifices and these disastrous afflictions? And this will be the answer: When the Spaniards, few in number, discovered the Western Indies and adjacent continental America, they needed labor to draw forth from its virgin stores some speedy return to the cupidity of the court and the bankers of Madrid. They enslaved the indolent, inoffensive, and confiding natives, who perished by thousands, and even by millions, under that new and unnatural bondage. A humane ecclesiastic advised the substitution of Africans reduced to captivity in their native wars, and a pious princess adopted the suggestion, with a dispensation from the Head of the Church, granted on the ground of the prescriptive right of the Christian to enslave the heathen, to effect his conversion. The colonists of North America, innocent in their unconsciousness of wrong, encouraged the slave traffic, and thus the labor of subduing their territory devolved chiefly upon the African race. A happy conjuncture brought on an awakening of the conscience of mankind to the injustice of slavery, simultaneously with the independence of the Colonies. Massachusetts, Connecticut, Rhode Island, New Hampshire, Vermont, New York, New Jersey, and Pennsylvania, welcomed and embraced the spirit of universal emancipation. Renouncing luxury, they secured influence and empire. But the States of the South, misled by a new and profitable culture, elected to maintain and perpetuate slavery; and thus, choosing luxury, they lost power and empire.

When this answer shall be given, it will appear that the question of dissolving the Union is a complex question; that it embraces the fearful issue whether the Union shall stand, and slavery, under the steady, peaceful action of moral, social, and political causes, be removed by gradual, voluntary effort, and with compensation, or whether the Union shall be dissolved, and civil wars ensue, bringing on violent but complete and immediate emancipation. We are now arrived at that stage of our national progress when that crisis can be foreseen, when we must foresee it. It is directly before us. Its shadow is upon us. It darkens the legislative halls, the temples of worship, and the home and the hearth. Every question, political, civil, or ecclesiastical, however foreign to the subject of slavery, brings up slavery as an incident, and the incident supplants the principal question. We hear of nothing but slavery, and we can talk of nothing but slavery. And now, it seems to me that all our difficulties, embarrassments, and dangers, arise, not out of unlawful perversions of the question of slavery, as some suppose, but from the want of moral courage to meet this question of emancipation as we ought. Consequently, we hear on one side demands—absurd, indeed, but yet unceasing—for an immediate and unconditional abolition of slavery—as if any power, except the people of the slave States, could abolish it, and as if they could be moved to abolish it by merely sounding the trumpet violently and proclaiming emancipation, while the institution is interwoven with all their social and political interests, constitutions, and customs.

On the other hand, our statesmen say that "slavery has always existed, and, for aught they know or can do, it always must exist. God permitted it, and He alone can indicate the way to remove it." As if the Supreme Creator, after giving us the instructions of His providence and revelation for the illumination of our minds and consciences, did not leave us in all human transactions, with due invocations of His Holy Spirit, to seek out His will and execute it for ourselves.

Here, then, is the point of my separation from both of these parties. I feel assured that slavery must give way, and will give way, to the salutary instructions of economy, and to the ripening influences of humanity; that emancipation is inevitable, and is near; that it may be hastened or hindered; and that whether it be peaceful or violent, depends upon the question whether it be hastened or hindered; that all measures which fortify slavery or extend it, tend to the consummation of violence; all that check its extension and abate its strength, tend to its peaceful extirpation. But I will adopt none but lawful, constitutional, and peaceful means, to secure even that end; and none such can I or will I forego. Nor do I know any important or responsible body that proposes to do more than this. No free State claims to extend its legislation into a slave State. None claims that Congress shall usurp power to abolish slavery in the slave States. None claims that any violent, unconstitutional, or unlawful measure shall be embraced. And, on the other hand, if we offer no scheme or plan for the adoption of the slave States, with the assent and co-operation of Congress, it is only because the slave States are unwilling as yet to receive such suggestions, or even to entertain the question of emancipation in any form.

But, sir, I will take this occasion to say that, while I cannot agree with the honorable Senator from Massachusetts in proposing to devote eighty millions of dollars to remove the free colored population from the slave States, and thus, as it appears to me, fortify slavery, there is no reasonable limit to which I am not willing to go in applying the national treasures to effect the peaceful, voluntary removal of slavery itself.

I have thus endeavored to show that there is not now, and there is not likely to occur, any adequate cause for revolution in regard to slavery. But you reply that, nevertheless, you must have guaranties; and the first one is for the surrender of fugitives from labor. That guaranty you cannot have, as I have already shown, because you cannot roll back the tide of social progress. You must be content with what you have. If you wage war against us, you can, at most, only conquer us, and then all you can get will be a treaty, and that you have already.

But you insist on a guaranty against the abolition of slavery in the District of Columbia, or war. Well, when you shall have declared war against us, what shall hinder us from immediately decreeing that slavery shall cease within the national capital?

You say that you will not submit to the exclusion of slaves from the new Territories. What will you gain by resistance? Liberty follows the sword, although her sway is one of peace and beneficence. Can you propagate slavery then by the sword?

You insist that you cannot submit to the freedom with which slavery is discussed in the free States. Will war—a war for slavery—arrest or even moderate that discussion? No, sir; that discussion will not cease; war would only inflame it to a greater height. It is a part of the eternal conflict between truth and error—between mind and physical force—the conflict of man against the obstacles which oppose his way to an ultimate and glorious destiny. It will go on until you shall terminate it in the only way in which any State or Nation has ever terminated it—by yielding to it—yielding in your own time, and in your own manner, indeed, but nevertheless yielding to the progress of emancipation. You will do this, sooner or later, whatever may be your opinion now; because nations which were prudent and humane, and wise as you are, have done so already.

Sir, the slave States have no reason to fear that this inevitable change will go too far or too fast for their safety or welfare. It cannot well go too fast or too far, if the only alternative is a war of races.

But it cannot go too fast. Slavery has a reliable and accommodating ally in a party in the free States, which, though it claims to be, and doubtless is in many respects, a party of progress, finds its sole security for its political power in the support and aid of slavery in the slave States. Of course, I do not include in that party those who are now co-operating in maintaining the cause of Freedom against Slavery. I am not of that party of progress which in the North thus lends its support to slavery. But it is only just and candid that I should bear witness to its fidelity to the interests of slavery.

Slavery has, moreover, a more natural alliance with the aristocracy of the North and with the aristocracy of Europe. So long as Slavery shall possess the cotton-fields, the sugar-fields, and the rice-fields of the world, so long will Commerce and Capital yield it toleration and sympathy. Emancipation is a democratic revolution. It is Capital that arrests all democratic revolutions. It was Capital that in a single year rolled back the tide of revolution from the base of the Carpathian mountains, across the Danube and the Rhine, into the streets of Paris. It is Capital that is rapidly rolling back the throne of Napoleon into the chambers of the Tuileries.

Slavery has a guaranty still stronger than these in the prejudices of caste and color, which induce even large majorities in all the free States to regard sympathy with the slave as an act of unmanly humiliation and self-abasement, although philosophy meekly expresses her distrust of the asserted natural superiority of the white race, and confidently denies that such a superiority, if justly claimed, could give a title to oppression.

There remains one more guaranty—one that has seldom failed you, and will seldom fail you hereafter. New States cling in closer alliance than older ones to the Federal power. The concentration of the slave power enables you for long periods to control the Federal Government with the aid of the new States. I do not know the sentiments of the representatives of California; but, my word for it, if they should be admitted on this floor to-day, against your most obstinate opposition, they would, on all questions really affecting your interests, be found at your side.

With these alliances to break the force of emancipation, there will be no disunion and no secession. I do not say that there may not be disturbance, though I do not apprehend even that. Absolute regularity and order in administration have not yet been established in any Government, and unbroken popular tranquillity has not yet been attained in even the most advanced condition of human society. The machinery of our system is necessarily complex. A pivot may fall out here, a lever may be displaced there, a wheel may fall out of gearing elsewhere, but the machinery will soon recover its regularity, and move on just as before, with even better adaptation and adjustment to overcome new obstructions.

There are many well-disposed persons who are alarmed at the occurrence of any such disturbance. The failure of a legislative body to organize is to their apprehension a fearful omen, and an extra-constitutional assemblage to consult upon public affairs is with them cause for desperation. Even Senators speak of the Union as if it existed only by consent, and, as it seems to be implied, by the assent of the Legislatures of the States. On the contrary, the Union was not founded in voluntary choice, nor does it exist by voluntary consent.

A Union was proposed to the colonies by Franklin and others, in 1754; but such was their aversion to an abridgment of their own importance, respectively, that it was rejected even under the pressure of a disastrous invasion by France.

A Union of choice was proposed to the colonies in 1775; but so strong was their opposition that they went through the war of Independence without having established more than a mere council of consultation.

But with Independence came enlarged interests of agriculture —absolutely new interests of manufactures—interests of commerce, of fisheries, of navigation, of a common domain, of common debts, of common revenues and taxation, of the administration of justice, of public defence, of public honor; in short, interests of common nationality and sovereignty—interests which at last compelled the adoption of a more perfect Union— a National Government.

The genius, talents, and learning of Hamilton, of Jay, and of Madison, surpassing perhaps the intellectual power ever exerted before for the establishment of a Government, combined with the serene but mighty influence of Washington, were only sufficient to secure the reluctant adoption of the Constitution that is now the object of all our affections and of the hopes of mankind. No wonder that the conflicts in which that Constitution was born, and the almost desponding solemnity of Washington, in his Farewell Address, impressed his countrymen and mankind with a profound distrust of its perpetuity! No wonder that while the murmurs of that day are yet ringing in our ears, we cherish that distrust, with pious reverence, as a national and patriotic sentiment!

But it is time to prevent the abuses of that sentiment. It is time to shake off that fear, for fear is always weakness. It is time to remember that Government, even when it arises by chance or accident, and is administered capriciously and oppressively, is ever the strongest of all human institutions, surviving many social and ecclesiastical changes and convulsions; and that this Constitution of ours has all the inherent strength common to Governments in general, and added to them has also the solidity and firmness derived from broader and deeper foundations in national justice, and a better civil adaptation to promote the welfare and happiness of mankind.

The Union, the creature of necessities, physical, moral, social, and political, endures by virtue of the same necessities; and these necessities are stronger than when it was produced—stronger by the greater amplitude of territory now covered by it—stronger by the sixfold increase of the society living under its beneficent protection—stronger by the augmentation ten thousand times of the fields, the workshops, the mines, and the ships, of that society; of its productions of the sea, of the plough, of the loom, and of the anvil, in their constant circle of internal and international exchange—stronger in the long rivers penetrating regions before unknown—stronger in all the artificial roads, canals, and other channels and avenues essential not only to trade but to defence—stronger in steam navigation, in steam locomotion on the land, and in telegraph communications, unknown when the Constitution was adopted—stronger in the freedom and in the growing empire of the seas—stronger in the element of national honor in all lands, and stronger than all in the now settled habits of veneration and affection for institutions so stupendous and so useful.

The Union, then, *is,* not because merely that men choose that it shall be, but because some Government must exist here, and no other Government than this can. If it could be dashed to atoms by the whirlwind, the lightning, or the earthquake, to-day, it would rise again in all its just and magnificent proportions to-morrow.

This nation is a globe, still accumulating upon accumulation, not a dissolving sphere.

I have heard somewhat here, and almost for the first time in my life, of divided allegiance—of allegiance to the South and to the Union—of allegiance to States severally and to the Union. Sir, if sympathies with State emulation and pride of achievement could be allowed to raise up another sovereign to divide the allegiance of a citizen of the United States, I might recognize the claims of the State to which, by birth and gratitude, I belong—to the State of Hamilton and Jay, of Schuyler, of the Clintons, and of Fulton—the State which, with less than two hundred miles of natural navigation connected with the ocean, has, by her own enterprise, secured to herself the commerce of the continent, and is steadily advancing to the command of the commerce of the world. But for all this I know only one country and one sovereign—the United States of America and the American People. And such as my allegiance is, is the loyalty of every other citizen of the United States. As I speak, he will speak when his time arrives. He knows no other country and no other sovereign. He has life, liberty, property, and precious affections, and hopes for himself and for his posterity, treasured up in the ark of the Union. He knows as well and feels as strongly as I do that this Government is his own Government; that he is a part of it; that it was established for him, and that it is maintained by him; that it is the only truly wise, just, free, and equal Government that has ever existed; that no other Government could be so wise, just, free, and equal; and that it is safer and more beneficent than any which time or change could bring into its place.

You may tell me, sir, that although all this may be true, yet the trial of faction has not yet been made. Sir, if the trial of faction has not been made, it has not been because faction has not always existed, and has not always menaced a trial, but because faction could find no fulcrum on which to place the lever to subvert the Union, as it can find no fulcrum now; and in this is my confidence. I would not rashly provoke the trial; but I will not suffer a fear, which I have not, to make me compromise one sentiment, one principle of truth or justice, to avert a danger that all experience teaches me is purely chimerical. Let, then, those who distrust the Union make compromises to save it. I shall not impeach their wisdom, as I certainly cannot their patriotism; but indulging no such apprehensions myself, I shall vote for the admission of California directly, without conditions, without qualifications, and without compromise.

For the vindication of that vote I look not to the verdict of the passing hour, disturbed as the public mind now is by conflicting interests and passions, but to that period, happily not far distant, when the vast regions over which we are now legislating shall have received their destined inhabitants.

While looking forward to that day, its countless generations seem to me to be rising up and passing in dim and shadowy review before us; and a voice comes forth from their serried ranks, saying: "Waste your treasures and your armies, if you will; raze your fortifications to the ground; sink your navies into the sea; transmit to us even a dishonored name, if you must; but the soil you hold in trust for us—give it to us free. You found it free, and conquered it to extend a better and surer freedom over it. Whatever choice you have made for yourselves, let us have no partial freedom; let us all be free; let the reversion of your broad domain descend to us unincumbered, and free from the calamities and the sorrows of human bondage."

ABRAHAM LINCOLN

THE HOUSE DIVIDED

Speech at the Republican State Convention, State House, Springfield, Illinois, June 16, 1858

[Abraham Lincoln was born in Hardin county, Kentucky, on February 12, 1809. In 1830 he moved with his father to Macon county, Illinois, and later to Coles county. From April to June, 1832, he served in the Black Hawk War. He was postmaster of New Salem, Illinois, from 1833 to 1836, and from 1834 to 1836 deputy county surveyor. He was a member of the Illinois House of Representatives from 1834 to 1840, was admitted to the bar in 1836, and moved to Springfield, Illinois, to begin the practice of law. He was a Whig member of Congress, 1847 to 1849; a representative in the state legislature, 1854; an unsuccessful Whig candidate for election to the United States Senate before the Legislature of 1855; and in 1858 the unsuccessful candidate of the Republican Party to oppose the re-election of Stephen A. Douglas to the United States Senate. From 1861 to April 15, 1865, he was President of the United States. On the night of April 14, 1865, while in Ford's Theatre, Washington, D. C., he was shot by J. Wilkes Booth, and died the following day.

The House Divided speech was delivered on the evening of the day during which the Convention had resolved "that Abraham Lincoln is the first and only choice of the Republicans of Illinois for the United States Senate, as the successor of Stephen A. Douglas." It had been prepared in advance of the nomination, and had been unfavorably criticised by several of his friends, most of whom thought it was political suicide to deliver it. Referring to the "house divided" phrase, Lincoln replied: "I want to use some universally known figure, expressed in simple language as universally well-known, that may strike home to the minds of men, in order to raise them up to the peril of the times. I do not believe I would be right in changing or omitting it. I would rather be defeated with this expression in the speech, and uphold and discuss it before the people, than be victorious without it." With regard to the whole speech, he said: "Friends, this thing has been retarded long enough. The time has come when these sentiments should be uttered; and if it is decreed that I should go down because of this speech, then let me go down linked to the truth—let me die in the advocacy of what is just and right."

A circumstantial account of the preparation, delivery, and effect of the speech is contained in Beveridge's Abraham Lincoln, 2: 573–586.]

Mr. President and Gentlemen of the Convention:

If we could first know where we are, and whither we are tending, we could better judge what to do, and how to do it. We are now far into the fifth year since a policy was initiated with the avowed object and confident promise of putting an end to slavery agitation. Under the operation of that policy, that agitation has not only not ceased but has constantly augmented. In my opinion, it will not cease until a crisis shall have been reached and passed. "A house divided against itself cannot stand." I believe this government cannot endure permanently half slave and half free. I do not expect the Union to be dissolved—I do not expect the house to fall—but I do expect it will cease to be divided. It will become all one thing, or all the other. Either the opponents of slavery will arrest the further spread of it, and place it where the public mind shall rest in the belief that it is in the course of ultimate extinction; or its advocates will push it forward till it shall become alike lawful in all the States, old as well as new, North as well as South.

Have we no tendency to the latter condition?

Let any one who doubts carefully contemplate that now almost complete legal combination—piece of machinery, so to speak—compounded of the Nebraska doctrine and the Dred Scott decision. Let him consider not only what work the machinery is adapted to do, and how well adapted; but also let him study the history of the construction, and trace, if he can, or rather fail, if he can, to trace the evidences of design and concert of action among its chief architects, from the beginning.

The new year of 1854 found slavery excluded from more than half the States by State constitutions, and from most of the national territory by congressional prohibition. Four days later commenced the struggle which ended in repealing that congressional prohibition. This opened all the national territory to slavery, and was the first point gained.

But, so far, Congress only had acted; and an indorsement by the people, real or apparent, was indispensable to save the point already gained and give chance for more.

This necessity had not been overlooked, but had been provided for, as well as might be, in the notable argument of "squatter

sovereignty," otherwise called "sacred right of self-government," which latter phrase, though expressive of the only rightful basis of any government, was so perverted in this attempted
use of it as to amount to just this: That if any one man choose
to enslave another, no third man shall be allowed to object. That
argument was incorporated into the Nebraska bill itself, in the
language which follows: "It being the true intent and meaning
of this act not to legislate slavery into any Territory or State,
nor to exclude it therefrom; but to leave the people thereof perfectly free to form and regulate their domestic institutions in
their own way, subject only to the Constitution of the United
States." Then opened the roar of loose declamation in favor of
"squatter sovereignty" and "sacred right of self-government."
"But," said opposition members, "let us amend the bill so as to
expressly declare that the people of the Territory may exclude
slavery." "Not we," said the friends of the measure; and down
they voted the amendment.

While the Nebraska bill was passing through Congress, a law
case involving the question of a negro's freedom, by reason of
his owner having voluntarily taken him first into a free State
and then into a Territory covered by the congressional prohibition, and held him as a slave for a long time in each, was passing
through the United States Circuit Court for the District of Missouri; and both Nebraska bill and lawsuit were brought to a
decision in the same month of May, 1854. The negro's name
was Dred Scott, which name now designates the decision finally
made in the case. Before the then next presidential election,
the law case came to and was argued in the Supreme Court of
the United States; but the decision of it was deferred until after the election. Still, before the election, Senator Trumbull, on
the floor of the Senate, requested the leading advocate of the
Nebraska bill to state his opinion whether the people of a Territory can constitutionally exclude slavery from their limits;
and the latter answered: "That is a question for the Supreme
Court."

The election came. Mr. Buchanan was elected, and the indorsement, such as it was, secured. That was the second point
gained. The indorsement, however, fell short of a clear popular majority by nearly four hundred thousand votes, and so,

perhaps, was not overwhelmingly reliable and satisfactory. The outgoing President, in his last annual message, as impressively as possible echoed back upon the people the weight and authority of the indorsement. The Supreme Court met again; did not announce their decision, but ordered a reargument. The presidential inauguration came, and still no decision of the court; but the incoming President in his inaugural address fervently exhorted the people to abide by the forthcoming decision, whatever it might be. Then, in a few days, came the decision.

The reputed author of the Nebraska bill finds an early occasion to make a speech at this capital indorsing the Dred Scott decision, and vehemently denouncing all opposition to it. The new President, too, seizes the early occasion of the Silliman letter to indorse and strongly construe that decision, and to express his astonishment that any different view had ever been entertained!

At length a squabble springs up between the President and the author of the Nebraska bill, on the mere question of fact, whether the Lecompton constitution was or was not, in any just sense, made by the people of Kansas; and in that quarrel the latter declares that all he wants is a fair vote for the people, and that he cares not whether slavery be voted down or voted up. I do not understand his declaration that he cares not whether slavery be voted down or voted up to be intended by him other than as an apt definition of the policy he would impress upon the public mind—the principle for which he declares he has suffered so much, and is ready to suffer to the end. And well may he cling to that principle. If he has any parental feeling, well may he cling to it. That principle is the only shred left of his original Nebraska doctrine. Under the Dred Scott decision "squatter sovereignty" squatted out of existence, tumbled down like temporary scaffolding—like the mold at the foundry, served through one blast and fell back into loose sand—helped to carry an election, and then was kicked to the winds. His late joint struggle with the Republicans against the Lecompton constitution involves nothing of the original Nebraska doctrine. That struggle was made on a point—the right of a people to make their own constitution—upon which he and the Republicans have never differed.

The several points of the Dred Scott decision, in connection with Senator Douglas's "care not" policy, constitute the piece of machinery in its present state of advancement. This was the third point gained. The working points of that machinery are:

(1) That no negro slave, imported as such from Africa, and no descendant of such slave, can ever be a citizen of any State, in the sense of that term as used in the Constitution of the United States. This point is made in order to deprive the negro in every possible event of the benefit of that provision of the United States Constitution which declares that "the citizens of each State shall be entitled to all the privileges and immunities of citizens in the several States."

(2) That, "subject to the Constitution of the United States," neither Congress nor a territorial legislature can exclude slavery from any United States Territory. This point is made in order that individual men may fill up the Territories with slaves, without danger of losing them as property and thus enhance the chances of permanency to the institution through all the future.

(3) That whether the holding a negro in actual slavery in a free State makes him free as against the holder, the United States courts will not decide, but will leave to be decided by the courts of any slave State the negro may be forced into by the master. This point is made not to be pressed immediately, but, if acquiesced in for a while, and apparently indorsed by the people at an election, then to sustain the logical conclusion that what Dred Scott's master might lawfully do with Dred Scott in the free State of Illinois, every other master may lawfully do with any other one or one thousand slaves in Illinois or in any other free State.

Auxiliary to all this, and working hand in hand with it, the Nebraska doctrine, or what is left of it, is to educate and mold public opinion, at least Northern public opinion, not to care whether slavery is voted down or voted up. This shows exactly where we now are, and partially, also, whither we are tending.

It will throw additional light on the latter, to go back and run the mind over the string of historical facts already stated. Several things will now appear less dark and mysterious than they did when they were transpiring. The people were to be left "perfectly free," "subject only to the Constitution." What the

Constitution had to do with it outsiders could not then see. Plainly enough now, it was an exactly fitted niche for the Dred Scott decision to afterward come in, and declare the perfect freedom of the people to be just no freedom at all. Why was the amendment expressly declaring the right of the people voted down? Plainly enough now, the adoption of it would have spoiled the niche for the Dred Scott decision. Why was the court decision held up? Why even a senator's individual opinion withheld till after the presidential election? Plainly enough now, the speaking out then would have damaged the "perfectly free" argument upon which the election was to be carried. Why the outgoing President's felicitation on the indorsement? Why the delay of a reargument? Why the incoming President's advance exhortation in favor of the decision? These things look like the cautious patting and petting of a spirited horse preparatory to mounting him, when it is dreaded that he may give the rider a fall. And why the hasty after-indorsement of the decision by the President and others?

We cannot absolutely know that all these exact adaptations are the result of preconcert. But when we see a lot of framed timbers, different portions of which we know have been gotten out at different times and places and by different workmen—Stephen, Franklin, Roger, and James, for instance—and we see these timbers joined together, and see they exactly make the frame of a house or a mill, all the tenons and mortises exactly fitting, and all the lengths and proportions of the different pieces exactly adapted to their respective places, and not a piece too many or too few, not omitting even scaffolding—or, if a single piece be lacking, we see the place in the frame exactly fitted and prepared yet to bring such piece in—in such a case we find it impossible not to believe that Stephen and Franklin and Roger and James all understood one another from the beginning, and all worked upon a common plan or draft drawn up before the first blow was struck.

It should not be overlooked that, by the Nebraska bill, the people of a State as well as Territory were to be left "perfectly free," "subject only to the Constitution." Why mention a State? They were legislating for Territories, and not for or about States. Certainly the people of a State are and ought to be subject to the Constitution of the United States; but why is mention of this lugged into this merely territorial law? Why are the people of a Territory and the people of a State therein lumped together, and their relation to the Constitution therein treated as being precisely the same? While the opinion of the court, by Chief Justice Taney, in the Dred Scott case, and the separate opinions of all the concurring judges, expressly declare that the Constitution of the United States neither permits Congress nor a territorial legislature to exclude slavery from any United States Territory, they all omit to declare whether or not the same Constitution permits a State, or the people of a State, to exclude it. Possibly, this is a mere omission; but who can be quite sure, if McLean or Curtis had sought to get into the opinion a declaration of unlimited power in the people of a State to exclude slavery from their limits, just as Chase and Mace sought to get such declaration, in behalf of the people of a Territory, into the Nebraska bill—I ask, who can be quite sure that it would not have been voted down in the one case as it had been in the other? The nearest approach to the point of declaring the power of a State over slavery is made by Judge Nelson. He approaches it more than once, using the precise idea, and almost the language too, of the Nebraska act. On one occasion his exact language is: "Except in case where the power is restrained by the Constitution of the United States, the law of the State is supreme over the subject of slavery within its jurisdiction." In what cases the power of the States is so restrained by the United States Constitution is left an open question, precisely as the same question as to the restraint on the power of the Territories was left open in the Nebraska act. Put this and that together, and we have another nice little niche, which we may, ere long, see filled with another Supreme Court decision declaring that the Constitution of the United States does not permit a State to exclude slavery from its limits. And this may especially be expected if the doctrine of "care not whether slavery be voted down or voted up" shall gain upon the public mind sufficiently to give promise that such a decision can be maintained when made.

Such a decision is all that slavery now lacks of being alike lawful in all the States. Welcome, or unwelcome, such decision is probably coming, and will soon be upon us, unless the power of the present political dynasty shall be met and overthrown. We shall lie down pleasantly dreaming that the people of Missouri are on the verge of making their State free, and we shall awake to the reality instead that the Supreme Court has made Illinois a slave State. To meet and overthrow the power of that dynasty is the work now before all those who would prevent that consummation. That is what we have to do. How can we best do it?

There are those who denounce us openly to their own friends, and yet whisper us softly that Senator Douglas is the aptest instrument there is with which to effect that object. They wish us to infer all from the fact that he now has a little quarrel with the present head of the dynasty; and that he has regularly voted with us on a single point upon which he and we have never differed. They remind us that he is a great man, and that the largest of us are very small ones. Let this be granted. But "a living dog is better than a dead lion." Judge Douglas, if not a dead lion for this work, is at least a caged and toothless one. How can he oppose the advances of slavery? He don't care anything about it. His avowed mission is impressing the "public heart" to care nothing about it. A leading Douglas Democratic newspaper thinks Douglas's superior talent will be needed to resist the revival of the African slave-trade. Does Douglas believe an effort to revive that trade is approaching? He has not said so. Does he really think so? But if it is, how can he resist it? For years he has labored to prove it a sacred right of white men to take negro slaves into the new Territories. Can he possibly show that it is less a sacred right to buy them where they can be bought cheapest? And unquestionably they can be bought cheaper in Africa than in Virginia. He has done all in his power to reduce the whole question of slavery to one of a mere right of property; and as such, how can he oppose the foreign slave-trade? How can he refuse that trade in that "property" shall be "perfectly free," unless he does it as a protection to the home production? And as the home producers will probably not ask the protection, he will be wholly without a ground of opposition.

Senator Douglas holds, we know, that a man may rightfully be wiser to-day than he was yesterday—that he may rightfully change when he finds himself wrong. But can we, for that reason, run ahead, and infer that he will make any particular change of which he, himself, has given no intimation? Can we safely base our action upon any such vague inference? Now, as ever, I wish not to misrepresent Judge Douglas's position, question his motives, or do aught that can be personally offensive to him. Whenever, if ever, he and we can come together on principle so that our great cause may have assistance from his great ability, I hope to have interposed no adventitious obstacle. But clearly, he is not now with us—he does not pretend to be—he does not promise ever to be.

Our cause, then, must be intrusted to, and conducted by, its own undoubted friends—those whose hands are free, whose hearts are in the work, who do care for the result. Two years ago the Republicans of the nation mustered over thirteen hundred thousand strong. We did this under the single impulse of resistance to a common danger, with every external circumstance against us. Of strange, discordant, and even hostile elements, we gathered from the four winds, and formed and fought the battle through, under the constant hot fire of a disciplined, proud, and pampered enemy. Did we brave all then to falter now?—now, when that same enemy is wavering, dissevered, and belligerent? The result is not doubtful. We shall not fail— if we stand firm, we shall not fail. Wise counsels may accelerate or mistakes delay it, but, sooner or later, the victory is sure to come.

JUDAH P. BENJAMIN

THE RIGHT OF SECESSION

SPEECH IN THE UNITED STATES SENATE, DECEMBER 31, 1860,
ON THE SECESSION OF SOUTH CAROLINA FROM THE UNION

[Judah Philip Benjamin was born on the Island of St. Croix, Danish West Indies, on August 6, 1811. In 1816 he moved with his parents to Savannah, Georgia, and from there to Wilmington, North Carolina. He attended Yale College from 1825 to 1827, but left without taking a degree. In 1831 he moved to New Orleans, where he taught school, studied law as a notary's clerk, and was admitted to the bar on December 16, 1832. He was a member of the Louisiana Constitutional Convention of 1844–45, was elected to the United States Senate in 1852, and served from 1853 to February 4, 1861, when he withdrew. He served successively as Attorney General, Acting Secretary of War, Secretary of War, and Secretary of State of the Confederate States. At the end of the Civil War he moved to England, studied law in Lincoln's Inn, and was called to the English bar. In 1868 he published Benjamin on Sales, which established his reputation as an English lawyer. He became Queen's Counsel in 1872, retired from practice in 1883, and died in Paris on May 6, 1884.

Tradition has it that Sir George Cornewall Lewis said of his speech of December 31, 1860: "It is better than our Benjamin (Disraeli) could have done."]

Mr. President, When I took the floor at our last adjournment I stated that I expected to address the Senate to-day in reference to the critical issue now before the country. I had supposed that by this time there would have been some official communication to the Senate in reference to the fact now known to all of the condition of affairs in South Carolina. I will assume, for the purposes of the remarks that I have to make, that those facts have been officially communicated, and address myself to them. And, Mr. President, probably never has a deliberative assembly been called upon to determine a question calculated to awaken a more solemn sense of responsibility than those that now address themselves to our consideration. We are brought at last, sir, directly forced, to meet promptly an issue produced by an irresistible course of events whose inevitable results some of us, at least, have foreseen for years. Nor, sir, have we failed in our duty of warning the Republicans that they were fast driving us to a point where the very instincts of self-preservation would impose upon us the certain necessity of separation. We repeated those warnings with a depth of conviction, with an earnestness of assertion that inspired the hope that we should succeed in imparting at least some faint assurance of our sincerity to those by whose aid alone could the crisis be averted. But, sir, our assertions were derided; our predictions were scoffed at; all our honest and patriotic efforts to save the Constitution and the Union sneered at and maligned, as dictated, not by love of country, but by base ambition for place and power.

Mr. President, it has been justly said that this is no time for crimination; and, sir, it is in no such spirit, but with the simple desire to free myself personally, as a public servant, from all responsibility for the present condition of affairs, that I desire to recall to the Senate some remarks made by me in debate more than four years ago, in which I predicted the precise state of public feeling now, and pointed out the two principal causes that were certain to produce that state. The first was the incessant attack of the Republicans, not simply on the interests, but on the feelings and sensibilities of a high-spirited people by the most insulting language, and the most offensive epithets; the other was their fatal success in persuading their followers that these constant aggressions could be continued and kept up with no danger; that the South was too weak and too conscious of weakness to dare resistance. Sir, on the 2d of May, 1856, after reviewing this subject at some length, I said:

"Now, Mr. President, when we see these two interests contrasted—the North struggling for the possession of a power to which she has no legitimate claim under the Constitution, for the sole purpose of abusing that power—the South struggling for property, honor, safety—all that is dear to man—tell me if the history of the world exhibits an example of a people occupying a more ennobling attitude than the people of the South? To vituperation they oppose calm reason. To menaces and threats of violence, and insulting assumptions of superiority, they disdain reply. To direct attacks on their rights or their honor, they appeal to the guarantees of the Constitution; and when those guarantees shall fail, and not till then, will the injured, outraged South throw her sword into the scale of her rights, and appeal to the God of battles to do her justice. I say her sword, because I am not one of those who believe in the possibility of a peaceful disruption of the Union. It cannot come until all possible means of conciliation have been exhausted; it cannot come until every angry passion shall have been roused; it cannot come until brotherly feeling shall have been converted into deadly hate; and then, sir, with feelings embittered by the consciousness of injustice, or passions high-wrought and inflamed, dreadful will be the internecine war that must ensue.

"Mr. President, among what I consider to be the most prominent dangers that now exist, is the fact that the leaders of the Republican party at the North have succeeded in persuading the masses of the North that there is no danger. They have finally so wrought upon the opinion of their own people at home by the constant iteration of the same false statements and the same false principles, that the people of the North cannot be made to believe that the South is in earnest, notwithstanding its calm and resolute determination which produces the quiet so ominous of evil if ever the clouds shall burst. The people of the North are taught to laugh at the danger of dissolution. One honorable Senator is reported to have said, with exquisite amenity, that the South could not be kicked out of the Union. The honorable Senator from New York says:

" 'The slaveholders, in spite of all their threats, are bound to it by the same bonds, and they are bound to it also by a bond *peculiarly their own—that of dependence on it for their own safety. Three million slaves are a hostile force constantly in their presence, in their very midst.* The servile war is always the most fearful form of war. *The world without sympathizes with the servile enemy.* Against that war the American Union is the only defense of the slaveholders—their *only* protection. If ever they shall, in a season of madness, secede from that Union, and provoke that war, they will—soon come back again.'

"The honorable Senator from Massachusetts [Mr. Wilson] indulges in the repetition of a figure of rhetoric that seems peculiarly to please his ear and tickle his fancy. He represents the southern mother as clasping her infant with convulsive and closer embrace, because the black avenger, with uplifted dagger, would be at the door, and he tells us that is a bond of Union which we dare not violate."

Mr. President, no man can deny that the words uttered four years and a half ago form a faithful picture of the state of things that we see around us now. Would to God, sir, that I could believe that the apprehensions of civil war, then plainly expressed, were but the vain imaginations of a timorous spirit. Alas, sir, the feelings and sentiments expressed since the commencement of this session, on the opposite side of this floor, almost force the belief that a civil war is their desire; and that the day is full near when American citizens are to meet each other in hostile array; and when the hands of brothers will be reddened with the blood of brothers.

Mr. President, the State of South Carolina, with a unanimity scarcely with parallel in history, has dissolved the union which connects her with the other States of the confederacy, and declared herself independent. We, the representatives of those remaining States, stand here to-day, bound either to recognize that independence, or to overthrow it; either to permit her peaceful secession from the confederacy, or to put her down by force of arms. That is the issue. That is the sole issue. No artifice can conceal it. No attempts by men to disguise it from their own consciences, and from an excited or alarmed public, can suffice to conceal it. Those attempts are equally futile and disingenuous. As for the attempted distinction between coercing a State, and forcing all the people of the State, by arms, to yield obedience to an authority repudiated by the sovereign will of the State, expressed in its most authentic form, it is as unsound in principle as it is impossible of practical application. Upon that point, however, I shall have something to say a little further on.

If we elevate ourselves, Mr. President, to the height from which we are bound to look in order to embrace all the vast consequence that must result from our decision, we are not permitted to ignore the fact that our determination does not involve the State of South Carolina alone. Next week, Mississippi, Alabama, and Florida, will have declared themselves independent; the week after, Georgia; and a little later, Louisiana;

soon, very soon, to be followed by Texas and Arkansas. I confine myself purposely to these eight States, because I wish to speak only of those whose action we know with positive certainty, and which no man can for a moment pretend to controvert. I designedly exclude others, about whose action I feel equally confident, although others may raise a cavil.

Now, sir, shall we recognize the fact that South Carolina has become an independent State, or shall we wage war against her? And first as to her right. I do not agree with those who think it idle to discuss that right. In a great crisis like this, when the right asserted by a sovereign State is questioned, a decent respect for the opinions of mankind at least requires that those who maintain that right, and mean to act upon it, should state the reasons upon which they maintain it. If, in the discussion of this question, I shall refer to familiar principles, it is not that I deem it at all necessary to call the attention of members here to them; but because they naturally fall within the scope of my argument, which might otherwise prove unintelligible.

From the time that this people declared its independence of Great Britain, the right of the people to self-government in its fullest and broadest extent has been a cardinal principle of American liberty. None deny it. And in that right, to use the language of the Declaration itself, is included the right whenever a form of government becomes destructive of their interests or their safety, "to alter or to abolish it, and to institute a new government, laying its foundation on such principles and organizing its powers in such form as to them shall seem most likely to effect their safety and happiness." I admit that there is a principle that modifies this power, to which I shall presently advert; but leaving that principle for a moment out of view, I say that there is no other modification which, consistently with our liberty, we can admit, and that the right of the people of one generation, in convention duly assembled, to alter the institutions bequeathed by their fathers is inherent, inalienable, not susceptible of restriction; that by the same power under which one Legislature can repeal the act of a former Legislature, so can one convention of the people duly assembled, repeal the acts of a former convention of the people duly assembled; and that it is in strict and logical deduction from this fundamental principle of American liberty, that South Carolina has adopted the form in which she has declared her independence. She has in convention duly assembled in 1860, repealed an ordinance passed by her people in convention duly assembled in 1788. If no interests of third parties were concerned, if no question of compact intervened, all must admit the inherent power—the same inherent power which authorizes a Legislature to repeal a law, subject to the same modifying principle, that where the rights of others than the people who passed the law are concerned, those rights must be respected and cannot be infringed by those who descend from the first Legislature or who succeed them. If a law be passed by a Legislature impairing a contract, that law is void, not because the Legislature under ordinary circumstances would not have the power to repeal a law of its predecessor but because by repealing a law of its predecessor involving a contract, it exercises rights in which third persons are interested, and over which they are entitled to have an equal control. So in the case of a convention of the people assuming to act in repeal of an ordinance which showed their adherence to the Constitution of the United States, the power is inherently in them, subject only to this modification: that they are bound to exercise it with due regard to the obligations imposed upon them by the compact with others.

Authorities, on points like this, are perfectly idle; but I fear that I may not have expressed the ideas which I entertain so well as I find them expressed by Mr. Webster in his celebrated argument in the Rhode Island case. He says:

"First and chief, no man makes a question that the people are the source of all political power. Government is instituted for their good, and its members are their agents and servants. He who would argue against this, must argue without an adversary. And who thinks there is any peculiar merit in asserting a doctrine like this, in the midst of twenty million people, when nineteen million nine hundred and ninety nine thousand nine hundred and ninety-nine of them hold it, as well as himself? There is no other doctrine of government here; and no man imputes to another, and no man should claim for himself, any particular merit for asserting what everybody knows to be true, and nobody denies."—Works of Daniel Webster, vol. 6, p. 221.

But he says in this particular case an attempt is made to establish the validity of the action of the people, organized in convention, without their having been called into convention by the exercise of any constituted authority of the State; and against the exercise of such a right of the people as that he protests. He says:

"Is it not obvious enough that men cannot get together and count themselves, and say they are so many hundreds and so many thousands, and judge of their own qualifications, and call themselves the people, and set up a government? Why, another set of men forty miles off, on the same day, with the same propriety, with as good qualifications, and in as large numbers, may meet and set up another government; one may meet at Newport and another at Chepachet, and both may call themselves the people."—Ibid., p. 226.

Therefore, he says, it is not a mere assemblage of the people, gathered together *sua sponte,* that forms that meeting of the people authorized to act in behalf of the people; but he says that—

"Another American principle growing out of this, and just as important and well settled as is the truth that the people are the source of power, is, that, when in the course of events it becomes necessary to ascertain the will of the people on a new exigency, or a new state of things or of opinion, the legislative power provides for that ascertainment by an ordinary act of legislation."

*   *   *   *   *   *   *   *

"All that is necessary here is, that the will of the people should be ascertained by some regular rule of proceeding prescribed by previous law. But when ascertained, that will is as sovereign as the will of a despotic prince, of the Czar of Muscovy, or the Emperor of Austria himself, though not quite so easily made known. A ukase or an edict signifies at once the will of a despotic prince; but that will of the people, which is here as sovereign as the will of such a prince, is not so quickly ascertained or known; and hence arises the necessity for suffrage, which is the mode whereby each man's power is made to tell upon the Constitution of the Government, and in the enactment of laws."

He concludes—

"We see, therefore, from the commencement of the Government under which we live, down to this late act of the State of New York"—

To which he had just referred—

"one uniform current of law, of precedent, and of practice, all going to establish the point that changes in government are to be brought about by the will of the people, assembled under such legislative provisions as may be necessary to ascertain that will truly and authentically."—Ibid., pp. 227, 229.

We have then, sir, in the case of South Carolina, so far as the duly organized convention is concerned, the only body that could speak the will of this generation in repeal of the ordinance passed by their fathers in 1788; and I say again, if no third interests intervened by a compact binding upon their faith, their power to do so is inherent and complete. But, sir, there is a compact, and no man pretends that the generation of to-day is not bound by the compacts of the fathers; but, to use the language of Mr. Webster, a bargain broken on one side is a bargain broken on all; and the compact is binding upon the generation of to-day only if the other parties to the compact have kept their faith.

This is no new theory, nor is practice upon it without precedent. I say that it was precisely upon this principle that this Constitution was formed. I say that the old Articles of Confederacy provided in express terms that they should be perpetual; that they should never be amended or altered without the consent of all the States. I say that the delegates of States unwilling that that Confederation should be altered or amended, appealed to that provision in the convention which formed the Constitution, and said: "If you do not satisfy us by the new provisions, we will prevent your forming your new government, because your faith is plighted, because you have agreed that there shall be no change in it unless with the consent of all." This was the argument of Luther Martin, it was the argument of Paterson, of New Jersey, and of large numbers of other distinguished members of the convention. Mr. Madison answered it. Mr. Madison said, in reply to that:

"It has been alleged that the Confederation having been formed by unanimous consent, could be dissolved by unanimous consent only. Does this doctrine result from the nature of compacts? Does it arise from any particular stipulation in the Articles of Confederation? If we consider the Federal Union as analogous to the fundamental compact by which individuals compose one society, and which must, in its theoretic origin at least, have been the unanimous act of the component members, it cannot be said that no dissolution of the compact can be effected without unanimous consent. A breach of the fundamental principles of the compact, by a part of the society, would certainly absolve the other part from their obligations to it."

*   *   *   *   *   *   *   *

"If we consider the Federal Union as analogous, not to the social compacts among individual men, but to the conventions among individual States, what is the doctrine resulting from these conventions? Clearly, according to the expositors of the law of nations, that a breach of any one article, by any one party, leaves all the other parties at liberty to consider the whole convention as dissolved, unless they choose rather to compel the delinquent party to repair the breach. In some treaties, indeed, it is expressly stipulated that a violation of particular articles shall not have this consequence, and even that particular articles shall remain in force during war, which is, in general, understood to dissolve all subsisting treaties. But are there any exceptions of this sort to the Articles of Confederation? So far from it, that there is not even an express stipulation that force shall be used to compel an offending member of the Union to discharge its duty."—Madison Papers of Debates in the Federal Convention, vol. 5., pp. 206, 207.

I need scarcely ask, Mr. President, if anybody has found in the Constitution of the United States any article providing, by express stipulation, that force shall be used to compel an offending member of the Union to discharge its duty. Acting on that principle, nine States of the Confederation seceded from the Confederation, and formed a new Government. They formed it upon the express ground that some of the States had violated their compact. Immediately after, two other States seceded and joined them. They left two alone, Rhode Island and North Carolina; and here is my answer to the Senator from Wisconsin [Mr. Doolittle], who asked me the other day, if thirty-three States could expel one, inasmuch as one had the right to leave thirty-three: I point him to the history of our country, to the acts of the fathers, as a full answer upon that subject. After this Government had been organized; after every department had been in full operation for some time; after you had framed your navigation laws, and provided what should be considered as ships and vessels of the United States, North Carolina and Rhode Island were still foreign nations, and so treated by you, so treated by you in your laws; and in September, 1789, Congress passed an act authorizing the citizens of the States of North Carolina and Rhode Island to enjoy all the benefits attached to owners of ships and vessels of the United States up to the 1st of the following January—gave them that much more time to come into the new Union, if they thought proper; if not, they were to remain as foreign nations. Here is the history of the formation of this Constitution, so far as it involves the power of the States to secede from a Confederation, and to form new confederacies to suit themselves.

Now, Mr. President, there is a difficulty in this matter, which was not overlooked by the framers of the Constitution. One State may allege that the compact has been broken, and others may deny it; who is to judge? When pecuniary interests are involved, so that a case can be brought up before courts of justice, the Constitution has provided a remedy within itself. It has declared that no act of a State, either in convention or by Legislature, or in any other manner, shall violate the Constitution of the United States, and it has provided for a supreme judiciary to determine cases arising in law or equity which may involve the construction of the Constitution or the construction of such laws.

But, sir, suppose infringements on the Constitution in political matters, which from their very nature cannot be brought before the court? That was a difficulty not unforeseen; it was debated upon propositions that were made to meet it. Attempts were made to give power to this Federal Government in all its departments, one after the other, to meet that precise case, and the convention sternly refused to admit any. It was proposed to enable the Federal Government, through the action of Congress, to use force. That was refused. It was proposed to give to the President of the United States the nomination of State Governors, and to give them a veto on State laws, so as to preserve the supremacy of the Federal Government. That was refused. It was proposed to make the Senate the judge of difficulties that might arise between States and the General Government. That was refused. It was finally proposed to give Congress a negative on State legislation interfering with the powers of the Federal Government. That was refused. At last, at the very last moment, it was proposed to give that power to Congress by a vote of two thirds of each branch; and that, too, was denied.

Now, sir, I wish to show, with some little detail—as briefly as I possibly can and do justice to the subject—what was said by the leading members of the convention on these propositions to subject the States, in their political action, to any power of the General Government, whether of Congress, of the judiciary, or of the Executive, and by any majorities whatever. The first proposition was made by Mr. Randolph, on the 29th of May, 1787; and it was, that power should be given to Congress—

"To negative all laws passed by the several States contravening, in the opinion of the National Legislature, the articles of Union, or any treaty subsisting under the authority of the Union; and to call forth the force of the Union against any member of the Union failing to fulfill its duty under the articles thereof."

To negative all laws violative of the articles of Union, and to employ force to constrain a State to perform its duty. Mr. Pinckney's proposition on the same day was:

"And to render these prohibitions effectual, the Legislature of the United States shall have the power to revise the laws of the several States that may be supposed to infringe the powers exclusively delegated by this Constitution to Congress, and to negative and annul such as do."

The proposition giving a power to negative the laws of the States, passed at first hurriedly, without consideration; but upon further examination, full justice was done to it. Upon the subject of force, Mr. Madison said, moving to postpone the proposition to authorize force:

"Mr. Madison observed, that the more he reflected on the use of force, the more he doubted the practicability, the justice, and the efficacy of it, when applied to people collectively, and not individually. A union of the States containing such an ingredient, seemed to provide for its own destruction. The use of force against a State would look more like a declaration of war than an infliction of punishment, and would probably be considered by the party attacked as a dissolution of all previous compacts by which it might be bound. He hoped that such a system would be framed as might render this resource unnecessary, and moved that the clause be postponed."—Madison Papers—Debates in the Federal Convention, vol. 5, p. 140.

Mr. Mason, the ancestor of our own distinguished colleague from Virginia, said:

"The most jarring elements of nature, fire and water, themselves, are not more incompatible than such a mixture of civil liberty and military execution. Will the militia march from one State into another in order to collect the arrears of taxes from the delinquent members of the Republic? Will they maintain an army for this purpose? Will not the citizens of the invaded State assist one another, till they rise as one man, and shake off the Union altogether? Rebellion is the only case in which the military force of the State can be properly exerted against its citizens. In one point of view, he was struck with horror at the prospect of recurring to this expedient. To punish the nonpayment of taxes with death was a severity not yet adopted by despotism itself; yet this unexampled cruelty would be mercy compared to a military collection of revenue, in which the bayonet could make no discrimination between the innocent and the guilty. He took this occasion to repeat, that, notwithstanding his solicitude to establish a national Government, he never would agree to abolish the State governments, or render them absolutely insignificant. They were as necessary as the general Government, and he would be equally careful to preserve them."—Madison Papers—Debates in the Federal Convention, vol. 5, p. 217.

Mr. Ellsworth, upon the same subject, said:

"Hence we see how necessary for the Union is a coercive principle. No man pretends the contrary: we all see and feel this necessity. The only question is, shall it be a coercion of law, or a coercion of arms? There is no other possible alternative. Where will those who oppose a coercion of law come out? Where will they end? A necessary consequence of their principles is a war of the States one against the other. I am for coercion by law—that coercion which acts only upon delinquent individuals. This Constitution does not attempt to coerce sovereign bodies, States, in their political capacity. No coercion is applicable to such bodies; but that of an armed force. If we should attempt to execute the laws of the Union by sending an armed force against a delinquent State, it would involve the good and bad, the innocent and guilty, in the same calamity."—Elliot's Debates, vol. 2, p. 197.

Alexander Hamilton said:

"It has been observed, to coerce the States is one of the maddest projects that was ever devised. A failure of compliance will never be confined to a single State. This being the case, can we suppose it wise to hazard a civil war? Suppose Massachusetts, or any large State, should refuse, and Congress should attempt to compel them, would they not have influence to procure assistance, especially from those States which are in the same situation as themselves? What picture does this idea present to our view? A complying State at war with a non-complying State; Congress marching the troops of one State into the bosom of another; this State collecting auxiliaries, and forming, perhaps, a majority against its Federal head. Here is a nation at war with itself. Can any reasonable man be well disposed toward a Government which makes war and carnage the only means of supporting itself—a Government that can exist only by the sword? Every such war must involve the innocent with the guilty. This single consideration should be sufficient to dispose every peaceable citizen against such a Government."—Elliot's Debates, vol. 2, p. 233.

But, sir, strong as these gentlemen were against giving the power to exert armed force against the States, some of the best and ablest members of the convention were in favor of giving

Congress control over State action by a negative. Mr. Madison himself was strongly in favor of that; and if that power had been granted, the first of the personal liberty bills that were passed would have been the last, for Congress would at once have annulled it, and the other States would have taken warning by that example. Mr. Pinckney's proposition was brought up, that "the national Legislature should have authority to negative all laws which they should judge to be improper." He urged it strongly. Mr. Madison said:

"A negative was the mildest expedient that could be devised for preventing these mischiefs. The existence of such a check would prevent attempts to commit them. Should no such precaution be engrafted, the only remedy would be in an appeal to coercion. Was such a remedy eligible? Was it practicable? Could the national resources, if exerted to the utmost, enforce a national decree against Massachusetts, abetted, perhaps, by several of her neighbors? It would not be possible. A small proportion of the community, in a compact situation, acting on the defensive, and at one of its extremities, might at any time bid defiance to the national authority. Any government for the United States, formed on the supposed practicability of using force against the unconstitutional proceedings of the States, would prove as visionary and fallacious as the government of Congress."—Madison Papers, Debates of Convention, vol. 5, p. 171.

That is, of the Congress of the Confederation. Well, sir, Mr. Butler said to that, he was "vehement against the negative in the proposed extent as cutting off all hope of equal justice to the distant States. The people there would not, he was sure, give it a hearing;" and on the vote, Mr. Madison, aided by Mr. Pinckney, got but three States for it, and of these three States one was Virginia, and he got Virginia only by a vote of three to two, General Washington in the chair not voting. The proposition, therefore, was directly put down, but it was not killed forever. On the 17th of July it was renewed, and Mr. Madison again urged the convention to give some power to the Federal Government over State action:

"Mr. Madison considered the negative on the laws of the States as essential to the efficacy and security of the General

Government. The necessity of a General Government proceeds from the propensity of the States to pursue their particular interests, in opposition to the general interest. This propensity will continue to disturb the system unless effectually controlled. Nothing short of a negative on their laws will control it. They will pass laws which will accomplish their injurious objects before they can be repealed by the General Legislature, or set aside by the national tribunals." * * * * * "A power of negativing the improper laws of the States is at once the most mild and certain means of preserving the harmony of the system. Its utility is sufficiently displayed in the British system," etc.

This was again negatived in July by the same vote. Finally, on the 23d of August, for the last time, an attempt was made to give that negative with a check upon it; and it was in these words:

"Mr. Charles Pinckney moved to add, as an additional power to be vested in the Legislature of the United States:

"'To negative all laws passed by the several States, interfering, in the opinion of the Legislature, with the general interests and harmony of the Union, provided that two thirds of the members of each House assent to the same.'"

Mr. Madison wanted it committed. Mr. Rutledge said:

"If nothing else, this alone would damn, and ought to damn, the Constitution. Will any State ever agree to be bound hand and foot in this manner? It is worse than making mere corporations of them, whose by-laws would not be subject to this shackle."

And thereupon Mr. Pinckney withdrew his proposition, and all control was abandoned. There was then to be no control on the part of the General Government over State legislation, otherwise than in the action of the Federal judiciary upon such pecuniary controversies as might be properly brought before them.

Notwithstanding all this jealousy, when this Constitution came to be discussed in the conventions of the States, it met formidable opposition, upon the ground that the States were not sufficiently secure. Its advocates by every possible means endeavored to quiet the alarms of the friends of State rights. Mr.

Madison, in Virginia, against Patrick Henry; Mr. Hamilton and Chief Justice Jay, in New York, against the opponents there; in all the States, eminent men used every exertion in their power to induce the adoption of the Constitution. They failed, until they proposed to accompany their ratifications with amendments that should prevent its meaning from being perverted, and prevent it from being falsely construed; and in two of the States especially—the States of Virginia and New York, the ratification was preceded by a statement of what their opinion of its true meaning was, and a statement that, on that construction, and under that impression, they ratified it. Some of the members of the Convention were for asking for these amendments in advance of ratification; but they were told it was unnecessary. In the Virginia convention, Mr. Randolph, who was General Washington's Attorney General, and Judge Nicholas, both expressed the opinion that it was not necessary, and that the ratification would be conditional upon that construction. Mr. Randolph said:

"If it be not considered too early, as ratification has not yet been spoken of, I beg to speak of it. If I did believe, with the honorable gentleman, that all power not expressly retained was given up by the people, I would detest this Government.

"But I never thought so; nor do I now. If, in the ratification, we put words to this purpose, 'And that all authority not given is retained by the people, and may be resumed when perverted to their oppression; and that no right can be canceled, abridged, or restrained, by the Congress, or any officer of the United States'—I say if we do this, I conceive that, as this style of ratification would manifest the principles on which Virginia adopted it, we should be at liberty to consider as a violation of the Constitution every exercise of a power not expressly delegated therein. I see no objection to this."

And Mr. Nicholas said the same thing:

"Mr. Nicholas contended that the language of the proposed ratification would secure everything which gentlemen desired, as it declared that all powers vested in the Constitution were derived from the people, and might be resumed by them whensoever they should be perverted to their injury and oppression; and that every power not granted thereby remained at their will. No danger whatever could arise; for [says he] these expressions will become a part of the contract. The Constitution cannot be binding on Virginia but with these conditions. If thirteen individuals are about to make a contract, and one agrees to it, but at the same time declares that he understands its meaning, signification, and intent to be (what the words of the contract plainly and obviously denote) that it is not to be construed so as to impose any supplementary condition on him, and that he is to be exonerated from it whensoever any such imposition shall be attempted, I ask whether, in this case, these conditions on which he has assented to it would not be binding on the other twelve? In like manner these conditions will be binding on Congress. They can exercise no power that is not expressly granted them."

So, sir, we find that not alone in these two conventions, but by the common action of the States, there was an important addition made to the Constitution by which it was expressly provided that it should not be construed to be a General Government over all the people, but that it was a Government of States, which delegated powers to the General Government. The language of the ninth and tenth amendments to the Constitution is susceptible of no other construction:

"The enumeration in the Constitution of certain rights shall not be construed to deny or disparage others retained by the people."

"The powers not delegated to the United States."

Gentlemen are fond of using the words "surrendered," abandoned, given up. That is the constant language on the other side. The language of the amendment intended to fix the meaning of the Constitution says that these powers were not abandoned by the State, not surrendered, not given up, but "delegated," and therefore subject to resumption:

"The powers not delegated to the United States by the Constitution, nor prohibited by it to the States, are reserved to the States respectively, or to the people."

Now, Mr. President, if we admit, as we must, that there are certain political rights guarantied to the States of this Union by the terms of the Constitution itself—rights political in their character, and not susceptible of judicial decision—if any State is deprived of any of those rights, what is the remedy? for it is idle to talk to us at this day in a language which shall tell us we have rights and no remedies. For the purpose of illustrating the argument upon this subject, let us suppose a clear, palpable case of violation of the Constitution. Let us suppose that the State of South Carolina having sent two Senators to sit upon this floor, had been met by a resolution of the majority here that, according to her just weight in the Confederacy, one was enough, and that we had directed our Secretary to swear in but one, and to call but one name on our roll as the yeas and nays are called for voting. The Constitution says that each State shall be entitled to two Senators, and each Senator shall have one vote. What power is there to force the dominant majority to repair that wrong? Any court? Any tribunal? Has the Constitution provided any recourse whatever? Has it not remained designedly silent on the subject of that recourse? And yet, what man will stand up in this Senate and pretend that if, under these circumstances, the State of South Carolina had declared, "I entered into a Confederacy or a compact by which I was to have my rights guarantied by the constant presence of two Senators upon your floor; you allow me but one; you refuse to repair the injustice; I withdraw;" what man would dare say that that was a violation of the Constitution on the part of South Carolina? Who would say that that was a revolutionary remedy? Who would deny the plain and palpable proposition that it was the exercise of a right inherent in her under the very principles of the Constitution, and necessarily so inherent for self-defense?

Why, sir, the North, if it has not a majority here to-day, will have it very soon. Suppose these gentlemen from the North with the majority think that it is no more than fair, inasmuch as we represent here States in which there are large numbers of slaves, that the northern States should have each three Senators; what are we to do? They swear them in. No court has the power of prohibition, of *mandamus* over this body in the exercise of its political powers. It is the exclusive judge of the elections, the qualifications, and the returns of its own members, a judge without appeal. Shall the whole fifteen southern States submit to that, and be told that they are guilty of revolutionary excess if they say, we will not remain with you on these terms;

we never agreed to it? Is that revolution, or is it the exercise of clear constitutional right?

Suppose this violation occurs under circumstances where it does not appear so plain to you, but where it does appear equally plain to South Carolina: then you are again brought back to the irrevocable point, who is to decide? South Carolina says, "You forced me to the expenditure of my treasure, you forced me to the shedding of the blood of my people, by a majority vote, and with my aid you acquired territory; now I have a constitutional right to go into that territory with my property, and to be there secured by your laws against its loss." You say, no, she has not. Now there is this to be said: that right is not put down in the Constitution in quite so clear terms as the right to have two Senators; but it is a right which she asserts with the concurrent opinion of the entire South. It is a right which she asserts with the concurrent opinion of one third or two fifths of your own people interested in refusing it. It is a right that she asserts, at all events, if not in accordance with the decision—as you may say no decision was rendered—in accordance with the opinion expressed by the Supreme Court of the United States; but yet there is no tribunal for the assertion of that political right. Is she without a remedy under the Constitution? If not, then what tribunal? If none is provided, then natural law and the law of nations tell you that she and she alone, from the very necessity of the case, must be the judge of the infraction and of the mode and measure of redress.

This is no novel doctrine; but it is as old as the law of nations, coeval in our system with the foundation of the Constitution; clearly announced over and over again in our political history. A very valued friend from New York did me the favor to send me an extract, which he has written out, from an address delivered by John Quincy Adams before the New York Historical Society in 1839, at the jubilee of the Constitution. His language is this:

"Nations acknowledge no judge between them upon earth, and their Governments, from necessity, must, in their intercourse with each other, decide when the failure of one party to a contract to perform its obligations absolves the other from the reciprocal fulfillment of his own. But this last of earthly powers is not necessary to the freedom or independence of States, connected together by the immediate action of the people, of whom they consist. To the people alone is there reserved, as well the dissolving as the constituent power, and that power can be exercised by them only under the tie of conscience, binding them to the retributive justice of heaven.

"With these qualifications, we may admit the same right as vested in the people of every State in the Union, with reference to the General Government, which was exercised by the people of the United Colonies with reference to the supreme head of the British Empire, of which they formed a part; and, under these limitations, have the people of each State in the Union a right to secede from the confederated Union itself?

"Thus stands the *right*. But the indissoluble link of union between the people of the several States of this confederated nation is, after all, not in the *right*, but in the *heart*. If the day should ever come (may Heaven avert it!) when the affections of the people of these States shall be alienated from each other; when the fraternal spirit shall give way to cold indifference, or collisions of interest shall fester into hatred, the bands of political association will not long hold together parties no longer attracted by the magnetism of conciliated interests and kindly sympathies; and far better will it be for the people of the *disunited* States to part in friendship from each other, than to be held together by constraint. Then will be the time for reverting to the precedent, which occurred at the formation and adoption of the Constitution, to form again a more perfect Union, by dissolving that which could no longer bind, and to leave the separated parts to be reunited by the law of political gravitation, to the center."

I am compelled to refer also, for the purpose of completing my argument, to the very familiar Virginia and Kentucky resolutions. They cannot, however, be too often repeated or held too reverently in memory. The first, drawn by Mr. Jefferson, is:

"*Resolved*, That the several States composing the United States of America are not united on the principle of unlimited submission to their General Government; but that, by compact, under the style and title of a Constitution for the United States, and of amendments thereto, they constituted a General Government for special purposes, delegated to that Government certain definite powers, reserving each State to itself the residuary mass of right to their own self-government; and that whensoever the General Government assumes undelegated powers its acts are unauthoritative, void, and of no force; that to this compact each State acceded as a State, and is an integral party; that this Government, created by this compact, was not made the exclusive or final judge of the extent of the powers delegated to itself, since that would have made its discretion, and not the Constitution, the measure of its power; but that, as in all other cases of compact among parties having no common judge, each party has an equal right to judge for itself as well of infractions as of the mode and measure of redress."

These resolutions of Virginia were submitted to all the States. They were commented upon; they were answered generally with contempt and disdain, because the people of the northern States never seem to have comprehended that the States had any rights at all. They have always gone astray in the heresy that this was one consolidated Government, governing subjects to the Federal Government, and not controlling States, and individuals in the States. These resolutions were returned in many cases with terms of contempt and contumely. They were, therefore, referred to Mr. Madison for further consideration and defense, and he produced upon that subject the best considered, the most perfect, the most compact argument upon the constitutional rights of the States of this Union, that has ever been delivered. It has never been answered to this day in any of its positions. No man can answer it. The proof is such that conviction is forced home upon the mind as by the enunciation of an axiom. A single passage I desire to quote. It has been often quoted, but I must read it again:

"It appears to your committee to be a plain principle, founded in common sense, illustrated by common practice, and essential to the nature of compacts, that, where resort can be had to no tribunal superior to the authority of the parties, the parties themselves must be the rightful judges, in the last resort, whether the bargain made has been pursued or violated. The Constitution of the United States was formed by the sanction

of the States, given by each in its sovereign capacity. It adds
to the stability and dignity, as well as to the authority, of the
Constitution, that it rests on this legitimate and solid foundation. The States, then, being the parties to the constitutional
compact, and in their sovereign capacity, it follows, of necessity,
that there can be no tribunal, above their authority, to decide,
in the last resort, whether the compact made by them be violated, and consequently, that, as the parties to it, they must
themselves decide, in the last resort, such questions as may be of
sufficient magnitude to require their interposition."

He goes on to state, not limitations upon the power, but considerations in regard to the mode of exercising it. He says:

"The resolution has, accordingly, guarded against any misapprehension of its object, by expressly requiring, for such an interposition, 'the case of a deliberate, palpable, and dangerous
breach of the Constitution, by the exercise of powers not granted
by it.' It must be a case not of light and transient nature, but
of a nature dangerous to the great purposes for which the Constitution was established."

Mr. Madison, in the debates in the Virginia convention,
seemed to take it for granted that any State had a right to secede at any time, without any condition or limitation. His later,
well-considered report, qualifies that doctrine, as I have just
shown; but at the time the debates occurred in the Virginia convention about adopting the Constitution, it was taken for granted
on all sides that Virginia could withdraw whenever she pleased;
nobody seems to have disputed that. After defending the grant
of power in relation to the militia, Mr. Madison said:

"An observation fell from a gentleman on the same side with
myself, which deserves to be attended to. If we be dissatisfied
with the National Government, if we should choose to renounce
it, this is an additional safeguard to our defense."—Elliot's Debates, vol. 3, p. 414.

Apparently taking it for granted that any State could renounce it when it pleased, and that the militia would already be
organized as a safeguard for its defense. I do not state this as
any particularly pertinent authority, but to show the impressions
that generally prevailed at the time of the adoption of the Constitution; but when the question was subsequently discussed in

1798 and 1799, upon the alien and sedition laws, not only did Mr. Madison make this report, but I have a reference here to a letter of Mr. Jefferson, which I have not on the table, and which I will annex to my speech when printed, showing that he deliberately examined this whole question, and came to the same conclusion.

But, Mr. President, the President of the United States tells us that he does not admit this right to be constitutional; that it is revolutionary. I have endeavored thus far to show that it results from the nature of the compact itself; that it must necessarily be one of those reserved powers which was not abandoned by it, and therefore grows out of the Constitution, and is not in violation of it. If I am asked how I will distinguish this from revolutionary abuse, the answer is prompt and easy. These States, parties to the compact, have a right to withdraw from it, by virtue of its own provisions, when those provisions are violated by the other parties to the compact, when either powers not granted are usurped, or rights are refused that are especially granted to the States. But, sir, there is a large class of powers granted by this Constitution, in the exercise of which a discretion is vested in the General Government, and, in the exercise of that discretion, these admitted powers might be so perverted and abused as to give cause of complaint, and finally, to give the right to revolution; for under those circumstances there would be no other remedy. Now, taking again the supposition of a dominant northern majority in both branches, and of a sectional President and Vice President, the Congress of the United States then, in the exercise of its admitted powers, and the President to back them, could spend the entire revenue of the Confederation in that section which had control, without violating the words or the letter of the Constitution; they could establish forts, light-houses, arsenals, magazines, and all public buildings of every character in the northern States alone, and, utterly refuse any to the South. The President, with the aid of his sectional Senate, could appoint all officers of the Navy and of the Army, all the civil officers of the Government, all the judges, attorneys, and marshals, all collectors and revenue officers, all postmasters—the whole host of public officers he might, under the forms and powers vested by the Constitution, appoint exclusively from the northern States, and quarter them in the southern States, to eat out the substance of our people, and assume an insulting superiority over them. All that might be done in the exercise of admitted constitutional power; and it is just that train of evils, of outrages, of wrongs, of oppressions long continued, that the Declaration of Independence says a people preserves the inherent right of throwing off by destroying their government by revolution. I say, therefore, that I distinguish the rights of the States under the Constitution into two classes: one resulting from the nature of their bargain; if the bargain is broken by the sister States, to consider themselves freed from it on the ground of breach of compact; if the bargain be not broken, but the powers be perverted to their wrong and their oppression, then, whenever that wrong and oppression shall become sufficiently aggravated, the revolutionary right—the last inherent right of man to preserve freedom, property, and safety—arises, and must be exercised, for none other will meet the case.

But, Mr. President, suppose South Carolina to be altogether wrong in her opinion that this compact has been violated to her prejudice; and that she has, therefore, a right to withdraw; take that for granted: what then? You still have the same issue to meet face to face. You must permit her to withdraw in peace, or you must declare war. That is, you must coerce the State itself, or you must permit her to depart in peace. There is nothing whatever that can render for an instant tenable the attempted distinction between coercing a State itself, and coercing all the individuals in the manner now proposed. Let me read a few lines upon that subject. First, Vattel, in speaking of States, and of their rights, and the rights of their citizens, uses this language;

"Every nation that governs itself, under what form soever, without dependence on any foreign Power, is a *sovereign State*. Its rights are naturally the same as those of any other State. Such are the moral persons who live together in a natural society, subject to the law of nations. To give a nation a right to make an immediate figure in this grand society, it is sufficient that it be really sovereign and independent; that is, that it govern itself by its own authority and laws."

Then, he speaks of those qualifications that may exist in relation to this sovereignty; and he says:

"Several sovereign and independent States may unite themselves together by a perpetual confederacy, without ceasing to be, each individually, a perfect State. They will together constitute a federal republic: their joint deliberations will not impair the sovereignty of each member, though they may, in certain respects, put some restraint on the exercise of it, in virtue of voluntary engagements. A person does not cease to be free and independent when he is obliged to fulfill engagements which he has voluntarily contracted."—Vattel's Law of Nations, book 1, chap. 1.

Here, then, we see that, under the law of nations, the State of South Carolina is a sovereign State, independently of all considerations drawn from the language of the Constitution itself, and as such is entitled to be treated, and as such has a right to protect and shield her citizens from all the consequences of obedience to her acts. The honorable Senator from Illinois [Mr. Trumbull] put to my friend from Virginia [Mr. Mason] the question what rebellion was, and put it with a triumphant air, as if he supposed that in case of rebellion the laws of war did not apply; that then it was a mere question of hanging traitors; that there could be no independence of the State of South Carolina, but a mere rebellion of the body of its citizens. Suppose it to be so; what does the law of nations say in that very case?

"When a party is formed in a State who no longer obey the sovereign, and are possessed of sufficient strength to oppose him —or when, in a Republic, the nation is divided into two opposite factions, and both sides take up arms—this is called a *civil war*. Some writers confine this term to a just insurrection of the subjects against their sovereign, to distinguish that lawful resistance from *rebellion*, which is an open and unjust resistance. But what appellation will they give to a war which arises in a republic torn by two factions—or in a monarchy, between two competitors for the crown? Custom appropriates the term 'civil war' to every war between the members of one and the same political society. If it be between part of the citizens on the one side, and the sovereign, with those who continue in obedience to him, on the other, provided the malcontents have any reason for taking up arms, nothing further is required to entitle such disturbance to the name of *civil war,* and not to that of *rebellion.* This latter term is applied only to such an insurrection against lawful authority as is void of all appearance of justice. The sovereign, indeed, never fails to bestow the appellation of *rebels* on all such of his subjects as openly resist him; but when the latter have acquired sufficient strength to give him effectual opposition, and oblige him to carry on the war against them according to the established rules, he must necessarily submit to the use of the term '*civil war.*'

"It is foreign to our purpose in this place to weigh the reasons which may authorize and justify a civil war; we have elsewhere treated of the cases wherein subjects may resist the sovereign. (Book 1, chap. iv.) Setting, therefore, the justice of the cause wholly out of the question, it only remains for us to consider the maxims which ought to be observed in a civil war, and to examine whether the sovereign in particular is, on such an occasion, bound to conform to the established rules of war.

"A civil war breaks the bands of society or government, or at least suspends their force and effect; it produces in the nation two independent parties, who consider each other as enemies, and acknowledge no common judge. These two parties, therefore, must necessarily be considered as thenceforward constituting, at least for a time, two separate bodies, two distinct societies."

How does that square with this notion about coercing individuals and not societies?

"Though one of the parties may have been to blame in breaking the unity of the State and resisting lawful authority, they are not the less divided in fact. Besides, who shall judge them? Who shall pronounce on which side the right or the wrong lies? On earth, they have no common superior. They stand, therefore, in precisely the same predicament as two nations who engage in a contest, and, being unable to come to an agreement, have recourse to arms."—Vattel's Law of Nations, book 3, chap. 18, p. 424.

So much for the question of rebellion under the law of nations. But, sir, I wish to call the attention of gentlemen to an authority which, on the other side, is seldom disputed upon questions of constitutional and international law. I refer to Mr. Webster. On the occasion of the disturbances on the Canada frontier, Alexander McLeod, a British subject, came across the line in time of profound peace, seized a steamboat called the Caroline, killed one of the men on board, moved it from its moorings, set fire to it, and it plunged over the Falls of Niagara. Some years afterwards he was found in the State of New York, arrested, and brought to trial for the crime. The Government of Great Britain communicated to this Government that, as a Government, it assumed the responsibility, and therefore, under the law of nations, required that the individual should be given up. Mr. Fox, in his letter to Mr. Webster, said:

"It would be contrary to the universal practice of civilized nations to fix individual responsibility upon persons who, with the sanction or by the orders of the constituted authorities of a State, engaged in military or naval enterprises in their country's cause; and it is obvious that the introduction of such a principle would aggravate beyond measure the miseries and would frightfully increase the demoralizing effects of wars, by mixing up with national exasperation the ferocity of personal passions, and the cruelty and bitterness of individual revenge.

"Her Majesty's Government cannot believe the Government of the United States can really intend to set an example so fraught with evil to the community of nations, and the direct tendency of which must be to bring back into the practice of modern war atrocities which civilization and Christianity have long since banished."—Works of Daniel Webster, vol. 6, p. 248.

To that, Mr. Webster made reply:

"The communication of the fact that the destruction of the Caroline was an act of public force by the British authorities, being formally made to the Government of the United States by Mr. Fox's note, the case assumes a decided aspect.

"The Government of the United States entertains no doubt, that after this avowal of the transaction as a public transaction, authorized and undertaken by the British authorities, individuals concerned in it ought not, by the principles of public law and the

general usage of civilized States, to be holden personally responsible in the ordinary tribunals of law for their participation in
it. And the President presumes that it can hardly be necessary
to say that the American people, not distrustful of their ability
to redress public wrongs by public means, cannot desire the punishment of individuals when the act complained of is declared to
have been an act of the Government itself."—Works of Daniel
Webster, vol. 6, p. 253.

Instructions to this effect were accordingly sent to the Attorney General. But Mr. Webster was subsequently attacked in
the Senate for his conduct in relation to this negotiation; and
he delivered a very elaborate speech in defense of the treaty of
Washington. This brings me to the point which I suggested to
the honorable Senator from Wisconsin, when he told us the other day that each citizen owed allegiance to two sovereignties,
and that he was bound at his peril to distinguish between their
orders; that he could commit treason, under the Constitution,
against the United States, and that the Constitution also recognizes that he could commit treason against the State; and yet the
honorable Senator went so far as to say, that if his State ordered him to do a thing, and the United States forbade him from
doing it, both under the penalty of death, it was his misfortune
to be placed in such a position that he might be hanged or executed by either, and under the law of nations have no redress,
no escape. I answer him in the language of Mr. Webster on
that very subject:

"In the next place, and on the other hand, General Harrison
was of the opinion that the arrest and detention of McLeod were
contrary to the law of nations. McLeod was a soldier, acting
under the authority of his Government, and obeying orders
which he was bound to obey. It was absurd to say that a soldier, who must obey orders or be shot, may still be hanged if
he does obey them."—Works of Daniel Webster, vol. 5, page
123.

I do not use the term "absurd"; it is Mr. Webster who uses it.
But perhaps gentlemen will say: Mr. Webster says that he was
acting under the authority of his Government, and obeying orders which he was bound to obey; but we deny that a citizen of
South Carolina is bound to obey the orders of his Government.

To that I reply, in the language of Vattel, that no citizen of any State has the right to question that; that it is a principle of the law of nations, that the citizen owes obedience to the command of his sovereign, and he cannot enter into the question whether the sovereign's order is lawful or unlawful, except at his peril. If his sovereign engages in war—if his State declares her independence—he is bound by the action of his State, and has no authority to control it. Why, Mr. President, how idle and absurd would be any other proposition! How idle and absurd to suppose that you can, in principle and in practice, separate each particular individual of a State and make him responsible for the collective act of his Government—each agent in turn. The honorable Senator from Ohio [Mr. Pugh], who delivered to us the other day so magnificent and patriotic an appeal, read you the language of the different Presidents of the United States upon that subject, and cited to you the language of Mr. Adams, in which he said that he had been forced to avoid making use of the power of the Federal Government, in the State of Georgia, against certain surveyors acting in defiance of the Federal authority, because he understood that they were ordered so to act by their State government, and believed themselves bound to obey the order.

Sir, if there was anything in this idea in theory, you might reduce it to practice; but what can be more absurd, more vague, more fanciful, than the suggestions put out by gentlemen here? You are going now, observe, to declare no war and to coerce no State; you are simply going to execute the laws of the United States against individuals in the State of South Carolina. That is your proposition. Is it serious? One gentleman says he will hang for treason. Ah, where is the marshal to seize, and where is the court to try, where is the district attorney to prosecute, and where is the jury to convict? Are you going to establish all these by arms? Perhaps you tell me you will remove him elsewhere for trial. Not so; our fathers have not left our liberties so unguarded and so unprotected as that. The Constitution originally provided that no man could be brought to trial for an offense out of the State where he committed it. The fathers were not satisfied with it, and they added an amendment that he should not be brought to trial out of the district even in which he had committed it. You cannot take him out of the district. You have got no judge, no marshal, no attorney, no jurors, there; and suppose you had: who is to adjudge, who is to convict? His fellow-citizens, unanimous in opinion with him, determine that he has done his duty, and has committed no guilt. That is the way you are going to execute the laws against treason!

What next? Oh, no, says the Senator from Ohio [Mr. Wade], that is what we will do; we will execute the laws to collect revenue by blockading your ports, and stopping them up. At first blush this seems a very amusing mode of collecting revenue in South Carolina, by allowing no vessels to come in on which revenue can be collected. It is the strangest of all possible fancies that that is the way of collecting revenue there, of enforcing the laws in the State against individuals. But first you are to have no war. And what is blockade? Does any man suppose that blockade can exist by a nation at peace with another; that it is a peace power; that it can be exercised on any other ground than that you are at war with the party whose ports you blockade, and that you make proclamation to all the Governments of the earth that their vessels shall not be authorized to enter into these ports, because you are reducing your enemy by the use of regular constituted, recognized, warlike means? Oh, but perhaps it is not a blockade that you will have; you will have an embargo, that is what you mean. We are guarded here again. The Constitution heads you off at every step in this Quixotic attempt to go into a State to exercise your laws against her whole citizens without declaring war or coercing the State. You cannot embargo the ports of one State without embargoing all your ports; you cannot shut up one without shutting up all; the Constitution of the United States expressly forbids it. If your blockade or your embargo were a peaceful measure, you are prohibited by the very words of the Constitution itself from forcing a vessel bound to or from one State to enter or clear or pay duties in another, or from making any regulations of commerce whatever, giving any preference to the ports of one State over the ports of another; and you have no more right to blockade or close the ports of South Carolina by embargo, even by act of Congress, than you have to declare that a sovereign State shall have no right to have more than one Senator on this floor. Your blockade is impracticable, unconstitutional, out of the power of the President.

What is this idea of executing the laws by armed force against individuals? Gentlemen seem to suppose—and they argue upon the supposition—that it is possible, under the Constitution of the United States, for the President to determine when laws are not obeyed and to force obedience by the sword, without the interposition of courts of justice. Does any man have such an idle conceit as that? Does he suppose that, by any possible construction, the power of the Federal Congress to call out the militia, and to use the Army and the Navy to suppress insurrection and to execute the laws, means that the President is to do it of his own volition and without the intervention of the civil power? The honorable Senator from Tennessee [Mr. Johnson], the other day, called upon us to look at the example of Washington, who put down rebellion in Pennsylvania. He said well that he was no lawyer, when he cited that General Washington called forth the militia of Pennsylvania and of other States to aid in executing the laws, upon a requisition by a judge of the Supreme Court of the United States certifying to him that the marshal was unable to carry out the judgments of the court.

Mr. Johnson, of Tennessee. I understood that very well.

Mr. Benjamin. Then what on earth do you mean by saying that you will go into a State and execute the laws of the United States against individuals, without a judge or jury there, without a marshal or attorney, with nobody to declare the violation of law, or to order its execution before you attempt to enforce it? The Senator may not have intended to assume such a position. He has been unfortunate in the impressions that he has produced upon the country.

But, sir, other means are suggested. We cannot go to war; we are not going to war; we are not going to coerce a State. "Why," says the Senator from Illinois, "who talks of coercing a State; you are attempting to breed confusion in the public mind; you are attempting to impose upon people by perverting the question; we only mean to execute the laws against individuals." Again, I say, where will be the civil process which must precede the action of the military force? Surely, surely it is not at this day that we are to argue that neither the President, nor the President and Congress combined, are armed with the powers of a military despot to carry out the laws, without the intervention of the courts, according to their own caprice and their own discretion, to judge when laws are violated, to convict for the violation, to pronounce sentence, and to execute it. You can do nothing of the kind with your military force.

But it is suggested, and the President is weak enough to yield to the suggestion, that you will collect your revenue by force— by the action of the power of the Federal Government on individuals. Has anybody followed this out practically? Is it possible? I remember that Mr. Webster once, as a mere figure of rhetoric, in his debate on the Foot resolutions, used some such threat as this against this same State of South Carolina; but it was looked upon as a mere beautiful figure of speech. No man ever paid any attention to it as really a threat of the use of constitutional power. You will put your collector on board of a vessel in the harbor. It shall be a man-of-war; it is in the port; and there you will make everybody pay duties before the goods are landed. That is the next proposition, that nobody sees any practical difficulty about. But, sir, it is totally impracticable— totally impossible. Take a case. A citizen of New York owns a vessel which loads with a cargo of assorted merchandise, part free, part owing duty, and consigns it to Charleston. He enters the harbor. Under the law he is obliged to make entry of his vessel, to produce his manifest, to go through certain other formalities. He goes on board your ship-of-war, sees the collector, and complies with the orders. What next? There are no duties paid yet, and the man who has a right to the free goods has no duties to pay. You cannot prevent him from going to the wharf and discharging them. There is no law to be executed there against an individual. But I will take it for granted that the whole cargo is a duty-paying cargo, and all belongs to one man, who does not mean to pay your duties. You are no better off. The man declines to enter his cargo. What is the law? The master of the vessel wants to go away. He is entitled by law to report to the collector that he is ready to deliver his cargo, that nobody is there to enter it, and that he demands that his cargo be discharged, and put in public store; and under that he may go upon his new voyage; and you cannot change that, unless you change the law for all the ports of the United States. Or he may go further; the importer may go to the collector, and say, "I want to enter my cargo in warehouse;" and he gives a bond signed by himself and a solvent fellow-citizen, that they will pay the duty when he takes the goods out of the warehouse. Then you must let him put those goods into the custom-house warehouse; and you cannot change that law either, without changing it for the whole United States; because you cannot, under the Constitution, by any regulation of commerce, give any preference to the ports of one State over those of another.

Mind you, you are at peace; you are not coercing a State; you are merely executing the laws against individuals! You cannot do it without breaking up your whole warehouse system; you cannot do it without breaking up your whole commercial system in every port of the Confederacy. Your goods are ashore; they are in Government warehouses; but you have not got the duties. A rush upon the warehouse, and the goods are taken out. You have got a bond, but you have no court to sue it in; and if you had, you would have no jury to forfeit it, because the jury would be told by the court, or at all events by the lawyers who defended the defendant, that the Government had no right to collect that bond; that it was a usurpation which required him to give the bond.

This whole scheme, this whole fancy, that you can treat the act of a sovereign State, issued in an authoritative form, and in her collective capacity as a State, as being utterly out of existence; that you can treat the State as still belonging collectively to the Confederacy, and that you can proceed, without a solitary Federal officer in the State, to enforce your laws against private individuals, is as vain, as idle, and delusive, as any dream that ever entered into the head of man. The thing cannot be done. It is only asserted for the purpose of covering up the true question, than which there is no other: you must acknowledge the independence of the seceding State, or reduce her to subjection by war.

Now, Mr. President, I desire not to enter in any detail into the dreary catalogue of wrongs and outrages by which South Carolina defends her position; that she has withdrawn from this Union because she has a constitutional right to do so, by reason of prior violations of the compact by her sister States. Before, however, making any statement—that statement to which we have been challenged, and which I shall make in but very few words—of the wrongs under which the South is now suffering, and for which she seeks redress, as the difficulty seems to arise chiefly from a difference in our construction of the Constitution, I desire to read one more, and a last, citation from Vattel, giving a rule in relation to the construction of treaties between sovereigns, and compacts between States. Among other things, he says:

"The rules that establish a lawful interpretation of treaties are sufficiently important to be made the subject of a distinct chapter. For the present, let us simply observe that an evidently false interpretation is the grossest imaginable violation of the faith of treaties. He that resorts to such an expedient, either imprudently sports with that sacred faith, or sufficiently evinces his inward conviction of the degree of moral turpitude annexed to the violation of it; he wishes to act a dishonest part, and yet preserve the character of an honest man; he is a puritanical impostor who aggravates his crime by the addition of a detestable hypocrisy. Grotius quotes several instances of evidently false interpretations put upon treaties. The Plateans having promised the Thebans to restore their prisoners, restored them after they had put them to death. Pericles, having promised to spare the lives of such of the enemy as laid down their arms, ordered all those to be killed that had iron clasps to their cloaks. A Roman general having agreed with Antiochus to restore him half his fleet, caused each of the ships to be sawed in two. All these interpretations are as fraudulent as that of Rhadamistus, who, according to Tacitus' account, having sworn to Mithridates that he would not employ either poison or steel against him, caused him to be smothered under a heap of clothes."—Vattel's Law of Nations, book 2, chap. 15, p. 234.

There is the text; now the commentary. You, Senators of the Republican party, assert, and your people whom you represent assert, that under a just and fair interpretation of the Federal Constitution, it is right that you deny that our slaves, which directly and indirectly involve a value of more than four thousand million dollars, are property at all, or entitled to protection in Territories owned by the common Government. You assume the interpretation that it is right to encourage, by all possible means, directly and indirectly, the robbery of this property, and to legislate so as to render its recovery as difficult and dangerous as possible; that it is right and proper and justifiable, under the Constitution, to prevent our mere transit across a sister State, to embark with our property on a lawful voyage, without being openly despoiled of it. You assert, and practice upon the assertion, that it is right to hold us up to the ban of mankind— in speech, writing, and print, with every possible appliance of publicity—as thieves, robbers, murderers, villains, and criminals of the blackest dye, because we continue to own property which we owned at the time that we all signed the compact; that it is right that we should be exposed to spend our treasure in the purchase, or shed our blood in the conquest, of foreign territory, with no right to enter it for settlement without leaving behind our most valuable property, under penalty of its confiscation. You practically interpret this instrument to me that it is eminently in accordance with the assurance that our tranquillity and welfare were to be preserved and promoted; that our sister States should combine to prevent our growth and development; that they should surround us with a cordon of hostile communities, for the express and avowed purpose of accumulating in dense masses, and within restricted limits, a population which you believe to be dangerous, and thereby force the sacrifice of property nearly sufficient in value to pay the public debt of every nation in Europe.

This is the construction of the instrument that was to preserve our security, promote our welfare, and which we only signed on your assurance that that was its object. You tell us that this is a fair construction—not all, some say one thing, some another; but you act, or your people do, upon this principle. You do not propose to enter into our States, you say, and what do we complain of? You do not pretend to enter into our States to kill or destroy our institutions by force. Oh, no. You imitate the faith of Rhadamistus; you propose simply to close us in an embrace that will suffocate us. You do not propose to fell the tree; you promised not. You merely propose to girdle it, that it dies. And then when we tell you that we did not understand this bargain this way, that your acting upon it in this spirit releases us from the obligations that accompany it; that under no circumstances can we consent to live together under that interpretation, and say, "we will go from you; let us go in peace;" we are answered by your leading spokesmen: "Oh, no; you cannot do that; we have no objection to it personally, but we are bound by our oaths; if you attempt it, your people will be hanged for treason. We have examined this Constitution thoroughly; we have searched it out with a fair spirit, and we can find warrant in it for releasing ourselves from the obligation of giving you any of its benefits, but our oaths force us to tax you; we can dispense with everything else; but our consciences, we protest upon our souls, will be sorely worried if we do not take your money." That is the proposition of the honorable Senator from Ohio, in plain language. He can avoid everything else under the Constitution, in the way of secession; but how is he to get rid of the duty of taking our money he cannot see.

Now, Senators, this picture is not placed before you with any idea that it will act upon any one of you, or change your views, or alter your conduct. All hope of that is gone. Our committee has reported this morning that no possible scheme of adjustment can be devised by them all combined. The day for the adjustment has passed. If you would give it now, you are too late.

And now, Senators, within a few weeks we part to meet as Senators in one common council chamber of the nation no more forever. We desire, we beseech you, let this parting be in peace. I conjure you to indulge in no vain delusion that duty or conscience, interest or honor, imposes upon you the necessity of invading our States or shedding the blood of our people. You have no possible justification for it. I trust it is in no craven spirit, and with no sacrifice of the honor or dignity of my own State, that I make this last appeal, but from far higher and holier motives. If, however, it shall prove vain, if you are resolved to pervert the Government framed by the fathers for the protection of our rights into an instrument for subjugating and enslaving us, then, appealing to the Supreme Judge of the universe for the rectitude of our intentions, we must meet the issue that

you force upon us as best becomes freemen defending all that
is dear to man.

What may be the fate of this horrible contest, no man can
tell, none pretend to foresee; but this much I will say: The fortunes of war may be adverse to our arms; you may carry desolation into our peaceful land, and with torch and fire you may
set our cities in flames; you may even emulate the atrocities of
those who, in the war of the Revolution, hounded on the blood-
thirsty savage to attack upon the defenseless frontier; you may,
under the protection of your advancing armies, give shelter to
the furious fanatics who desire, and profess to desire, nothing
more than to add all the horrors of a servile insurrection to the
calamities of civil war; you may do all this—and more too, if
more there be—but you never can subjugate us; you never can
convert the free sons of the soil into vassals, paying tribute to
your power; and you never, never can degrade them to the level
of an inferior and servile race. Never! Never!

JUDAH P. BENJAMIN

FAREWELL TO THE SENATE

Speech in the United States Senate, February 4, 1861, on the Occasion of His Withdrawal from the Senate

[By Ordinance, Louisiana seceded from the Union on January 26, 1861. On February 4 a copy of this Ordinance was read by the Secretary of the Senate, after which Senators Slidell and Benjamin made their farewell addresses.]

Mr. President, if we were engaged in the performance of our accustomed legislative duties, I might well rest content with the simple statement of my concurrence in the remarks just made by my colleague. Deeply impressed, however, with the solemnity of the occasion, I cannot remain insensible to the duty of recording, amongst the authentic reports of your proceedings, the expression of my conviction that the State of Louisiana has judged and acted well and wisely in this crisis of her destiny.

Sir, it has been urged, on more than one occasion, in the discussions here and elsewhere, that Louisiana stands on an exceptional footing. It has been said that whatever may be the rights of the States that were original parties to the Constitution—even granting *their* right to resume, for sufficient cause, those restricted powers which they delegated to the General Government in trust for their own use and benefit—still Louisiana can have no such right, because *she* was acquired by purchase. Gentlemen have not hesitated to speak of the sovereign States formed out of the territory ceded by France as property bought with the money of the United States, belonging to them as purchasers; and, although they have not carried their doctrine to its legitimate results, I must conclude that they also mean to assert, on the same principle, *the right of selling for a price that which for a price was bought.*

I shall not pause to comment on this repulsive dogma of a party which asserts the right of property in free-born white men, in order to reach its cherished object of destroying the right of

[94]

property in slave-born black men—still less shall I detain the Senate in pointing out how shadowy the distinction between the condition of the servile African and that to which the white freemen of my State would be reduced, if it indeed be true that they are bound to this Government by ties that cannot be legitimately dissevered, without the consent of that very majority which wields its powers for their oppression. I simply deny the fact on which the argument is founded. I deny that the province of Louisiana, or the people of Louisiana, were ever conveyed to the United States for a price as property that could be bought or sold at will. Without entering into the details of the negotiation, the archives of our State department show the fact to be, that although the domain, the public lands, and other property of France in the ceded province, were conveyed by absolute title to the United States, *the sovereignty was not conveyed otherwise than in trust.*

A hundred fold, sir, has the Government of the United States been reimbursed by the sales of public property, of public lands, for the price of the acquisition; but not with the fidelity of the honest trustee has it discharged the obligations as regards the sovereignty.

I have said that the Government assumed to act as trustee or guardian of the people of the ceded province, and covenanted to transfer to them the sovereignty thus held in trust for their use and benefit, as soon as they were capable of exercising it. What is the express language of the treaty?

"The inhabitants of the ceded Territory *shall be incorporated in the Union* of the United States, and admitted *as soon as possible,* according to the principles of the Federal Constitution, to the enjoyment of *all* the rights, advantages, and immunities of citizens of the United States; and in the mean time they shall be maintained and *protected* in the enjoyment of their liberty, *property,* and the religion which they profess."

And, sir, as if to mark the true nature of the cession in a manner too significant to admit of misconstruction, the treaty stipulates no price; and the sole consideration for the conveyance, as stated on its face, is the desire to afford a strong proof of the friendship of France for the United States. By the terms of a separate convention stipulating the payment of a sum of money, the precaution is again observed of stating that the payment is to be made, not as a consideration or a price or a condition precedent of the cession, but it is carefully distinguished as being a consequence of the cession. It was by words thus studiously chosen, sir, that James Monroe and Thomas Jefferson marked their understanding of a contract now misconstrued as being a bargain and sale of sovereignty over freemen. With what indignant scorn would those staunch advocates of the inherent right of self-government have repudiated the slavish doctrine now deduced from their action!

How were the obligations of this treaty fulfilled? That Louisiana at that date contained slaves held as property by her people through the whole length of the Mississippi valley—that those people had an unrestricted right of settlement with their slaves under legal protection throughout the entire ceded province—no man has ever yet had the hardihood to deny. Here is a treaty promise to *protect* that property, that *slave property,* in that *Territory, before* it should become a State. That this promise was openly violated, in the adjustment forced upon the South at the time of the admission of Missouri, is matter of recorded history. The perspicuous and unanswerable exposition of Mr. Justice Catron, in the opinion delivered by him in the Dred Scott case, will remain through all time as an ample vindication of this assertion.

If, then, sir, the people of Louisiana had a right, which Congress could not deny, of the admission into the Union with *all* the rights of *all* the citizens of the United States, it is in vain that the partisans of the right of the majority to govern the minority with despotic control, attempt to establish a distinction, to her prejudice, between her rights and those of any other State. The only distinction which really exists is this: that she can point to a breach of treaty stipulations expressly guarantying her rights, as a wrong superadded to those which have impelled a number of her sister States to the assertion of their independence.

The rights of Louisiana as a sovereign State, are those of Virginia; no more, no less. Let those who deny her right to resume delegated powers, successfully refute the claim of Virginia to the same right, in spite of her express reservation made and notified to her sister States when she consented to enter the Union. And, sir, permit me to say that, of all the causes which justify the action of the southern States, I know none of greater gravity and more alarming magnitude than that now developed of the denial of the right of secession. A pretension so monstrous as that which perverts a restricted agency, constituted by sovereign States for common purposes, into the unlimited despotism of the majority, and denies all legitimate escape from such despotism, when powers not delegated are usurped, converts the whole constitutional fabric into the secure abode of lawless tyranny, and degrades sovereign States into provincial dependencies.

It is said that the right of secession, if conceded, makes of our Government a mere rope of sand; that to assert its existence imputes to the framers of the Constitution the folly of planting the seeds of death in that which was designed for perpetual existence. If this imputation were true, sir, it would merely prove that their offspring was not exempt from that mortality which is the common lot of all that is not created by higher than human power. But it is not so, sir. Let facts answer theory. For two thirds of a century this right has been known by many of the States to be, at all times, within their power. Yet, up to the present period, when its exercise has become indispensable to a people menaced with absolute extermination, there have been but two instances in which it has been even threatened seriously: the first, when Massachusetts led the New England States in an attempt to escape from the dangers of our last war with Great Britain; the second, when the same State proposed to secede on account of the admission of Texas as a new State into the Union.

Sir, in the language of our declaration of secession from Great Britain it is stated, as an established truth, that "all experience has shown that mankind are more disposed to suffer while evils are sufferable, than to right themselves by abolishing the forms to which they have been accustomed." And nothing can be more obvious to the calm and candid observer of passing events than that the disruption of the Confederacy has been due, in great measure, not to the existence, but to the denial of this right. Few candid men would refuse to admit that the Republicans of the North would have been checked in their mad career, had they been convinced of the existence of this right, and the intention to assert it. The very knowledge of its existence, by preventing occurrences which alone could prompt its exercise, would have rendered it a most efficient instrument in the preservation of the Union. But, sir, if the fact were otherwise—if all the teachings of experience were reversed—better, far better, a rope of sand, ay, the flimsiest gossamer that ever glistened in the morning dew, than chains of iron, and shackles of steel; better the wildest anarchy, with the hope, the chance, of one hour's inspiration of the glorious breath of freedom, than ages of the hopeless bondage and oppression to which our enemies would reduce us.

We are told that the laws must be enforced; that the revenues must be collected; that the South is in rebellion without cause, and that her citizens are traitors.

Rebellion! The very word is a confession; an avowal of tyranny, outrage, and oppression. It is taken from the despot's code, and has no terror for other than slavish souls. When, sir, did millions of people, as a single man, rise in organized, deliberate, unimpassioned rebellion against justice, truth, and honor? Well did a great Englishman exclaim on a similar occasion:

"You might as well tell me that they rebelled against the light of heaven; that they rejected the fruits of the earth. Men do not war against their benefactors; they are not mad enough to repel the instincts of self-preservation. I pronounce fearlessly that no intelligent people ever rose, or ever will rise, against a sincere, rational, and benevolent authority. No people were ever born blind. Infatuation is not a law of human nature. When there is a revolt by a free people, with the common consent of all classes of society, there must be a *criminal* against whom that revolt is aimed."

Traitors! Treason! Ay, sir, the people of the South imitate and glory in just such treason as glowed in the soul of Hampden; just such treason as leaped in living flame from the impassioned lips of Henry; just such treason as encircles with a sacred halo the undying name of Washington!

You will enforce the laws. You want to know if we have a Government; if you have any authority to collect revenue; to wring tribute from an unwilling people? Sir, humanity desponds, and all the inspiring hopes of her progressive improvement vanish into empty air at the reflections which crowd on the mind at hearing repeated, with aggravated enormity, the sentiments against which a Chatham launched his indignant thunders nearly a century ago. The very words of Lord North and his royal master are repeated here in debate, not as quotations, but as the spontaneous outpourings of a spirit the counterpart of theirs.

In Lord North's speech, on the destruction of the tea in Boston harbor, he said:

"We are no longer to dispute between legislation and taxation; *we are now only to consider whether or not we have any authority there.* It is very clear we have none, if we suffer the property of our subjects to be destroyed. We must punish, control, or yield to them."

And thereupon he proposed to close the port of Boston, just as the Representatives of Massachusetts now propose to close the port of Charleston, *in order to determine whether or not you have any authority there.* It is thus that, in 1861, Boston is to pay her debt of gratitude to Charleston, which, in the days of her struggle, proclaimed the generous sentiment that "the cause of Boston was the cause of Charleston." Who, after this, will say that Republics are ungrateful? Well, sir, the statesmen of Great Britain answered to Lord North's appeal, "yield." The courtiers and the politicians said, "punish," "control." The result is known. History gives you the lesson. Profit by its teachings.

So, sir, in the address sent under the royal sign-manual to Parliament, it was invoked to take measures "for better securing the execution of the laws," and acquiesced in the suggestion. Just as now, a senile Executive, under the sinister influence of insane counsels, is proposing, with your assent, "to secure the better execution of the laws," by blockading ports and turning upon the people of the States the artillery which they provided at their own expense for their own defense, and intrusted to you

and to him for that and for no other purpose. Nay, even in
States that are now exercising the undoubted and most precious
rights of a free people; where there is no secession; where the
citizens are assembling to hold peaceful elections for considering what course of action is demanded in this dread crisis by
a due regard for their own safety and their own liberty; ay,
even in Virginia herself, the people are to cast their suffrages
beneath the undisguised menaces of a frowning fortress. Cannon are brought to bear on their homes, and parricidal hands are
preparing weapons for rending the bosom of the mother of
Washington.

Sir, when Great Britain proposed to exact tribute from your
fathers against their will, Lord Chatham said:

"Whatever is a man's own is absolutely his own; no man
has a right to take it from him without his consent. Whoever
attempts to do it, attempts an injury. Whoever does it, commits a robbery. You have no right to tax America. I rejoice
that America has resisted." * * * "Let the sovereign authority of this country over the colonies be asserted in as strong
terms as can be devised, and be made to extend to every point
of legislation whatever, so that we may bind their trade, confine
their manufactures, and exercise every power, *except that of
taking money out of their own pockets without their consent.*"

It was reserved for the latter half of the nineteenth century,
and for the Congress of a Republic of freemen, to witness the
willing abnegation of all power, save that of exacting tribute.
What imperial Britain, with the haughtiest pretensions of unlimited power over dependent colonies, could not even attempt
without the vehement protest of her greatest statesmen, is to be
enforced in aggravated form, if you can enforce it, against independent States.

Good God! sir, since when has the necessity arisen of recalling to American legislators the lessons of freedom taught in
lisping childhood by loving mothers; that pervade the atmosphere we have breathed from infancy; that so form part of
our very being, that in their absence we would lose the consciousness of our own identity? Heaven be praised that all
have not forgotten them; that when we shall have left these

familiar Halls, and when force bills, blockades, armies, navies, and all the accustomed coercive appliances of despots shall be proposed and advocated, voices shall be heard from this side' of the Chamber that will make its very roof resound with the indignant clamor of outraged freedom. Methinks I still hear ringing in my ears the appeal of the eloquent Representative [Hon. George H. Pendleton, of Ohio] whose northern home looks down on Kentucky's fertile borders: *"Armies, money, blood, cannot maintain this Union; justice, reason, peace, may."*

And now to you, Mr. President, and to my brother Senators, on all sides of this Chamber, I bid a respectful farewell; with many of those from whom I have been radically separated in political sentiment, my personal relations have been kindly, and have inspired me with a respect and esteem that I shall not willingly forget; with those around me from the southern States, I part as men part from brothers on the eve of a temporary absence, with a cordial pressure of the hand and a smiling assurance of the speedy renewal of sweet intercourse around the family hearth. But to you, noble and generous friends, who, born beneath other skies, possess hearts that beat in sympathy with ours; to you, who, solicited and assailed by motives the most powerful that could appeal to selfish natures, have nobly spurned them all; to you who, in our behalf, have bared your breasts to the fierce beatings of the storm, and made willing sacrifice of life's most glittering prizes in your devotion to constitutional liberty; to you, who have made our cause your cause,' and from many of whom I feel I part forever, what shall I, can I say? Nought, I know and feel, is needed for myself; but this I will say for the people in whose name I speak to-day: whether prosperous or adverse fortunes await you, one priceless treasure is yours—the assurance that an entire people honor your names, and hold them in grateful and affectionate memory. But with still sweeter and more touching return shall your unselfish devotion be rewarded. When, in after days, the story of the present shall be written; when history shall have passed her stern sentence on the erring men who have driven their unoffending brethren from the shelter of their common home, your names will derive fresh luster from the contrast; and when your children shall hear repeated the familiar tale, it will be with glowing cheek and kindling eye, their very souls will stand a-tiptoe as their sires are named, and they will glory in their lineage from men of spirit as generous and of patriotism as high-hearted as ever illustrated or adorned the American Senate.

ABRAHAM LINCOLN

THE GETTYSBURG ADDRESS

ADDRESS AT THE DEDICATION OF THE GETTYSBURG NATIONAL
CEMETERY, NOVEMBER 19, 1863

[This masterpiece among the world's orations was thought by Lincoln, before he delivered it, to be a "flat failure." "The people won't like it," he said. There were three versions of the speech; the third, printed below, being the one finally approved by Lincoln.]

Fourscore and seven years ago our fathers brought forth on this continent a new nation, conceived in liberty, and dedicated to the proposition that all men are created equal.

Now we are engaged in a great civil war, testing whether that nation, or any nation so conceived and so dedicated, can long endure. We are met on a great battle-field of that war. We have come to dedicate a portion of that field as a final resting-place for those who here gave their lives that that nation might live. It is altogether fitting and proper that we should do this.

But, in a larger sense, we cannot dedicate—we cannot consecrate—we cannot hallow—this ground. The brave men, living and dead, who struggled here, have consecrated it far above our poor power to add or detract. The world will little note nor long remember what we say here, but it can never forget what they did here. It is for us, the living, rather, to be dedicated here to the unfinished work which they who fought here have thus far so nobly advanced. It is rather for us to be here dedicated to the great task remaining before us—that from these honored dead we take increased devotion to that cause for which they gave the last full measure of devotion; that we here highly resolve that these dead shall not have died in vain; that this nation, under God, shall have a new birth of freedom; and that government of the people, by the people, and for the people, shall not perish from the earth.

SUSAN B. ANTHONY

THE ENFRANCHISEMENT OF WOMEN

Speech in the United States District Court, Northern
District of New York, Canandaigua, New York,
June 18, 1873

[Susan Brownell Anthony was born in South Adams, Massachusetts, on February 15, 1820. In 1826 her family moved to Battensville, New York. After studying in private schools, she became a teacher, and from 1846 to 1849 was head of the Female Department of Canajoharie Academy. In 1850 her home near Rochester, New York, became a meeting place for reformers, among whom were Amelia Bloomer, Lucretia Mott, Lucy Stone, and Elizabeth Cady Stanton. She organized the Woman's State Temperance Society of New York, and was a leader in the movement for the abolition of slavery. She was the first militant woman suffragist, and in 1868, with Mrs. Stanton and Parker Pillsbury, published *The Revolution*, a periodical devoted to woman suffrage. She became chairman of the Executive Committee of the National Woman Suffrage Association when it was formed in 1869, and was President of the National American Woman Suffrage Association from 1892 to 1900. She died in Rochester, New York, on March 13, 1906.

In 1872 Miss Anthony and fourteen other women carried out a plan to test their right to vote, relying on section 1 of the Fourteenth Article of the Amendments to the United States Constitution, which reads: "All persons born or naturalized in the United States, and subject to the jurisdiction thereof, are citizens of the United States and of the State wherein they reside. No State shall make or enforce any law which shall abridge the privileges or immunities of citizens of the United States; nor shall any State deprive any person of life, liberty, or property, without due process of law; nor deny to any person within its jurisdiction the equal protection of the laws." Having previously registered, Miss Anthony and her companions voted at Rochester, New York, in the congressional election of November, 1872. Two weeks later she was indicted under the United States Act of May 31, 1870, for having illegally voted. Her trial was deferred and she voted again in the city elections of the following March.

In the trial before Judge Ward Hunt and a jury, on June 17–18, 1873 (11 Blatchford, 200), she was ably defended by Henry R. Selden and John Van Voorhis. After argument, the Court directed that the jury find a verdict of guilty. A motion for a new trial was denied, and then the colloquy occurred which is printed below. Miss Anthony never paid her fine.]

Mr. Justice Hunt. The prisoner will stand up. Has the prisoner anything to say why sentence shall not be pronounced?

Miss Anthony. Yes, your Honor, I have many things to say; for in your ordered verdict of guilty, you have trampled under foot every vital principle of our government. My natural rights, my civil rights, my political rights, my judicial rights, are all alike ignored. Robbed of the fundamental privilege of citizenship, I am degraded from the status of a citizen to that of a subject; and not only myself individually, but all of my sex are, by your Honor's verdict, doomed to political subjection under this, so-called, form of government.

Mr. Justice Hunt. The Court cannot listen to a rehearsal of arguments the prisoner's counsel has already consumed three hours in presenting.

Miss Anthony. May it please your Honor, I am not arguing the question, but simply stating the reasons why sentence cannot in justice be pronounced against me. Your denial of my citizen's right to vote, is the denial of my right of consent as one of the governed, the denial of my right of representation as one of the taxed, the denial of my right to a trial by a jury of my peers as an offender against law, therefore the denial of my sacred rights to life, liberty, property and—

Mr. Justice Hunt. The Court cannot allow the prisoner to go on.

Miss Anthony. But your Honor will not deny me this one and only poor privilege of protest against this high-handed outrage upon my citizen's rights. May it please the Court to remember that since the day of my arrest last November, this is the first time that either myself or any person of my disfranchised class has been allowed a word of defense before judge or jury.

Mr. Justice Hunt. The prisoner must sit down—the Court cannot allow it.

Miss Anthony. All my prosecutors, from the Eighth ward corner grocery politician, who entered the complaint, to the United States Marshal, Commissioner, District Attorney, District Judge, your Honor on the bench, not one is my peer, but each and all are my political sovereigns; and had your Honor submitted my case to the jury, as was clearly your duty, even then I should have had just cause of protest, for not one of those men was my peer; but, native or foreign born, white or black, rich or poor, educated or ignorant, awake or asleep, sober or drunk, each and every man of them was my political superior; hence, in no sense, my peer. Even, under such circumstances, a commoner of England, tried before a jury of Lords, would have far less cause to complain than should I, a woman, tried before a jury of men. Even my counsel, the Hon. Henry B. Selden, who has argued my cause so ably, so earnestly, so unanswerably before your Honor, is my political sovereign. Precisely as no disfranchised person is entitled to sit upon a jury, and no woman is entitled to the franchise, so, none but a regularly admitted lawyer is allowed to practice in the courts, and no woman can gain admission to the bar—hence, jury, judge, counsel, must all be of the superior class.

Mr. Justice Hunt. The Court must insist—the prisoner has been tried according to the established forms of law.

Miss Anthony. Yes, your Honor, but by forms of law all made by men, interpreted by men, administered by men, in favor of men, and against women; and hence, your Honor's ordered verdict of guilty, against a United States citizen for the exercise of that citizen's right to vote simply because that citizen was a woman and not a man. But yesterday the same man-made forms of law declared it a crime punishable with $1,000 fine and six months' imprisonment, for you, or me, or any of us, to give a cup of cold water, a crust of bread, or a night's shelter to a panting fugitive as he was tracking his way to Canada. And every man or woman in whose veins coursed a drop of human sympathy violated that wicked law, reckless of consequences, and was justified in so doing. As then, the slaves who got their freedom must take it over, or under, or through the unjust forms of law, precisely so, now, must women, to get their right to a voice in this government, take it; and I have taken mine, and mean to take it at every possible opportunity.

Mr. Justice Hunt. The Court orders the prisoner to sit down. It will not allow another word.

Miss Anthony. When I was brought before your Honor for trial, I hoped for a broad and liberal interpretation of the Constitution and its recent amendments, that should declare all United States citizens under its protecting ægis—that should declare equality of rights the national guaranty to all persons born or naturalized in the United States. But failing to get this justice—failing, even, to get a trial by a jury not of my peers—I ask not leniency at your hands—but rather the full rigors of the law.

Mr. Justice Hunt. The Court must insist—

(Miss Anthony sat down.)

Mr. Justice Hunt. The prisoner will stand up. (Miss Anthony arose again.) The sentence of the Court is that you pay a fine of one hundred dollars and the costs of the prosecution.

Miss Anthony. May it please your Honor, I shall never pay a dollar of your unjust penalty. All the stock in trade I possess is a $10,000 debt, incurred by publishing my paper—*The Revolution*—four years ago, the sole object of which was to educate all women to do precisely as I have done, rebel against your man-made, unjust, unconstitutional forms of law, that tax, fine, imprison and hang women, while they deny them the right of representation in the government; and I shall work on with might and main to pay every dollar of that honest debt, but not a penny shall go to this unjust claim. And I shall earnestly and persistently continue to urge all women to the practical recognition of the old revolutionary maxim, that resistance to tyranny is obedience to God.

Mr. Justice Hunt. Madam, the Court will not order you committed until the fine is paid.

ROBERT G. INGERSOLL

THE PLUMED KNIGHT

SPEECH AT THE REPUBLICAN NATIONAL CONVENTION, CINCINNATI, OHIO, JUNE 15, 1876, NOMINATING JAMES G. BLAINE AS A CANDIDATE FOR THE PRESIDENCY

[Robert Green Ingersoll was born in Dresden, Yates county, New York, on August 11, 1833. In 1843 he moved with his father to Illinois, and after being admitted to the bar in 1854 began the practice of the law at Shawneetown. Having moved to Peoria, he was in 1860 an unsuccessful Democratic candidate for Congress. He served with distinction in the Civil War from 1862 to 1864, and in 1866 became Attorney General of Illinois. In 1877 he declined the post of United States Minister to Germany; in 1878 he moved to Washington, D. C., and in 1885 to New York City. He died in Dobbs Ferry, New York, on July 21, 1899.

He was one of the greatest orators of his generation, both on the platform and in the courtroom. "The zenith of his fame," says Chauncey Depew, "was reached by his 'plumed knight' speech, nominating James G. Blaine for President at the National Republican Convention in 1876. It was the testimony of all the delegates that, if the vote could have been taken immediately at the conclusion of the speech, Mr. Blaine would have been elected."]

Massachusetts may be satisfied with the loyalty of Benjamin H. Bristow; so am I; but if any man nominated by this convention cannot carry the State of Massachusetts, I am not satisfied with the loyalty of that State. If the nominee of this convention cannot carry the grand old Commonwealth of Massachusetts by seventy-five thousand majority, I would advise them to sell out Faneuil Hall as a Democratic headquarters. I would advise them to take from Bunker Hill that old monument of glory.

The Republicans of the United States demand as their leader in the great contest of 1876 a man of intelligence, a man of integrity, a man of well-known and approved political opinions. They demand a statesman; they demand a reformer after as well as before the election. They demand a politician in the highest, broadest and best sense—a man of superb moral cour-

[108]

age. They demand a man acquainted with public affairs—with the wants of the people; with not only the requirements of the hour, but with the demands of the future. They demand a man broad enough to comprehend the relations of this Government to the other nations of the earth. They demand a man well versed in the powers, duties and prerogatives of each and every department of this Government. They demand a man who will sacredly preserve the financial honor of the United States; one who knows enough to know that the national debt must be paid through the prosperity of this people; one who knows enough to know that all the financial theories in the world cannot redeem a single dollar; one who knows enough to know that all the money must be made, not by law, but by labor; one who knows enough to know that the people of the United States have the industry to make the money, and the honor to pay it over just as fast as they make it.

The Republicans of the United States demand a man who knows that prosperity and resumption, when they come, must come together; that when they come, they will come hand in hand through the golden harvest fields; hand in hand by the whirling spindles and the turning wheels; hand in hand past the open furnace doors; hand in hand by the flaming forges; hand in hand by the chimneys filled with eager fire, greeted and grasped by the countless sons of toil.

This money has to be dug out of the earth. You cannot make it by passing resolutions in a political convention.

The Republicans of the United States want a man who knows that this Government should protect every citizen, at home and abroad; who knows that any government that will not defend its defenders, and protect its protectors, is a disgrace to the map of the world. They demand a man who believes in the eternal separation and divorcement of church and school. They demand a man whose political reputation is spotless as a star; but they do not demand that their candidate shall have a certificate of moral character signed by a Confederate congress. The man who has, in full, heaped and rounded measure, all these splendid qualifications, is the present grand and gallant leader of the Republican party—James G. Blaine.

Our country, crowned with the vast and marvelous achievements of its first century, asks for a man worthy of the past, and prophetic of her future; asks for a man who has the audacity of genius; asks for a man who is the grandest combination of heart, conscience and brain beneath her flag—such a man is James G. Blaine.

For the Republican host, led by this intrepid man, there can be no defeat.

This is a grand year—a year filled with recollections of the Revolution; filled with proud and tender memories of the past; with the sacred legends of liberty—a year in which the sons of freedom will drink from the fountains of enthusiasm; a year in which the people call for the man who has preserved in Congress what our soldiers won upon the field; a year in which they call for the man who has torn from the throat of treason the tongue of slander—for the man who has snatched the mask of Democracy from the hideous face of rebellion; for the man who, like an intellectual athlete, has stood in the arena of debate and challenged all comers, and who is still a total stranger to defeat.

Like an armed warrior, like a plumed knight, James G. Blaine marched down the halls of the American Congress and threw his shining lance full and fair against the brazen foreheads of the defamers of his country and the maligners of his honor. For the Republican party to desert this gallant leader now, is as though an army should desert their general upon the field of battle.

James G. Blaine is now and has been for years the bearer of the sacred standard of the Republican party. I call it sacred, because no human being can stand beneath its folds without becoming and without remaining free.

Gentlemen of the convention, in the name of the great Republic, the only republic that ever existed upon this earth; in the name of all her defenders and of all her supporters; in the name of all her soldiers living; in the name of all her soldiers dead upon the field of battle, and in the name of those who perished in the skeleton clutch of famine at Andersonville and Libby, whose sufferings he so vividly remembers, Illinois—Illinois nominates for the next President of this country, that prince of parliamentarians—that leader of leaders—James G. Blaine.

JAMES G. BLAINE

THE IRISH QUESTION

SPEECH IN PORTLAND, MAINE, JUNE 1, 1886, AT A MEETING
IN SUPPORT OF GLADSTONE'S FIRST HOME RULE
BILL FOR IRELAND

[James Gillespie Blaine was born in West Brownsville, Washington county, Pennsylvania, on January 31, 1830. He was graduated from Washington College, Washington, Pennsylvania, in 1847, and taught school in Philadelphia, while studying law. In 1854 he moved to Maine and began a journalistic career, which, except for politics, remained his chief interest. He was a founder of the Republican Party, and in 1856 a delegate to the first Republican National Convention. From 1859 to 1881 he was chairman of the Republican State Committee of Maine. He was a member of the Maine House of Representatives from 1859 to 1862, and its Speaker during his last two terms. From 1863 to 1876 he was a Representative in Congress and from 1869 to 1875 Speaker of the House. He was the leading, but unsuccessful, candidate for the Republican nomination for President in 1876 (see Ingersoll's Plumed Knight speech, *ante*), and from July, 1876, to 1881, he was a United States Senator. Again failing to be nominated for President in 1880, he served as Secretary of State under Garfield from March 5 to December 19, 1881. He was nominated for President in 1884, but was defeated by President Cleveland. He held no office from 1884 to 1889, lived in Washington, and devoted himself to writing and speaking. His two volumes, *Twenty Years of Congress*, were published in 1884 and 1886. After the election of President Benjamin Harrison, he served as Secretary of State from 1889 to June 4, 1892. He died in Washington, D. C., on January 27, 1893.

Blaine is said to have been perhaps the most thrilling speaker of his day, despite the fact that he habitually filled his speeches with carefully prepared exact information. The speech printed below illustrates these two qualities, and is of special interest because of its subject. Blaine's foreign policy in 1881, especially its supposed anti-British side, had pleased the Irish voters of the United States. Late in his campaign for President in 1884, many Irish Catholics were alienated from him by the slogan invented by one of his supporters that he was fighting "rum, Romanism, and rebellion." The meeting in Portland in 1886 in support of Gladstone's First Home Rule Bill, gave him the occasion for a speech in which to justify himself before the Irish Catholic electorate by squarely stating his position on a question already agitating all Irishmen.]

[111]

Your Excellency and Fellow-Citizens—Directly after the published notice of this meeting I received a letter from a venerable friend in an adjacent county asking me, as I was announced to speak, to explain if I could, just what the "Irish question" is. I appreciate this request, for on an issue that calls forth so much sympathy and so much sentiment among those devoted to free government throughout the world, and evokes so much passion among those who are personally concerned in the contest, there may be danger of not giving sufficient attention to the simple, elementary facts which enter into the subject.

What then is Home Rule? It is nothing more and nothing less than that which is enjoyed among us by every State and every Territory of the Union. Negatively it is what the people of Ireland do not enjoy. In a Parliament of 670 members Great Britain has 567 and Ireland has 103. Except with the consent of this Parliament, in which the Irish members are outnumbered by more than five to one, the people of Ireland possess no Legislative power whatever. They cannot incorporate a horse railroad company, or authorize a ferry over a stream, or organize a gas company to light the streets of a city. Apply that to yourselves. Suppose the State of Maine were linked with the State of New York in a joint Legislature in which New York had five members to Maine's one. Suppose you could not take a step for the improvement of your beautiful city, or this State organize an association of any kind, or adopt any measure for its own advancement, unless by the permission of the overwhelming majority of the New York members! How long do you think the people of Maine would endure such a condition of affairs? Yet that illustrates the position which Ireland holds with respect to England, except that there is one irritating feature in addition which would not apply to New York and Maine—the centuries of oppression which have inspired the people of Ireland with a deep sense of wrong on the part of England.

If the Anglo-Celtic contention were left to the people of the United States to adjust, I suppose we should say—adopt the Federal system! Let Ireland have her legislature, let England have her legislature, let Scotland have her legislature, let Wales have her legislature, and then let the Imperial Parliament legislate for the British Empire. Let questions that are Irish be settled by Irishmen, questions that are English be settled by Englishmen, questions that are Welsh be settled by Welshmen, and questions that are Scotch be settled by Scotchmen. Let questions that affect the whole Empire of Great Britain be settled in a Parliament in which the four great constituent elements shall be impartially represented. That would be our direct, shorthand method of settling the question. Under that system we have lived and grown and prospered for more than two hundred years in the United States, continually expanding and continually strengthening our institutions.

I do not forget that it would be political empiricism to attempt to give the details of any measure that would settle this prolonged strife between Great Britain and Ireland. To prescribe definite measures for a British Parliament would be a presumption on our part as much as for the English people to prescribe definite measures for the American Congress. I have noticed so many errors, even among the leading men of Great Britain, concerning the Congress of the United States, that I have been taught modesty in attempting to criticise the processes and the specific measures of the British Parliament. I well remember that Lord Palmerston on a grave occasion during our Civil War informed the House of Commons that "the President of the United States could not of his own power declare war; that it required the assent of the Senate." Every school-boy in America knows that it is the Congress of the United States, both Senate and House, to which the war power is given by the Constitution of the Republic, and not to the President at all. But Lord Palmerston's error was slight compared with another which is said to have occurred in Parliament. A member in an authoritative manner assured the House that no law in the United States was valid until it had received the assent of the Legislatures of two-thirds of the several States; and a fellow-member corrected him, saying, "You are wrong; the American Congress cannot discuss any measure until two-thirds of the Legislatures of the States shall have already approved it." Admonished by these and like instances, I refrain from any discussion of the details of Mr. Gladstone's Home Rule Bill. It may

not be perfect.   It may not give to Ireland all that she is entitled
to.   I only know that it is a step in the right direction, and
that the long-oppressed people of Ireland hail it as a great and
beneficent measure of relief.   They and their representatives
understand it; and more than all Mr. Gladstone understands it.

On the occasion of Lord John Russell's somewhat famous
motion in the House of Commons in 1844 to inquire into the
condition of Ireland, Lord Macaulay said, in one of his most
eloquent speeches, "You admit that you govern Ireland not as
you govern England, not as you govern Scotland, but as you
govern your new conquests in Scinde; not by means of the
respect which the people feel for the law, but by means of
bayonets and artillery and intrenched camps."   If that were
true in 1844 I am sure I do not exaggerate when I say that the
long period of forty-two years which has intervened has served
to strengthen rather than to diminish the truth of Macaulay's
words.   And now without in any way denying the facts set
forth in Macaulay's extraordinary statement, Lord Salisbury
comes forward with a remedy of an extremely harsh character.
He says in effect that "the Irish can remain as they are now
situated, or they can emigrate."   But the Irish have been in Ireland as long as Lord Salisbury's ancestors have been in England
and I presume much longer.   His Lordship's lineage is not
given in Burke's Peerage beyond the illustrious Burleigh of
Queen ·Elizabeth's day, and possibly his remote ancestry may
have been Danish pirates or peasants in Normandy before the
Conquest, and centuries after the Irish people were known in
Ireland.   I repeat, therefore, Lord Salisbury's proposition is
extremely harsh.   Might we not, indeed, with good reason call
it impudent?   Would it transgress courtesy if we called it
insolent?   Should we violate truth if we called it brutal in its
cruelty?   We have had occasion in this country to know Lord
Salisbury too well.   He was the bitterest foe that the Government of the United States had in the British Parliament during
our Civil War.   He coldly advocated the destruction of the
American Union simply as a measure of increasing the commerce and prosperity of Great Britain.   His policy for Ireland
and his policy towards the United States are essentially alike
in spirit and in temper.

Another objection to Mr. Gladstone's policy comes from the Presbyterians of Ulster in the form of an appeal to the Presbyterians of the United States against granting the boon of Home Rule to Ireland. As a Protestant I deplore this action. I was educated under Presbyterian influences, in a Presbyterian college. I have connections with that church by blood and affinity that began with my life and shall not cease until my life ends. And yet I am free to say that I should be ashamed of the Presbyterian Church of America if it responded to an appeal which demands that five millions of Irish people shall be perpetually deprived of free government because of the remote and fanciful danger that a Dublin Parliament might interfere with the religious liberty of Presbyterians in Ulster. Mr. Chairman, if the Home Rule Bill shall pass, the Dublin Parliament will assume power with a greater responsibility to the public opinion of the world than was ever before imposed upon a Legislative body, because if the Dublin Parliament is formed it will be formed by reason of the pressure of public opinion from the liberty-loving people of the world. If the Irishmen who compose it should take one step against perfect liberty of conscience, or against any Protestant form of worship, they would fall under a condemnation even greater in its intensity than the friendship and sympathy which their own sufferings have so widely called forth. But I have not the remotest fear that any such result will happen. The Catholics and the Presbyterians of Ireland will live and do just as the Presbyterians and Catholics of the United States live and do. They will accord perfect liberty of conscience each to the other, and will be mutually governed by the greatest of Christian virtues, which is charity.

Mr. Gladstone's policy includes another measure. It proposes to do something to relieve the Irish from the intolerable oppression of absentee landlordism. Let me here quote Lord Macaulay again. Speaking of Ireland whose territory is less than the territory of the State of Maine, less than thirty-three thousand square miles in extent, Lord Macaulay in the same speech from which I have already quoted, says, "In natural fertility Ireland is superior to any area of equal size in Europe, and is far more important to the prosperity, the strength, the dignity of the British Empire than all our distant dependencies together; more important than the Canadas, the West Indies, South Africa, Australasia, Ceylon and the vast dominions of the Moguls." I am sure that if any Irish orator had originally made that declaration in America he would have been laughed at for Celtic exaggeration and imagination.

This extraordinary statement from Lord Macaulay led me to a practical examination of Ireland's resources. I went at it in a direct, farmer-like way, and examined the statistics relating to Ireland's production. I gathered all my information from trustworthy British authority, and I give you the result of my examination, frankly confessing that I was astounded at the magnitude of the figures. In the year 1880 Ireland produced four million bushels of wheat. But wheat has ceased to be the crop of Ireland. She produced eight million bushels of barley. But barley is not one of the great crops of Ireland. She produced seventy million bushels of oats, a very extraordinary yield considering Ireland's small area. The next item I think every one will recognize as peculiarly adapted to Ireland; of potatoes, she produced one hundred and ten millions of bushels—within sixty millions of the whole product of the United States for the same year. In turnips and mangels together she produced one hundred and eighty-five million bushels—vastly greater in weight than the largest cotton crop of the United States. She produced of flax sixty millions of pounds, and of cabbage eight hundred and fifty millions of pounds. She produced of hay three million eight hundred thousand tons. She had on her thousand hills and in her valleys over four million head of cattle, and in the same pasturage she had three million five hundred thousand head of sheep. She had five hundred and sixty thousand horses, and two hundred and ten thousand asses and mules. During the year 1880 she exported to England over seven hundred thousand cattle, over seven hundred thousand sheep, and nearly half a million swine. Pray remember all these came from a territory not quite so large as the State of Maine, and from an area of cultivation less than twenty millions of acres in extent! But with this magnificent abundance on this fertile land, rivaling the richness of the ancient land of Goshen, there are men in want of food, and appealing to-day to the charity of the stranger—compelled to ask alms through their blood and kindred in America. Why should this sad condition occur in a land that overflows with plenty, and exports millions of produce to other countries? According to the inspired command of the great Lawgiver of Israel, "Thou shalt not muzzle the ox that treadeth out the corn," and St. Paul, in quoting this text in his first epistle to Timothy, added, "The laborer is worthy of his reward." Yet many of the men engaged in producing these wonderful harvests are to-day lacking bread.

Mr. Gladstone believes, and we hope more than half of Great Britain believes with him, that the cause of this distress in Ireland is to be traced in large part to the absentee ownership of the land. Seven hundred and twenty-nine Englishmen own half the land in Ireland. Three thousand other men own the majority of the other half of the agricultural land of Ireland. Counting all the holdings there are but nineteen thousand two hundred and eighty-eight owners of land in Ireland, and this in a population of more than five million souls. Produce that condition of affairs in Maine or in all New England and the distress here in a few years would be as great as the distress in Ireland to-day. Mr. Gladstone, speaking as a statesman and a Christian, says that this intolerable wrong must cease, and that the men who till the land in Ireland must be permitted to purchase and to hold it.

But the story is not half told. The tenants and the peasantry of this little island, not so large, mind you, as Maine, pay a rental of sixty-five millions of dollars per annum upon the land. Besides this, Ireland pays an imperial tax of thirty-five millions of dollars annually, and a local tax of fifteen millions more. Thus the enormous sum of one hundred and fifteen millions of dollars is annually wrought out of the bone and flesh and spirit of the Irish people! No wonder that under this burden many lie crushed and down-trodden.

I believe the day has dawned for deliverance from these great oppressions; but from the experience of Ireland's past, it is not wise to be too sanguine of a speedy result. For one, therefore, I shall not be disappointed to see Mr. Gladstone's measures defeated in this Parliament. The English members can do it. But there is one thing which the English members cannot do.

They cannot permanently defy the public opinion of the lovers
of justice and liberty throughout the civilized world. Lord
Hartington made a very significant admission when in a complaining tone he accused Mr. Gladstone of having conceded so
much in his measure that Irishmen would never take less. I
do not know the day, whether it be this year or next year or
the year after that, or even years beyond, when a final settlement shall be made; but I have confidence that if Mr. Gladstone's bills are defeated the settlement will never be made on
as easy terms for English landlords as the Premier now proposes.

They complain sometimes in England of such meetings as
we are now holding. They say we are transcending the just
and proper duties of a friendly nation. Even if that were true,
the Englishman who remembers 1862–63–64 should maintain
a discreet silence. Yet I freely admit that misconduct of Englishmen during our war would by no means justify misconduct
on our part now. I do not refer to that as any palliation or
as any ground for justification if we were doing wrong. I do
not adopt the flippant cry of *tit* for *tat,* or the illogical taunt
of *tu quoque.* Indeed, there has been nothing done in America
that is not strictly within the lines of justice and strictly within
the limits of international obligation. Nor is any thing done
in the United States with the intention of injuring or with
the remotest desire to injure Great Britain. The English people
themselves are divided, and the American people sympathize
with what they believe to be the liberal and just side of English
opinion. We are no more sympathizing with Ireland as against
the England of the past than we are sympathizing with Gladstone against Salisbury in the England of the present. Nor
must it be forgotten that England herself, apparently not ap-
preciating her own course towards Ireland, has never failed
in the last fifty years to extend sympathy and sometimes the
helping-hand to nationalities in Europe struggling to be freed
from the clutch of tyranny. When Hungary resisted the rule
of Austria, Kossuth was as much a hero in England as he was
in America. When Lombardy raised the standard of revolt
against the House of Hapsburg, the British Ministry could
scarcely be held back from open expression of sympathy. When

Sicily revolted against the reign of the Neapolitan Bourbons, English sympathy was so active that Lord Palmerston was openly accused of permitting guns from Woolwich Arsenal to be smuggled to the Island of Sicily to aid the insurrection against King Bomba.

The American people are therefore justified by the example of England, and apart from any consideration except the broad one of human fellowship, stand forth as the friends of Ireland in her present distress. They do not stand forth as Democrats. They do not stand forth as Republicans. They do not stand forth as Protestants. They do not stand forth as Catholics. But they stand forth as citizens of a Free Republic, sympathizing with freedom throughout the world.

If I had a word of personal advice to give, or if I were in a position to give authoritative counsel, it would be this: the time is coming that will probably try the patience and the self-control of the Irish people more severely than they have been tried in any other stage in the progress of their long struggle. My advice is that by all means and with every personal and moral influence which can be used, all acts of violence be suppressed. Irishmen have earned the approving opinion of that part of the Christian world which believes in free government. Let them have a care that nothing be done to divide this opinion. Let no act of imprudence or rashness or personal outrage or public violence produce a re-action. Never has a cause been conducted with a clearer head or with better judgment in its parliamentary relations than that which has been conducted by Mr. Parnell. I regard it as a very fortunate circumstance that Mr. Parnell is a Protestant. It has been the singular, and in many respects the happy fortune of Ireland in every trouble to be so led that generous-minded men the world over might see that it was not sectarian strife, but a struggle for freedom and good government. How often has the leader in Irish agitation been a Protestant:—Dean Swift, Molyneux, Robert Emmet, Theobald Wolf Tone, Lord Edward Fitzgerald, Henry Grattan, and I might add many names to the list. These patriots carried the Irish cause high above and beyond all considerations of sectarian difference and founded it on "the rights of human nature," as Jefferson defined the American cause in our own

Revolutionary period. Thus led and thus guarded the Irish cause must prevail. There has never been a contest for liberty by any section of the British Empire composed of white men that was not successful in the end, if the white men were united. By union the Thirteen Colonies gained their independence. By union Canada gained every concession she wished upon the eve of a revolution, and there is nothing to-day which Canada could ask this side of absolute separation that would not be granted for the asking.

I have only one more word to say, and that again is a word of advice. The men of Irish blood in this country should keep this question as it has been kept thus far, out of our own political controversies. They should mark any man as an enemy who seeks to use it for personal or for partisan advancement. To the sacredness of your cause conducted in this spirit, in the lofty language of the most eloquent of Irishmen, Edmund Burke—"you can attest the retiring generations, you can attest the advancing generations, between whom we stand as a link in the great chain of eternal order." Conducted in that spirit you can justify your cause before earthly tribunals, and you can carry it with pure heart and strong faith before the judgment seat of God.

HENRY GEORGE

THE MASSES AGAINST THE CLASSES

SPEECH IN COOPER INSTITUTE, NEW YORK CITY, OCTOBER 5, 1886, ACCEPTING THE NOMINATION AS CANDIDATE FOR MAYOR OF NEW YORK CITY, IN OPPOSITION TO ABRAM S. HEWITT

[Henry George was born in Philadelphia, Pennsylvania, on September 2, 1839. As a boy he sailed before the mast to India, and finally settled in California. He worked at the printing trade, became a reporter, and in 1867 editor of the San Francisco *Times*. In 1879, he published the book which made him famous, *"Progress and Poverty."* In it, say Charles and Mary Beard, he drew "the deadly parallel of riches and misery, sun and shadow," and advocated a single tax, "designed to absorb unearned increment in land values and strike at the root of gross inequalities of wealth." In 1880 he moved to New York City. He traveled extensively from 1881 to 1885, lecturing on his tax theory. In 1886 he was the unsuccessful candidate of the Union Labor Party for mayor of New York. In the next year he founded *The Standard*, a weekly paper, and ran on the Labor ticket for the office of Secretary of State. He was a delegate to the Land Reform Conference in Paris in 1889, visited Australia and New Zealand in 1890, was an independent candidate for Mayor of New York in 1897, and died from overexertion during the campaign, on October 28, 1897.

The speech, printed below, was the first of more than a hundred delivered by him during the campaign for Mayor of New York in October, 1886. It is the version taken down by the stenographer for the *Irish World*, and published in *The George-Hewitt Campaign*, by Post and Leubuscher. George agreed to accept the nomination on the Labor ticket only after a petition signed by 34,460 voters had been presented to him. On the night of his speech, in Cooper Union, the "huge rolls containing the signatures and tied with blue ribbon were stacked in a pyramid in full view of the vast audience." The vote on November 2 resulted in the election of Mr. Hewitt, with 90,552 votes, as compared to 68,110 for Henry George, and 60,435 for Theodore Roosevelt.]

The step I am about to take has not been entered upon lightly. When my nomination for Mayor of New York was first talked of I regarded it as a nomination which was not to be thought about. I did not desire to be Mayor of New York. I have had in my time political ambition, but years ago I gave it up. I saw what practical politics meant; I saw that under the conditions as they were a man who would make a political career must cringe and fawn and intrigue and flatter, and I resolved that I would not so degrade my manhood. Another career opened to me; the path that I had laid before me—that my eyes were fixed upon—was rather that of a pioneer—that of the men who go in advance of politics, the men who break the road that after they have gone will be trod by millions. It seemed to me that there lay duty and that there lay my career, and since this nomination has been talked about my friends here and through the country and beyond the seas have sent me letter after letter, asking me not to lower, as they are pleased to term it, the position I occupied by running for a municipal office. But I believe, and have long believed, that working-men ought to go into politics. I believe, and I have long believed, that through politics was the way, and the only way, by which anything real and permanent could be secured for labor. In that path, however, I did not expect to tread. That, I thought, would devolve upon others, but when the secretary of this nominating convention came to me and said, "You are the only man upon whom we can unite, and I want you to write me a letter either accepting or refusing to accept, and giving your reasons," that put a different face on the matter. When it came that way I could not refuse. But I made my conditions. I asked for a guarantee of good faith; I asked for some tangible evidence that my fellow-citizens of New York really wanted me to act. That evidence you have given me. All I asked, and more.

John McMackin, Chairman of the Convention of Organized Labor, I accept your nomination, and in grasping your hand I grasp in spirit the hand of every man in this movement. From now henceforward let us stand together.

Working-men of New York—organized laborers of New York—I accept your nomination. For weal or for woe, for failure or for success, henceforward I am your candidate. I am proud of it from the bottom of my heart. I thank you for the compliment you have paid me. Never in my time has any American citizen received from his fellow-citizens such a compliment as has been consummated to-night; never shall any act of mine bring discredit upon that compliment.

Working-men of New York, I am your candidate; now it devolves upon you to elect me. In your name I solicit the suffrages of all citizens, rich or poor, white or black, native or foreign-born; if any organization of citizens sees fit to indorse your nomination, well and good; but as you have asked me for no pledges, so you may rely on me; I will make no pledge to any man. As you have nominated me unsolicited, I will solicit the indorsement of no other party. Whoever accepts me must accept me as the candidate of organized labor standing alone. And now it devolves upon you to elect me. You can; but look in the face what is against us. This, in my opinion, will be one of the fiercest contests that ever took place in this or any other American city. If money can beat me, I shall be beaten. Every influence that can be arrayed against me will be used. There will be falsehood and slanders, everything that money and energy and political knowledge and experience can command. Don't imagine that those who have their hands in the pockets of this city through their control of the municipal departments will give up easily; don't imagine that the politicians will allow the working-men to smash their machines without trying their utmost to prevent it. But I do believe, as your chairman has said, that we shall win in spite of all. And I believe it because I see, in this gathering enthusiasm—a power that is stronger than money, more potent than trained politicians; something that will meet and throw them aside like chaff before a gale.

Standing now as your candidate for the Mayoralty of New York City, it is meet and fitting that I should say something with regard to the office to which you propose to elect me. It is an important office; it is a powerful position, but any man who obtains it will be fettered by a system which is bad. Our system of government here is very bad. What we should have is one similar to that of the United States—one executive, responsible to the people, and the heads of the various departments appointed by him removable at his pleasure and responsible to him. Then you will have somebody to call to account. Under our present system you have dual commissions, commissions of three, or four, or five persons, and the consequence is you can fix no responsibility anywhere. These men have to provide for their friends, and therefore there are all sorts of trading and dickering. Nevertheless the Mayor of New York has large powers; he has absolute power in appointing commissioners, though he has no power, as he ought to have, to remove them, with the exception of two very important commissioners—the Commissioners of Accounts; these he may appoint and remove at pleasure. Their business is to go through the departments and see that everything is all correct. But the Mayor has a greater power, the power of visitation and inquisition, finding out how things are going; and he has another great power, that of appealing to public opinion. If elected, as I believe I shall be elected, Mayor, I will do my utmost to discharge its duties faithfully and well—I will do my utmost to give you an honest and a clean government. I will do my utmost to bring about such changes in legislation as will remedy defects which have been proved, and I will enforce the laws.

I want this to be distinctly understood—that when I take the oath of office as Mayor of New York I will be Mayor of the whole city. I will preserve order at all risks; I will enforce the law against friends as fully as against enemies. But there are some things that, if I am Mayor of New York, I shall stop if I can prevent them. There will be no more policemen acting as censors of what shall be said at public meetings. I will support to the utmost of my power and my influence the peace officers of the city, but if it is in my power to put a stop to it I will put a stop to the practice which seems to be common among many of the hoodlums of the force, of turning themselves into judge, jury, and executioner, and clubbing anybody who they think ought to be clubbed. Without fear and without favor I will try to do my duty. I will listen as readily to the complaint of the richest man in this city as I will to the complaint of the poorest. (A voice—"The rich have nothing to complain of.") Some of them are under the impression that if I am elected they may have. No; you are right about it. The rich in this city have very little to complain of. Corrupt government always is and always must be the government of the men who have money. Under our republican forms, while we profess to believe in the equality of all men, the rich have virtually ruled the administration of the law. It reminds me of an old fable I used to read in a French book. There was a terrible pestilence among the animals once upon a time. The lion made proclamation and called all the beasts together. They were suffering for their sins, he said, and ought to investigate who it was that provoked the wrath of Heaven, and then offer him up as a sacrifice. And so all the animals met. They elected the fox as chairman. The lion said he was a great sinner; that he had eaten many flocks of sheep, and even once eaten a shepherd. The fox said to the lion that the sheep ought to feel complimented to be eaten by his majesty, and as for the shepherd, it served him right, "for evidently," went on the fox, "he had been throwing stones at your majesty." And then the wolf and the hyena and the tiger and so on confessed their several sins, until it came to the fox, who said he had eaten a great many chickens, but they crowed so in the morning that they disturbed him very much. Lastly came the donkey, who said that as he was carrying a load of hay to the market for his master he turned around and took a mouthful. "Wicked monster," cried the fox. "But I was hungry," continued the ass; "he had forgotten to give me my breakfast." "That makes no difference," cried the fox, and it was unanimously decided that it was the sin of the ass that brought the pestilence, and all the animals fell on him and tore him to pieces by way of sacrifice. It is so with many rich criminals. The Theiss boycotters are still in prison. Is there not something in the State of New York that recalls that battle of the animals?

The politicians whom you have disturbed by your nomination, and a good many of the respectable journals, think very poorly of this movement, because they term it, "class movement." They dislike to see class movements in our politics; they would rather you would go on in the old way voting for Tammany Hall, or the County Democracy, or the Republicans. Class movement! What class is it? The working class! Do you ever ask yourselves how it is that the working-men came to constitute a class? In the beginning all men had to work. Is it not the dictate of Scripture: "Thou shalt earn thy bread by the sweat of thy brow?" Nature gives to man nothing. Without work nothing can be produced. Work is the producer of all wealth. How, then, is it that there came to be distinctively a working class? How is it that that working class is everywhere the poorer class? It is that some men devise schemes by which they can live without working, by throwing the burden of their work upon their fellows. An English writer has divided all men into three classes—working-men, beggar-men, and thieves—and this is correct. There are only three ways of getting the product of labor—by working for it, by having it given to you, and by stealing it. If this is a class movement, then it is a movement of the working class against the beggarmen and the thieves. A class movement! No. It is what Gladstone said of that great movement on the other side of the water—it is a movement of the masses against robbery by the classes, and is it not time that there should be in this city of New York some such movement as this? The political condition of this city is a reproach in all the monarchies of Europe. Go on the other side and venture to say one word against their aristocratic institutions, and see how quickly you will be met with the reproach that there is nowhere such open-faced corruption as in the City of New York. This government of New York City—our whole political system—is rotten to the core. It needs no investigation to discover it. An assemblyman ordinarily "puts up" more than he can honestly expect to get back in salary. The ordinary expenditure of a candidate for Congress, I am told, is about $10,000, and he can make the expenses of his campaign go as high as $80,000. Even our judges pay some $20,000 for the privilege of running. It is well understood that a candidate for Mayor must be prepared to spend $75,000, and it is said that, in a recent campaign, the candidate spent something like $200,000. Look how money flows everywhere. This morning we read of Alderman Divver barbecuing an ox and letting beer run like water—and this distance from election, too! Is this vast amount of money thrown out for simple salaries? The money that is habitually spent in campaigning in this city is put in as a business investment—money out to get money in. Corruption! Just consider, for a moment, the contemptuous manner in which this movement of our working class is treated. And why? Just because they think we haven't the "sinews of war." Because, as Mr. "Fatty" Walsh says, "Those labor fellows ain't got no inspectors of election." And, under the beautiful system of local politics here, one rogue is

turned out and another let in. Does that improve things? Do
you suppose that Mr. Rollin M. Squire was a sinner above all
other office-holders in this city? Is not the present incumbent
applying the same old official axe—chopping off Tammany heads
and putting in County Democrats in the same good old fashion? Is it not well understood that without some such deal
tickets cannot be got up nor candidates run? Look at the out-
cry that has gone up over this movement. The cry of alarm,
"The Democracy must unite," is heard everywhere. How has
the party of Jefferson and of Jackson fallen when its two local
wings must be called upon to unite, and even the power of the
National Administration brought in to help that unity! And
against what? Against the working-man! Why don't they
unite, then, when the obligation is so imperative? Because the
difficulty lies in parcelling out the spoils—in giving out the offices and getting the proper kind of pledges. As to the principle of the thing, they care nothing for that. Isn't it time that
fresh breath was infused into this corruption?

In this movement of ours there is hope of better things. In
a city where it has long been held that a man must be rich, very
rich, to hold its highest office, you have put up a poor man. In
a city where it is a standing rule that a candidate must disburse
money, you propose to furnish your own money. And you have
a candidate who is free from pledges. Can your Johnny O'Bri-
ens say that when their candidate is nominated? If the much
hoped for union of Tammany Hall and Irving Hall and the
County Democracy does take place, can it be said of their candidate that he stands free of pledges as to how he will parcel
out the jobs in his gift? Remember that until you can elect
men who are free you cannot expect an unfettered administration. This movement aims at political reform; but that is not
all. That is not the entire significance of my candidacy. We
aim, too, at social reform. As declared in the platform you
heard here to-night we aim at equal rights for all men. Chattel
slavery is dead, but there devolves upon us the task of removing
industrial slavery. That is the meaning of our movement. This
is at once a revolt against political corruption and social injustice. Look over our vast city, and what do we see? On one
side a very few men richer by far than it is good for men to be,

and on the other side a great mass of men and women struggling and worrying and wearying to get a most pitiful living. In this big metropolis in this year of grace 1886, we have a vast surging class of so-called free and independent citizens, with none of whom the wild, Red Indian, in anything like his native state, could afford to exchange. We have hordes of citizens living in want and in vice born of want, existing under conditions that would appall a heathen. Is this by the will of our Divine Creator? No. It is the fault of men, and as men and citizens on us devolves the duty of removing this wrong; and in that platform that the convention has adopted and on which I stand the first step is taken. Why should there be such abject poverty in this city? There is one great fact that stares in the face anyone who chooses to look at it. That fact is that the vast majority of men and women and children in New York have no legal right to live here at all. Most of us—ninety-nine per cent. at least—must pay the other one per cent. by the week or month or quarter for the privilege of staying here and working like slaves. See how we are crowded here. London has a population of 15,000 to the square mile. Canton, in crowded China, has 35,000 inhabitants within the same area. New York has 54,000 to the square mile, and leaving out the uninhabited portion it has a population of 85,000 to the square mile. In the Sixth Ward there is a population of 149,000 to the square mile; in the Tenth Ward, 276,000; in the Thirteenth, 224,000, including roads, yards, and all open places. Why, there is one block in this city that contains 2,500 living beings and every room in it a workshop. Nowhere else in the civilized world are men and women and children packed together so closely. As for children, they die almost as soon as they enter the world. In the district known as the Mulberry Bend, according to Commissioner Wingate's report, there is an infant death-rate of sixty-five per cent., and in the tenement district he says that a large percentage of the children die before they are five years of age. Now, is there any reason for such overcrowding? There is plenty of room on this island. There are miles and miles and miles of land all around this nucleus. Why cannot we take that and build houses upon it for our accommodation? Simply because it is held by dogs in the manger who will not use it themselves, nor allow anybody else to use it, unless they pay an enormous price for it—because what the Creator intended for the habitation of the people whom He called into being is held at an enormous rent or an enormous price. Did you ever think, men of New York, what you pay for the privilege of living in this country? I do not ask what you pay for bricks and mortar and wood, but for rent; and the rent is mainly the rent of the land. Bricks and mortar and wood are of no greater value here than they are in Long Island or in Iowa. When what is called real estate advances it is the land that is getting more valuable; it is not the houses. All this enormous value that the growth of population adds to the land of this city is taken by the few individuals and goes for the benefit of the idle rich, who look down upon those who earn their living by their labor.

But what do we propose to do about it? We propose, in the first place, as our platform indicates, to make the buildings cheaper by taking the tax off buildings. We propose to put that tax on land exclusive of improvements, so that a man who is holding land vacant will have to pay as much for it as if he was using it, just upon the same principle that a man who goes to a hotel and hires a room and takes the key and goes away would have to pay as much for it as if he occupied the room and slept in it. In that way we propose to drive out the dog in the manger who is holding from you what he will not use himself. We propose in that way to remove this barrier and open the land to the use of labor in putting up buildings for the accommodation of the people of the city. I am called a Socialist. I am really an individualist. I believe that every individual man ought to have an individual wife, and is entitled to an individual home. I think it is monstrous, such a state of society as exists in this city. Why, the children, thousands and thousands, have no place to play. It is a crime for them to play ball in the only place in which they can play ball. It is an offence for them to fly their kites. The children of the rich can go up to Central Park, or out into the country in the summer time; but the children of the poor, for them there is no playground in the city but the streets; it is some charity excursion which takes them out for a day, only to return them again to the same sweltering condition.

Hicks' Sp.A.S.—9

There is no good reason whatever why every citizen of New York should not have his own separate house and home; and the aim of this movement is to secure it. We hold that the land belongs to the entire people. We hold that the value of the land of this city, by reason of the presence of this great population, belongs to us to apply to the welfare of the people. Everyone should be entitled to share in it. It should be for the use of the whole people, and for the beautifying and adornment of the city, for providing public accommodations, playgrounds, schools, and facilities for education and recreation. Why, here is this building in which we are assembled, the Cooper Institute; its superintendent told me only a little while ago they accommodated only about one-tenth of the young people who are flocking here to get an education to enable them to make a livelihood. Instead of relying upon the beneficence of individuals, we, the people of New York, ought to furnish the institutions ourselves. We ought to have in this city of New York twenty such institutions as this. What the platform aims at is the taking for the use of the people all that value and benefit which result from social growth. We believe that the railroads of this city ought to be taken properly and legally by the people and run for the benefit of the people of New York. Why should it not be so? Any individual putting up a big building, such as the Morse building, the Cyrus Field building, the Western Union building, puts in an elevator. But he does not put in that elevator a man with a bell-punch strung around his neck to collect fares. He gains the advantage in the increased value of his building. So we could take their railroads and run them. We could take those railroads and run them free, let everybody ride who would, and we could pay for it out of the increased value of the people's property in consequence. These are but steps, but the aim of this movement, and this is its significance, is the assertion of the equal rights of man—the assertion of his equal and inalienable right to life and to all the elements that the Creator has furnished for the maintenance of that life.

Here is the heart of the labor question, and until we address ourselves to that the labor question never can be solved. These little children who die in our tenement districts, have they no business here? Do they not come into life with equal rights from their Creator? In the early days of New Zealand, when the English colonists bought land from the natives, they encountered a great difficulty. After they had bought and paid for a piece of land, the women would come with babes in their arms and would say: "We want something for these babes." The reply was: "We paid you for your land!" Then they who had parted with the land answered: "Yes, yes, yes, but you did not pay these babes. They were not born then."

I expect, my friends, to meet you many times during this campaign, and expect to make my voice heard in all parts of this city. I am ready to meet any questions that may be addressed to me, and to do whatever in me lies for the success of our ticket. I am your candidate for Mayor of New York. It is something that a little while ago I never dreamt of. Years ago I came to this city from the West, unknown, knowing nobody, and I saw and recognized for the first time the shocking contrast between monstrous wealth and debasing want. And here I made a vow, from which I have never faltered, to seek out and remedy, if I could, the cause that condemned little children to lead such a life as you know them to lead in the squalid districts. It is because of that that I stand before you to-night, presenting myself for the chief office of your city—espousing the cause, not only of your rights but of those who are weaker than you. Think of it! Little ones dying by thousands in this city; a veritable slaughter of the innocents before their time has come. Is it not our duty as citizens to address ourselves to the adjustment of social wrongs that force out of the world those who are called into it almost before they are here—that social wrong that forces girls upon the streets and our boys into the grogshops and then into penitentiaries? We are beginning a movement for the abolition of industrial slavery, and what we do on this side of the water will send its impulse across the land and over the sea, and give courage to all men to think and act. Let us, therefore, stand together. Let us do everything that is possible for men to do from now until the second of next month, that success may crown our efforts, and that to us in this city may belong the honor of having led the van in this great movement.

J. C. S. BLACKBURN

RETORT TO INGALLS

SPEECH IN THE UNITED STATES SENATE, MARCH 6, 1888, IN REPLY TO SENATOR JOHN J. INGALLS

[Josephus Clay Stiles Blackburn was born in Woodford county, Kentucky, on October 1, 1838. He was graduated from Centre College, Danville, Kentucky, in 1857; studied law; and in 1858 was admitted to the bar in Lexington, Kentucky. From 1858 to 1860 he practiced law in Chicago, Illinois, and in Woodford county, Kentucky. He entered the Confederate army in 1861 as a private, and had attained the rank of Lieutenant Colonel at the end of the war. He settled in Desha county, Arkansas, as a planter, but in 1868 returned to Kentucky and opened an office in Versailles. From 1871 to 1875, he was a member of the Kentucky House of Representatives; from 1875 to 1885 he was a Democratic Representative in the United States Congress; from 1885 to 1897, and from 1901 to 1907, United States Senator; and from 1907 to 1909, Governor of the Panama Canal Zone, on the appointment of President Roosevelt. He died in Washington, D. C., on September 12, 1918.

On March 6, 1888, the Senate, as in Committee of the Whole, resumed consideration of the Dependent Pension Bill. In the course of the debate, Senator Ingalls, President pro tempore of the Senate, took the floor and made an intemperate speech, in which he attacked President Grover Cleveland, Senator Vest of Missouri, and Senator Blackburn of Kentucky, imputing to them sectional partisan opposition to the pension bill; Horace Greeley; General Winfield Scott Hancock, and General George B. McClellan, whom he accused of having been allies of the Confederacy; and Henry W. Grady, whose speech at the unveiling of a monument to Benjamin Harvey Hill in Atlanta, Georgia, he characterized as sacrilegious and blasphemous. At the close of the speech, Senator Blackburn rose and made the following remarkable extempore reply.]

Mr. President, I am at a loss to account for the course that the Senator from Kansas [Mr. Ingalls] has seen fit to adopt in lugging me into the tirade in which he has just indulged, for I am sure that I had never made boast of identification with any military service in my life. I had never referred to the fact of having been a Confederate soldier. Unlike the Senator from Kansas, I thought my military record was too modest and too humble to prove a subject of interest to the galleries that have assembled to listen to his political harangue.

I did not need to be told by him that I stood here a representative from a State that had never seceded from the Union. I did not need to be reminded that Kentucky had always been loyal. I knew then, as he should know now, that I represent a constituency that are entitled to draw more pensions than the State so ably represented by the Senator who has just preceded me. The records of this country, I believe, show that the State of Kentucky furnished three men to the Union Army for every one that Kansas furnished; and in passing I may assure the Senator that it is not without pride that I recall the fact that of the thirty-odd States then in this Union the one from which I came is the only one that, without the application of a conscript law, furnished more than her quota of men to both sides during that struggle.

Now, why he should travel out of his way to have made an onslaught upon me I do not know. I do not understand that I was a necessary text for his speech of acceptance of the Presidential nomination of which he complained. I shall not undertake to answer for the Senator from Missouri [Mr. Vest]. The Senator from Kansas doubtless knew that illness in his family had taken him a long distance from this city, and that he is to be absent for some time on that account.

I do not intend to be involved in any controversy with the Senator from Kansas, but I do intend to protest against the lack of fairness which he employs when he undertakes to deal after such a fashion with men who have but simply stated facts and submitted data for the consideration of the Senate upon a bill that is pending.

What connection had the speech made at Atlanta by a gentleman who never was a member of either House of Congress in his life, or the speech made by that same gentleman in Brooklyn or New York, with the bill that is pending here?

When the Senator from Kansas undertakes to speak of the Chief Executive of this country in the terms that he has seen fit to employ in a deliberately prepared and conned effort, he surely will not take issue with me if I conclude that it is not entitled to response or reply in this or any other decent presence.

What cause of grievance he has that warrants him in employing language that would not be permissible upon the hustings—I will not say it would be disgraceful even if employed by fish-women—but when he undertakes to denounce the Chief Executive of the United States after such a fashion as to deliberately declare that no man is afflicted with antecedents so degraded, or ignorance so profound, or obscurity so unfathomable as to preclude him from becoming that man's successor, it does seem to me that the dignity of the Senate Chamber refuses permission for response. I am not here to defend the President from such unwarranted attacks. I know but one sin that he has committed in the eyes of the Senator from Kansas, and that may be the unpardonable offense of not only having defeated his party at the polls but having given to the American people for three years past so efficient, so honest, so clean-handed an administration as to doom the last of that party's aspirations to disaster.

If it be possible, the Senator from Kansas has gone further and done worse. In his intemperate zeal he has not hesitated to invade graves. In his frantic efforts to stir prejudice between sections that have already been reunited he goes into the trenches of the soldiery, and not on my side but on his side, and drags up for abuse and vilification before the American Senate such men as traced with their own unblemished swords in blood the brightest pages of American history. McClellan and Hancock are to be denounced upon this floor as allies of Confederates. Might it not have been in better taste, more creditable, at least, to the courage and to the candor of that Senator, if he had made that charge before both of these men were dead?

Mr. Ingalls. I did, often.

Mr. Blackburn. Then so much the worse for the Senator from Kansas. What warrant or ground had he for that, except that they were both different from himself, at least in political faith, if we may not hope in many other regards?

Hancock an ally of the Confederates! Was he so regarded and believed when, weltering in his blood upon Cemetery Heights, he refused to be taken from the field, and yet persisted in giving orders to check the last advance of Longstreet's irresistible veterans? Was it this man who was honored up to the very day that he accepted the nomination at the hands of the Democratic party, honored alike by the American people, whether they were Republicans or Democrats?

He travels on to berate the Commissioner of Pensions, and he speaks in terms certainly as little complimentary, if he does not, as in the other two cases, impeach his loyalty. Mr. President, that crippled and maimed Commissioner of Pensions, himself a general in the Federal Army from 1861 to 1865, would hesitate to have the contrast or comparison, as he may term it, drawn between himself and the Senator from Kansas. Whilst he was earning his military reputation when the flag was flying upon the borders of the Senator's own State, and bleeding upon every battle-field upon which he went, what great service was the Senator from Kansas rendering?

He complains of the Senator from Missouri, and says that he rests his complaints upon that Senator's autobiography. I believe that it is generally assumed that a gentleman writes that bit of interesting history for himself. Now, in looking over the short but conspicuously brilliant autobiography of the Senator from Kansas, I find that he was not in the Army in 1861.

He surely was not in the Army in 1862, because he says that he was in the State Senate of Kansas, "a member of the State Senate of Kansas from Atchison County in 1862." But he would have us believe that he was in the Army from 1863 to 1865. 'Tis not true. He never was in the Federal Army. Why, to have sat and listened to the Senator one would have imagined that he was controlling the great armies that were operating in the West at least, if not in the East.

I saw the bronzed and weather-beaten commander of the American Armies sit there in that chair and blush in modesty at the humble part that he found that he had played in the war of the rebellion; and what was the Senator from Kansas doing whilst he was earning his reputation? What was his occupation in a military capacity? He tells you himself that he was "a judge-advocate to Kansas militia volunteers." Whilst Black was bleeding on Kansas soil, whilst McClellan was commanding the armies of the Potomac, whilst Hancock was weltering in his blood upon Cemetery Heights at Gettysburg, the Senator from Kansas, away behind in the rear of the Army, was prosecuting Kansas jay-hawkers for robbing hen-roosts! [Great laughter.]

Mr. President, what are we to think of the recklessness of a Senator who will leave that place now occupied by yourself and come to the floor in the illustration of a partisan zeal that I am glad to say I have never seen equaled, to attack everybody, all decent people, from the President of the United States down, civilians and military men, living and dead? No object can be found that escapes the venom of his tongue—a cynic, one would say, despising mankind because perhaps he has a suspicion that mankind is not enamored with him; malignant even toward himself; and there doubtless are some who would agree that he has cause; but neither President nor soldier, living nor dead, Confederate nor Federal, unless he accords with him in political conviction, is safe from his unwarranted, unjust, and unfounded attacks.

I do not want to be put in the position of an opponent or an enemy to the pensioning of honest Federal soldiers. I have never opposed the pensioning, whether by private act or public act, of any man that ever bore service in the Union Army and was incapacitated to support himself either by disease or by wounds contracted in that service. And I do not know the Confederate that ever did, and I trust that none ever will.

But to illustrate the accuracy of the Senator's statements, he tells us in the haste with which he rushes to his conclusions that no Democratic constituency in the South ever elected a Union soldier to either House of Congress. I do not know that it is material to answer that assertion; but, like most of the material that enters into his late utterances, there is not a particle of foundation in fact for the statement. The State of Texas sent to the Halls of Congress term after term, and until recently, a distinguished Union soldier during the war in the person of Governor Hancock. The State of Arkansas sent here in recent years from a Democratic constituency a Union soldier during the war to represent her in the other House of Congress. I would like to know whether the late governor of Virginia, Governor Walker, was not a Union soldier and an honored Representative in the other branch of Congress from an overwhelmingly Democratic district in the Old Dominion?

Mr. Riddleberger. He was not a soldier.

Mr. Blackburn. I thought that he was.

Mr. Riddleberger. He was a Northern man who came to Virginia.

Mr. Blackburn. He certainly was a loyal man during the war.

Mr. Riddleberger. He came to Virginia during the war.

Mr. Blackburn. I should like to know why the Senator from Kansas, when he was studying that record so closely and blundered so badly when he undertook to state what the facts were, did not remember that within the last six years, and for four years, the State of Kentucky kept continuously in the other House of Congress a distinguished Federal general who was shot out of his saddle more than half a dozen times, and he came there always as the candidate of the Democratic party, and elected in a Democratic district.

I do not care to follow the Senator, for time forbids, through all the inaccuracies of his utterances, but this much I do propose to say before I close. Mr. President, party man as I am, partisan as I confess myself to be, I do sincerely trust that I may never find my term of public service prolonged to that day, nor my life extended to that hour when, without warrant, without fact to support me, without truth at my back, I shall deliberately traduce and abuse the dead who whilst living were honored by all honorable men.

HENRY W. GRADY

THE RACE PROBLEM

SPEECH AT THE ANNUAL BANQUET OF THE MERCHANTS'
ASSOCIATION, BOSTON, MASSACHUSETTS,
DECEMBER 13, 1889

[Henry Woodfin Grady was born in Athens, Georgia, on May 17, 1851. In 1864 his father, who was an officer in the Confederate army, was killed at Petersburg, Virginia. He was graduated from the University of Georgia in 1868, and received his Bachelor's degree from the University of Virginia in 1871. He immediately engaged in newspaper work and in 1880 became managing editor and part owner of the Atlanta *Constitution*. He never sought office, but was influential in politics through his writing and speaking. His speech on December 21, 1886, was received with great acclaim and made him a national figure. This was the beginning of a series of speeches, all of which were noteworthy. He died in Atlanta, Georgia, on December 23, 1889.

Grady was generally accepted as the embodiment of the spirit of the New South. The fixed and solemn purpose of his life was to aid in the reconciliation of the North and the South, and he was acknowledged as the "national pacificator," except by a few irreconcilables like Senator Ingalls. In a speech in the United States Senate, March 6, 1888, Ingalls contrasted a speech by Grady delivered in the South with one delivered in the North, and intimated that the latter was a pouring out of "treacle, cold cream, honey and maple sirup all over the North." The Boston speech, printed below, was delivered ten days before Grady's death and is regarded as the culmination of his career. "He prepared his Boston speech with great care," wrote Joel Chandler Harris, "not merely to perfect its form, but to make it worthy of the great cause he had at heart, and in its preparation he departed widely from his usual methods of composition. He sent his servants away, locked himself in Mrs. Grady's room, and would not tolerate interruptions from any source. His memory was so prodigious that whatever he wrote was fixed in his mind, so that, when he had once written out a speech, he needed the manuscript no more. Those who were with him say that he did not confine himself to the printed text of the Boston speech, but made little excursions suggested by his surroundings. Nevertheless, that speech, as it stands, reaches the high-water mark of modern oratory. It was his last, as it was his best, contribution to the higher politics of the country—the politics that are above partisanry and self-seeking.]

Mr. President: Bidden by your invitation to a discussion of the race problem—forbidden by occasion to make a political speech—I appreciate in trying to reconcile orders with propriety the predicament of the little maid who, bidden to learn to swim, was yet adjured, "Now, go, my darling, hang your clothes on a hickory limb, and don't go near the water."

The stoutest apostle of the church, they say, is the missionary, and the missionary, wherever he unfurls his flag, will never find himself in deeper need of unction and address than I, bidden to-night to plant the standard of a Southern Democrat in Boston's banquet hall, and discuss the problem of the races in the home of Phillips and of Sumner. But, Mr. President, if a purpose to speak in perfect frankness and sincerity; if earnest understanding of the vast interests involved; if a consecrating sense of what disaster may follow further misunderstanding and estrangement, if these may be counted to steady undisciplined speech and to strengthen an untried arm—then, sir, I find the courage to proceed.

Happy am I that this mission has brought my feet at last to press New England's historic soil, and my eyes to the knowledge of her beauty and her thrift. Here, within touch of Plymouth Rock and Bunker Hill—where Webster thundered and Longfellow sang, Emerson thought and Channing preached—here in the cradle of American letters, and almost of American liberty, I hasten to make the obeisance that every American owes New England when first he stands uncovered in her mighty presence. Strange apparition! This stern and unique figure—carved from the ocean and the wilderness—its majesty kindling and growing amid the storms of winters and of wars—until at last the gloom was broken, its beauty disclosed in the sunshine, and the heroic workers rested at its base—while startled kings and emperors gazed and marveled that from the rude touch of this handful, cast on a bleak and unknown shore, should have come the embodied genius of human government, and the perfected model of human liberty! God bless the memory of those immortal workers—and prosper the fortunes of their living sons—and perpetuate the inspiration of their handiwork.

Two years ago, sir, I spoke some words in New York that caught the attention of the North. As I stand here to reiterate, as I have done everywhere, every word I then uttered—to declare that the sentiments I then avowed were universally approved in the South—I realize that the confidence begotten by that speech is largely responsible for my presence here to-night. I should dishonor myself if I betrayed that confidence by uttering one insincere word, or by withholding one essential element of the truth. Apropos of this last, let me confess, Mr. President—before the praise of New England has died on my lips—that I believe the best product of her present life is the procession of 17,000 Vermont Democrats that for twenty-two years, undiminished by death, unrecruited by birth or conversion, have marched over their rugged hills, cast their Democratic ballots, and gone back home to pray for their unregenerate neighbors, and awake to read the record of 26,000 Republican majority. May the God of the helpless and the heroic help them—and may their sturdy tribe increase!

Far to the south, Mr. President, separated from this section by a line, once defined in irrepressible difference, once traced in fratricidal blood, and now, thank God, but a vanishing shadow, lies the fairest and richest domain of this earth. It is the home of a brave and hospitable people. There, is centered all that can please or prosper humankind. A perfect climate, above a fertile soil, yields to the husbandman every product of the temperate zone. There, by night the cotton whitens beneath the stars, and by day the wheat locks the sunshine in its bearded sheaf. In the same field the clover steals the fragrance of the wind, and the tobacco catches the quick aroma of the rains. There, are mountains stored with exhaustless treasures; forests, vast and primeval, and rivers that, tumbling or loitering, run wanton to the sea. Of the three essential items of all industries—cotton, iron and wood—that region has easy control. In cotton, a fixed monopoly—in iron, proven supremacy—in timber, the reserve supply of the Republic. From this assured and permanent advantage, against which artificial conditions cannot much longer prevail, has grown an amazing system of industries. Not maintained by human contrivance of tariff or capital, afar off from the fullest and cheapest source of supply, but resting in Divine assurance, within touch of field and mine and forest—not set amid costly farms from which competition has driven the farmer in despair, but amid cheap and sunny lands, rich with agriculture, to which neither season nor soil has set a limit—this system of industries is mounting to a splendor that shall dazzle and illumine the world.

That, sir, is the picture and the promise of my home—a land better and fairer than I have told you, and yet but fit setting, in its material excellence, for the loyal and gentle quality of its citizenship. Against that, sir, we have New England, recruiting the Republic from its sturdy loins, shaking from its overcrowded hives new swarms of workers and touching this land all over with its energy and its courage. And yet, while in the Eldorado of which I have told you, but 15 per cent. of lands are cultivated, its mines scarcely touched and its population so scant that, were it set equidistant, the sound of the human voice could not be heard from Virginia to Texas—while on the threshold of nearly every house in New England stands a son, seeking with troubled eyes some new land in which to carry his modest patrimony, the strange fact remains that in 1880 the South had fewer Northern-born citizens than she had in 1870— fewer in '70 than in '60. Why is this? Why is it, sir, though the sectional line be now but a mist that the breath may dispel, fewer men of the North have crossed it over to the South than when it was crimson with the best blood of the Republic, or even when the slaveholder stood guard every inch of its way?

There can be but one answer. It is the very problem we are now to consider. The key that opens that problem will unlock to the world the fairest half of this Republic, and free the halted feet of thousands whose eyes are already kindling with its beauty. Better than this, it will open the hearts of brothers for thirty years estranged, and clasp in lasting comradeship a million hands now withheld in doubt. Nothing, sir, but this problem, and the suspicions it breeds, hinders a clear understanding and a perfect union. Nothing else stands between us and such love as bound Georgia and Massachusetts at Valley Forge and Yorktown, chastened by the sacrifices at Manassas and Gettysburg, and illumined with the coming of better work and a nobler destiny than was ever wrought with the sword or sought at the cannon's mouth.

If this does not invite your patient hearing to-night—hear one thing more. My people, your brothers in the South—brothers in blood, in destiny, in all that is best in our past and future —are so beset with this problem that their very existence depends upon its right solution. Nor are they wholly to blame for its presence. The slave-ships of the Republic sailed from your ports—the slaves worked in our fields. You will not defend the traffic, nor I the institution. But I do hereby declare that in its wise and humane administration, in lifting the slave to heights of which he had not dreamed in his savage home, and giving him a happiness he has not yet found in freedom— our fathers left their sons a saving and excellent heritage. In the storm of war this institution was lost. I thank God as heartily as you do that human slavery is gone forever from the American soil. But the freedman remains. With him a problem without precedent or parallel. Note its appalling conditions. Two utterly dissimilar races on the same soil—with equal political and civil rights—almost equal in numbers, but terribly unequal in intelligence and responsibility—each pledged against fusion—one for a century in servitude to the other, and freed at last by a desolating war—the experiment sought by neither, but approached by both with doubt—these are the conditions. Under these, adverse at every point, we are required to carry these two races in peace and honor to the end.

Never, sir, has such a task been given to mortal stewardship. Never before in this Republic has the white race divided on the rights of an alien race. The red man was cut down as a weed, because he hindered the way of the American citizen. The yellow man was shut out of this Republic because he is an alien and inferior. The red man was owner of the land—the yellow man highly civilized and assimilable—but they hindered both sections and are gone! But the black man, affecting but one section, is clothed with every privilege of government and pinned to the soil, and my people commanded to make good at any hazard, and at any cost, his full and equal heirship of American privilege and prosperity. It matters not that every other race has been routed or excluded, without rhyme or reason. It matters not that wherever the whites and blacks have touched, in any era or in any clime, there has been irreconcilable violence.

It matters not that no two races, however similar, have lived anywhere at any time on the same soil with equal rights in peace! In spite of these things we are commanded to make good this change of American policy which has not perhaps changed American prejudice—to make certain here what has elsewhere been impossible between whites and blacks—and to reverse, under the very worst conditions, the universal verdict of racial history. And driven, sir, to this superhuman task with an impatience that brooks no delay—a rigor that accepts no excuse—and a suspicion that discourages frankness and sincerity. We do not shrink from this trial. It is so interwoven with our industrial fabric that we cannot disentangle it if we would—so bound up in our honorable obligation to the world, that we would not if we could. Can we solve it? The God who gave it into our hands, He alone can know. But this the weakest and wisest of us do know; we cannot solve it with less than your tolerant and patient sympathy—with less than the knowledge that the blood that runs in your veins is our blood—and that when we have done our best, whether the issue be lost or won, we shall feel your strong arms about us and hear the beating of your approving hearts.

The resolute, clear-headed, broad-minded men of the South—the men whose genius made glorious every page of the first seventy years of American history—whose courage and fortitude you tested in five years of the fiercest war—whose energy has made bricks without straw and spread splendor amid the ashes of their war wasted homes—these men wear this problem in their hearts and their brains, by day and by night. They realize, as you cannot, what this problem means—what they owe to this kindly and dependent race—the measure of their debt to the world in whose despite they defended and maintained slavery. And though their feet are hindered in its undergrowth, and their march encumbered with its burdens, they have lost neither the patience from which comes clearness, nor the faith from which comes courage. Nor, sir, when in passionate moments is disclosed to them that vague and awful shadow, with its lurid abysses and its crimson stains, into which I pray God they may never go, are they struck with more of apprehension than is needed to complete their consecration!

Such is the temper of my people. But what of the problem itself? Mr. President, we need not go one step further unless you concede right here the people I speak for are as honest, as sensible, and as just as your people, seeking as earnestly as you would in their place, to rightly solve the problem that touches them at every vital point. If you insist that they are ruffians, blindly striving with bludgeon and shotgun to plunder and oppress a race, then I shall sacrifice my self-respect and tax your patience in vain. But admit that they are men of common sense and common honesty—wisely modifying an environment they cannot wholly disregard—guiding and controlling as best they can the vicious and irresponsible of either race—compensating error with frankness, and retrieving in patience what they lose in passion—and conscious all the time that wrong means ruin— admit this, and we may reach an understanding to-night.

The President of the United States in his late message to Congress, discussing the plea that the South should be left to solve this problem, asks: "Are they at work upon it? What solution do they offer? When will the black man cast a free ballot? When will he have the civil rights that are his?" I shall not here protest against the partisanry that, for the first time in our history in time of peace, has stamped with the great seal of our government a stigma upon the people of a great and loyal section, though I gratefully remember that the great dead soldier who held the helm of state for the eight stormiest years of reconstruction never found need for such a step; and though there is no personal sacrifice I would not make to remove this cruel and unjust imputation on my people from the archives of my country! But, sir, backed by a record on every page of which is progress, I venture to make earnest and respectful answer to the questions that are asked. I bespeak your patience, while with vigorous plainness of speech, seeking your judgment rather than your applause, I proceed step by step. We give to the world this year a crop of 7,500,000 bales of cotton, worth $45,000,000, and its cash equivalent in grain, grasses and fruit. This enormous crop could not have come from the hands of sullen and discontented labor. It comes from peaceful fields, in which laughter and gossip rise above the hum of industry, and contentment runs with the singing plow.

It is claimed that this ignorant labor is defrauded of its just hire. I present the tax-books of Georgia, which show that the negro, 25 years ago a slave, has in Georgia alone $10,000,000 of assessed property, worth twice that much. Does not that record honor him, and vindicate his neighbors? What people, penniless, illiterate, has done so well? For every Afro-American agitator, stirring the strife in which alone he prospers, I can show you a thousand negroes, happy in their cabin homes, tilling their own land by day, and at night taking from the lips of their children the helpful message their State sends them from the schoolhouse door. And the schoolhouse itself bears testimony. In Georgia we added last year $250,000 to the school fund, making a total of more than $1,000,000—and this in the face of prejudice not yet conquered—of the fact that the whites are assessed for $368,000,000, the blacks for $10,000,000, and yet 49 per cent. of the beneficiaries are black children—and in the doubt of many wise men if education helps, or can help, our problem. Charleston, with her taxable values cut half in two since 1860, pays more in proportion for public schools than Boston. Although it is easier to give much out of much than little out of little, the South with one-seventh of the taxable property of the country, with relatively larger debt, having received only one-twelfth as much public land, and having back of its tax-books none of the half billion of bonds that enrich the North—and though it pays annually $26,000,000 to your section as pensions—yet gives nearly one-sixth of the public school-fund. The South since 1865 has spent $122,000,000 in education, and this year is pledged to $37,000,000 for state and city schools, although the blacks paying one-thirtieth of the taxes get nearly one half of the fund.

Go into our fields and see whites and blacks working side by side. On our buildings in the same squad. In our shops at the same forge. Often the blacks crowd the whites from work, or lower wages by the greater need or simpler habits, and yet are permitted because we want to bar them from no avenue in which their feet are fitted to tread. They could not there be elected orators of the white universities, as they have been here, but they do enter there a hundred useful trades that are closed

against them here. We hold it better and wiser to tend the
weeds in the garden than to water the exotic in the window. In
the South, there are negro lawyers, teachers, editors, dentists,
doctors, preachers, multiplying with the increasing ability of
their race to support them. In villages and towns they have
their military companies equipped from the armories of the
State, their churches and societies built and supported largely
by their neighbors. What is the testimony of the courts? In
penal legislation we have steadily reduced felonies to misdemeanors, and have led the world in mitigating punishment for
crime, that we might save, as far as possible, this dependent race
from its own weakness. In our penitentiary record 60 per cent.
of the prosecutors are negroes, and in every court the negro
criminal strikes the colored juror, that white men may judge
his case. In the North, one negro in every 65 is in jail—in the
South only one in 446. In the North the percentage of negro
prisoners is six times as great as native whites—in the South,
only four times as great. · If prejudice wrongs him in southern
courts, the record shows it to be deeper in northern courts.

I assert here, and a bar as intelligent and upright as the bar
of Massachusetts will solemnly indorse my assertion, that in
the southern courts, from highest to lowest, pleading for life,
liberty or property, the negro has distinct advantage because
he is a negro, apt to be overreached, oppressed—and that this
advantage reaches from the juror in making his verdict to the
judge in measuring his sentence. Now, Mr. President, can it
be seriously maintained that we are terrorizing the people from
whose willing hands come every year $1,000,000,000 of farm
crops? Or have robbed a people, who twenty-five years from
unrewarded slavery have amassed in one State $20,000,000 of
property? Or that we intend to oppress the people we are arming every day? Or deceive them when we are educating them
to the utmost limit of our ability? Or outlaw them when we
work side by side with them? Or re-enslave them under legal
forms when for their benefit we have even imprudently narrowed the limit of felonies and mitigated the severity of law?
My fellow countryman, as you yourself may sometimes have
to appeal to the bar of human judgment for justice and for

right, give to my people to-night the fair and unanswerable conclusion of these incontestible facts.

But it is claimed that under this fair seeming there is disorder
and violence. This I admit. And there will be until there is one
ideal community on earth after which we may pattern. But
how widely it is misjudged! It is hard to measure with exact-
ness whatever touches the negro. His helplessness, his isolation, his century of servitude, these dispose us to emphasize and
magnify his wrongs. This disposition, inflamed by prejudice
and partisanry, has led to injustice and delusion. Lawless
men may ravage a county in Iowa and it is accepted as an incident—in the South a drunken row is declared to be the fixed
habit of the community. Regulators may whip vagabonds in
Indiana by platoons, and it scarcely arrests attention—a chance
collision in the South among relatively the same classes is gravely accepted as evidence that one race is destroying the other.
We might as well claim that the Union was ungrateful to the
colored soldiers who followed its flag, because a Grand Army
post in Connecticut closed its doors to a negro veteran, as for
you to give racial significance to every incident in the South, or
to accept exceptional grounds as the rule of our society. I am
not one of those who becloud American honor with the parade
of the outrages of either section, and belie American character
by declaring them to be significant and representative. I prefer
to maintain that they are neither, and stand for nothing but the
passion and the sin of our poor fallen humanity. If society, like
a machine, were no stronger than its weakest part, I should
despair of both sections. But, knowing that society, sentient
and responsible in every fibre, can mend and repair until the
whole has the strength of the best, I despair of neither. These
gentlemen who come with me here, knit into Georgia's busy life
as they are, never saw, I dare assert, an outrage committed on
a negro! And if they did, not one of you would be swifter to
prevent or punish. It is through them, and the men who think
with them—making nine-tenths of every southern community—
that these two races have been carried thus far with less of
violence than would have been possible anywhere else on earth.
And in their fairness and courage and steadfastness—more

than in all the laws that can be passed or all the bayonets that can be mustered—is the hope of our future.

When will the black cast a free ballot? When ignorance anywhere is not dominated by the will of the intelligent; when the laborer anywhere casts a vote unhindered by his boss; when the vote of the poor anywhere is not influenced by the power of the rich; when the strong and the steadfast do not everywhere control the suffrage of the weak and shiftless—then and not till then will the ballot of the negro be free. The white people of the South are banded, Mr. President, not in prejudice against the blacks—not in sectional estrangement, not in the hope of political dominion—but in a deep and abiding necessity. Here is this vast ignorant and purchasable vote—clannish, credulous, impulsive and passionate—tempting every art of the demagogue, but insensible to the appeal of the statesman. Wrongly started, in that it was led into alienation from its neighbor and taught to rely on the protection of an outside force, it cannot be merged and lost in the two great parties through logical currents, for it lacks political conviction and even that information on which conviction must be based. It must remain a faction—strong enough in every community to control on the slightest division of the whites. Under that division it becomes the prey of the cunning and unscrupulous of both parties. Its credulity is imposed on, its patience inflamed, its cupidity tempted, its impulses misdirected—and even its superstition made to play its part in a campaign in which every interest of society is jeopardized and every approach to the ballot-box debauched. It is against such campaigns as this—the folly and the bitterness and the danger of which every southern community has drunk deeply—that the white people of the South are banded together. Just as you in Massachusetts would be banded if 300,000 black men, not one in a hundred able to read his ballot—banded in race instinct, holding against you the memory of a century of slavery, taught by your late conquerors to distrust and oppose you, had already travestied legislation from your statehouse, and in every species of folly or villainy had wasted your substance and exhausted your credit.

But admitting the right of the whites to unite against this tremendous menace, we are challenged with the smallness of our vote. This has long been flippantly charged to be evidence, and has now been solemnly and officially declared to be proof of political turpitude and baseness on our part. Let us see. Virginia—a State now under fierce assault for this alleged crime—cast in 1888 75 per cent. of her vote. Massachusetts, the State in which I speak, 60 per cent. of her vote. Was it suppression in Virginia and natural causes in Massachusetts? Last month Virginia cast 69 per cent. of her vote, and Massachusetts, fighting in every district, cast only 49 per cent. of hers. If Virginia is condemned because 31 per cent. of her vote was silent, how shall this State escape in which 51 per cent. was dumb? Let us enlarge this comparison. The sixteen southern States in 1888 cast 67 per cent. of their total vote—the six New England States but 63 per cent. of theirs. By what fair rule shall the stigma be put upon one section, while the other escapes? A congressional election in New York last week, with the polling-place in touch of every voter, brought out only 6,000 votes of 28,000—and the lack of opposition is assigned as the natural cause. In a district in my State, in which an opposition speech has not been heard in ten years, and the polling-places are miles apart—under the unfair reasoning of which my section has been a constant victim—the small vote is charged to be proof of forcible suppression. In Virginia an average majority of 10,000, under hopeless division of the minority, was raised to 42,000; in Iowa, in the same election, a majority of 32,000 was wiped out, and an opposition majority of 8,000 was established. The change of 42,000 votes in Iowa is accepted as political revolution—in Virginia an increase of 30,000 on a safe majority is declared to be proof of political fraud. I charge these facts and figures home, sir, to the heart and conscience of the American people, who will not assuredly see one section condemned for what another section is excused!

If I can drive them through the prejudice of the partisan, and have them read and pondered at the fireside of the citizen, I will rest on the judgment there formed and the verdict there rendered!

It is deplorable, sir, that in both sections a larger percentage of the vote is not regularly cast, but more inexplicable that this should be so in New England than in the South. What invites the negro to the ballot-box? He knows that, of all men, it has promised him most and yielded him least. His first appeal to suffrage was the promise of "forty acres and a mule." His second, the threat that Democratic success meant his re-inslavement. Both have proved false in his experience. He looked for a home, and he got the freedman's bank. He fought under the promise of the loaf, and in victory was denied the crumbs. Discouraged and deceived, he has realized at last that his best friends are his neighbors, with whom his lot is cast, and whose prosperity is bound up in his—and that he has gained nothing in politics to compensate the loss of their confidence and sympathy that is at last his best and his enduring hope. And so, without leaders or organization—and lacking the resolute heroism of my party friends in Vermont that makes their hopeless march over the hills a high and inspiring pilgrimage—he shrewdly measures the occasional agitator, balances his little account with politics, touches up his mule and jogs down the furrow, letting the mad world jog as it will!

The negro vote can never control in the South, and it would be well if partisans in the North would understand this. I have seen the white people of a State set about by black hosts until their fate seemed sealed. But, sir, some brave man, banding them together, would rise, as Elisha rose in beleaguered Samaria, and touching their eyes with faith, bid them look abroad to see the very air "filled with the chariots of Israel and the horsemen thereof." If there is any human force that cannot be withstood, it is the power of the banded intelligence and responsibility of a free community. Against it, numbers and corruption cannot prevail. It cannot be forbidden in the law or divorced in force. It is the inalienable right of every free community—and the just and righteous safeguard against an ignorant or corrupt suffrage. It is on this, sir, that we rely in the South. Not the cowardly menace of mask or shotgun; but the peaceful majesty of intelligence and responsibility, massed and unified for the protection of its homes and the preservation of its liberty. That, sir, is our reliance and our hope, and against it all the powers of the earth shall not prevail. It was just as certain that Virginia would come back to the unchallenged control of her white race—that before the moral and material power of her people once more unified, opposition would crumble until its last desperate leader was left alone vainly striving to rally his disordered hosts—as that night should fade in the kindling glory of the sun. You may pass force bills, but they will not avail. You may surrender your own liberties to Federal election law, you may submit, in fear of a necessity that does not exist, that the very form of this government may be changed—this old State that holds in its charter the boast that "it is a free and independent commonwealth"—it may deliver its election machinery into the hands of the government it helped to create—but never, sir, will a single State of this Union, North or South, be delivered again to the control of an ignorant and inferior race. We wrested our State government from negro supremacy when the Federal drumbeat rolled closer to the ballot-box and Federal bayonets hedged it deeper about than will ever again be permitted in this free government. But, sir, though the cannon of this Republic thundered in every voting district of the South, we still should find in the mercy of God the means and the courage to prevent its re-establishment!

I regret, sir, that my section, hindered with this problem, stands in seeming estrangement to the North. If, sir, any man will point out to me a path down which the white people of the South divided may walk in peace and honor, I will take that path though I took it alone—for at the end, and nowhere else, I fear, is to be found the full prosperity of my section and the full restoration of this Union. But, sir, if the negro had not been enfranchised, the South would have been divided and the Republic united. His enfranchisement—against which I enter no protest—holds the South united and compact. What solution, then, can we offer for the problem? Time alone can disclose it to us. We simply report progress and ask your patience. If the problem be solved at all—and I firmly believe it will, though nowhere else has it been—it will be solved by the people most deeply bound in interest, most deeply pledged in honor to its solution. I had rather see my people render back this question lightly solved than to see them gather all the spoils over which faction has contended since Catiline conspired and Cæsar fought. Meantime we treat the negro fairly, measuring to him justice in the fullness the strong should give to the weak, and leading him in the steadfast ways of citizenship that he may no longer be the prey of the unscrupulous and the sport of the thoughtless. We open to him every pursuit in which he can prosper, and seek to broaden his training and capacity. We seek to hold his confidence and friendship, and to pin him to the soil with ownership, that he may catch in the fire of his own hearth-stone that sense of responsibility the shiftless can never know. And we gather him into that alliance of intelligence and responsibility that, though it now runs close to racial lines, welcomes the responsible and intelligent of any race. By this course, confirmed in our judgment and justified in the progress already made, we hope to progress slowly but surely to the end.

The love we feel for that race you cannot measure nor comprehend. As I attest it here, the spirit of my old black mammy from her home up there looks down to bless, and through the tumult of this night steals the sweet music of her croonings as thirty years ago she held me in her black arms and led me smiling into sleep. This scene vanishes as I speak, and I catch a vision of an old Southern home, with its lofty pillars, and its white pigeons fluttering down through the golden air. I see women with strained and anxious faces, and children alert yet helpless. I see night come down with its dangers and its apprehensions, and in a big homely room I feel on my tired head the touch of loving hands—now worn and wrinkled, but fairer to me yet than the hands of mortal woman, and stronger yet to lead me than the hands of mortal man—as they lay a mother's blessing there while at her knees—the truest altar I yet have found—I thank God that she is safe in her sanctuary, because her slaves, sentinel in the silent cabin or guard at her chamber door, puts a black man's loyalty between her and danger.

I catch another vision. The crisis of battle—a soldier struck, staggering, fallen. I see a slave, scuffling through the smoke, winding his black arms about the fallen form, reckless of the hurtling death—bending his trusty face to catch the words that tremble on the stricken lips, so wrestling meantime with agony that he would lay down his life in his master's stead. I see him by the weary bedside, ministering with uncomplaining patience, praying with all his humble heart that God will lift his master up, until death comes in mercy and in honor to still the soldier's agony and seal the soldier's life. I see him by the open grave, mute, motionless, uncovered, suffering for the death of him who in life fought against his freedom. I see him when the mound is heaped and the great drama of his life is closed, turn away and with downcast eyes and uncertain step start out into new and strange fields, faltering, struggling, but moving on, until his shambling figure is lost in the light of this better and brighter day. And from the grave comes a voice saying: "Follow him! Put your arms about him in his need, even as he puts his about me. Be his friend as he was mine." And out into this new world—strange to me as to him, dazzling, bewildering both—I follow! And may God forget my people—when they forget these!

Whatever the future may hold for them—whether they plod along in the servitude from which they have never been lifted since the Cyrenian was laid hold upon by the Roman soldiers and made to bear the cross of the fainting Christ—whether they find homes again in Africa, and thus hasten the prophecy of the psalmist who said: "And suddenly Ethiopia shall hold out her hands unto God"—whether, forever dislocated and separated, they remain a weak people beset by stronger, and exist as the Turk, who lives in the jealousy rather than in the conscience of Europe—or whether in this miraculous Republic they break through the caste of twenty centuries and, belying universal history, reach the full stature of citizenship, and in peace maintain it—we shall give them uttermost justice and abiding friendship. And whatever we do, into whatever seeming estrangement we may be driven, nothing shall disturb the love we bear this Republic, or mitigate our consecration to its service. I stand here, Mr. President, to profess no new loyalty. When General Lee, whose heart was the temple of our hopes and whose arm was clothed with our strength, renewed his allegiance to the government of Appomattox, he spoke from a heart too great to be false, and he spoke for every honest man from Maryland to Texas. From that day to this, Hamilcar has nowhere in the South sworn young Hannibal to hatred and vengeance—but everywhere to loyalty and to love. Witness the soldier standing at the base of a Confederate monument above the graves of his comrades, his empty sleeve tossing in the April wind, adjuring

the young men about him, to serve as honest and loyal citizens
the government against which their fathers fought. This message, delivered from that sacred presence, has gone home to
the hearts of my fellows! And, sir, I declare here, if physical
courage be always equal to human aspiration, that they would
die, sir, if need be, to restore this Republic their fathers fought
to dissolve!

Such, Mr. President, is this problem as we see it; such is the
temper in which we approach it: such the progress made. What
do we ask of you? First, patience; out of this alone can come
perfect work. Second, confidence; in this alone can you judge
fairly. Third, sympathy; in this you can help us best. Fourth,
give us your sons as hostages. When you plant your capital in
millions, send your sons that they may help know how true are
our hearts and may help to swell the Anglo-Saxon current until
it can carry without danger this black infusion. Fifth, loyalty
to the Republic—for there is sectionalism in loyalty as in estrangement. This hour little needs the loyalty that is loyal to
one section and yet holds the other in enduring suspicion and
estrangement. Give us the broad and perfect loyalty that loves
and trusts Georgia alike with Massachusetts—that knows no
south, no north, no east, no west; but endears with equal and
patriotic love every foot of our soil, every State in our Union.

A mighty duty, sir, and a mighty inspiration impels every
one of us to-night to lose in patriotic consecration whatever
estranges, whatever divides. We, sir, are Americans—and we
fight for human liberty. The uplifting force of the American
idea is under every throne on earth. France, Brazil—these are
our victories. To redeem the earth from kingcraft and oppression—this is our mission. And we shall not fail. God has sown
in our soil the seed of his millennial harvest, and he will not
lay the sickle to the ripening crop until his full and perfect day
has come. Our history, sir, has been a constant and expanding
miracle from Plymouth Rock and Jamestown all the way—
aye, even from the hour when, from the voiceless and trackless
ocean, a new world rose to the sight of the inspired sailor. As
we approach the fourth centennial of that stupendous day—
when the old world will come to marvel and to learn, amid our
gathered treasures—let us resolve to crown the miracles of our

past with the spectacle of a Republic compact, united, indissoluble in the bonds of love—loving from the lakes to the Gulf—the wounds of war healed in every heart as on every hill—serene and resplendent at the summit of human achievement and earthly glory—blazing out the path, and making clear the way up which all the nations of the earth must come in God's appointed time!

JOHN P. ALTGELD

THE CHILDREN OF TOIL

Address at Kuhn's Park, Chicago, Illinois, on Labor Day, September 8, 1893

[John Peter Altgeld was born in Nieder Selters, Nassau, Germany, on December 30, 1847. While he was an infant his parents emigrated to Richland county, Ohio, where he grew up, without formal education, working at hard labor, until he was twenty-one. In 1869 he left home, worked as a laborer, then as a school-teacher, and finally studied law. In 1874 he was elected State's Attorney of Andrew county, Missouri. He moved to Chicago, Illinois, in 1875, practiced law, and was Judge of the Superior Court of Cook county from 1886 to 1891. When he resigned he was Chief Justice. He was the first Democratic Governor of Illinois after the Civil War, serving from 1892 to 1896. He died in Chicago on March 12, 1902.

"Words fitly spoken are like apples of gold in pictures of silver," wrote the St. Louis *Republic*, commenting on the speech printed below. "Nowhere of late have such words been spoken with more force and with promise of more good effect than by Governor Altgeld, at Chicago, on Labor Day." He had been savagely scored throughout the country for his pardon, in June, 1893, of the three "anarchists" who had been in prison since the Haymarket riot of May 4, 1886. He had been denounced as "the crowned hero and worshiped deity of the anarchists of the Northwest." Three months afterward, he surprised the country by rejecting the demagogue's opportunity and delivering this conservative speech, noteworthy both in substance and in form.]

Mr. President, Ladies and Gentlemen:

You are to be congratulated on the success of your celebration. Two great demonstrations in Chicago alone are vying with each other in honoring Labor Day. These vast assemblages represent sturdy manhood and womanhood. They represent honest toil of every kind, and they represent strong patriotism and desirable citizenship. The law has set apart this day in recognition of the nobility of labor, and as the Governor of this great State, I have come to pay homage to that force which lays the foundation of empires, which builds cities, builds railroads, develops agriculture, supports schools, founds industries, creates commerce, and moves the world. It is wisely directed

labor that has made our country the greatest ever known, and
has made Chicago the wonder of mankind. I say wisely directed labor; for without wise direction labor is fruitless. The
pointing out and the doing are inseparably connected. More
than this, ahead of the directing, there must go the genius which
originates and conceives, the genius which takes the risk and
moves a league forward. All three are necessary to each other.
Weaken either, and there are clouds in the sky. Destroy either,
and the hammer of industry ceases to be heard. Glance over
this majestic city, see its workshops, its warehouses, its commercial palaces, its office temples, and the thousand other structures that show the possibilities of human achievement and tell
who did all this. You say the laboring men; yes, that is correct; but I tell you that if the gods keep a record of our doings,
they have set down the men who originated all this, and then
dared to make a forward step in building, as among the greatest
of laborers. We are at present in the midst of a great industrial
and commercial depression. Industry is nearly at a stand-still
all over the earth. The consumptive power, or rather the purchasing power, of the world has been interfered with, producing
not only a derangement but a paralysis, not only stopping further production, but preventing the proper distribution of what
there is already created; so that we have the anomalous spectacle of abundant food products on the one hand, and hungry men
without bread on the other. Abundant fabrics on the one hand,
and industrious, frugal men going half clad on the other. Employer and employé are affected alike.

There are thousands of honest, industrious and frugal men
who walk the streets all day in search of work, and even bread,
and there are many hundreds of the most enterprising employers
who sweat by day and walk the floor by night trying to devise
means to keep the sheriff away from the establishment. You
are not responsible for this condition. Men here and in Europe,
who call themselves statesmen, have inaugurated policies of
which this is a natural result. Considering the increase in population, the increase in the industries and commercial activity of
the world, as well as the increased area over which business was
done, there has in recent years been a practical reduction in the
volume of the money of the world of from thirty-three to forty

per cent., and there had of necessity to follow a shrinkage in the value of property to a corresponding extent. This has been going on for a number of years, and as it has progressed it has become harder and harder for the debtor to meet his obligations. For the value of his property kept falling while his debt did not fall. Consequently, every little while a lot of debtors, who could no longer stand the strain, succumbed. The result was that each time there was a flurry in financial circles. By degrees these failures became more frequent, until finally people who had money took alarm, and withdrew it from circulation. This precipitated a panic and with it a harvest of bankruptcy. No doubt there were secondary causes that contributed, but this one cause was sufficient to create the distress that we see. If for some years to come there should not be sufficient blood in the industrial and commercial world to make affairs healthy, then you must console yourselves with the thought that our country, with all the other great nations, has been placed on a narrow gold basis, and you will not be troubled with any of these cheap dollars that the big newspapers claim you did not want. The present depression, resulting from a lack of ready money in the world, shows how indispensable capital is to labor—all the wheels of industry stand still the moment it is withdrawn. It also shows that while the interests of the employer and the employé may be antagonistic on the subject of wages, they are the same in every other respect; neither can do anything without the other—certain it is that the employé cannot prosper unless the employer does. On the other hand, if the purchasing power of the employé is destroyed, the employer must soon be without a market for his goods. The great American market was due to the purchasing power of the laboring classes. If this should in the end be destroyed it will change entirely the character of our institutions. Whenever our laboring classes are reduced to a condition where they can buy only a few coarse articles of food and clothing, then our glory will have departed. Still another thing has been made more clear than before, and that is, that the employers, as a rule, are not great capitalists of the country. As a rule, they are enterprising men who borrow idle capital, and put it to some use, and whenever they are suddenly called on to pay up and are not able to borrow elsewhere, they are obliged to shut down.

There are many advanced thinkers who look forward to a new industrial system that shall be an improvement on the present, and under which the laborer shall come nearer getting his share of the benefits resulting from invention and machinery, than under the present system. All lovers of their kind would hail such a system with joy. But we are forced to say that it is not yet at hand. As we must have bread and must have clothing, we are obliged to cling to the old system for the present, and probably for a long time to come, until the foundations can be laid for a better one by intelligent progress. Classes, like individuals, have their bright and their dark days, and just now there seems to be a long dark day ahead of you. It will be a day of suffering and distress, and I must say to you there seems to be no way of escaping it, and I therefore counsel you to face it squarely and bear it with that heroism and fortitude with which an American citizen should face and bear calamity. It has been suggested that the State and different branches of government should furnish employment during the winter to idle men. Certainly everything that can be done in this line will be done, but I must warn you not to expect too much from this source. The powers of government are so hedged about with constitutional provisions that much cannot be done. The State at present has no work to do. The parks can employ only a few men. The city has work for more men, but it is also limited in its funds. The great drainage canal may, and probably will, give employment to a considerable number of men, but, after all, you must recognize that these things will be only in the nature of makeshifts; only to tide over; only to keep men and their families from starving. And on this point let me say it will be the duty of all public officials to see to it that no man is permitted to starve on the soil of Illinois, and provision will be made to that end. But all this is temporary. The laborer must look to ways and means that are permanent for the improvement of his condition when the panic is over, and these measures must be along the line of and in harmony with the institutions of this century, and must move by a gradual and steady development. Nothing that is violently done is of permanent advantage to the working man. He can only prosper when his labor is in demand, and his labor can be in demand only when his employer prospers and there is nothing to interfere with consumption.

The world has been slow to accord labor its due. For thousands of years pillage, plunder and organized robbery, called warfare, were honorable pursuits, and the man who toiled, in order that all might live, was despised. In the flight of time, it was but yesterday that the labor of the earth was driven with the lash, and either sold on the block like cattle, or tied by an invisible chain to the soil, and was forbidden to even wander outside his parish. In the yesterday of time, even the employers of labor were despised. The men who conducted great industries, who carried on commerce, who practiced the useful arts, the men who made the earth habitable, were looked down upon by a class that considered it honorable to rob the toiler of his bread, a class which, while possessing the pride of the eagle, had only the character of the vulture. Great has been the development since then. This century brought upon its wings higher ideas, more of truth and more of common sense, and it announced to mankind that he is honorable who creates; that he should be despised who can only consume; that he is the benefactor of the race who gives it an additional thought, an additional flower, an additional loaf of bread, an additional comfort; and he is a curse to his kind who tramples down what others build, or, without compensation, devours what others create. The century brought with it still greater things. Not only did it lift the employer to a position of honor, influence and power, but it tore away parish boundaries, it cut the chains of the serf, it burned the auction block, where the laborer and his children were sold; and it brought ideas; it taught the laboring man to extend his hand to his fellow-laborer; it taught him to organize, and not only to read but to investigate, to inquire, to discuss, to consider and to look ahead; so that, to-day, the laborer and his cause, at least theoretically, command the homage of all civilized men, and the greatest States in christendom have set apart a day to be annually observed as a holiday in honor of labor.

The children of Israel were forty years in marching from the bondage of Egypt to the freer atmosphere of Palestine, and a halo of glory envelops their history. In the last forty years the children of Toil have made a forward march which is greater than any ever made in the wilderness. True, the land is not conquered. You have simply camped upon that higher plane where you can more clearly see the difficulties of the past, and where, in the end, you may hope for a higher justice and a happier condition for yourselves and your children, but a great deal remains to be done. In a sense, you are just out of the wilderness. You ask, along what lines, then, shall we proceed when the times get better in order to improve our condition? I answer, along lines which harmonize, not only with nature's laws, but with the laws of the land. Occupying, as I do, a position which makes me in a sense a conservator of all interests and classes, I desire to see the harmonious prosperity of all; and let me say to you that, until all the active interests of the land prosper again, there can be no general demand for your services, and, consequently, no healthy prosperity. What I wish to point out is the absolute necessity of each class or interest being able to take care of itself in the fierce struggle for existence. You have not yet fully reached this state. In the industrial world, as well as in the political world, only those forces survive which can maintain themselves, and which are so concentrated that their influence is immediately and directly felt. A scattered force, no matter how great, is of no account in the sharp contests of the age. This is an age of concentration. Everywhere there is concentration and combination of capital and of those factors which to-day rule the world. The formation of corporations has greatly accelerated this movement, and no matter what is said about it, whether we approve it or not, it is the characteristic feature of our civilization, and grows out of increased invention, the speedy communication between different parts of the world, and the great industrial generalship and enterprise of the time. It is questionable whether this tendency to combination could have been stopped in any way. It is certain, without this concentration of force, the gigantic achievements of our times would have been an impossibility. Combination and concentration are the masters of the age. Let the laborer learn from this and act accordingly. Fault-finding and idle complaint are useless. Great

HICKS' SP.A.S.—11

forces, like great rivers, cannot be stopped. You must be able
to fight your own battles. For the laborer to stand single-
handed before giant combinations of power means annihilation.
The world gives only when it is obliged to, and respects only
those who compel its respect.

Government was created by power and has always been
controlled by power. Do not imagine that it is sufficient if
you have justice and equity on your side, for the earth is covered with the graves of justice and equity that failed to receive recognition, because there was no influence or force to
compel it, and it will be so until the millennium. Whenever
you demonstrate that you are an active, concentrated power,
moving along lawful lines, then you will be felt in government.
Until then you will not. This is an age of law as well as of
force, and no force succeeds that does not move along legal lines.
The laboring men of the world always have been, and are to-day,
the support and principal reliance of the government. They
support its flags in time of war, and their hands earn the taxes
in time of peace. Their voice is for fair play, and no great government was ever destroyed by the laboring classes. Treason
and rebellion never originated with them, but always came from
the opposite source. Early in our history there occurred what
was called Shay's Rebellion, but they were not wage-workers
who created it. Then came the so-called Whisky Rebellion, created not by day laborers. During the War of 1812, a convention
was held in the East which practically advocated a dissolution
of the Union, but wage-workers were not among its members.
The great rebellion of 1861 was not fomented by the laboring
classes, but by those classes which ate the bread that others
toiled for. It was a rebellion by those who had long been prominent as leaders, who largely controlled the wealth of the country, who boasted of aristocratic society, and many of whom had
been educated at the expense of the country whose flag they fired
on. While, on the other hand, the great armies which put down
this rebellion and supported the flag were composed of men who
had literally earned their bread by the sweat of their brows.
It is true that at times a number of laborers, more or less ignorant, who thought they were being robbed of the fruits of their
toil, have indulged in rioting; and, while they have always lost

by it, and while they cannot be too severely condemned, yet they do not stand alone in this condemnation, for there have been many broadcloth mobs in this country and in different sections of it, whose actions were lawless and as disgraceful as that of any labor mob that ever assembled. I must congratulate organized labor upon its freedom from turbulence. Rioting is nearly always by an ignorant class outside of all organizations, and which, in most cases, was brought into the community by conscienceless men to defeat organized labor. There should be a law compelling a man who brings this class of people into our midst to give bond for their support and their good behavior, for at present they are simply a disturbing element. They threaten the peace of society and bring reproach on the cause of labor. The lesson I wish to impress upon you is that in business, in the industries, in government, everywhere, only those interests and forces survive that can maintain themselves along legal lines, and if you permanently improve your condition it must be by intelligently and patriotically standing together all over the country. Every plan must fail unless you do this.

At present you are to a great extent yet a scattered force, sufficiently powerful, if collected, to make yourselves heard and felt; to secure, not only a fair hearing, but a fair decision of all questions. Unite this power and you will be independent; leave it scattered and you will fail. Organization is the result of education as well as an educator. Let all the men of America who toil with their hands once stand together and no more complaints will be heard about unfair treatment. The progress of labor in the future must be along the line of patriotic association, not simply in localities, but everywhere. And let me caution you that every act of violence is a hindrance to your progress. There will be men among you ready to commit it. They are your enemies. There will be sneaks and Judas Iscariots in your ranks, who will for a mere pittance act as spies and try to incite some of the more hot-headed of your number to deeds of violence, in order that these reptiles may get the credit of exposing you. They are your enemies. Cast them out of your ranks. Remember that any permanent prosperity must be based upon intelligence and upon conditions which are permanent. And let me say to you again, in conclusion: This fall and this winter will be a trying time to you. The record of the laborers of the earth is one of patriotism. They have maintained the government, they have maintained the schools and churches, and it behooves you now to face the hardships that are upon you and see that your cause is not injured by grave indiscretions. Make the ignorant understand that government is strong and that life and property will be protected and law and order will be maintained, and that, while the day is dark now, the future will place the laborer in a more exalted position than he has ever occupied.

CARL SCHURZ

HILL AND HILLISM

SPEECH AT COOPER UNION, NEW YORK CITY, OCTOBER 29, 1894, IN SUPPORT OF EVERETT P. WHEELER, REFORM DEMOCRATIC CANDIDATE FOR GOVERNOR OF NEW YORK

[Carl Schurz was born in Liblar, near Cologne, Germany, on March 2, 1829. Educated at the Cologne Gymnasium and at the University of Bonn, he fled from Germany in consequence of his participation in the Revolution of 1848, later supporting himself as a newspaper correspondent in Paris and as a school-teacher in London. In 1852 he emigrated to the United States and settled in Philadelphia. In 1855 he moved to Wisconsin, studied law, was admitted to the bar and began practice in Milwaukee. In 1861 he was appointed United States Minister to Spain, but resigned to enter the Union army, in which he was a Brigadier General of Volunteers. After the war he engaged in newspaper work in St. Louis, Missouri. From 1869 to 1875 he was a Republican member of the United States Senate, and from 1877 to 1881, Secretary of the Interior in the Cabinet of President Hayes. From then until his death he was engaged chiefly in literary work, and was editor of the New York *Evening Post* from 1881 to 1884. From 1892 to 1901 he was president of the National Civil Service Reform League. He died in New York City on May 14, 1906.

The campaign speech printed below is a characteristic example of the reform speeches made in the periodic bitter contests with Tammany Hall. In this instance neither David B. Hill nor Everett P. Wheeler was elected, but the Republican candidate, Levi P. Morton, became Governor.]

As a private citizen not engaged in active politics, but taking a warm interest in the public welfare, I am here to tell you why I think that David B. Hill should not be elected governor, and that the movement which has put forward Everett P. Wheeler as its standard-bearer deserves support. This being no time for sweet circumlocution, I shall speak to you in plain language and endeavor to call things by their right names. Let me begin with a chapter of contemporaneous history which, although well known, needs constant repetition.

There is in this municipality a great struggle going on which is to decide whether the city of New York shall be owned by

the inhabitants thereof or by Tammany Hall. It has long been
popularly believed that Tammany Hall is a nest of rapacious
freebooters. But recent disclosures of corruption, of blackmail, of robbery, of vice and crime planted and protected for
revenue, of terrorism, of cruel oppression practiced upon the
poor, the weak and the helpless, have gone far beyond popular
expectation. I know Tammany Hall disclaims responsibility
for some of these atrocities. But they were inspired by the
Tammany spirit; they found in the Tammany "pull" their encouragement and assurance of impunity; they filled Tammany
pockets; they helped to keep Tammany in power, and they are
properly charged to the Tammany system of government. I
have seen something of the world, and affirm that in no civilized
country, and hardly in any uncivilized, is there a government
which, in foulness of corruption, in insatiable rapacity, in criminal practices, in cruel oppression of the lowly, equals Tammany
rule.

The good citizens of New York concluded at last that it was
time to make an end of this. They organized a City Club, Good
Government clubs, a German-American Reform Union and various other bodies, and from day to day the call grew louder for
a union of all honest men without distinction of party—all
against Tammany. The Tammany chiefs became alarmed.
They saw a day of judgment coming. Their head chief, Dick
Croker, took to his heels. He gathered up the princely fortune
he had saved from his revenues as king of New York and retired as a Tammany "sage," complacently conscious of having
secured his harvest in season. But the other Tammany chiefs
were not so comfortably settled. They had to brave the coming
storm. How could they avoid defeat at the municipal election?
They found themselves put to their wits, and tried various devices. They sang the song of harmony as sweetly as any suck-
ing dove. They would forswear all selfish designs. They would
nominate a high-toned citizen for mayor. They would even
endorse a ticket nominated by reform Democrats. They would
do anything to make people forget the Tiger's teeth and claws
until after election. But it was all in vain.

In their extremity they remembered that in their kind of politics the shortest way from one point to another is a crooked line.

The salvation they could not expect to win directly in New York city they might secure by a flank march via Albany. They bethought themselves of their lifelong friend, their trusty confederate, David B. Hill. If they could only make Hill governor again, they need not trouble themselves about a defeat in a mayor's election. As a leading Tammany man said in a reported interview: "Tammany can afford to give up the mayoralty for a couple of years. It would give up a great deal more if it could thereby prevent the election of a Republican governor and legislature." Of course, with Hill in the governor's chair there would be no removals of Tammany heads of departments; no anti-Tammany laws would escape his veto. And with a legislature to match there would be no annoying investigations. Tammany, substantially remaining in possession of all its power, save the mayoralty, would laugh at the impotent wrath of the anti-Tammany mayor, and after two years of fostering care by friend Hill turn up as good as new and get back all it had before. Such was the calculation, and it was excellent. The Tammany mind is eminently practical.

But would friend Hill be willing to accept the nomination for the governorship? Hardly. Comfortably ensconced for several years in the Senate, he would not like to take unnecessary risks. If asked beforehand, he would refuse. Tammany therefore resolved to nominate without asking, and the game succeeded. It is universally known, and not contradicted, that the stampede in the Democratic State convention, which thrust the nomination upon Hill, was planned and managed by Tammany, and that Hill had been nominated and virtually accepted and found himself harnessed to the Tammany cart ere he had time to rub his eyes. That so sly a fox should be caught by surprise may seem ludicrous. But it is more than a joke. It is the revenge of fate; it is the sin of the evil-doer coming home to roost; it is the devil claiming his own. So often had Hill ridden into place and power on the backs of Tammany and the State machine that Tammany and its allies have a right to jump upon his back and say: "Now we will ride you for our salvation! We have done your work; now you will do ours!" All this is perfectly fit and proper. Hill and Tammany are bound together by natural ties. They are of one flesh and blood. Their principles are the same, their methods the same, their aims the same and they know, as Benjamin Franklin once said, that they will have to hang together, or they will hang separately. As Tammany has always fought Hill's battles, so Hill now fights the battles of Tammany.

Can any sane man doubt it? What does it mean when the Tammany Mayor Gilroy never grows tired of protesting: "The State ticket is paramount! Never mind the city"? What does it mean when Mr. Straus—altogether too good a man to be seen in such company—relinquished his candidacy because the city ticket was openly sacrificed to Hill? What does it mean that the shouts for Hill in Tammany meetings are so much louder than those for Grant? It means that the battle against Tammany is really fought in the contest for the governorship. It means that every vote for Hill is a vote for protecting Tammany Hall against any legislation unfavorable to its interests. It means that every vote for Hill is a vote for shielding the Tammany chiefs of the municipal departments from any effective interference by the reform mayor. It means that every vote for Hill is a vote for stripping the reform mayor of the power necessary to clean out the Augean stables of Tammany corruption. It means that every vote for Hill is a vote for enabling Tammany to preserve the substance of its power for a resumption of its nefarious business when the storm of indignant excitement will have blown over. It means that every vote for Hill is a vote for defrauding this patriotic uprising of the good citizens of New York of its most valuable fruit. It means, in one word, that every vote for Hill is a vote for Tammany Hall, and all that it implies.

That a Tammany man should vote for Hill with zest is natural. That an unreasoning, bigoted partisan, or a person ignorant of his record, should vote for him, I can understand. But when I hear professed anti-Tammany Democrats, men who have preached political morality and reform, men who have with burning words held up Hill's villainies to public scorn, men who have denounced him for demoralizing and disgracing his party, men who have called upon their fellow-Democrats to organize against the scandals of his leadership, and who stood at the very head of the organization so formed—when I hear such men appeal to that very organization, at this solemn crisis, to support him for the governorship—thus seeking to unsettle the righteous public sentiment they themselves have labored to call forth, and thus putting in wanton jeopardy everything that has been gained and all we are striving for—when I hear this, then, I must confess, I stand appalled and perplexed. I am far from throwing suspicion upon the motives of any one incurring so fearful a responsibility. But I inquire anxiously into the reasons they can possibly have for such amazing conduct. Permit me to pass in review all that these new converts to Hill may have to say for him. It is with the utmost reluctance that I descend to the discussion of personalities in politics. But in this case where the person forms so important a part of the political issue, I must be pardoned for regarding it as a commanding duty to tear off the mask of the most audacious pretender among living public men.

In the first place it is said that David B. Hill has shown himself an able man. Yes; and how able!

How ably, after he had once risen to political prominence, did he manage to attach to himself the mercenary elements of his party and form out of them the worst political machine this State has ever seen!

How ably he used this machine to undermine Mr. Cleveland in the Democratic organization of this State!

How ably he strove to belittle the tariff issue brought forward by Mr. Cleveland until that issue was generally accepted!

How ably he contrived, when Mr. Cleveland in 1888 was a second time a candidate for the Presidency, to get for himself in this State, as a candidate for governor, a plurality of many thousands, while Mr. Cleveland was sacrificed!

How ably he used his power as governor to nullify the civil service law and to keep in the ballot-reform law openings for corrupt practices!

How ably he took $15,000 out of a public contract, and, therefore, out of the people's pockets, for his campaign expenses!

How ably he instigated and directed the crime of abstracting an election return, falsifying an election and stealing the Senate!

How ably he championed the crime, advocated the elevation of the criminal to the highest tribunal of the State "as an act of

simple justice" and set down our foremost lawyers, who had
some respect for the honor of the judicial ermine, as a "brain-
less set of namby-pambys"!

How ably he led his party, after having insulted the people
of the State with such a nomination, into a humiliation and defeat by more than a hundred thousand votes!

How ably he got up his famous snap convention, thus stealing for himself the Democratic delegation of the State and falsifying the public sentiment of its people!

How ably he managed, at Mr. Cleveland's second election in
1892, to make the Cleveland vote fall behind the ordinary party
strength in almost all the counties in which Hill's personal influence was especially strong!

How ably he afterwards claimed for himself the honors of the
campaign!

How ably he labored as a member of the Senate to baffle the
Democratic Administration in every public measure in which it
took a special interest!

How ably he coupled with his vote for the repeal of the sil-
ver-purchase law a speech enabling him to slide easily down on
the free-coinage side of the fence!

How ably he managed to defeat in the Senate the nominations
for the Federal Supreme bench of some of the best jurists of
his own State and robbed New York of the honor of a seat on
the highest Federal tribunal!

How ably he fought day in and day out to keep the McKinley
tariff on the statute book as the law of the land under the pretext of demanding an amendment to the Wilson tariff bill which
he knew would not be adopted!

How ably is he now playing himself off as the champion of
the self-same tariff act which he struggled to the last by hook
or crook to defeat, and which he was the only Democrat in the
Senate to vote against!

Able! I should say so. There is no abler genius of mischief
in the Democratic ranks. There is no abler traitor to Democratic principles and policies, no abler demoralizer of Democratic
virtue, no abler enemy of the Democratic Administration.
There are few rogues in politics whom David B. Hill cannot

easily beat at their trade. And he is still able to pull the wool over the eyes of lots of credulous citizens.

I leave it to you to think out what will become of the country and of your party, if such ability is to rule their destinies!

It is said that of late David B. Hill has much "broadened." To be sure he has. He is broad enough to be for good money and for the free coinage of silver at the same time. He is broad enough to fight bitterly against the tariff bill and then to extol it as a beneficent Democratic measure. If he goes on "broadening," he will soon be broad enough to be on every side of every public question, always with the keen eye of the statesman firmly fixed upon the interests of David B. Hill.

And he is broadly generous too. He even went so far at one time in the Senate as to defend the hated Cleveland—when he thought he could thereby most effectually kill the tariff bill. And he was hot for killing the tariff bill because he thought he could thereby most effectually kill Mr. Cleveland.

He is, indeed, generous to us all. He tells us that if he had had his way he would have admitted the delegates of the State Democracy and of the Brooklyn reform Democrats to the late State convention. I should not wonder, for, being sure of an immense machine majority in that convention anyhow, which would have made the reformers absolutely powerless and at the same time harmless, the spider could generously invite the fly into his net. And now he is so generous as to permit all his opponents to vote for him. What more can you ask for?

It is said that he is courageous. No more courageous man in his circumstances than he. Only think of it; after all he has done, he still has the courage to call himself a Democrat! He still has the courage to show his face among decent people and actually to ask for the suffrages of patriotic and self-respecting men. Human intrepidity can hardly rise higher.

It is said—Mr. Coudert says so—that David B. Hill "represents in this contest everything we have fought for these last ten years." I do not know whom Mr. Coudert means by "we." For his own sake I hope he does not include himself. If he means by "we" such men as Dick Croker and Bill Sheehan and Barney Martin and Paddy Divver, and that ilk of patriots, then I agree. What *they* have fought for these last ten years could indeed find no more brilliant representative than Dave Hill. To represent political methods which resulted in the building up of the most corrupt and despotic machine this State has ever known, and in such audacious frauds as the famous snap convention; to represent a political morality which flowered in the falsification of an election and a theft of the Senate majority, and in an attempt to seat a criminal on the highest State tribunal; to represent a Democratic partisanship which consists in systematic treachery to Democratic principles and measures, and in malignant attempts to break down a Democratic Administration—all this to further the most selfish and devouring of personal ambitions—to represent such things David B. Hill, of all others, is your man. But to say that David B. Hill truly represents what *the Democratic party* has fought for these last ten years, is far worse than anything the bitterest enemies of the Democratic party can say against it. The Democratic party may be able to endure much obloquy. But as soon as the people generally believe that, good Heavens! what will become of the Democracy then? And David B. Hill's election now would go very far to make the people believe it.

Look the situation squarely in the face. There is an anti-Democratic current sweeping over the land. We all know it. Democratic defeats crowd one another. What is the trouble? No doubt the hard times have something to do with it. But in spite of the hard times the Democracy would have a good fighting chance did it stand before the country with a character commanding respect and confidence. Why does it not? Because of its professed principles and its leading measure? No. If the choice between the McKinley tariff and the Wilson tariff were, purely on their merits, submitted to a popular vote, I am confident the McKinley tariff would be voted down by a decisive majority. Even thousands of Republicans would vote against it. What, then, is the trouble? It is corrupt and treacherous leadership. It is your Tammany, your Hills, your Gormans, your Murphys, your Brices, your Smiths, that have disgusted decent men and made them doubtful whether the Democratic party is capable of conducting the Government honestly and for the general good. This is the trouble.

What, then, would David B. Hill's defeat in this election

signify? He himself tries to frighten Democratic children with the pretense that it would mean the adoption of the apportionment amendment to the State constitution, and the disfranchisement of Democrats. Nonsense. I shall vote, and so will you, against that amendment, and with entire consistency we can put him and it into the same grave.

He pretends also that his defeat will mean a victory of the American Protective Association. Nonsense again. That proscriptive secret society is a waning power already, and we shall all coöperate to put it into the same grave as a good third. He further pretends that a defeat of the regular Democratic organization in New York State this year will necessarily draw after it defeat in the Presidential election two years hence. More nonsense. It is history that several times the party defeated in New York one year was victorious in the National field one or two years afterwards.

This is Hill's cry, and it is Tammany's cry likewise. Being one and the same, they have an equal right to it. They cannot be expected to remember that the numerical strength of a party always depends in the long run upon its moral strength. It is, nevertheless, an overruling truth. And in order to recover the necessary moral strength, the Democratic party needs not more Tammany and more Hill, but a good deal less of them. To make the Democratic ship swim again, the party must throw its Jonahs overboard. It must bury them in the waves, out of sight, and, if that be possible, out of memory. This is what Hill's defeat will mean.

Now let us see what his victory would signify. Listen to me a moment, Democrats, who constantly affirm their zeal for reform, clean politics and good government, but now tell us that the good of the Democratic party requires Hill's election. Have you considered what the consequences would be if you succeeded in seducing a sufficient number of anti-Tammany and anti-Hill Democrats to give him a majority? As to our municipal struggle, do you really mean merely to hit Tammany without hurting it? Or to hurt it only a little, and at the same time to furnish the surgeon who will surely set it upon its legs again, and restore its power for mischief? And this at the very moment when by thorough action that hideous nest of corruption and despotism may be stamped out! Have you considered what an awful responsibility you take in trying to deprive the present great uprising of good citizenship of its ultimate and most valuable fruit, to frustrate this rare opportunity and to discredit nonpartisan reform movements for years to come? Have you considered what curses will follow you, curses of the betrayed and the robbed and the oppressed, if you succeed?

But more. Only recently the rascally and tyrannical methods of the Democratic State machine excited you to righteous indignation. You declared that the Democratic party could not live under it; you declared it incompatible with your character as gentlemen to submit to it. You protested; you got up the anti-snapper movement; you organized the State Democracy— all against the machine. Well, who is the State machine? David B. Hill. And if you make him governor again—what then? Why, the machine will be stronger, and, after having victoriously passed through such a crisis, more arbitrary and despotic than ever. And will you then organize other anti-machine movements? Oh, no; for after this year's pro-Hill performance no self-respecting man will again trust the sincerity of your leadership. You will be what David B. Hill wishes his Democratic opponents to be: impotent and despised.

But still more. You call yourselves Cleveland Democrats and supporters of his patriotic purposes. Consider what you are now about to do for him and for the aims he represents. You elect Hill and you give him a prestige of personal strength and success such as he never had before, and as is enjoyed at present by no other Democrat. It has been said that the election to the governorship of New York this year will be the sure stepping-stone to the nomination for the Presidency two years hence. Whether this be so in fact or not, it will certainly be believed by the crowd of those who are always inclined to turn their faces towards the rising sun; and their number is legion in every party. Hill's election now against unusual odds would make him the most unprincipled and most dangerous politician brought forth by New York politics since the days of Aaron Burr, the most powerful personal force in the Democratic organization. He would, by all the pushing ambitions in the Democratic camp in Congress as well as outside of it, be looked upon

as the man of the future, and Cleveland as the man of the past.
They would court the coming man's favor and go to him for orders. From that moment on Mr. Cleveland will, in the pursuit of his principles and policies, find himself confronted by
an insidious power which, added to the opposition he has already
to meet, may be strong enough to turn the second half of his
Administration into a slow funeral of laudable endeavors.
This is what, by electing Hill, you will do for our National politics; but, pray, call yourselves Cleveland Democrats no longer.

We are told that Mr. Cleveland himself may support Hill.
I trust not. I should greatly deplore it if President Cleveland
were weak enough to consider it his duty, as head of the party,
to support every tainted character regularly nominated. But it
would not alter the situation. If Mr. Cleveland asked me personally to deliver him bound hand and foot into the hands of
his worst enemy, I would answer: "I will not do it!" As a
true friend I would consider it my duty to defend him against
himself.

This is not all. When last year the moral sense of the people
rose in revolt against the nomination of Maynard for the court
of appeals, we heard it commonly said that the proper place for
such a criminal was the penitentiary and not the judicial bench.
You said so yourselves. And in your righteous wrath you buried Maynard under a majority of over 100,000 votes. But let
me ask you, if Maynard, the tool, deserved such a crushing condemnation, what does Hill deserve, who, as the principal, employed the tool in the execution of the crime instigated by himself? Will you virtuous men of last year make that principal
this year governor of the State? If you find it in your consciences to do this, then you must admit that you have grievously
wronged Maynard and owe him apology and reparation. You
are in duty bound to go to him and say: "Worthy sir, we have
done you injustice. Pardon us, for we repent. What we called
a crime we have since discovered to have been a commendable
deed. We have expressed our appreciation of it by rewarding
its instigator with the highest office in the State. And you, in
bravely helping him to perform the meritorious act of abstracting an election return, falsifying an election and stealing the
Senate majority, deserved honor instead of punishment. We

come to put a civic crown upon your head, and shall be happy to carry you at the earliest opportunity in triumph to a seat in our highest tribunal, that you may sit as a judge over us, to support and strengthen by your decisions, if you can, the patriotic efforts of our great and virtuous governor!" When this interesting ceremony takes place, will Mr. Ellery Anderson marshal the procession, and will Mr. Coudert pronounce the eulogy? For my part, if I did such a thing as support Hill after having condemned Maynard, I would feel as if I could no longer look straight into the eyes of my children. I certainly should not wish my sons to follow my example. Do you feel differently, my anti-Maynard, pro-Hill friends?

And now I ask you to open your eyes and look, as sensible, self-respecting and patriotic men, at the miserable plight of your party. What has brought it to this? What a wicked fraud it is, this vaunted political smartness of the Hill school, which pretends to strengthen a party by organizing machines that would rather fit a band of marauders than an association of honest men, and must inevitably provoke the indignation of the public conscience; which will steal a Senate one year only to lose a whole legislature the next; which seeks party victory with political sharpers at its head, and runs the good aims of the party, and with it the party itself, into certain ruin and disgrace!

What a contemptible humbug it is, this so-called statesmanship which equivocates and shifts and dodges and squirms about every principle and public policy, and schemes and plots and intrigues for no higher object than personal advancement and power and plunder!

What a farcical spectacle it is, this so-called heroic campaign, Hill himself, the Great Mogul of the machine, with the brand of fate already upon his forehead, a sick devil in the monk's cowl, rushing from place to place, praising the tariff act he voted against, fawning upon Cleveland, whom he has been constantly stabbing in the back, whining about his self-sacrifice in taking the nomination, peddling around his canting promise as to what a good boy he will be, with the impudent assumption that, if he is defeated, the party will die!

And what a calamitous weakness it is, this so-called party loyalty of respectable men, which, when the party is led into iniquity and dishonor, indulges itself in highly moral protests; but then, when the test comes, supports, "for the good of the party," the very leader in iniquity, and thus serves to nurse and encourage and propagate the very wickedness protested against!

Gentlemen of the Reform Organization of the Democratic party, I turn to you with a feeling of relief and hope. It is a joy to meet once more with men who dare to look the truth squarely in the face, and to call their souls their own. Your clearness of mind amid so much mental confusion, your firmness amid so much wavering, your courage amid so much pusillanimity, entitle you to the respect of friend and foe. You have manfully declined to kneel before the idol of a party organization serving bad ends. You have scorned to stultify and disgrace yourselves by honoring to-day what you denounced as a crime yesterday. You have justly repelled the leadership of the evil genius of the party nominated by Tammany Hall for its purposes. You have done more. You have shown the Democratic party in its distress the way of salvation. You have proclaimed the principle that, if it is to be the party of tariff reform, it must be led by tariff reformers, and that if it is to be the party of good government, it must be led by honest men.

Your acts have been as good as your words. Your platform is the model Democratic platform, indeed the model platform of the day. And your standard-bearer, Everett P. Wheeler, is by his principles and his public and private virtues the model candidate of whom any party might be proud.

I invite the Democrats of this State and of the whole country to look at this. What would the position of your party be to-day, what its power and its prestige, if it had constantly stood true to such a platform with such leaders at its head? It would be irresistible in the confidence of the people. Well, what has not been may be. Before us is a great opportunity. Now is the time, in this State at least, to crush the powers of evil and to clear the field for a power of good. Boldly plant your flag as the flag of true Democracy. Around it will rally not only hosts of true Democrats, but, after this election, thousands of Republicans too, who are impatient with the tendencies and abuses of their own party, but were kept in it because Tammany and

Hillism disgusted and repelled them.   An organization like this, with such principles and such men, will solve their doubts.   It will be a gathering of new forces.

It is objected that this will not be the regular organization of the State.   The answer is that the true Democracy must not rest until it becomes the regular Democracy.   It is objected also that this will involve Democratic defeat.   The answer is that great reforms are never accomplished by those whom the thought of defeat can frighten from their purpose.   Besides, there will, in all likelihood, be Democratic defeat anyhow.   The question is only what kind of defeat.   The worst defeat of Democratic principles, Democratic morals and Democratic prospects would be David B. Hill's election.   This, however, I am glad to say, is hardly to be apprehended.   But the defeat of a bad Democratic leader may be turned into a triumph of good Democratic principles if emphasized by Democratic votes.   And here is the great duty the true Democrats of New York have to perform.   Every vote for Hill is a vote for corruption and machine politics and for the demoralization and decay of the Democratic party.   Every vote for Everett P. Wheeler is a vote for fidelity to the principles of good government and for party purification and rejuvenation.

May the citizens of New York when they go to the ballot-box not forget the true saying which has passed into a proverb: He serves his party most who serves his country best.

WILLIAM J. BRYAN

THE CROSS OF GOLD

SPEECH DELIVERED AT THE DEMOCRATIC NATIONAL CONVENTION, CHICAGO, ILLINOIS, JULY 8, 1896, CLOSING THE DEBATE ON THE ADOPTION OF THE PLATFORM

[William Jennings Bryan was born in Salem, Marion county, Illinois, on March 19, 1860. He was graduated from Illinois College, Jacksonville, Illinois, in 1881, and from the Union College of Law, Chicago, in 1883. At first he practiced in Jacksonville, but in 1887 moved to Lincoln, Nebraska. He was a Democratic member of Congress from 1891 to 1895, and was a delegate to the Democratic National Conventions of 1896, 1904, 1912, 1920, and 1924. He was the unsuccessful Democratic Candidate for President of the United States in 1896, 1900, and 1908. He was Secretary of State in President Wilson's cabinet from 1913 to June 9, 1915. While attending the Scopes trial in Dayton, Tennessee, he died on July 26, 1925.

The speech printed below, sometimes called the "Crown of Thorns" speech, won him the Democratic Presidential nomination in 1896. Bryan, in his speeches on Free Silver, had already used all of the arguments in this speech except that relating to the definition of a business man. Being in charge of the debate in support of the platform, and realizing that he was "more effective in a brief speech in conclusion than in a longer speech that simply laid down propositions for another to answer," he saved himself for the closing speech. In his Memoirs, he says that, between the preliminary conference and the convening of the Convention, he had taken part in a debate at Crete, Nebraska, with John Irish of Iowa. In that debate, he says, "I used the sentence with which I closed my Chicago speech—the sentence which refers to 'the cross of gold and the crown of thorns.' I had used it a few times before that time, recognizing its fitness for the conclusion of a climax, and had laid it away for a proper occasion."]

I would be presumptuous, indeed, to present myself against the distinguished gentlemen to whom you have listened if this were a mere measuring of abilities; but this is not a contest between persons. The humblest citizen in all the land, when clad in the armor of a righteous cause, is stronger than all the hosts of error. I come to speak to you in defense of a cause as holy as the cause of liberty—the cause of humanity.

When this debate is concluded, a motion will be made to lay upon the table the resolution offered in commendation of the administration, and also the resolution offered in condemnation of the administration. We object to bringing this question down to the level of persons. The individual is but an atom; he is born, he acts, he dies; but principles are eternal; and this has been a contest over a principle.

Never before in the history of this country has there been witnessed such a contest as that through which we have just passed. Never before in the history of American politics has a great issue been fought out as this issue has been, by the voters of a great party. On the fourth of March, 1895, a few Democrats, most of them members of Congress, issued an address to the Democrats of the nation, asserting that the money question was the paramount issue of the hour; declaring that a majority of the Democratic party had the right to control the action of the party on this paramount issue; and concluding with the request that the believers in the free coinage of silver in the Democratic party should organize, take charge of, and control the policy of the Democratic party. Three months later, at Memphis, an organization was perfected, and the silver Democrats went forth openly and courageously proclaiming their belief, and declaring that, if successful, they would crystallize into a platform the declaration which they had made. Then began the conflict. With a zeal approaching the zeal which inspired the crusaders who followed Peter the Hermit, our silver Democrats went forth from victory unto victory until they are now assembled, not to discuss, not to debate, but to enter up the judgment already rendered by the plain people of this country. In this contest brother has been arrayed against brother, father against son. The warmest ties of love, acquaintance and association have been disregarded; old leaders have been cast aside when they have refused to give expression to the sentiments of those whom they would lead, and new leaders have sprung up to give direction to this cause of truth. Thus has the contest been waged, and we have assembled here under as binding and solemn instructions as were ever imposed upon representatives of the people.

We do not come as individuals. As individuals we might have been glad to compliment the gentleman from New York (Senator Hill), but we know that the people for whom we speak would never be willing to put him in a position where he could thwart the will of the Democratic party. I say it was not a question of persons; it was a question of principle, and it is not with gladness, my friends, that we find ourselves brought into conflict with those who are now arrayed on the other side.

The gentleman who preceded me (ex-Governor Russell) spoke of the State of Massachusetts; let me assure him that not one present in all this convention entertains the least hostility to the people of the State of Massachusetts, but we stand here representing people who are the equals, before the law, of the greatest citizens in the State of Massachusetts. When you (turning to the gold delegates) come before us and tell us that we are about to disturb your business interests, we reply that you have disturbed our business interests by your course.

We say to you that you have made the definition of a business man too limited in its application. The man who is employed for wages is as much a business man as his employer, the attorney in a country town is as much a business man as the corporation counsel in a great metropolis; the merchant at the crossroads store is as much a business man as the merchant of New York; the farmer who goes forth in the morning and toils all day—who begins in the spring and toils all summer—and who by the application of brain and muscle to the natural resources of the country creates wealth, is as much a business man as the man who goes upon the board of trade and bets upon the price of grain; the miners who go down a thousand feet into the earth, or climb two thousand feet upon the cliffs, and bring forth from their hiding places the precious metals to be poured into the channels of trade are as much business men as the few financial magnates who, in a back room, corner the money of the world. We come to speak for this broader class of business men.

Ah, my friends, we say not one word against those who live upon the Atlantic coast, but the hardy pioneers who have braved all the dangers of the wilderness, who have made the desert to blossom as the rose—the pioneers away out there (pointing to the West), who rear their children near to Nature's heart, where they can mingle their voices with the voices of the birds —out there where they have erected schoolhouses for the education of their young, churches where they praise their Creator, and cemeteries where rest the ashes of their dead—these people, we say, are as deserving of the consideration of our party as any people in this country. It is for these that we speak. We do not come as aggressors. Our war is not a war of conquest; we are fighting in the defense of our homes, our families, and posterity. We have petitioned, and our petitions have been scorned; we have entreated, and our entreaties have been disregarded; we have begged, and they have mocked when our calamity came. We beg no longer; we entreat no more; we petition no more. We defy them.

The gentleman from Wisconsin has said that he fears a Robespierre. My friends, in this land of the free you need not fear that a tyrant will spring up from among the people. What we need is an Andrew Jackson to stand, as Jackson stood, against the encroachments of organized wealth.

They tell us that this platform was made to catch votes. We reply to them that changing conditions make new issues; that the principles upon which Democracy rests are as everlasting as the hills, but that they must be applied to new conditions as they arise. Conditions have arisen, and we are here to meet these conditions. They tell us that the income tax ought not to be brought in here; that it is a new idea. They criticize us for our criticism of the Supreme Court of the United States. My friends, we have not criticized; we have simply called attention to what you already know. If you want criticisms, read the dissenting opinions of the court. There you will find criticisms. They say that we passed an unconstitutional law; we deny it. The income tax law was not unconstitutional when it was passed; it was not unconstitutional when it went before the Supreme Court for the first time; it did not become unconstitutional until one of the judges changed his mind, and we cannot be expected to know when a judge will change his mind. The income tax is just. It simply intends to put the burdens of government justly upon the backs of the people. I am in favor of an income tax. When I find a man who is not willing to bear his share of the burdens of the government which protects him, I find a man who is unworthy to enjoy the blessings of a government like ours.

They say that we are opposing national bank currency; it is true. If you will read what Thomas Benton said, you will find he said that, in searching history, he could find but one parallel to Andrew Jackson; that was Cicero, who destroyed the conspiracy of Cataline and saved Rome. Benton said that Cicero only did for Rome what Jackson did for us when he destroyed the bank conspiracy and saved America. We say in our platform that we believe that the right to coin and issue money is a function of government. We believe it. We believe that it is a part of sovereignty, and can no more with safety be delegated to private individuals than we could afford to delegate to private individuals the power to make penal statutes or levy taxes. Mr. Jefferson, who was once regarded as good Democratic authority, seems to have differed in opinion from the gentleman who has addressed us on the part of the minority. Those who are opposed to this proposition tell us that the issue of paper money is a function of the bank, and that the Government ought to go out of the banking business. I stand with Jefferson rather than with them, and tell them, as he did, that the issue of money is a function of government, and that the banks ought to go out of the governing business.

They complain about the plank which declares against life tenure in office. They have tried to strain it to mean that which it does not mean. What we oppose by that plank is the life tenure which is being built up in Washington, and which excludes from participation in official benefits the humbler members of society.

Let me call your attention to two or three important things. The gentleman from New York says that he will propose an amendment to the platform providing that the proposed change in our monetary system shall not affect contracts already made. Let me remind you that there is no intention of affecting those contracts which according to present laws are made payable in gold; but if he means to say that we cannot change our monetary system without protecting those who have loaned money before the change was made, I desire to ask him where, in law or in morals, he can find justification for not protecting the debtors when the act of 1873 was passed, if he now insists that we must protect the creditors.

He says he will also propose an amendment which will provide for the suspension of free coinage if we fail to maintain the parity within a year. We reply that when we advocate a policy which we believe will be successful, we are not compelled to raise a doubt as to our own sincerity by suggesting what we shall do if we fail. I ask him, if he would apply his logic to us, why he does not apply it to himself. He says he wants this country to try to secure an international agreement. Why does he not tell us what he is going to do if he fails to secure an international agreement? There is more reason for him to do that than there is for us to provide against the failure to maintain the parity. Our opponents have tried for twenty years to secure an international agreement, and those are waiting for it most patiently who do not want it at all.

And now, my friends, let me come to the paramount issue. If they ask us why it is that we say more on the money question than we say upon the tariff question, I reply that, if protection has slain its thousands, the gold standard has slain its tens of thousands. If they ask us why we do not embody in our platform all the things that we believe in, we reply that when we have restored the money of the Constitution all other necessary reforms will be possible; but that until this is done there is no other reform that can be accomplished.

Why is it that within three months such a change has come over the country? Three months ago, when it was confidently asserted that those who believe in the gold standard would frame our platform and nominate our candidates, even the advocates of the gold standard did not think that we could elect a President. And they had good reason for their doubt, because there is scarcely a State here to-day asking for the gold standard which is not in the absolute control of the Republican party. But note the change. Mr. McKinley was nominated at St. Louis upon a platform which declared for the maintenance of the gold standard until it can be changed into bimetalism by international agreement. Mr. McKinley was the most popular man among the Republicans, and three months ago everybody in the Republican party prophesied his election. How is it to-day? Why, the man who was once pleased to think that he looked like Napoleon—that man shudders to-day when he remembers that he was nominated on the anniversary of the battle of Waterloo. Not only that, but as he listens he can hear with ever-increasing distinctness the sound of the waves as they beat upon the lonely shores of St. Helena.

Why this change? Ah, my friends, is not the reason for the change evident to any one who will look at the matter? No private character, however pure, no personal popularity, however great, can protect from the avenging wrath of an indignant people a man who will declare that he is in favor of fastening the gold standard upon this country, or who is willing to surrender the right of self-government and place the legislative control of our affairs in the hands of foreign potentates and powers.

We go forth confident that we shall win. Why? Because upon the paramount issue of this campaign there is not a spot of ground upon which the enemy will dare to challenge battle. If they tell us that the gold standard is a good thing, we shall point to their platform and tell them that their platform pledges the party to get rid of the gold standard and substitute bimetalism. If the gold standard is a good thing, why try to get rid of it? I call your attention to the fact that some of the very people who are in this convention to-day and who tell us that we ought to declare in favor of international bimetalism—thereby declaring that the gold standard is wrong and that the principle of bimetalism is better—these very people four months ago were open and avowed advocates of the gold standard, and were then telling us that we could not legislate two metals together, even with the aid of all the world. If the gold standard is a good thing, we ought to declare in favor of its retention and not in favor of abandoning it; and if the gold standard is a bad thing why should we wait until other nations are willing to help us to let go? Here is the line of battle, and we care not upon which issue they force the fight; we are prepared to meet them on either issue or on both. If they tell us that the gold standard is the standard of civilization, we reply to them that this, the most enlightened of all the nations of the earth, has never declared for a gold standard and that both the great parties this year are declaring against it. If the gold standard is the standard of civilization, why, my friends, should we not have it? If they come to meet us on that issue we can present the history of our nation. More than that; we can tell them that they will search the pages of history in vain to find a single instance where the common people of any land have ever declared themselves in favor of the gold standard. They can find where the holders of fixed investments have declared for a gold standard, but not where the masses have.

Mr. Carlisle said in 1878 that this was a struggle between "the idle holders of idle capital" and "the struggling masses, who produce the wealth and pay the taxes of the country"; and, my friends, the question we are to decide is: Upon which side will the Democratic party fight; upon the side of "the idle holders of idle capital" or upon the side of "the struggling masses"? That is the question which the party must answer first, and then it must be answered by each individual hereafter. The sympathies of the Democratic party, as shown by the platform, are on the side of the struggling masses who have ever been the foundation of the Democratic party. There are two ideas of government. There are those who believe that, if you will only legislate to make the well-to-do prosperous, their prosperity will leak through on those below. The Democratic idea, however, has been that if you legislate to make the masses prosperous, their prosperity will find its way up through every class which rests upon them.

You come to us and tell us that the great cities are in favor of the gold standard; we reply that the great cities rest upon our broad and fertile prairies. Burn down your cities and leave our farms, and your cities will spring up again as if by magic; but destroy our farms and the grass will grow in the streets of every city in the country.

My friends, we declare that this nation is able to legislate for its own people on every question, without waiting for the aid or consent of any other nation on earth; and upon that issue we expect to carry every State in the Union. I shall not slander the inhabitants of the fair State of Massachusetts nor the inhabitants of the State of New York by saying that, when they are confronted with the proposition, they will declare that this nation is not able to attend to its own business. It is the issue of 1776 over again. Our ancestors, when but three millions in number, had the courage to declare their political independence of every other nation; shall we, their descendants, when we have grown to seventy millions, declare that we are less independent than our forefathers? No, my friends, that will never be the verdict of our people. Therefore, we care not upon what lines the battle is fought. If they say bimetalism is good, but that we cannot have it until other nations help us, we reply that, instead of having a gold standard because England has, we will restore bimetalism, and then let England have bimetalism because the United States has it. If they dare to come out in the open field and defend the gold standard as a good thing, we will fight them to the uttermost. Having behind us the producing masses of this nation and the world, supported by the commercial interests, the laboring interests, and the toilers everywhere, we will answer their demand for a gold standard by saying to them: You shall not press down upon the brow of labor this crown of thorns, you shall not crucify mankind upon a cross of gold.

ALBERT J. BEVERIDGE

THE MARCH OF THE FLAG

SPEECH OPENING THE INDIANA REPUBLICAN CAMPAIGN,
TOMLINSON HALL, INDIANAPOLIS, SEPTEMBER 16, 1898

[Albert Jeremiah Beveridge was born in Highland county, Ohio, on October 6, 1862. He was graduated from Indiana Asbury (now De Pauw) University, Greencastle, Indiana, in 1885, was admitted to the bar in 1887, and practiced law in Indianapolis, Indiana, for twelve years. At the age of thirty-six, in January, 1899, he was elected to the United States Senate as a Republican, and served from 1899 to 1911. Thereafter he held no office, although he was active in the Progressive Party, and later was a candidate for Senator on the Republican ticket. After retirement from political life, he distinguished himself as a historian, his most important works being the *Life of John Marshall*, and *Abraham Lincoln*. Of the latter only two volumes had been completed when he died in Indianapolis on April 27, 1927.

From his college days, Mr. Beveridge was a noted public speaker, and for fifteen years he spoke in every political campaign in his state. He was an ardent nationalist and an advocate of the doctrine "America first." The speech printed below, which became the Republican campaign document for Indiana, Iowa, and other states, was delivered during the Spanish-American war, just before he was elected United States Senator. It was the forerunner of the so-called imperialistic policy upon which the country soon afterward embarked.]

It is a noble land that God has given us; a land that can feed and clothe the world; a land whose coastlines would inclose half the countries of Europe; a land set like a sentinel between the two imperial oceans of the globe, a greater England with a nobler destiny.

It is a mighty people that He has planted on this soil; a people sprung from the most masterful blood of history; a people perpetually revitalized by the virile, man-producing working-folk of all the earth; a people imperial by virtue of their power, by right of their institutions, by authority of their Heaven-directed purposes—the propagandists and not the misers of liberty.

It is a glorious history our God has bestowed upon His chosen people; a history heroic with faith in our mission and our future; a history of statesmen who flung the boundaries of the

Republic out into unexplored lands and savage wilderness; a history of soldiers who carried the flag across blazing deserts and through the ranks of hostile mountains, even to the gates of sunset; a history of a multiplying people who overran a continent in half a century; a history of prophets who saw the consequences of evils inherited from the past and of martyrs who died to save us from them; a history divinely logical, in the process of whose tremendous reasoning we find ourselves to-day.

Therefore, in this campaign, the question is larger than a party question. It is an American question. It is a world question. Shall the American people continue their march toward the commercial supremacy of the world? Shall free institutions broaden their blessed reign as the children of liberty wax in strength, until the empire of our principles is established over the hearts of all mankind?

Have we no mission to perform, no duty to discharge to our fellow-man? Has God endowed us with gifts beyond our deserts and marked us as the people of His peculiar favor, merely to rot in our own selfishness, as men and nations must, who take cowardice for their companion and self for their deity—as China has, as India has, as Egypt has?

Shall we be as the man who had one talent and hid it, or as he who had ten talents and used them until they grew to riches? And shall we reap the reward that waits on our discharge of our high duty; shall we occupy new markets for what our farmers raise, our factories make, our merchants sell—aye, and, please God, new markets for what our ships shall carry?

Hawaii is ours; Porto Rico is to be ours; at the prayer of her people Cuba finally will be ours; in the islands of the East, even to the gates of Asia, coaling stations are to be ours at the very least; the flag of a liberal government is to float over the Philippines, and may it be the banner that Taylor unfurled in Texas and Fremont carried to the coast.

The Opposition tells us that we ought not to govern a people without their consent. I answer: The rule of liberty that all just government derives its authority from the consent of the governed, applies only to those who are capable of self-government. We govern the Indians without their consent, we govern our territories without their consent, we govern our children without their consent. How do they know that our government would be without their consent? Would not the people of the Philippines prefer the just, humane, civilizing government of this Republic to the savage, bloody rule of pillage and extortion from which we have rescued them?

And, regardless of this formula of words made only for enlightened, self-governing people, do we owe no duty to the world? Shall we turn these peoples back to the reeking hands from which we have taken them? Shall we abandon them, with Germany, England, Japan, hungering for them? Shall we save them from those nations, to give them a self-rule of tragedy?

They ask us how we shall govern these new possessions. I answer: Out of local conditions and the necessities of the case methods of government will grow. If England can govern foreign lands, so can America. If Germany can govern foreign lands, so can America. If they can supervise protectorates, so can America. Why is it more difficult to administer Hawaii than New Mexico or California? Both had a savage and an alien population; both were more remote from the seat of government when they came under our dominion than the Philippines are to-day.

Will you say by your vote that American ability to govern has decayed; that a century's experience in self-rule has failed of a result? Will you affirm by your vote that you are an infidel to American power and practical sense? Or will you say that ours is the blood of government; ours the heart of dominion; ours the brain and genius of administration? Will you remember that we do but what our fathers did—we but pitch the tents of liberty farther westward, farther southward—we only continue the march of the flag?

The march of the flag! In 1789 the flag of the Republic waved over 4,000,000 souls in thirteen states, and their savage territory which stretched to the Mississippi, to Canada, to the Floridas. The timid minds of that day said that no new territory was needed, and, for the hour, they were right. But Jefferson, through whose intellect the centuries marched; Jefferson, who dreamed of Cuba as an American state; Jefferson, the first Imperialist of the Republic—Jefferson acquired that imperial territory which swept from the Mississippi to the mountains, from Texas to the British possessions, and the march of the flag began!

The infidels to the gospel of liberty raved, but the flag swept on! The title to that noble land out of which Oregon, Washington, Idaho and Montana have been carved was uncertain; Jefferson, strict constructionist of constitutional power though he was, obeyed the Anglo-Saxon impulse within him, whose watchword then and whose watchword throughout the world to-day is, "Forward!": another empire was added to the Republic, and the march of the flag went on!

Those who deny the power of free institutions to expand urged every argument, and more, that we hear, to-day; but the people's judgment approved the command of their blood, and the march of the flag went on!

A screen of land from New Orleans to Florida shut us from the Gulf, and over this and the Everglade Peninsula waved the saffron flag of Spain; Andrew Jackson seized both, the American people stood at his back, and, under Monroe, the Floridas came under the dominion of the Republic, and the march of the flag went on! The Cassandras prophesied every prophecy of despair we hear, to-day, but the march of the flag went on!

Then Texas responded to the bugle calls of liberty, and the march of the flag went on! And, at last, we waged war with Mexico, and the flag swept over the southwest, over peerless California, past the Gate of Gold to Oregon on the north, and from ocean to ocean its folds of glory blazed.

And, now, obeying the same voice that Jefferson heard and obeyed, that Jackson heard and obeyed, that Monroe heard and obeyed, that Seward heard and obeyed, that Grant heard and obeyed, that Harrison heard and obeyed, our President to-day plants the flag over the islands of the seas, outposts of commerce, citadels of national security, and the march of the flag goes on!

Distance and oceans are no arguments. The fact that all the territory our fathers bought and seized is contiguous, is no argument. In 1819 Florida was farther from New York than Porto Rico is from Chicago to-day; Texas, farther from Washington in 1845 than Hawaii is from Boston in 1898; California, more inaccessible in 1847 than the Philippines are now. Gibraltar is farther from London than Havana is from Washington; Melbourne is farther from Liverpool than Manila is from San Francisco.

The ocean does not separate us from lands of our duty and desire—the oceans join us, rivers never to be dredged, canals never to be repaired. Steam joins us; electricity joins us—the very elements are in league with our destiny. Cuba not contiguous! Porto Rico not contiguous! Hawaii and the Philippines not contiguous! The oceans make them contiguous. And our navy will make them contiguous.

But the Opposition is right—there is a difference. We did not need the western Mississippi Valley when we acquired it, nor Florida, nor Texas, nor California, nor the royal provinces of the far northwest. We had no emigrants to people this imperial wilderness, no money to develop it, even no highways to cover it. No trade awaited us in its savage fastnesses. Our productions were not greater than our trade. There was not one reason for the land-lust of our statesmen from Jefferson to Grant, other than the prophet and the Saxon within them. But, to-day, we are raising more than we can consume, making more than we can use. Therefore we must find new markets for our produce.

And so, while we did not need the territory taken during the past century at the time it was acquired, we do need what we have taken in 1898, and we need it now. The resources and the commerce of these immensely rich dominions will be increased as much as American energy is greater than Spanish sloth. In Cuba, alone, there are 15,000,000 acres of forest unacquainted with the ax, exhaustless mines of iron, priceless deposits of manganese, millions of dollars' worth of which we must buy, to-day, from the Black Sea districts. There are millions of acres yet unexplored.

The resources of Porto Rico have only been trifled with. The riches of the Philippines have hardly been touched by the fingertips of modern methods. And they produce what we consume, and consume what we produce—the very predestination of reciprocity—a reciprocity "not made with hands, eternal in the heavens." They sell hemp, sugar, cocoanuts, fruits of the tropics, timber of price like mahogany; they buy flour, clothing, tools, implements, machinery and all that we can raise and make. Their trade will be ours in time. Do you indorse that policy with your vote?

Cuba is as large as Pennsylvania, and is the richest spot on the globe. Hawaii is as large as New Jersey; Porto Rico half as large as Hawaii; the Philippines larger than all New England, New York, New Jersey and Delaware combined. Together they are larger than the British Isles, larger than France, larger than Germany, larger than Japan.

If any man tells you that trade depends on cheapness and not on government influence, ask him why England does not abandon South Africa, Egypt, India. Why does France seize South China, Germany the vast region whose port is Kaouchou?

Our trade with Porto Rico, Hawaii and the Philippines must be as free as between the states of the Union, because they are American territory, while every other nation on earth must pay our tariff before they can compete with us. Until Cuba shall ask for annexation, our trade with her will, at the very least, be like the preferential trade of Canada with England. That, and the excellence of our goods and products; that, and the convenience of traffic; that, and the kinship of interests and destiny, will give the monopoly of these markets to the American people.

The commercial supremacy of the Republic means that this Nation is to be the sovereign factor in the peace of the world. For the conflicts of the future are to be conflicts of trade—struggles for markets—commercial wars for existence. And the golden rule of peace is impregnability of position and invincibility of preparedness. So, we see England, the greatest strategist of history, plant her flag and her cannon on Gibraltar, at Quebec, in the Bermudas, at Vancouver, everywhere.

So Hawaii furnishes us a naval base in the heart of the Pacific; the Ladrones another, a voyage further on; Manila another, at the gates of Asia—Asia, to the trade of whose hundreds of millions American merchants, manufacturers, farmers, have as good right as those of Germany or France or Russia or England; Asia, whose commerce with the United Kingdom alone amounts to hundreds of millions of dollars every year; Asia, to whom Germany looks to take her surplus products; Asia, whose doors must not be shut against American trade. Within five decades the bulk of Oriental commerce will be ours.

No wonder that, in the shadows of coming events so great, free-silver is already a memory. The current of history has swept past that episode. Men understand, to-day, that the greatest commerce of the world must be conducted with the steadiest standard of value and most convenient medium of exchange human ingenuity can devise. Time, that unerring reasoner, has settled the silver question. The American people are tired of talking about money—they want to make it. Why should the farmer get a half-measure dollar of money any more than he should give a half-measure bushel of grain?

Why should not the proposition for the free coinage of silver be as dead as the proposition of irredeemable paper money? It is the same proposition in a different form. If the Government stamp can make a piece of silver, which you can buy for 45 cents, pass for 100 cents, the Government stamp can make a piece of pewter, worth one cent, pass for 100 cents, and a piece of paper, worth a fraction of a cent, pass for 100 cents. Free-silver is the principle of fiat money applied to metal. If you favor fiat silver, you necessarily favor fiat paper.

If the Government can make money with a stamp, why does the Government borrow money? If the Government can create value out of nothing, why not abolish all taxation?

And if it is not the stamp of the Government that raises the value, but the demand which free coinage creates, why has the value of silver gone down at a time when more silver was bought and coined by the Government than ever before? Again, if the people want more silver, why do they refuse what we already have? And if free silver makes money more plentiful, how will *you* get any of it? Will the silver-mine owner give it to you? Will he loan it to you? Will the Government give or loan it to you? Where do you or I come in on this free-silver proposition?

The American people want this money question settled for ever. They want a uniform currency, a convenient currency, a currency that grows as business grows, a currency based on science and not on chance.

And now, on the threshold of our new and great career, is the time permanently to adjust our system of finance. The American people have the mightiest commerce of the world to conduct. They can not halt to unsettle their money system every time some ardent imagination sees a vision and dreams a dream. Think of Great Britain becoming the commercial monarch of the world with her financial system periodically assailed! Think of Holland or Germany or France bearing their burdens, and, yet, sending their flag to every sea, with their money at the mercy of politicians-out-of-an-issue. Let us settle the whole financial system on principles so sound that no agitation can shake it. And then, like men and not like children, let us on to our tasks, our mission and our destiny.

There are so many real things to be done—canals to be dug, railways to be laid, forests to be felled, cities to be builded, fields to be tilled, markets to be won, ships to be launched, peoples to be saved, civilization to be proclaimed and the flag of liberty flung to the eager air of every sea. Is this an hour to waste upon triflers with nature's laws? Is this a season to give our destiny over to word-mongers and prosperity-wreckers? No! It is an hour to remember our duty to our homes. It is a moment to realize the opportunities fate has opened to us. And so it is an hour for us to stand by the Government.

Wonderfully has God guided us. Yonder at Bunker Hill and Yorktown His providence was above us. At New Orleans and on ensanguined seas His hand sustained us. Abraham Lincoln was His minister and His was the altar of freedom the Nation's soldiers set up on a hundred battle-fields. His power directed Dewey in the East and delivered the Spanish fleet into our hands, as He delivered the elder Armada into the hands of our English sires two centuries ago. The American people can not use a dishonest medium of exchange; it is ours to set the world its example of right and honor. We can not fly from our world duties; it is ours to execute the purpose of a fate that has driven us to be greater than our small intentions. We can not retreat from any soil where Providence has unfurled our banner; it is ours to save that soil for liberty and civilization.

CHARLES J. BONAPARTE

OUR NATIONAL DANGERS, REAL AND UNREAL

ORATION DELIVERED IN SANDERS THEATRE, BEFORE THE
HARVARD CHAPTER OF PHI BETA KAPPA,
THURSDAY, JUNE 29, 1899 *

[Charles Joseph Bonaparte, grandson of Jerome Bonaparte, King of Westphalia, was born in Baltimore, Maryland, on June 9, 1851. He was graduated from Harvard College in 1872, and from the Harvard Law School in 1874. He practiced law in Baltimore, but devoted much of his efforts to the cause of good government. He was a founder of the Baltimore Reform League; the *Civil Service Reformer*, organ of the Maryland Civil Service League; the National Municipal League; and the National Civil Service Reform League. In 1905, he was appointed Secretary of the Navy by President Roosevelt, and he served as Attorney General of the United States from December, 1906, to March, 1909, when he returned to the practice of the law. He died at his country home near Baltimore on June 28, 1921.

In college and law school, Mr. Bonaparte was active as a debater, and throughout his life he was an effective speaker, especially in advocacy of reform in public life. The speech printed below, a good example of his style, reflects the uneasiness of mind that was common in the United States after the Spanish-American war.]

Less than half a year's space separates us to-day from the one hundredth anniversary of Washington's death. Of the great services of that great man to his and our country, I deem none greater than the wise counsel of his Farewell Address. There may be, it would seem that there are, some among us who think this out of date and believe themselves qualified to furnish a substitute. I do not pause to compare such men with its author, or to speculate whether any one of them will live in the memory of his countrymen a hundred days after his body shall be laid in the grave; I content myself with saying that I do not agree with them. In the Farewell Address we are reminded that "in proportion as the structure of a government gives force to public opinion, it is essential that public opinion

---

* Reprinted by permission from the Harvard Graduates' Magazine, September, 1899.

should be enlightened." Of no government is this more eminently characteristic than of that which Washington, perhaps more than any other man, aided to frame for the nation to which he, certainly more than any other man, gave being. I may, then, claim the warrant of his authority when I ask of this old and honored learned society, as the fulfilment of a patriotic duty, its aid in enlightening public opinion at a moment when our government must deal with new and grave problems, when our country is threatened by new and grave dangers.

These dangers are in no small measure the penalties for our neglect of Washington's warnings. He tells us: "Of all the dispositions and habits which lead to political prosperity, religion and morality are indispensable supports. * * * The mere politician equally with the pious man ought to respect and cherish them." In these latter days we have listened patiently, if not with approval, to those who declared that "the purification of politics is an iridescent dream. The Decalogue and the Golden Rule have no place in a political campaign." What is worse, we have suffered such things in our government as gave to their words no little semblance of truth. He warns us, "in the most solemn manner, against the baneful effect of the spirit of party. * * * It exists under different shapes in all governments, * * * but in those of the popular form it is seen in its greatest rankness, and is truly their worst enemy. * * * The common and continual mischiefs of the spirit of party are sufficient to make it the interest and duty of a wise people to discourage and restrain it. * * * A fire not to be quenched, it demands a uniform vigilance to prevent its bursting into a flame." To this advice we now prefer a doctrine preached by the thousands of politicians and the hundreds of newspapers who tell us daily that to attain party success, to perfect party organization, to strengthen party discipline, good citizens should give their votes to unworthy candidates; support policies they believe disastrous; see with complacency, or at least with resignation, the public service used to furnish bribes or rewards for partisan service, and admit that every office, however responsible or however humble, that of Chief Justice of the Supreme Court or that of a village lamplighter, shall be filled in the interest and at the dictation of that very "spirit of party" which it is "the interest and duty of a wise people to discourage and restrain." He deems it most important "that the habits of thinking in a free country should inspire caution in those intrusted with its administration, to confine themselves within their respective constitutional spheres, avoiding in the exercise of the powers of one department to encroach upon another." Would one who thus wrote, think ye, see with contentment senators and representatives dividing among themselves, not only with impunity, but almost as a matter of unquestioned prerogative, thousands of appointments committed to his successor in the Presidency, as part of that "office of President of the United States" which the latter has "solemnly sworn" to "faithfully execute," by the express words of that Constitution which he has likewise sworn to "preserve, protect, and defend"?

Finally, Washington affirms that "virtue or morality is a necessary spring of popular government." We have abandoned the government he founded to the Boss and the Ring. These powers of darkness would have men ignorant and vicious, pressed by want and rebellious to law, because of such men they make their dupes and tools. They are the common enemies of all who war against sin and suffering, for amid a people happy through righteousness they could not live. They protect and foster every degrading pursuit, every noxious industry, every dangerous and shameful calling, as training-schools for their followers and resources for their fisc. We know them and their works, yet we endure them as our rulers, and we have endured them for many weary years: it is as true now as it was when Burke said it, that "there never was *long* a corrupt government of a virtuous people."

Had we, however, proved mindful of Washington's words, we must yet have now encountered new perils and undertaken new tasks. The Farewell Address says: "Europe * * * must be engaged in frequent controversies, the causes of which are essentially foreign to our concerns. * * * Our detached and distant situation invites and enables us to pursue a different course. * * * Why forego the advantages of so peculiar a situation? Why quit our own to stand upon foreign ground?" Fortunately or unfortunately, as it may seem to different minds, but, in either event, certainly, our situation is no longer "detached and distant." Mount Vernon is nearer, for any purpose, to London or Paris or Berlin to-day than it was to Cambridge when these words were written: for some purposes it is nearer to Pekin or Calcutta or Cape Town. We can hardly realize how vast a change has been made in our relations to men of other lands by submarine cables: when the newspapers began to place beside our breakfast plates daily epitomes of the world's history for each yesterday, the area of our attention and sympathy was more widely expanded than it would be if a telescope were constructed many thousandfold stronger than any yet known, through which astronomers could contemplate the good or ill fortunes of intelligent beings on our sister planets; the causes of European, even of Asiatic or African, controversies are not always now, in future they may be seldom, "essentially foreign to our concerns." Moreover, it should not be, although it often is, forgotten that, in a military sense, our isolation is already a thing of the past. With our shores but six days' space from the harbors of the Old World, the transportation hither of an army larger than Washington ever commanded, even on paper, would be a less task for the navy and mercantile marine of any one of several among the Great Powers than was that of General Ross's brigade in 1814. Washington looked for a time "when we may choose peace or war, as our interest, guided by justice, shall counsel." That time came, but there is reason to ask whether it has not also gone, for the greatest change of all in our situation is that we have become an object of fear. This is a change of but yesterday. Our prodigious growth, our immense resources, were indeed known abroad, but few foreigners had ever thought of the infant giant as a conqueror, or even as an enemy. To this possibility the booming of Dewey's guns awakened the world, and their answer throughout Continental Europe and Spanish America was a growl of popular hatred imperfectly smothered by diplomacy. These wrathful mutterings were not prompted, they were even, so far as might be, stifled by foreign governments; but, for thoughtful Americans, this made them but the graver symptom of a national danger: a nation dreaded, and therefore hated, from the heart by surrounding peoples, however sincerely pacific its purposes, is condemned to sleep on its arms.

We cannot escape perils by ignoring them. The pilgrims in the "Vision of Theodore," who had been gathering flowers under the protection of Innocence, were by no means happy when that gentle guardian soon left them to toil up the Mountain of Existence under sterner guides and by rough and narrow paths. "Some went back to the first part of the Mountain, and seemed desirous of continuing busied in plucking flowers, but they were no longer guarded by Innocence;" and it fared ill with them. I am as far apart as any one can be from those "statesmen" who would attest and celebrate our national maturity by an uproarious display of national vanity and folly, much like a boy who smokes and gets tight to show that he is a man: but our national maturity has come, and with it, in a material sense, national greatness; and although we may determine in some measure *how* we shall meet the attendant dangers, we cannot choose *not* to meet them. The question is not now whether we would have them come sooner or later; such was the question before us eighteen months ago, and I, at least, was fully prepared to answer with Lord Wellington then, "I prefer them later." But to-day they are here: we can no more dissipate them by shutting our eyes than the ostrich eludes its enemy when it buries its head in the sand. As Moses to Joshua, let us then say: "Be strong and of a good courage; fear not, nor be afraid of them;" and to these ends let us calmly and truthfully tell ourselves what they are.

However great my regard for them, I see a serious danger in the presence among us of many philanthropists, humanitarians, and social reformers, eminently well-meaning and generally intelligent people, but to whom could be appropriately addressed Saint Paul's words to the Thessalonians: "We beseech ye, brethren, * * * that ye study to be quiet, and to do your own business." I would not be misunderstood as to this class of persons: I do not say that the country would be better off if we hadn't them; on the contrary, I think them a meritorious and a valuable element in the community; the good they do outweighs the risks they cause, but these are grave risks, and we should guard against them. The citizens I have in mind, of all things, like least "to be quiet and to do their own business," or, at all events, to admit that anything can happen anywhere which is not their business. They are always in a state of ebullient sympathy with reported wrong or suffering in whatever out-of-the-way place rumor may locate it, and always ready to tell foreign rulers how to do what is undeniably *their* business,— the Czar how to deal with Siberia or Finland, the Sultan and the Powers how to pacify Armenia or Crete, South American republics how to secure liberty of conscience, Italians how to quell bread riots, Englishmen how to treat the Mahdi's tomb,—and are angry when these will not hear.

I have read many descriptions and criticisms of our country and people by foreigners, often carefully, even elaborately, prepared by men of marked ability and learning; in all, without exception, I have detected, or supposed that I detected, notable misapprehensions of fact and consequent errors in reasoning: I always hesitate therefore to express, or even form, decided opinions respecting the problems which may confront public men in other lands, and especially to pronounce sweeping and uncharitable condemnations on their supposed shortcomings. But no suspicion that their zeal may not be according to knowledge ever seems to trouble the good men and women to whom I have referred; they enjoy, apparently, a boundless and invincible confidence in their own omniscience:

"I number the sands; I measure the sea;
What's hidden to others is known to me;"

and they express themselves with corresponding assurance and emphasis.

It might be a matter of little moment what such people said and did were the world, or even the United States, peopled by philosophers or saints: unfortunately our nation and the nations around us are as yet, and probably will continue to be, made up of very human men; and while this remains true, those who thus awaken angry passions and inflame bitter prejudices play with fire. The consequences of their activity may be vastly more far-reaching than they themselves propose,—may be even the very opposite of their wishes. To turn again to the Farewell Address: "Antipathy in one nation against another disposes each more readily to offer insult and injury, to lay

hold of slight causes of umbrage, and to be haughty and intrac-
table when accidental or trifling occasions of dispute occur.
Hence frequent collisions, obstinate, envenomed, and bloody
contests. The nation, prompted by ill-will and resentment,
sometimes impels to war the government, contrary to the best
calculations of policy." In the last few words is suggested the
momentous query: How far can our public men be trusted to
resist and turn back a tide of misguided popular sentiment setting strongly towards a needless war, "contrary to the best calculations of policy?" It must be admitted that in one respect
they are well qualified for the duty: an American politician
repeats with such parrot-like fidelity and assiduity his party's
shibboleth, whatever this may be, that he may half persuade
himself he believes it; but beyond this he has no opinions, and
since he considers all enthusiasm no less factitious, and all professions no less insincere than he knows his own to be, he is
protected from the contagion of a visionary fanaticism. With
a government made up of such men that risk is not imminent
to which Washington alludes in saying: "The government
sometimes participates in the national propensity, and adopts
through passion what reason would reject." But there is a far
greater, indeed a very great, danger that in such a case American politicians may sacrifice their country's prosperity and safety, not, indeed, to their passions, but to their real or supposed
selfish interests. With some honorable exceptions, which do but
prove the rule, our present public men are profoundly indifferent to the prosperity, the dignity, the safety of the country they
govern; too many members of our federal legislature might
ask with astonishment, "What are we here for?" should any
one suggest that they give time or thought to questions of diplomacy or national defense, or, indeed, to anything beside
office-mongering and vote-hunting. Their hearts and lives are
given up to the noble work of quartering for support on the
taxpayers as many as possible of their relatives and dependents
and political henchmen, preferably such of these as may be too
stupid or lazy or vicious to make a living for themselves; to
any other task, unless perhaps it be electioneering to retain their
own places, they can give but the leavings of their time and
the dregs of their energy. Moreover, they are notoriously in-

competent to gauge public opinion, and peculiarly clumsy and unlucky in their efforts to forecast a popular verdict. The blunders made by some of the most prominent among them as to the results of impending elections (a subject on which, of all others, they might be supposed entitled to speak with authority) have been so gross and frequent of late years as to seem at once incredible and incomprehensible to observers who know public men in other countries, or knew our public men in other days. As a consequence, not only do they never dream of resisting a genuine though mistaken and mischievous popular clamor, but, as the old lady thought her pastor must have mistaken "some other loud noise" for his divine call to the ministry, however closely they glue their ears to the telephone to catch an inkling of the people's wishes, it is even chances or less that they can make these out. For the cackling of geese may make a loud noise; a crowd of idlers may be easily gathered in stirring times to stare at a noted person, and what a casual crowd will shout for is in great measure matter of chance at best, and may be readily determined by artifice. It ought to be, but I do not think it, incredible that a resolution of Congress actually or virtually declaring war may be one day signed by a President who himself believes war "contrary to the best calculations of policy" for this country, but has been led to think it also, and perhaps to think it falsely, necessary or advisable to assure his party's victory at the polls, possibly to assure his own reëlection to office.

I say this, fully recognizing the moral obliquity involved in his act. A heavier weight could hardly rest on any man's conscience, a more formidable indictment could hardly await any man at the bar of history, than must fall to the lot of one who knows he has bartered the lives of his fellow-countrymen, the security of his country, the peace of the world, for partisan advantage to gratify personal ambition. Washington may have reasonably believed that no man capable of such conduct would ever sit in the chair he first filled; for us, this belief is to my mind no longer reasonable.

The national danger lurking in the degeneracy of our public men may become yet more manifest after war has become a fact. Treason in such form as Benedict Arnold's is too unusual to be greatly feared, but a failure in official duty which would differ from it morally less in kind than in degree is, to say the least, by no means inconceivable. Can we be assured that some future President will not "give aid and comfort" to the public enemy by placing or retaining in some position of the highest responsibility, even as the administrative head of the army itself, some influential politician grossly and notoriously unfit to be thus employed? And if this be possible, is it any the less possible that at critical times high military command may be unworthily held as the fruit of political intrigue or personal favoritism? May it not happen that our soldiers shall be shamefully neglected, that recognized abuses shall remain without remedy, that detected misconduct shall be condoned, because to right these wrongs may be, or may be thought, "bad politics"? Painful as is this odious picture, even to the imagination, we must endure its contemplation if we would do our part, as good citizens, as honest men, to make certain that our country shall never hereafter offer it to a disgusted world.

To some of my hearers the thought may occur that for these evils and indeed for all those springing from warfare, an obvious and sufficient safeguard is a policy of peace, and that scandals in the organization or administration of our army would be surely avoided had we no army at all; they, and perchance others not quite so trenchant in their views, may also see in "militarism" one of the gravest of those impending dangers now overshadowing the United States. The suggestion that we escape abuses in our army by disbanding it seems to me like telling a dyspeptic that nothing he eats will disagree with him if he eats nothing. I can indeed conceive of a world wherein there should be no need of soldiers, as I can conceive of one wherein policemen and jailers and executioners, judges and lawyers, physicians and nurses, would be likewise superfluous; but it is not the world I live in, and I gravely doubt whether it would be a world for the habitation of men. With all my heart I echo the words of the Farewell Address: "Observe good faith and justice towards all nations; cultivate peace and harmony with all: religion and morality enjoin this conduct; and can it be that good policy does not equally enjoin it?" But the great writer tells us to do these things, "taking care always to keep

ourselves by suitable establishments on a respectable defensive
posture," and "remembering also that timely disbursements to
prepare for danger frequently prevent much greater disbursements to repel it." I have already said that I think the time
has passed when we could rely with reasonable confidence upon
our isolation as a sufficient protection; the time has also passed
when we could avoid the responsibilities, the enmities, the perils
incident to our national strength: that such are the facts is
certainly no cause for vainglorious rejoicing, but, on the other
hand, the facts should be resolutely accepted: we may regret
past days, but it were unworthy to whimper over them, and
foolish to strive to doubt that they are beyond recall: "suitable
establishments" sustained by "timely disbursements" we must
have; not only to maintain "a respectable defensive posture,"
and "prepare for danger" inseparable from our prospective, indeed our present, position as one of the world's great powers,
but also that we may, in case of need, "choose peace or war, as
our interest, guided by justice, shall counsel:" does this necessity involve any real danger from "militarism"?

· What is "militarism"? The word is English, if it be English
at all, only by recent naturalization, and the thing is no less
unfamiliar than distasteful to the English-speaking folk. It is
often loosely used as though it signified a martial spirit, a popular interest in military matters, or a general readiness throughout the people to accept with alacrity a soldier's duties: as a
matter of fact, if employed with any accuracy, it denotes very
nearly the reverse of all these things; speaking broadly, we may
say that a nation almost inevitably becomes less warlike as it
becomes more "militaristic," if a barbarous word may be coined
for the occasion. No monarch of modern times was so essentially and thoroughly a crowned drill-sergeant as Frederick I
of Prussia; in him militarism amounted, not merely to a passion, but to a mania; yet he was also one of the most pacific of
sovereigns. His reign illustrated the saying attributed to the
Grand Duke Constantine, a prince and soldier of somewhat
the same type, that he "hated war because it spoiled the troops."
In a healthy state of public opinion, the army is a mere living
weapon: it stands to the nation as a horse to its rider; it asks,
with the mute eloquence of obvious justice and humanity, that

its toil and blood be not wasted; no right-thinking man can hear without indignation of faithful soldiers uselessly sacrificed in worse than useless enterprises; but, after all, it is, as is the horse, a thing to spend and to be spent; if it must be ridden to death in its master's service, to the death it obeys the spur. When, however, the means becomes an end; when the welfare of the instrument is allowed to weigh against, even to outweigh, that of the owner; when, in other words, the army grows, or rather decays, into something indulged and pampered and finally feared; when its selfish interests are consulted, its prejudices are inflamed, its passions are gratified at the country's cost,— we have "militarism," and unless some source of national regeneration be found, we are fairly on the highroad to a military tyranny. In this wretched system one finds all that is small, paltry, harmful in military life, its frippery, its pedantry, its petty abuses of authority, its callousness to suffering, its indifference to rights, but less and ever less, as the miserable order endures, of its heroism in obedience, of the noble humility of its self-surrender; as the civic virtues die out in the people, the military virtues die out in the army; and when the latter has become all-powerful in the state, for its proper work it is almost invariably worthless. Rome under the Prætorians, the days of *pronunciamento* in Spanish America, have furnished pictures, Haïti has furnished the caricature, of a people and an army alike the prey of militarism developed into military despotism.

Once, and once only, have people of English speech been subject for a few years to the yoke of their own army: the Protectorate of Cromwell was a period of prosperity at home, of victory abroad; the ruler was an extraordinary man, the army which sustained his rule was a yet more extraordinary army; nevertheless, so hostile to the habits, the temperament, the traditions of the people, was the virtual though disguised reign of the sword, that the man of genius who upheld it was hardly cold in his grave before the entire nation had called back from exile a frivolous, selfish, and dissolute prince, and welcomed him enthusiastically to the throne as deliverer from a seemingly intolerable bondage. To my mind, there is little fear lest their children by blood or adoption, on either side of the Atlantic,

shall ever feel or act otherwise. For his countrymen at least,
Byron had no cause to dread

> "That spell upon the minds of men
> * * * * *
> Which led them to adore
> Those pagod things of sabre sway
> With fronts of brass and feet of clay."

On the other hand, in the readiness with which, a year since,
so many thousands of our young men left their homes for a
war whereof many, probably most, of them regretted the outbreak and doubted the need, I saw, and still see, a great cause
for encouragement. It proved that they remembered a truth
some older men have appeared since then inclined to forget,
namely, that the duties of a good citizen in time of war in no
wise depend on his opinion regarding the merits of the controversy which has ended in war or the necessity or expediency of
the conflict,—that a man who thought the late war a criminal
folly was under precisely the same obligation to enlist as one
who thought it a noble crusade in the cause of enlightenment
and humanity. In every community there must evidently be
some authority which shall finally determine all questions of
international relations, and, in last resort, the momentous question of peace or war. By our Constitution, this latter power is
intrusted to Congress; it may have been in this instance exercised wisely or foolishly, from good motives or from bad; but
when it had been exercised, whatever each of us might think
of the decision or of those who made it, that decision fixed the
duty of every American citizen. He had no more right to refuse his aid in giving it effect because he questioned its rightful-
ness than a sheriff or a jailer would have to release a prisoner
whom he believed to have been unjustly convicted by a stupid or
prejudiced, or even by a bribed, jury. For any nation to permit
each one of its subjects to decide such questions for himself
and act on his decision would be suicidal, and no nation does
this: the nearest approach to such legalized anarchy known to
history was furnished by the *liberum veto* and "Confederations"
of Poland, and there such institutions bore their legitimate fruit.
When Stephen Decatur gave the sentiment, "Our country, right

or wrong," he used words unfortunately liable to serious misconstruction, but which, in the sense he unquestionably ascribed
to them, express a most significant truth. It is not true that
a good man will promote his country's prosperity *per fas aut
nefas;* it is not true that, in international or any other human
relations, "Might is right and conscience nought but fear;"
but it is true, and of vital moment to be owned as truth, that the
grave responsibilities for what must follow an appeal to arms
rest wholly on the country's statesmen, and in no wise on her
soldiers. Our young men remembered also that, in law and
conscience, every American citizen is always a soldier in reserve: the duties of a soldier rest upon him in time of war, even,
if need be, in time of peace as well, not by his special choice, but
as a result of birth or residence, as a return for the privilege of
citizenship and the protection of the laws; and although, under
the circumstances then existing, the question whether each one
of them should assume the active discharge of those duties was
wisely left, in the first instance, to his own election, it was well
for them and for the country that so many chose as they did.
After all has been said, at the Hague or elsewhere, as to the
wickedness of warfare, Washington's profession can hardly be
one unbecoming a civilized or a Christian man, or one to be
shunned by an American. A Byzantine of the Lower Empire,
an Italian of the Renaissance, may have regarded soldiers and
their work with a large measure of unaffected disgust and contempt, but those were not times and countries in which were
developed high and sound types of human character. That nation is diseased which answers a call to arms sluggishly and
with reluctance.

I am even prepared to find some compensation for the sacrifices made inevitable by the no less inevitable dangers of our
new position in the vivid consciousness of national existence,
in the antidote to partisan and sectional prejudices and to enmities of class or race or creed, which will be furnished by some
experience of military life common to the entire country. In
war time it may be true of a self-governing people

"That none are for a party, but all are for the state;
  That the great man loves the poor man, and the poor man loves
      the great."

Comrades on the firing line will never be truly strangers. No one knew better than Washington that it was the Revolution's baptism of blood which made Americans really a nation. He tells them: "You have, in a common cause, fought and triumphed together; the independence and liberty you possess are the work of joint counsels and joint efforts, of common dangers, sufferings, and successes." There is the less reason to regret the increased interest in matters pertaining to the national defense, awakened by the war, among our people, because Congress had so long, so culpably, and so grievously failed to make for this any reasonable provision whatever. When Washington, in the words I have quoted, declared a respectable military establishment necessary to the safety and dignity of the nation, he did not doubtless expect or desire our army ever to rival those maintained to-day by Russia, Germany, or France, Austria or Italy, or even England; he might have been content with but a fraction of the force deemed needful by such powers as Spain, Turkey, and Japan: but he could have hardly imagined that a time would come when the United States could boast of seventy millions of inhabitants, and an area as large as Europe, and yet rest satisfied with an "establishment" immeasurably weaker than that of Holland or of Portugal, of Sweden or of Switzerland; yet such was the sober fact when Congress declared the recent war. Our regular army consisted of barely 27,000 troops, scattered all over a vast continent, and even these, as the event soon made painfully apparent, were altogether unprepared for the field. Beside this, we had about 105,000 organized militia, not subject as a body to federal authority, and neither intended nor fit for active, and especially for foreign, service: this force was completely disorganized and well-nigh destroyed by its use as the nucleus for an army of invasion. With an improvidence and levity which would be incredible had not our eyes witnessed their exhibition, Congress actually rushed into a war of aggression with nothing which could be called, by the widest stretch of imagination or courtesy, "an army" at its command. We may well be devoutly thankful that the weakness of our enemy gave us then the precious time we so sorely needed, but we should remember that Providence may not send us *two* such warnings.

The vital danger, however, lies rather in possible fruits of victory than in any ills to flow from defeat. The corruption and incapacity of our politicians in high office, their negligence in preparation, recklessness in provocation, unblushing readiness ever to sacrifice their country's interests to their own, may expose us to humiliating disasters and grievous losses; but, in my belief, no *foreign* foe will imperil our national unity or orderly freedom: these were so won and so saved for us that only our own vices can destroy them: the tablets on yonder walls are warrants to assure them from domestic revolt or outward violence, while a nation worthy to live shall live to defend them.

> "By our children's golden future,
> By our fathers' stainless shield,
> That which God and heroes left us
> We shall never, never yield!"

But will that escutcheon remain untarnished, will that future be still unclouded, if the sordid vices of our political life are allowed to spread with all the rank luxuriance of noxious weeds in the abuses of some vast vassal empire which we may hold by the sword? Imagine the dumb, helpless millions of the East, the passive prey for ages of rapacity and oppression, at the mercy of proconsuls chosen among the bosses of our cities and States; picture to yourselves these vulgar tyrants employing the treasures which their shameless greed has amassed abroad to further debauch our politics, to further degrade our government: think of these things as possible, nay, as not unlikely, and I do not say tremble at the thought, but let it banish any levity and any presumption.

I know there are those who hope to find a remedy in the very gravity of the threatened evils; who tell us Civil Service Reform came from Calcutta to London, and look for good government and pure politics to come from Manila to New York. God grant, in His Mercy, which has been so often and so signally shown us, which we have so ill deserved, that these may prove true prophets! But did any such passengers ever cross the seas from Manila to Madrid? And at Manila we are but on the threshold of our threatening destiny. Our optimists tell us also, when a great burden seems about to be laid upon him, a brave man will not pray that it pass, but that he be given strength to bear it: have we not the best of all possible authority to ask both blessings? Yes, it is not for such as we are to choose; but may we not well, in all submission to God's Will, with all confidence in God's Goodness, yet pray that our country be not tried unduly, be not tempted beyond her strength?

WHITELAW REID

A CONTINENTAL UNION—CIVIL SERVICE FOR THE ISLANDS

ADDRESS AT THE MASSACHUSETTS CLUB, YOUNG'S HOTEL, BOSTON, MARCH 3, 1900

[Whitelaw Reid was born in Xenia, Ohio, on October 27, 1837. He was graduated from Miami University, Oxford, Ohio, in 1856, and during his life received honorary degrees from nine institutions. He began a journalistic career, which lasted until 1905, as editor of the *Xenia News*. From 1861 to 1862 he was a war correspondent, and from 1862 to 1868, Washington correspondent of the *Cincinnati Gazette*. He was aide-de-camp to General Thomas A. Morris and to General W. S. Rosecrans in West Virginia, was clerk of the Military Committee of the House of Representatives, 1862 to 1863, and Librarian of the House, from 1863 to 1866. In 1868 he joined the editorial staff of the *New York Tribune*, the next year becoming managing editor; and from 1872 to 1905, he was chief proprietor and editor in chief. From 1889 to 1892 he was United States Minister to France; in 1898 he was a member of the Commission which concluded the peace of Paris at the end of the Spanish-American war; and from 1905 to December 15, 1912, when he died in London, he was United States Ambassador to England.

His speech printed below reflects a strong defense reaction to the problems arising out of the Spanish-American war, and helps to complete the picture presented in preceding pages by the speeches of Senator Beveridge and Mr. Bonaparte.]

A third of a century ago or more, I had the honor to be a guest at this club, which met then, as now, in Young's Hotel. It has ever since been a pleasure to recall the men of Boston who gathered about the board, interested, as now, in the affairs of the Republic to which they were at once ornament and defence. Frank Bird sat at the head. Near him was Henry Wilson. John M. Forbes was here, and John A. Andrew, and George S. Boutwell, and George L. Stearns, and many another, eager in those times of trial to seek and know the best thing to be done to serve this country of our pride and love. They were practical business men, true Yankees in the best sense; and they spent no time then in quarrelling over how we got into

[212]

our trouble. Their one concern was how to get out, to the greatest advantage of the country.

Honored now by another opportunity to meet with the club, I can do no better than profit by this example of your earlier days. You have asked me to speak on some phase of the Philippine question. I would like to concentrate your attention upon the present and practical phase; and to withdraw it for the time from things that are past and cannot be changed.

Stare decisis. There are some things settled. Have we not a better and more urgent use for our time now than in showing why some of us would have liked them settled differently? In my State there is a dictum by an eminent Judge of the Court of Appeals, so familiar now as to be a commonplace, to the effect that when that Court has rendered its decision, there are only two things left to the disappointed advocate. One is to accept the result attained, and go to work on it as best he can; the other, to go down to the tavern and "cuss" the Court. I want to suggest to those who dislike the past of the Philippine question that there is more important work pressing upon you at this moment than to cuss the Court. You cannot change the past, but you may prevent some threatened sequences, which even in your eyes would be far greater calamities.

There is no use bewailing the war with Spain. Nothing can undo it, and its results are upon us. There is no use arguing that Dewey should have abandoned his conquest. He didn't. There is no use regretting the Peace of Paris. For good or for ill, it is a part of the supreme law of the land. There is no use begrudging the twenty millions. They are paid. There is no use depreciating the islands, East or West. They are the property of the United States, by an immutable title, which, whatever some of our own people say, the whole civilized world recognizes and respects. There is no use talking about getting rid of them;—giving them back to Spain, or turning them over to Aguinaldo, or simply running away from them. Whoever thinks that any one of these things could be done, or is still open to profitable debate, takes his observations—will you pardon me the liberty of saying it?—takes his observations too closely within the horizon of Boston bay to know the American people.

They have not been persuaded and they cannot be persuaded that this is an inferior Government, incapable of any duty Providence (through the acts of a wicked Administration, if you choose) may send its way—duties which other nations could discharge, but we cannot. They do not and will not believe that it was any such maimed, imperfect, misshapen cripple from birth for which our forefathers made a place in the family of Nations. Nor are they misled by the sudden cry that, in a populous region, thronged by the ships and traders of all countries, where their own prosecution of a just war broke down whatever guarantees for order had previously existed, they are violating the natural rights of man, by enforcing order. Just as little are they misled by the other cry that they are violating the right of self-government, and the Declaration of Independence, and the Constitution of the United States by preparing for the distracted, warring tribes of that region, such local government as they may be found capable of conducting, in their various stages of development from pure barbarism toward civilization. The American people know they are thus proceeding to do just what Jefferson did in the vast region he bought from France—without the consent, by the way, either of its sovereign or its inhabitants. They know they are following in the exact path of all the constructive statesmen of the Republic, from the days of the man who wrote the Declaration, and of those who made the Constitution, down to the days of the men who conquered California, bought Alaska, and denied the right of self-government to Jefferson Davis. They simply do not believe that a new light has been given to Mr. Bryan, or to the better men who are aiding him, greater and purer than was given to Washington, or to Jefferson, or to Lincoln.

And so I venture to repeat, without qualification or reserve, that what is past cannot be changed. Candid and dispassionate minds, knowing the American people of all political shades and in all sections of the country, can see no possibility that any party in power, whether the present one or its opponent, would or could now or soon, if ever, abandon or give back one foot of the territory gained in the late war, and ours now by the supreme law of the land and with the assent of the civilized world. As well may you look to see California, which your own

Daniel Webster, quite in a certain modern Massachusetts style, once declared in the Senate to be not worth a dollar, now abandoned to Mexico.

It seems to me then idle to thresh over old straw when the grain is not only winnowed but gone to the mill. And so I am not here to discuss abstract questions, as for example whether in the year 1898 the United States was wise in going to war with Spain, though on that I might not greatly disagree with the malcontents; or as to the wisdom of expansion; or as to the possibility of a republic's maintaining its authority over a people without their consent. Nor am I here to apologize for my part in making the nation that was in the wrong and beaten in the late war pay for it in territory. I have never thought of denying or evading my own full share of responsibility in that matter. Conscious of a duty done, I am happily independent enough to be measurably indifferent as to a mere present and temporary effect. Whatever the verdict of the men of Massachusetts to-day, I contentedly await the verdict of their sons.

But, on the other hand, I am not here either to launch charges of treason against any opponent of these policies, who nevertheless loves the institutions founded on these shores by your ancestors, and wishes to perpetuate what they created. Least of all would it occur to me to utter a word in disparagement of your senior Senator [Mr. Hoar], of whom it may be said with respectful and almost affectionate regard that he bears a warrant as authentic as that of the most distinguished of his predecessors to speak for the conscience and the culture of Massachusetts. Nor shall any reproach be uttered by me against another eminent son of the Commonwealth and servant of the Republic, who was expected, as one of the officers of your Club told me, to make this occasion distinguished by his presence. He has been represented as resenting the unchangeable past so sternly that he hopes to aid in defeating the party he has helped to lead through former trials to present glory. If so, and if from the young and unremembering reproach should come, be it ours, silent and walking backward, merely to cast over him the mantle of his own honored service.

No, no! Let us have a truce to profitless disputes about what cannot be reversed. Censure us if you must. Even strike at your old associates and your own party if you will, and when you can, without harming causes you hold dear. But for the duty of this hour, consider if there is not a common meeting ground and instant necessity for union in a rational effort to avert present perils. This, then, is my appeal. Disagree as we may about the past, let us to-day at least see straight—see things as they are. Let us suspend disputes about what is done and cannot be undone, long enough to rally all the forces of goodwill, all the undoubted courage and zeal and patriotism that are now at odds, in a devoted effort to meet the greater dangers that are upon us.

For the enemy is at the gates. More than that, there is some reason to fear that, through dissensions from within, he may gain the citadel. In their eagerness to embarrass the advocates of what has been done, and with the vain hope of in some way undoing it, and so lifting this Nation of seventy-five millions bodily backward two years on its path, there are many who are still putting forth all their energies in straining our Constitution and defying our history, to show that we have no possessions whose people are not entitled to citizenship and ultimately to Statehood. Grant that, and instead of reversing engines safely in mid-career, as they vainly hope, they must simply plunge us over the precipice. The movement began in the demand that our Dingley tariff—as a matter of right, not of policy, for most of these people denounce the tariff itself as barbarous—that our Dingley tariff should of necessity be extended over Puerto Rico as an integral part of the United States. Following an assent to this must have come inevitably all the other rights and privileges belonging to citizenship, and then no power could prevent the admission of the State of Puerto Rico.

Some may think that in itself would be no great thing; though it is for you to say how Massachusetts would relish having this mixed population, a little more than half colonial Spanish, the rest negro and halfbreed, illiterate, alien in language, alien in ideas of right, interests and government, send in from the mid-Atlantic, nearly a third of the way over to Africa, two Senators to balance the votes of Mr. Hoar and Lodge; for you to say how Massachusetts would regard the spectacle of her Senatorial vote nullified, and one-third of her representation in the

House offset on questions, for instance, of sectional and tropical interest, in the government of this Continent, and in the
administration of this precious heritage of our fathers.

Or, suppose Massachusetts to be so little Yankee (in the best
sense still) that she could bear all this without murmur or objection; is it to be imagined that she can lift other States in this
generation to her altruistic level? How would Kansas for example enjoy being balanced in the Senate, and nearly balanced
in the House, on questions relating to the irrigation of her arid
plains, or the protection of her beet-root industry, or on any
others affecting the great central regions of this continent by
these voices from the watery waste of the ocean? Or how
would West Virginia or Oregon or Connecticut, or half a dozen
others of similar population, regard it, to be actually outvoted
in their own home, on their own continent, by this Spanish and
negro waif from the mid-Atlantic?

All this, in itself, may seem to some unimportant, negligible,
even trivial. At any rate it would be inevitable; since no one
is wild enough to believe that Puerto Rico can be turned back
to Spain, or bartered away, or abandoned by the generation that
took it. But make its people citizens now, and you have already
made it, potentially, a State. Then behind Puerto Rico stands
Cuba, and behind Cuba, in time, stand the whole of the West
Indies, on whom that law of political gravitation which John
Quincy Adams described, will be perpetually acting with re-
doubled force. And behind them,—no, far ahead of them,—
abreast of Puerto Rico itself, stand the Philippines! The
Constitution which our Fathers reverently ordained for the
United States of *America* is thus tortured by its professed
friends into a crazy quilt, under whose dirty folds must huddle
the United States of America, of the West Indies, of the East
Indies, and of Polynesia; and Pandemonium is upon us.

I implore you, as thinking men, pause long enough to realize
the degradation of the Republic thus calmly contemplated by
those who proclaim this to be our Constitutional duty toward
our possessions. The Republican institutions I have been
trained to believe in were institutions founded, like those of New
England, on the Church and the School House. They constitute a system only likely to endure among a people of high virtue

and high intelligence. The Republican Government built up on this continent, while the most successful in the history of the world, is also the most complicated, the most expensive and often the slowest. Such are its complications and checks and balances and interdependencies, which tax the intelligence, the patience and the virtue of the highest Caucasian development, that it is a system absolutely unworkable by a group of Oriental and tropical races, more or less hostile to each other, whose highest type is a Chinese and Malay halfbreed, and among whom millions, a majority possibly, are far below the level of the pure Malay.

What holds a nation together, unless it be community of interests, character and language, and contiguous territory? What would more thoroughly insure its speedily flying to pieces than the lack of every one of these requisites? Over and over the clearest-eyed students of history have predicted our own downfall even as a continental Republic, in spite of our measurable enjoyment of all of them. How near we all believed we came to it once or twice! How manifestly under the incongruous hodge-podge of additions to the Union thus proposed, we should be organizing with Satanic skill the exact conditions which have invariably led to such downfalls elsewhere!

Before the advent of the United States, the history of the world's efforts at Republicanism was a monotonous record of failure. Your very schoolboys are taught the reason. It was because the average of intelligence and morality was too low; because they lacked the self-restrained, self-governing quality, developed in the Anglo-Saxon bone and fibre through all the centuries since Runnymede; because they grew unwieldy and lost cohesion by reason of unrelated territory, alien races and languages, and inevitable territorial and climatic conflicts of interest.

On questions vitally affecting the welfare of this Continent it is inconceivable, unthinkable, that even altruistic Massachusetts should tolerate having two Senators and thirteen Representatives neutralized by as many from Mindanao. Yet Mindanao has a greater population than Massachusetts, and its Mahometan Malays are as keen for the conduct of public affairs, can talk as much—and look as shrewdly for the profit of it!

There are cheerful, happy-go-lucky public men, who assure us that the National digestion has been proved equal to anything. Has it? Are we content, for example, with the way we have dealt with the negro problem in the Southern States? Do we think the suffrage question there is now on a permanent basis, which either we, or our Southern friends can be proud of, while we lack the courage either honestly to enforce the rule of the majority, or honestly to sanction a limitation of suffrage within lines of intelligence and thrift? How well would our famous National digestion probably advance, if we filled up our Senate with twelve or fourteen more Senators, representing conditions incomparably worse?

Is it said this danger is imaginary? At this moment some of the purest and most patriotic men in Massachusetts, along with a great many of the very worst in the whole country, are vehemently declaring that our new possessions are already a part of the United States, that in spite of the treaty which reserved the question of citizenship and political status for Congress, their people are already citizens of the United States, and that no part of the United States can be arbitrarily and permanently excluded from Statehood.

The immediate contention, to be sure, is only about Puerto Rico, and it is only a very little island. But who believes he can stop the avalanche? What wise man at least will take the risk of starting it? Who imagines that we can take in Puerto Rico and keep out nearer islands when they come? Powerful elements are already pushing Cuba. Practically everybody recognizes now that we must retain control of Cuba's foreign relations. But beyond that, the same influences that came so near hurrying us into a recognition of the Cuban Republic and the Cuban debt are now sure that Cuba will very shortly be so "Americanized" (that is, overrun with American speculators) that it cannot be denied admission—that in fact it will be as American as Florida! And, after Cuba, the deluge! Who fancies that we could then keep Santo Domingo and Hayti out; or any West India island that applied; or our friends, the Kanakas? Or who fancies that after the baser sort have once tasted blood in the form of such rotten-borough States, and have learned to form their larger combinations with them, we shall still be able to admit as a matter of right a part of the territory exacted from Spain, and yet deny admission as a matter of right to the rest?

The Nation has lately been renewing its affectionate memories of a man who died in his effort to hold on, with or without their consent, to the States we already have on this continent, but who never dreamed of casting a dragnet over the world's archipelagoes for more. Do we remember his birthday and forget his words? "This Government (meaning that under the Constitution ordained for the United States of *America*), this Government cannot permanently endure, half slave, half free." Who disputes it now? Well, then, can it endure half civilized and enlightened, half barbarous and pagan; half white, half black, brown, yellow and mixed; half northern and western, half tropical and Oriental; one half a homogeneous Continent, the other half in myriads of islands, scattered halfway around the globe, but all eager to participate in ruling this Continent which our fathers with fire and sword redeemed from barbarism and subdued to the uses of the highest civilization.

I will not insult your intelligence or your patriotism by imagining it possible that in view of such considerations you could consent to the madman's policy of taking these islands we control into full partnership with the States of this Union. Nor need you be much disturbed by the interested outcries as to the injustice you do by refusing to admit them.

When it is said you are denying the natural rights Mr. Jefferson proclaimed, you can answer that you are giving these people, in their distant islands, the identical form of government Mr. Jefferson himself gave to the territories on this continent which he bought. When it is said you are denying our own cardinal doctrine of self-government, you can point to the arrangements for establishing every particle of self-government with which these widely different tribes can be safely trusted, consistently with your responsibility for the preservation of order and the protection of life and property in that archipelago; and the pledge of more, the moment they are found capable of it. When you are asked, as a leading champion asked the other night at Philadelphia, "Does your liberation of one people give you the right to subjugate another?" you can answer him: "No, nor to allow and aid Aguinaldo to subjugate them either, as you proposed." When the idle quibble that after Dewey's victory Spain had no sovereignty to cede is repeated, it may be asked why acknowledge then that she did cede it in Cuba and Puerto Rico, and deny that she could cede it in the Philippines? Finally, when they tell you in mock heroics, appropriated from the great days of the anti-slavery struggle for the cause now of a pinchbeck Washington, that no results of the irrevocable past two years are settled, that not even the title to our new possessions is settled, and never will be until it is settled according to their notions, you can answer that then the title to Massachusetts is not settled, nor the title to a square mile of land in most of the States from ocean to ocean. Over practically none of it did we assume sovereignty by the consent of the inhabitants.

Quite possibly these controversies may embarrass the Government and threaten the security of the party in power. New and perplexing responsibilities often do that. But is it to the interest of the sincere and patriotic among the discontented to produce either result? The one thing sure is that no party in power in this country will dare abandon these new possessions. That being so, do those of you who regret it prefer to lose all influence over the outcome? While you are repining over what is beyond recall, events are moving on. If you do not help shape them, others, without your high principle and purity of motive, may. Can you wonder if, while you are harassing the Administration with impracticable demands for an abandonment of territory which the American people will not let go, less unselfish influences are busy presenting candidates for all the offices in its organization? If the friends of a proper Civil Service persist in chasing the ignis fatuus of persuading Americans to throw away territory, while the politicians are busy crowding their favorites into the territorial offices, who will feel free from self-reproach at the results? Grant that the situation is bad. Can there be a doubt of the duty to make the best of it? Do you ask how? By being an active patriot, not a passive one. By exerting, and exerting now, when it is needed, every form of influence, personal, social, political, moral—the influence of the Clubs, the Chambers of Commerce, the manufactories, the Colleges and the Churches, in favor of the purest, the ablest, the most scientific, the most disinterested—in a word the best possible Civil Service for the new possessions that the conscience and the capacity of America can produce, with the most liberal use of all the material available from native sources.

I have done. I have no wish to argue, to defend or to attack. I have sought only to point out what I conceive to be the present danger and the present duty. It is not to be doubted that all such considerations will summon you to the high resolve that you will neither shame the Republic by shirking the duty its own victory entails, nor despoil the Republic by abandoning its rightful possessions, nor degrade the Republic by admissions of unfit elements to its Union; but that you will honor it, enrich it, ennoble it, by doing your utmost to make the administration of these possessions worthy of the Nation that Washington founded and Lincoln preserved. My last word is an appeal to stand firm and stand all together for the Continental Union and for a pure Civil Service for the Islands.

JONATHAN P. DOLLIVER

THE COW

SPEECH IN THE UNITED STATES SENATE, MARCH 26, 1902, ON
THE OLEOMARGARINE BILL

[In March and April, 1902, the United States Senate vigorously
debated a bill to make oleomargarine and other imitation dairy products subject to the laws of any State or Territory into which they
might be transported, to change the tax on oleomargarine, and to
amend an act entitled "An act defining butter, also imposing a tax upon and regulating the manufacture, sale, importation and exportation
of oleomargarine, approved August 2, 1886."

The three speeches which follow, by Senators Dolliver, Bailey, and
Depew, are taken from the debate which occurred on March 26 and
April 1 and 2. They well represent the respective styles of these three
men, all of whom were noted as orators.

Jonathan Prentiss Dolliver was born in Preston county, Virginia
(now West Virginia), on February 6, 1858. He was graduated from
the University of West Virginia, in Morgantown, in 1876; in 1878
was admitted to the bar and began the practice of law in Ft. Dodge,
Iowa. He was solicitor of that city from 1880 to 1887; was a Republican Representative in Congress from 1889 to August 22, 1900;
and thereafter was United States Senator, until his death in Ft.
Dodge, on October 15, 1910.]

Mr. President, I would not venture to ask anybody to listen
to me on this bill if it were not for the fact that for many years
in the other House of Congress I had some modest connection
with the legislation which had for its object the prevention of
the adulteration of cheese and flour and other agricultural products; and while the subject is rather a lowly one from some
standpoints, it has nevertheless become, in my humble judgment,
one of the pressing and important questions with which we have
to deal.

I was very much interested in the discourse delivered here
yesterday by the honorable Senator from Mississippi [Mr.
Money], and I regret that in stating the object of this measure
he failed altogether to get the standpoint of those who have felt
an interest in the passage of this bill. His idea seemed to be
that the object of this measure is to suppress the legitimate in-

dustry of manufacturing oleomargarine, whereas in truth the object of this measure and the only object which it has is so to amend the oleomargarine act of 1886 as to more effectually prevent the imposition which has been practiced upon the community in the manufacture and sale of imitation dairy products.

That statute levied a tax of 2 cents a pound on oleomargarine and provided means for identifying the article in the market place. It was thought at the time to be adequate for that purpose, and would have been in all probability if its promoters had not deliberately chosen for their industry a career of lawlessness and false pretenses. At that time the annual production of oleomargarine was comparatively small, and few people could be found to eat it if they knew it, but since then the number of factories has greatly increased, the chemical processes of its manufacture have been vastly improved, and the annual output multiplied beyond a hundred million pounds.

If those who have invested their money in the business had chosen to deal in good faith with the community, observing the act of Congress and the laws of the States in which three-fourths of our population live, no additional legislation would have been necessary. But year after year this business has played into the hands of men who have nullified the act of Congress in every particular save only the payment of the tax, and have trampled under foot the local enactments of thirty-two States in the Union; all for the purpose of selling its product to those who are unable to distinguish it from butter.

The result of this is that the business has become fraudulent through and through, and unless its promoters are willing to co-operate with the law-making power, State and Federal, in the effort to lift it above the general reputation of a cheat at common law, the time will come, however many millions are invested in it, when it will be unfit for the countenance of any honest man.

Before I go any further I will point out what this bill proposes to do. The first section subjects original packages of all imitation dairy products entering any State through the channels of interstate commerce to the police regulations of that State in respect to such articles. This section is drawn for the purpose of preventing people in one State from sending these articles into another under conditions which exempt them from the operation of the laws of the State to which they are sent.

There was a time when most lawyers would have said that whenever an article of commerce enters a State it becomes immediately subject to the police powers of that State, for the opinion of Chief Justice Taney in the license cases of 1847, notably the case of Peirce et al. v. State of New Hampshire, reported in 5 How. 504, 12 L. Ed. 256, would appear to settle the right of any State to fix the status of articles of commerce brought into it from another State.

But at the October term, 1889, that ancient landmark of our jurisprudence was removed by the opinion of the court in the case of Leisy v. Hardin, reported in 135 U. S. page 100, 10 S. Ct. 681, 34 L. Ed. 128. That case arose in the State of Iowa. The Legislature of Iowa, in its discretion, had prohibited the manufacture and sale of intoxicating liquors within its borders under the usual penalties of seizure and condemnation.

The firm of Leisy & Co., citizens of Illinois, transported to Keokuk original packages of intoxicating liquors and undertook to sell them there notwithstanding the statutes of Iowa in such cases made and provided. They were seized by the constable of the township, and in an action of replevin to recover them the Supreme Court of Iowa held that they were in all respects subject to the laws of the State.

The case was brought here on writ of error, and the Supreme Court, with a dissenting opinion by Mr. Justice Harlan, in which Mr. Justice Gray and Mr. Justice Brewer joined, held that the liquors in controversy being articles of interstate commerce, had not, when sold for the first time in their original packages, so commingled with the common stock of goods subject to State jurisdiction as to feel the weight of State laws intended to prevent the traffic in intoxicating liquors.

This decision of the court would undoubtedly have produced universal confusion in every State where the law had undertaken to subject the liquor traffic to police regulations, whether by license or prohibition, if Congress had not promptly acted upon a suggestion of the Chief Justice, repeatedly made in the decision, in which its right is recognized to permit by express enactment the exercise by the States of the power to interfere by seizure or any other action with the importation or sale of goods brought in by foreign or nonresident importers.

Acting upon this suggestion, the original-package law of 1890, applicable only to intoxicating liquors, was passed—a law since fully sustained by the court in re Rohrer (140 U. S.)—and the first section of this bill repeats verbatim the language of that law, extending it to include the imitation dairy products with which we are now concerned. I regard the first section of this bill, therefore, as an important step in the direction of effectually managing the oleomargarine question.

It will be observed that the committee has struck out an amendment added by the House. We did that for two reasons. In the first place it is not necessary and therefore of no value, and in the next place it is ambiguous and therefore likely to produce controversy. Without the amendment nobody will be constrained in taking oleomargarine into States where the law permits its sale, provided the tax is paid, while with the amendment left in a question of construction may arise in which the rule of uniformity in the levy of taxes may be invoked to invalidate the whole statute.

I found great pleasure in urging the committee to leave it out because I heard the advocates of oleomargarine boasting that they had secured an amendment in the House which, while innocent in its appearance, would operate to cripple if not to nullify the statute. So much for the first section.

The second section extends the definition of the words "manufacturer of oleomargarine" so as to include everybody who sells it for money. It does not include those who are in possession of it for their own use. So the bill enables the purchaser, the poor workingman, who seemed to disturb the feelings of the Senator from Mississippi [Mr. Money] so much, to buy the article in its natural appearance and color it to suit himself, a thing which was shown to the committee to be very much more simple in the economy of the household than the somewhat complex process of salting mashed potatoes, for example.

But the bill extends that definition so as to include boarding houses, dining cars, hotels, restaurants, and everybody who handles the article for the purpose of disposing of it to others.

The next section of the bill may be described as the battle-ground of the controversy. It increases the tax on oleomargarine from 2 cents to 10 in case the article is colored in imitation of butter, and it reduces the tax from 2 cents to a quarter of a cent in case the article is put upon the market without an artificial coloring which brings it into the similitude of butter.

The final section of the bill is administrative—concerns only the relations of wholesale dealers to the Treasury Department.

The Senator from Mississippi [Mr. Money] undertook to state the purpose of the bill, and I am afraid that, without intending it, he did so with a certain lack of that fairness which usually characterizes his utterances here. He said that it was the object of the bill to kill the oleomargarine industry.

I will say to the Senator from Mississippi that the object of this bill, if I have understood it correctly, is to put a stop to an abuse which has long existed in the American market place—an abuse which has worked a very special hardship upon a great agricultural industry of the country, and in a lesser degree upon the whole community.

Mr. Money. Mr. President, will the Senator permit me?

Mr. Dolliver. Certainly.

Mr. Money. I desire to state to the Senator that I did not intend to impute any dishonesty of purpose to the members of the committee particularly, but I quoted the men who are here urging the bill and whose pockets are interested in the result, who declared before the committee and are in print to the effect that they intended to exterminate this industry, and if this bill did not do it they would come with another. That was the reason why I said it was the object of the bill to extinguish the industry.

Mr. Dolliver. I do not desire to raise any personal question with my honorable friend from Mississippi, although I could not help being somewhat impressed with the cheerful way in which he stated that this bill would receive a majority of the votes cast in the open Senate, but would be left with only a bare dozen if a secret ballot could be had.

Mr. Money. I want to say to the Senator that since I made that statement I have had assurance on the other side of the House that that is the case.

Mr. Dolliver. I do not wish to get the Senate into such a controversy as any further pursuit of that subject might involve. I desire, however, by the kindness of your attention, to discuss this question both from the standpoint of the American farm and from the point of view of everybody who takes an interest in the integrity of the market place itself.

What is oleomargarine? My friend from Mississippi gave a beautiful and classic definition of it yesterday; a definition very valuable in this discussion, when he pointed out that it is derived from a word signifying pearl, and that it means a pearl-colored oil. It was the invention of a French chemist, who, in 1869, I think, under the patronage of the Government of Napoleon III, found a way to remove the fat of beef from its cellular tissue by the action of carbonate of potash under a temperature of 115° F. and then by hydraulic pressure to separate the stearin, leaving a neutral residuum of oil.

That product he churned in milk and water, and after a careful washing it was ready for use. The process was a very simple one, and produced an article nutritious and in a degree wholesome, which could be used as a cheap substitute for butter, but did not deceive anybody on account of its similarity.

Very soon the formula fell into the hands of enterprising persons both here and in other countries, who set out to produce an article so nearly akin to butter chemically as to need only a few unscrupulous commercial arts to convert it into the most elaborate swindle that has ever been contrived against the rule of square dealing among men.

The originators of it did not at first perceive the actual possibilities of the swindle, for the industry passed through stages of development so crude, both in the materials employed and in the methods used, that for many years it needed the surveillance of the board of health rather than the attention of the legislature.

Indeed, if a man will go through the debates which accompanied the oleomargarine act of 1886 he will see at once that the chief ground of complaint against the article was based upon the natural repugnance that men everywhere feel toward articles of food suspicious in their appearance and doubtful in their origin.

The tax of 2 cents a pound would in all probability have totally wiped out the business if the managers of it, in order to save its life, had not taken two steps—one in the right direction, and the other in a direction which, whatever may be the fate of this bill, will leave it one day outcast and discredited everywhere in the United States.

They set out by the aid of science to remove from it all elements deleterious to the public health; and for the purposes of this debate, though for no other purpose, the claim need not be disputed that the oleo factory of to-day at its best is able to produce, and if the hope of unnatural profits were taken away would uniformly produce, an article of food which, whatever its merits as a substitute for butter, would at least give rise to no questions of mere sanitation and hygiene.

I do not go quite as far as my honorable friend from Wisconsin [Mr. Spooner], who intimated yesterday that in his judgment the article is unhealthy. I do not know whether it is or not, although I am convinced that if it produces any diseases at all they are likely to be chronic in their character and such as might be expected to arise from a gradual impairment of the human system. I heard a gentleman say the other day—a colleague of mine from the Fifth congressional district of Iowa, Representative Cousins—that he had examined the subject with very great care and he found only one real difference between oleomargarine and butter, and that difference a mere question of time, a question of twenty-four hours, butter having the peculiar property of melting in you in the same day.

I do not know whether that covers the whole case or not; but for the purposes of this argument, though for no other purpose, I am willing to concede that oleo in its best estate is no longer subject to the suspicion which, twenty years ago, made its most reputable headquarters mysterious with the secrets of the garbage plant and the soap factory. I make this admission freely for the purposes of this debate, reserving only the right of further inquiry under proper guidance as to where the visible supply of oleo oil, now known to pass annually through the channels of our commerce, domestic and foreign, actually comes from.

Unfortunately, even yet the manufacturers of oleomargarine seem to hesitate about taking the public into their confidence. There is a little book bearing the title of Facts about Butterine, presented with the compliments of William J. Moxley, a leading manufacturer of the goods in Chicago. Now, you would expect to find in a book like that a statement of what the article is made of.

It gives the composition of butter on the authority of those who have analyzed it, but says nothing about oleomargarine except that it contains a fraction less of acids, leaving the impression upon the mind that this shortage is intentional in order to make the goods more acceptable to the popular taste. We are not, however, without the means of finding out what the thing is made of, and we can not fail to admire the ingenuity with which the oleomargarine trade has inveigled into its defense the various industries which supply, or are said to supply, its raw materials.

Mr. John H. Garber, an expert special agent of the Twelfth Census, has just finished his bulletin upon the oleomargarine industry, and in the course of that bulletin he gives exactly the composition of the three grades of oleomargarine known to the trade. If you will let me, although I hate to do it, I will read what he says:

Formula 1.—Cheap grade.

	Pounds.
Oleo oil	495
Neutral lard	265
Cotton-seed oil	315
Milk	255
Salt	120
Color	1¼
Total	1,451¼

Formula 2.—Medium high grade.

	Pounds.
Oleo oil	315
Neutral lard	500
Cream	280
Milk	280
Salt	120
Color	1½
Total	1,496½

Formula 3.—High grade.

	Pounds.
Oleo oil	100
Neutral lard	130
Butter	95
Salt	32
Color	½
Total	357½

Mr. Money. Mr. President—

The Presiding Officer. Does the Senator from Iowa yield to the Senator from Mississippi?

Mr. Money. I do not want to interrupt the Senator—

Mr. Dolliver. I do not object to the Senator's interruption.

Mr. Money. Except that as long as he is on that line I beg to call his attention to the report made by the Commissioner of Internal Revenue to the Secretary of the Treasury, the report for 1900. He gives the table in full here of the ingredients of oleomargarine. The Senator will find it on the eighty-eighth page of Mr. Springer's argument, if he has it there.

Mr. Dolliver. I am familiar with that. I read this simply because it appears to me that the expert examination made by the Director of the Census would probably be more accurate than the analyses of specimens by people who are not familiar with the business connected with the Internal Revenue Department of the Government.

Mr. Money. The report the Senator read, if he will pardon me, was made by a special employee of the Census Bureau.

Mr. Dolliver. I so stated.

Mr. Money. The other was made by the Internal Revenue inspection department. I had supposed each one of them to be charged with the duty of finding out exactly what it was. But I do not intend to interrupt the Senator to set off one table against the other, by any means, or to make any conflict of authority on that point; I simply direct attention to the fact that there is a variation.

Mr. Dolliver. I recognize the slight variation, but I have felt more security in Mr. Garber's report, in view of his expert knowledge of the oleomargarine industry, than I would feel in an Internal Revenue report, even if the Commissioner had signed it himself.

Now, what will be the effect of this bill upon this article? It will have no effect at all unless it induces the manufacturers in preparing these goods for the market to leave out the coloring matter, and in the highest grade to leave out that admixture of butter or other ingredient which by reason of its natural shade would be likely to dominate the appearance of the finished product. It gives to these manufacturers, with the tax reduced almost to nothing, the whole field of supplying the world with a cheap substitute for butter, and takes away from them only one opportunity which they now enjoy—the opportunity of filling the channels of a long-established trade in the United States with an unlimited output of bogus merchandise.

Now, what will be the effect of this bill upon the manufacture of this product? Will it go on as at present? The framers of this bill think not, and for this reason: The addition of 8 cents a pound to the retail price of the goods brings it up so near the usual price of butter as to take away altogether the temptations of the trade to mislead its customers as to the character of the article; for after all the least tolerable feature of the oleomargarine swindle is its habitual assumption of the price of butter as well as its appearance. In fact the fraud could not exist if it did not do that.

If a householder found himself buying creamery butter, everywhere known to be worth 30 cents, for 15, he would instantly perceive that there was something the matter with the transaction, just exactly as a man would be put on his guard if he was offered a Perfecto cigar for a nickel. Therefore this assumption of price goes side by side with the oleomargarine business. The trade itself understands this perfectly, for I find here preserved in the hearings before the committee a circular letter by the Capital City Dairy Company, of Columbus, Ohio, in which they distinctly point out the importance of selling their prime butterine at 25 or 30 cents, and also suggest that they have mixed packs or country rolls always in stock.

This means that they are preparing for the market in the State of Ohio not only an imitation of the color of butter, but of the humble efforts of the country housewife to put it up in packages, noticeable on account of the limitation of her situation. They deliberately copy the infirmities and defects incident to her situation, and then send peddlers, dressed as farmers, through the streets of the cities of Ohio selling this article as genuine butter.

The other day I was in the city of Cleveland and I found there a universal turmoil going on about the discovery that everybody was eating oleomargarine. The courts were getting in action and indictments were being found, and the food commissioner of the State, in an interview printed in an evening newspaper, said "that most of the oleomargarine cases are cases of peddlers who rig themselves up as farmers" and proceed to peddle this butter through the streets of that city. I have no doubt that the same business is going on all over the United States. I know that it is going on in the city of Chicago, which is the headquarters of this swindle in the United States.

I have here [exhibiting] the sign of one of the leading oleomargarine grocery houses in the city of Chicago, which was presented in evidence before the Senate committee at the last session of Congress: "Try our best Elgin creamery butter; five pounds for a dollar." The gentleman who secured the sign asked for butter and got oleomargarine, though there was none for sale in there for less than 25 cents a pound.

The other day, in order just to satisfy myself as to whether this business was still going on, I caused to be purchased in the city of Chicago, of a very famous butter dealer there, who never had a pound of real butter in his place, a little package of butter, and I have it here unopened. [Exhibiting.] Everybody in the Senate will remember what the provisions are of the oleomargarine law of 1886 as to the marketing of this product. There is a package of the article, and I intend to exhibit to the Senate the skill with which that law is nullified.

I will unwrap that package and tell you in advance that it is marked in plain letters "Oleomargarine." I would be willing to contribute something to the happiness of any Senator in this Chamber who will within five minutes discover the mark upon that package. In order to have the business well and faithfully attended to I will ask my friend from the State of South Carolina, which has the most stringent laws on this subject of any State in the Union, to try to find the mark "Oleomargarine" which the law of 1886 requires to be written upon the covering of that package [handing package to Mr. Tillman].

Mr. Tillman. Do you mean this package?

Mr. Dolliver. Yes; the outside wrapping paper.

Mr. Tillman. This is the wrapper in which the grocer gave it to you?

Mr. Dolliver. Exactly; but the law of 1886 requires this mark to be made upon the wrapper. It will engage any man's ingenuity to discover it, although if he knows exactly how that business is practiced in the city of Chicago, and removes all the folds around the imitation butter, he might before nightfall find the word "oleomargarine" printed in dim letters on the package.

Mr. Tillman. Does the Senator leave the package on my desk because he wants me to get introduced to this article?

Mr. Dolliver. I hope to introduce the Senator to the genuine goods before I am through.

Mr. Tillman. I wish to say to the Senator that a couple of years ago I was in the town of Elgin, and they gave me oleomargarine at the hotel table. I recognized it.

Mr. Dolliver. You recognized the goods?

Mr. Tillman. That is supposed to be the leading dairy market in the West.

Mr. Dolliver. If the Senator will remember that this retail grocer, who never had a pound of butter in his great establishment, advertised in his windows "New Elgin butter."

Mr. Tillman. Why do you not try him?

Mr. Dolliver. He has been in the courts half the time in the last five years, but he never got in without finding at his side the attorneys of the oleomargarine manufacturers and their representatives ready to sign his bail bonds. I see by the Chicago newspapers of yesterday that he is in court again, along with about 15 or 20 other slippery gentlemen there.

Mr. Money. Mr. President—

The Presiding Officer. Does the Senator from Iowa yield to the Senator from Mississippi?

Mr. Dolliver. Certainly.

Mr. Money. I fear that the Senator in his good nature has been imposed upon by my interruptions.

Mr. Dolliver. Not at all.

Mr. Money. Since the Elgin creamery has been brought in, are you quite sure that the oleomargarine dealer when he advertises Elgin butter was not giving it its proper name?

Mr. Dolliver. I think not—

Mr. Money. I should just like to say, then—

Mr. Dolliver. As will be developed in the course of my remarks, I have not that supreme confidence in these manufacturers which the Senator from Mississippi manifested here on the floor yesterday.

Mr. Money. I have not a bit more confidence in them than I have in the butter men, but I desire to say that a very high and responsible gentleman, and very high in the Republican party, told me he went to market here to get pure butter, made a little scarce by this investigation. He went to the principal butter man in town and asked him, "Do you sell oleomargarine?" He said, "No; I do not; I sell butter, but I can take you to a man who sells oleomargarine." He asked him, "Where do you get your butter?" And he said, "I get it from the Elgin Creamery." The gentleman happened to be the correspondent or agent here of the Armour Company, and he told me the Elgin Creamery was the biggest customer Armour had for the butterine which the retail dealers are selling us.

Mr. Dolliver. I do not want to get into a side controversy with the Senator from Mississippi. His remarks only indicate the bewildering mystery of the business with which we are dealing. I have personally gone into at least a score of stores on a single street in the city of Chicago and stood there as an observer while the workingmen, whom my friend from Mississippi was disturbed about yesterday, were asking for butter and carrying away with them, at the price of butter, a spurious article which they did not come there to buy.

Of course it is too much to expect a dealer, whether in Washington or Chicago, when he has once embarked upon piracy like that, to reduce any of his margins as a voluntary concession to the rights of anybody else. The only way to break up a nest like that is to reduce to a minimum the profits of the rascality, and I will say to my friend from Mississippi that if the 10-cent tax proposed in this bill is not sufficient to do that he will find me ready to vote to make it high enough to accomplish that result.

What, then, does this bill leave for these manufacturers to do? It leaves them to put upon the market the article which they are making in its natural color. It leaves them still at liberty to copy the smell of butter by capturing and colonizing our microbes and permitting them to starve to death in an unfriendly environment. They may simulate the taste of butter, but this bill will require them to give to me and to you and to everybody else at least one unmistakable and authentic way to find out what kind of a lubricant we are actually spreading upon ou. bread.

Mr. Tillman. Mr. President—

The Presiding Officer. Does the Senator from Iowa yield?

Mr. Dolliver. Certainly.

Mr. Tillman. Then will the Senator be ready when he sees a white article in the market to declare that it is oleomargarine?

Mr. Dolliver. That will certainly make it easier to locate.

Mr. Tillman. Does not the Senator know that during eight months of the year you can not get yellow butter?

Mr. Dolliver. Like my friend, I ought to know something about butter. Out in our part of the country, where cows are fed on nutritious food, we manage to get up a little color all the year round.

Mr. Tillman. Very little, however, during the winter months.

Mr. Dolliver. But I do not intend to waste the time of the Senate in taking lessons to-day on the subject of what the color of butter is if I can help it.

Mr. Tillman. I do not want to intrude on the Senator unless it is agreeable to him.

Mr. Dolliver. It is perfectly agreeable.

Mr. Tillman. If white becomes the flag of oleomargarine and yellow becomes the flag of butter, I simply want to know how you are going to keep the people from being deceived by white butter?

Mr. Dolliver. It is impossible to entirely avoid that difficulty; but if any misguided man should be entrapped into buying good butter when he is looking for something in the nature of oleomargarine I think he is entitled neither to the Senator's sympathy nor to mine. [Laughter.]

Mr. Tillman. If, on the contrary, you get something that is not good butter, but is colored in imitation of good butter, as oleo is said to be artificially and fraudulently colored, thus deceiving the customer, would that have the Senator's indorsement?

Mr. Dolliver. Not at all. I agree entirely with the suggestion made here yesterday by the chairman of the committee in respect of all falsifications of butter.

Mr. Tillman. Will the Senator vote for an amendment forbidding the coloring of genuine butter—good butter?

Mr. Dolliver. I do not think I will.

Mr. Tillman. Why not?

Mr. Dolliver. There is no reason why I should do so. Cow butter has been colored from time immemorial.

Mr. Tillman. By what?

Mr. Dolliver. By everybody who has been engaged in making it. At certain seasons of the year, as my friend says, it falls off from the natural color.

Mr. Tillman. I suppose when the cow herself can not color it, it is permissible to color it?

Mr. Dolliver. That is permissible. That has been the practice for many years, and I know of nobody who has been wronged by it.

Mr. President, if the operation of this bill results as we hope it will, instead of doing the manufacturers of oleomargarine an injury, as the Senator from Mississippi seems to think, in point of fact we would be doing them more good service than all the attorneys they have ever employed and all the witnesses that have filled the courts of 32 States with the atmosphere of its disrepute; for the way in which this business is now managed, notwithstanding its investment of millions, has made it a defendant in the criminal courts of nearly every State in the Union.

As the distinguished Senator from North Dakota [Mr. Hansbrough] said a moment ago, the testimony of those who have spoken before the Senate committee in behalf of labor revealed the fact that this article has attached to itself the badge of a disgrace so complete that even among the mining villages of

Pennsylvania it is impossible for anybody to call its name in a store without running the risk of social ostracism and reproach.

Not even the modern liquor traffic at the point of its worst degradation has ever lived in such a storm of indictments and motions for a new trial. This article, so far as its manufacture and sale are concerned, has been put under the ban of the law in nearly every State in the Union; and yet the business out of its unjust profits has gone steadily forward, executing the most far-reaching conspiracy that we have ever known in the United States against the administration of justice.

The law's delays in thousands of cases pending all over the United States; organized relays of hired attorneys carrying their thumb-worn briefs from one court-house to another, leaving behind them the trail of appeal bonds and assignments of error; jury fixers in all the stages of moral decay; professional witnesses graduated in the arts of perjury—these, and such as these, are the influences with which the food commissioners of 32 States in the Union have for years been waging an almost hopeless conflict.

They have come before the committee of the Senate charged with this business, and as they have told us—faithful officers of the law, as they are—their story of this unequal warfare, I have not permitted myself to doubt that if the managers of these misguided commercial enterprises are looking for a fight to a finish with the American farm, they will be accommodated by the allied agricultural industries of the United States.

But my friend from Mississippi says, Why do you emphasize the wrong of the manufacturers when the fraud belongs altogether to the grocery trade? Why do you, on account of this unseemly carnival of petit larceny in the retail stores, want to disturb the happiness of the noble band of men who are engaged in this industry and who are turning out upon the tender mercies of a very cold world these 100,000,000 pounds of wholesome and nutritious food product?

I wish I could take the view that my friend from Mississippi takes. I wish I could acquit these manufacturers of the misdemeanors which are now being committed in their name; but the evidence in this case prevents me from doing that, because I find that these reputable gentlemen, standing a little in the background, are even now guiding the course of this traffic, are offering their counsel and their money and their help to everybody who gets into the pitfalls of the retail oleomargarine trade, and are following to-day with vigilant attention the covert and devious passage of this article throughout the whole market place.

What is the evidence of that? Fortunately the evidence is clearly upon record. If you will open the little volume containing the hearings, you will find stated in the circular of the trade itself the origin of these retail frauds. It may be said that the whole scheme of committing the color fraud has been perfected under the direct guidance and supervision of these reputable manufacturers for whom my friend was so eloquently speaking only yesterday; and in order to show that I will read this circular, dated Chicago, April 5, 1899, and signed by a leading manufacturer of these goods there.

Notice to the Trade.

"Inclosed find a color card, which is as near the color of our butterine as the printer's art can represent. Our aim in sending you this card is to aid you in selecting the proper color suitable to your trade."

Not a palatable color that would be cheerful to the eye, as my friend said, but "the proper color suitable to your trade."

"Mistakes are easily made, but hard to remedy."

There is a profound truth.

"In nearly every section of the country there is a difference in the color of butter, and even in certain seasons of the year there is a change—"

These people seem to be onto this, if the Senator from South Carolina will take note of this language—

"In certain seasons of the year there is a change, as you will have noticed. In winter butter is of a lighter color than in summer. In many sections this is the result of the difference in feed or pasture."

This man seems to be familiar with that aspect of suburban life. He continues:

"We can give you just what you want at all seasons if we know your requirements. As an example, No. 1 has no coloring matter; No. 2 has a little coloring, and so on to No. 8, which is the highest colored goods we turn out. Preserve this card, order the color you want by number, and we will send you just what you want."

It is in vain for these reputable manufacturers to cry out that they are being persecuted simply because they put upon their product a palatable and cheerful color. If that is so, what does it mean when these trade circulars go out advising and exhorting their customers to watch the changing color of butter in particular markets and at particular seasons of the year?

But my friend from Mississippi says they have the same right to color their oleomargarine that the butter manufacturer has to color butter. I deny it. They are without the legal authority to do it in 32 States of the Union, and they are without the moral right to do it anywhere in the United States. Why? Because the coloring of butter, whether the practice be good or bad, misleads nobody, wrongs nobody, injures nobody; whatever its color, it is still butter and nothing else. The maker of it in adding a harmless vegetable dye to his product at those seasons of the year when the natural color of butter differs from the bright yellow produced by green pastures, modifies, in a way of which nobody can complain, the appearance of the article, without in any way disturbing the rights of anybody else.

I hope to see the color fashion of butter so changed as to no longer require a resort to this cheap device; but if that good day should ever come the literature of the oleomargarine business contains ample evidence that its promoters, as the Senator from Mississippi candidly admitted yesterday, would follow such a change with a skill so perfect as to perpetuate the scheme which they have been working for twenty years. The thing I protest against is not the coloring of oleomargarine, but the selling of it in the market under the false pretense that it is butter, and this bill strikes the color only because it is the instrument of that crime.

I have not come here as an adviser of these 27 oleomargarine factories scattered here and there over the United States, but I will say to them—and I wish my voice could reach the ear of some worthy and honest man connected with the business, which has in it to-day an investment of more than $3,000,000—

if my voice could reach the men engaged in this business, I would say to them that I am a better friend to them than those in Congress or out who would counsel them to go on trying to perpetuate the license which they are now enjoying to prey upon the entire community.

Already the demand for oleomargarine in its natural color is seen in the markets of the United States, and it has long been seen in Denmark, in France, in Holland, and in Italy, and it needs, in my judgment, only the encouragement of a moderate integrity—only a moderate integrity—to increase to the proportions at least of a decent commerce.

There must be something fatally wrong about an investment that spends more of its time dodging police than it does in the other departments of the business, and I for one hope the time is come when we shall have in the United States a state of things such as exists in Denmark to-day. If that time should come, it would at least make this business respectable, whether it remained profitable or not.

I do not therefore agree with those who think that the enactment of this law will disturb for any length of time the manufacture of a suitable substitute for butter, made in its own likeness and presented to the public on its own merits in a legitimate way. It is on account of this belief that I have listened without alarm to the representations that have been made before the Committee on Agriculture of both Houses of Congress in behalf of great interests which are said to be threatened by this measure.

If it operated to entirely extinguish the oleomargarine business by shutting up these factories, I would not even then have very much fear on account of any damage to American agriculture; for those who have given the profoundest thought to the problems of the farm are united in the opinion that the dairy stands for more in all sections of the United States than all the interests that contribute to the oleomargarine trade added together.

In the last session of Congress the Secretary of Agriculture appeared before the Senate committee at their request. It is no disparagement of others to say that he stands to-day unapproached in his own country and unrivaled in any other country of the world as a student of the questions with which the farm has to deal. And not the least of his qualifications for the great work which he is now doing is his talent for surrounding himself with men who, like Major Alvord and his young assistant in the Dairy Division, Raymond A. Pearson, have become independent workers and constant contributors to the sum of the allied sciences to which they have devoted their lives.

No man can doubt his devotion to the interest of the American farmer, whether on the scattered quarter sections of the Mississippi Valley, or in the region where cotton was king, or on the remote frontiers where the cowboys, watching over their herds, take their first lessons in the curriculum of the strenuous life.

While Secretary Wilson was making his statement to the committee on the occasion to which I have referred, a telegram was handed to me from a dealer in my own State saying that this bill was likely to very greatly damage the value of beef cattle. I took occasion to read the telegram to the Secretary in order to get his opinion about it, and without hesitation he answered in these words:

"He does not know what he is talking about, that same cattleman."

He showed that the total amount of beef fat used in making oleomargarine is, in the nature of the case, so insignificant as to find no expression in the market price of cattle.

But under his brief statement was a suggestion still more important than that, for he pointed out that the days of the range herd are numbered, as the Senator from Mississippi himself admits, and that the very life of that business even now depends upon the individual homestead, with its bona fide settlers, and the creamery near at hand.

I can not help admiring the success of the oleomargarine industry in putting itself into partnership with the Stock Growers' Association, and I can easily understand the satisfaction with which one of its chief spokesmen, in a letter which I have had an opportunity of seeing, congratulates the contributors to the oleomargarine campaign fund that in securing the services of the attorney of the Stock Growers' Association they had acquired a standing here which an undisguised oleo barrister could never have secured.

I claim not only the right to speak, but I exercise an official duty in speaking for the live-stock industry of a State that is first in swine, first in beef cattle, and first in the production of milch cows. Our people can not be shut out of a first-class live-stock association or any other well-regulated institution. [Laughter.]

Mr. Tillman. They raise a pretty good crop of politicians out there.

Mr. Dolliver. Maybe that is so. There is a little pork fat which in the form of neutral oil is used in making oleomargarine, and nearly everybody in Iowa is raising pigs, but nobody wants to sell them for butter, so far as I have ever heard. Some fat of beef is used, and nearly everybody in Iowa is raising steers, magnificent specimens, tracing their ancestry through the herd books of the Old World, but you never meet anybody there who wants to sell them for butter.

With hogs so corpulent that we have to put casters under them to move them around the feed yard [laughter] and shorthorns that balance the weight of a ton on scales at Chicago, I have heard from only one man who appears to think that the live-stock industry has anything to gain by crippling the butter trade of the United States; for that whole community long ago learned from the counsel of James Wilson that at the threshold of all permanent agricultural prosperity stands the cow with her calf by her side.

More grotesque even is the effort of the oleomargarine partisans to enlist in their support the cotton belt of the United States on the theory that this bill, by wiping out oleomargarine, cuts off an important cotton-seed market. That is an argument put forth with only the dimmest comprehensions of the facts. Little or no cotton-seed oil is used in the manufacture of oleomargarine and none at all except in the cheapest grade. There are several reasons for this. In the first place, no possible refinement of cotton-seed oil takes away from it entirely its characteristic taste. I do not say that the taste is unpleasant or disagreeable, only that it is peculiar, and no article desiring to enjoy the undisturbed experience of butter in the market can afford to carry with it the taste of cotton-seed oil.

Besides that, cotton-seed oil resumes its liquid state within the temperature which butter is called on to endure. Therefore any considerable admixture of it softens the product, not indeed past the point of use, but past the point of keeping up the appearance of butter. For these two reasons incidentally pointed out in the Census bulletin to which I have before referred, the employment of cotton-seed oil in this product has wholly disappeared except in the cheapest grades; and the only possible way to reinstate it in the chemical formula of oleomargarine is to bring back the business to its legitimate channels, since in its masquerade as butter it is compelled, in order to keep its disguise on straight, to part company with cotton-seed oil even in its most refined forms.

But if it were true as some have claimed that the oleomargarine factories have opened a great and growing market for this product, there are two far-reaching reasons which ought to disassociate the cotton fields from this lawless invasion of the rights of the American dairyman. The cotton belt gets more money by the sale of cotton-seed meal to butter-producing States than it does from the sale of cotton-seed oil to the oleomargarine factories, many times over, so that, from the purely business point of view, it has an interest far more distinct in the prosperity of the dairy farm than in the scandalous programme of its enemies. If our friends of the South want to get the riches of cotton seed into butter why not put it in by feeding the animal, because she has within the only chemistry that can assimilate that product.

Beside that, as Secretary Wilson stated before the committee out of the abundance of his wisdom and his undoubted good will toward the South, the redemption of its worn-out fields must come from the widest variation in their tillage, combined with such specialties in production as have made the modern creamery a universal and unfailing sign of thrift and wealth.

There are almost unnumbered reasons why the State of Mississippi, for example, distinguished on this floor by the public services of my friend and colleague on the committee, should have as much interest in the dairy as the State of Vermont, in

which our honored chairman pursues the quiet tasks that belong
to country life. I venture to predict that within twenty years
the States of the Middle South will be the center of the butter-
making industry of America, and that the children of its present representatives will be laughing at the folly of their fathers,
who for the sake of selling a few gallons of cotton-seed oil are
lending the influence of their honored names to the most destructive fraud ever devised against American agriculture.

Mr. Bate. I beg to say to the Senator from Iowa that we are
moved by a principle in this matter and not that we may make
a few dollars by the sale of cotton-seed oil. I am sorry the Senator has made such a reflection. I can not believe he means it—

Mr. Dolliver. I make no reflection. On the contrary, it is
inspiring to know that the representatives of any section of the
country for the sake of principle are willing to sacrifice so much.

I have so far spoken mainly of the rights of the people at
large to be defended against the adulteration and falsification of
their food. If this is not the most important aspect of the oleomargarine question, it is at least the aspect which invites the attention of the most people, for it can not be denied that we live
in a time when greed and avarice have filled the world with a
thousand plausible inventions intended to deceive and rob the
unfortunate and the unwary.

Neither the clothing that we wear nor the food we eat has
escaped the strategy of the counterfeiter. Wherever we go and
whatever we buy, we are not for a moment free from the uneasy
feeling that we are likely to be entrapped and fleeced on every
hand. And if this measure, dealing with the most conspicuous
swindle of them all, shall operate to deliver our market place
from this notorious offense against sound morality, it will be
a notable step in fulfillment of the law of self-protection, which
in nearly every country except our own has become part of the
general code of civilized life.

Even those who like to eat oleomargarine have a right to know
what they are eating, and those who are just able to stand it
when they can not afford anything else are entitled to have it
served in such a way that both the price of it and the looks of it
will put them on their guard as to its actual character. A free
people ought not to be asked to surrender the right to know what

kind of a dose is being administered to them. The American people have done nothing to deserve such a fate.

In the course of his joint debate with Job, Zophar, the comforter, undertakes to show the state and final portion of the wicked. Curse after curse he utters as he tries to reach an adequate statement of their misfortunes. "He shall suck the poison of asps, and the vipers' tongues shall slay him." But that is not all: the climax of loss and penalty is not yet reached. It is no sudden retribution; no swift judgment from the skies. He hastens to present it to the imagination of the afflicted patriarch. "He shall not see the rivers, the floods, the brooks of honey and butter." Not even the brooks. A pictorial way, obviously, of saying that the worst thing that can happen to a man is to be sentenced to eat glucose and oleomargarine all the days of his life. [Laughter.]

Much has been said in the course of this controversy—and just now reiterated by the honorable Senator from Nevada [Mr. Stewart]—intended to disparage the butter trade by pointing out the conditions of negligence and filth which are said to surround farm life in the United States and which result in making butter an undesirable and even dangerous article of diet. I do not recognize the necessity of defending the home life of the American farm against these contemptuous comments. They have no application to the great butter-producing communities of the United States, and I do not believe that they describe conditions existing, certainly not above the line of abject poverty, even in the most remote backwood neighborhoods.

And I have not been able to listen to those sneering descriptions of dirt and destitution surrounding the old-fashioned family churn without going back in my own memory to the cellar doorway of an humble farmhouse yonder among the mountains of West Virginia, where, in the shadow of climbing roses, with a spring of living water at hand, colder than ice and clearer than crystal, I took my turn in counting the strokes which at length brought forth the yellow luxury, which waited only the sleight of patient fingers to transform it into a work of art and beauty.

"Surely the churning of milk bringeth forth butter," said the royal sage of Israel, ages ago. I do not believe that any butter brought forth by the methods mentioned in the Scriptures ever did the world any serious harm. The market has an unerring way of measuring its value by its quality and condition, so that the incentive is always present to correct its faults by care and labor. It always has been true, and is still true, that those who make bad butter eat the most of it themselves, and therefore the general market never has had and does not now have anything more than a sympathetic interest in the subject.

I am aware that in recent years means have been invented to renovate grades of homemade butter not before available. But whatever may be said against the sale of renovated butter, one thing must not be overlooked—it is butter. Surely the churning of milk has brought it forth. I do not believe that it appears in the butter market under any subterfuges of the trade. It is bought for cooking and for other immediate uses. It does not bear the price of butter of the first quality, and no merchant with a fixed place of business seeks to deceive his customers in its sale.

It reveals its character to the senses, and if its taste does not betray it the first day its smell will the next. It can not hide itself. Therefore it stands upon the counters on the butter market in its true character and at its true price. Some people like it, others tolerate it, while others reject it altogether. In some tropical markets it finds great favor, being consumed in a melted form like the goat butter of the ancients, of which Pliny says in the twenty-eighth book of his natural history, "The more rank it is in smell the more highly it is esteemed."

The mere reworking of butter to cleanse and solidify it and to give it uniformity of color and specific gravity can arouse no reasonable complaint. But if it is true, as the evidence appears to show, that in recent years the butter market has been invaded by goods heretofore unmerchantable, collected into factories and resurrected by questionable chemical processes in order to remove the evidences of decay, there can be no objection to putting such a business under the same supervision with which we propose to surround the sale of oleomargarine.

The House of Representatives, in the bill before us, made an effort in that direction. That amendment your committee struck out, not for the want of sympathy with the purpose in view, but because the House amendment contained no definition of renovated butter and provided no effective machinery for approaching the subject; and at the proper time it is the purpose of your committee to offer an amendment more completely covering that subject. I assent to this, not because I believe it involves in any appreciable degree the rights of the public, except in so far as sound commercial policy ought to encourage thrift and enterprise, leaving goods hopelessly unmarketable without profitable access to the channels of the trade.

My friend from Mississippi seemed to find it against this bill because it is intended really to help the farmer. I do not mind confessing to my honorable friend that I, for one, do not regard it as necessary to conceal the fact that the American farmer has probably more interest in the suppression of these abuses than anybody else.

A country like ours, which not only feeds itself but stands ready to answer calls for bread and meat and all other food from every part of the world, does not need to apologize for a vigilant national policy guarding the welfare of the farming population. Whatever intrudes upon the privileges of the farm, disturbing its business, limiting its opportunities, and wasting its ancient estate, is a proper subject for notice even in the Senate of the United States.

There are 30,000,000 people in this country living upon farms, actually making their homes, bringing up their families, going about their daily business in the midst of the surroundings which were described here by the Senator from Nevada as a miserable landscape of squalor and disease. They are not alone in their miseries, because they have sent out the best vigor of their blood into every center of American energy to win the prizes of the great professions, to master the problems of national life, to conquer the mysteries of the arts and sciences, and to win the laurels of all great achievements.

Not very long ago the late President of the United States crossed the State of Iowa with a distinguished party on a train which carried him into the Northwest, where he went to receive the returning volunteer regiments of the Philippine army. There were present with him in the car all the members of his Cabinet, the governors of several great States, and nearly a score of Senators and Representatives, all of them famous and honored in the public life of these times.

As they were all sitting one morning in the smoking car, just after an early breakfast, everybody noticed the President laughing benevolently to himself as he watched the antics of two boys who appeared to be warming their feet by the roadside in a place, a sort of oasis in the desert of frost, where an old cow had been lying down all night; and turning to his company, the President said, "Gentlemen, do you know that one of the most delightful recollections of my boyhood is the solid comfort of the experience that those boys are now having, warming frost-bitten feet in the place where cows had been lying down?"

Turning to his company, he said: "I wonder how many of you here have had the same experience." One after another the members of his Cabinet gave in their experience. My honored colleague, the senior Senator from Iowa, was present upon the occasion and heard every member of the Cabinet bear the same witness, beginning with John Hay, who did his foot warming partly in Ohio and partly on the prairies of Illinois, and ending with James Wilson, "Tama Jim," as we affectionately call the Secretary of Agriculture out in Iowa, who did his on the heather in Scotland. Everyone gave the same testimony, and one after another all the governors and the Senators and Representatives of great States followed, every one of them bearing the same witness, a manly testimony to the recollection of the luxuries of their own boyhood.

I heard a man say the other day that he was surprised that a few milk dealers could get the attention of the Congress of the United States, as they evidently have had it on the oleomargarine question. He seemed to think they did not amount to anything. He made one mistake in his calculations. He did not count the reserve corps, for when the old homestead calls for volunteers in its defense, millions of men and women are ready to answer the call as they go back again to the far-off happy days when, after sundown, boys and girls together, with laughter and with song, they followed the procession through the barnyard gate as the cows came home. And so gentlemen need not be surprised that an attack like this, carried on for twenty years against American agriculture, has excited a little attention even here in the Senate of the United States.

Mr. President, the American farm, whatever my friend from Nevada may say, whatever the learned Senator from Mississippi may say or think, asks no advantage over its competitors if you will give it a market place that is on the square. We have no fear of competition that is straight. We do not believe that the natural fruits of the earth's bounty are ever going to be cast away to make room for the secrets of the laboratory or the patent rights of the chemist.

We have no anxiety—none at all—for fear the simple bill of fare which Abraham and Sarah set before angels from heaven at the very dawn of history as they held a picnic together under a friendly tree will ever lose its place in the menu of civilized man. [Laughter.] We have no fear of that. But if I have interpreted the resolution of the farmers of the United States correctly, very interesting events are in progress.

The Senator from Nevada complains that they are counterfeiting one thing. Other gentlemen complain that they are counterfeiting another. I serve notice on the whole race of counterfeiters that the day of reckoning with public opinion in the United States is at hand.

It used to be thought that the cow jumped over the moon. That was not true. It used to be said that the dish had run away with the spoon. That was a harmless fiction of the nursery; but if the little dog will keep his eyes open he will see some interesting exercises yet [laughter], for if I have interpreted aright the purpose and the resolution of the American farmers, they do not intend to permanently allow a horde of sneak thieves to follow them through the streets of cities, here and abroad, forging their trade-mark, purloining their profits, and degrading their merchandise in markets where it has been respected through uncounted centuries.

The American farmer does not come here to beg anything. He makes a plea here directly to the sense of fairness and of justice, never absent from the American character. He prays for nothing. He pleads nothing. He does not ask Congress to give him anything. His appeal here is a petition of right; and representing 2,000,000 of them, now hopefully going about their spring work, sorting their seed corn between the great rivers which throw the arms of their loving kindness about the Commonwealth of Iowa, I desire to thank you for the patience and attention with which you have listened to the inadequate statement which I have made of their case in equity against the oleomargarine fraud.

JOSEPH W. BAILEY

COMPETITION

SPEECH IN THE UNITED STATES SENATE, APRIL 1 AND 2, 1902,
ON THE OLEOMARGARINE BILL

[Joseph Weldon Bailey was born in Copiah county, Mississippi, on October 6, 1863. He attended the public schools and Cumberland University, Lebanon, Tennessee, studied law, was admitted to the bar in 1883, and began practice in Hazlehurst, Mississippi. In 1885 he moved to Gainesville, Texas, and continued the practice of law. In 1884 and again in 1888 he was a presidential elector. From 1891 to 1901 he was a Democratic member of Congress, and from 1901 to January 8, 1913, when he resigned, he was a United States Senator. He practiced law in Washington, D. C., until 1921, when he moved to Dallas, Texas. He died in Sherman, Texas, on April 13, 1929, while engaged in a lawsuit in the District Court.

When he died, the newspaper accounts referred to him as "one of the last of the State's old-time silver-tongued orators and fiery political campaigners." He was a vigorous, militant speaker, of picturesque personality. His speech printed below was one of the features of the Oleomargarine debate.]

Mr. President, I have been suffering with a very troublesome irritation of my throat for several days, and I had, on that account, abandoned my intention of addressing the Senate, because I felt that it would be impossible for me to speak in the manner and at the length which I desired. But the speech of the Senator from Wisconsin [Mr. Spooner], so interesting in all of its parts, and commanding my unqualified assent on almost every legal proposition which he submitted to the Senate, differs so widely from what I understand to be the facts, both as asserted by scientific experts, and as accepted by practical men, that I have been prompted to reconsider my determination, and I shall detain the Senate for at least a brief time. If the condition of my throat renders it impossible for me to conclude this afternoon, I shall crave the indulgence of the Senate at tomorrow's session.

For the sake of clearness, as well as for the sake of brevity, I shall attempt to consider this bill first in its legal aspects, and next upon its merit, or rather upon its lack of merit as an economic measure. Of course I perfectly understand how impossible it is in a discussion of this kind to prevent these two questions from blending at certain points; but I believe it is possible, and I know it is desirable, to keep them reasonably well separated. The Senator from Wisconsin, who is not only one of the most skillful debaters, but is also one of the most accomplished lawyers in this body, has stated his propositions of law so clearly and so forcibly that I shall adopt them substantially as he laid them down. Only at one point in the course of his entire speech did I think he evaded a question of law, and that was as to the power of Congress to abdicate its control over perfectly wholesome articles of interstate and foreign commerce. It is very true, as asserted by the Senator from Wisconsin, that the Supreme Court of the United States in the Rahrer case has affirmed the power of Congress to subject interstate commerce in certain articles to the law of the several States.

But, Mr. President, that court did not say, even in the Rahrer case, and I sincerely hope it will never say in any case, that as to articles not involving the question of police power Congress can abdicate its function of regulating commerce among the several States and with foreign nations. The Senator from Wisconsin must agree with me in this opinion, because when I broadened the question so as to leave out the particular subject now under consideration and asked him if he believed that Congress could enact a general law submitting all articles of interstate and foreign commerce to the jurisdiction of the several States, he answered with a most emphatic negative. He said that no sane man—I do not repeat his exact words, but I do represent his literal meaning—would contend for such a proposition. I agree with him, and if we are both right in the opinion that Congress could not by a single enactment subject all articles of interstate and foreign commerce to the jurisdiction of the several States, then certainly it has no power to subject one article after another until it has subjected them all and completely divested itself of that very power for the exercise of which, as has so often been said, the present Government was originally established. This difference of opinion, if it really be a difference, between the Senator from Wisconsin and myself is, however, of no practical importance in this discussion, in view of other questions of law on which we are at agreement.

Purpose of the Bill.

Mr. President, let us first consider the purpose of this bill, and inquire whether Congress can find any warrant in the Constitution for serving such a purpose. I am thoroughly convinced that its sole and only purpose is to destroy the oleomargarine industry in order to relieve the butter industry of its competition; but as its advocates disclaim this purpose I shall not ask the Senate to accept my view, and I will allow those who have framed and who support the measure to state its object. The Senator from Vermont [Mr. Proctor], who is chairman of the committee which reported it to the Senate, and who opened the debate in favor of it, declares in the very first paragraph of his speech that—

"This bill proposes to put a tax of 10 cents a pound on oleomargarine when it is colored so as to make it pass for an entirely different and more valuable product, and to reduce the present tax of 2 cents per pound to one-fourth of 1 cent per pound when it is not colored so as to deceive purchaser and consumer. It also subjects it to the laws of any State into which it may come, although it may have been introduced therein in original packages. It may be claimed that this is a measure to tax a legitimate industry out of existence. We claim that it only affects the fraud; that it may and should prevent this product from masking under false colors, and that the legitimate industry will be benefited rather than injured as the present tax is reduced."

The Senator from Iowa, whose brilliant oration is easily the feature of the debate, and who is himself a member of the committee which reported the bill, as well as one of its most earnest advocates, declared:

"I will say to the Senator from Mississippi that the object of this bill, if I have understood it correctly, is to put a stop to an abuse which has long existed in the American market place—an abuse which has worked a very special hardship upon a great agricultural industry of the country, and in a lesser degree upon the whole community."

The Senator from Wisconsin [Mr. Quarles], who is also a member of the committee having charge of the bill, and therefore qualified to speak of its purpose, used these words:

"As is well known, Congress has jurisdiction to punish fraud in its public service, but has no authority within one of the sovereign States, as an original matter of jurisdiction, to entertain a complaint of that kind. But what have we done? For the purpose of throwing the influence of this great Government against fraud, we have enacted penalties for the use of our mails by fraudulent enterprises. A rigid enforcement of that enactment, which has penalties adequate to punish the fraud, has rid many a State of fraudulent nuisances that might otherwise have escaped the State jurisdiction. So that it may almost be said that this Government has been ingenious in its efforts to acquire jurisdiction to rebuke fraudulent practices."

The Senator from New Hampshire [Mr. Gallinger] said:

"As I understand the bill, it is precisely the opposite of that, its chief aim and purpose being to compel the manufacturers of and dealers in oleomargarine to be just, moral, and honest; to discontinue the perpetration of fraud, and conduct their business squarely and legitimately. That seems to be the underlying principle of the bill, and surely that is commendable."

In addition to these explicit and repeated declarations, made by these distinguished Senators in the presence of the Senate, I could produce many as strong, or even stronger, declarations to the same effect coming from gentlemen outside of Congress, who are the real originators and promoters of this legislation; but I prefer to try this phase of the question, at least, upon the statement of Senators, and I will reserve these other instances for another place. In the face of what these distinguished Senators have said when speaking to that very point, can any man entertain an honest doubt that the purpose of this bill is to suppress and punish fraudulent practices in the sale of oleomargarine? If there be any here who doubt that purpose, it can only be those of us who believe that there is a deeper and more unlawful purpose still in the minds of those who support this measure. I shall feel compelled further on in what I have to say to speak of that deeper and more unlawful purpose and to impeach the candor of the Senators, or the candor of those outsiders who are behind this legislation and who have either imposed upon the Senators or else have induced these Senators to impose upon the Senate.

But leaving all of that for its proper time in this discussion, and coming to the point which is now at issue, the question is: Has Congress any constitutional power to define and punish fraudulent practices in the sale of oleomargarine? What will the lawyers of this body say on that question? We all remember the pointed manner in which the Senator from Massachusetts denied the existence of such a power. I well recall that just after the brilliant Senator from Iowa had concluded his magnificent oration, the eloquence of which delighted us all, but the logic of which some of us could not follow, the Senator from Massachusetts arose in his place and declared that if the arguments advanced with so much eloquence by the Senator from Iowa were all that could be offered in behalf of this bill, he could not support it. The Senator from Massachusetts does not happen at this time to be in his seat, and in order to avoid all possibility of anyone supposing that I have misstated his position, I will take the liberty of reading his exact words from the Record. They were these:

"So if all the arguments which have been stated with so much eloquence and force against the abuses of the manufacture of this spurious article were all that existed I not only could not give it my support, but I should be bound to resist the measure as one carrying with it an extreme danger."

Although I deemed this of itself sufficient, I was delighted this afternoon to hear the Senator from Wisconsin [Mr. Spooner] add his authority—I will not say to the greater authority of the Senator from Massachusetts, because no authority is greater on a question of the law than that of the Senator from Wisconsin; but I will say that I was delighted to hear him add his equal authority in denying the right of the Federal Government to assume jurisdiction and control over fraudulent sales of food products in the States.

Not only did the Senator from Massachusetts explicitly declare that Congress has no such power as the advocates of this bill assert, but he declared that the assertion of such a power was fraught with the greatest possible danger. Here are his words, and I earnestly commend them to the thoughtful members of this body, and still more earnestly to thoughtful men throughout the country:

"I think one of the greatest dangers to the country now is the danger that the principle will be established that we may use the taxing power of the Government as a means either of punishing or suppressing vice and all crime or any form of wrongdoing. We have, in my judgment, no right under the Constitution to use the taxing power for that purpose. If we have, we can usurp into the hands of Congress the entire power of criminal and penal legislation in this country. We can punish polygamy or murder or burglary or any form of offense against the safety of business like stockjobbing and attempt to reach it in a way by which the measure, on the part of the State, can be defeated, and so get all the powers which belong to the States indirectly into our hands."

It seems, Mr. President, that I could rest my contention against the power of Congress to punish fraudulent sales within a State upon the practically unanimous judgment of this side of the Chamber, re-enforced by the judgment of the Senator from Wisconsin [Mr. Spooner] and the Senator from Massachusetts [Mr. Hoar], of whom I can say, without any invidious comparison, there are not two greater lawyers in this body.

But, sir, there is a stronger and a more conclusive argument than all of this to be found in the decisions of the Supreme Court of the United States. In the very first paragraph of the Rahrer case that court, speaking through Chief Justice Fuller, declares:

"The power of the State to impose restraints and burdens upon persons and property in conservation and promotion of the public health, good order, and prosperity is a power originally and always belonging to the States, not surrendered by them to the General Government nor directly restrained by the Constitution of the United States, and essentially exclusive."

Again, in the case of Plumley v. Massachusetts the court met this precise question, and laid down the following doctrine:

"If there be any subject over which it would seem the States ought to have plenary control and the power to legislate in respect to which it ought not to be supposed was intended to be surrendered to the General Government, it is the protection of the people against fraud and deception in the sale of food products. Such legislation may, indeed, indirectly or incidentally affect trade in such products transported from one State to another State. But that circumstance does not show that laws of the character alluded to are inconsistent with the power of Congress to regulate commerce among the States."

Could anything be clearer or more exactly in point? It is here expressly declared that the power to deal with the question of fraudulent sales is a power reserved to the States and not surrendered to the Federal Government, and Senators who support this bill must not only answer the argument of the Senator from Massachusetts and the Senator from Wisconsin, but they must also ignore the plain decision of the Supreme Court. It is true enough that three justices dissented in the Plumley case; but their dissenting opinion gives no comfort to the advocates of this bill, because it was based upon the explicit declaration that oleomargarine is a perfectly healthful product. The language of the court is this:

"Upon this record oleomargarine is conceded to be a wholesome, palatable, and nutritious article of food in no way deleterious to the public health or welfare. It is of the natural color of butter, and looks like butter, and is often colored, as butter is, by harmless ingredients, a deeper yellow, to render it more attractive to consumers."

I do not countenance the sale of oleomargarine for butter, and these decisions do not sanction it; but I contend, and they decide, that under our form of government such frauds must be prohibited and punished by the States, and are not within the reach of Federal jurisdiction.

The Right to Regulate Commerce.

But, while the Senator from Wisconsin and the Senator from Massachusetts join us in completely repudiating the right of Congress to deal with fraudulent sales, they both declare that Congress has the right to pass this bill upon two other grounds. The first one is that under the power to regulate commerce among the several States and with foreign nations the Federal

Government has a right to control the sale of oleomargarine as a deleterious food product. Here are the words of the Senator from Massachusetts, and I read them rather than the words of the Senator from Wisconsin simply because the speech of the Senator from Massachusetts has already been printed while the speech of the Senator from Wisconsin, having only just been delivered, is not, of course, yet before us. All of us, however, who heard both speeches know that they agree, and therefore the contention of one is substantially the contention of the other. The Senator from Massachusetts said:

"We have undoubtedly under our right to regulate interstate commerce the right to suppress commerce in deleterious articles."

I need not controvert that proposition of law, and indeed, under the recent decisions, it probably can not be successfully controverted. If the original doctrine that all articles affecting the health and morals of the people are completely within the police powers of the States still prevailed, there would be no necessity for asserting Federal power over such articles; but since the decision in what is known as the original-package case the States would in many instances be powerless to enforce their police regulations without some action on the part of Congress.

I shall not ask the Senate to hear me complain at the decision in Leisy v. Harden, but I will be permitted to say that, in common with many other lawyers, I have always felt that the dissenting opinion in that case is the sounder and better view of the law. I have always deeply regretted that the court felt compelled to overrule its former decisions, and thus produce some confusion as to the relations between the States and the Federal Government upon matters of purely police regulations. My judgment is that it would have been much better for the country, much safer for the States, and much less perplexing for Congress if the court, following the earlier cases, had held that, in all matters affecting the health, morals, and good order of the people, the police power of the States is supreme.

Accepting that decision, and considering the consequences which might grow out of it, I freely concede that if oleomargarine is a deleterious product, then Congress has the power to regulate it as an article of interstate commerce, and that if Congress fails to supplement the legislation of the States with some suitable provision, it would fail to perform a most important duty. By conceding this much I reduce the whole contention as to this point between the Senator from Massachusetts and the Senator from Wisconsin on the one hand and myself on the other hand to a mere difference of opinion upon a question of fact.

Is oleomargarine deleterious? The Senator from Massachusetts professes no knowledge upon that subject, while the Senator from Wisconsin, conscious that the overwhelming weight of testimony is against him, declares that no amount of scientific evidence can satisfy him that oleomargarine is a wholesome product, and yet, Mr. President, in almost the next sentence he quoted an eminent chemist in support of his view on another phase of the question. If we can not accept the testimony of scientific experts upon matters like this, then we might as well have lived in the Middle Ages, and Congress must legislate blindfold and in the dark. As for my part, I believe in the progress of science, as I believe in the progress of art and invention, and I readily accept the testimony of eminent and educated scientists when they all concur. If driven to choose amongst their varying and conflicting opinions I might hesitate, and, indeed, in an important matter I would hesitate, but when they all agree in expressing the same opinion it is not creditable to the intelligence of a Senator to say that he utterly rejects their evidence.

The chief proponent of this bill, the president of the American Dairymen's Association, says they do not press the question of the wholesomeness of oleomargarine because it is immaterial. His language was this:

"In pressing Congress for protection against the fraudulent sale of oleomargarine, the dairymen have refrained from discussing to any extent the wholesomeness of the article, for the simple reason that we regarded that immaterial."

I can not refrain in passing from calling attention to the fact that Governor Hoard confesses this to be a question of fraudulent sales, and considers the health of the consumers as entirely immaterial.

In the cases reported from the Supreme Court of the United States the defendant in every instance, I believe, offered to prove that oleomargarine is a wholesome and palatable food product; and in the Schollenberger case, to which the Senator from Wisconsin referred, the decision was based upon the ground that it is a merchantable and wholesome article of food. With the experts both in this and in other countries testifying to its purity, its palatability, and its healthfulness, with the courts of the country basing their decisions upon that as a truth, will Senators blindly persist in rejecting the testimony of the men who must be presumed to understand the question in order to find a justification before their conscience for a vote like this?

I believed for years that oleomargarine was unclean and unwholesome, because I accepted the statement made so recklessly and by so many people. But there can be no good excuse for any man whose duty it is to legislate with reference to this article to be ignorant about it now.

The learned professor of chemistry at Columbia College, Prof. C. F. Chandler, says:

"I have studied the question of its use as food in comparison with the ordinary butter made from cream, and have satisfied myself that it is quite as valuable as the butter from the cow. The product is palatable and wholesome, and I regard it as a most valuable article of food."

Professor Alvord, formerly of the Massachusetts College of Agriculture, says practically the same thing. Doubtless Professor Alvord would accept, without hesitation, the legal opinion of the Senator from Massachusetts, and will not the Senator from Massachusetts accept the scientific opinion of Professor Alvord? Professor Alvord says:

"The great bulk of butterine and its kindred products is as wholesome, cleaner, and in many respects better than the low grades of butter of which so much reaches the market."

Professor Schweitzer, professor of chemistry at the University of the State of Missouri, says:

"As a result of my examination, made both with the microscope and the delicate chemical tests applicable to such cases, I pronounce butterine to be wholly and unequivocally free from any deleterious or in the least objectionable substances. Carefully made physiological experiments reveal no difference whatever in the palatability and digestibility between butterine and butter."

Mr. President, I could multiply these evidences until I had exhausted my own strength and the patience of the Senate, and I could not then recite all of the testimony to the same effect. There is, however, one other expert opinion which I desire to quote at some greater length, and as I also desire to call the attention of the Senate to an extract from a decision of the Supreme Court of the United States, if it is agreeable to the Senate I would prefer to yield the floor now and resume my remarks at to-morrow's session.

I discover that my throat begins to give me a little trouble. I desire to analyze the decision in the Plumley case more closely than I will be able to do this afternoon. I hesitate, however, to ask that this matter shall go over until to-morrow for my convenience, because I said to the chairman of the Committee on Agriculture that I thought we could reach a vote this afternoon.

Mr. Proctor. I shall be very glad, Mr. President, to accommodate the Senator from Texas.

Mr. Bailey. Then I believe I will, with the permission of the Senate, resume the floor when this bill is taken up to-morrow.

[On April 2, 1902, Mr. Bailey resumed his speech.]

Mr. President, when I yielded the floor yesterday afternoon I had reached that point in the argument where, after admitting as a matter of law the contention of the Senator from Massachusetts [Mr. Hoar] that if oleomargarine is a deleterious food product, it falls within the power of Congress to control it as an article of interstate and foreign commerce, I was considering whether as a matter of fact oleomargarine is deleterious. I had read to the Senate the opinions of three distinguished scientific experts, all asserting that oleomargarine is a wholesome, a palatable, and a digestible article of food; and I now desire to supplement those statements by one somewhat more extended and, if possible, more convincing than those which I read on yesterday.

Prof. Charles Harrington, who is the assistant professor of hygiene in the medical school of Harvard University, has published an excellent work entitled "Practical Hygiene," in which he discusses this very question of oleomargarine, and as a matter of saving my voice I will ask the Secretary to read that part which I have indicated by pencil marks, beginning on page 112.

The Presiding Officer. No objection being made, the Secretary will read as requested.

The Secretary read as follows:

"Oleomargarine has been misrepresented to the public to a greater extent probably than any other article of food. From the time of its first appearance in the market as a competitor of butter, there has been a constant attempt to create and foster a prejudice against it as an unwholesome article, made from unclean refuse of various kinds, a vehicle for diseased germs, and a disseminator of tapeworms and other unwelcome parasites. It has been said to be made from soap grease, from the carcasses of animals dead of disease, from grease extracted from sewer sludge, and from a variety of other articles equally unadapted to its manufacture.

"The most absurd statement which the author has seen appeared in the annual report of the board of health of a community large enough and rich enough to be enabled to afford better service; this was that a large part of the annual output was made from the grease of dogs shot while suffering from rabies by the police in the streets of large cities.

"The publication of a great mass of untruth can not fail to have its desired effect, not solely on the minds of the ignorant, but even of some of those of over average intelligence. So it is that a prejudice was created against this valuable food product, but it is gradually becoming less and less pronounced.

"The truth concerning oleomargarine is that it is made only from the cleanest materials in the cleanest possible manner, that it is quite as wholesome as butter, and that when sold for what it is and at its proper price it brings into the dietary of those who can not afford the better grades of butter an important fat food much superior in flavor and keeping property to the cheaper grades of butter which bring a better price. Oleomargarine can not be made from rancid fat, and in its manufacture great care must be exercised to exclude any material, however slightly tainted.

"It is not and can not be made from fats having a marked or distinctive taste, and its flavor is derived wholly from the milk or genuine butter employed in its manufacture. It contains, as a rule, less water than does genuine butter, and consequently any difference in food value is in its favor. It undergoes decomposition much more slowly, and, indeed, may be kept many months without becoming rancid. Much has been said concerning its digestibility, and alarmists have gone so far as to claim that it is quite indigestible and likely to prove a prolific cause of dyspepsia, quite forgetting that the materials from which it is made have held a place in the dietaries of all civilized peoples since long before butter was promoted from its position as an ointment to that of an article of food. Many comparative studies have been made on this point, and results in general have shown that there is little if any difference. H. Lührig has proved by careful experiment that the two are to all intents and purposes exactly alike in point of digestibility."

Mr. Bailey. Now, Mr. President, I will add to these scientific opinions an extract from a case decided by the Supreme Court of the United States. Quoting from a New York case this highest judicial tribunal of the land says:

"It appears from the opinion that on the trial of that action it was proved on the part of the defendant by distinguished chemists that oleomargarine was composed of the same elements as dairy butter. That the only difference between them was that it contained a smaller proportion of fatty substance known as butterine. That this butterine exists in dairy butter only in a small proportion, from 3 to 6 per cent.

" 'That it exists in no other substance than butter made from milk, and it is introduced to oleomargarine butter by adding to oleomargarine stock some milk, cream, or butter, and churning, and when this is done it has all the elements of natural butter; but there must always be a smaller percentage of butterine in the manufactured product than in the butter made from milk. The only effect of the butterine is to give flavor to the butter, having nothing to do with its wholesomeness. That the oleaginous substances in the oleomargarine are substantially identical with those produced from milk or cream. Professor Chandler testified that the only difference between the two articles was that dairy butter had more butterine; that oleomargarine contained not over 1 per cent of that substance, while dairy butter might contain 4 or 5 per cent, and that if 4 or 5 per cent of butterine were added to the oleomargarine there would be no difference. It would be butter, irrespective of the sources; they would be the same substances."

And so, Mr. President, the almost unbroken authority of every disinterested witness who has considered the question is that oleomargarine is a wholesome, palatable, and a digestible food product, and they fully dispose of so much of the argument of both the Senator from Massachusetts and the Senator from Wisconsin as predicated the power of Congress over this article upon the theory that it is deleterious to health.

The Taxing Power.

Besides the right based upon the deleterious character of the article, the only other ground, according to both the Senator from Wisconsin and the Senator from Massachusetts, upon which this bill can be defended as a constitutional exercise of power on the part of Congress is that we have a right to tax uncolored oleomargarine for the purpose of raising revenue, and, resulting from that, we have a right to tax colored oleomargarine as a means of preventing the evasion of the tax upon the uncolored article. I prefer, however, that the Senator from Massachusetts should state his own position, and consequently I shall read his words from the printed Record. After maintaining, as I have stated above, the right of Congress over oleomargarine upon the theory that it is deleterious, he then proceeds:

"We have another right which is well settled, and that is in selecting objects upon which we shall put the tax in raising revenue. We have the right to select objects the burdening of which is not a public injury, and to omit or pass by objects which are a clear benefit, and every burden, or load, or condition placed upon which is a public disadvantage.

"We might, I suppose, for the mere purpose of raising a revenue, tax the production of wheat, or of milk, or of honest and wholesome butter as an excise, but we do not do that because we do not want to put any burden upon such products, which are absolutely and unquestionably beneficial. So we take brandy, whisky, tobacco, beer, and articles which, while they yield us a revenue, we do not mean to prohibit their sale if we could. Still nobody claims that if the sale or use of beer, or tobacco, or brandy, or whisky be burdened the public has suffered any disadvantage.

"Now, that being true, and it being a sound Constitutional principle and a sound principle in the exercise of legislative discretion, we have undertaken to tax oleomargarine under the use of our taxing power on the same principles and for a like reason, and moderately, just as we have undertaken to tax beer and whisky and brandy.

"This fraudulent and spurious butter is not only, if the gentlemen who have spoken are right, as I suppose they are, an injury to the farmers' butter, *but it is an escape by fraud or forgery from exhibiting and laying open for purposes of taxation a genuine product of oleomargarine which we have a right to tax. Just as we had the right to tax out of existence the State-bank currency because it interfered with our national currency, which we had a right to provide, to establish, and to regulate, we have a right to tax out of existence spurious oleomargarine, because it interferes with the genuine oleomargarine, which is a genuine and legitimate object of taxation."*

To all of this I readily assent as a matter of law. Nobody doubts the power of Congress to select such articles as its wisdom may dictate from which to raise the money necessary to support the Government; nor do I doubt that in the selection of the articles upon which to levy a tax Congress may be governed by considerations of expediency, and may levy the impost upon oleomargarine rather than upon butter, because it may believe that the oleomargarine manufacturers can better afford to pay it than the butter makers. I also assent to what appears to be the subordinate, but what, here, is really the principal statement, that when Congress lays a tax on a given article it has the perfect right to lay a tax upon another article for the purpose of more effectively collecting the tax first levied. In other words, and applying the rule to the case at bar, if the tax on uncolored oleomargarine is intended to raise revenue for the Government, and if the greater tax on colored oleomargarine is intended to better insure the collection of the tax on uncolored oleomargarine, then that ends the argument with me, and must end it with every sensible man.

But, Mr. President, does any Senator here believe that this bill lays a tax of one-fourth of 1 cent per pound on uncolored oleomargarine for the sake of the revenue it will bring into the Treasury? Or, if there be one so blind as to believe in that, is there one who is blinder still and believes that the tax of 10 cents per pound on colored oleomargarine is levied in order to more effectively collect the tax of one-fourth of 1 cent per pound upon the uncolored article? I will not hazard giving offense to my associates by declaring that no man can believe either statement to be true, and as two distinguished Senators have advanced these legal propositions in justification of the bill I shall assume that, as to them, at least, there must appear some facts to which they can apply their law. Granting that they must believe that the bill carries such a purpose, I desire to show them, as well as all other members of this body, that such a purpose is not even pretended by the originators and promoters of this legislation. I will go further, and from the lips of the most eminent and influential advocates of this measure, I will show that they have admitted that the taxation is a subterfuge and a false pretense.

Ex-Governor Hoard, in a hearing before a committee of the House of Representatives, declared in answer to a question:

"The Government taxed State banks out of existence. Federal legislation can proceed only along that line. We unfortunately have not a form of government in that respect like Canada. In Canada they can put a fraud or a cheat out of existence; but we have to proceed along the lines we can."

In another place, and in reply to practically the same question in a different form, ex-Governor Hoard again replied:

"I have to do business with the things I have, with the machinery I have. I can not approach it from the Federal standpoint except through taxation."

Governor Hoard was not talking about raising revenue to support the Government when he says he "can not approach it from a Federal standpoint except through taxation," but he is talking about discouraging the sale of colored oleomargarine. If anything could make his meaning plainer than his testimony before the House committee this year, it would only be necessary to refer to his testimony before the House committee in 1901, when he unequivocally and unhesitatingly stated why a tax was levied by this bill. He was not then under cross-examination; but in his direct and voluntary statement he says:

"To give added force to the first section of the bill it is also provided in the second section that a tax of 10 cents a pound shall be imposed on all oleomargarine in the color or semblance of butter. *In plain words, this is repressive taxation.*"

Mr. Hoard's friends and associates in all of this agitation have been more candid than some of the Senators in this discussion, and have not hesitated to declare that the tax was levied not for revenue, but, as they describe it, to destroy a fraud. In his testimony before a committee of the Senate at its last session, Mr. George L. Flanders, the assistant commissioner of agriculture of the State of New York, speaking of this bill, declared:

"I hope it will tax fraud out of oleomargarine. That is all I want."

Mr. Flanders made no pretense that he expected or desired the tax to raise revenue, but only that it should tax the fraud out of oleomargarine. Before the same committee and during the same year Mr. H. G. Adams, who is, I believe, the food and dairy commissioner of Wisconsin, declared:

"We are here, as Mr. Flanders said, to, if possible, legislate fraud out of oleomargarine."

Mr. Adams, with a candor which some of his Senatorial friends would do well to imitate, declares that the tax is not intended to raise revenue, but purely and only *to legislate fraud out of oleomargarine.*

We know perfectly well that though the original act of 1886 has contributed to the support of the Government, it was not intended to do so, and in that respect it has proved a great disappointment to its authors. Governor Hoard, who has been more prominent in this whole agitation than any other one man, and who is perfectly familiar with the plans of those who are urging this legislation, made this statement before a committee of the Senate:

"This law of 1886 was enacted as the only remedy the General Government could afford to check the enormous frauds being practiced in the sale of oleomargarine at that time. The tax was placed at 2 cents per pound, this being regarded as about the figure needed to raise sufficient revenue to enable the Government to enforce the other provisions of the bill."

In plain words, Governor Hoard avowed before a committee of the Senate that the original act of 1886 was intended to suppress commercial frauds, and that a tax was levied because only in that way could Federal jurisdiction be sustained, and that the rate was fixed not with a view of helping to support the Government, but merely with the view of raising money enough to execute the provisions of a law which Congress confessedly had no power to pass except upon the false pretense that it was a revenue measure. The Senator from North Dakota [Mr. McCumber] declared in his speech:

"Everyone knows that this bill is intended to tax oleomargarine out of existence, although it is under the guise of a revenue bill."

I might here again repeat those passages from the speeches of Senators which I have already quoted in discussing another branch of the question; but it will be sufficient for me to remark that in quoting those Senators to show that they, like Governor Hoard, were supporting this bill in order to correct certain trade abuses, they in effect, of course, admitted that they were not supporting it for the purpose of raising revenue. It is, however, Mr. President, a waste of time for me to pursue this line any further. It is an affront to the intelligence of the Senate for me to stand in its presence and argue that this bill is not a revenue measure. Everybody knows that it is not; and nobody supports it because it is believed to be.

Does any Senator here believe that this tax of one-fourth of 1 cent per pound on uncolored oleomargarine is levied for the sake of revenue? Does any Senator further believe that the tax of 10 cents per pound on colored oleomargarine is levied for the purpose of better insuring the collection of the tax of one-fourth of 1 cent per pound on uncolored oleomargarine?

And yet, sir, the Senator who does not believe both propositions can not conscientiously vote for this bill under the taxing clause of the Constitution. The courts will not, I grant you, declare it unconstitutional, because our theory of government wisely forbids the judiciary to examine the motives of the legislative department, and though the judge might be convinced as a man that our object was different from what the law professes, he dare not as a judge declare it so. But while the court can not look into our hearts and minds and determine the motive which controlled our votes, the rule is different with the Senator himself. He knows the motive which controls him, and he ought not to be governed by one which he dares not avow before the world. Mr. President, it is extremely disagreeable to question the candor of men, but I will venture to say that if you will put the question not in the usual form of "Shall this bill pass?" but state it, "As many Senators as believe this bill is intended to raise revenue vote 'aye,'" it would not receive a single vote in the Senate.

But, Mr. President, turning from these questions as to the power of Congress to regulate interstate commerce and to levy taxes, we find in section 3 a more palpable and, if possible, a grosser violation of the Constitution than the others to which I have already called attention. One of the few questions concerning the law or the Constitution of this country upon which men of every shade of political opinion have agreed is that the Federal Government is entirely powerless to regulate the manufacture and sale of articles within a State. Indeed, the Supreme Court in the case of The United States v. Knight has expressly decided that manufacture is not commerce, and that the Federal Government can pass no law regulating it. There was in that case one dissenting opinion, based upon reasons which it is not necessary to consider in this connection; but there has never been, either in the courts or in the Senate, any lawyer of respectable attainments who has asserted the power of Congress over the domestic commerce of any State in this Union. Keeping that universally recognized rule of law in our minds, let us examine this third section for a moment, and see how utterly indefensible it is.

The friends of this bill, of course, do not pretend that it

makes any exception in favor of an article that may be sold and consumed entirely within the State where it was manufactured. Indeed, sir, they boldly declare that it is their purpose to subject colored oleomargarine to the prohibitory laws of States which prohibit its manufacture and sale, and to burden it with onerous taxation with the intention of suppressing its manufacture where its manufacture and sale are permitted. That a law purely regulatory in its provisions would be unconstitutional and void no Senator in this body will deny; and it was because this is true that these gentlemen have summoned to their aid the subterfuge of taxation. I subscribe to the doctrine of the Senator from Massachusetts [Mr. Hoar] that when the Federal Government has a right to regulate or prohibit any given thing it may do so by means of a tax as well as by a direct and specific regulation or prohibition. But, sir, the converse of this proposition must be just as correct as the proposition itself; and I am sure that the Senator from Massachusetts will agree with me that when the Government has no right to regulate or prohibit a given thing it can not constitutionally levy a tax for the purpose of regulating or prohibiting it.

And so, Mr. President, we are again brought back to our old question of fact: Is this tax on oleomargarine laid for revenue? That it is not must be apparent to all who have heard this debate; and if any doubt remains in the mind of any Senator it must be dispelled when he recalls the statement of ex-Governor Hoard, who declared before a committee of the House of Representatives that if colored oleomargarine continues to be sold after the passage of this bill the same as now, he will "come before Congress and demand a still higher tax." Here, Mr. President, the atmosphere is somewhat clearer than it was in dealing with this question from the standpoint of interstate commerce, and a Senator who votes for this bill, knowing that its purpose is to regulate the manufacture and sale of an article wholly within a State, can not acquit himself to his conscience by allowing his mind to be confused by the somewhat contradictory decisions in respect to the regulation of interstate and foreign commerce.

Economic Fallacy of the Bill.

Mr. President, I have not by any means presented all that can be said against this bill from a constitutional point of view; and I have condensed what I have said as much as possible, because I do not desire to detain the Senate too long, and I do desire to consider the bill in another aspect. I therefore dismiss its ill-concealed and dangerous violation of sound legal principles to consider briefly the economic fallacies which it embodies; and I maintain, sir, that if the founders of this Government had been so unwise as to permit such a perversion of its powers, and even if we had a perfect and constitutional right to pass this bill, it would neither be just nor wise for us to do so. It is not necessary, in looking at this bill as a practical or economic measure, to misrepresent or to ignore its real purpose. Here Senators are not embarrassed by their oath to support the Constitution, for having laid that question aside for the time to consider this other question, or rather having conceded for the purpose of this particular branch of the argument that Congress has the power to pass such a law as this, and the only question being as to its justice and its wisdom, surely there will be no further attempt either to conceal the object or to deny the effect of this legislation.

I have stated it as my opinion that the purpose of this bill is to destroy the oleomargarine industry in order to relieve butter of its competition; and I call as my witness for this statement Mr. H. G. Adams, the food and dairy commissioner of Wisconsin. Before a committee of the House which was considering this very bill Mr. Adams declared in the usual, but rather inelegant, phrase:

"There is no use beating about the bush in this matter. We want to pass this law and drive the oleomargarine manufacturers out of the business."

It is true that this bold and candid avowal as to the real purpose of this legislation alarmed its advocates, and Mr. Adams afterwards declared that his testimony had been misunderstood; but the chairman of the House committee declares unequivocally that Mr. Adams did make the statement just as I have quoted it, and other members of the committee are equally as positive that he did. I do not desire to be understood as saying that this law will accomplish what its authors and promoters desire and expect; because my judgment is that it will not, and that it will result somewhat the same as the act of 1886. Those financially interested in this legislation have calculated that the difference in the cost of producing oleomargarine and butter is about 10 cents per pound, and they think that by taxing the substitute—I prefer to call it a substitute rather than an imitation, because it was devised originally as a substitute and not as an imitation—until they bring its price to a level with the price of the principle article, everybody will purchase butter, and oleomargarine will be driven out of the market.

Undoubtedly it is true that if by legislation you force the price of the substitute up to the price of the principal article, consumers will all take the principal article, although it may not be one whit better than the substitute. But the vice in the calculation of these gentlemen is that under this bill the price of butter will advance somewhat when relieved from the competition of oleomargarine, and as the price of butter advances oleomargarine will still be cheaper with the tax of 10 cents per pound than creamery butter. Or, if that does not happen, then, sir, the oleomargarine and butterine manufacturers by taking something from the price which they now pay for their raw material and by adding something to the price which they charge for the finished product will be able to preserve their trade. But, sir, if this bill fails to accomplish its object of suppression, we will be confronted in the next Congress by another which will not fail.

Perhaps, Mr. President, in considering the morality in this proposition, we ought to treat it as if it will accomplish the object of its promoters, and consequently we ought to deal with it upon the supposition that it will destroy every oleomargarine factory in this country. For whose benefit shall this be done? The Senator from Iowa [Mr. Dolliver] and all others who have followed him in this discussion on that side would lead us to believe that it is for the benefit of the farmer; but, sir, any man who has given the slightest attention to this subject knows that it will be the creameries, and not the farmers, of this country who will enjoy the benefit of this legislation. These gentlemen have spoken as if the farmers and the creameries are one and the same; but the proprietor of a creamery is no more a farmer because he manufactures butter out of the farmer's milk than a pork packer is a farmer because he makes pork out of a farmer's hog. He is no more a farmer than the manufacturer of cotton goods because he manufactures goods out of the farmer's cotton. Conducting a creamery is as separate and distinct from the farmer's vocation as is the manufacture of any other article out of the raw produce of the farm.

The creamery business has been one of the most profitable in the United States during the last ten years. I have here an advance bulletin from the Census Office, and it shows that in the year 1900 upon an investment of $36,000,000 the creameries and cheese factories of the United States, after paying their wages and paying for their raw material, netted a profit of over $16,000,000. And still they are not satisfied. With a profit of 40 per cent. as now operated, they are organizing a trust for more, and still not satisfied with a combination among themselves to protect each from the competition of the other they seek to destroy their oleomargarine competitors with a law of Congress.

For the benefit of the farmer? Gentlemen, you forget that the ingredients of oleomargarine and butterine come from the farm just as well as the ingredients of creamery butter. And they come from farmers who do not realize a profit of 40 per cent. on their investment. Senators appeal to the dairymen; but the dairymen will not be benefited by this law. Listen to what Consul Roosevelt says about the effect of oleomargarine factories upon dairy interest and upon cattle raising:

"Some time since France sent a delegation to Holland for the purpose of studying the methods employed there for the suppression of frauds in butter making, and also to ascertain if the manufacture of margarin has been favorable to agricultural interests. The report contains the attestation of seven mayors of communes in southern Holland, showing that since the introduction of the margarin industry in that country not only has the price of milk increased, but also the number of cattle, which plainly shows that the industry in question has become a source of profit to the farmers."

That is the disinterested report of an American consul; and it is entirely reasonable to suppose that, as the oleomargarine manufactories are purchasers of milk for the purpose of making their product, their demand will increase the price of milk. The oleomargarine manufacturers become competitors against the creameries for the dairymen's milk, and it is small wonder that this American consul should report that the establishment and extension of an enterprise which consumes milk to the extent of 25 per cent. of its entire product should enlarge the demand and therefore increase the price of milk.

If you drive the oleomargarine industry out of existence and then organize the creameries into a trust, the dairyman who sells his milk to be manufactured into butter has but one customer where otherwise he would have many.

But, Mr. President, I beg the Senate's pardon for descending in the discussion of a question like this to the mere consideration of private interests. It would signify nothing to me whether this bill was for or against the material interests of the people who have honored me with a seat in this Chamber. The question is, Is it right or wrong? If it is right it ought to pass no matter who suffers or who profits by it. If it is wrong it ought not to pass, and no appeal of a special class ought to influence the Senate in its favor. My constituents can have my seat in this body, but they can not drive me to vote for a measure as pernicious as this.

I have been somewhat amused at the helpless bewilderment of our friends on the other side. They complain that oleomargarine is sold for butter, and insist that the purchaser can not distinguish it from butter either by looking at it or by eating it. If this be true—and undoubtedly it is true, as it is also true that its effect upon the human system is precisely the same as butter—then they bring the case within that class which the law would call an innocent fraud, or a damage without an injury. I believe that every man is entitled to get exactly what he buys, and I do not believe that a trader has any right to give his customer an article different from that for which he pays, even though the different article might be equally as good as the other. But surely, Mr. President, the evil to be remedied here is not so great as to justify what even the moderate and conservative Senator from Wisconsin admits to be a kind of pious fraud upon the taxing power of Congress.

If we are to believe the advocates of this bill, they entertain no very great prejudice against oleomargarine; but they pour out the vials of their wrath upon the practice of coloring it. If uncolored oleomargarine is pure and wholesome, and the ingredients used to color it are entirely harmless, then certainly the men who color oleomargarine perpetrate no greater fraud than that committed by the butter makers when they color their product. Why is butter colored? The chairman of the Committee on Agriculture in the House of Representatives, an upright and honorable man of great ability, has a large experience in this business, and I will first let him answer that question. He says:

"I am a manufacturer of butter. I color every pound of butter because I get from 5 to 10 cents more for the butter by reason of its being colored."

Immediately following this statement by the chairman, which was made at a meeting of his committee, ex-Governor Hoard said:

"I am a manufacturer of butter myself. I do this because, as I have said, I have to do all of the things necessary to make the butter attractive to the customer, make it palatable and healthful, and sweet and wholesome—all of the things that belong to it in the technique of the business."

Thus, according to Governor Hoard, they color butter to make it attractive to the buyer, and he calls it the "technique of the business." But when the oleomargarine manufacturer colors his product with precisely the same ingredients we must understand that this is done with a fraudulent design. If it requires coloring to make creamery butter attractive to the customer, palatable and wholesome, then what violence to logic is there in concluding that the oleomargarine manufacturers color their product for the same reason? I confess, Mr. President, that I have no prejudice against making anything attractive as long as it is not made harmful. I do not believe that because our wives and daughters array themselves in the most attractive dress that they are practicing a fraud upon us, or that because they sometimes touch their cheeks with a deeper glow than nature gave that they are trying to deceive us to our harm.

Mr. President, is it not a matter of common knowledge that there is nothing upon our tables more prolific of disease than butter? It sometimes communicates tuberculosis, and it has been demonstrated by more than one experiment that it conveys typhoid fever.

Mr. Stewart. I have the report here.

Mr. Bailey. Certainly; that fact is uncontested. But while the advocates of this bill acknowledge that the least desirable quality of butter can be colored until it is attractive to the customer, still they exclaim with indignant vehemence because the cleaner and more wholesome oleomargarine is colored.

Mr. President, not only do these special advocates of the creamery greatly misrepresent the character of oleomargarine as a food product, but they also greatly misrepresent the extent to which it is sold and consumed. If we were to believe what they say, the retail butter dealers of this country are the most consummate set of rascals unhung, for we are told that almost every man who tries to purchase butter is cheated by being given oleomargarine. According to their exaggerated statements, genuine butter has practically disappeared from our market places and a spurious imitation has taken its place.

As an American citizen somewhat acquainted with the retail merchants of my country I was not prepared to believe them as a rule dishonest. I, therefore, set myself at work to ascertain as nearly as possible how extensive are the frauds of which they stand accused; and I was amazed to find that while the overzealous friends on the other side have talked as if everybody who wanted butter was deceived into taking oleomargarine, the truth is that the butter sold and consumed in the United States is more than eighteen times greater than the entire output of the oleomargarine factories; and, consequently, there can be no good foundation for this wholesale charge of fraud against the retail merchants of this land.

The present Secretary of Agriculture, who is an ardent advocate of this legislation, and whose large experience with this and kindred subjects has been so strongly vouched for by the Senator from Iowa, has testified before a committee of the Sen-

ate that the consumption of butter in the United States amounts
to 18½ pounds per capita, while only a pound per capita of
oleomargarine is consumed. This testimony will be found on
page 424 of the hearings before the committee in 1901. Testifying as to the consumption of butter, he said:

"*Secretary Wilson.* * * * My statement was 18½
pounds per capita."

That is the consumption of butter.

"*Mr. Springer.* You stated, however, that the consumption
of oleomargarine amounted to but a little over 1 pound per
capita.

"*Secretary Wilson.* A little over 1 pound per capita in the
United States; yes."

Mr. Bate. Was that before the House or the Senate committee?

Mr. Bailey. Before the Senate committee. Governor Hoard
in his testimony, when trying to minimize the importance of the
oleomargarine industry to our cattle growers and cotton-seed
producers, declared that during 1899 there were but 83,000,000
pounds of oleomargarine manufactured in the United States.
Our people then numbered 75,000,000, and if every ounce of it
was consumed here and not a pound exported, it would have
been but a fraction more than a pound per capita. But as a
matter of fact we know that for years the United States has
been largely engaged in exporting this article. Mr. Roosevelt,
the American consul to Belgium, in a special report on butter
and oleomargarine, states:

"Very little oleomargarine is manufactured in this country
(meaning Belgium). Large quantities are produced in Austria
and France, but nearly the entire continent of Europe receives
its supply from New York and Chicago. Importation is almost
exclusively via the port of Rotterdam, which received, in 1893,
72,651,800 pounds."

And as is suggested by my distinguished friend, the Senator
from Kentucky [Mr. Blackburn], Mr. Roosevelt has been our
consul there for sixteen years.

Mr. Harris. Was that oleo oil or oleomargarine?

Mr. Bailey. Oleomargarine. But I think what it means is
not that the 72,000,000 pounds came from this country alone,

but that 72,000,000 pounds were received at the port of Rotterdam from all countries.

Mr. Harris. We exported in 1900, 140,720,000 pounds of oleo oil.

Mr. Bailey. But this says:

"Very little *oleomargarine* is manufactured in this country. Large quantities are produced in Austria and France, but nearly the entire continent of Europe receives its supply from New York and Chicago."

He is not talking about oleo oil. He is talking about oleomargarine, and he adds:

"Importation is almost exclusively via the port of Rotterdam, which received"—

Not necessarily from the United States—

"in 1893, 72,651,800 pounds."

And if it is true, as Consul Roosevelt says, that New York and Chicago enjoyed a profitable export trade in oleomargarine, then we had much less than 1 pound per capita for home consumption.

Mr. Hansbrough. Mr. President—

The Presiding Officer (Mr. Quarles in the chair). Does the Senator from Texas yield to the Senator from North Dakota?

Mr. Bailey. With great pleasure.

Mr. Hansbrough. I desire to call the attention of the Senator to the fact that according to his statement the butter men and creamery men have made a tremendous profit on their business. Statistics show that the production of butter in the United States last year amounted to about fifteen hundred million pounds. The Senator states that their profits amounted to about $16,000,000. The statistics also show that the amount of oleomargarine manufactured last year was 104,000,000 pounds; that the cost of production was about 9 cents a pound and it was sold at an average price of 22 cents a pound—sold as butter. These figures would give the oleomargarine men a profit of about $13,000,000 on a total product of 104,000,000 pounds as against $16,000,000 profit for the butter men on a total product of fifteen hundred million pounds. I simply desire to call the attention of the Senator to the fact that there is a wide disparity between the two profits.

Mr. Bailey. And the purpose of this 10-cent tax per pound is to diminish the profits of the oleomargarine manufacturers?

Mr. Hansbrough. Oh, not at all.

Mr. Bailey. Governor Hoard says it is intended to take the enormous profit of the oleomargarine business and put it into the Treasury, and that is practically what the Senator from Wisconsin [Mr. Quarles] argued in his speech which I hold in my hand.

Mr. Hansbrough. The question of profits and the constitutional question which the Senator so ably discusses are two different propositions altogether.

Mr. Bailey. I had left one, and the Senator from North Dakota was not attending closely to what I was saying or else he would remember that I called attention to the enormous profit of the creameries merely to show that these were not the farmers; or at least not that ideal farmer of whom the Senator from Iowa [Mr. Dolliver] drew such an entrancing picture. Nor did I call attention to the fact that the creameries in the country are making such profits in the way of complaining about their prosperity. I rather like to see them as I like to see everybody else prosper, and I never try to lay a tax simply to subtract from anybody's proper prosperity. I think that all men and every enterprise ought to be compelled to contribute out of what they make their fair proportion toward supporting the Government, but not one penny more.

New and Dangerous Doctrine.

I can understand the Republican theory that in order to build up great and useful industries among us everybody shall be compelled by the necessities of the case to pay a little more for a particular article when they buy it, by reason of a law which keeps the foreign article out of our markets and leaving the domestic one free from outside competition allows it to command a higher price. I can understand how great and wise men have believed that to be a proper policy, but I can not understand this new departure, alike undemocratic and unrepublican, that asks us to lay a tax intended to destroy an industry that produces a clean and wholesome article of food for the toiling millions. When this bill goes upon the statute book it will invite a train of other and similar ones; and if some of us are spared, as I hope we will be, to serve as long as my distinguished friend from Nevada [Mr. Stewart] has served, we will see a hundred measures akin to this coming here for recognition and indorsement.

Oleomargarine is not the only thing that is pressing established industries by competition; others are pressing, and pressing hard, and they are entitled to their day in Congress the same as the creameries have. Now is the time to shut the door in the face of all this impudent class who in order to successfully compete with their competitors are crying out for help from Congress. Deny these people this, and there will be no more trouble; grant this, and next year, and the next, and in all the years to come, others will demand like treatment at your hands.

I have heard it proclaimed in this debate that the people of all classes demand the enactment of this bill into a law. I do not believe it; but even if it were true the bill ought not to pass. I do not mean to say that a Senator ought to ignore the public sentiment of his State; far from it. Indeed, I am one of those old-fashioned Democrats who believe in the doctrine of obedience or resignation. But all the people of my State could not instruct me to vote for a bill that I believed against the Constitution of my country. All the people of every State have no right to make such a demand upon a single Senator in this body. Even if this demand came from an enlightened public opinion, you have no right to heed it; because, when you pass this bill upon the theory that you intend it to raise revenue, you incorporate a falsehood in the records of this Congress.

Farmers Ask No Special Favors.

Those of us who can not support this bill have been assailed with the reproach that we are unfriendly to the American farm, and the Senator from Iowa portrayed, with exquisite pathos, the early scenes of rural life; but, sir, he profanes the memories of those earlier and better days when he invokes them in a cause like this. I know the farmers of this country, and in my association with them I have found them our equal in everything except, perhaps, in opportunity. They love their country, they cherish its institutions, they pay its taxes in times of peace, and fight its battles in times of war. But they ask for no laws except just, equal ones, and they will resent the demand made in their name for unjust and repressive legislation.

I am myself as enthusiastic in my love of agricultural pursuits as the Senator from Iowa can possibly be. I spend all of my spare time and money in raising horses and cattle, and it is one of my peculiar ideas that every American citizen with money enough to buy it ought to own a farm and ought to live on it a part of every year. A contact with the soil renews our strength, confirms our purposes if they be high, and elevates them if they be low. Among its fields and meadows lofty ideals and noble thoughts find entertainment, and the virtues which make statesmen as well as heroes are developed and cultivated.

From the strife and the tumult of our great cities, where the violence of anarchy and the avarice of corporate power are holding high carnival, we must turn to the rural homesteads of this land for the simple faith and habits that shall yet enable this Republic to fulfill the high and sacred mission to which our fathers dedicated it; and, sir, I repel the suggestion that these sturdy and unselfish patriots are clamoring for a law that shall destroy an industry which consumes the products of their farms in providing a cheap and wholesome article of food for the millions who earn subsistence in workshops and in factories.

Will Senators follow the logic of this legislation? If in the providence of God the drought should come, and with failing crops in this country, there should still be abundant crops in other lands to depress the price of agricultural products again below the cost of production, will you tell the farmers that, as Congress has already made the precedent, they should come here and clamor at our doors until we pass a law to abolish these electrical vehicles that have so greatly curtailed the demand for horses. To abolish the use of electricity in operating the street-car systems of our great cities and return again to the horse, would almost double the demand for as well as the price of horses; and in this way you can not only increase the demand for horses, but you will vastly increase the demand for the farmers' hay and grain to feed them. When that proposition comes before us, as come it may if this character of legislation is to be encouraged, will the Senator from Iowa draw glowing pic-

tures of the horse and plead for him against the use of electricity? It will be so easy to describe these new motor carriages as
fit only for millionaires and dudes to ride in.

The farmers and their friends would have a stronger argument considered only with reference to its selfishness in that
case than they have in this, because electrical appliances not only
first destroy the demand for the horses the farmers raise, but
subsequently destroy the demand for the grain and hay to feed
those horses. Tell him it is wrong, he will point you to the law
of Congress. Tell him two wrongs never made one right, he
will tell you that it is not a question of right or wrong that controls you, but a question of votes and influence.

If this kind of legislation is safe, prudent, and wise, then no
man in this country will dare to invest his capital in a new enterprise, because in doing so he takes the chance that an old and
established one will come to Congress for a law taxing his
new enterprise to death.

Progress v. Repression.

Mr. President, I believe that the material progress of the
world finds its highest and most beneficent achievement in bringing to the toiling millions, whose hard lot is work and want,
better food and better raiment; but if we are to accept the new
philosophy, which finds expression in this bill, then it is a crime,
to be punished by imprisonment, for any man to devise a cheaper but healthful substitute for an article now in use. If men
shall not have oleomargarine because it looks like butter, then
we may extend the principle, and next week declare they shall
not wear cloth that looks like wool, and that every manufacturer
in this country who strives by improved processes to make
better cloth from cotton until it is almost as good as wool, shall
be a criminal; and then follow that with another statute, every
man who makes from the farmer's fleece a higher quality of
woolen goods until it almost resembles silk, shall likewise be
sent to jail to keep company with the man who is said to have
counterfeited the product of his woolen mill.

Once enter upon this kind of legislation and where will it
end? It will end only after the Congress of the United States
has become a kind of board to settle the rivalries between com-

peting manufacturers, and it will settle them, not according to their justice, but according to the power and influence of the rivals. The weak, though they have the better product, must fall, and the strong, though their product be higher in its price and lower in its quality, will survive.

I believe in the philosophy of my childhood, when I was taught that competition is the life of trade. I believe in leaving every man—merchant, manufacturer, or trader—out in the open market with his wares, and if he have more sagacity or better merchandise than his competitor, let him prosper and with his profits he will establish new industries to employ more men and bring new blessings to mankind. Let us not drive him from his pursuits with penal statutes; let us not stifle genius and deny enterprise its just reward; but rather let us offer premiums for it, until every heart and brain in all the land shall be quickened with an impulse to do something for his kind and country.

But, Mr. President, I waste my time and I waste the time of the Senate in prolonging this discussion. I did not hope in the beginning that anything I could say would change a single vote, for I fear very much that we have reached that lamentable condition which was described by a Scotch member of the British Parliament, who declared that he had heard many speeches that had changed his mind, but never a single speech that had changed his vote. [Laughter.] The vote, when it shall be taken to-morrow, will probably be the same as it would have been if it had been taken the day the bill was first reported. Nor have I detained the Senate in any hope that I could contribute anything to its knowledge on this subject any more than I have detained it in the hope that I could change its vote. I simply desired to record my protest against a species of legislation that is without warrant in the Constitution and without justification in the natural laws of trade.

CHAUNCEY M. DEPEW

THE COW AND HONEST COMPETITION

SPEECH IN THE UNITED STATES SENATE, APRIL 2, 1902, ON
THE OLEOMARGARINE BILL

[Chauncey Mitchell Depew was born in Peekskill, New York, on
April 23, 1834. He was graduated from the Peekskill Military Academy in 1852, and from Yale College in 1856. He was admitted to the
bar in 1858 and began the practice of law in Peekskill. From 1861 to
1862 he was a member of the state Assembly; in 1863 he was Secretary of State; and in 1865 he declined an appointment as United
States Minister to Japan. He was Colonel and Judge Advocate of
the Fifth Division, New York National Guard, 1873 to 1881, and
regent of the University of the State of New York, 1877 to 1904. He
was a Republican member of the United States Senate from 1899 to
1911. For sixty years he was associated with the New York Central
& Hudson River Railroad, first as director and attorney, then as
President from 1885 to 1898, and finally as Chairman of the Board
of Directors. He died on April 5, 1928, in New York City.

Mr. Depew was widely known as an orator, after-dinner speaker,
and lecturer. His published addresses fill many volumes. The speech
printed below, delivered immediately after the previous speaker, Senator Bailey, took his seat, is a good example of his speeches in lighter
vein, suggestive of an after-dinner speech, but answering a serious
argument in an effective way.]

Mr. President, I desire to say that I shall be compelled to be
absent to-morrow, and therefore shall not have an opportunity
to record my vote on this measure. If here, however, I should
vote for the bill of the committee with the amendments which
they have proposed.

I say this notwithstanding the very eloquent and entrancing
speech which has just been made by the Senator from Texas
[Mr. Bailey]. In my brief experience as a Senator I certainly
never have heard any effort in this Chamber which has so affected my imagination, has so fired my fancy, and has had so little
influence upon my judgment. [Laughter.] Unlike the Scotch
member of Parliament, whom the Senator mentioned, in stating
how I should vote if present here to-morrow, I am stating both

how I would talk, think, and act if called upon to answer the roll call.

I have been a student and somewhat of a practitioner all my life of that kind of oratory, which appeals to my imagination as much as it does to anyone, of the progress of our country and the opportunities of its citizens; but the speech of the Senator from Texas was the finest tribute to which I have listened in many a day to the opportunities which will exist if this bill does not pass, but which will be forever destroyed if it becomes a law. If I understand aright the Senator from Texas, this bill will defeat the opportunities for progress of the young man of the future, because the growth of our country is built upon oleomargarine [laughter] ; the growth of our country is built upon some kind of a misrepresentation, and all success is due to fraud.

I am a thorough believer in the doctrine, which the Senator advanced, that competition is the life of trade and that the growth of business, the perfection of our machinery, and the creation of communities which have become the happy homes of artisans and the places where prosperity dwells, have been due to that principle that competition is the life of trade, but I have been taught, also, that competition must be honest. Where an honest merchant is selling honest flour and the man on the next block is saying that his flour is just as good when it is half plaster of Paris, that is not honest competition; and if the man who sells flour which is half plaster of Paris or ground earth, or what not, is to be commended because he drives the honest merchant out of business, then I say that the honest merchant should be protected by law and that the dishonest merchant should be punished for fraud.

A friend of mine, who knows the secret test by which oleomargarine can be detected, was in a fashionable restaurant recently, and when a beautiful pat of butter was placed before him, he subjected it to his test, and then he said to the waiter, "How do you pronounce, sir, o-l-e-o-m-a-r-g-a-r-i-n-e?" And that intelligent servitor of that magnificent place of pleasure responded, "I pronounce it, sir, butter; else I lose my job." [Laughter.] This legislation is to protect the conscience of that waiter; **it** is to prevent his being driven out of employment, reduced to poverty, and his family reduced to great distress unless he lies.

This waiter probably came to us from a foreign land. He probably never learned our language until he arrived upon our shores, and then, in order to earn an honest living, he applied himself diligently, as all our adopted citizens do, to learn the only language in the world in which God's truth can be clearly and perfectly expressed, and then he discovers that in this great and glorious country, where he has come for the enjoyment of every privilege and every liberty, upon the principle which my eloquent friend from Texas advocates, he has got to pronounce a word in the English language entirely different from anything that he has been taught in the books or learned in his family, or what it means, in order to retain a position where he is earning an honest living.

My friend from Texas says that he has talked with the farmer, and that the farmer never has expressed a desire for this measure. The farmer says, "Let me alone; I want to let everybody else alone." My impression is that my eloquent friend has been talking with the agriculturist, and not with the farmer. The agriculturist does not raise butter, unless it be the bull butter which my friend is so anxious to have presented to the public. I have received thousands of appeals for this measure from the farmers of New York.

We have no objection to oleomargarine sold as such; we have no objection to filled cheese sold as such; we have no objection to flour which has in it a substance that will never digest, if people want to put in their stomachs things which will constitute monuments over their graves after they are dead. But what we do object to is that the citizen who pays a dollar for a good article, an honest and reputable article, to take home to his wife and children, should be deluded by getting something else.

The cow does not complain of oleomargarine. The cow complains that oleomargarine, which she does not produce and can not produce unless she is killed and carved and then put into a pot and boiled, should be called that delightful substance which comes out of the wonderful chemistry which God has given the cow for the delight of the world and for the sustenance of children.

Mr. President, it seems to me that the line comes very clear on this class of legislation, not only on this article, but on all others. There is no legislature in the United States which has not had before it at one time or another, and which has not passed at one time or another, bills which have been enacted into law for the purpose of protecting the public against these chemical horrors which the ordinary household has not the means of detecting.

Nobody objects to competition when it is free from fraud. Nobody objects to competition when it is free from deceit. On the contrary, under such circumstances and conditions, let the best brain, the best energy, the best industry, the best grasp of the situation win. But there is no ability, no capacity for business, no energy, and no industry which can successfully compete with a good article against a fraudulent article where the public and the customers are deceived and where they can not detect the fraud.

I believe that if this legislation becomes a law there will be no diminution in the sales of oleomargarine or in the profits of its manufacture. I believe that it has been so long before the public that it can be sold upon its merits and that there will be a growing constituency who would prefer it to a poor article of butter, if their circumstances are such that they can buy nothing but a poor article of butter.

It is a strong point which my eloquent friend made that butter is colored, and therefore why not color oleomargarine? But colored butter is still butter, and colored oleomargarine is not still oleomargarine, according to what its seller says. To color butter does not destroy its taste, does not destroy its chemical properties, does not destroy its wholesomeness. It is still butter, with that particular color given to it which the customer wants in his butter. But when the oleomargarine is colored, it is colored not to sell it as oleomargarine, but in order to follow butter as butter through all the grades of the article.

There was one part of my eloquent friend's speech which shocked me—absolutely shocked me. It would not seem possible that a gentleman who has such a command of the English language, who is so chivalrous, who talks and thinks and acts upon such a high plane as does my eloquent friend, the Senator from Texas, could shock me. But he did. When he compared the color of oleomargarine to the art by which a young lady wins the heart of her lover, I felt that the American girl had been put in a wrong position before the American people. [Laughter.]

Mr. Bailey. I forgot for the moment a recent occurrence in the life of the Senator from New York or I should not have said it. [Laughter and applause.]

Mr. Depew. And but for that occurrence I should have left it for a younger man to come to the defense of the American girl. It was the Senator's youth and beauty which astonished me when he made that remark. [Laughter.] If he had been sour and acrid, if he had been disappointed in love, if the sex had treated him in any way which would lead him to speak of them in that way, then I could understand it. But no one can meet the Senator, no one can meet him socially or in his grave and dignified position as a Senator in this Chamber, no one can see his photograph on Pennsylvania avenue, no one can come in that contact with him which is always a pleasure without knowing that his geniality, his happiness, his eloquence have come because the American girl has loved and has admired him. [Laughter.] And he never ought, so soon after she appeared so entrancing in her Easter hat and gown in the churches and on the avenues of Washington, to have gone back on her to-day by saying that she is a fraudulent specimen of living oleomargarine. [Laughter.] With all her finery, flowers, and ribbons and colors, she was still the incomparable American girl.

Mr. President, I did not rise to make a speech, but I have been betrayed into it because of the peculiar, as well as eloquent way in which my distinguished friend, the Senator from Texas, presented in most attractive form the proposition that fraud and misrepresentation stand on the same plane with truth, and honesty, and open-mindedness; that fraud and misrepresentation are the honest competitors of truth and virtue. Up in Peekskill, where I was born, that was not taught in the old-school Presbyterian Church in which I was reared. It may be that in the wilds of Texas that is the way the people think, but along

HICKS' SP.A.S.—19

the Hudson River we people of Dutch ancestry learned to call a spade a spade.

We learned to call butter butter and milk milk, and we do not learn to call anything else, made in some other way, by the wonders of chemistry, whether it is better or worse, by an honest name; but we learned to call an article just what it is, and then we take it or reject it upon a full understanding. of what we are buying. We are not brought up in the belief that one of the enterprising citizens of the metropolis who discovers. an honest yeoman from Texas—not an agriculturist, but a farmer —in New York, and then, appealing to his cupidity, sells him a gold brick, is an honest competitor with the jeweler across the way. On the contrary, in the State of New York we have laws by which this active, energetic, and enterprising business man of our State, who, accepting the Senator's views of competition, captures this innocent agriculturist from Texas and sells him a gold brick, is seized and punished, not for selling the gold brick, but because he sold it as gold. If he had sold it as a gold brick, as amounting to nothing but brass outside and sand in, and got a gold price for it from a farmer from Texas, then the laws of New York say that that is honest competition. It is the deceit which we punish; not the art.

Mr. President, this debate has gone into many fields, and especially this evening. It is fortunate for modern eloquence that it has led on the one side and the other to two of the most attractive speeches I have ever heard in a legislative body—the Senator from Iowa [Mr. Dolliver] on the cow, and the Senator from Texas [Mr. Bailey] on competition. The cow and competition will live in the annals of American oratory as presented under the forms of rhetoric, of eloquence, of fancy, and of flights of imagination which place these two Senators along with the Miltons and the Byrons of the English language.

GEORGE F. HOAR

THE FILIPINO WAR

SPEECH IN THE UNITED STATES SENATE, MAY 22, 1902, ON
A BILL TO PROVIDE FOR CIVIL GOVERNMENT
IN THE PHILIPPINE ISLANDS

[George Frisbie Hoar was born in Concord, Massachusetts, on August 29, 1826. He was graduated from Harvard College in 1846, and from the Dane Law School in 1849, was admitted to the bar in the same year, and began practice in Worcester, Massachusetts. He was successively member of the Massachusetts House of Representatives, 1852, State Senator, 1857, Republican member of Congress, 1869 to 1877, and United States Senator, 1877 to 1904. In 1876 he was a manager for the House of Representatives to conduct the impeachment proceedings against Secretary of War Belknap, and he was a member of the Presidential Election Commission of 1877. He died on September 30, 1904, in Worcester, Massachusetts.

Senator Hoar was a Republican of the old school, who led the fight against the annexation of the Philippines, and never became reconciled to the action that was taken. The "Filipino war," the capture of Aguinaldo, and "atrocities" practiced by both sides in the contest, all served to confirm his opinion. The speech printed below is an example of his courageous, outspoken style of oratory.]

Mr. President: I have something to say upon the pending bill. I will say it as briefly and as compactly as I may. We have to deal with a territory 10,000 miles away, 1,200 miles in extent, containing 10,000,000 people. A majority of the Senate think that people are under the American flag and lawfully subject to our authority. We are not at war with them or with anybody. The country is in a condition of profound peace as well as of unexampled prosperity. The world is in profound peace, except in one quarter, in South Africa, where a handful of republicans are fighting for their independence, and have been doing better fighting than has been done on the face of the earth since Thermopylæ, or certainly since Bannockburn.

Yet the Filipinos have a right to call it war. They claim to be a people and to be fighting for their rights as a people. The Senator from Ohio [Mr. Foraker] admits that there is a people there, although he says they are not one people, but there are several. But we can not be at war under the Constitution without an act of Congress.

We are not at war. We made peace with Spain on the 14th day of February, 1899. Congress has never declared war with the people of the Philippine Islands. The President has never asserted nor usurped the power to do it. We are only doing on a large scale exactly what we have done at home within a few years past, where the military forces of the United States have been called out to suppress a riot or a tumult or a lawless assembly, too strong for the local authorities. You have the same right to administer the water torture, or to hang men by the thumbs, to extort confession, in one case as in the other. You have the same right to do it in Cleveland or Pittsburg or at Colorado Springs as you have to do it within the Philippine Islands. I have the same right as an American citizen or an American Senator to discuss the conduct of any military officer in the Philippine Islands that I have to discuss the conduct of a marshal or a constable or a captain in Pittsburg or in Cleveland if there were a labor riot there.

That duty I mean to perform to the best of my ability, fearlessly as becomes an American citizen, and honestly as becomes an American Senator.

But I have an anterior duty and an anterior right to talk about the action of the American Senate, both in the past and in the present, for which, as no man will deny, I have my full share of personal responsibility.

The Senator from Ohio, in his very brilliant and forcible speech, which I heard with delight and instruction, said that we were bound to restore order in the Philippine Islands, and we can not leave them till that should be done. He said we were bound to keep the faith we pledged to Spain in the treaty, and that we were bound, before we left, to see that secured. He said we were bound, especially, to look out for the safety of the Filipinos who had been our friends, and that we could not, in honor, depart until that should be made secure.

All that, Mr. President, is true. So far as I know, no man has doubted it. But these things are not what we are fighting for; not one of them. There never was a time when, if we had

declared that we only were there to keep faith with Spain, and
that we only were there to restore order, that we were only there
to see that no friend of ours should suffer at the hands of any
enemy of ours, that the war would not have ended in that
moment.

You are fighting for sovereignty. You are fighting for the
principle of eternal dominion over that people, and that is the
only question in issue in the conflict. We said in the case of
Cuba that she had a right to be free and independent. We affirmed in the Teller resolution, I think without a negative voice,
that we would not invade that right and would not meddle with
her territory or anything that belonged to her. That declaration
was a declaration of peace as well as of righteousness; and we
made the treaty, so far as concerned Cuba, and conducted the
war and have conducted ourselves ever since on that theory—
that we had no right to interfere with her independence; that
we had no right to her territory or to anything that was Cuba's.
So we only demanded in the treaty that Spain should hereafter
let her alone. If you had done to Cuba as you have done to the
Philippine Islands, who had exactly the same right, you would
be at this moment, in Cuba, just where Spain was when she
excited the indignation of the civilized world and we compelled
her to let go. And if you had done in the Philippines as you did
in Cuba, you would be to-day or would soon be in those islands
as you are in Cuba.

But you made a totally different declaration about the Philippine Islands. You undertook in the treaty to acquire sovereignty over her for yourself, which that people denied. You declared not only in the treaty, but in many public utterances in
this Chamber and elsewhere, that you had a right to buy sovereignty with money, or to treat it as the spoils of war or the
booty of battle. The moment you made that declaration the
Filipino people gave you notice that they treated it as a declaration of war. So your generals reported, and so Aguinaldo expressly declared. The President sent out an order to take forcible possession, by military power, of those islands. General
Otis tried to suppress it, but it leaked out at Iloilo through General Miller. General Otis tried to suppress it and substitute
that they should have all the rights of the most favored provinc-

es. He stated that he did that because he knew the proclamation would bring on war. And the next day Aguinaldo covered the walls of Manila with a proclamation stating what President McKinley had done, and saying that if that were persisted in he and his people would fight, and General MacArthur testified that Aguinaldo represented the entire people. So you deliberately made up the issue for a fight for dominion on one side and a fight for liberty on the other.

Then when you had ratified the treaty you voted down the resolution in the Senate, known as the Bacon resolution, declaring the right of that people to independence, and you passed the McEnery resolution, which declared that you meant to dispose of those islands as should be for the interest of the United States. That was the origin of the war, if it be war. That is what the war is all about, if it be war; and it is idle for my brilliant and ingenious friend from Ohio to undertake to divert this issue to a contest on our part to enable us to keep faith with our friends among the Filipinos, or to restore order there, or to carry out the provisions of the treaty with Spain.

Now, Mr. President, when you determined to resort to force for that purpose, you took upon yourself every natural consequence of that condition. The natural result of a conflict of arms between a people coming out of subjection and a highly civilized people—one weak and the other strong, with all the powers and resources of civilization—is inevitably, as everybody knows, that there will be cruelty on one side and retaliation by cruelty on the other. You knew it even before it happened, as well as you know it now that it has happened; and the responsibility is yours.

If, in a conflict between a people fighting for independence and liberty, being a weak people, and a people striving to deprive them of their independence and liberty, being a strong people, always, if the nature of man remains unchanged, the war is converted in the end into a conflict in which bushwhacking, treachery, and cruelty have to be encountered, the responsibility is with the men who made the war. Conflicts between white races and brown races or red races or black races, between superior races and inferior races, are always cruel on both sides, and the men who decree with full notice that such

conflict shall take place are the men on whom the responsibility
rests. When Aguinaldo said he did not desire the conflict to go
on, and that it went on against his wish, he was told by our general that he would not parley with him without total submission.
My friend from Wisconsin declared in the Senate that we would
have no talk with men with arms in their hands, whether we
were right or wrong. The responsibility of everything that has
happened since, which he must have foreseen if he knew anything of history and human nature, rests upon him and the men
who acted with him.

We can not get rid of this one fact, we can not escape it, and
we can not flinch from it. You chose war instead of peace. You
chose force instead of conciliation, with full notice that everything that has happened since would happen as a consequence
of your decision. Had you made a declaration to Aguinaldo
that you would respect their title to independence, and that all
you desired was order and to fulfill the treaty and to protect
your friends, you would have disarmed that people in a moment. I believe there never has been a time since when a like
declaration made by this Chamber alone, but certainly made by
this Chamber and the other House, with the approval of the
President, would not have ended this conflict and prevented
all these horrors.

Instead of that gentlemen talked of the wealth of the Philippine Islands, and about the advantage to our trade. They sought
to dazzle our eyes with nuggets of other men's gold. Senators
declared in the Senate Chamber and on the hustings that the flag
never shall be hauled down in the Philippine Islands, and those
of you who think otherwise keep silent and enter no disclaimer.
The Senator from Ohio says our policy has not been in the dark,
but it has been a policy published to the world. Has it? Has
it? I want to ask: What was it which created the war, which
keeps it up, and which created and keeps up the hatred, and
will make war break out again and again for centuries to come,
unless human nature be changed or be different in their bosoms
from what it is in ours? It is because our policy has not been
published to the world. It is because you keep a padlock on
your lips.

This debate for the last three years has contained many audacities. One thing, however, no Senator has been audacious enough to affirm, and that is that if he were a Filipino, as he is an American, he would not do exactly, saving only acts of cruelty, as the Filipino has done.

I find myself beset with one difficulty whenever I undertake to debate this question. I am to discuss and denounce what seems to me one of the most foolish and wicked chapters in history. Yet I am compelled to admit that the men who are responsible for it are neither foolish nor wicked. On the contrary, there are no men on the face of the earth with whom on nearly all other subjects I am in general more in accord, to whose sound judgment or practical sagacity I am more willing to defer, or to whose patriotism or humanity I am more willing to commit the honor or the fate of the Republic.

It may be that it is presumption to act on my own judgment against that of my valued and beloved political friends. But we do not settle questions of righteousness or justice on any man's authority. Still less do we settle them by a show of hands. Each man is responsible only to his own conscience, which is the only authority he must obey. Besides, Mr. President, I have on my side in this great debate the fathers of the Republic, the statesmen who adorned its first century, the founders of the Republican party, every one of whom declared and lived by and died by the doctrine you are now repudiating. I have also your own authority, your own declaration, made only three years ago, at the beginning of the Spanish war. When you declared that Cuba of right—of right—ought to be a free and independent State, and that the United States would not acquire her territory as the result of the war with Spain, you settled as a matter of duty and of justice this whole Philippine question.

I have, however, at least, to congratulate my friends who differ from me on an increased sobriety in dealing with this matter.

We are not flourishing nuggets of gold in the Senate just now. The devil imperialism is not promising us all the kingdoms of this world and the glory thereof, if we will fall down and worship him. You have just hauled down the American flag in China where it once floated, and you have just hauled it down day before yesterday in Cuba where it has floated for three years.

For the words, "interests of the United States," which the McEnery resolution declared were to determine our actions in governing these islands, you substitute in this bill the declaration that "the rights acquired in the Philippine Islands under the treaty with Spain are to be administered for the benefit of the inhabitants of those islands."

"Sec. 10. That all the property and rights which may have been acquired in the Philippine Islands by the United States under the treaty of peace with Spain, 1898, are hereby placed under the control of the government of the Philippine Islands, to be administered for the benefit of inhabitants of the islands."

"Sec. 7. There are to be municipal and provincial governments as far and as fast as the governments are capable, fit, and ready for the same, with popular representative government."

The share to which you propose to admit these people in your scheme of government, is an admission that a large number of them are fit for self-government. You propose for them—to take effect in the near future—a constitution, not very different from that of Canada, where the Crown of England appoints the Governor-General, and the Governor-General appoints the senate, and there is a veto on every provincial law by the Governor-General, and a veto on every law of the Canadian congress, not only by the Governor-General, but by the Government at home.

The Senator from New Hampshire called a witness the other day to the effect that every Filipino would take a bribe. Sir Robert Walpole said that of England. I acquit the majority of the Senate and the committee who report this bill from believing the charge made by my honorable friend from New Hampshire. They affirm that there are many Filipinos who are sincerely our friends. They admit, if I understand them, that there are in those islands many citizens accomplished and well educated, lawyers and merchants, conducting large affairs in trade, and they themselves propose to commit to these people at once, as soon as may be, large powers of government, retaining for us little more than the power of a veto.

What you have been fighting for all this time as your right, if

you expect to enact this bill into law and to carry it out in practice, is to substitute a constitution of your making for one of
their making; to have a dependency, which is what you want,
instead of a republic, which is what they want; to have fitness
for the elective franchise determined by an authority which has
its source 10,000 miles away, instead of with the people at home;
and to deny them independence, even if they are fit for it, so
long as you please, without any regard to their desire.

This investigation, I suppose, is yet upon the threshold. Your
chief witnesses, so far, have been soldiers and governors who are
committed to policies of subjugation. The investigation has
been conducted by a committee of that way of thinking.

Yet we have got already some pregnant admissions, and some
remarkable facts have already come to light. Governor Taft,
if I understood him, concedes that nothing so far indicates that
the existing policy has been good for the United States. It is
only the benefit of the people of the Philippine Islands, in saving them from anarchy, or from foreign nations, in establishing
schools for them, that vindicates what you have done so far.
What you have done so far has been to get some few thousand
children actually at school in the whole Philippine dominion.
To get this result, you have certainly slain many times that
number of parents.

It would be without avail to repeat in the Senate to-day what
was said at the time of the Spanish treaty, and afterwards when
you determined to reduce the Philippine people by force to submission. .

What your fathers said when they founded the Republic; the
declarations of the great leaders of every generation; our century of glorious history, were appealed to in vain. Their lessons fell upon the ears of men dazzled by military glory and
delirious with the lust of conquest. I will not repeat them now.
My desire to-day is simply to call attention to the practical working of the two doctrines—the doctrine of buying sovereignty or
conquering it in battle, and the doctrine of the Declaration of
Independence. For the last three years you have put one of
them in force in Cuba and the other in the Philippine Islands.
I ask you to think soberly which method, on the whole, you like
better. I ask you to compare the cost of war with the cost of

peace, of justice with that of injustice, the cost of empire with
the cost of republican liberty, the cost of the way of America
and the way of Europe, of the doctrine of the Declaration of
Independence with the doctrine of the Holy Alliance. You have
tried both, I hope, to your heart's content. But before I do
that I want to call attention to one important fact in our history
not generally known. It is very interesting in its connection
with this debate.

John Quincy Adams, as everybody knows, was the father of
what we call the Monroe doctrine. He secured its adoption
through the weight of his great influence, by a hesitating President, and a reluctant Cabinet. It is not so well known that he
placed the Monroe doctrine solely upon the doctrine that just
governments must rest upon the consent of the governed. That,
he declared to be its only foundation, and that so founded it
rested upon the eternal principle of righteousness and justice.

A thorough examination has lately been made by an accomplished historical scholar, Mr. Worthington C. Ford, aided by
Mr. Charles Francis Adams, grandson of John Quincy Adams,
of the unpublished Adams manuscripts at Quincy, the archives
of the Department of State, and the papers of President Monroe, lately published by Congress.

I can relate this story in a moment. I think it an important
contribution to this debate.

Mr. President, I discussed some time ago, and more than once,
this attempt to buy sovereignty with money of a dispossessed
tyrant, or to get it as booty or spoils of battle. I showed that it
is in contradiction of the great American doctrine that just governments rest only on the consent of the governed—in flat contradiction of the doctrine on which this Government is founded
and of the uniform tradition of all our statesmen from 1776 to
the adoption of the Spanish treaty. I do not mean to repeat that
argument now. It was met by the affirmation that Jefferson
disregarded it when we bought Louisiana, and that John Quincy
Adams disregarded it when we acquired Florida, and that Abraham Lincoln disregarded it when he put down the rebellion, and
that Charles Sumner disregarded it when he urged the purchase
of Alaska.

It was never denied that we could acquire territory and that we could govern it after it was acquired. The doctrine was that if the territory be inhabited by that vital and living being we call a people, as distinct from a few scattered and unorganized inhabitants, neither controlling it nor governing themselves, that people have a right to govern themselves and to determine their own destiny after their own fashion. This is the American exposition of the law of nations. Thomas Jefferson never departed from it. He regarded the Louisiana Territory as something not worth taking. He declared that it would not be inhabited for a thousand years. He only wanted New Orleans. The rest of the Territory was forced upon him by Napoleon. There was no people, in the sense of the law of nations, either in New Orleans or in the Louisiana Territory. There was no people there that could make a government or a treaty.

Abraham Lincoln put down the rebellion, because by his and our interpretation of the Constitution we were one people and not two—to which doctrine the Southern people had consented when they adopted the Constitution; and besides, if you had counted the whole people, black and white, there was never a majority on the side of secession in any single Southern State. Sumner again and again declared that there was nothing in Alaska which could be called a people, and that if there were the United States would never be willing to acquire them without their consent; and that we would never take Canada, if we could get it, except with the full approbation of her people. If my friends of the press or in the Senate who still stick to this ten hundred times refuted fallacy are not content, they will never be persuaded, though Thomas Jefferson and John Quincy Adams and Abraham Lincoln and Charles Sumner rise from the dead.

I do not wish to detain the Senate by renewing that debate. But I wish to cite a chapter of the history of this country, which shows that your present policy is in contradiction of the Monroe doctrine, as it is in contradiction of the Declaration of Independence. It is well known that John Quincy Adams was the author of the Monroe doctrine. He carried his point over the opposition of the Cabinet and reluctance on the part of the President.

When Canning proposed that the United States join England in asserting that the Holy Alliance should not reduce any South American country under the dominion of Spain, Mr. Adams said that we would not join England, although she asked us to do it. He said we were not to be a little cockboat in the wake of the British man-of-war. He counseled the President, and his advice was taken, that this country should make its declaration to Russia, the head and strength of the Holy Alliance, and he put that declaration expressly and solely on the doctrine of the consent of the governed, affirmed in our Declaration of Independence. He declared that doctrine was a doctrine of absolute right and righteousness.

. It will take but a moment to tell the story as it appears in the archives in our Department of State, in the Monroe papers lately published, in Adams's Diary, and in the Adams manuscripts at Quincy, which have been made public within a few days.

In August, September, and October, 1823, there came to the State Department of Washington from Mr. Rush dispatches containing letters from Mr. Canning. These letters suggested designs of the Holy Alliance against the independence of the South American colonies, and proposed co-operation between Great Britain and the United States against that alliance.

President Monroe asked the advice of Mr. Jefferson and Mr. Madison, and suggested that we should make it known that we should view an attack by the European powers upon the colonies of Spain as an attack upon ourselves. But in the meantime the Russian minister, Baron Tuyll, on the 16th of October, communicated to the Secretary of State a declaration of the Emperor of Russia that the political principles of that Power would not permit him to recognize the independence of the revolted colonies of Spain.

Mr. Adams saw and seized his opportunity. He gave this advice to President Monroe, as appears by his diary, on November 7, 1823:

"I remarked that the communications recently received from the Russian minister, Baron Tuyll, afforded, as I thought, a very suitable and convenient opportunity for us to take our stand against the Holy Alliance, and at the same time decline the overtures of Great Britain. It would be more candid and more dignified to avow our principles explicitly to Baron Tuyll than to go in as a cockboat in the wake of the British man-of-war. This idea was acquiesced in on all sides."

At the Cabinet meeting of November 15, 1823, the subject was again discussed.

"Letters were read from Mr. Jefferson, who was for acceding to the pending proposal. Mr. Madison was less decisively pronounced, but thought the movement on the part of Great Britain impelled more by her interest than by a principle of general liberty. President Monroe was quite despondent."

Adams proceeds:

"I soon found the source of the President's despondency with regard to South American affairs. Calhoun is perfectly moonstruck by the surrender of Cadiz, and says the Holy Allies, with 10,000 men, will restore all Mexico and all South America to the Spanish dominion. I did not deny that they might make a temporary impression for three, four, or five years, but I no more believe that the Holy Allies will restore the Spanish dominion upon the American continent than that Chimborazo will sink beneath the ocean. But, I added, if the South Americans were really in a state to be so easily subdued, it would be but a more forcible motive for us to beware of involving ourselves in their fate. I set this down as one of Calhoun's extravaganzas. He is for plunging into a war to prevent that which, if his opinion of it is correct, we are utterly unable to prevent. He is for embarking our lives and fortunes in a ship which he declares the very rats have abandoned. Calhoun reverts again to his idea of giving discretionary power to our minister to accede to all Canning's proposals, if necessary, but not otherwise. After much discussion, I said I thought we should bring the whole answer to Mr. Canning's proposals to a test of right and wrong. *Considering the South Americans as independent nations, they themselves, and no other nation, had the right to dispose of their condition. We have no right to dispose of them,* either alone or in conjunction with other nations. Neither have any other nations the right of disposing of them without their consent. This principle will give us a clue to answer all Mr. Canning's questions with candor and confidence, and I am to draft a dispatch accordingly." (Adams' Memoirs, p. 186.)

Before Mr. Adams prepared the draft, two more dispatches were received from Rush, dated the 2d and 10th of October, indicating a decided change in Canning's tone, and almost an indifference on his part to pursue his project of united action. Meantime, there came a new communication from Russia, which gave Adams his opportunity. He put his reply on the express and impregnable ground of the consent of the governed, as declared in our Declaration of Independence. On the 25th of November, he made, for the President's use, a draft of observations upon the communications recently received from the Russian minister. The paper begins as follows:

"The Government of the United States of America is essentially republican. By their Constitution it is provided that 'the United States shall guarantee to every State in this Union a republican form of government, and shall protect them from invasion.'

"The principles of this polity are: 1. That the institution of government to be lawful, must be pacific, that is, *founded upon the consent and by the agreement of those who are governed;* and 2, that each nation is exclusively the judge of the government best suited to itself, and that no other nation can justly interfere by force to impose a different government upon it. The first of the principles may be designated as the principle of liberty, the second as the principle of national independence; they are both principles of peace and of good will to men.

"A necessary consequence of the second of these principles is that the United States recognize in other nations the right which they claim and exercise for themselves of establishing and modifying their own governments, according to their own judgments and views of their interests, not encroaching upon the rights of others. (Ford, p. 38.)"

Mr. Adams states later in the same document:

"In the general declarations that the allied monarchs will never compound and never will even treat with the revolution, and that their policy has only for its object by forcible interposition to guarantee the tranquillity of all the States of which the civilized world is composed, the President wishes to perceive the sentiments, the application of which is limited, and intended in their results to be limited to the affairs of Europe. (Ford, p. 40.)"

Mr. Monroe and Mr. Calhoun hesitated in regard to the insertion of this paragraph in the answer to Russia, but neither of them, as appears from the full narrative in Mr. Adams's diary, objected to the doctrine. They thought it might be offensive to Russia. Accordingly Mr. Adams read the paper to Baron Tuyll, omitting that paragraph, but received a letter from the President a little later, yielding his objections and consenting to its retention.

Mr. Worthington C. Ford, in an interesting paper contained in the Proceedings of the Massachusetts Historical Society for January, 1902, narrates the whole story, and says in conclusion:

"That the timidity of the President was awakened, that record shows; but the persistence of Adams and the very weighty arguments he advanced in its favor induced Monroe to yield, but not until it was too late for the purpose intended. (Ford, p. 40.)"

Mr. Ford adds, after citing the Russian minister's communication:

"This gave Adams his opening. If the Emperor set up to be the mouthpiece of Divine Providence it would be well to intimate that this country did not recognize the language spoken and had a destiny of its own, also under the guidance of Divine Providence. If Alexander could exploit his political principles, those of a brutal repressive policy, the United States could show that another system of government, remote and separate from European traditions and administration, could give rise to a new and more active political principle—the consent of the governed—between which and the Emperor there could not exist even a sentimental sympathy. (Ford, p. 15.)"

So, Mr. President, if you have your own way, and keep on in the path you are treading, you have not only repealed the Declaration of Independence, but you have left for the Monroe doctrine only the principle of brutal selfishness. You have taken from that doctrine, which is the chief glory of this country, from the time of the treaty of peace in 1783 till the inauguration of Abraham Lincoln in 1861, its foundation in righteousness and freedom, and you found it only upon selfishness. You say not that it is right, but only that it is for our interest. If hereafter you go to war for it—if you have your way—it will not be for the glory of the liberator or for the principle on which the Republic is founded. You will only have Ancient Pistol's solace:

> "I shall sutler be unto the camp,
> And profits will accrue."

John Quincy Adams lived to see the great doctrine he had been taught from his cradle, which he had drawn in with his mother's milk, derided and trampled under foot by a people drunk with conquest and dazzled by military glory. He lived to see the President take soldiers and not statesmen for his counselors. He lived to see slavery entrenched in every department of the Government—in the White House, in court, in Congress, in trade, and in the pulpit. But he never wavered nor faltered in his sublime faith. He faced the stormy and turbulent waves of the House of Representatives at eighty. He took for his motto: Alteri Seculo—a motto which his son inscribed at his burial place at Quincy.

But the new age came sooner even than the faith of John Quincy Adams had predicted. In less than thirteen years from his death, Abraham Lincoln, whom the people sent to the White House, had declared on his way thither the sublime doctrine of the consent of the governed to be that on which the Republic is founded, and for which, if need be, he was willing to be assassinated. I think, therefore, modestly I hope and humbly, that the men who differ from their political associates, and even from majorities, may find something of consolation and something of hope in the company of John Quincy Adams and in the company of Abraham Lincoln.

When we ratified the treaty of Paris we committed ourselves to one experiment in Cuba and another in the Philippine Islands. We had said already that Cuba of right ought to be free and independent. So when in the treaty Spain abandoned her sovereignty the title of Cuba became at once complete. We were only to stay there to keep order until we could hand over Cuba to a government her people had chosen and established.

HICKS' SP.A.S.—20

By the same treaty we bought the Philippine Islands for $20,-
000,000 and declared and agreed that Congress shall dispose of
them. So, according to those who held that treaty valid, it became the duty of the President to reduce them to submission,
and of Congress to govern them.

Here the two doctrines are brought into sharp antagonism.

In Cuba, of right, just government, according to you, must
rest on the consent of the governed. Her people are to "institute a new government, laying its foundation on such principles,
and organizing its powers in such form as to them shall seem
most likely to effect their safety and happiness."

In the Philippine Islands a government is to be instituted by a
power 10,000 miles away, to be in the beginning a despotism, established by military power.

It is to be a despotism where there is treason without an overt
act and elections, if they have them, without political debate, and
schools where they can not teach liberty. It is to be established
by military power, and to be such, to use the language of the
McEnery resolution, such as shall seem "for the interest of the
United States."

You have given both doctrines a three years' trial. Three
years is sometimes a very long time and sometimes a very short
time in human affairs. I believe the whole life of the Savior,
after He first made His divine mission known, lasted but three
years. Three years has wrought a mighty change in Cuba, and
it has wrought a mighty change in the Philippine Islands. We
have had plenty of time to try both experiments.

President Roosevelt a day or two ago very truly and eloquently recited the story of what we had done for Cuba, and claimed,
and surely he was right, that it was one of the chief glories of
the Republic in all our glorious history. When he had finished
the recital he said, "That is one deed consummated to-day; and
now for the other." I do not believe that brave and honest man
will content himself to match this glorious instance of self-
denial and good faith, which has so stirred his enthusiasm, by
putting against it the gift of $200,000 from the Treasury to re-
lieve suffering Martinique, a gift which, in proportion to our
resources, is as if a man with $60,000 had given a two-dollar
bill. There can be but one other deed which his Administration

can do which can match the glories of the liberation of Cuba, and that will be the liberation of the Philippine Islands.

Now, what has each cost you, and what has each profited you?

In stating this account of profit and loss I hardly know which to take up first, principles and honor or material interests—I should have known very well which to have taken up first down to three years ago—what you call the sentimental, the ideal, the historical on the right side of the column; the cost or the profit in honor or shame and in character and in principle and moral influence, in true national glory; or the practical side, the cost in money and gain, in life and health, in wasted labor, in diminished national strength, or in prospects of trade and money getting.

I should naturally begin where our fathers used to begin. But somehow the things get so inextricably blended that we can not keep them separate. This world is so made that you can not keep honesty, and sound policy, and freedom, and material property, and good government, and the consent of the governed, apart. Men who undertake to make money by cheating pay for it by failure in business. If you try to keep order by military despotism you suffer from it by revolution and by barbarity in war. If a strong people try to govern a weak one against its will, the home government will get despotic, too. You can not maintain despotism in Asia and a republic in America. If you try to deprive even a savage or a barbarian of his just rights you can never do it without becoming a savage or a barbarian yourself.

Gentlemen talk about sentimentalities, about idealism. They like practical statesmanship better. But, Mr. President, this whole debate for the last four years has been a debate between two kinds of sentimentality. There has been practical statesmanship in plenty on both sides. Your side have carried their sentimentalities and ideals out in your practical statesmanship. The other side have tried and begged to be allowed to carry theirs out in practical statesmanship also. On one side have been these sentimentalities. They were the ideals of the fathers of the Revolutionary time, and from their day down till the day of Abraham Lincoln and Charles Sumner was over. The sentimentalities were that all men in political right were created equal; that governments derive their just powers from the consent of the governed, and are instituted to secure that equality; that every people—not every scattering neighborhood or settlement without organic life, not every portion of a people who may be temporarily discontented, but the political being that we call a people—has the right to institute a government for itself and to lay its foundation on such principles and organize its powers in such form as to it and not to any other people shall seem most likely to effect its safety and happiness. Now, a good deal of practical statesmanship has followed from these ideals and sentimentalities. They have builded forty-five States on firm foundations. They have covered South America with republics. They have kept despotism out of the Western Hemisphere. They have made the United States the freest, strongest, richest of the nations of the world. They have made the word republic a name to conjure by the round world over. By their virtue the American flag—beautiful as a flower to those who love it; terrible as a meteor to those who hate it—floats everywhere over peaceful seas, and is welcomed everywhere in friendly ports as the emblem of peaceful supremacy and sovereignty in the commerce of the world.

Has there been any practical statesmanship in our dealing with Cuba? You had precisely the same problem in the East and in the West. You knew all about conditions in Cuba. There has been no lack of counselors to whisper in the ear of the President and Senate and House the dishonorable counsel that we should hold on to Cuba, without regard to our pledges or our principles, and that the resolution of the Senator from Colorado [Mr. Teller] was a great mistake. "Ye shall not surely die," said the serpent—

"Squat like a toad, close at the ear of Eve."

I do not know how other men may feel, but I think that the statesmen who have had something to do with bringing Cuba into the family of nations, when they look back on their career, that my friends who sit around me, when each comes to look back upon a career of honorable and brilliant public service, will count the share they had in that as among the brightest, the greenest, and the freshest laurels in their crown.

I do not think I could honestly repeat all the compliments which the Senator from Wisconsin is in the habit of paying to the Senator from Colorado. The Senator from Colorado has gone against my grain very often, especially when he voted for the Spanish treaty and when his vote defeated the Bacon resolution. But I doubt whether any man who has sat in this Chamber since Charles Sumner died, or whether all who sit here now put together, have done a more important single service to the country than he did in securing the passage of the resolution which pledged us to deal with Cuba according to the principles of the Declaration of Independence.

You also, my imperialistic friends, have had your ideals and your sentimentalities. One is that the flag shall never be hauled down where it has once floated. Another is that you will not talk or reason with a people with arms in their hands. Another is that sovereignty over an unwilling people may be bought with gold. And another is that sovereignty may be got by force of arms, as the booty of battle or the spoils of victory.

What has been the practical statesmanship which comes from your ideals and your sentimentalities? You have wasted six hundred millions of treasure. You have sacrificed nearly 10,000 American lives—the flower of our youth. You have devastated provinces. You have slain uncounted thousands of the people you desire to benefit. You have established reconcentration camps. Your generals are coming home from their harvest, bringing their sheaves with them, in the shape of other thousands of sick and wounded and insane to drag out miserable lives, wrecked in body and mind. You make the American flag in the eyes of a numerous people the emblem of sacrilege in Christian churches, and of the burning of human dwellings, and of the horror of the water torture. Your practical statesmanship, which disdains to take George Washington and Abraham Lincoln or the soldiers of the Revolution or of the Civil War as models, has looked in some cases to Spain for your example. I believe—nay, I know—that in general our officers and soldiers are humane. But in some cases they have carried on your warfare with a mixture of American ingenuity and Castilian cruelty.

Your practical statesmanship has succeeded in converting a people who three years ago were ready to kiss the hem of the garment of the American and to welcome him as a liberator, who thronged after your men when they landed on those islands with benediction and gratitude, into sullen and irreconcilable enemies, possessed of a hatred which centuries can not eradicate.

The practical statesmanship of the Declaration of Independence and the Golden Rule would have cost nothing but a few kind words. They would have bought for you the great title of liberator and benefactor, which your fathers won for your country in the South American Republics and in Japan and which you have won in Cuba. They would have bought for you the undying gratitude of a great and free people and the undying glory which belongs to the name of liberator. That people would have felt for you as Japan felt for you when she declared last summer that she owed everything to the United States of America.

What have your ideals cost you, and what have they bought for you?

1. For the Philippine Islands you have had to repeal the Declaration of Independence.

For Cuba you have had to reaffirm it and give it new luster.

2. For the Philippine Islands you have had to convert the Monroe doctrine into a doctrine of mere selfishness. •

For Cuba you have acted on it and vindicated it.

3. In Cuba you have got the eternal gratitude of a free people.

In the Philippine Islands you have got the hatred and sullen submission of a subjugated people.

4. From Cuba you have brought home nothing but glory.

From the Philippines you have brought home nothing of glory.

5. In Cuba no man thinks of counting the cost. The few soldiers who came home from Cuba wounded or sick carry about their wounds and their pale faces as if they were medals of honor.

What soldier glories in a wound or an empty sleeve which he got in the Philippines?

6. The conflict in the Philippines has cost you $600,000,000, thousands of American soldiers—the flower of your youth—the health and sanity of thousands more, and hundreds of thousands of Filipinos slain.

Another price we have paid as the result of your practical statesmanship. We have sold out the right, the old American right, to speak out the sympathy which is in our hearts for people who are desolate and oppressed everywhere on the face of the earth. Has there ever been a contest between power and the spirit of liberty, before that now going on in South Africa, when American Senators held their peace because they thought they were under an obligation to the nation in the wrong for not interfering with us? I have heard that it turned out that we had no great reason for gratitude of that kind. But I myself heard an American Senator, a soldier of the Civil War, declare in this Chamber that, while he sympathized with the Boers, he did not say so because of our obligation to Great Britain for not meddling with us in the war with Spain. Nothing worse than that was said of us in the old slavery days. A great English poet before the Civil War, in a poem entitled "The Curse," taunted us by saying that we did not dare to utter our sympathy with freedom so long as we were the holders of slaves. I remember, after fifty years, the sting and shame I felt in my youth when that was uttered. I had hoped that we had got rid of that forever before 1865.

> Ye shall watch while kings conspire
> Round the people's smouldering fire,
>   And, warm for your part,
> Shall never dare, O, shame!
> To utter the thought into flame
>   Which burns at your heart.
>
> Ye shall watch while nations strive
> With the bloodhounds—die or survive—
>   Drop faint from their jaws,
> Or throttle them backward to death,
> And only under your breath
>   Shall ye bless the cause.

Sometimes men are affected by particular instances who are not impressed by statistics of great numbers.

Sterne's starling in its cage has moved more hearts than were ever stirred by census tables.

Let me take two examples out of a thousand with which to contrast the natural result of the doctrine of your fathers with yours.

I do not think there ever was a more delightful occurrence in the history of Massachusetts since the Puritans or the Pilgrims landed there, than the visit to Harvard two years ago of the Cuban teachers to the Harvard Summer School. The old University put on her best apparel for the occasion. The guests were manly boys and fair girls, making you think of Tennyson's sweet girl graduates, who came to sit at the feet of old Harvard to learn something which they could teach to their pupils, and to carry back to their country and teach their own children undying gratitude to the great Republic. It was one of the most delightful lessons in all history of the gratitude of a people to its liberator, and of the affection of the liberator-Republic to the people it had delivered. Was there ever a more fitting subject for poetry or for art than the venerable President Eliot, surrounded with his staff of learned teachers and famous scholars, the foremost men in the Republic of letters and science, as he welcomed them, these young men and women, to the delights of learning and the blessings of liberty?

Contrast this scene with another. It is all you have to show, that you have brought back, so far, from the Philippine Islands. You have no grateful youth coming to sit at your feet. You do not dare to bring here even a friendly Filipino to tell you, with unfettered lips, what his people think of you, or what they want of you. I read the other day in a Nebraska paper a terrible story of the passage through Omaha of a carload of maniacs from the Philippine Islands.

The story, I believe, has been read in the Senate. I telegraphed to Omaha to the editor of a paper, of high reputation, I believe, a zealous supporter of the policy of Imperialism, to learn if the story was authentic. I am told in reply, and I am glad to know it, that the picture is sensational and exaggerated, but the substantial fact is confirmed that that load of young soldiers passed through that city lately, as other like cargoes have passed through before, maniacs and broken in mental health as the result of service in the Philippine Islands.

It is no answer to tell me that such horrors exist everywhere; that there are other maniacs at St. Elizabeth, and that every State asylum is full of them. Those unhappy beings have been

visited, without any man's fault, by the mysterious Providence
of God, or if their affliction comes from any man's fault it is our
duty to make it known and to hold the party guilty responsible.
It is a terrible picture that I have drawn. It is a picture of men
suffering from the inevitable result which every reasonable man
must have anticipated of the decisions made in this Chamber
when we elected to make war for the principle of despotism instead of a policy of peace, in accordance with the principles of
the Declaration of Independence.

Mr. President, every one of these maniacs, every one of the
many like freights of horror that come back to us from the
Philippine Islands, every dead soldier, every wounded or
wrecked soldier was once an American boy, the delight of some
American home, fairer and nobler in his young promise, as we
like to think, than any other the round world over. Ah! Mr.
President, it was not $20,000,000 that we paid as the price of
sovereignty. It was the souls of these boys of ours that entered
into the cost. When you determined by one vote to ratify the
Spanish treaty; when you determined by one vote to defeat the
Bacon resolution; when you declared, in the McEnery resolution, that we would dispose of that people as might be for the
interest of the United States; when the Senator from Wisconsin
said we would not talk to a people who had arms in their hands,
although they begged that there should be no war, and that we
would at least hear them; when some of you went about the
country declaring that the flag never should be hauled down
where it once floated, you did not know, because in your excitement and haste your intellectual vision was dazzled with empire, you did not know that this was to come. But you might
have known it. A little reflection and a little reason would have
told you. I wonder if the Republican editor who made that
known was attacking the American Army. I wonder if those
of us who do not like that are the friends or the enemies of the
American soldier.

I can not understand how any man, certainly how any intelligent student of history, could have failed to foretell exactly
what has happened when we agreed to the Spanish treaty.
Everything that has happened since has been the natural, inevitable, inexorable result of the policy you then declared.

If you knew anything of human nature you knew that the great doctrine that just government depends on the consent of the governed, as applied to the relation of one people to another, has its foundation in the nature of man itself. No people will submit, if it can be helped, to the rule of any other people. You must have known perfectly well, if you had stopped to consider, that so far as the Philippine people were like us they would do exactly what we did and would do again in a like case. So far as they were civilized they would resist you with all the power of civilized war. So far as they were savage they would resist you by all the methods of savage warfare.

You never could eradicate from the hearts of that people by force the love of liberty which God put there.

> For He that worketh high and wise,
> Nor pauseth in His plan,
> Will take the sun out of the skies
> Ere freedom out of man.

This war, if you call it war, has gone on for three years. It will go on in some form for three hundred years, unless this policy be abandoned. You will undoubtedly have times of peace and quiet, or pretended submission. You will buy men with titles, or office, or salaries. You will intimidate cowards. You will get pretended and fawning submission. The land will smile and smile and seem at peace. But the volcano will be there. The lava will break out again. You can never settle this thing until you settle it right.

I think my friends of the majority, whatever else they may claim—and they can rightly claim a great deal that is good and creditable for themselves—will not claim to be prophets. They used to prophesy a good deal two years ago. We had great prophets and minor prophets. All predicted peace and submission, and a flag followed by trade, with wealth flowing over this land from the Far East, and the American people standing in the Philippine Islands looking over with eager gaze toward China. Where are now your prophets which prophesied unto you? I fear that we must make the answer that was made to the children of Israel: "They prophesied falsely, and the prophets have become wind, and the word is not in them."

An instance of this delusion, which seems to have prevailed everywhere, is stated by Mr. Andrew Carnegie in the May number of the North American Review. He says:

"The writer had the honor of an interview with President McKinley before war broke out with our allies, and ventured to predict that if he attempted to exercise sovereignty over the Filipinos—whom he had bought at $2.50 a head—he would be shooting these people down within thirty days. He smiled, and, addressing a gentleman who was present, said: 'Mr. Carnegie doesn't understand the situation at all.' Then turning to the writer, he said: 'We will be welcomed as their best friends.' 'So little,' says Mr. Carnegie, 'did dear, kind, loving President McKinley expect ever to be other than the friendly co-operator with these people.' "

A guerrilla warfare, carried on by a weaker people against a stronger, is recognized and legitimate. Many nations have resorted to it. Our war of the Revolution in many parts of the country differed little from it. Spain carried it on against Napoleon when the French forces overran her territory, and mankind sympathized with her. The greatest of English poets since Milton, William Wordsworth, described that warfare in a noble sonnet, which will answer, with scarcely the change of a word, as a description of the Filipino people:

"Hunger, and sultry heat, and nipping blast
From bleak hilltop, and length of march by night
Through heavy swamp or over snow-clad height—
These hardships ill-sustained, these dangers past,
The roving Spanish bands are reached at last,
Charged, and dispersed like foam; but as a flight
Of scattered quails by signs do reunite,
So these—and, heard of once again, are chased
With combination of long-practiced art
And newly kindled hope; but they are fled,
Gone are they, viewless as the buried dead:
Where now? Their sword is at the foeman's heart!
And thus from year to year his walk they thwart,
And hang like dreams around his guilty bed."

I believe the American Army, officers and soldiers, to be made up of as brave and humane men, in general, as ever lived. They have done what has always been done, and until human nature shall change, always will be done in all like conditions. The chief guilt is on the heads of those who created the conditions.

One thing, however, I am bound to say in all frankness. I do not know but my statement may be challenged. But I am sure that nearly every well-informed man who will hear it or read it will know that it is true. That is, that you will never get officers or soldiers in the standing Army, as a rule, to give testimony which they think will be disagreeable to their superiors or to the War Department.

I have letters in large numbers myself. I believe every Senator in this body, who is expected to do anything to inquire into these atrocities, has had abundant letters to the effect which I state. The same evil of which we are all conscious, which leads men in public life to be unwilling to incur unpopularity or the displeasure of their constituents by frankly uttering and acting upon their opinions, applies with a hundredfold more force when you summon a soldier or an officer to tell facts which will bear heavily on the administration of the war. I have had letters shown me by members of this body who vouched personally for the absolute trustworthiness of the writers, who detailed the horrors of the water torture and other kindred atrocities, which no inducement would lead them to make public.

The private soldier who has ended his term of service or who expects to end it and return to private life, is under less restraint. But when he tells his story he is met by the statement of an officer, in some cases, that it is well known that private soldiers are in the habit of "drawing the long bow," to use the phrase of one general whose name has been brought into this discussion. In other words, these generals are so jealous of the honor of the Army, and their own, that they confine their jealousy to the honor of the officers, and expect you to reject these things on the assertion that the soldier is an habitual liar, and then they reproach the men who complain with being indifferent to the honor of the Army.

Was it ever heard before that a civilized, humane, and Christian nation made war upon a people and refused to tell them what they wanted of them? You refuse to tell these people this year or next year or perhaps for twenty years, whether you mean in the end to deprive them of their independence, or no. You say you want them to submit. To submit to what? To mere military force? But for what purpose or what end is that military force to be exerted? You decline to tell them. Not only you decline to say what you want of them, except bare and abject surrender, but you will not even let them tell you what they ask of you.

The Senator from Ohio [Mr. Foraker] says it is asserted with a show of reason that a majority of the people favor our cause. General MacArthur denies this statement, and says they were almost a unit for Aguinaldo. Mr. Denby and Mr. Schurman, two of the three commissioners of the first Filipino Commission, deny the statement. General Bell, in his letter of December 13, 1901, says "a majority of the inhabitants of his province have persistently continued their opposition during the entire period of three years, and that the men who accept local office from the governor and take the oath of allegiance do it solely for the purpose of improving their opportunity for resistance." That statement is concurred in by every department commander there. Certainly Major Gardener's apparently temperate and fair statement—about which we are to have no opportunity to examine him until Congress adjourns—does not say any such thing as that suggested by the Senator from Ohio.

But what is your cause? What is your cause that they favor? Do you mean that a majority of the Filipino people favor your killing them? Certainly not. Do you mean that a majority of the Filipino people, or that any one man in the Philippine Islands, according to the evidence of Governor Taft himself, favors anything that you are willing to do?

The evidence is that some of them favor their admission as an American State and others favor a government of their own under your protection. Others would like to come in as a Territory under our Constitution. But is there any evidence that one human being there is ready to submit to your government without any rights under our Constitution, or without any prospect of coming in as an American State? Or is there any evidence that any single American citizen, in the Senate or out of it, is willing that we should do anything that a single Filipino is ready to consent to?

I have no doubt they will take the oath of allegiance. Undoubtedly they will go through the form of submission. Undoubtedly you have force enough to make the whole region a howling wilderness, if you think fit. Undoubtedly you can put up a form of government in which they will seem to take some share, and they will take your offices and your salaries. But when you come to getting anything which is not merely temporary; when you come to announce anything in principle, such as those on which governments are founded, you have not any evidence of any considerable number of people there ready to submit to your will unless they are compelled by sheer brutal force.

I do not wish to dwell at length on the circumstances which attended the capture of Aguinaldo. But as they have been elaborately defended in this body, and it is said that the officer who captured him had a good record before, and especially as he has been decorated by a promotion by the advice and consent of the Senate, I can not let it pass in silence.

I understand the facts to be that that officer disguised the men under his command in the dress of Filipino soldiers; wrote, or caused to be written, a forged letter to Aguinaldo, purporting to come from one of his officers, stating that he was about to bring him some prisoners he had captured, and in that way got access to Aguinaldo's headquarters. As he approached he sent a message to Aguinaldo that he and his friends were hungry; accepted food at his hands, and when in his presence threw down and seized him; shot some of the soldiers who were about Aguinaldo, and brought him back a prisoner into our lines. That is the transaction which is so highly applauded in imperialistic quarters.

I do not believe that the Senate knew what it was doing when it consented to General Funston's promotion. The nomination came in with a list of Army and Navy appointments and promotions—2,038 in all—and the Senate assented to that at the same time with 1,828 others. I doubt very much whether there were 10 Senators in their seats or whether one of them listened to the list as it was read. It is, I suppose, betraying no secret to say that these lists are almost never read to the Senate when they come in or when they are reported from the committee; that the only reading they get is at the time of the confirmation, when they commonly attract no attention whatever. I do not mean to say that if the Senate had had its attention called to the transaction the result would have been different. I only mean to say that I believe many Senators did not know it. I suppose the question whether the Senate would have approved it might have depended on the character and the quality of the general service of that officer and not on the estimate we formed of this particular transaction, which seems to have been done under orders. I did not know myself that the nomination had been made till long after the Senate had assented. But I incline to think, with General MacArthur's testimony before the investigating committee that the act was done by his direction and with his approval, I should not have thought it fair to hold the officer responsible for it by denying him an otherwise deserved promotion.

I think we are bound in justice to General Funston to take the declaration of General MacArthur that he ordered and approved everything that officer did. If that be true we have no right to hold the subordinate responsible, however odious the act. If it turn out that that still higher authority has approved the act, then it becomes still more emphatically our duty to point out its enormity.

*   *   *   *   *   *

Mr. President, we have two guides for the conduct of military officers in such circumstances. They apply not only to this act of General Funston, but they apply to most of the conduct of our military officers, of which complaint has been made. One of these is Instructions for the Government of Armies of the United States in the Field, prepared by Dr. Francis Lieber and promulgated by order of Abraham Lincoln.

The other is the convention at The Hague, agreed upon by the representatives of this Government with the others on the 29th day of July, 1899, and ratified by the Senate on the 14th of March, 1902.

Observe that this convention was agreed upon before all these acts happened, and was unanimously adopted after they had all happened.

I extract from the Instructions for the Government Regulation of Armies in the Field the following paragraphs:

Paragraph 148 is this:

"The law of war does not allow proclaiming either an individual belonging to the hostile army or a citizen or a subject of the hostile government an outlaw, who may be slain without trial by any captor, any more than the modern law of peace allows such intentional outlawry. On the contrary, it abhors such outrage. The sternest retaliation should follow the murder committed in consequence of such proclamation, made by whatever authority. Civilized nations look with horror upon offers of rewards for the assassination of enemies as relapses into barbarism."

Now, Mr. President, is it denied that hundreds upon hundreds of Filipinos have been put to death without trial? Has any soldier or officer been brought to trial by our authority for these offenses? Now, if it be an outrage upon which "nations look with horror," to use the language of that paragraph, and which "the law of war * * * abhors," is it any less a crime to be abhorred when it is done without such proclamation? The proclamation does not, according to this authority, justify the officer or soldier who acts in obedience to it. On the contrary, his conduct is abhorrent to all civilized mankind. And yet these things pass without condemnation, without punishment, without trial. Gentlemen seem to be impatient when they are asked to investigate them, or even to hear the story told in the Senate of the United States.

Paragraph 16 is:

"Military necessity does not admit of cruelty—that is, the infliction of suffering for the sake of suffering or for revenge, nor of maiming or wounding except in fight, nor of torture to extort confession. It does not admit of the use of poison in any way nor of the wanton devastation of a district. It admits of deception, but disclaims acts of perfidy, and, in general, military necessity does not include any act of hostility which makes the return to peace unnecessarily difficult."

The rule says:

"It admits of deception, but disclaims acts of perfidy."

That also follows the prohibition of the use of poison, with which it is associated.

Now, perfidy is defined later in paragraph 117, which declares:

"It is justly considered an act of bad faith, of infamy, or fiendishness to deceive the enemy by flags of protection. * * *"

Paragraph 65 is:

"The use of the enemy's national standard, flag, or other emblem of nationality for the purpose of deceiving the enemy in battle is an act of perfidy. * * *"

Is not the uniform an emblem of nationality? If it be an act of perfidy—the use of that emblem of nationality to deceive the enemy in battle—is it any less an act of perfidy to use it to steal upon him and deceive him when he is not in battle and is in his own quarters?

This is also prohibited by the convention of The Hague, which must have been well known to all our officers, which had been signed by the representatives of this Government, although its formal approval by the Senate took place this winter.

I suppose if it be perfidy now, according to the unanimous opinion of the Senate, and was perfidy before, according to the concurrent action of 24 great nations, the question when we formally ratified the treaty becomes unimportant.

Article 23 of the convention declares:

"(f) To make improper use of a flag of truce, the national flag, or military ensigns, and the enemy's uniform"— is specially prohibited. That is classed in that article also with the use of poison and poisoned arms.

So, Mr. President, the act of General Funston—not General Funston himself, if he acted under orders of his superior—but the act of General Funston is stamped with indelible infamy by Abraham Lincoln's articles of war, to which the Secretary of War appeals, and the concurrent action of 24 great nations, and the unanimous action of the Senate this winter.

Let me repeat a little: What is an act of perfidy, as distinguished from the deception which General MacArthur thinks appropriate to all war, as defined by both these great and commanding authorities?

That is defined in paragraph 65, which declares that—

"The use of the enemy's national standard, flag, or other emblem of nationality for the purpose of deceiving the enemy in battle is an act of perfidy, by which they lose all claim to the protection of the law of war."

If that be true, is it less an act of perfidy to use the uniform of the enemy—his emblem of nationality—to steal upon him when no battle is going on?

One hundred and seventeen is to like effect:

"It is justly considered an act of bad faith, of infamy, or fiendishness to deceive the enemy by a flag of protection. Such act of bad faith may be good cause for refusing to respect such flag."

Such deception is of the same kind as that practiced on the unsuspecting Aguinaldo, which the rule "justly," as it declares, "considers an act of infamy or fiendishness."

Rule 60 is:

"It is against the usage of modern war to resolve, in hatred and revenge, to give no quarter."

Observe this is not justified even by revenge.

"No body of troops has the right to declare that it will not give, and therefore will not accept, quarter.

"56. A prisoner of war is subject to no punishment for being a public enemy, nor is any revenge wreaked upon him by the intentional infliction of any suffering or disgrace, by cruel imprisonment, want of food, by mutilation, death, or any other barbarity."

So, Mr. President, in this attempt to force your sovereignty by this process of benevolent assimilation, we have been brought to the unexampled dishonor of disregarding our own rules for the conduct of armies in the field and to disregard the rules to which our national faith has just been pledged to substantially all the civilized powers of the earth.

I understand the facts to be that this officer, with the approval of his superior officer, disguised himself or some of his men in the Filipino uniform, stole upon Aguinaldo unawares under that guise, deceived him by a forged letter representing that they were hungry, received food at his hands, and then threw him down and made him captive.

Now, if that be not the perfidy twice denounced and expressly ranked with poisoning and other like barbarities I can not understand the meaning of human language or the force of human conduct.

But this act of General Funston's, approved by his superior officer, was in violation, not only of the laws of war, but of that law of hospitality which governs alike everywhere the civilized Christian or pagan wherever the light of chivalry has penetrated. He went to Aguinaldo under the pretense that he was ahungered, and Aguinaldo fed him. Was not that an act of perfidy? It violated the holy rite of hospitality which even the Oriental nations hold sacred?

In Scott's immortal romance of the Talisman, the Sultan Saladin interposes to prevent a criminal who had just committed a treacherous murder from partaking of his feast by striking off his head as he approached the banquet. "Had he murdered my father," said the Saladin to Richard Cœur de Lion, "and afterwards partaken of my bowl and cup, not a hair of his head could have been injured by me."

In this case it was not the host sparing the guest, it was not Conrad de Montserat partaking of the bowl and the cup of Saladin, but it was the guest who had partaken of the hospitality of the host who betrayed his benefactor, and in doing it represented the United States of America in the Philippines.

Mr. President, the story of what has been called the water torture has been, in part, told by other Senators. I have no inclination to repeat the story. I can not help believing that not a twentieth part of it has yet been told. I get letters in large numbers from officers, or the friends of officers, who repeat what they tell me, all testifying to these cruelties. And yet as in the case cited by the Senator from Georgia [Mr. Bacon] the other day the officer, or the officer's friends or kindred, who send the letters to me, send them under a strict injunction of secrecy. Other Senators tell me they have a like experience. These brave officers, who would go to the cannon's mouth for honor, who never flinch in battle, flinch before what they deem the certain ruin of their prospects in life if they give the evidence which they think would be distasteful to their superiors. I do not undertake to judge of this matter. Other Senators can judge as well as I can. The American people can do it better.

I suppose, Mr. President, that those of us who are of English descent like to think that the race from which we come will compare favorably with most others in the matter of humanity. Yet history is full of the terrible cruelties committed by Englishmen when men of other races refused to submit to their authority. I think my friends who seek to extenuate this water torture, or to apologize for it, may perhaps like to look at the precedent of the dealings with the Irish rebels in 1799.

In Howell's State Trials there will be found the proceedings in a suit by Mr. Wright against James Judkin Fitzgerald, a sheriff, who ordered a citizen to be flogged for the purpose of extorting information. I believe 50 lashes were administered and then 50 more by Fitzgerald, and in many other cases the same course was taken. It was wholly to extract information, as this water torture has been to get information. Fitzgerald, the sheriff, told his own story. He pointed out the necessity of his system of terror. He said he got one man he had flogged to confess that the plaintiff was a secretary of the United Irishmen, and this information he could not get from him before; that Mr. Wright himself had offered to confess, but his memory had been so impaired by the flogging that he could not command the faculty of recollection. Notwithstanding he had by the terror of his name and the severity of his flogging succeeded most astonishingly, particularly in one instance, where, by the flogging of one man, he and 36 others acknowledged themselves United Irishmen.

Now, that was abundantly proved; and the sheriff who had tortured and flogged these men who were only fighting that Ireland should not be ruled without the consent of the governed had the effrontery to ask for an act of indemnity from the House of Commons against the damages which had been recovered against him, and that claim found plenty of advocates. The ministry undertook to extenuate the action of this monster by citing the cruelties which the Irish people had inflicted in their turn, and by saying that very material discoveries were made relative to concealed arms as the result of these tortures. The defenders of the administration said the most essential service had been rendered to the State and to the country by Mr. Fitzgerald. The Attorney General trusted the House would cheerfully accede to the prayer of the petition. Mr. Wright, the man who had been tortured, was a man of excellent character and education, and a teacher of the French language. As soon as he knew there were charges against him he went to the house of the defendant to give himself up and demand a trial. I will not take the time of the Senate to read the debates. The argument for the Government would do very well for some of the arguments we have heard here, and the arguments we have heard here would have done very well there. The House passed a general bill to indemnify all sheriffs and magistrates who had acted for the suppression of the rebellion in a way not warranted by law, and to secure them against actions at law for so doing. The sole question at stake was the right of torture to extort information. The bill passed the House, and afterwards Fitzgerald got a considerable pension, and was created a baronet of the United Kingdom.

Now, I agree that this precedent, so far as it may be held to have set an example for what has been done in the Philippine Islands, may be cited against me. I cite it only to show that such things are inevitable when you undertake by brute force to reduce to subjection an unwilling people, and that, therefore, when you enter upon that undertaking you yourselves take the responsibility for everything that follows.

Mr. President, it is said that these horrors which never would have come to the public knowledge had not the Senate ordered this investigation, were unknown to our authorities at home. I hope and believe they were unknown to the War Department. I know they were unknown to President Roosevelt, and I know they were unknown to President McKinley. But I can not think, perhaps I am skeptical, that the recent declaration of that honorable gentleman, the Secretary of War, made on a memorable occasion, that the war on our part has been conducted with unexampled humanity, will be accepted by his countrymen.

Let us not be diverted from the true issue. We are not talking of retaliation. We are not talking of the ordinary brutalities of war. We are not talking about or inquiring into acts of vengeance committed in the heat of battle. We are talking about torture, torture—cold-blooded, deliberate, calculated torture; torture to extort information. Claverhouse did it to the Scotch Covenanters with the boot and thumb-screw. It has never since

till now been done by a man who spoke English except in Ireland. The Spanish inquisition did it with the slow fire and the
boiling oil. It is said that the water torture was borrowed from
Spain. I am quite ready to believe it. The men who make the
inquiry are told that they are assailing the honor of the American Army. How do the defenders of the American Army meet
the question? By denying the fact? No. By saying that the
offenders have been detected and punished by military power?
Some of these facts were reported to the War Department more
than a year ago. So far as I can find there have been but two
men tried for torture to extort information. They were two
officers who hung up men by the thumbs, and they were found
guilty. The general officer who approved the finding said "that
they had dishonored and degraded the American Army," and
then they were sent back to their command with a reprimand.
I agree with the Senator from Wisconsin that the men who have
stolen, and committed assaults for the gratification of brutal
lusts have been punished, and punished severely.

My honorable friend from Wisconsin [Mr. Spooner] said
something about this matter the other day. That is the only
case of a punishment to be found in our records so far as I have
seen them. I agree with my friend from Wisconsin that the
men who have stolen and committed assaults for the gratification
of brutal lusts have been punished, and punished severely, but
what we are talking about is torture.

Mr. Spooner. Did I say anything about the number?

Mr. Hoar. The Senator said there were two or three hundred
cases, quoting the record before him.

Mr. Carmack. Was it not the Senator from Iowa [Mr.
Dolliver]?

Mr. Hoar. No; it was the Senator from Wisconsin, unless
my memory deceives me. I will change it if I am mistaken, but
I think I am not mistaken.

We are talking about torture committed in the open day by
men who were not drunk, but sober; men who had not just come
out of battle, but torture for the purpose of getting information, on which, according to one of this committee, the tribunals
acted.

What we are talking about is the torture committed in the presence of numerous witnesses for the purpose of extorting information, and orders from high authority to depopulate whole districts, and to slay all inhabitants, including all boys over 10 years old.

Is it denied that these things have been done? Is it denied that although you are still on the threshold of this inquiry, and have only called such witnesses as you happen to find 10,000 miles away from the scene, that these things have been proved to the satisfaction of the majority of the committee, and that no man has yet been punished, although they were going on considerably more than a year ago? Now, how do our friends who seek, I will not say to defend, but to extenuate them, deal with the honor of the American Army? Why, they come into the Senate and say that there have been other cruelties and barbarities and atrocities in war. When these American soldiers and officers are called to the bar our friends summon Nero and Torquemada and the Spanish inquisition and the sheeted and ghostly leaders of the Ku Klux Klan and put them by their side. That is the way you defend the honor of the American Army. It is the first time the American soldier was put into such company by the men who have undertaken his defense.

It has been shown, I think, in the investigation now going on that the secretary of the province of Batangas declared that one-third of the 300,000 of the population of that province have died within two years—100,000 men and women.

The *Boston Journal,* an eminent Republican paper and a most able supporter of the imperialistic policy, printed on the 3d of May, 1901, an interview with Gen. James M. Bell, given to the *New York Times*—not the General Bell who has been discussed here, but Gen. James M. Bell is his name, an officer who came back from the Philippines in May, 1901.

Mr. Spooner. James F. Bell is the one there now.

Mr. Lodge. James Franklin Bell.

Mr. Hoar. This one is James M. Bell, unless I have the initials wrong. I have taken great pains to make inquiry. I have heard from the man to whom the interview was given, a newspaper correspondent of high character, and I have applied to the gentlemen of the *Boston Journal* to know if they ever heard it contradicted. He said in May, 1901, and he advocated the policy in the interview, too, that one-sixth of the natives of Luzon have either been killed or have died of the dengue fever in the last two years. Now, what is the population of Luzon? It is about 3,000,000, is it not?

Mr. Allison. That or thereabouts.

Mr. Hoar. Then one-sixth is 500,000.

I suppose that this dengue fever and the sickness which depopulated Batangas is the direct result of the war, and comes from the condition of starvation and bad food which the war has caused. The other provinces have not been heard from. If this be true we have caused the death of more human beings in the Philippines than we have caused to our enemies, including insurgents in the terrible Civil War, in all our other wars put together. The general adds that "the loss of life by killing alone has been very great, but I think not one man has been slain except where his death served the legitimate purposes of war. It has been necessary to adopt what in other countries would probably be thought harsh measures, for the Filipino is tricky and crafty and has to be fought in his own way."

I have made careful inquiry and I am satisfied that this interview is genuine. Now, all this is because you will not tell what you mean to do in the future, as I understand it.

Where did this order to make Samar a howling wilderness originate? The responsibility unquestionably, according to the discipline of armies in the field, rests with the highest authority from which it came.

We used to talk, some of us, about the horrors of Andersonville, and other things that were done during the Civil War. We hope, all of us, never to hear them mentioned again. But is there anything in them worse than that which an officer of high rank in the Army, vouched for by a Senator on this floor, from personal knowledge, as a man of the highest honor and veracity, writes about the evils of these reconcentrado camps in the Philippine Islands? Now all this cost, all these young men gone to their graves, all these wrecked lives, all this national dishonor, the repeal of the Declaration of Independence, the overthrow of the principle on which the Monroe doctrine was placed by its author, the devastation of provinces, the shooting of captives, the torture of prisoners and of unarmed and peaceful citizens, the hanging men up by the thumbs, the carloads of maniac soldiers that you bring home are all because you would not tell and will not tell now whether you mean in the future to stand on the principles which you and your fathers always declared in the past.

The Senator from Ohio says it is not wise to declare what we will do at some future time. Mr. President, we do not ask you to declare what you will do at some future time. We ask you to declare an eternal principle good at the present time and good at all times. We ask you to reaffirm it, because the men most clamorous in support of what you are doing deny it. That principle, if you act upon it, prevents you from crushing out a weak nation, because of your fancied interest now or hereafter. It prevents you from undertaking to judge what institutions are fit for other nations on the poor plea that you are the strongest. We are asking you at least to go no further than to declare what you would not do now or hereafter, and the reason for declaring it is that half of you declare you will hold this people in subjection and the other half on this matter are dumb. You declared what you would not do at some future time when you all voted that you would not take Cuba against the will of her people, did you not? We ask you to declare not at what moment you will get out of the Philippine Islands, but only on what eternal principle you will act, in them or out of them. Such declarations are made in all history. They are made in every important treaty between nations.

The Constitution of the United States is itself but a declaration of what this country will do and what it will not do in all future times. The Declaration of Independence, if it have the practical meaning it has had for a hundred years, is a declaration of what this country would do through all future times. The Monroe Doctrine, to which sixteen republics south of us owe their life and their safety, was a declaration to mankind of what we would do in all future time. Among all the shallow pretenses of imperialism this statement that we will not say what we will do in the future is the most shallow of all. Was there ever such a flimsy pretext flaunted in the face of the American people as that of gentlemen who say, If any other nation on the

face of the earth or all other nations together attempt to overthrow the independence of any people to the south of us in this
hemisphere, we will fight and prevent them, and at the same time
think it dishonorable to declare whether we will ever overthrow
the independence of a weaker nation in another hemisphere.

If we take your view of it we have crushed out the only republic in Asia and put it under our heel and we are now at war
with the only Christian people in the East. Even, as I said, the
Senator from Ohio admits they are a people, he only says there
are several peoples and not one, as if the doctrine that one people
has no right to buy sovereignty over another, or to rule another against its will, did not apply in the plural number. You
can not crush out an unwilling people, or buy sovereignty over
them, or treat them as spoils of conquest, or booty of battle in
the singular, or at retail, but you have a perfect right to do it
by wholesale. Suppose there are several peoples in the Philippines. They have population enough to make a hundred and
twelve States of the size of Rhode Island or Delaware when
they adopted the Constitution.

I suppose, according to this modern doctrine, that if, when the
Holy Alliance threatened to reduce the colonies which had
thrown off the yoke of Spain in South America, not a whit more
completely than the Philippine people had thrown off the yoke
of Spain in Asia, if they had undertaken to subdue them all at
once, John Quincy Adams and James Monroe would have held
their peace and would at least have said it was not wise to say
what we would do in the future. If we had the right to protect
nascent republics from the tyranny of other people and to declare that we would do it in the future, and if need be would
encounter the whole continent of Europe single-handed in that
case, is it any less fitting to avow that we will protect such peoples from ourselves? How is it that these gentlemen who will
not tell you what they will do in the future in regard to the
Philippine Islands were so eager and greedy to tell you what
they would do and what they would not do in the case of Cuba
when we first declared war on Spain? You can make no distinction between these two cases except by having a motive,
which I do not for one moment impute, that when you made

war upon Spain you were afraid of Europe, if you did not make the declaration.

These people are given to us as children, to lead them out of their childhood into manhood. They were docile and affectionate in the beginning. But they needed your kindness and justice, and a respect in them for the rights we claimed for ourselves, and the rights we had declared always were inherent in all mankind. You preferred force to kindness, and power to justice, and war to peace, and pride to generosity.

You said you would not treat with a man with arms in his hands. You have come, instead, to torture him when he was unarmed and defenseless. Yet you said you would make his conduct the measure of your own; that if he lied to you, you would lie to him; that if he were cruel to you, you would be cruel to him; that if he were a savage, you would be a savage also. You held an attitude toward him which you hold to no strong or to no civilized power. You decorate an officer for the capture of Aguinaldo by treachery, and the next week ratify The Hague convention and denounce such action, and classify it with poisoning and breaking of faith.

You tell us, Mr. President, that the Philippine people have practiced some cruelties themselves. The investigation has not yet gone far enough to enable you to tell which side began these atrocities. One case which one of the members of the majority of the committee told the Senate the other day was well established by proving that it occurred long before April, 1901, and was so published, far and wide, in the press of this country at that time. I do not learn that there was any attempt to investigate it, either by the War Department or by Congress, until the beginning of the present session of Congress. But suppose they did begin it. Such things are quite likely to occur when weakness is fighting for its rights against strength. Is their conduct any excuse for ours? The Philippine people is but a baby in the hands of our Republic. The young athlete, the giant, the Hercules, the Titan, forces a fight upon a boy 10 years old and then blames the little fellow because he hits below the belt.

I see that my enthusiastic friend from North Carolina seeks to break the force of these revelations by saying that they are only what some Americans are wont to do at home. It is benevolent assimilation over again. It is just what the junior Senator from Indiana predicted. He thought we should conduct affairs in the Philippine Islands so admirably that we should pattern our domestic administration on that model. But did I understand that the Senator from North Carolina proposes, if his charge against the Democrats there is true, to make North Carolina a howling wilderness, or to burn populous towns of 10,000 people, to get the people of North Carolina into reconcentration camps, and to slay every male child over 10 years old? I know nothing about the truth of the Senator's charges. They have never been investigated by the Senate so far. We had some painful investigations years ago by committees in this body and of the other House, notably one of which the senior Senator from Colorado was chairman. But I never heard that you undertook to apply to Americans the methods which, if not justified, at least are sought to be extenuated, in the Philippine Islands.

Mr. President, if the stories which come to me in private from officers of the Army and from the kindred and friends of soldiers are to be trusted; if the evidence which seems to be just beginning before the Senate Committee can be trusted, there is nothing in the conduct of Spain in Cuba worse than the conduct of Americans in the Philippine Islands. If this evidence be true, and nobody is as yet ready to deny it, and Spain were strong enough, she would have the right to-morrow to wrest the Philippine Islands from our grasp on grounds as good, if not better, than those which justified us when we made war upon her. The United States is a strong and powerful country—the strongest and most powerful on earth, as we love to think. But it is the first time in the history of this people for nearly three hundred years when we had to appeal to strength and not to the righteousness of our cause to maintain our position in a great debate of justice and liberty.

Gentlemen tell us that the Filipinos are savages, that they have inflicted torture, that they have dishonored our dead and outraged the living. That very likely may be true. Spain said the same thing of the Cubans. We have made the same charges against our own countrymen in the disturbed days after the war. The reports of committees and the evidence in the documents in our library are full of them. But who ever heard before of an American gentleman, or an American, who took as a rule for his own conduct the conduct of his antagonist, or who claimed that the Republic should act as savages because she had savages to deal with? I had supposed, Mr. President, that the question, whether a gentleman shall lie or murder or torture, depended on his sense of his own character, and not on his opinion of his victim. Of all the miserable sophistical shifts which have attended this wretched business from the beginning, there is none more miserable than this.

You knew—men are held to know what they ought to know in morals and in the conduct of States—and you knew that this people would resist you; you knew you were to have a war; you knew that if they were civilized, so far as they were civilized and like you, the war would be conducted after the fashion of civilized warfare, and that so far as they were savage the war would be conducted on their part after the fashion of savage warfare; and you knew also that if they resisted and held out, their soldiers would be tempted to do what they have done, and would yield to that temptation.

And I tell you, Mr. President, that if you do not disregard the lessons of human nature thus far, and do not retrace your steps and set an example of another conduct, you will have and those who follow you will have a like experience hereafter. You may pacify this country on the surface; you may make it a solitude, and call it peace; you may burn towns; you may exterminate populations; you may kill the children or the boys over 10, as Herod slew the firstborn of the Israelites. But the volcano will be there. You will not settle this thing in a generation or in a century or in ten centuries, until it is settled right. It never will be settled right until you look for your counselors to George Washington and Thomas Jefferson and John Quincy Adams and Abraham Lincoln, and not to the reports of the War Department.

There is much more I should like to say, but I have spoken too long already. I have listened to what many gentlemen have said—gentlemen whom I love and honor—with profound sorrow. They do over again in the Senate what Burke complained of to the House of Commons.

"In order to prove that the Americans have no right to their liberties we are every day endeavoring to subvert the maxims which preserve the whole spirit of our own. To prove that the Americans ought not to be free we are obliged to depreciate the value of freedom itself; and we never seem to gain a paltry advantage over them in debate without attacking some of those principles or deriding some of those feelings for which our ancestors have shed their blood."

I wish to cite another weighty maxim from Burke:

"America, gentlemen say, is a noble object—it is an object well worth fighting for. Certainly it is, if fighting a people be the best way of gaining them. Gentlemen in this respect will be led to their choice of means by their complexions and their habits. Those who understand the military art will of course have some predilection for it. Those who wield the thunder of the state may have more confidence in the efficacy of arms. But I confess, possibly for the want of this knowledge, my opinion is much more in favor of prudent management than of force— considering force not as an odious, but a feeble instrument, for preserving a people so numerous, so active, so growing, so spirited as this, in a profitable connection with us."

"There is nothing," says Gibbon, the historian of the Decline and Fall of the Roman Empire, "more adverse to nature and reason than to hold in obedience remote countries and foreign nations in opposition to their inclination and interest. A torrent of barbarians may pass over the earth, but an extensive empire must be supported by a refined system of policy and oppression; in the center, an absolute power, prompt in action and rich in resources; a swift and easy communication with the extreme parts; fortifications to check the first effort of rebellion; a regular administration to protect and punish; and a well-disciplined army to inspire fear, without provoking discontent and despair."

Lord Elgin, Governor-General of India and formerly Governor-General of Canada, well known and highly esteemed in the United States, declared as the result of his experience in the East: "It is a terrible business, however—this living among inferior races. I have seldom from man or woman since I came to the East heard a sentence which was reconcilable with the hypothesis that Christianity had ever come into the world. Detestation, contempt, ferocity, vengeance, whether Chinamen or Indians be the object. One moves among them with perfect indifference, treating them not as dogs, because in that case one would whistle to them and pat them, but as machines with which one can have no communion or sympathy. When the passions of fear and hatred are ingrafted on this indifference, the result is frightful—an absolute callousness as to the sufferings of the objects of those passions, which must be witnessed to be understood and believed."

The glowing narrative of Macaulay, the eloquence of Burke and Sheridan have made the crimes committed in India under the rule of Warren Hastings familiar to mankind. Yet I believe the verdict of history has acquitted Hastings, as the tribunal that tried him acquitted him. He was dismissed, exculpated, from the bar of the House of Lords, and decorated. He was sworn of the Privy Council and received at court. A large purse was made up for him by the East India Company. Yet no man doubts the truth of Burke's terrible indictment. He was acquitted because England, and not he, was the criminal. When England undertook to assert her rule in India what followed was the inevitable consequence of the decision.

Lord Erskine, the foremost advocate who ever spoke the English tongue on English soil, placed with unerring sagacity the defense of Hastings on this ground alone. He admitted that Hastings, in ruling India, "may, and must, have offended against the laws of God and nature." "If he was the faithful viceroy of an empire wrested in blood from the people to whom God and nature had given it, he may and must have preserved that unjust dominion over timorous and abject nations by a terrifying superiority." "A government having no root in consent or affection, no foundation in similarity of interests, nor support from any one principle which cements men in society together could only be upheld by alternate stratagem and force." Erskine adds: "To be governed at all, they must be governed with a rod of iron; and our empire in the East would long since have been lost to Great Britain if civil skill and military prowess had not united their efforts to support an authority which Heaven never gave—by means which it never can sanction."

Mr. President, this is the eternal law of human nature. You may struggle against it, you may try to escape it, you may persuade yourself that your intentions are benevolent, that your yoke will be easy and your burden will be light, but it will assert itself again and again. Government without the consent of the governed—an authority which Heaven never gave—can only be supported by means which Heaven never can sanction.

The American people have got this one question to answer. They may answer it now; they can take ten years, or twenty years, or a generation, or a century to think of it. But it will not down. They must answer it in the end—Can you lawfully buy with money, or get by brute force of arms, the right to hold in subjugation an unwilling people, and to impose on them such constitution as you, and not they, think best for them?

We have answered this question a good many times in the past. The fathers answered it in 1776, and founded the Republic upon their answer, which has been the corner stone. John Quincy Adams and James Monroe answered it again in the Monroe doctrine, which John Quincy Adams declared was only the doctrine of the consent of the governed. The Republican party answered it when it took possession of the forces of Government at the beginning of the most brilliant period in all legislative history. Abraham Lincoln answered it when, on that fatal journey to Washington in 1861, he announced that the doctrine of the consent of the governed was the cardinal doctrine of his political creed, and declared, with prophetic vision, that he was ready to be assassinated for it if need be. You answered it again yourselves when you said that Cuba, who had no more title than the people of the Philippine Islands had to their independence, of right ought to be free and independent.

The question will be answered again hereafter. It will be answered soberly and deliberately and quietly as the American people are wont to answer great questions of duty. It will be answered, not in any turbulent assembly, amid shouting and clapping of hands and stamping of feet, where men do their thinking with their heels and not with their brains. It will be answered in the churches and in the schools and in the colleges; and it will be answered in fifteen million American homes, and it will be answered as it has always been answered. It will be answered right.

A famous orator once imagined the nations of the world uniting to erect a column to Jurisprudence in some stately capital. Each country was to bring the name of its great jurist to be inscribed on the side of the column, with a sentence stating what he and his country through him had done toward establishing the reign of law in justice for the benefit of mankind.

Rome said, "Here is Numa, who received the science of law from the nymph Egeria in the cavern and taught its message to his countrymen. Here is Justinian, who first reduced law to a code, made its precepts plain, so that all mankind could read it, and laid down the rules which should govern the dealing of man with man in every transaction of life."

France said, "Here is D'Aguesseau, the great chancellor, to whose judgment seat pilgrims from afar were wont to repair to do him reverence."

England said, "Here is Erskine, who made it safe for men to print the truth, no matter what tyrant might dislike to read it."

Virginia said, "Here is Marshall, who breathed the vital principle into the Constitution, infused into it, instead of the letter that killeth, the spirit that maketh alive, and enabled it to keep State and nation each in its appointed bounds, as the stars abide in their courses."

I have sometimes fancied that we might erect here in the capital of the country a column to American Liberty which alone might rival in height the beautiful and simple shaft which we have erected to the fame of the Father of the Country. I can fancy each generation bringing its inscription, which should recite its own contribution to the great structure of which the column should be but the symbol.

The generation of the Puritan and the Pilgrim and the Huguenot claims the place of honor at the base. "I brought the torch of Freedom across the sea. I cleared the forest. I subdued the savage and the wild beast. I laid in Christian liberty and law the foundations of empire."

The next generation says: "What my fathers founded I build-

ed. I left the seashore to penetrate the wilderness. I planted
schools and colleges and courts and churches."

Then comes the generation of the great colonial day. "I
stood by the side of England on many a hard-fought field. I
helped humble the power of France. I saw the lilies go down
before the lion at Louisburg and Quebec. I carried the cross
of St. George in triumph in Martinique and the Havana. I
knew the stormy pathways of the ocean. I followed the whale
from the Arctic to the Antarctic seas, among tumbling mountains of ice and under equinoctial heat, as the great English orator said, 'No sea not vexed by my fisheries; no climate not witness to my toils.' "

Then comes the generation of the Revolutionary time. "I
encountered the power of England. I declared and won the
Independence of my country. I placed that declaration on the
eternal principles of justice and righteousness which all mankind
have read, and on which all mankind will one day stand. I affirmed the dignity of human nature and the right of the people
to govern themselves. I devised the securities against popular
haste and delusion which made that right secure. I created the
Supreme Court and the Senate. For the first time in history I
made the right of the people to govern themselves safe, and established institutions for that end which will endure forever."

The next generation says, "I encountered England again. I
vindicated the right of an American ship to sail the seas the wide
world over without molestation. I made the American sailor as
safe at the ends of the earth as my fathers had made the American farmer safe in his home. I proclaimed the Monroe doctrine
in the face of the Holy Alliance, under which sixteen republics
have joined the family of nations. I filled the Western Hemisphere with Republics from the Lakes to Cape Horn, each controlling its own destiny in safety and in honor."

Then comes the next generation: "I did the mighty deeds
which in your younger years you saw and which your fathers
told. I saved the Union. I put down the rebellion. I freed the
slave. I made of every slave a freeman, and of every freeman a
citizen, and of every citizen a voter."

Then comes another who did the great work in peace, in which
so many of you had an honorable share: "I kept the faith. I

paid the debt. I brought in conciliation and peace instead of
war. I secured in the practice of nations the great Doctrine of
Expatriation. I devised the Homestead system. I covered the
prairie and the plain with happy homes and with mighty States.
I crossed the continent and joined together the seas with my
great railroads. I declared the manufacturing independence of
America, as my fathers affirmed its political independence. I
built up our vast domestic commerce. I made my country the
richest, freest, strongest, happiest people on the face of the
earth."

And now what have we to say? What have we to say? Are
we to have a place in that honorable company? Must we engrave
on that column, "We repealed the Declaration of Independence.
We changed the Monroe doctrine from a doctrine of eternal
righteousness and justice, resting on the consent of the governed,
to a doctrine of brutal selfishness, looking only to our own advantage. We crushed the only republic in Asia. We made war
on the only Christian people in the East. We converted a war
of glory to a war of shame. We vulgarized the American flag.
We introduced perfidy into the practice of war. We inflicted
torture on unarmed men to extort confession. We put children
to death. We established reconcentrado camps. We devasted
provinces. We baffled the aspirations of a people for liberty."

No, Mr. President. Never! Never! Other and better counsels will yet prevail. The hours are long in the life of a great
people. The irrevocable step is not yet taken.

Let us at least have this to say: We too have kept the faith
of the Fathers. We took Cuba by the hand. We delivered her
from her age-long bondage. We welcomed her to the family of
nations. We set mankind an example never beheld before of
moderation in victory. We led hesitating and halting Europe
to the deliverance of their beleaguered ambassadors in China.
We marched through a hostile country—a country cruel and barbarous—without anger or revenge. We returned benefit for
injury, and pity for cruelty. We made the name of America
beloved in the East as in the West. We kept faith with the
Philippine people. We kept faith with our own history. We
kept our national honor unsullied. The flag which we received
without a rent we handed down without a stain.

CHAUNCEY M. DEPEW

THE PANAMA CANAL

SPEECH IN THE UNITED STATES SENATE, JANUARY 14, 1904,
ON THE CONSTRUCTION OF A CANAL ACROSS
THE ISTHMUS OF PANAMA

[The speech printed below was part of the debate on the ratification
of the Hay-Varilla Treaty with the Republic of Panama, by which
the United States acquired jurisdiction over the Canal Zone, and the
right to construct the canal. The independence of Panama from Colombia was proclaimed on November 3, 1903, and the new republic was
recognized by the United States on November 6. On November 18
the representatives of the two countries signed the treaty in Washington, D. C., and Panama ratified it on December 2. Meanwhile,
American troops were in Panama, and American warships in her harbors. Explaining the procedure, President Roosevelt afterwards
said: "If I had followed traditional, conservative methods, I would
have submitted a dignified state paper of probably two hundred pages
to Congress and the debate on it would have been going on yet; but
I took the Canal Zone and let Congress debate; while the debate
goes on the Canal does also." The immediate occasion for Mr. Depew's
speech was a Senate resolution introduced by Senator Gorman, calling upon President Roosevelt for information concerning the relations
between the United States and Colombia. The debate on the treaty
lasted until February 23, 1904, when the Senate advised the President
to ratify the treaty. This he did on February 25, and on the next day
ratifications were exchanged in Washington, and the treaty proclaimed.]

Mr. President: The most interesting and vitally important
question to the American people is the construction of the Isth-
mian Canal. There is absolute unanimity of opinion for the
work to be begun, prosecuted and completed at the earliest possible moment. The opponents of the treaty are really aiding the
enemies of the canal. If there ever has been a concert of action
among any great railway corporations to defeat this most beneficent work of commerce and civilization, I am not aware of
it; but if such a combination does exist, then its allies and its
most efficient assistants are to be found among those who, un-

der any device or excuse, are endeavoring to defeat the treaty
with the Republic of Panama.

Piercing the Isthmus of Darien is no new idea. It has appealed to statesmen for hundreds of years, and now, four centuries after Columbus sailed along the coast of the Isthmus trying to find the opening which would let him into the Pacific, the
completion of his dream is near at hand. Charles V. was the
ablest ruler of his century. The power of Spain under him and
his successor included Cuba and Porto Rico, territories on the
Gulf of Mexico and the Pacific Ocean, and the Isthmus of
Darien and the Philippine Islands. His knowledge of geography was limited because of the meager discoveries of his period, but he did see that here was an opportunity for an Eastern
and Western empire by connecting the two oceans, and set about
energetically to accomplish the task.

Before his plans had matured he was succeeded by his son,
that phenomenal bigot and tyrant, Philip II. He declared that
it was sacrilege to undo what God had created, and therefore
wicked to cut through the mountains for a canal. For three
hundred years the wall of superstition built by this monarch
prevented the union of the oceans. The initiative was with the
United States, whose people are opposed to the opinions of King
Philip, and believe the duty of man is to exploit, develop, utilize, and improve the waste places of the world, the air, the water
and the earth. As early as the Administration of John Quincy
Adams, our statesmen saw the necessity for this work. It was
encouraged by almost every succeeding Administration. It
originated the American idea of Henry Clay and has always
been a bulwark of the Monroe Doctrine.

In the past fifty years our Government has repeatedly asserted the necessity for the canal, and that it would look with extreme hostility upon its being built, or owned, or dominated by
a foreign power. The discovery of gold in California and the
rush of our people to the Pacific Coast in 1849 opened the eyes
of all Americans to the necessity of the United States controlling this highway between our Eastern and Western States.
We made treaties with Great Britain to encourage private enterprise to do this work, and to prevent any European power
from undertaking it. Our necessity was so great that we per-

mitted without protest the French Canal Company of De Lesseps to proceed with their work. After the failure of that company and of private enterprises on the Nicaragua route, the duty of our Government became clear.

When we succeeded to the inheritance of Charles V., by the acquisition of Porto Rico, by the establishment of a friendly republic in Cuba and by the possession of California on our Pacific Coast, of Hawaii midway and the Philippines at the gates of the Orient, the responsibility upon us to construct this canal was as much greater than it was upon that monarch as has been the growth of commerce and civilization from the fifteenth to the nineteenth century. For national defense, as well as national unity, there must be an unbroken line of coast from the northernmost limits of Maine to the northernmost limits of Alaska. For the employment of our capital and our labor in the ever-increasing surplus of our productions, we must reach, with the advantages which the canal would give us, the republics of South America and the countless millions in the old countries across the Pacific.

The Republic of Colombia recognizing this need sent here a diplomatic representative carrying a proposition. With scarcely any modification on our part this tentative agreement presented by Colombia was embodied in the Hay-Herran Treaty. In that instrument was the most generous treatment of all interests to be acquired. We were to buy the plant and the properties of the French Company for $40,000,000. We were to give to Colombia $10,000,000 for a franchise which would be of incalculable benefit to that country. While we were permitted to exercise certain powers within a zone, six miles wide, for the protection of the canal, yet the sovereignty over that strip was recognized in every line of the treaty as remaining with Colombia. This concession was a weakness in the treaty for our interests.

The excuse for this concession was that our power was so great our interests could never be imperiled. There is no enlightened government in the world whose financial condition is not strong enough to construct through its territories a public improvement of such vast moment to its people, which would not grant freely the right to build to any company or govern-

ment which would spend their millions to confer upon its citizens commerce, trade, industries, and development. This Colombian treaty, agreed to by the President, approved by the Secretary of State, and ratified by the Senate of the United States,
was carried back to Bogota by the Colombian minister. Then
began upon the stage of that capital a drama of unequaled interest, whether we look upon it as tragedy, comedy or opera
bouffe. Marroquin, the Vice-president, had three years before,
by a revolution, imprisoned the President, suspended the constitution, established martial law and begun ruling as dictator.

After many revolts against his authority, in a final revolution
he defeated the liberals in a great battle, and they fled from the
field, leaving upon it 7,000 of their dead. Marroquin was now
absolute master of the constitution, the laws, the lives, and the
property of the people of Colombia. He evidently proposed
this treaty to secure $10,000,000 from the United States Gov-
ernment. He wanted money, and ten millions in gold, reckoned
by the value of Colombian currency, would be about fifty millions in that Republic. But the speed and alacrity with which
his offer was accepted opened his mind to visions of boundless
wealth. He certainly developed, in his effort to compass these
riches, Machiavellian statesmanship of a high order.

He declared the constitution operative, ordered an election
and summoned a Congress. He had the army and absolute
power; he controlled the machinery of elections, and brought
to the capital his own representatives. He was in a position at
any moment to again suspend the constitution, prorogue Congress or send them to jail. But he said, "This is my treaty,
which I sent up to Washington when I was the government,
which the United States has agreed to, and there must be some
excuse which will appeal to the powers at Washington for more
money. I must create an opposition to my government." So
he granted for the first time in three years a restricted liberty to
the press, he liberated the editors and permitted the confiscated
newspapers to resume. The "cue" given to them was to assail
the treaty and the United States. This was to create the impression that there was a violent opposition, in a country where only
five per cent. of the people can read, against the Hay-Herran

settlement. Next he created an opposition to the Government in Congress.

The orators to whom this rôle was assigned, with all the tropical luxuriance of Latin eloquence, denounced this infamous agreement, this frightful surrender of the rights and interests of Colombia. Marroquin, as Vice-president, presiding over the Senate, listened with pleasure to these fusilades upon his own statesmanship prearranged by himself. Every citizen of Colombia who had any intelligence, and every member of either House of that Congress knew that Marroquin had but to lift his finger and the vote for the treaty would be unanimous. This drama, accurately reported by our Minister Beaupré to the Secretary of State, closed with Vice-President Marroquin saying to us substantially: "You see the trouble I have in this uncontrollable opposition. Of course I want to carry out my treaty, but unless concessions are made, not to me, but to the pride and sentiments of my country, I am helpless. But if the United States will give $10,000,000 more, I think I can satisfy this opposition; at least I will risk my popularity, reputation and power in the effort."

The answer of the United States was an unmistakable and emphatic no. That answer has the unanimous approval of the public sentiment of our country. The Vice-president then said to the French company, "If you will pay that $10,000,000 extra out of your $40,000,000, we will ratify the treaty." The French company rejected the proposition. Then both the minister of Great Britain and the minister of Germany were approached to see whether a "dicker" could not be arranged and a sort of auction set up, with Great Britain, Germany and the United States as the bidders. The folly of this proposition was in its violation of the Monroe Doctrine by a Republic which had been many times its beneficiary, a Republic which now has quarrels upon its hands with Great Britain and France because of outrages committed upon the citizens of those countries, which would lead to summary and drastic measures of reprisals except for the Monroe Doctrine.

No better illustration of the understanding by the European governments of the sanctity of this article of American international law has been shown of late than this action of the representatives of these powers. No stronger proofs have been given of the interest of every great commercial nation in the construction of this canal in the interest of commerce and civilization and its construction and control by the United States. These patriotic efforts of the Vice-president and dictator to secure more money by many methods of holdup were discouraging, but he did not despair. He had received an emphatic negative from the United States, had been refused by the French Panama Canal Company, and turned down by Great Britain and Germany. But he had been trained in many revolutions where money had to be raised by other processes than the orderly ones of assessments and taxation upon all the people and properties of the country upon an equal basis. His resourceful genius was equal to the occasion.

He had called together his Congress, to carry out his programme of exploiting this asset of Colombia for many times more than the price at which he had agreed to sell it. Then occurred to him an idea of high finance which ought to make the most imaginative and audacious of our promoters blush at their incapacity. The Panama Canal Company had received from him while dictator upon the payment of a million dollars and 5,000,000 francs at par of stock of the new company, a concession which ran until 1910. The old concession expired in October, 1904, and for this the French company had paid Colombia 12,000,000 francs. With every concession, where vast amounts of money had been expended in good faith and large sums paid for the franchise, there are always equities to the defaulting party, but the new scheme dismissed the equities, the extension of the charter and the million dollars consideration paid, which had been spent.

The Congress, to the tearful regret and over the wishes of the dictator and Vice-president, rejected the treaty by an almost unanimous vote and then adjourned. But Congressmen talk after adjournment. It is their habit in all countries, and the Senators and Representatives who participated in this picturesque drama of national aggrandizement said that the object of the adjournment was to wait until the old concession of the Panama Canal Company had expired, in October, then to recall Congress in extraordinary session in November, declare the concession canceled and seize upon the property of the French Canal Company. Then, they said, we will offer to the United States the properties of the French Canal Company for the $40,000,000 which are to be paid that corporation and the ten million which are coming to us. "Of course," they argued, "the United States will be quite willing to enter upon an agreement of this kind, because the sum which they pay will be the same in amount as they have agreed upon under the terms of the Hay-Herran Treaty and the contract with the French Canal Company."

There are two considerations in this choice bit of financiering which seemed never to have occurred to the statesman who guides the destinies of Colombia and the orators whom he placed in various rôles to play their instructed parts. The first was an utter indifference or ignorance of the fact that the United States had a national conscience. We are a commercial nation. Our people are trained to all the refinements of business obligations and all the reciprocal relations of contracts. Much as we want the canal, we never could have taken it by becoming a partner in this highway robbery of the property of the citizens of France. The Panama Canal scheme has been unpopular in France for many years, and French statesmen and politicians have been afraid to have any connections with it.

It is because of the millions of dollars lost by the French people in the investment and the scandals caused by the corrupt use, by the officers of the company, of much of the money subscribed. But here would be a case which no government could neglect. The French Canal Company, representing its several hundred thousands of French citizens, could say to the French Government, "Here are equities of great value, and here is a property for which we have paid our money that has been arbitrarily confiscated." Then we would have had upon our hands difficulties, compared with which the present ones are infinitesimal. We could not deny the justice of the demand of the French Government to land its army upon the Isthmus and enforce its claims. Here again the shrewd and able leader of Colombia—for he is both shrewd and able—counted first upon the cupidity of the United States to become a party to this robbery of the French, and then to the assertion of the Monroe

Doctrine to prevent France from demanding and maintaining the rights of her citizens.

Colombia, after failing to confiscate the French property in the canal, now appeals as a stockholder in the French Canal Company, to prohibit the transfer of the canal property to the United States without the consent of Colombia. France has recognized the Republic of Panama. In so doing she is committed to the transfer to the new sovereignty of all public property within its jurisdiction. The Colombian Government has no better claim to the Panama Canal, or jurisdiction over it, than Great Britain has over Bunker Hill. The same rule and construction will apply in case Colombia should, as has been suggested here, commence an action in New York against the Panama Railroad Company, a New York corporation, to compel a continuance of the subsidy of $250,000 a year to Colombia, instead of to Panama.

Up to this time, it will be said, no matter what was the conduct, no matter what the double dealing, no matter what the breaches of faith, no matter what the character of the hold up by the responsible Government of Colombia, that Government could act as it pleased upon granting rights, franchises, and properties within its own jurisdiction. This leads us at once to the new phase of the problem presented by the organization of the Republic of Panama. Panama was one of the first settlements made in the Western Hemisphere. After the city of Panama had been raided, robbed, and burned by Morgan and his pirates it was moved about seven miles, to the present site. It was the depot for hundreds of years for the commerce going between the Atlantic and Pacific oceans. The province was one of the last to throw off the yoke of Spain.

When General Bolivar succeeded in the revolution which he organized, he formed a loose-jointed republic out of the States of Colombia, Venezuela, Ecuador, and Panama. There was little in common, territorially, commercially, or industrially between these States. After a few years Venezuela seceded and formed a separate government. Three years afterwards Ecuador did the same. Panama remained to all intents and purposes an independent Republic. In the new arrangement which was made Panama joined Colombia under a constitution which distinctly recognized the right of secession for any cause, and bound the several parts only to federal contributions according to their judgment. It was almost a counterpart of the Articles of Federation in our own country which were succeeded by the Federal Constitution. This relation continued practically from 1861 to 1886.

Then a dictator arose by the name of Nunez and got control of the army and navy and all the resources of the country. He suspended the constitution, the Congress, and the laws, and governed the country according to his own despotic will for a number of years. He subjugated the several States, overturned their sovereignty and forced them to become mere departments of the centralized power of Bogota. He adopted a system, under a so-called constitution, by which they were ruled as Spain governed Cuba—by governors, who were really captain-generals, with absolute power.

His enemies in the several States, and the patriots who resisted this suppression of liberty, were punished by imprisonment, exile or execution. From the time of this arbitrary destruction of the rights and liberties of the independent State of Panama that Republic has been in a continued condition of unrest and revolt. The duties collected at its ports of Panama and Colon were transmitted to Bogota. The taxes levied all went to Bogota. Of the subsidy of $250,000 a year paid by the Panama Railroad Company, $225,000 went to Bogota and $25,000 to the governor of Panama, appointed by the President of Colombia, to distribute in his judgment in the Department of Panama. Though Panama had only one-fifteenth of the population of the Republic, she contributed a large part of its revenues, but under this arbitrary constitution to which Panama never assented and never accepted, a constitution imposed by force and maintained by an army and an alien governor, she received during all these years practically no moneys for highways, for development, for education or for any of the needs of a live and growing State.

It is an interesting and picturesque view of the situation that the obligation of the United States to keep free transit across the Isthmus has worked both ways with Colombia. There have been many revolts in Panama in the effort on the part of tyrannized, plundered and patriotic citizens to regain their liberties and rights. Every one of them has been sternly and ruthlessly suppressed by the central Government at Bogota. The success of the Bogotan Government was due in nearly every instance to the fact that the United States would not permit interruption of transit across the Isthmus. When the revolutionists would have seized the railroad which connected the oceans, the United States was the ally of the Bogotan Government to keep that open.

The result was that it was easy for the Government forces every time to put down a rebellion because the recruits of the State could not be gathered into a successful army. But lo! the working of this provision the other way. Citizens of Panama in November of this year, without a dissenting voice, reasserted the sovereignty of the State, which they had never surrendered, and proclaimed a Republic. The Colombian army joined the revolution. With the military forces of the Bogotan Government enlisting under the flag of the new Republic, the authority of Panama was complete throughout all its borders. When, therefore, some time after the Republic had been established and was in working order, and had at Panama its army, a Colombian army landed at Colon for the purpose of invasion and battle, the United States took toward it the same position that it had toward the revolutionists in the many efforts made by them for the freedom of Panama.

Our Government simply said to these soldiers, "You can not take possession of this railroad and interrupt traffic across the Isthmus. You can not engage in a battle or a series of battles which would stop communication for an indefinite period." At this point occurs an episode of which I find no parallel in ancient or modern history. The generals of the invading army said to the authorities of the new Republic, "We are here to suppress you, arrest you, carry you prisoners to Bogota and overthrow the Republic, but what will you give us to quit?" The sum of $8,000 was paid to the general, $5,000 for the officers and $3,000 for the men, and the invading army sailed away with the proud consciousness of having become the possessors of a part of the assets of the new Republic.

The story of the rule of Panama by these arbitrary satraps,

sent down from Bogota, reads like the history of the rule of a Roman proconsul or the story of the methods of a Turkish governor. Arbitrary arrests and imprisonments without trial were common. Arbitrary assessments of shopkeepers and people of property were of everyday occurrence. These victims have been afraid heretofore to speak, but now the newspapers are filled with their stories. The price of life and liberty, after forcible seizure of person and property, was dependent upon the amount that the citizen disgorged. Under this tyrannical rule he was helpless before the courts or upon appeal to the central Government. Panama had as much right to revolt as did Greece from Turkey in the early part of the nineteenth century or Bulgaria in the latter part, and even more, for she had never consented to surrender her sovereignty to Colombia.

The people of Colombia outside of Panama number about 4,000,000, of which 2,000,000 are of Spanish descent and 2,000,000 a mixture of Caucasian, Indian and negro. There are few or no railroads or other highways in the country, there is no system of general education, and dense ignorance prevails. A very small proportion of the people—a few thousand—are educated in the United States or in Europe, and form the governing class. Colombia is separated from Panama by hundreds of miles of mountains and impenetrable forests and swamps, inhabited by hostile Indians. Panama, on the other hand, has every facility, under good government, for a prosperous State. It is about as large as Maine. It has the same agricultural possibilities as the other Central American republics. It is rich in minerals and timber. Great cities, thriving populations and varied industries have always grown along the lines of commercial highways.

While the Panama Canal is being constructed and $150,000,000 spent within the Republic, there will be a wonderful industrial development. When the canal is opened and the commerce of the world is passing to and fro, the population of Panama will speedily rise above the million point. Merchandise of every kind for the supply of the ships sailing through it will bring capital and business talent to the cities on either side and through the interior. Sanitation, which has done so much for Cuba, will make the Isthmus as healthy as any part of the United States. With American ideas and American sovereignty over the large strip between the two seas, and American influence and example, schoolhouses will dot the land and the people become educated to an appreciation of their liberties and the proper exercise of them and of their marvelously favorable commercial, fiscal and industrial position.

But, it is said, the position of the United States in recognizing the Republic of Panama is a reversal of our national position on the subject of secession. I can not conceive of the argument by which comparison is made between the States of the American Commonwealth and Panama and Colombia. One hundred and seventeen years ago our forefathers saw that a nation could not be held together by such a rope of sand as the Articles of Federation. They met in convention, not under the rule of a dictator, not under the guidance of an autocrat, but as the accredited representatives of the people of the various States. When their labors were completed the country read, and the world was astonished by, the marvelous instrument which they had prepared.

The opening sentence of this great charter tells the story of the perpetuity of our national life: "We, the people of the United States, in order to form a more perfect union, establish justice, insure domestic tranquillity, provide for the common defense, promote the general welfare and secure the blessings of liberty to ourselves and our posterity, do ordain and establish this Constitution for the United States of America." For eighty years the national sovereignty was questioned only in debate. To preserve the institution of slavery, which was alien to our Declaration of Independence and a stain upon the spirit of our institutions, the Civil War was inaugurated. To-day in every part of the country public sentiment is unanimous of its approval of the verdict which came from the arbitrament of arms. Our Union is sustained by a continued series of decisions of our highest court, by the judgment of our Presidents and Congresses and by the results of war, and, unimpaired by the passions of the conflict, will continue on forever. It is sacrilege to compare this majestic and impregnable fabric of government with the position of Panama in the Republic of Colombia.

In 1886 Mr. V. O. King, United States minister to Colombia, in a dispatch to Mr. Bayard, Secretary of State, tells precisely how the Colombian constitution was formed. He says:

"At the close of the late revolution President Nunez, whose term of office had then nearly expired and whose reelection was forbidden by the constitution then in force, issued a proclamation annulling that instrument and declaring an interregnum in the Government. He appointed provisional governors in all of the nine states, and directed them to nominate two delegates each, who, together, should constitute a national council to convene at the capital."

And this is the convention which is compared with that which formed our Constitution!

"On assembling in November, 1885, the first acts of this body were to ratify the conduct of Doctor Nunez and to confirm his appointments. It then elected him as chief magistrate of the nation for the term of six years, and proceeded to formulate a *projet* of fundamental principles for a new constitution to be submitted to the corporate vote of the municipal boards of aldermen throughout the country. Upon canvassing the returns of the council"—this council of his own—"declared a majority of such votes to be in favor of the new constitution, and thereupon proceeded to elaborate the instrument that is herewith submitted, which, from the number, fullness, and precision of the precepts enunciated, has left but little of the machinery to be devised by the executive or legislative power."

It will thus be seen that President Nunez, who was both a usurper and dictator, arbitrarily annulled the constitution under which Panama consented to become a part of the Republic of Colombia, retaining, however, her entire sovereignty and right of secession. The tremendous difference between the formation of our Constitution and that of Colombia in 1886 is in the fact that this so-called convention, which framed the constitution destructive of the State, was composed of the instruments of the dictator, appointed by himself, and that neither in the election of delegates to the convention nor the ratifying of the treaty did the people of Panama or their representatives have any voice whatever.

Panama, an independent State, robbed by armies of her liberties, tyrannically and arbitrarily governed without her consent, suffering under intolerable tyranny and threatened with the confiscation of a public improvement upon which depended her existence, simply retakes, and demonstrates her ability to hold, the sovereignty of which she had been despoiled. But, say the critics of the President, the officers of the United States inaugurated this rebellion and ships were dispatched to aid the revolt before it was ever intended. No one doubts that it was the duty of the President to keep the highway open across the Isthmus. No one doubts that if the rights of American citizens were in peril because of revolution or anarchy the United States must have a force on the spot sufficient for their protection. The dispatches of Minister Beaupré are illuminating on this subject.

The forces of the United States arrived at the Isthmus on November 3. The revolution broke out on November 4. The building of the canal was vital to Panama. Except for the money to be distributed at Bogota for the concession, its construction was of little account to the Republic over the mountains. The delegates from Panama to the Congress were apparently the only independent members of that body. When they arrived on July 5 they immediately notified Vice-President Marroquin that if the treaty was rejected Panama would revolt. This notification was so public that the minister of the United States was enabled to write it to our Government.

On August 17 the treaty was rejected and the representatives from Panama expressed their purpose so emphatically that our minister was able to inform the Secretary of State that they had determined to break loose from the Bogota Government and form an independent republic. Two things are evident: One, Marroquin believed his forces upon the Isthmus were sufficient to prevent the revolt from succeeding. He evidently thought it would be the old process by which the patriots would organize at different places and could not come together without having a conflict along the line of the railroad with the forces of the central Government, that such a conflict would interrupt travel and communication and that the United States would, as

HICKS' SP.A.S.—23

before, prevent the revolutionary army from concentrating or making any headway. It never occurred to him that his own army would go over to the revolutionists, and then he would be outside the breastworks.

It is perfectly plain that these delegates, on returning in August to Panama, were joined by all the leading citizens, and that they had plenty of time between the middle of August and November 4 to perfect their plans for a successful revolution. So the President knew perfectly well by advice from our minister at Bogota, from our naval officers at Panama and Colon and from newspaper reports which were the common property of everyone, that such an uprising would occur as to require of the United States the presence of a force sufficient to protect our citizens and to carry out our treaty obligations.

The farcical character of the action of the Colombian Congress and its complete control by Marroquin, together with the fact that Colombia could not subdue the revolution in Panama without the aid of the United States, are demonstrated by the following dispatch, sent November 6, two days after the revolution in Panama, by our Minister Beaupré:

"Knowing that the revolution has already commenced in Panama, ——— says that if the Government of the United States will land troops to preserve Colombian sovereignty and the transit, if requested by the Colombian chargé d'affaires, this Government will declare martial law, and by virtue of vested constitutional authority, when public order is disturbed, will approve by decree the ratification of the canal treaty as signed; or, if the Government of the United States prefers, will call extra session of Congress and new and friendly members next May to approve the treaty."

Because it was a telegram the name was indicated by a blank. The blank undoubtedly meant Marroquin, for no one else could have made such pledges.

Mr. President, that is an exhibition of arbitrary power, of the confidence of the dictator of his ability to do whatever he pleases, of which I think there is no parallel anywhere. He says, in effect, to the United States: "A revolution has broken out in Panama, my army has gone over to the Republic and I am helpless. Now, if you will put down that revolution at my request I will abandon the claim of $10,000,000 more than agreed to which our Congress made. I will dismiss all pretense that this Congress had any 'power or was other than myself. I will do everything you want. I will suspend the constitution. Then I can do anything and will ratify this treaty—the Hay-Herran treaty—or do any other old thing you may desire; or, if you have constitutional lawyers in the Senate who doubt my ability or' power to act under a suspension of the constitution, I will put the constitution again in force and summon the members of Congress here. Each one of them will do what I tell him, and Congress will ratify the treaty in any form that you. suggest."

Yet our friend the Senator from Nevada [Mr. Newlands] has just eloquently and at great length proved—to his own satisfaction—that war exists between the United States and Colombia; that war exists by the act of the United States landing 42 marines on the Isthmus, when Marroquin had 1,500 soldiers who deserted his standard and 400 others who left for home when their general got $8,000; that war exists between the United States and Colombia when, during all the time from the first telegram of President Roosevelt until now, the Colombian minister has been here, having daily communication with the Secretary of State. When every diplomatic condition which means peace, and continuing peace, exists between the United States and Colombia, the Senator from Nevada says we have war. There must be lurid imaginings among Senators who, instead of living within the limits of the city, where they are in contact with hard facts, reside and muse in the rural outskirts of the capital.

Our diplomatic history bristles with recognitions of de facto governments formed by revolutions. Where the sympathies of our people were with the revolt, Presidents have paid little attention to the possibilities of success or the offensive or defensive means of the revolting provinces or states. The principle of international law that recognition is wholly in the discretion of the power which makes it and is not a cause for war is too elementary to discuss. Our position with Cuba went far beyond this. We warned the Spanish Government to get out of Cuba when there was no war between us simply because of intolerable internal conditions on that island. We finally drove the Spanish army out of Cuba and then governed it for two years. We refused to let Cuba recognize the Cuban debt, the bonds of which had been sold in Europe based for security upon Cuban revenues.

Our obligation for forty-eight years to Colombia, to Panama, to our citizens and the world has been to keep communication and transit open and unmolested between the oceans. It is a territorial burden and runs with the land. It binds the United States to keep off the premises all hostile trespassers, whether they are the armies of the great powers of Europe, of Colombia, or of the contiguous people of Panama.

Marroquin, amidst the ruins of his scheme by the successful revolt of Panama, is not discouraged. He rises gaily and hopefully to new efforts. He proposes, notwithstanding his machine Congress has adjourned, to give us now the canal on our own terms if we will suppress the Panama Republic. When that is rejected, he has another resource. It appears in a dispatch in the Washington *Post* of January 10, dated January 8, from Bogota, from Clifford Smythe, former consul at Cartagena, Colombia. Mr. Smythe says he is authorized by President Marroquin to quote him as follows: "The people of Colombia"—that is delightful from Marroquin—"the people of Colombia still hope that actual conflict may be averted through Democratic intervention in the Senate. Personally, I count on the assistance of the Democratic Party and the great American people to save the sacred rights of Colombia, which have been so scandalously wounded."

The trouble with President Marroquin is, in the first place, he does not understand that the Democratic Party is not in a majority in the two Houses of Congress and that it has not the Presidency; he does not understand that it is not likely in the near future to have either; he does not understand that the relations between the Democratic Party and the people are such that if he did understand he would not couple them in the way he has in this authorized dispatch.

Then he does not understand another thing, Mr. President— I say this not to do injustice to the Democratic Party—that the Democratic State of Louisiana has unanimously, by its Legislature, directed its Senators to vote in favor of the ratification of this treaty; that the Democratic State of Mississippi has, through its Legislature, directed its Senators to vote to ratify this treaty; and that in all probability if the other Southern States, who will be more benefited a hundred times over than all the rest of the United States by the construction of this canal, should meet in their Legislatures, they would not stand in the position of saying, "We keep the goods while we denounce the method by which they were secured."

The Republic of Panama had absolute authority over its territory without any pretense of opposition from outside or inside of the Republic at the time of its recognition by our President, and has still. Our Government recognized the Republic of Panama on November 13. Certainly there had been no change in the conditions there when three days afterwards France did the same, nor when eleven days afterwards Austria-Hungary also extended its recognition; nor, still more significant, when, fourteen days afterwards, Germany—most particular and scrupulous about anything occurring on this hemisphere—extended her diplomatic recognition. In less than fifty days sixteen of the powers of the world had established relations with the young Republic. If these old countries—Great Britain, Germany, France, Russia, China, Japan, Sweden and Norway, Belgium, Switzerland, Italy, and Denmark—find the conditions such upon the Isthmus that they can take a step which in the chancelleries of the Old World means so much, surely our younger and more progressive diplomacy has ample excuse for preceding them by a few days.

Now, sir, we had no other hand nor part in this revolution than the example of the American colonies and the successful application of the principles of liberty in the United States, which have created republics and undermined thrones all over the world. The advantages of the treaty with Panama over that with Colombia to the United States are incalculable. Instead of six miles for the canal zone, there are ten on each side of the waterway. Instead of a limited sovereignty, which would necessarily lead to endless complications, this territory is ceded outright and in perpetuity to the United States. At the termini of the canal it is vital that there should be unquestioned jurisdiction of the United States. In this territory the Government has complete authority for three marine leagues from Panama into the Pacific Ocean and three leagues from Colon into the Caribbean Sea. The Republic of Panama surrenders the right to impose port dues or duties of any kind upon ships and goods in transit across the Isthmus. The sole power to impose tolls and collect them rests with the United States.

Every nation and the people of all countries are interested in this great work. There is a unanimity unequaled in history that it should be constructed, operated and owned by the United States. We are distant by 3,000 miles of ocean from Europe. We are not in conflict and can not be embroiled in the jealousies or conflicts of the great 'powers. They trust our honor to keep this waterway inviolate as the highway of the nations. They see that the problem which Columbus sought to solve will so find its solution under the auspices of the United States and it will not be, as it would under the auspices of Charles V., a Spanish canal, nor will it be, as under De Lesseps, a French canal, but for all the purposes of commerce and of intercourse between the East and the West it will be an open sea, subject only to such restrictions as are admitted by all the world necessary for the protection of the waterway or for the protection or defense of the United States.

In the providence of the creation and decay of nations no State ever became independent so completely, so righteously, or so timely as Panama. The hour struck for her when the world was watching the clock. No President ever did a more timely or patriotic act than did President Roosevelt in his recognition and defense of the Republic of Panama.

BOOKER T. WASHINGTON

ABRAHAM LINCOLN

<small>ADDRESS AT THE TWENTY-THIRD ANNUAL DINNER OF THE
REPUBLICAN CLUB OF THE CITY OF NEW YORK,
FEBRUARY 12, 1909 *</small>

[Booker Taliaferro Washington was born of slave parents in the
year 1859, near Hale's Ford, Virginia. After the Civil War he went
to Malden, West Virginia, and worked in the coal mines, meanwhile
attending night school. In 1872, he entered the Hampton Normal and
Agricultural Institute, at Hampton, Virginia, from which he was
graduated in 1875. He taught school in Malden for two years, studied
in Wayland Academy, Washington, D. C., and in 1879 returned to
Hampton Institute as a teacher. In 1881 he was selected by General
S. C. Armstrong, of Hampton, on the application of the citizens of
Tuskegee, Alabama, to start a school for negroes there. During the
first year he was the only instructor and had thirty pupils. His successful founding and development of the Tuskegee Normal and Industrial Institute, of which he was President until his death, made
him a figure of national importance, and his influence was felt throughout the South. In 1900, he organized the National Negro Business
League. Honorary degrees were conferred upon him by Harvard
University and by Dartmouth College. He was an effective writer, his
most noted book being "Up from Slavery," and he was a forceful
public speaker, much in demand. He died on November 14, 1915.]

President Young and Gentlemen: You ask that which he
found a piece of property and turned into a free American citizen to speak to you to-night of Abraham Lincoln. I am not
fitted by ancestry, nor by training, to be your teacher to-night,
for, as I have stated, I was born a slave. My first knowledge
of Abraham Lincoln came in this way: I lay sleeping one
morning on the dirt floor of our slave cabin; I was awakened
by the prayers of my mother kneeling over my bed as I lay
wrapped in a bundle of rags, earnestly praying that one day
Abraham Lincoln might succeed and that one day she and her
boy might be free. You give me the chance, Gentlemen of the

---

* Reprinted by permission from *Addresses Delivered at the Lincoln
Dinner of the Republican Club.* Copyright, 1909.

Republican Club, to celebrate with you and the nation to-night the answer to that prayer. Says the Great Book somewhere, "Though a man die, yet shall he live." If this be true of the ordinary man, how much more is it true of the hero of the hour and the hero of the century, Abraham Lincoln. One hundred years of the life and influence of Lincoln is the story of the struggle, the trials, the triumphs, the success of the people of our complex American civilization. Interwoven into the warp and woof of this story is the moving story of the people of all races and colors in their struggles from weakness to power, from poverty to wealth, from slavery to freedom. Knit into the story of the life of Lincoln also is the story of the success of the nation, and the welding of all creeds, colors and races into one great composite nation, leaving each individual, separate group free to lead and live its own special social life, yet each a part of a great whole. If a man die, shall he live? Answering this question as applied to my race perhaps you expect me to confine my words of appreciation to the great boon that our martyred president conferred upon my race. My undying gratitude and that of ten millions of my race for that, and yet more. To have been the instrument which was used by Providence to confer freedom upon four millions of African slaves, now grown into ten millions of free American citizens, would within itself have brought eternal fame to any name. But, my friends, this is not the only claim that Lincoln has upon our sense of gratitude and our sense of appreciation. To-day by the side of General S. C. Armstrong, and by the side of William Lloyd Garrison, Lincoln lives. In the very highest sense he lives in the present more potently than fifty years ago. If that which is seen is temporal, that which is unseen is eternal. He lives in the thirty-two thousand young men and women of the negro race learning trades and other useful occupations, in the two hundred thousand farms acquired by those that he freed, in the more than four hundred thousand homes built, in the forty-six banks established and ten thousand stores owned, in the five hundred and fifty millions of dollars worth of taxable property in hand, in the twenty-eight thousand public schools with thirty thousand teachers, in the one hundred and seventy industrial schools, colleges and universities, and in the twenty-three thousand churches and twenty-six thousand ministers. But, my friends, above and beyond all this he lives in the steady, unalterable determination of these millions of black citizens to continue to climb the ladder of the highest success, to perfect themselves in the highest usefulness and to perfect themselves year by year in strong, robust American characters. For making all this possible, Lincoln lives to-night. But again, for a higher reason, he lives to-night in every corner of the Republic. To set the physical man free means much; to set the spiritual man free means more, for so often the keeper is on the inside of the prison bars and the prisoner on the outside. As an individual, as grateful as I am to Lincoln for freedom of body, my gratitude is still greater for freedom of soul, the liberty which permits one to live up in that atmosphere where he refuses to permit sectional or racial hatred to drag down and warp and narrow his soul. The signing of the Emancipation Proclamation was a great event, and yet it was but the symbol of another still greater and more momentous. We who celebrate this anniversary should not forget that the same pen that gave freedom to four millions of African slaves at the same time struck the shackles of slavery from the souls of twenty-seven millions of American citizens of another color.

In any country, regardless of what its laws may say, wherever people act upon the principle that the disadvantage of one man is the good of another, there slavery exists. Wherever in any country the whole people feel that the happiness of all is dependent upon the happiness of the weakest individual, there freedom exists. In abolishing slavery Lincoln proclaimed the principle that even in the case of the humblest and lowest of mankind, the welfare of each is still the good of all. In re-establishing in this country the principle that at bottom the interests of humanity and the individual are one, he freed men's souls from spiritual bondage and he freed them to mutual helpfulness. Henceforth no man or no race in the North or in the South need feel constrained to hate or fear his brother. By the same token that Lincoln made America free, he pushed back the boundaries of freedom everywhere, gave the spirit of liberty a wider influence throughout the world and re-established the dignity of man as a man. By the same act that freed my race he said to the civilized and uncivilized world that man everywhere must be free, that man everywhere must be enlightened, and the Lincoln spirit of freedom and fair-play will never cease to spread and grow in power until throughout the world men everywhere shall know the truth and the truth shall make them free.

Lincoln was wise enough to recognize that which is true in the present and true for all time, that in a state of slavery man renders the lowest and most costly form of service to his fellows. In a state of freedom and enlightenment he renders the highest and most helpful form of service. The world is fast learning that of all forms of slavery there is none that is so degrading, that is so hurtful, as that form of slavery which makes one human being to hate another by reason of his race or by reason of his color. One man, my friends, cannot hold another man down in the ditch without remaining down in the ditch with him. When I was a boy I used to have a great reputation for fighting. I could whip every boy with whom I fought and I was careful to maintain that reputation as long as possible, but the people about me did not know how I maintained it. I was always careful in my selection of the boy with whom I fought. I was always sure that he was smaller than I was, weaker than I was. As I grew older I used to take pleasure, as I thought, in getting hold of those little fellows and holding them down in the ditch, but when I grew to manhood I soon learned that when I held those little fellows down in the ditch I had to remain down there with them as long as they remained, and to let them up I had to get up myself.

My friends, one who goes through life with his eyes closed against all that is best in another race is as narrow and as circumscribed as one who fights in battle with one hand tied behind him.

Lincoln was in the truest sense great because he unfettered himself. He climbed up out of the valley where his vision was narrowed and weakened by the fog and miasma onto the mountain top, where in pure and unclouded atmosphere he could see the truth which enabled him to rate all men at their true worth. Growing out of his universal ascent and atmosphere may there crystallize throughout the nation a resolve that on such a mountain the American people will strive to live. We owe then to Lincoln, physical freedom, moral freedom, and yet not all. There is a debt of gratitude which we as individuals, no matter to what race or nation we may belong, must recognize as due to Abraham Lincoln. Not for what he did as Chief Magistrate of a nation, for what he did as a man. In his rise from the most abject poverty and ignorance to a position of the highest usefulness and power, he taught one of the greatest of all lessons. In fighting his own battle from obscurity and squalor he fought the battle of every other individual and every other race that was down, and so helped to pull up every other man that was down, no matter where he lived. People so often forget that by every inch that the lowest man crawls up he makes it easier for every other man to get up. To-day throughout the world, because Lincoln lived and struggled and triumphed, every boy who is ignorant, every boy who is in poverty, every boy who is despised, every boy who is discouraged holds his head a little higher, his heart beats a little faster, his ambition to be something and to do something is a little stronger, because Lincoln blazed the way.

To my own race at this point in its career there are special lessons for us in the life of Abraham Lincoln. In so far as his life emphasizes patience, long-suffering, sincerity, naturalness, dogged determination and courage, courage to avoid the superficial, courage to persist insistently and seek after the substance instead of the shadow, so far as it emphasizes these elements, the character, the life of Lincoln points the road that my race is to travel to success. As a race we are learning more and more, I believe, in an increasing degree, that the best way for us to honor the memory of our great emancipator is in trying to be like him. Like him, the negro should seek to be simple, without bigotry and without ostentation. That is great power, not simplicity. Great men are always simple men, great races are those that strive for simplicity. We, as a race, should, like Lincoln, have moral courage to be what we are and not pretend to be what we are not. We should keep in mind that no one can degrade us except ourselves, and that if we are worthy no influence can defeat us. Like other races we shall meet with obstacles. The negro will often meet with stumbling blocks, often be sorely tried, often be sorely tempted, but he should remember that freedom in its highest and broadest sense has never been a bequest, it is always a conquest. In the final test the success of our race will be in proportion to the service that it renders to the world. In the long run the badge of service is the badge of sovereignty.

With all his other elements of strength, Lincoln possessed in the highest degree, patience, and, as I have said, courage. The highest form of courage is not that which is always exhibited on the battlefield in the midst of the flare of trumpets and the waving of flags. The highest courage is of the Lincoln kind; it is the same kind of courage that is daily manifested by the thousands of young men and young women who are going out from Hampton and Tuskegee and Atlanta, and similar institutions, without thought of salary, without thought of personal comfort, and are giving up their lives in the erection of a school system, the building of schoolhouses, the prolonging of school terms, the teaching of our people how to build decent, clean homes and live honorable, clean lives. And, my friends, those young men and young women who are going out in this simple way are fighting the battles of this country just as truly, just as bravely, as any man who goes out to do battle against a foreign foe.

In paying my tribute of respect to the martyred president I desire to say a word further in behalf of an element of brave and true white men of the South, who, though they thought they saw in Lincoln's policy the ruin of all that they believed in and hoped for, have nevertheless loyally accepted the results of the Civil War and to-day are working with a courage that few people in the North can understand or appreciate to uplift the negro, and thus complete the emancipation which Lincoln began. And here I am almost tempted, my friends, even in this presence, to add that it would require almost as high a degree of courage for men of the type of J. M. L. Curry, John E.

Gordon and Robert E. Lee to accept in the manner and the spirit that they did the results of the Civil War as the courage displayed on the battlefield, by Lincoln, by Grant and Sherman in saving the Republic.

And in this connection, my friends, forgive me for adding this in this presence: I am glad to meet here the Bishop of the City of New York; I am glad to meet here the senator-elect from the great State of Ohio; I am glad to meet the president of your club; I am glad to greet and to shake hands with all the noble men who surround this banquet board, but, my friends, there is one man in this room whom I am glad most of all to meet, and that is the young man who played with me when I was a slave, the grandson of the man who owned my body on a Virginia farm—I refer to my friend, Mr. A. H. Burroughs, whom I met for the first time this week since the day of slavery, and who is now an honored lawyer in your city. How well do I remember that in the days of slavery we played together in my master's yard, and perhaps fought together. But, my friends, I recall also the picture early one morning of the slaves gathering around the master's house and about hearing for the first time the Emancipation Proclamation read to us that declared us free. The same proclamation that declared me a freeman declared my boyhood friend and the grandson of my former owner a free man at the same time.

Lincoln also, my friends, let me add, was a Southern man by birth, but he was one of those white men of whom there is a large and growing class who resented the idea that in order to assert and maintain the superiority of the Anglo-Saxon race it was necessary that another group of human beings should be kept in ignorance. Lincoln was not afraid or ashamed to come in contact with the lowly of all races. His reputation and social standing were not of such a transitory and transparent kind that he was afraid that he would lose them by being kind and just even to a man of dark skin. I always pity from the bottom of my heart any man who feels that somebody else must be kept down and kept in ignorance in order that he may appear great by comparison. It requires no courage for a strong man to keep a weak man down. Lincoln lives to-day because he had a courage that made him refuse to hate the man at the North or the man at the South when they did not agree with him. He had the courage, as well as the patience and foresight, to suffer the silence to be misunderstood, to be abused, to refuse to revile when reviled, because he knew if he was right the ridicule of to-day would mean the applause of to-morrow. He knew, too, that in some distant day our nation would repent of the folly of cursing its public servants while they live and blessing them only when they die. In this connection I cannot refrain from suggesting the question to the millions of voices raised to-day in his praise: "Why didn't you say it yesterday? Just that one word of gratitude, one word of appreciation would have gone so far in strengthening his heart and his hand." As we recall to-night his words and deeds we can do so with grateful hearts and strong faith in the future for the spread of righteousness. The civilization of the world is going forward, not backward. Here and there, for a little season, progress may seem to halt or tarry by the wayside, or even slide backwards, but the trend is ever onward and upward and will be so until some man invent and enforce a law to stop the progress of civilization. In goodness and in liberality the world moves forward. It moves forward beneficently, but it moves forward relentlessly. In the last analysis the forces of nature are behind the progress of the world, and those forces will crush into powder any group of humanity that resists this progress.

As we gather here to-night, brothers all in common joy and thanksgiving for the life of Lincoln, can I not ask that you, the worthy representatives of seventy millions of white Americans, join heart and hand with the ten millions of black Americans, these ten millions who speak your tongue, profess your religion and have never lifted their voices or their hands except in defense of their country's honor and their country's flag, and with us swear eternal fealty to the traditions and to the memory of the sainted Lincoln? I repeat, may I not ask that you join with us and let us all here highly resolve that justice, good will and peace shall be the motto of our lives? And if this be true, my friends, Lincoln shall not have lived and died in vain. And, finally, gathering inspiration and encouragement from this hour

and Lincoln's life, I pledge to you and to the nation that my
race, in so far as I can speak for it, which, in the past, whether
in slavery or in freedom, whether in ignorance or intelligence,
has always been true to the highest and best interests of this
country, has always been true to the stars and stripes, will strive
so to deport itself that it will reflect nothing but the highest
credit upon the whole people in the North and in the South.

CARRIE CHAPMAN CATT

THE WORLD MOVEMENT FOR WOMAN SUFFRAGE

PRESIDENTIAL ADDRESS AT THE SIXTH CONVENTION OF THE
INTERNATIONAL WOMAN SUFFRAGE ALLIANCE,
STOCKHOLM, SWEDEN, JUNE 13, 1911

[Mrs. Carrie Lane Chapman Catt was born in Ripon, Wisconsin, on January 9, 1859. She attended the Iowa State College, and was for three years principal of the High School in Mason City, Iowa. There in 1884 she married Leo Chapman, editor of the *Republican*, who died in 1886. In 1891, she married George W. Catt, American engineer. Since 1890, Mrs. Catt has devoted herself to woman suffrage work. She has been President of the National American Woman Suffrage Association since 1916, and President of the International Woman Suffrage Alliance since 1904. Her home is in New York City.]

In the debate upon the Woman Suffrage Bill in the Swedish Parliament, a few weeks ago, a University Professor said, in a tone of eloquent finality: "The Woman Suffrage movement has reached and passed its climax; the suffrage wave is now rapidly receding." To those who heard the tone of voice and saw the manner with which he spoke, there was no room for doubt that he believed what he said. "Men believe for the most part that which they wish," wrote Julius Cæsar. With patronising air, more droll than he could know, the gentleman added: "We have permitted this movement to come thus far, but we shall allow it to go no further." Thus another fly resting upon the proverbial wheel of progress has commanded it to turn no more. This man engages our attention because he is a representative of a type to be found in all our lands: wise men on the wrong side of a great question—modern Joshuas who command the sun to stand still and believe that it will obey.

Long centuries before the birth of Darwin an old-time Hindoo wrote: "I stand on a river's bank. I know not from whence the waters come or whither they go. So deep and silent is its current that I know not whether it flows north or south; all is mystery to me; but when I climb yon summit the river becomes a silver thread weaving its length in and out among the hills and over the plains. I see it all from its source in yonder mountains to its outlet in yonder sea. There is no more mystery." So these university professors buried in school books, these near-sighted politicians, fail to note the meaning of passing events. To them, the woman movement is an inexplicable mystery, an irritating excrescence upon the harmonious development of society. But to us, standing upon the summit of international union, where we may observe every manifestation of this movement in all parts of the world, there is no mystery. From its source, ages ago, amid the protests which we now know barbaric women must have made against the cruel wrongs done their sex, we clearly trace the course of this movement through the centuries, moving slowly but majestically onward, gathering momentum with each century, each generation; until just before us lies the golden sea of woman's full liberty. Others may theorise about the woman movement but to us has been vouchsafed positive knowledge. Once, this movement represented the scattered and disconnected protests of individual women. In that period women as a whole were blinded by ignorance, because society denied them education; they were compelled to silence, for society forbade them to speak. They struggled against their wrongs singly and alone, for society forbade them to organise; they dwelt in poverty, for the law denied them the control of property and even the collection of wages. Under such conditions of sexual serfdom, what wonder that their cries for justice were stifled, and that their protests never reached the ears of the men who wrote the history of those times? Happily those days are past; and out of that incoherent and seemingly futile agitation, which extended over many centuries, there has emerged a present-day movement possessing a clear understanding and a definite, positive purpose.

This modern movement demands political rights for women. It demands a direct influence for women upon the legislation which concerns the common welfare of all the people. It recognises the vote as the only dignified and honourable means of securing recognition of their needs and aspirations.

It pins its faith to the fact that in the long run man is logical. There may be a generation, or even a century, between premise and conclusion, but when the premise is once stated clearly and truthfully, the conclusion follows as certainly as the night the day. Our premise has been stated. The world has jeered at it, stormed at it, debated it; and now what is its attitude toward it? In the secret councils of every political party and every Parliament in the civilised world, this question is recognised as a problem which sooner or later must be solved; and the discussion is no longer upon the justice of our claims, but how to avert final action. Our opponents may not recognise this fact, but we who have watched the progress of this movement for many years, we who are familiar with every symptom of change, have seen the opposing forces abandon, one by one, each and every defence, until nothing remains but pitiable pleas for postponement. Such developments are not signs of a receding wave.

To follow up the advantages already won, there is to-day an army of women, united, patient, invincible. In every land there are trained pens in the hands of women, eloquence and wit on women's lips to defend their common cause. More, there is an allied army of broad-minded, fearless, unyielding men who champion our reform. The powers of opposition, armed as they are with outworn tradition and sickly sentiment *only,* are as certain to surrender to these irresistible forces as is the sun to rise to-morrow.

These are the things *we know.* That others may share the faith that is ours, permit me to repeat a few familiar facts. A call for the first International Conference was issued nine years ago, and it was held in the City of Washington. At that time the Woman Suffrage agitation had resulted in nationally organised movements in five countries only. In chronological order of organisation these were: The United States, Great Britain, Australia, Norway, the Netherlands. Two years later, in 1904, the organisation of the Alliance was completed in Berlin, and associations in Canada, Germany, Denmark, and Sweden were ready to join. These nine associations comprised the world's organised movement, and there was small prospect of immediate further extensions. To-day, seven years later, however, our Alliance counts 24 auxiliary national associations, and correspondence groups in two additional countries. Are these evidences of a wave rapidly receding? It would be more in accordance with facts should we adopt the proud boast of the British Empire, and say that the sun *now* never sets upon Woman Suffrage activities. More, the subscribing membership in the world has increased seven times in the past seven years, and it has doubled since the London Congress. Even in Great Britain, where the opposition declared at that time very confidently that the campaign had reached its climax, the National Union, our auxiliary, has tripled its individual membership, tripled its auxiliary societies, and doubled its funds since then. A similar increase of members and funds has come to the two militant groups, and twelve independent suffrage societies have been organised in that country. The membership and campaign funds have likewise tripled in the United States, and every president of an auxiliary national society has reported increase in numbers, funds, and activity. This army of Suffragists is augmented by new and enthusiastic converts every month and every week. We welcome to this Congress fraternal delegates from men's leagues of five countries, four of which have been organised within the past two years. The movement grows everywhere by surprising leaps and bounds. Two things are certain: first, Woman Suffrage is not a receding wave—it is a mighty in-coming tide which is sweeping all before it; second, no *human* power, no university professor, no Parliament, no Government, can stay its coming. It is a step in the evolution of society, and the eternal verities are behind it.

Those unfamiliar with our work may ask, what does this great body of men and women do? They do everything which human ingenuity can devise and human endurance carry out, to set this big, indifferent world to thinking. When John Stuart Mill made his famous speech in the British Parliament, in 1867, he said: "I admit that one practical argument is wanting in the case of women: they do not hold great meetings in Hyde Park nor demonstrations at Islington"; and the Parliament roared with amusement at the droll idea of women doing such things. But John Bull and Uncle Sam, and all the rest of the brotherhood of lawmakers, are slow and stubborn. They have scorned the reasonable appeals of women and have spurned their signed petitions. So demonstrations of numbers and earnestness of demand had to be made in some other form. In consequence, Hyde Park has witnessed many a demonstration for Woman Suffrage, one being larger than any other in the history of England, and on Saturday of this week a procession longer than any which has yet upheld the standard of an aspiring cause will pass through the streets of London. There are no examples among men in their long struggle to secure suffrage rights of such devotion, self-denial, and compelling earnestness as has been shown by the British women. I believe more money has been contributed, more workers enlisted, more meetings held, more demonstrations made in Great Britain alone in behalf of Woman Suffrage than in the entire world's movement for man suffrage. Certainly the man suffrage movement never brought forth such originality of campaign methods, such superb organisation, such masterly alertness. Yet it is said in all countries that women do not want to vote. It is to be devoutly hoped that the obstinacy of no other Government will drive women to such waste of time, energy, and money, to such sacrifice and suffering, as has that of Great Britain.

Nor are demonstrations and unusual activities confined to Great Britain. Two thousand women swarmed to the Parliament of Canada last winter, thousands flocked to the Legislatures of the various capitals in the United States. A procession of the best womanhood in New York a few weeks ago marched through that city's streets in protest against legislative treatment. Sweden has filled the great Circus building in Stockholm to overflowing. Hungary, Germany, France, "demonstrate," and in my opinion no campaign is moved by more self-sacrificing devotion, more passionate fervour, than that in Bohemia. Teachers and other trained women workers are holding meetings night after night, willingly carrying this burden in addition to their daily work that the women of Bohemia may be free. In our combined countries many thousands upon thousands of meetings are held every year, and millions of pages of leaflets are distributed, carrying our plea for justice into the remotest corners of the globe.

There are doubtless hard encounters ahead, but there are now educated women's brains ready to solve every campaign prob-lem. There are hands willing to undertake every wearisome task; yea, and women's lives ready for any sacrifice. It is be-cause they know the unanswerable logic behind our demands and the irresistible force of our growing army that Suffragists throughout the world repeat in unison those thrilling words of the American leader, Susan B. Anthony, "Failure is impos-sible."

It is not the growing strength of our campaign forces alone which has filled us with this splendid optimism; there are ac-tual gains which in themselves should tell the world that the goal of this movement is near. Of the nine associations uniting to form this Alliance in 1904, eight have secured a permanent change in the law, which is a step nearer the political suffrage. Of the 24 nations represented in this Congress the women of 15 have won more political rights than they had seven years ago. These gains vary all the way from the repeal of the law which forbade women to form political organisations in Ger-many; ecclesiastical suffrage in Switzerland, suffrage in Trade Councils in France, Italy, and Belgium, up to municipal suffrage in Denmark, and political suffrage and eligibility in Australia, Finland, Norway, and the State of Washington.

Among our delegates we count women members of Parlia-ment from Finland, a proxy member from Norway, a factory inspector from each of these two countries, and several town councillors from different countries; and to none of these po-sitions were women eligible seven years ago. There are vic-tories, too, quite outside our own line of activities.

A new organisation has arisen in Portugal which has con-ducted its campaign in novel fashion. Observing that the new constitution did not forbid the vote to women, Carolina Angelo, a doctor of medicine, applied for registration as a voter, and when denied appealed her case to the highest Court. The judge, Dr. Affonso Costa, sustained her demand, and one woman in that country possesses the same political rights as men. This lady has just cast her first vote. She was accompanied by ten ladies and was received with respectful applause by all the men present. This movement developed out of an organisation com-posed of 1,000 women members whose work was to further the cause of republicanism in Portugal. The suffrage organisation is small and new, but the President of the Republic and three members of the Cabinet are favourable to a further extension of political rights to women, and the new workers are confident of favourable action by the Parliament. It would be curious indeed if the women of Portugal, without a struggle, should be crowned with the political power so long withheld from the long-suffering women of other lands. But justice, like the physical forces of nature, always moves on by the "paths of least resistance," and therefore it is the unexpected which happens. It is with especially affectionate and tender cordiality that we welcome this newly organised and already victorious group into our Alliance. With pride and gratitude we have ordered a Portuguese flag to be added to our international collection, and hope to number Portuguese women in our future Congresses.

In Bosnia and Herzegovina, by the new constitution of February 20th, 1910, authorised by the Austrian and Hungarian Empire, four classes of men may qualify to vote. The first is composed of landowners who pay a tax of 140 crowns on their estate, and widows and spinsters are included in this class. They vote by proxy only, but that is a mere detail. The first election took place in May, 1910. Seventy-eight women voted, seventy-six being Mohammedans, one Servian, one Roman Catholic. When it is remembered that this Mohammedan land has so far forgotten the injunctions of the Koran as to extend this small portion of justice to women, this achievement, though seemingly unimportant, becomes a very significant straw which unmistakably shows the way the wind is blowing in this twentieth century.

As the direct result of our organised movement there has been an important triumph to celebrate at each International Congress. The most significant gain of the past year comes from the United States. In point of wealth, population, and political influence, Washington is the most important American State yet won. It will be remembered that in the United States Woman Suffrage must be secured by the vote of a majority of the men voters in each State. The question in Washington was carried by a vote of three to one. The most gratifying factor in this victory was the common testimony that this remarkable vote was due to the influence of men and women who had formerly lived in one of the adjoining suffrage States, notably Idaho and Wyoming, and who met the theoretical opposition advanced upon every side with facts and figures drawn from experience.

Undoubtedly the five full suffrage States of the United States seem insignificant gains to people of other lands. It is true these States are new and the population small. So new are they that when I was a child the greater part of the territory covered by these States was indicated on my geography map as "The Great American Desert." But a generation has wrought wonderful changes. Modern irrigation has transformed the desert into fertile land, and its delicious fruits have found their way into the markets of the world. Bread made from its grain may be eaten upon the tables of any land. Its mines send gold and silver to the mints of the world; its mountains supply semi-precious stones to all countries; its coal and iron give thousands of factories work and enterprise. Masts from the great forests of Washington are found upon all seas, and a network of railways covers the territory and carries its vast produce to the ocean, where one of the largest and deepest harbours in the world receives it. All the elements which in other lands have contributed to the upbuilding of cities and the support of great populations are to be found there. Even now the total number of voting women in these sparsely settled States is half the number of women who would receive the Parliamentary vote by the Conciliation Bill in Great Britain! The territory of these five States is equal to that of England, Scotland, Ireland, Wales, the Isle of Man, Norway, Sweden, Denmark, and half of the Netherlands. So unlimited are its resources that time will surely bring a population as large as that found in these older countries. Remember that the vote is guaranteed to all those generations of unborn women, and realise that these victories are of mighty significance.

It is impossible to think of that far-off future without bringing to mind an antipodal empire, that island continent, our best beloved suffrage achievement—Australia. Old monarchies may scoff at its newness, but look to its future. Its territory is nearly as large as that of all Europe; its resources are as varied and rich. Mankind, ever restless, and ever seeking fresh fields with easier undertakings in its struggle for existence, will not fail to supply a population as large. Asia held the cradle of civilisation; Europe was the teacher and guide of its youth; but its manhood is here. It looks no longer to Europe *alone* for guidance. The newest developments come from new lands, where traditions and long-established custom have least influence. As Europe supplanted Asia, so it is not only possible, but quite probable, that Australia, with its new democracy, its equality of rights, its youthful virility, its willingness to experiment, may yet supplant Europe as the leader of civilisation. Look to the future, and remember that over these new lands "the glad spirit of human liberty" will rest for centuries to come; and be convinced that our victories already won are colossal with meaning.

These are the achievements of our cause reached within the past seven years. From history we may turn to prophecy, and ask what are the prospects of our cause? In Great Britain, the United States, and the four Scandinavian countries further extensions of suffrage to women are sure to come soon. It is not easy to make prophecy concerning the outcome of the Woman Suffrage campaigns on the Continent. Certain it is that the victories which are near in England and Scandinavia will greatly accelerate the rate of progress there, and since the surprising developments in Portugal, prophecy becomes impossible.

As all the world knows, an obstinate and recalcitrant Government alone stands between the women of Great Britain and their enfranchisement. A campaign which will always be conspicuous among the world's movements for human rights for its surpassing fervour, sacrifice, and originality has been maintained without a pause. Ninety towns and county councils, including the chief cities of Great Britain, have petitioned Parliament to pass the Bill, the Lord Mayor of Dublin appearing at the bar of the House of Commons to present the petition in person. Three hundred thousand men during the late elections petitioned Parliament to the same end, and complete evidence has been presented that there is a tremendous public sentiment demanding Parliamentary action. The chief men of Australia and New Zealand have sent their strongest and unreserved approval of the results of Woman Suffrage in their respective countries. The Parliament of Australia has cabled its endorsement to the British Parliament, and now Australian and New Zealand women voters are organising to aid their English sisters. The Government evidently nurses a forlorn hope that by delay it may tire out the workers and destroy the force of the campaign. It little comprehends the virility of the movement. When a just cause reaches its flood-tide, as ours has done in that country, whatever stands in the way must fall before its overwhelming power. Political parties, governments, constitutions must yield to the inevitable or take the consequences of ruin. Which horn of the dilemma the English Government will choose is the only question remaining. Woman Suffrage in Great Britain is inevitable.

In the United States five Legislatures have submitted the question to the voters, and we await the result. One decision will be given this year in October, the others next year.

In Iceland, one Parliament has already passed an amendment to the national constitution, and it now only awaits the action of the next Parliament to become law. In Denmark, there are two suffrage organisations whose combined membership make the suffrage organisation of that country, in proportion to population, the largest in the world. A few weeks ago, I had the pleasure of visiting the Parliament, and speaking with many men representing all the political parties. The Premier, the speakers of both Chambers, the leaders of parties, and many others, assured me that the Parliamentary vote for women would not be long delayed. It requires three years to amend the constitution in Denmark, and the question is confused with other problems, and we must therefore be patient. The women have voted wisely and well; they are serving with dignity and public spirit in town councils; they are doing womanly and intelligent political work, and the evidence presented by the actual experiment has destroyed nearly all the serious opposition. The final step cannot in reason be long delayed.

It was my pleasure also to visit Norway. I wish every doubting Thomas could see what I saw in Norway. More than all else, I wish the Parliaments of all nations could pay that country a visit. One feels the difference between the enfranchised and unenfranchised countries rather in the spirit of things than in tangible form. That sex antagonism which everywhere exists, whether we like to admit it or not, is gone, and in its place has come a comradeship on a high moral plane. It seems like the peace and relief of mind which is always manifest after the satisfactory adjustment of an irritating difference of opinion. The men have been just to the women, and they are proud of their act; the women have had justice done, and they are grateful. In this state of mutual good feeling, the men promise that they will remove the tax qualification and make the suffrage universal for women as it is for men. The Prime Minister assured me that the four political parties differed widely on many questions, but they were quite of one mind in their approval of Woman Suffrage. Norway presents an ideal example of Woman Suffrage in practice, and is an achievement of which we may boast with no reservation of doubt. Two hundred and ten women sit in its town and county councils and three hundred and seventy-nine serve as alternates for councillors. Everywhere, women as officers, as jurors, as voters are patriotically and intelligently working for the public welfare of their country in dignified and womanly fashion.

I have reserved Sweden, the land of our hostesses, as the last country to be mentioned. Sweden has had a Saint Birgitti, a woman who was canonised because of her goodness and religious work. The guide books tell us that she was the first woman's rights woman in the world, for she was outspoken and emphatic in her demand for Woman's freedom. Later Fredrike Bremer, well known in all lands, advocated rights for women. She was a woman ahead of her times. Her last book, "Herta," published in 1865, set forth the reforms she considered necessary in order to establish a correct and fair status for women. Many of these proposed changes have now been made, but so new were these ideas then that the book was received with a storm of disapproval. Her former admirers became critics, and her friends thought she had lost her balance of mind. Two weeks before her death she wrote a friend, "I have lost all my popularity, my countrymen no longer approve of me, my friends are lost, and I am deserted and alone; nevertheless I wrote that book in response to the highest duty I know, and I am glad I did it." It is sad to think of that wonderful woman dying in this enlightened land, with possibly no true companion of her great soul to understand the service she had rendered woman-kind, or the motive which inspired it. But her "prophecy of yesterday" has "become the history of to-day." Municipal or communal suffrage was granted to taxpaying widows and spinsters in 1862, undoubtedly as the result of her teaching. Later the Fredrike Bremer Association was organised, and cultivated education and independence among women. In 1899 two of its members petitioned the Parliament for an extension of suffrage rights, and when our first international conference was held in Washington, it sent a delegate. Measures concerning women were pending in Parliament, and it was determined to organise an association which should have Woman Suffrage as its sole purpose. That was in 1902, and from that date the movement has made amazing progress. The municipal suffrage has been extended to married women, and eligibility secured. Organisations exist in 170 towns, some of them north of the Polar Circle, and there is a paying membership of 12,000; 1,550 meetings have been held since the London Congress. A member of Parliament tells me it is the most thoroughly organised under-taking in Sweden. Does this history indicate a receding wave? Instead, from the days of St. Birgitta this movement has been marching forward to certain victory. No country has made such progress in so short a time. Two political parties now boldly espouse the cause, and the third merely pleads that the times are not ripe for it. It requires three years to amend the constitution here, as it does in Denmark. The women are intelligent, sympathetic, alert and active; worthy descendants of Birgitta and Fredrike Bremer. They will not desert the cause, nor pause in their campaign. It is not difficult to predict the outcome.

The Suffrage Association is not the only force at work in Sweden for the desired end. It has an interesting ally in the many curious inconsistencies in the law which defines the status of women. These must appeal powerfully to the common sense of the people, and thus hasten the conversion of the country to political suffrage. I shall name a few.

1. Women may vote for town and county councils, and these bodies elect the Upper House of Parliament. Women, therefore, have as much suffrage for the Upper House as most men, but they are accounted wholly unworthy by the House they help to elect to vote for members of the Lower House.

2. Women are eligible to municipal councils, and thirty-seven women are now serving as town councillors. Eleven women are members of Councils which have a direct vote for the Upper House, and these women, therefore, have a higher suffrage right than most men; but these same women may not vote at all for members of the Lower House.

3. A gifted woman who will speak at our Congress has secured the Nobel prize in recognition of her rare endowments. Her name and her quaint stories are known the world over. She may vote for a municipal or county councillor, but with all her genius Selma Lagerlöf is not permitted to vote for a member of Parliament.

4. The President of the Swedish Suffrage Association is a learned lady. By the ancient ceremony at Uppsala she has been crowned with a laurel wreath in acknowledgment of her wisdom. Yet with all her learning she is not considered by her Government intelligent enough to cast a vote for a member of Parliament.

5. In Sweden people possessed of a certain income may qualify to cast many votes, the highest number of votes allowable being forty. There are many women who have 40 votes in the municipal elections, and I have myself met several who started in life with nothing in their pockets, but who, by their own initiative and enterprise, have accumulated enough to entitle them to 40 votes. Yet these same women cannot cast one vote for Parliament. A Parliament which sees nothing amusing in these illogical discriminations has no sense of humour.

The Scandinavian peoples represent a race which does not forget that its ancestors were Vikings, who sailed the seas without chart or compass. There are modern Vikings in all these lands as fearlessly ready to solve modern problems as were those of old. It is unlikely that all the people were bold and courageous in those ancient times. There were undoubtedly pessimistic croakers who declared the ships would never return, that the men would be lost at sea, and that the enterprises were foolhardy and silly. It is the antitype of this class which we find in the university professor, but we recall that it is the Vikings who are remembered to-day.

In order to learn the whole truth concerning our movement I sent a questionnaire to all our presidents. Among the questions was this: "What are the indications that the woman movement is growing in your country?" Not one president of our 24 countries found signs of backward steps. Instead, such volumes of evidence of onward progress were received that it is quite impossible to give any adequate idea of its far-reaching character. In a number of countries the entire code of laws affecting women are under revision, and liberal measures are proposed to take the places of the old. Denmark will take the oath of obedience out of the marriage ceremony. The Bishop of Iceland has supported a Bill to make women eligible to ecclesiastical offices, and declared St. Paul himself would have favoured the change were he here. In Silesia, where women landowners have the right of a proxy vote in the communal election, which, however, has not been usually exercised, nearly 2,000 women availed themselves of this privilege in the recent elections, to the amazement of the people. Unusual honours have been given women in all lands. Simultaneously women were elected presidents of the National Teachers' Associations in Great Britain and the United States for the first time. Positions heretofore closed have opened their doors to women. Equal pay for equal work has been granted the 13,000 women teachers of New York City after a splendid campaign of several years. The Press is everywhere more friendly. Distinguished people are joining our ranks. The argument has changed ground, and the evidence is complete that women are no longer the forgotten sex. King George, in his accession speech, spoke of his wife as "a helpmate in every endeavour for our people's good." It is believed that no other King in English history has thus publicly acknowledged his Queen Consort as sharing responsibility. I can only say that evidence is overwhelming that the walls of the opposition all along the line are falling down like those of Jericho of old before the blare of our suffrage trumpets.

Some may ask why we are not now content to wait for the processes of reason and evolution to bring the result we want. Why do we disturb ourselves to hasten progress? I answer, because we refuse to sit idly by while other women endure hideous wrongs. Women have suffered enough of martyrdom through the false position they have been forced to occupy for centuries past. We make our protest now hotly and impatiently, perhaps, for we would bequeath to those who come after us a fair chance in life. Modern economic conditions are pushing hundreds of thousands of women out of their homes into the labour market. Crowded into unskilled employments for want of proper training, they are buffeted about like a cork upon a sea. Everywhere paid less than men for equal work, everywhere discriminated against, they are utterly at the mercy of forces over which they have no control. Law-making bodies, understanding neither women nor the meaning of this woman's invasion of modern industry, are attempting to regulate the wages, the hours, the conditions under which they shall work. Already serious wrong has been done many women because of this ill-advised legislation. Overwhelmed by the odds against them in this struggle for existence, thousands are driven to the streets. There they swell that horrid, unspeakably unclean peril of civilisation, prostitution—augmented by the White Slave Traffic and by the machinations of male parasites who live upon the earnings of women of vice. Inaction is no longer pardonable. Prostitution is no longer a moral outcast to be mentioned with bated breath or treated as a subject too indelicate for discussion. It has become a problem actual with an entirely new significance, and demands immediate attention. It is now well known to be the breeding-ground of dangerous and insidious diseases which are surely and steadily deteriorating the race. They enter the palaces of kings and the hovels of the poor. Something must be done; the race must be preserved, while there is time. In accordance with modern discoveries concerning tuberculosis the nations have organised campaigns against it; we women, armed with ballots, must attack this far more serious foe. These wretched women, designed by nature for the sacrament of motherhood, have been told off by distorted, unnatural conditions and degraded into a class which is slowly destroying the race. We must be merciful, for they are the natural and inevitable consequence of centuries of false reasoning concerning women's place in the world. We may, perhaps, draw the curtain of obscurity over those women who because of inherent evil have voluntarily sought this life, but investigation has proved that at least two-thirds of them have been driven to this last despairing effort to live by economic conditions. Upon these women we have no right to turn our backs. Their wrongs are our wrongs. Their existence is part of our problem. They have been created by the very injustices against which we protest.

It is the helpless cry of these lost women who are the victims of centuries of wrong; it is the unspoken plea of thousands of women now standing on the brink of similar ruin; it is the silent appeal of the army of women in all lands who in shops and factories are demanding fair living and working conditions; it is the need to turn the energies of more favoured women to public service; it is the demand for a complete revision of women's legal, social, educational, and industrial status all along the line, which permits us no delay, no hesitation. The belief that we are defending the highest good of the mothers of our race and the ultimate welfare of society makes every sacrifice seem trivial, every duty a pleasure. The pressing need spurs us on, the certainty of victory gives us daily inspiration.

We have come upon a new time, which has brought new and strange problems. Old problems have assumed new significance. In the adjustment of the new order of things we women demand an equal voice; we shall accept nothing less. So

> To the wrong that needs resistance,
> To the right that needs assistance,
> To the future in the distance

we give ourselves.

WILLIAM H. TAFT

THE JUDICIARY AND PROGRESS

ADDRESS AT TOLEDO, OHIO, FRIDAY EVENING, MARCH 8, 1912

[William Howard Taft was born in Cincinnati, Ohio, on September 15, 1857. He was graduated from Yale University in 1878, from the Cincinnati Law School in 1880, has honorary degrees from thirteen institutions, and is an Honorary Bencher of the Middle Temple, London. He was admitted to the bar in 1880; was Assistant Prosecuting Attorney of Hamilton county, Ohio, from 1881 to 1883; Assistant County Solicitor, 1885 to 1887; Judge of the Superior Court in Cincinnati, 1887 to 1890; Solicitor General of the United States, 1890 to 1892; United States Circuit Judge for the Sixth Circuit, 1892 to 1900; Professor of Law and Dean of the Cincinnati Law School, 1896–1900; Kent Professor of Law, Yale Law School, 1913–1921; and since June 30, 1921, has been Chief Justice of the United States. He was President of the United States Philippine Commission, 1900 to 1901; first Civil Governor of the Philippine Islands, 1901 to 1904; Secretary of War of the United States, 1904–1908; and President of the United States, 1909 to 1913.

The speech printed below was delivered while Mr. Taft was still President, at a time when the stage was being set for the presidential election of November, 1912. Adherents to the Progressive Party, then in process of formation, were vigorously advocating the necessity of providing for the recall of judges and of judicial decisions. Mr. Taft, in this speech, replied to their arguments with particular reference to constitutional questions. In the election of 1912 both Mr. Taft, the Republican candidate, and Mr. Roosevelt, the Progressive candidate, were defeated by Woodrow Wilson.]

In the last year or two we have heard much of radical methods of changing the judiciary system. If we would properly consider these proposals and stand on solid and safe ground we must re-examine the fundamental principles of stable popular government. The history of the world seems to show that our form of government is more enduring and satisfactory than any other. We began as a small Union of 13 States, strung along the Atlantic coast, of 3,000,000 of people, and under the same Constitution we have enlarged to be a world power of 48 sovereign States, bound into one, of more than 90,000,000 of people, and with a humane guardianship of ten million more—nine

[384]

in the Pacific and one in the Atlantic. We have fought, beginning with the Revolution, four foreign wars, and we have survived a Civil War of the greatest proportions recorded in history, and have united the battling sections by an indissoluble tie. From our body politic we have excised the cancer of slavery, the only thing protected by the Constitution which was inconsistent with that liberty the preservation of which was the main purpose of establishing the Union. We have increased our business and productive activities in every direction; we have expanded the development of our natural resources to be continent wide, and all the time we have maintained sacred those inalienable rights of man—the right of liberty, the right of private property, and the right to the pursuit of happiness.

For these reasons we believe in popular government. Government is a human instrumentality to secure the greatest good to the greatest number, and the greatest happiness to the individual. Experience, and especially the growth of popular government in our own history has shown, that in the long run every class of the people, and by that I mean those similarly situated, are better able to secure attention to their own welfare than any other class, however altruistic the latter class may be. Of course, this assumes that the members of the class have reasonable intelligence and capacity for knowing their own rights and interest. Hence, it follows that the best government, in the sense of the government most certain to provide for and protect the rights and governmental needs of every class, is that one in which every class has a voice. In recognition of this, the tendency from earliest times in our history has been the enlargement of the electorate to include in the ultimate source of governmental power as many as possible of those governed. But even to-day the electorate is not more in number than one-fourth of the total number of those who are citizens of the Nation and are the people for whom the Government is maintained, and whose rights and happiness the Government is intended to secure. More than this, government by unanimous vote of the electorate is impossible, and therefore the majority of the electorate must rule. We find, therefore, that government by the people is, under our present system, government by a majority of one-fourth of those whose rights and happiness are to be affected by the course and conduct of the Government. This is the nearest to a government by the whole people we have ever had. Woman's suffrage will change this, and it is doubtless coming as soon as the electorate can be certain that most women desire it and will assume its burden and responsibility. But even then the electorate will only be part of the whole people. In other words, the electorate is a representative governing body for the whole people for which the Government was established and the controlling majority of the electorate is a body still less numerous. It is thus apparent that ours is a Government of all the people by a representative part of the people.

Now, the object of government is not only to secure the greatest good to the greatest number, but also to do this as near as may be by securing the rights of each individual in his liberty, property, and pursuit of happiness. Hence, it was long ago recognized that the direct action of a temporary majority of the existing electorate must be limited by fundamental law; that is, by a constitution intended to protect the individual and the minority of the electorate and the nonvoting majority of the people against the unjust or arbitrary action of the majority of the electorate. This made it necessary to introduce into the Constitution certain declarations as to the rights of the individual which it was the purpose of the whole people to maintain through the Government against the aggression of any temporary majority of the electorate and to provide in the same instrument certain procedure by which the individual might assert and vindicate those rights. Then, to protect against the momentary impulse of a temporary majority of the electorate to change the fundamental law and deprive the individual or the voting minority or the nonvoting majority of inalienable rights, the Constitution provided a number of checks and balances whereby every amendment to the Constitution must be adopted under forms and with delays that are intended to secure much deliberation on the part of the electorate in adopting such amendments.

I can not state the necessity for maintaining the checks and balances in a constitution to secure the guaranty of individual rights and well-ordered liberty better than by quoting from Daniel Webster. He said:

"The first object of a free people is the preservation of their liberty; and liberty is only to be preserved by maintaining constitutional restraints and just divisions of political power. Nothing is more deceptive or more dangerous than the pretense of a desire to simplify government. The simplest governments are despotism; the next simplest, limited monarchies; but all republics, all governments of law, must impose numerous limitations and qualifications of authority and give many positive and many qualified rights. In other words, they must be subject to rule and regulation. This is the very essence of free political institutions. The spirit of liberty is, indeed, a bold and fearless spirit; but it is also a sharp-sighted spirit; it is a cautious, sagacious, discriminating, far-seeing intelligence; it is jealous of encroachment, jealous of power, jealous of man. It demands checks; it seeks for guards; it insists on securities; it intrenches itself behind strong defenses and fortifies itself with all possible care against the assaults of ambition and passion. It does not trust the amiable weaknesses of human nature, and therefore it will not permit power to overstep its prescribed limits, though benevolence, good intent, and patriotic purpose come along with it. Neither does it satisfy itself with flashy and temporary resistance to illegal authority. Far otherwise. It seeks for duration and permanence. It looks before and after; and, building on the experience of ages which are past, it labors diligently for the benefit of ages to come. This is the nature of constitutional liberty; and this is our liberty, if we will rightly understand and preserve it.

"Every free government is necessarily complicated, because all such governments establish restraints, as well on the power of government itself as on that of individuals. If we will abolish the distinction of branches, and have but one branch; if we will abolish jury trials, and leave it all to the judge; if we will then ordain that the legislator shall himself be that judge; and if we will place the executive power in the same hands, we may readily simplify government. We may easily bring it to the simplest of all possible forms—a pure despotism. But a separation of departments, so far as practical, and the preservation of clear lines of division between them, is the fundamental idea in the creation of all our constitutions; and doubtless the continuance of regulated liberty depends on maintaining these boundaries."

These checks and balances, as has been pointed out, include the division of the Government into three independent branches —the legislative, executive, and the judiciary—and the provisions by which usurpation by one of the functions of another is forbidden. The Executive, while he is bound to act in behalf of all the people and to regard their rights, is properly influenced by that discretionary policy which he was elected by his constituents to carry out. In that sense he represents the majority of the electorate. So, too, the legislative members elected to uphold certain governmental views of the majority will properly favor the embodiment of such views in valid legislation.

But the judiciary are not representative in any such sense, whether appointed or elected. The moment they assume their duties they must enforce the law as they find it. They must not only interpret and enforce valid enactments of the legislature according to its intention, but when the legislature in its enactments has transgressed the limitations set upon its power in the Constitution the judicial branch of the Government must enforce the fundamental and higher law by annulling and declaring invalid the offending legislative enactment. Then the judges are to decide between individuals on principles of right and justice. The great body of the law is unwritten, determined by precedent, and founded on eternal principles of right and morality. This the courts have to declare and enforce. As between the individual and the state, as between the majority and the minority, as between the powerful and the weak, financially, socially, politically, courts must hold an even hand and give judgment without fear or favor. In so doing they are performing a governmental function, but it is a complete misunderstanding of our form of government or any kind of government that exalts justice and righteousness to assume that judges are bound to follow the will of the majority of an electorate in respect of the issue for their decision. In many cases before the judges that temporary majority is a real party to the controversy to be decided. It may be seeking to deprive an individual or a minority of a right secured by the fundamental law. In such a case, if the judges were mere representatives or agents of the majority to carry out its will, they would lose their judicial character entirely, and the so-called administration of justice would be a farce.

Having made clear what the function of our courts is under our form of government in maintaining the constitutional guaranties of rights, and in preserving against the usurpation of the majority the rights of the nonvoting part of the people and of the voting minority and of the individual, we come now to examine the charges made against the existing system. I concede that the system is not perfect or as good as it can and ought to be made. I have been preaching for reform, especially in the enforcement of the criminal law, for years. Then, too, I have pointed out in addresses and presidential messages the great need for cheapening the cost of civil litigation and expediting it so as to put as little a burden on the poor litigant as possible. The defects in our judiciary have not been in the corruption of the judges, but mainly in the procedure and in the helplessness of the judges in jury cases to assist in reaching right conclusions. The popular impulse has been to take away the power from the judge and to give it all to the jury, and this has not been for the public good in the enforcement of the criminal law. Such defects as I have described are completely within the control of the legislatures of the States and Congress; and I am glad to say that the movement for reform has been accelerated by action of the State and National bar associations, and we may look for decided progress in the near future.

But these humdrum defects and their tedious remedies are not of the spectacular character to call for political discussion or to attract effort from politicians in the passage of remedial legislation. The formidable attack upon our judiciary now is that the judges do not respond sufficiently to popular opinion. It is said that courts are interposing their obstructive power to the enforcement of legislation looking to the relief of the oppressed by declaring laws unconstitutional and by so-called judicial legislation in interpreting into statutes words not intended by the legislature. I do not intend to discuss these charges, although if reduced to specific cases it would be easy to show many of them to be unfounded. For the purposes of this discussion, I may admit that courts have erred in this regard, have unduly broadened constitutional restrictions in order to invalidate useful statutes, or have given such statutes a wrong construction. Indeed, I do not hesitate to say that I do not concur in the reasoning of certain courts of last resort as to the constitutional validity of certain social reform statutes, and I am very anxious that the remedies proposed in those statutes should be given effective operation. How is it proposed to remedy these wrongs? In one of two ways, either by the judicial recall or by the recall of judicial decisions. Let us examine these remedies separately.

In the remedy by judicial recall it is proposed to provide by law that whenever a judge has so discharged his duties as to induce a certain percentage of the electorate to deem it wise to remove him, and that percentage sign a petition asking his recall, an election shall take place in which the incumbent shall stand against other candidates; and if he does not secure a plurality of votes, he is ipso facto removed. I have pointed out that under our form of government and Constitution many of the issues arising before our courts are in effect issues between the State and the individual, between the majority and the minority—cases in which the popular interest might be greatly excited to secure a favorable judgment. By this system the question whether the judge is to be removed or not is to be left to that majority that may be greatly aroused to secure from him a judgment favorable to them. Could a system be devised better adapted to deprive the judiciary of that independence without which the liberty and other rights of the individual can not be maintained against the Government and the majority?

But it is said we may have corrupt judges. How are we going to get rid of them? They can be impeached under our present system. But that is said to be too cumbersome. Well, amend the procedure of impeachment. Create a tribunal for removal of judges for cause. Give them an opportunity to be heard, and by an impartial tribunal; but do not create a system by which, in the heat of disappointment over a lost cause, the defeated litigants are to decide without further hearing or knowledge whether the judge who decides against them is to continue in office. It would be hard to devise a more unjust and ineffective method of purifying the judiciary or one less likely to promote courage of honest conviction.

Let us examine the other method proposed for the reform of the judiciary. That is a recall of decisions. By this method, when a supreme court has found a law, intended to secure public benefit, to be invalid because it infringes some constitutional limitation, the decision is to be submitted to a vote of the qualified electors, and if a majority of them differ with the court and reverse the decision, the law is to be regarded and enforced as valid and constitutional.

This is a remarkable suggestion, and one which is so contrary to anything in government heretofore proposed that it is hard to give it the serious consideration which it deserves because of its advocates and of the conditions under which it is advanced.

What the court decides, is that the enacted law violates the fundamental law and is beyond the power of the legislature to enact. But when this issue is presented to the electorate, what will be the question uppermost in the minds of most of them and forced upon them by the advocates of the law? Will it not necessarily be whether the law is on its merits a good law rather than whether it conflicts with the Constitution? The interpretation of the Constitution and the operation of a law to violate some limitation of that instrument are often nice questions to be settled by judicial reasoning and farsighted experience, which are not to be expected of the electorate, or welcomed by it. If the issue is transferred to them the simple question will be of the approval or disapproval of the law. What this recall of decisions will then amount to, if applied to constitutional questions, is that there will be a suspension of the Constitution to enable a temporary majority of the electorate to enforce a popular but invalid act.

Suppose the act to be invalid because it infringes the rights of liberty of a certain unpopular class and by indirect means suspends the writ of habeas corpus in their cases. I ask any candid, fair-minded man if the decision of such a question when submitted to a popular majority is not likely to turn rather upon the popular disfavor of those affected than upon the possible infraction of the constitutional liberty of a citizen. Let another law involving other classes who could make themselves heard be submitted and would not the court's decision be likely to be sustained by the majority?

Take another case, instances of which have frequently arisen in our history: suppose, in the early development of a State, the question arises whether a series of special privileges shall be granted to a rich company willing to invest if only the privileges are exclusive and certain. Suppose the court finds the law unconstitutional, and the decision is submitted to the people. In an early state of development the popular yearning is for capital and expansion, and the popular vote might well fasten such a burden on the State and people forever. Of course, in this day and generation, such danger will be said to be remote; but in a business and political atmosphere, like that in Alaska of to-day, the popular view is different. Later on, of course, the people might and probably would change in respect to another but similar law.

A most serious objection to the recall of decisions is that it destroys all probability of consistency in constitutional interpretation. The majority which sustains one law is not the same majority that comes to consider another, and the obligation of consistency of popular decision is one which would sit most lightly on each recurring electorate, and the operation of the system would result in suspension or application of constitutional guaranties according to popular whim. We would then have a system of suspending the Constitution to meet special cases. The greatest of all despotisms is a government of special instances.

But the main argument used to sustain such a popular review of judicial decisions is that if the people are competent to establish a constitution they are competent to interpret it, and that this recall of decisions is nothing but the exercise of the power of interpretation. This is clearly a fallacious argument. The approval of general principles in a constitution, on the one hand, and the interpretation of a statute and consideration of its probable operation in a particular case and its possible infringement of a general principle, on the other hand, are very different things. The one is simple, the latter complex; and the latter when submitted to a popular vote, as already pointed out, is much more likely to be turned into an issue of general approval or disapproval of the act on its merits for the special purpose of its enactment than upon its violation of the constitution. Moreover, a popular majority does not adopt a constitution, or any principle of it, or amend its terms, until after it has been adopted by a constitutional convention or a legislature, and the final adoption is, and ought to be, surrounded with such checks and delays as to secure deliberation. In other words, the course of procedure in the adoption of constitution or amendment is very different from what the proposed vote of a majority on constitutional interpretation would be.

Constitutions ought to be protected by such requirements as to their amendment as to insure great deliberation by the people in making them—much greater than one vote of a mere temporary majority. This method of amending the constitution would give it no more permanence than that of an ordinary legislative act and would give to the inalienable rights of liberty, private property, and the pursuit of happiness no more sanction than that of an annual appropriation bill. Can it be that the power of a temporary majority of the electorate by a single popular vote to do away with rights secured to individuals, which have been inviolable for seven hundred years since the days of Magna Charta, approves itself to those who love liberty and who hold dear its sacred guaranties? Would we not in giving such powerful effect to the momentary impulse of a majority of an electorate prepare the way for the possible exercise of the grossest tyranny?

Finally, I ask what is the necessity for such a crude, revolutionary, fitful, and unstable way of reversing judicial construction of the constitution? Why, if the construction is wrong, can it not be righted by a constitutional amendment? The securing of that, it is true, is usually hedged about by checks and balances devised to secure delay, deliberation, discussion before a change of the fundamental law; but such amendments can be made, and if so, the effect of the decision can be reversed in respect to a new law by an amendment with express terms of authority to enact such a law. An answer made to this is that the same judges will construe the amendment and defeat the popular will as in the first instance. This assumes dishonesty and a gross violation of their oaths of duty on the part of judges, a hypothesis utterly untenable. If the meaning of the amendment is made plain, as it readily can be, of course the court will follow it.

I have examined this proposed method of reversing judicial decisions on constitutional questions with care. I do not hesitate to say that it lays the ax at the foot of the tree of well-ordered freedom and subjects the guaranties of life, liberty, and property without remedy to the fitful impulse of a temporary majority of an electorate.

Mr. Justice Miller, of Iowa, was one of the greatest jurists that ever adorned the Supreme Bench of the United States. Speaking for that great court in the case of Loan Association v. Topeka (20 Wall., 655), in a case presenting the question of the constitutionality of a law imposing a general tax on all citizens to pay for a factory to be run and owned by a private company, after referring to the act as "an invasion of private right," he said:

"It must be conceded that there are such rights in every free government beyond the control of the State. A government which recognized no such rights, which held the lives, the liberty, and the property of its citizens subject at all times to the absolute disposition and unlimited control of even the most democratic repository of power, is, after all, but a despotism. It is true it is a despotism of the many—of the majority, if you choose to call it so. But it is none the less a despotism. It may well be doubted if a man is to hold all that he is accustomed to call his own, all in which he has placed his happiness and the security of which is essential to that happiness, under the unlimited dominion of others, whether it is not wiser that this power should be exercised by one man than by many.

"The theory of our Governments, State and National, is opposed to the deposit of unlimited power anywhere. The executive, the legislative, and the judicial branches of these Governments are all of limited and defined powers.

"There are limitations on such power, which grow out of the essential nature of all free governments—implied reservations of individual rights, without which the social compact could not exist, and which are respected by all governments entitled to the name. * * *

"To lay with one hand the power of the Government on the property of the citizen, and with the other to bestow it upon favored individuals to aid private enterprises and build up private fortunes, is none the less a robbery because it is done under the forms of law and is called taxation. This is not legislation. It is a decree under legislative forms."

Do not the words and illustrations of this case bring before us what we might expect from the exercise of the power of a popular majority to reverse a solemn judgment of a court in favor of an individual against a measure that, for the time being, seemed to the people something that would help all and yet which was plainly a trespass upon individual rights?

I agree that we are making progress and ought to make progress in the shaping of governmental action to secure greater equality of opportunity, to destroy the undue advantage of special privilege and of accumulated capital, and to remove obstructions to the pursuit of human happiness; and in working out these difficult problems we may possibly have, from time to time, to limit or narrow the breadth of constitutional guaranties in respect of property by amendment. But if we do it, let us do it deliberately, understanding what we are doing, and with full consideration and clear weighing of what we are giving up of private right for the general welfare. Let us do it under circumstances which shall make the operation of the change uniform and just, and not depend on the feverish, uncertain, and unstable determination of successive votes on different laws by temporary and changing majorities. Such a proposal as this is utterly without merit or utility, and, instead of being progressive, is reactionary; instead of being in the interest of all the people and of the stability of popular government is sowing the seeds of confusion and tyranny.

THEODORE ROOSEVELT

THE RIGHT OF THE PEOPLE TO RULE

Address under the Auspices of the Civic Forum, Carnegie Hall, New York City, March 20, 1912

[Theodore Roosevelt was born in New York City on October 27, 1858. He was graduated from Harvard College in 1880, was a member of the New York Legislature from 1882 to 1884, was United States Civil Service Commissioner, 1889 to 1895, President of the Board of Police Commissioners of New York City, 1895 to 1897, and Assistant Secretary of the Navy, 1897 to 1898. After organizing Roosevelt's Rough Riders and serving in the war with Spain, he was Governor of New York, 1899 to 1900. Elected Vice-President of the United States for the term 1901 to 1905, he succeeded to the Presidency on the death of William McKinley, September 14, 1901, and he was elected to succeed himself for the term from 1905 to 1909. Being unable to control the Republican National Convention of June, 1912, he withdrew from it, was nominated for President by the Progressive Party, and was defeated for election by Woodrow Wilson.

The speech printed below, while discussing other planks in the Progressive Party platform, is chiefly an answer to Mr. Taft's Toledo speech, twelve days earlier, which was devoted to the proposed recall of judges and of judicial decisions.]

The great fundamental issue now before the Republican Party and before our people can be stated briefly. It is, Are the American people fit to govern themselves, to rule themselves, to control themselves? I believe they are. My opponents do not. I believe in the right of the people to rule. I believe that the majority of the plain people of the United States will, day in and day out, make fewer mistakes in governing themselves than any smaller class or body of men, no matter what their training, will make in trying to govern them. I believe, again, that the American people are, as a whole, capable of self-control and of learning by their mistakes. Our opponents pay lip loyalty to this doctrine; but they show their real beliefs by the way in which they champion every device to make the nominal rule of the people a sham.

I have scant patience with this talk of the tyranny of the majority. Whenever there is tyranny of the majority, I shall protest against it with all my heart and soul. But we are to-day suffering from the tyranny of minorities. It is a small minority that is grabbing our coal deposits, our water powers, and our harbor fronts. A small minority is fattening on the sale of adulterated foods and drugs. It is a small minority that lies behind monopolies and trusts. It is a small minority that stands behind the present law of master and servant, the sweatshops, and the whole calendar of social and industrial injustice. It is a small minority that is to-day using our convention system to defeat the will of a majority of the people in the choice of delegates to the Chicago convention. The only tyrannies from which men, women, and children are suffering in real life are the tyrannies of minorities.

If the majority of the American people were in fact tyrannous over the minority, if democracy had no greater self-control than empire, then indeed no written words which our forefathers put into the Constitution could stay that tyranny.

No sane man who has been familiar with the government of this country for the last 20 years will complain that we have had too much of the rule of the majority. The trouble has been a far different one—that, at many times and in many localities, there have held public office in the States and in the Nation men who have, in fact, served not the whole people, but some special class or special interest. I am not thinking only of those special interests which by grosser methods, by bribery and crime, have stolen from the people. I am thinking as much of their respectable allies and figureheads, who have ruled and legislated and decided as if in some way the vested rights of privilege had a first mortgage on the whole United States, while the rights of all the people were merely an unsecured debt. Am I overstating the case? Have our political leaders always. or generally recognized their duty to the people as anything more than a duty to disperse the mob, see that the ashes are taken away, and distribute patronage? Have our leaders always or generally worked for the benefit of human beings, to increase the prosperity of all the people, to give to each some

opportunity of living decently and bringing up his children well?
The questions need no answer.

Now there has sprung up a feeling deep in the hearts of the
people—not of the bosses and professional politicians, not of
the beneficiaries of special privilege—a pervading belief of
thinking men that when the majority of the people do in fact,
as well as theory, rule, then the servants of the people will come
more quickly to answer and obey, not the commands of the special interests, but those of the whole people. To reach toward
that end the Progressives of the Republican Party in certain
States have formulated certain proposals for change in the form
of the State government—certain new "checks and balances"
which may check and balance the special interests and their allies. That is their purpose. Now turn for a moment to their
proposed methods.

First, there are the "initiative and referendum," which are
so framed that if the Legislatures obey the command of some
special interest, and obstinately refuse the will of the majority,
the majority may step in and legislate directly. No man would
say that it was best to conduct all legislation by direct vote of
the people—it would mean the loss of deliberation, of patient
consideration—but, on the other hand, no one whose mental
arteries have not long since hardened can doubt that the proposed changes are needed when the Legislatures refuse to carry
out the will of the people. The proposal is a method to reach
an undeniable evil. Then there is the recall of public officers—
the principle that an officer chosen by the people who is unfaithful may be recalled by vote of the majority before he finishes
his term. I will speak of the recall of judges in a moment—
leave that aside—but as to the other officers I have heard no
argument advanced against the proposition, save that it will
make the public officer timid and always currying favor with
the mob. That argument means that you can fool all the people
all the time, and is an avowal of disbelief in democracy. If it
be true—and I believe it is not—it is less important than to stop
those public officers from currying favor with the interests.
Certain States may need the recall, others may not; where the
term of elective office is short it may be quite needless; but

there are occasions when it meets a real evil, and provides a needed check and balance against the special interests.

Then there is the direct primary—the real one, not the New York one—and that, too, the Progressives offer as a check on the special interests. Most clearly of all does it seem to me that this change is wholly good—for every State. The system of party government is not written in our constitutions, but it is none the less a vital and essential part of our form of government. In that system the party leaders should serve and carry out the will of their own party. There is no need to show how far that theory is from the facts, or to rehearse the vulgar thieving partnerships of the corporations and the bosses, or to show how many times the real government lies in the hands of the boss, protected from the commands and the revenge of the voters by his puppets in office and the power of patronage. We need not be told how he is thus intrenched nor how hard he is to overthrow. The facts stand out in the history of nearly every State in the Union. They are blots on our political system. The direct primary will give the voters a method, ever ready to use, by which the party leader shall be made to obey their command. The direct primary, if accompanied by a stringent corrupt-practices act, will help break up the corrupt partnership of corporations and politicians.

My opponents charge that two things in my program are wrong because they intrude into the sanctuary of the judiciary. The first is the recall of judges, and the second, the review by the people of judicial decisions on certain constitutional questions. I have said again and again that I do not advocate the recall of judges in all States and in all communities. In my own State I do not advocate it or believe it to be needed, for in this State our trouble lies not with corruption on the bench, but with the effort by the honest but wrongheaded judges to thwart the people in their struggle for social justice and fair dealing. The integrity of our judges from Marshall to White and Holmes—and to Cullen and many others in our own State—is a fine page of American history. But—I say it soberly—democracy has a right to approach the sanctuary of the courts when a special interest has corruptly found sanctuary there; and this is exactly what has happened in some of the States where the recall of the judges is a living issue. I would far more willingly trust the whole people to judge such a case than some special tribunal—perhaps appointed by the same power that chose the judge—if that tribunal is not itself really responsible to the people and is hampered and clogged by the technicalities of impeachment proceedings.

I have stated that the courts of the several States—not always but often—have construed the "due-process" clause of the State constitutions as if it prohibited the whole people of the State from adopting methods of regulating the use of property so that human life, particularly the lives of the workingmen, shall be safer, freer, and happier. No one can successfully impeach this statement. I have insisted that the true construction of "due process" is that pronounced by Justice Holmes in delivering the unanimous opinion of the Supreme Court of the United States, when he said:

"The police power extends to all the great public needs. It may be put forth in aid of what is sanctioned by usage, or held by the prevailing morality or strong and preponderant opinion to be greatly and immediately necessary to the public welfare."

I insist that the decision of the New York Court of Appeals in the Ives case, which set aside the will of the majority of the people as to the compensation of injured workmen in dangerous trades, was intolerable and based on a wrong political philosophy. I urge that in such cases where the courts construe the due-process clause as if property rights, to the exclusion of human rights, had a first mortgage on the Constitution, the people may, after sober deliberation, vote, and finally determine whether the law which the court set aside shall be valid or not. By this method can be clearly and finally ascertained the preponderant opinion of the people which Justice Holmes makes the test of due process in the case of laws enacted in the exercise of the police power. The ordinary methods now in vogue of amending the Constitution have in actual practice proved wholly inadequate to secure justice in such cases with reasonable speed, and cause intolerable delay and injustice, and those who stand against the changes I propose are champions of wrong and injustice, and of tyranny by the wealthy and the strong over the weak and the helpless.

So that no man may misunderstand me, let me recapitulate:

1. I am not proposing anything in connection with the Supreme Court of the United States, or with the Federal Constitution.

2. I am not proposing anything having any connection with ordinary suits, civil or criminal, as between individuals.

3. I am not speaking of the recall of judges.

4. I am proposing merely that in a certain class of cases involving the police power, when a State court has set aside as unconstitutional a law passed by the Legislature for the general welfare, the question of the validity of the law—which should depend, as Justice Holmes so well phrases it, upon the prevailing morality or preponderant opinion—be submitted for final determination to a vote of the people, taken after due time for consideration. And I contend that the people, in the nature of things, must be better judges of what is the preponderant opinion than the courts, and that the courts should not be allowed to reverse the political philosophy of the people. My point is well illustrated by a recent decision of the Supreme Court, holding that the court would not take jurisdiction of a case involving the constitutionality of the initiative and referendum laws of Oregon. The ground of the decision was that such a question was not judicial in its nature, but should be left for determination to the other co-ordinate departments of the Government. Is it not equally plain that the question whether a given social policy is for the public good is not of a judicial nature, but should be settled by the Legislature or, in the final instance, by the people themselves?

The President of the United States, Mr. Taft, devoted most of a recent speech to criticism of this proposition. He says that it "is utterly without merit or utility, and, instead of being * * * in the interest of all the people, and of the stability of popular government, is sowing the seeds of confusion and tyranny." (By this he, of course, means the tyranny of the majority; that is, the tyranny of the American people as a whole.) He also says that my proposal (which, as he rightly sees, is merely a proposal to give the people a real instead of only a nominal chance to construe and amend a State constitution with reasonable rapidity) would make such amendment and interpretation "depend on the feverish, uncertain, and unstable determination of successive votes on different laws by temporary and changing majorities"; and that "it lays the ax at the foot of the tree of well-ordered freedom, and subjects the guarantees of life, liberty, and property without remedy to the fitful impulse of a temporary majority of an electorate."

This criticism is really less a criticism of my proposal than a criticism of all popular government. It is wholly unfounded, unless it is founded on the belief that the people are fundamentally untrustworthy. If the Supreme Court's definition of due process in relation to the police power is sound, then an act of the Legislature to promote the collective interests of the community must be valid, if it embodies a policy held by the prevailing morality or a preponderant opinion to be necessary to the public welfare. This is the question that I propose to submit to the people. How can the prevailing morality or a preponderant opinion be better and more exactly ascertained than by a vote of the people? The people must know better than the court what their own morality and their own opinion is. I ask that you, here, you and the others like you, you the people, be given the chance to state your own views of justice and public morality, and not sit meekly by and have your views announced for you by well-meaning adherents of outworn philosophies, who exalt the pedantry of formulas above the vital needs of human life.

The object I have in view could probably be accomplished by an amendment of the State constitutions taking away from the courts the power to review the Legislature's determination of a policy of social justice, by defining due process of law in accordance with the views expressed by Justice Holmes for the Supreme Court. But my proposal seems to me more democratic and, I may add, less radical. For, under the method I suggest, the people may sustain the court as against the Legislature, whereas, if due process were defined in the constitution, the decision of the Legislature would be final.

Mr. Taft's position is the position that has been held from the beginning of our Government, although not always so openly held, by a large number of reputable and honorable men who, down at bottom, distrust popular government, and, when they must accept it, accept it with reluctance, and hedge it around with every species of restriction and check and balance, so as to make the power of the people as limited and as ineffective as possible. Mr. Taft fairly defines the issue when he says that our Government is and should be a government of all the people by a representative part of the people. This is an excellent and moderate description of an oligarchy. It defines our Government as a government of all of the people by a few of the people. Mr. Taft, in his able speech, has made what is probably the best possible presentation of the case for those who feel in this manner. Essentially this view differs only in its expression from the view nakedly set forth by one of his supporters, Congressman Campbell. Congressman Campbell, in a public speech in New Hampshire, in opposing the proposition to give the people real and effective control over all their servants, including the judges, stated that this was equivalent to allowing an appeal from the umpire to the bleachers. Doubtless Congressman Campbell was not himself aware of the cynical truthfulness with which he was putting the real attitude of those for whom he spoke. But it unquestionably is their real attitude. Mr. Campbell's conception of the part the American people should play in self-government is that they should sit on the bleachers and pay the price of admission, but should have nothing to say as to the contest which is waged in the arena by the professional politicians. Apparently Mr. Campbell ignores the fact that the American people are not mere onlookers at a game, that they have a vital stake in the contest, and that democracy means nothing unless they are able and willing to show that they are their own masters.

I am not speaking jokingly, nor do I mean to be unkind; for I repeat that many honorable and well-meaning men of high character take this view, and have taken it from the time of the formation of the Nation. Essentially this view is that the Constitution is a strait-jacket to be used for the control of an unruly patient—the people. Now I hold that this view is not only false but mischievous, that our constitutions are instruments designed to secure justice by securing the deliberate but effective expression of the popular will, that the checks and balances are valuable as far, and only so far, as they accomplish that deliberation, and that it is a warped and unworthy and improper construction of our form of government to see in it only a means of thwarting the popular will and of preventing justice. Mr. Taft says that "every class" should have a "voice" in the Government. That seems to me a very serious misconception of the American political situation. The real trouble with us is that some classes have had too much voice. One of the most important of all the lessons to be taught and to be learned is that a man should vote, not as a representative of a class, but merely as a good citizen, whose prime interests are the same as those of all other good citizens. The belief in different classes, each having a voice in the Government, has given rise to much of our present difficulty; for whosoever believes in these separate classes, each with a voice, inevitably, even though unconsciously, tends to work, not for the good of the whole people, but for the protection of some special class—usually that to which he himself belongs.

The same principle applies when Mr. Taft says that the judiciary ought not to be "representative" of the people in the sense that the Legislature and the executive are. This is perfectly true of the judge when he is performing merely the ordinary functions of a judge in suits between man and man. It is not true of the judge engaged in interpreting, for instance, the due-process clause—where the judge is ascertaining the preponderant opinion of the people (as Judge Holmes states it). When he exercises that function he has no right to let his political philosophy reverse and thwart the will of the majority. In that function the judge must represent the people or he fails in the test the Supreme Court has laid down. Take the workmen's compensation act here in New York. The legislators gave us a law in the interest of humanity and decency and fair dealing. In so doing they represented the people, and represented them well. Several judges declared that law constitutional in our State, and several courts in other States declared similar laws constitutional, and the Supreme Court of the Nation declared a similar law affecting men in interstate business constitutional; but the highest court in the State of New York, the court of appeals, declared that we, the people of New York,

could not have such a law. I hold that in this case the legislators
and the judges alike occupied representative positions; the difference was merely that the former represented us well and the
latter represented us ill. Remember that the legislators promised
that law, and were returned by the people partly in consequence
of such promise. That judgment of the people should not have
been set aside unless it were irrational. Yet in the Ives case the
New York Court of Appeals praised the policy of the law and
the end it sought to obtain; and then declared that the people
lacked power to do justice.

Mr. Taft again and again, in quotations I have given and elsewhere through his speech, expresses his disbelief in the people
when they vote at the polls. In one sentence he says that the
proposition gives "powerful effect to the momentary impulse of
a majority of an electorate and prepares the way for the possible exercise of the grossest tyranny." Elsewhere he speaks of
the "feverish uncertainty" and "unstable determination" of laws
by "temporary and changing majorities"; and again he says
that the system I propose "would result in suspension or application of constitutional guaranties according to popular whim,"
which would destroy "all possible consistency" in constitutional
interpretation. I should much like to know the exact distinction
that is to be made between what Mr. Taft calls "the fitful impulse of a temporary majority" when applied to a question such
as that I raise and any other question. Remember that under
my proposal to review a rule of decision by popular vote, amending or construing, to that extent, the Constitution, would certainly take at least two years from the time of the election of
the Legislature which passed the act. Now only four months
elapse between the nomination and the election of a man as
President to fill for four years the most important office in the
land. In one of Mr. Taft's speeches he speaks of "the voice
of the people as coming next to the voice of God." Apparently,
then, the decision of the people about the Presidency, after four
months' deliberation, is to be treated as "next to the voice of
God"; but if after two years of sober thought they decide that
women and children shall be protected in industry, or men protected from excessive hours of labor under unhygienic conditions, or wage workers compensated when they lose life or limb

in the service of others, then their decision forthwith becomes a "whim," and "feverish," and "unstable," and an exercise of "the grossest tyranny," and the "laying of the ax to the foot of of the tree of freedom." It seems absurd to speak of a conclusion reached by the people after two years' deliberation, after thrashing the matter out before the Legislature, after thrashing it out before the governor, after thrashing it out before the court and by the court, and then after full debate for four or six months, as "the fitful impulse of a temporary majority." If Mr. Taft's language correctly describes such action by the people, then he himself and all other Presidents have been elected by "the fitful impulse of a temporary majority"; then the constitution of each State and the Constitution of the Nation have been adopted and all amendments thereto have been adopted by "the fitful impulse of a temporary majority." If he is right, it was "the fitful impulse of a temporary majority" which founded and another fitful impulse which perpetuated this Nation. Mr. Taft's position is perfectly clear. It is that we have in this country a special class of persons wiser than the people, who are above the people, who can not be reached by the people, but who govern them and ought to govern them, and who protect various classes of the people from the whole people.

That is the old, old doctrine which has been acted upon for thousands of years abroad; and which here in America has been acted upon, sometimes openly, sometimes secretly, for 40 years by many men in public and in private life, and, I am sorry to say, by many judges; a doctrine which has in fact tended to create a bulwark for privilege, a bulwark unjustly protecting special interests against the rights of the people as a whole. This doctrine is to me a dreadful doctrine; for its effect is, and can only be, to make the courts the shield of privilege against popular rights. Naturally, every upholder and beneficiary of crooked privilege loudly applauds the doctrine. It is behind the shield of that doctrine that crooked clauses creep into laws, that men of wealth and power control legislation. The men of wealth who praise this doctrine, this theory, would do well to remember that to its adoption by the courts is due the distrust so many of our wage workers now feel for the courts. I deny that that theory has worked so well that we should continue it.

I most earnestly urge that the evils and abuses it has produced cry aloud for remedy; and the only remedy is in fact to restore the power to govern directly to the people, and to make the public servant directly responsible to the whole people—and to no part of them, to no "class" of them.

Mr. Taft is very much afraid of the tyranny of majorities. For 25 years here in New York State, in our efforts to get social and industrial justice, we have suffered from the tyranny of a small minority. We have been denied, now by one court, now by another, as in the bakeshop case, where the courts set aside the law limiting the hours of labor in bakeries—the "due process" clause again—as in the workmen's compensation act, as in the tenement-house cigar factory case—in all these and many other cases we have been denied by small minorities, by a few worthy men of wrong political philosophy on the bench, the right to protect our people in their lives, their liberty, and their pursuit of happiness. As for "consistency"—why, the record of the courts, in such a case as the income tax, for instance, is so full of inconsistencies as to make the fear expressed of "inconsistency" on the part of the people seem childish.

Well-meaning, shortsighted persons have held up their hands in horror at my proposal to allow the people themselves to construe the Constitution which they themselves made. Yet this is precisely what the association of the bar of the city of New York proposed to do in the concurrent resolution which was introduced at their request into our Legislature on January 16 last, proposing to amend the State constitution by a section reading as follows: "Nothing contained in this constitution shall be construed to limit the powers of the Legislature to enact laws" such as the workmen's compensation act. In other words, the New York Bar Association is proposing to appeal to the people to construe the constitution in such a way as will directly reverse the court. They are proposing to appeal from the highest court of the State to the people. That is just what I propose to do; the difference is only one of method, not of purpose; my method will give better results, and will give them more quickly. The bar association by its action admits that the court was wrong, and sets to work to change the rule which it laid down. As Lincoln announced of the Dred Scott decision in his debates with Douglas: "Somebody has to reverse that decision, since it is made, and we mean to reverse it, and we mean to do it peaceably." Was Lincoln wrong? Was the spirit of the Nation that wiped out slavery "the fitful impulse of a temporary majority"?

Remember, I am not discussing the recall of judges, although I wish it distinctly understood that the recall is a mere piece of machinery to take the place of the unworkable impeachment which Mr. Taft in effect defends, and that if the days of Maynard ever came back again in the State of New York I should favor it. I have no wish to come to it; but our opponents, when they object to all efforts to secure real justice from the courts, are strengthening the hands of those who demand the recall. In a great many States there has been for many years a real recall of judges as regards appointments, promotions, reappointments, and re-elections; and this recall was through the turn of a thumbscrew at the end of a long-distance rod in the hands of great interests. I believe that a just judge would feel far safer in the hands of the people than in the hands of those interests.

I stand on the Columbus speech. The principles there asserted are not new, but I believe that they are necessary to the maintenance of free democratic government. The part of my speech in which I advocated the right of the people to be the final arbiters of what is due process of law in the case of statutes enacted for the general welfare will ultimately, I am confident, be recognized as giving strength and support to the courts instead of being revolutionary and subversive. The courts today owe the country no greater or clearer duty than to keep their hands off such statutes when they have any reasonably permissible relation to the public good. In the past the courts have often failed to perform this duty, and their failure is the chief cause of whatever dissatisfaction there is with the working of our judicial system. One who seeks to prevent the irrevocable commission of such mistakes in the future may justly claim to be regarded as aiming to preserve and not to destroy the independence and power of the judiciary.

My remedy is not the result of a library study of constitutional law, but of actual and long-continued experience in the use of governmental power to redress social and industrial evils. Again and again earnest workers for social justice have said to me that the most serious obstacles that they have encountered during the many years that they have been trying to save American women and children from destruction in American industry have been the courts. That is the judgment of almost all the social workers I know and of dozens of parish priests and clergymen, and of every executive and legislator who has been seriously attempting to use government as an agency for social and industrial betterment. What is the result of this system of judicial nullification? It was accurately stated by the Court of Appeals of New York in the Employers' Liability case, where it was calmly and judicially declared that the people under our republican government are less free to correct the evils that oppress them than are the people of the monarchies of Europe. To any man with vision, to any man with broad and real social sympathies, to any man who believes with all his heart in this great democratic Republic of ours, such a condition is intolerable. It is not government by the people, but mere sham government in which the will of the people is constantly defeated. It is out of this experience that my remedy has come; and let it be tried in this field.

When, as the result of years of education and debate, a majority of the people have decided upon a remedy for an evil from which they suffer, and have chosen a Legislature and executive pledged to embody that remedy in law, and the law has been finally passed and approved, I regard it as monstrous that a bench of judges shall then say to the people: "You must begin all over again. First amend your Constitution [which will take four years]; second, secure the passage of a new law [which will take two years more]; third, carry that new law over the weary course of litigation [which will take no human being knows how long]; fourth, submit the whole matter over again to the very same judges who have rendered the decision to which you object. Then, if your patience holds out and you finally prevail, the will of the majority of the people may have its way." Such a system is not popular government, but a mere mockery of popular government. It is a system framed to maintain and perpetuate social injustice, and it can be defended only by those who disbelieve in the people, who do not trust them, and, I am afraid I must add, who have no real and living sympathy with them as they struggle for better things. In lieu of it I propose a practice by which the will of a majority of the people, when they have determined upon a remedy, shall, if their will persists for a minimum period of two years, go straight forward until it becomes a ruling force of life. I expressly propose to provide that sufficient time be taken to make sure that the remedy expresses the will, the sober and well-thought-out judgment, and not the whim, of the people; but, when that has been ascertained, I am not willing that the will of the people shall be frustrated. If this be not a wise remedy, let those who criticize it propose a wise remedy, and not confine themselves to railing at government by a majority of the American people as government by the mob. To propose, as an alternative remedy, slight modifications of impeachment proceedings is to propose no remedy at all—it is to bid us be content with chaff when we demand bread.

The decisions of which we complain are, as a rule, based upon the constitutional provision that no person shall be deprived of life, liberty, or property without due process of law. The terms "life, liberty, and property" have been used in the constitutions of the English-speaking peoples since Magna Charta. Until within the last 60 years they were treated as having specific meanings; "property" meant tangible property; "liberty" meant freedom from personal restraint, or, in other words, from imprisonment in its largest definition. About 1870 our courts began to attach to these terms new meanings. Now "property" has come to mean every right of value which a person could enjoy, and "liberty" has been made to include the right to make contracts. As a result, when the State limits the hours for which women may labor, it is told by the courts that this law deprives them of their "liberty"; and when it restricts the manufacture of tobacco in a tenement, it is told that the law deprives the landlord of his "property." Now I do not believe that any people, and especially our free American people, will long consent that the term "liberty" shall be defined for them by a bench of judges. Every people has defined that term for itself in the course of its historic development.

Of course it is plain enough to see that in a large way the political history of man may be grouped about these three terms, "life, liberty, and property." There is no act of government which can not be brought within their definition, and if the courts are to cease to treat them as words having a limited, specific meaning, then our whole Government is brought under the practically irresponsible supervision of judges. As against that kind of a Government I insist that the people have the right and can be trusted to govern themselves. This our opponents deny, and the issue is sharply drawn between us.

If my critics would only show the same sober judgment of which they declare the people at large to be incapable, they would realize that my proposal is one of moderation and common sense. I wish to quote the remarks of William Draper Lewis, dean of the Law School of the University of Pennsylvania:

"To a lawyer the most interesting suggestion Col. Roosevelt has made is to allow the people, after consideration, to re-enact legislation which a court decision has declared is contrary to some clause in the existing State constitution.

"Anyone who has been asked to draft specific amendments to State constitutions will hesitate to condemn, without serious consideration, the suggestion made by Col. Roosevelt. To take a concrete instance: The New York Court of Appeals declared the workmen's compensation act passed by the New York Legislature unconstitutional, as depriving in its operation the employer of his property without due process of law. A number of amendments to the New York constitution, designed to validate a compensation act, have been drafted, and it is not unlikely that one of them will be adopted. Personally, one or more of these amendments having been shown to me, I can not but feel that constitutional amendments designed to meet particular cases run the danger of being so worded as to produce far-reaching results not anticipated or desired by the people. Col. Roosevelt's suggestion avoids this difficulty and danger. If a persistent majority of the people of New York State want a workmen's compensation act, they should have it. But in order to obtain it they should not be driven to pass an amendment to their State constitution which may have effects which they do not anticipate or desire. Let them pass on the act, as passed by the legislature, after a full knowledge that their highest court has unanimously expressed its opinion that the act is contrary to the constitution which the people at a prior election have declared to be their fundamental law.

"I may not always approve of what the persistent majority wants. I might sometimes think the measure unwise. But that doesn't alter the right of that majority to enforce its will in government. The Roosevelt idea, it seems to me, supplies an instrument by which that majority can enforce its will in the most conservative way. It makes explosions unnecessary.

"I would have been very proud to have been the author of that plan, although I want to emphasize the fact that it involves no new principle, only a new method.

"I don't mind saying, however, that I think it unfortunate that it should have been proposed by Col. Roosevelt. He is a man of such marked characteristics and his place in the political world is such that he arouses intense enthusiasm on the one hand and intense animosity on the other. Because of this the great idea which he has propounded is bound to be beclouded and its adoption to be delayed. It is a pity that anything so important should be confounded with any man's personality."

As regards the dean's last paragraph, I can only say that I wish somebody else whose suggestions would arouse less antagonism had proposed it; but nobody else did propose it, and so I had to. I am not leading this fight as a matter of æsthetic pleasure. I am leading because somebody must lead or else the fight would not be made at all.

I prefer to work with moderate, with rational, conservatives, provided only that they do in good faith strive forward toward the light. But when they halt and turn their backs to the light and sit with the scorners on the seats of reaction, then I must part company with them. We, the people, can not turn back. Our aim must be steady, wise progress. It would be well if our people would study the history of a sister republic. All the woes of France for a century and a quarter have been due to the folly of her people in splitting into the two camps of unreasonable conservatism and unreasonable radicalism. Had pre-Revolutionary France listened to men like Turgot and backed them up all would have gone well. But the beneficiaries of privilege, the

Bourbon reactionaries, the shortsighted ultraconservatives, turned down Turgot; and then found that instead of him they had obtained Robespierre. They gained 20 years' freedom from all restraint and reform at the cost of the whirlwind of the red terror; and in their turn the unbridled extremists of the terror induced a blind reaction; and so, with convulsion and oscillation from one extreme to another, with alternations of violent radicalism and violent Bourbonism, the French people went through misery toward a shattered goal. May we profit by the experiences of our brother republicans across the water and go forward steadily, avoiding all wild extremes; and may our ultraconservatives remember that the rule of the Bourbons brought on the Revolution, and may our would-be revolutionaries remember that no Bourbon was ever such a dangerous enemy of the people and of freedom as the professed friend of both, Robespierre. There is no danger of a revolution in this country; but there is grave discontent and unrest, and in order to remove them there is need of all the wisdom and probity and deep-seated faith in and purpose to uplift humanity we have at our command.

Friends, our task as Americans is to strive for social and industrial justice, achieved through the genuine rule of the people. This is our end, our purpose. The methods for achieving the end are merely expedients, to be finally accepted or rejected according as actual experience shows that they work well or ill. But in our hearts we must have this lofty purpose, and we must strive for it in all earnestness and sincerity, or our work will come to nothing. In order to succeed we need leaders of inspired idealism, leaders to whom are granted great visions, who dream greatly and strive to make their dreams come true; who can kindle the people with the fire from their own burning souls. The leader for the time being, whoever he may be, is but an instrument, to be used until broken and then to be cast aside; and if he is worth his salt he will care no more when he is broken than a soldier cares when he is sent where his life is forfeit in order that the victory may be won. In the long fight for righteousness the watchword for all of us is spend and be spent. It is of little matter whether any one man fails or succeeds; but the cause shall not fail, for it is the cause of mankind. We, here in America, hold in our hands the hope of the world, the fate of the coming years; and shame and disgrace will be ours if in our eyes the light of high resolve is dimmed, if we trail in the dust the golden hopes of men. If on this new continent we merely build another country of great but unjustly divided material prosperity, we shall have done nothing; and we shall do as little if we merely set the greed of envy against the greed of arrogance, and thereby destroy the material well-being of all of us. To turn this Government either into government by a plutocracy or government by a mob would be to repeat on a larger scale the lamentable failures of the world that is dead. We stand against all tyranny, by the few or by the many. We stand for the rule of the many in the interest of all of us, for the rule of the many in a spirit of courage, of common sense, of high purpose, above all in a spirit of kindly justice toward every man and every woman. We not merely admit, but insist, that there must be self-control on the part of the people, that they must keenly perceive their own duties as well as the rights of others; but we also insist that the people can do nothing unless they not merely have, but exercise to the full, their own rights. The worth of our great experiment depends upon its being in good faith an experiment—the first that has ever been tried—in true democracy on the scale of a continent, on a scale as vast as that of the mightiest empires of the old world. Surely this is a noble ideal, an ideal for which it is worth while to strive, an ideal for which at need it is worth while to sacrifice much; for our ideal is the rule of all the people in a spirit of friendliness, brotherhood toward each and every one of the people.

OLIVER WENDELL HOLMES
EDUCATION IN THE OBVIOUS

SPEECH DELIVERED AT A DINNER OF THE HARVARD LAW
ASSOCIATION OF NEW YORK CITY, FEBRUARY 15, 1913

[Oliver Wendell Holmes, son of the poet of the same name, was
born in Boston, Massachusetts, on March 8, 1841. He was graduated
from Harvard College in 1861, entered the Union army as a Lieutenant, was three times wounded, and at the end of the war was a Lieutenant Colonel. He then studied law at Harvard, graduating in 1866,
was admitted to the bar in 1867, and began the practice of law in
Boston. He continued in practice until 1882, at the same time being
instructor in constitutional law at Harvard College, editor of the
American Law Review, and lecturer on the Common Law at Lowell
Institute. In 1882, he was appointed Professor of Law in Harvard
Law School, and in the same year he became Associate Justice of
the Supreme Judicial Court of Massachusetts, of which he was Chief
Justice from 1889 to 1902. Since December 4, 1902, he has been an
Associate Justice of the United States Supreme Court.

The speech printed below is a philosophical commentary on the
gospel of discontent preached during the Bull Moose campaign which
ended, in November, 1912, in the election of Woodrow Wilson as President of the United States.]

Mr. Chairman and gentlemen, Vanity is the most philosophical of those feelings that we are taught to despise. For vanity
recognizes that if a man is in a minority of one we lock him up,
and therefore longs for an assurance from others that one's
work has not been in vain. If a man's ambition is the thirst for
a power that comes not from office but from within, he never
can be sure that any happiness is not a fool's paradise—he never
can be sure that he sits on that other bench reserved for the
masters of those who know. Then, too, at least until one draws
near to seventy, one is less likely to hear the trumpets than the
rolling fire of the front. I have passed that age, but I still am
on the firing line, and it is only in rare moments like this that
there comes a pause, and for half an hour one feels a trembling
hope. They are the rewards of a lifetime's work.

[415]

But let me turn to more palpable realities—to that other visible court to which for ten now accomplished years it has been my opportunity to belong. We are very quiet there, but it is the quiet of a storm center, as we all know. Science has taught the world skepticism, and has made it legitimate to put everything to the test of proof. Many beautiful and noble reverences are impaired, but in these days no one can complain if any institution, system, or belief is called on to justify its continuance in life. Of course we are not excepted, and have not escaped. Doubts are expressed that go to our very being. Not only are we told that when Marshall pronounced an act of Congress unconstitutional he usurped a power that the Constitution did not give, but we are told that we are the representatives of a class —a tool of the money power. I get letters, not always anonymous, intimating that we are corrupt. Well, gentlemen, I admit that it makes my heart ache. It is very painful, when one spends all the energies of one's soul in trying to do good work, with no thought but that of solving a problem according to the rules by which one is bound, to know that many see sinister motives and would be glad of evidence that one was consciously bad. But we must take such things philosophically and try to see what we can learn from hatred and distrust, and whether behind them there may not be some germ of inarticulate truth.

The attacks upon the court are merely an expression of the unrest that seems to wonder vaguely whether law and order pay. When the ignorant are taught to doubt they do not know what they safely may believe. And it seems to me that at this time we need education in the obvious more than investigation of the obscure. I do not see so much immediate use in committees on the high cost of living and inquiries how far it is due to the increased production of gold, how far to the narrowing of cattle ranges and the growth of population, how far to the bugaboo, as I do in bringing home to people a few social and economic truths. Most men think dramatically, not quantitatively, a fact that the rich would be wise to remember more than they do. We are apt to contrast the palace with the hovel, the dinner at Sherry's with the workingman's pail, and never ask how much or realize how little is withdrawn to make the prizes of success. (Subordinate prizes—since the only prize much cared for by the powerful is power. The prize of the general is not a bigger tent, but command.) We are apt to think of ownership as a terminus, not as a gateway—and not to realize that except the tax levied for personal consumption large ownership means investment, and investment means the direction of labor toward the production of the greatest returns, returns that so far as they are great show by that very fact that they are consumed by the many, not alone by the few. If I might ride a hobby for an instant, I should say we need to think things instead of words—to drop ownership, money, etc., and to think of the stream of products; of wheat and cloth and railway travel. When we do, it is obvious that the many consume them; that they now as truly have substantially all there is, as if the title were in the United States; that the great body of property is socially administered now, and that the function of private ownership is to divine in advance the equilibrium of social desires—which socialism equally would have to divine, but which, under the illusion of self-seeking, is more poignantly and shrewdly foreseen.

I should like to see it brought home to the public that the question of fair prices is due to the fact that none of us can have as much as we want of all the things we want; that as less will be produced than the public wants, the question is how much of each product it will have and how much go without; that thus the final competition is between the objects of desire, and therefore between the producers of those objects; that when we oppose labor and capital, labor means the group that is selling its product and capital all the other groups that are buying it. The hated capitalist is simply the mediator, the prophet, the adjuster according to his divination of the future desire. If you could get that believed, the body of the people would have no doubt as to the worth of law.

That is my outside thought on the present discontents. As to the truth embodied in them, in part it can not be helped. It can not be helped, it is as it should be, that the law is behind the times. I told a labor leader once that what they asked was favor, and if a decision was against them they called it wicked. The same might be said of their opponents. It means that the law is growing. As law embodies beliefs that have triumphed in the battle of ideas and then have translated themselves into action; while there still is doubt, while opposite convictions still keep a battle front against each other, the time for law has not come; the notion destined to prevail is not yet entitled to the field. It is a misfortune if a judge reads his conscious or unconscious sympathy with one side or the other prematurely into the law, and forgets that what seem to him to be first principles are believed by half his fellow men to be wrong. I think that we have suffered from this misfortune, in State courts at least, and that this is another and very important truth to be extracted from the popular discontent. When twenty years ago a vague terror went over the earth and the word socialism began to be heard, I thought and still think that fear was translated into doctrines that had no proper place in the Constitution or the common law. Judges are apt to be naif, simple-minded men, and they need something of Mephistopheles. We, too, need education in the obvious—to learn to transcend our own convictions and to leave room for much that we hold dear to be done away with short of revolution by the orderly change of law.

I have no belief in panaceas and almost none in sudden ruin. I believe with Montesquieu that if the chance of a battle—I may add, the passage of a law—has ruined a State, there was a general cause at work that made the State ready to perish by a single battle or law. Hence I am not much interested one way or the other in the nostrums now so strenuously urged. I do not think the United States would come to an end if we lost our power to declare an act of Congress void. I do think the Union would be imperiled if we could not make that declaration as to the laws of the several States. For one in my place sees how often a local policy prevails with those who are not trained to national views and how often action is taken that embodies what the commerce clause was meant to end. But I am not aware that there is any serious desire to limit the court's power in this regard. For most of the things that properly can be called evils in the present state of the law I think the main remedy, as for the evils of public opinion, is for us to grow more civilized.

If I am right, it will be a slow business for our people to reach rational views, assuming that we are allowed to work peaceably to that end. But as I grow older I grow calm. If I feel what are perhaps an old man's apprehensions, that competition from new races will cut deeper than workingmen's disputes and will test whether we can hang together and can fight; if I fear that we are running through the world's resources at a pace that we cannot keep, I do not lose my hopes. I do not pin my dreams for the future to my country or even to my race. I think it probable that civilization somehow will last as long as I care to look ahead—perhaps with smaller numbers, but perhaps also bred to greatness and splendor by science. I think it not improbable that man, like the grub that prepares a chamber for the winged thing it never has seen but is to be, that man may have cosmic destinies that he does not understand. And so beyond the vision of battling races and an impoverished earth I catch a dreaming glimpse of peace.

The other day my dream was pictured to my mind. It was evening. I was walking homeward on Pennsylvania Avenue near the Treasury, and as I looked beyond Sherman's statue to the west the sky was aflame with scarlet and crimson from the setting sun. But, like the note of downfall in Wagner's opera, below the sky line there came from little globes the pallid discord of the electric lights. And I thought to myself the Götterdämmerung will end, and from those globes clustered like evil eggs will come the new masters of the sky. It is like the time in which we live. But then I remembered the faith that I partly have expressed, faith in a universe not measured by our fears, a universe that has thought and more than thought inside of it, and as I gazed, after the sunset and above the electric lights, there shone the stars.

NICHOLAS MURRAY BUTLER

THE SPIRIT OF LOCARNO

ADDRESS AT THE LEAGUE OF NATIONS NON-PARTISAN ASSO-
CIATION DINNER, HOTEL ASTOR, NEW YORK CITY, JANU-
ARY 10, 1927, IN CELEBRATION OF THE SEVENTH BIRTHDAY
OF THE LEAGUE OF NATIONS

[Nicholas Murray Butler was born in Elizabeth, New Jersey, on
April 2, 1862. He was graduated from Columbia College in 1882, received the Doctorate of Philosophy in 1884, and has had honorary degrees conferred upon him by twenty-five institutions. He was a
Fellow in Philosophy at Columbia University from 1882 to 1885, and
for two years studied in Berlin and Paris. From 1886 to 1891 he was
President of the New York College for the Training of Teachers (now
Teachers' College), and from 1889 to 1920, he was editor of the *Educational Review.*

At Columbia University he has been in succession, Assistant in Philosophy, Tutor, Adjunct Professor, Dean of the Faculty of Philosophy,
and, since 1902, President. He has been a delegate to seven Republican National Conventions, was chairman of the New York State Republican Convention in 1912, and was an unsuccessful candidate for
the Republican Presidential nomination in 1920. Since 1924, he has
been President of the Carnegie Corporation, and, since 1925, President
of the Carnegie Endowment for International Peace. He has been
honored by many foreign governments, is a member of many learned
societies and clubs, has a long list of books to his credit, and is a
public speaker much in demand.]

Mr. Chairman, Ladies and Gentlemen:

My concern is for my country, for its good repute today and
in history, for its influence and for its moral leadership in these
great days of twentieth century democracy.

Toward the close of the summer holiday, I sat with an interested congregation in a little church by the sea and listened to
a very striking sermon. Its opening sentences were somewhat
like this: "The reason why Christianity no longer makes appeal to men is that they are too prosperous. They have discovered a new god, Comfort, and they are so concerned with wor-
shipping him that they have no time for the God of their
fathers." Then the preacher went on to say that the modern

American ideal of life seemed to be to put a comfortable baby into a comfortable crib to be watched over by a comfortable nurse until it was able to go to a comfortable school; then to send it to a comfortable college, where comfortable teachers would see that it did not work too hard; to find its way into a comfortable profession, to marry a wife with a comfortable fortune (laughter); to spend twenty or thirty comfortable years, and finally to pass through a comfortable opiate to a comfortable grave. (Laughter.) It was rather a striking picture, and not without its lessons for some of us.

As a people we seem just now not to be able to grasp the fact that it is given to us to stand at one of the turning points of human history and to watch the great procession of the ages as it changes its line of march and alters its objective. One wonders whether when Ancient Greece was passing, the leaders of Greek thought and letters knew that it was passing. When the Roman Empire was tottering to its fall, did the men of light and leading really understand that a stupendous change was going on? Did the men of the Renaissance have any conception of the period through which they lived and to which they made such powerful contribution? Did the political philosophers of England and France of the 17th and 18th centuries realize that they were teaching ideas and thoughts that were to make a new political and social and economic world? Do we know—do we realize—that the long process of nation-building that has been going on in the western world now for more than a thousand years has come to a substantial end, and that those nations—built many of them on strong and firm foundations, others still in the first flush of youth—are seeking, some of them in the darkness, for ways and means to clasp hands together to make a new form of human unity, of human co-operation, of expression of human effort, that shall destroy no nation but enrich them all? (Applause.)

He must be blind and deaf who cannot see and hear the signs of the times. Locarno, from being only the name of a little town by a mountain lake, has become a significant symbol that will take its place in the long list of names that mark the progress of man's march, first toward liberty, then toward that fine and noble and lofty use of liberty which is human co-operation and international peace. (Applause.)

This is not the place, this is not the time, to recount details, many of which are so familiar to you all. But when we speak of Locarno, we must never forget what three sterling personalities, three true leaders of men, did there for their countries and for the world, and what they did to place us all everlastingly in their debt. (Applause.) If you will let your mind run back twelve years to those dreadful days of 1914–15, does it not seem unthinkable that the Ministers of Foreign Affairs of France and Germany and Great Britain should in that short time be sitting together around a table, talking as friends and comrades and companions, in a sincere and, thank God, a successful effort to bring their nations into association and into harmony? (Applause.)

M. Briand is easily one of the most remarkable personalities of our time, if not *the* most remarkable. (Applause.) You must remember that France and Germany, and even Great Britain, have their stoutly recalcitrant elements which have to be dragged by main force up to any council table where peace and international association are to be considered and discussed. Aristide Briand, eight times Prime Minister of France, walked no pathway of roses when he went to Locarno, and he took in his hand his own political reputation and future perhaps, and, as many think, the security of the Government of France. M. Briand is not only a most accomplished orator with astounding power of eloquence and skill in presentation of argument and of fact, but a fascinatingly subtle personality with a temperament of so great charm that it disarms while it seduces. M. Briand brings you to his side with a smile, with a shrewd and kindly word, and then with a formula, the kind of formula that the French mind loves—simple, brief, clear, precise—he states his problem. Argument is made almost impossible.

Doctor Stresemann has become Monsieur Briand's warm personal friend. Tell me, if you please, whether anything so astonishing as that could have been foreseen in 1914? Doctor Stresemann has his own ultra-nationalists to deal with. They have no overweening desire to build on the foundations that the present offers. They keep pointing day by day to the occupation of the Rhineland, to the Silesian partition, to the Polish corridor, and they say to Doctor Stresemann and his parliamentary supporters, "How can you ask us to sit down with France and Great Britain, and proceed to formulate new policies of co-operation on the basis that those things are to remain *faits accomplis*." But Doctor Stresemann shrugs his somewhat square Prussian shoulders, raises his fine head and smiles, and goes to Locarno.

Let me tell you a story of Locarno that will illustrate far better than any words of mine could what the spirit of Locarno was and what these men were able to accomplish there. Last March the question of the admission of Germany to the Council of the League was at issue, and the word had come that Brazil was to use its legal power of veto to prevent the necessary unanimous consent. The night before the decision was to be taken, Monsieur Briand and Doctor Stresemann were closeted together in a back room, smoking vigorously and discussing how to meet the situation that had developed. Outside was an anxious group of fifty representatives of the world's newspaper press waiting for some indication of what France and Germany were going to do at this great crisis.

M. Briand said: "Dr. Stresemann, I do not see what we can do. Brazil has the power, if she chooses to exercise it, and it appears that she does. I do not see what we can do, do you?"

Dr. Stresemann replied, "No, I do not; we have come to an impasse. Brazil blocks the way, and we can apparently do nothing." "I will tell you what to do," said M. Briand, "Let us go to bed." (Laughter.) "Let us sleep over it, and perhaps something will come to us in our dreams and we shall get light." Dr. Stresemann said, "Splendid!" The door was thrown open. Briand and Stresemann went out to face the waiting newspaper men, arm in arm. Briand took his cigar from his mouth and he said, "Gentlemen, I have pleasure in saying to you that Germany and France are in absolute agreement as to the next steps to be taken." (Laughter.)

That was telegraphed from Japan to Chili, and the world was gratified beyond expression at the obvious co-operation and rapprochement between Germany and France. That story is authentic.

What I wish to emphasize is two things: First, the element of leadership that exists, and second, the cordial trust and confidence between men who traditionally represent long-standing bitter enmities. I submit, Mr. Chairman, that the association between these three men—M. Briand, Dr. Stresemann and Sir Austen Chamberlain—with their friendly understanding, their intimate personal touch, their complete confidence, is the key to an understanding of what is going on in Western Europe. Their countries, delighted, have risen to their support, and each man is stronger today with the public opinion of his nation than he ever was before in his long parliamentary career.

Locarno, Mr. Chairman, means much more than a series of treaties. Locarno is a spirit, a point of view, a determination that, come what will, the old order shall not be restored. (Applause.) What I wish to see, Mr. Chairman, is that my country shall share that spirit and that determination. (Prolonged applause.)

Unhappily, the policies as to international affairs—or perhaps the lack of policies—that have been pursued by our government since the Armistice, have made this nation of ours a dangerous derelict adrift on the high seas of international intercourse, and lying straight across the path of every ship that sails laden with the precious cargo of international friendship and concord. (Prolonged applause; audience rises.)

Has not the time come, is it not already late in the afternoon, for our people to rouse themselves from their lethargy, dulled by what Iago called the "drowsy syrups" of a material prosperity, possibly temporary, into a sullen and cynical indifference to those great causes, those great appeals, those noble ideals, which in other days stirred the soul of Americans, and which our fathers sent Franklin and Adams and Jefferson overseas to explain to the Old World from which we sprang? (Applause.) Surely we make a sorry spectacle to ourselves, to the on-looking and mystified world, and to the historian who some day will tell the story of it all.

When Jefferson put his pen to the Declaration of Independence, what was it that gave distinction and unique character to his preamble? It was his "decent respect for the opinions of mankind." (Applause.) We were not isolated and aloof then.

We were not isolated and aloof when Washington sent Jay to negotiate that great treaty with Britain. We were not isolated and aloof when Jefferson pursued the Barbary pirates that were preying upon the world's commerce. We were not isolated and aloof when Henry Clay's voice from the floor of the House of Representatives made that appeal which called South American nations into being. We were not isolated and aloof when we offered welcome and distinction to Louis Kossuth, the Hungarian revolutionary. We were not isolated and aloof when Secretary Blaine penned his first call for a Pan-American Conference. We were not isolated and aloof when John Hay wrote his note as to the open door in China. We were not isolated and aloof when Mr. McKinley and Secretary Hay sent that great delegation to the first Hague Conference, and when they saved that Conference from disaster by inventing and carrying to completion the Court of International Arbitration. We were not isolated and aloof when Mr. Secretary Root wrote his truly notable instructions to our delegates to the Second Hague Conference, instructing them as representatives of the Government of the United States to leave no stone unturned to bring into being a permanent Court of International Justice (applause), and distinguishing, as he so well knows how to do, between the possibility and duty of international association and co-operation in respect of common ends and the avoidance of interference with the internal policies and concerns of any nation. We were not isolated and aloof then, and we were not isolated and aloof when the awful blow fell in 1914, when the world staggered. We were not isolated and aloof in France and Belgium and on the seas. We were not isolated and aloof when the time came for the great settlement.

And Mr. Chairman, in the months of June, July and August, 1919, the representatives of our two great political parties were so nearly at one that the tragedy which followed is multiplied many times in its sadness and its horror. A little bending here, a little yielding there—a change of this phrase or a change of that—and the history of these last years would have been strangely and splendidly different.

In anticipation of meeting this company, I have examined today certain files and records covering those months of intimate confidential negotiations. I can only say that I am not going to write a book, and I can give the same excuse that Lord Beatty is said to have given when he was asked in London whether he proposed to write a volume or two containing his memoirs of the war. He said, "No, because so far as I can remember, I have done nothing that needs explanation or apology."

Now we are confronted, Mr. Chairman, with a practical situation. A great many of our people seem to be satisfied to sit toying with their taboos and their totems and counting their comforting coins. (Laughter.) One of their taboos is that somewhere there is concealed an American tradition that we never have anything to do with anybody. (Laughter.) Where it came from I do not know. The phrase, ascribed to Washington, on which it usually is based, Washington never saw. He died before it was written. It was used by Thomas Jefferson in his first inaugural, and it had no more reference to the sort of thing of which we are now speaking than it would have to equipment of a Polar exploration expedition. Our entire tradition, our entire historic development, has been absolutely the opposite. Why, it was only the other day that this isolated nation and aloof, was, through hundreds of boards of aldermen, scores of legislatures, and I think the Congress itself, passing resolutions calling for the dismemberment of the British Empire. That was at a time when the Irish vote was important. What would they think if the Common Council of the City of Prague, for example, should pass a resolution demanding that the City of New York, being downtrodden and oppressed by the upper part of the State, should be set up into a separate government?

No, Mr. Chairman, the tradition, the history, is exactly the opposite. The only way in which damage of this kind can be repaired is by the slow process of the re-education of public opinion. There is no possible use in trying to pass statutes, acts, resolutions—meaningless words all of them—unless public sentiment and public opinion support and practically compel them. From this day on with Locarno's name upon our lips and its symbol and significance in our hearts, the appeal should be in season and out of season, to our American people to leave off talking about things that do not matter; to stop this chatter about a prosperity which never can be more than a means to an end, and to set ourselves to the great task of rebuilding our intellectual and moral leadership and taking hold of these situations, to the world's betterment, and to our own best interests. Why, every ant-hill is prosperous!

I have no hesitation in meeting our adversaries on the field of interest. Only I prefer to appeal from that interest which is of the stomach and the pocket to that interest which is of the head and the heart. The nations of the world, excepting ourselves and Soviet Russia and one or two more, have established the League of Nations. Before the campaign of 1920, I signed with thirty or forty men of my party a statement that we believed that the election of the candidate whom we favored would lead to our support of that movement, and we based it upon his own words (applause), in which he said "call it society, call it league, call it association, call it what you will, we are concerned not with the form but with the substance." And what I signed in October, 1920, I honor with my signature now. (Applause.)

If times have changed, those of us with convictions have not changed; but the facts are now wholly different, and the problems must be approached by new methods. We are now ready and should be ready by formal treaty or engagement, to accept as our own the Locarno definition of aggression (applause), and we should then be ready to say that if war breaks out in this world by aggression on the part of any power signatory to that definition, we shall recognize no neutrality right on the part of our citizens to participate in that war by providing materials with which to carry it on. (Applause.)

> New occasions teach new duties,
> Time makes ancient good uncouth,

said Lowell. Some of our old and precious doctrines, excellent in the eighteenth century and well down into the nineteenth, have been legislated by fact into the realm of the morally impossible. Surely it should require no treaty, it should require no formal engagement, to keep the American people from being drawn, by reason of an attachment to a doctrine of neutrality that is now outworn, into even indirect participation in a war of aggression. We may define aggression as an act in defiance of the will or against the interest of another government or people without first submitting the issue to the impartial examination of a competent authority to determine what the facts may be and what are the equities involved. If that definition of aggression be accepted—and I know of none better—then for us to say that under the terms of a legal doctrine now quite out of harmony with modern progress, we demand for our citizens the right to participate indirectly in such a war by furnishing munitions and supplies to the aggressive belligerent, is a grotesque travesty on our common sense. (Applause.) We must quickly and publicly take the contrary stand.

If we were to do that, Mr. Chairman, clouds that still rest over the head and heart of Europe would quickly roll away. Believe me, they are afraid that in an aggressive war among themselves, arms and destructive implements would be obtained from this neutral country.

Mr. Chairman, in an aggressive war there can no longer be neutrality. We must stand with the nation that keeps its word, and we must not side, even indirectly, with a nation that, through temper, through ambition, through wrong feeling, or for any one of a hundred reasons, violates its pledge and proceeds once again to bring down upon us such an avalanche as 1914 let loose.

From the standpoint of security, Western Europe is content. There are problems in the Central and Eastern portions, grave problems. There are nations not schooled in self-government, with no long background of order and economic prosperity behind them, with a great many inherited and traditional animosities which the stronger and the older peoples must help hold quietly in check while instructing them in the art of peaceful co-operation and self-development.

For myself I believe that the key to the elimination of the Balkan problem is to be found in an economic union of those peoples. Let them begin to work together in economic co-operation and let that economic co-operation be successful, and we shall have come a long way from conditions that have disturbed Europe, and through Europe the world, for a hundred years.

In the Northeast of Europe there are new nations in the making. They were torn suddenly from the side of an old historic empire. They are feeling their way, trying to come to national self-consciousness and to arrive at and protect national independence, to participate in these international conferences as equals, to do their part, to give their counsel, to get their benefit. We have no immediate contact with them, to be sure, but our concern is that through any of them there may not be lighted once more the torch of fire that shall reach inflammable material lying loose in that section of the world.

But if I were the foreign minister of a Balkan state or the foreign minister of one of the new nations in Northeastern Europe I should be disposed to ask my country's diplomatic representative in Washington to suggest that the processes of arbitration and judicial settlement need not be confined in their operation to European nations. (Applause.) That could hardly be deemed an act of intrusion, but it would suggest something which, to the best of my knowledge, has been largely overlooked up to the moment in certain places. (Laughter and applause.)

One thing more: There could be no more inappropriate moment than this to talk about enlarging our naval forces. (Long applause and cries of "Right.") It makes no difference whether the ratio ought to be 5-5-3 or 5-5-3.9 or 5-4-3.2, this is not the time to talk about it. There is such a thing as a psychological moment, and now when the eyes of the world are fixed on what is to follow Locarno, how that is to be made permanent and built into the institutional and intellectual life of Europe, what could be more distressing, what more disheartening than to find the American Republic concerned, not with Locarno, but with the pre-war psychology of armaments? (Applause.)

It suggests once more the recurring question which it is so difficult satisfactorily to answer: Can men learn? (Laughter and applause.)

Abraham Lincoln, in his great debate with Douglas, used words about public sentiment which have come ringing down the decades since they were spoken. "Public sentiment," said Lincoln, "is everything. With public sentiment nothing can fail; without it, nothing can succeed." Public sentiment reached from the platform, from the press, through the personal contacts of men and women with mind and vision and heart and feeling, public sentiment is the objective upon which those of us must move in our concern for our country's fame and repute, for her highest interest and for her place in history as a builder. (Applause.)

To the public sentiment of the American people I would say tonight, using words that have come across the ages, "Choose ye this day whom ye will serve"—the pagan idols of destruction and desolation and war, or the God of righteousness and progress and peace!

JOHN SHARP WILLIAMS

JEFFERSON DAVIS

ADDRESS IN BEHALF OF THE STATE OF MISSISSIPPI, PRESENT-
ING TO THE UNITED STATES THE JEFFERSON DAVIS MONU-
MENT, IN THE NATIONAL MILITARY PARK, VICKSBURG,
MISSISSIPPI, OCTOBER 13, 1927

[John Sharp Williams was born in Memphis, Tennessee, on July 30, 1854. He was educated at the Kentucky Military Institute at Frankfort, at the University of the South, Sewanee, Tennessee, at the University of Virginia, at the University of Heidelberg, Germany, and in the Law Department of the University of Virginia. After being admitted to the bar, he moved to Yazoo City, Mississippi, where he engaged in cotton planting and practiced law. He was a Democratic member of Congress from 1893 to 1909, and a United States Senator from 1911 to 1923. He is a man of originality, vigor, and honesty, of whom it has been said that his "brilliance in debate on the Democratic side, in both House and Senate at Washington, shone through many stirring years of the nation's history." He is now living in retirement on his plantation, "Cedar Grove," near Yazoo City.]

Mr. Chairman; Your Excellency, the Governor of Mississippi; General Cheatham; Veterans of the Federal and Confederate Armies; Ladies and Gentlemen:

Somebody has said that the sublimest spectacle which can be presented by man to humanity is that of a "great man greatly falling with a falling state." Surely it may be said, with historic truth, that Jefferson Davis presented this picture to his beloved Southland, and to the world. Whatever faults of temperament or policy critics may find in him, he indubitably possessed the virtues of sincerity; honesty; loyalty to friends, principles, and a cause; courage to endeavor; fortitude to bear defeat and suffering; unvarying truthfulness and self-devotion. If these be the cardinal and foundation virtues for man to possess, or to admire in other men, as I think they are, they were all impact in Mr. Davis.

The Southern Confederacy had but one President. That "storm-cradled Nation, that rose and fell," itself went down in ruin and ashes, and, seemingly, "its people's hopes were dead," even before the expiration of the six years' term of office of that "one chosen one."

There is nothing in the character or bearing of that one for any son of the South, or of the North, to be ashamed of.

There are many things in him, as in the history of that short and bloody struggle, on both sides, for all sons of both sections to commemorate as glorious and as worthy of the American people at their best.

It is harder for the successful majority of a people, once divided into angry and warring parts, to do justice to the political leaders of the defeated minority, than it is to praise its military and naval heroes.

The genius of Stonewall Jackson, the nobility of Robert E. Lee, have long since received unstinted praise from former foes, as from all the world. Even Raphael Semmes, after deep and loud cursing, has had justice done his enterprise, ingenuity, and intelligence as a "sailorman."

Justice is beginning to be done by Northern writers, to the character, ability, and memory of Jefferson Davis. Gamaliel Bradford—his antagonistic heredity and environment considered—has done it nobly well. Captain Schaff of the Northern army, in his *Life and Personality of Jefferson Davis,* pays admiring tribute to him. The first book that I read coming from the North, and seeking to portray him as he was, entitled *The Real Jefferson Davis,* was written by Landon Knight of Ohio. It pays generous and just tribute to his private character and public record.

This is well, because the Southern side of "The War Between the States" is as much a part of the history of *our* United States, as is the Northern side of it.

It is a mistake of *fact* to say that the Southern States rebelled against, or even fought against, "the United States."

The plain, palpable, historical truth is that two groups of the theretofore United, then temporarily Disunited, and subsequently Reunited States, were at war with one another. The fact that, in order to avoid confusion in battle and otherwise, the minority group had *per* force to assume for their new union a new name and a different flag, and that the majority group naturally retained the old, has led to the confusion of *ideas and of things*.

Every drop of blood inherited by Jefferson Davis, and by most of the soldiers who fought under him, was of the blood once shed, or offered to be shed, for the independence of the colonies and the establishment of "the old Union." He had himself been an officer in its Regular Army and later, during the Mexican War, in its Volunteer Army. He retained to the day of his death an intense devotion to the memory of "the old service." This devotion to the old and voluntary union of all the States he carried over to the new union, or Confederation, of his part of those States—"the Confederate States of America." He became, by virtue of his office as President of this group, the "Commander in Chief" of its armies and, officially therefore, one of its soldiers. Upon this fact and his ante-bellum army service rests the claim to erect here on United States property this monument—a claim generously accorded by the Federal Government of these States, against the major part of which he had waged relentless war in behalf of the independence of the minor part of them.

He waged war, relentless until the fabric which he commanded had hopelessly collapsed and he himself had become a prisoner of war. After the first natural ebulition of war-passion and hate, he was *unconfessedly,* but *really,* treated as a prisoner of war. That is what his release on bail and the ultimate dismissal of the absurd "treason" charge against him really meant.

When helpless and shackled—and then only—did he cease the struggle against "the stars in their courses," and like Robert E. Lee—also a prisoner, though on parole—advised his followers to cease unavailing resistance and to reconcile themselves, as best they might, to the new order of things. Worthily had he borne his part in that brilliant and heroic Southern defense. Most worthily did he bear his part in that overwhelming defeat—worse than defeat—that collapse by exhaustion of all a people's resources, including the decimation of its man-power.

In every act and thought he had borne witness to the eternal truth that "it is better to have loved and lost than not to have loved at all"—better to have fought and lost than not to have fought at all.

HICKS' SP.A.S.—28

He had loved the old union of all the States; he had loved the new union of that part of the States to which his State had adhered; he had performed honest, brave, brilliant, and enduring service for both.

In retirement—unpardoned and not seeking pardon—he sought to explain "the why" and "the what" of it all, in order that the motives, and deeds, and suffering of those he had led might become a part of the understanding of the world; nor is his *Rise and Fall of the Confederacy* a book of small value, either as history, or as literature, or as constitutional law, though naturally written from the viewpoint of a counsel for the defense.

His fate was not as fortunate as was that of the other Chief Magistrate of the other group of our American Commonwealths —his great antagonist, Lincoln—who died assassinated in the very afterglow of the hour of victory and before the radical part of his party could attempt his impeachment, as they did attempt that of his successor—for trying, without his popularity, to carry out his policies.

American history will not be written accurately until it frankly records, that for a short period—short in time, though long in suffering, heroic deeds and high courage—these States and this people had contemporaneously two governments and two Presidents—Abraham Lincoln and Jefferson Davis. They were born in homes within present long-distance artillery fire of one another—in the border State of Kentucky—a State which sought to be a "neutral" State in a "War *Between* the States" —a thing impossible—and succeeded only in seeing her sons fight and die on both sides.

The family of Davis, being slaveholders, when it migrated, went naturally further South; that of Lincoln, being too poor to own slaves, when it migrated, went naturally further North, where environment was more inviting to white labor. Both were of Southern blood. Each proved fitted to the environment, which directed and made destiny for him. Each devoted to the policies he came in time to espouse, and to the people of the section he came in time to love, all that was in him.

No two disunited and warring parts of any people ever furnished two opposing chieftains of sincerer purpose, cleaner life, or more persevering fortitude.

It is given to men to *be true,* if only they *will;* it rests with God to order results.

In that fierce war between the cause of community self-government and independence on the one side, and the cause of what had, by historical evolution, come to be "the sanctity of the Union," on the other side, the cause of the one chieftain—Lincoln—could hardly, by any fault of his own, however gross, have been lost, and the cause of the other—Davis—could by no now conceivable virtue or strength of his own have been won. All that either could do was to give himself—body, mind and soul—to the utmost—for the right, "as God gave it to him to see the right." This both did—without stint.

No Southerner now would impeach the character of Lincoln; and no "generous soul," to use a phrase of Demosthenes, will now deny that Jefferson Davis is the outstanding American instance, in civil life, of "a great man greatly falling with a falling State."

He was worthy to be associated in his people's hearts, with "the Sword of Lee," with the military genius of Stonewall Jackson, and with the enduring fortitude of that Southern Soldiery, which, "with tattered uniforms, bare feet and bright muskets bore on their bayonets" for four years, the Southern cause. He was worthy to be associated in history with those other Americans, who finally overwhelmed them.

He was "a man faithful unto death." Indeed, so prone was he never to desert a friend, a principle, or a cause, that his enemies in the South—and let it be remembered that he had bitter, though not many, enemies there—gave to his faithfulness the name of "obstinacy." Even Landon Knight falls into this error. Courage at its best he had; physical, mental, political, and moral courage; courage of initiative to dare; courage of fortitude to suffer. Poise he had; for him success did not entail recklessness, nor defeat despair.

He was great as a soldier. Buena Vista early illustrated it and his military counsels during the war, as General Lee himself testified before Congress, confirmed it. He was a great Senator. He was a great War Secretary. He was at times a

great orator. Witness his Farewell Address to the United States
Senate and the Richmond speech near the close of the war,
which "fired the Southern heart" to renewed effort.

In private life, in all its relations, he was as nearly blame-
less as mere man can be. Especially was he so in the difficult
relation of master and slave—the most difficult of all relations
for the master. In his justness, humaneness and consideration
for his slaves, he was exemplary. He bore that part of "the
white man's burden" as only the noble white man can. The
Northern writers whom I have cited all bear witness to that
fact, and all here in Mississippi, who knew him, knew that he
was "a good master."

What was in his mind—because it is by what is in a man's
mind that you must judge him—what was, then, in his mind,
the *Cause* to which he so stubbornly sacrificed his health and
for which he would so gladly have given his life? Was it slavery? Then it is indeed a "Lost Cause." But there are, in God's
providence, no lost causes—permanently lost—except unfit
causes, just as there are in nature no survivals of the unfit.
Slavery was not the cause—though it was the occasion.

Was secession the cause? It was only the allegedly "constitutional remedy" resorted to, to assert the cause.

The real cause was something back of all that. Behind all
the talk about slavery as a condition and about secession as a
remedy, there laid in the minds of the Southern men, and even
more in the minds of the Southern women of that generation,
as any one may know who will seek their feeling and thought
in their private and public utterances, the cause of White Racial
Supremacy. That was in their Souls, the real cause—the vital
thing menaced. That cause it was which, in the slave States,
was thought—mistakenly, as we now know—to be inextricably
involved in the maintenance of slavery, unless abolition were
accompanied by the deportation of the Negro race, and for that
nobody was ready—South or North. Deportation spelled then,
to Southern minds, agricultural ruin; to Northern minds, National Bankruptcy.

The cause of White Racial Supremacy, which was thought
to involve, and does involve, white racial life itself, is not a
"Lost Cause." It is a Cause Triumphant! It was never as

safe as now since the Missouri Compromise discussion, which Thomas Jefferson—himself an emancipationist—said "broke upon his ears like the alarum of a fire bell in the night." What war failed to avert, the slow but sure processes of human thought and experience—North and South—under difficulties at times seemingly insuperable, have finally averted, and averted, let us hope, for good and forever.

The white man's family life, his code of social ethics, his racial integrity—in a word his civilization—the destruction of which in the slave states was dreaded, as the involved racial result of the abolition of slavery without deportation, are safe. All the dire results which had been seen at our very door in Haiti and San Domingo and other West Indies and in Mexico have been avoided by us. They were averted because, first, of the stern resolution, and the discipline and "the shoulder to shoulder touch" which four years of war and hardship had implanted in the old easy-going and pleasure-loving Southerners; and because, second, of the respect for Southern courage and endurance, which the war had taught the Northern People; and because, third, of the sympathy for the South in her humiliation and poverty under Negro and carpet-bag rule—a sympathy which was at last aroused in "generous souls" of late foes. How narrowly averted these dreaded results were, and how dangerously and long the white man's civilization was menaced in the South, few now realize.

My friends, this man—this Jefferson Davis—was no pygmy among men; he was a Giant.

Long may this bronze endure as a memorial to him and as a monument to the magnanimity of the majority of a Great People, reunited and never again to be disunited, and determinedly oblivious of past hatreds and bloody arbitrament of differences!

This monument by the "Father of Waters," in the historic "Seige City" of Vicksburg, on the soil of his beloved adopted State, to "the Greatest Mississippian," can neither add to nor subtract from his fame, but it can be, and will be, a witness of the opinion of true men, that it is not success, nor failure, which measures the worth of a man; but that brave endeavor, honest purpose persevered in, and forgetfulness of self are the essentials, which fill the measure of God's demand, and constitute the standard for true men's judgments. May such ever be our rule of final judgment of one another in this "Republic of Lesser Republics," consecrated to one flag, one government, one Constitution and one Civilization; now and forever!

JANE ADDAMS

WOMEN AND WAR

PRESIDENTIAL ADDRESS AT THE INTERNATIONAL CONGRESS
OF WOMEN AT THE HAGUE, MAY 1, 1915

[Jane Addams was born at Cedarville, Illinois, on September 6, 1860. She was graduated from Rockford College, Illinois, in 1881, and studied in Europe from 1883 to 1885. She is famed as a settlement worker, having been head resident of the Social Settlement of Hull House, Chicago, since 1889, when she founded it in collaboration with Miss Ellen Gates Starr. In 1909 she was President of the National Conference of Charities and Corrections, and since 1915 has been President of the Woman's International League for Peace. She presided at international congresses of the League in 1915, 1919, 1921, 1922, 1924, and 1926. She has written and spoken extensively on social and political reform, her most widely known book being *Twenty Years of Hull House*. Her speech, printed below, is noteworthy, not only as literature, but because of the unusual circumstances under which it was delivered.]

At this last evening of the International Congress of Women, now drawing to its successful conclusion, its president wishes first to express her sincere admiration for the women who have come here from the belligerent nations. They have come from home at a moment when the national consciousness is so welling up from each heart and overflowing into the consciousness of others that the individual loses, not only all concern for his personal welfare, but for his convictions as well and gladly merges all he has into his country's existence.

It is a high and precious moment in human experience; war is too great a price to pay for it but it is worth almost anything else. I therefore venture to call the journey of these women, many of them heartsick and sorrowful, to this Congress, little short of an act of heroism. Even to appear to differ from those she loves in the hour of their affliction or exaltation, has ever been the supreme test of woman's conscience.

For the women coming from neutral nations there have also been supreme difficulties. In some of these countries, woman has a large measure of political responsibility and, in all of them, women for long months have been sensitive to the complicated political conditions which may also easily compromise a neutral nation and jeopardize the peace and safety of its people. At a Congress such as this, an exaggerated word may easily be spoken or reported as spoken which would make a difficult situation still more difficult; but these women have bravely taken that risk and made the moral venture. We from the United States, who have made the longest journey and are therefore freest from these entanglements, can speak out our admiration for these fine women from the neutral as well as from the fighting nations.

Why then were women from both the warring and the neutral nations ready to come to this Congress to the number of one thousand five hundred? By what profound and spiritual forces were they impelled, at this moment when the spirit of Internationalism is apparently broken down, to believe that the solidarity of women would hold fast and that through them, as through a precious instrument, they would be able to declare the reality of those basic human experiences ever perpetuating and cherishing the race, and courageously to set them over against the superficial and hot impulses which have so often led to warfare.

Those great underlying forces, in response to which so many women have come here, belong to the human race as a whole and constitute a spiritual internationalism which surrounds and completes our national life, even as our national life itself surrounds and completes our family life; they do not conflict with patriotism on one side any more than family devotion conflicts with it upon the other.

We have come to this International Congress of women not only to protest from our hearts and with the utmost patience we can command, unaffrighted even by the "difficult and technical," to study this complicated modern world of ours now so sadly at war itself; but furthermore we would fain suggest ways by which this large internationalism may find itself and dig new channels through which it may flow.

At moments it appears as if the excessive nationalistic feeling expressing itself during these fateful months through the exaltation of warfare in so many of the great nations, is due to the accumulation within their own borders of those higher human affections which should have had an outlet into the larger life of the world but could not, because no international devices had been provided for such expression. No great central authority could deal with this sum of human will, as a scientist deals with the body of knowledge in his subject irrespective of its national origins, and the nations themselves became congested, as it were, and inevitably grew confused between what was legitimate patriotism and those universal emotions which have nothing to do with national frontiers.

We are happy that the Congress has met at The Hague. Thirty years ago I came to this beautiful city, full fifteen years before the plans for international organization had found expression here. If I can look back to such wonderful beginnings in my own lifetime, who shall say that the younger women on this platform may not see the completion of an international organization which shall make war impossible because good will and just dealing between nations shall have found an ordered method of expression?

We have many evidences at the present moment that, inchoate and unorganized as it is, it may be found even in the midst of this war constantly breaking through its national bounds. The very soldiers in the opposing trenches have to be moved about from time to time lest they come to know each other, not as the enemy but as individuals, and a sense of comradeship overwhelm their power to fight.

This totally unnecessary conflict between the great issues of internationalism and of patriotism rages all about us even in our own minds so that we wage a veritable civil war within ourselves. These two great affections should never have been set one against the other; it is too late in the day for war. For decades, the lives of all the peoples of the world have been revealed to us through the products of commerce, news agencies, through popular songs and novels, through photographers and cinematographs, and last of all through the interpretations of the poets and artists.

Suddenly all these wonderful agencies are applied to the hideous business of uncovering the details of warfare.

Never before has the world known so fearfully and so minutely what war means to the soldier himself, to women and children, to that civilization which is the common heritage of all mankind. All this intimate and realistic knowledge of war is recorded upon human hearts more highly sensitized than ever before in the history of man and filled with a new and avid hunger for brotherhood.

In the shadow of this intolerable knowledge, we, the women of this International Congress, have come together to make our solemn protest against that of which we know.

Our protest may be feeble but the world progresses, in the slow and halting manner in which it does progress, only in proportion to the moral energy exerted by the men and women living in it; social advance must be pushed forward by the human will and understanding united for conscious ends. The slow progress towards juster international relations may be traced to the distinguished jurist of the Netherlands, Grotius, whose honored grave is but a few miles from here; to the great German, Immanuel Kant, who lifted the subject of "Eternal Peace" high above even philosophical controversy; to Count Tolstoy, of Russia, who so trenchantly set forth in our own day, and so on from one country to another.

Each in his own time, because he placed law above force, was called a dreamer and a coward, but each did his utmost to express clearly the truth that was in him and beyond that human effort can not go.

These mighty names are but the outstanding witnesses among the host of men and women who have made their obscure contributions to the same great end.

Conscious of our own shortcomings and not without a sense of complicity in the present war, we women have met in earnestness and in sorrow to add what we may to this swelling tide of purpose.

It is possible that the appeal for the organization of the world upon peaceful lines has been made too exclusively to man's reason and sense of justice, quite as the eighteenth century enthusiasm for humanity was prematurely founded on intellectual sentiment. Reason is only a part of the human endowment; emotion and deep-set racial impulses must be utilized as well—

those primitive human urgings to foster life and to protect the hopeless, of which women were the earliest custodians, and even the social and gregarious instincts that we share with the animals themselves. These universal desires must be given opportunities to expand and the most highly trained intellects must serve them rather than the technique of war and diplomacy.

They tell us that wounded lads lying in helpless pain and waiting too long for the field ambulance, call out constantly for their mothers, impotently beseeching them for help; during this Congress we have been told of soldiers who say to their hospital nurses, "We can do nothing for ourselves, but go back to the trenches again and again so long as we are able. Can not the women do something about this war? Are you kind to us only when we are wounded?"

The time may come when the exhausted survivors of the war may well reproach women for their inaction during this terrible time. It is possible they will then say that when devotion to the ideals of patriotism drove thousands of men into international warfare, the women refused to accept the challenge and in that moment of terror failed to assert clearly and courageously the sanctity of human life, the reality of things of the spirit.

For three days we have met together, so conscious of the bloodshed and desolation surrounding us, that all irrelevant and temporary matters fell away and we spoke solemnly to each other of the great and eternal issues, as do those who meet around the bedside of the dying.

We have formulated our message and given it to the world to heed when it will, confident that at last the great Court of International Opinion will pass righteous judgment upon all human affairs.

ELIHU ROOT

INVISIBLE GOVERNMENT

SPEECH IN THE NEW YORK STATE CONSTITUTIONAL CON-
VENTION, ALBANY, AUGUST 30, 1915, ON THE
SHORT BALLOT AMENDMENT

[Elihu Root was born in Clinton, New York, on February 15, 1845.
He was graduated from Hamilton College, Clinton, New York, in 1864;
taught in the academy in Rome, New York, in 1865; and in 1867 was
graduated from New York University Law School, was admitted to
the bar, and began practice in New York City. From 1883 to 1885
he was United States District Attorney for the Southern District of
New York, and has since maintained a law office in New York City.
Among the numerous public services that he has rendered are the
following: Delegate at large to the New York State Constitutional
Convention of 1894, and Chairman of its Judiciary Committee; Secretary of War, 1899 to 1904; member of the Alaskan Boundary Tribunal, 1903; Secretary of State, 1905 to 1909; United States Senator,
1909 to 1915; counsel for the United States in the North Atlantic
Fisheries Arbitration at The Hague, 1910; member of the Permanent Court of Arbitration at The Hague since 1910; President of the
New York State Constitutional Convention, 1915; head of the special
United States diplomatic mission to Russia, 1917; member of the
International Commission of Jurists on a World Court, 1921; Commissioner Plenipotentiary at the Conferences on Limitation of Arma-
ments, Washington, D. C., 1921 and 1922; member of an International
Commission of Jurists appointed by the League of Nations to consider
the revision of the statute of the Permanent Court of International
Justice, Geneva, March, 1929.

The speech printed below is on the executive reorganization plan,
commonly called the Short Ballot Amendment, which was incorporated into the draft constitution of New York by the Convention of
1915. It proposed to consolidate 150 loose-lying government agencies
into seventeen designated departments, each agency to be accountable
to the head of the department, and each head of a department except
two, to be accountable to the Governor. Mr. Root, who was President
of the Convention, took the floor in support of this measure and made
what has been called the greatest speech of his career.

The proposed constitution of 1915 was not adopted by the electorate;
but the Short Ballot Amendment was incorporated into the Constitution, as article V, section 2, at the election of November, 1925.]

[444]

I have had great doubt whether or not I should impose any remarks on this bill upon the Convention, especially after my friend, Mr. Quigg, has so ingeniously made it difficult for me to speak; but I have been so long deeply interested in the subject of this bill, and I shall have so few opportunities hereafter, perhaps never another, that I cannot refrain from testifying to my faith in the principles of government which underlie the measure that is before us, and putting upon this record, for whatever it may be worth, the conclusion which I have reached upon the teachings of long experience in many positions, through many years of participation in the public affairs of this State and in observation of them.

I wish, in the first place, to say something suggested by the question of my friend, Mr. Brackett, as to where this short ballot idea came from. It came up out of the dark, he says. Let us see. In 1910, Governor Hughes, in his annual message, said this to the Legislature of the State: "There should be a reduction in the number of elective officers. The ends of democracy would be better attained to the extent that the attention of the voters may be focussed upon comparatively few offices, the incumbents of which can be strictly accountable for administration. This will tend to promote efficiency in public office by increasing the effectiveness of the voter and by diminishing the opportunities of political manipulators to take advantage of the multiplicity of elective officers to perfect their schemes at the public expense. I am in favor of as few elective officers as may be consistent with proper accountability to the people, and the short ballot. It would be an improvement, I believe, in the state administration if the executive responsibility was centered in the governor who should appoint a cabinet of administrative heads, accountable to him and charged with the duties now devolved upon elective state officers." Following that message from Governor Hughes, to whom a large part of the people of this State look with respect and honor, a resolution for the amendment to the Constitution was introduced in the Assembly of 1910. That resolution provided for the appointment of all State officers, except the Governor and the Lieutenant-Governor. There was a hot contest upon the floor. Speaker Wadsworth, "Young Jim," came down from the Speak-

er's chair to advocate the measure, and Jesse Phillips, sitting
before me, voted for it. And so, in the practical affairs of this
State, the movement out of which came this bill had its start
upon the floor of the State Legislature.

Hughes and Wadsworth, one drawing from his experience
as Governor, and the other from his observations of public affairs while Speaker of the Assembly, were its sponsors. Time
passed, and in 1912 the movement had gained such headway
among the people of the State that the Republican Convention
of that year declared its adherence to the principle of the short
ballot, and the Progressive Convention, in framing its platform,
under which 200,000—it is safe, is it not, to say 200,000—of
the Republican voters of this State followed Roosevelt as their
leader, rather than Taft—the Progressive Convention, in framing its platform, declared: "We favor the short ballot principle
and appropriate constitutional amendments." So two parties,
and all branches of the Republican party committed themselves
to the position that Hughes and Wadsworth took in the Assembly of 1910.

In 1913, after the great defeat of 1912, when the Republicans
of the State were seeking to bring back to their support the
multitudes that had gone off with the Progressive movement,
when they were seeking to offer a program of constructive forward movement in which the Republican party should be the
leader, Republicans met in a great mass meeting in the city of
New York, on the fifth of December of that year, 1913. Nine
hundred and seventy Republicans were there from all parts of
the State. It was a crisis in the affairs of the Republican party.
The party must commend itself to the people of the State, or it
was gone. Twenty-eight members of this Convention were
there, and in that meeting, free to all, open to full discussion,
after amendments had been offered, discussed and voted upon,
this resolution was adopted:

"Whereas this practice (referring to the long ballot) is also
in violation of the best principles of organization which require
that the governor, who, under the constitution, is the responsible chief executive, should be so in fact and that he should
have the power to select his official agents;

"Therefore, be it Resolved, That we favor the application to the state government of the principle of the short ballot, which is that only those offices shall be elective which are important enough to attract and deserve public attention;

"And be it further Resolved, That in compliance with this principle we urge the representatives of the Republican party of this state, in the senate and assembly, to support a resolution providing for the submission to the people of an amendment to the constitution, under which amendment it will be the duty of the Governor to appoint the secretary of the state, the state treasurer, the comptroller, the attorney-general, and the state engineer and surveyor, leaving only the governor and lieutenant-governor as elective executive officers."

That resolution, I say, after full discussion was unanimously adopted by the nine hundred and seventy representative Republicans who had met there to present to the people of the State a constructive program for the party. Mr. Frederick C. Tanner is chairman of this Committee on Governor and Other State Officers to-day, because it was he who offered the resolution in that meeting that was unanimously approved by the nine hundred and seventy Republicans. He is executing a mandate. He is carrying out a policy. He is fulfilling a pledge to the people.

The time went on and the following winter, in the Assembly of 1914, a new resolution was introduced following the terms of this resolution of the mass meeting, following the terms of the Hughes-Wadsworth resolution of 1910, providing that all these State officers except the 'Governor and Lieutenant-Governor should be appointed. That resolution passed the Assembly and every Republican in the Assembly voted for it. It never came to a vote in the Senate. Voting for that resolution were four members of the Assembly, who now sit in this Convention; Mr. Bockes, Mr. Eisner, Mr. Hinman, and Mr. Mathewson. Time passed on and in the autumn of 1914 a Republican Convention met at Saratoga; an unofficial convention, we are told. Unofficial? Negligible! Here is the law under which it was called, Section 45 of the Election Law:

"Nothing contained in this chapter shall prevent a party from holding party conventions to be constituted in such manner and to have such powers in relation to formulating party platforms and policies and the transaction of business relating to party affairs as the rules and regulations of the party may provide, not inconsistent with the provisions of this chapter."

That convention was thus called more specifically and solemnly to frame a platform than any other convention that ever met in this State, for that was its sole business. That is what it was there for, to define, to declare, to set before the people the faith and policies of the Republican party; and in that convention there was a report from the Committee on Rules, which embodied deliberation, full discussion and mature judgment, such as no report that ever came to a political convention within my experience ever had. The great mass meeting of December 5, 1913, had directed the appointment of a Committee of Thirty to meet and consider and prepare for submission to the convention a statement of the views of the Republican party regarding the new Constitution. That Committee was appointed; it met two or three days before the convention in the city of Saratoga. It met in the office of my friend, Mr. Brackett, and there day after day it discussed the subject, reached and voted upon its conclusions and framed a report. Let me say here, that Senator Brackett never agreed with the committee. He has been consistent and honest and open in the declaration of his views from first to last, but he was voted down in the Committee of Thirty. Their report favoring a short ballot, among other things, was presented to the convention. That report was referred to the Committee on Resolutions of the convention, a committee of forty-two members; among them were twelve members of this Convention, and that Committee on Resolutions took up the report of the Committee of Thirty and discussed it all day, and they voted upon it and again Mr. Brackett's view was voted down; and the Committee on Resolutions reported to the convention the plank in favor of the short ballot that has been read to you.

Mr. Brackett—Will the Senator permit an interruption? I know you have not intentionally made a misstatement, but you will recall that a report of the Committee of Thirty was not presented to the Committee on Platform until an hour before the convention, in the little room at the end of the piazza—before the convention met.

Mr. Root—It is a fact, and that room was the scene of excited and hot controversy for a long period over the adoption of that report, which was in part adopted and in part rejected.

Mr. Brackett—If you will pardon a suggestion, you said for a long period. It was, I think, about an hour and a half.

Mr. Deyo—I think that lasted until the following day.

Mr. Root—It did. Now, when it came to the convention there was no doubt about the subject we were talking on. The temporary chairman of the convention had said to the convention, "The reflections which arise from considering the relations of the Executive and the Legislature lead inevitably to another field of reform in State government. That is the adoption of the short ballot. That is demanded both for the efficiency of our elective system and the efficiency of government after election." And then, after stating the first, he proceeded: "The most obvious step toward simplifying the ballot in this State is to have the heads of executive departments appointed by the Governor, etc." Still more important would be the effect of such a change upon the efficiency of government. The most important thing in constituting government is to unite responsibility with power, so that a certain known person may be definitely responsible for doing what ought to be done; to be rewarded if he does it, punished if he does not do it, and that the person held responsible shall have the power to do the thing. Under our system we have divided executive power among many separately elected heads of departments, and we have thus obscured responsibility, because in the complicated affairs of our government it is hard for the best informed to know who is to be blamed, or who is to be praised, who ought to be rewarded and who punished. At the same time that the Governor is empowered to appoint the heads of executive departments and made responsible for their conduct, there ought to be a general reorganization of the executive branch of our government. After that, Mr. Chairman, came the report of the Committee on Resolutions, and Mr. Brackett submitted a minority report, taking substantially the position which he has taken here. That minority report was read, and it was argued at length. Amendments were offered and discussed. Mr. Brackett, I repeat, was heard at length upon it in what he then called the "great council of the party"—the convention elected and organized to make a platform—and he was beaten; beaten fighting manfully for his opinions, but he was beaten. The Republican party went to the people at the coming election upon the declaration that it was in favor of applying the principle of the short ballot to the selection of executive officers.

Now, let me turn to the other side of the story. When the resolution for the short ballot, simon-pure, making all the State officers but the Governor and Lieutenant Governor appointive, was before the Assembly of 1914, Mr. A. E. Smith, the member of this Convention whose attractive personality has so impressed itself upon every member, moved an amendment to limit the change to appointment of the Secretary of State, State Engineer and Surveyor, and State Treasurer, leaving the Comptroller and Attorney General elective. Upon that amendment the Democrats of the Assembly stood, voting with him. When the Democratic convention met in that autumn they put themselves on Mr. Smith's platform, approved his action and that of the Democrats in the Assembly and declared in favor of exactly what he called for in his amendment—the election of the Comptroller and the Attorney General and the appointment of all the other officers.

So you have this movement, not coming up out of the dark, but begun by a great Governor and advocated by a great Speaker, both of whom have received the approval of their country, one by being elevated to the bench of the Supreme Court of the United States and the other to the Senate of the United States. You have the movement progressing step by step until it has received the almost universal assent, the final and decisive action of the party to which that Governor and that Speaker belong, repeated over and over again, fully thought out and discussed; and you have the other party accepting the principle, agreeing to the application of it, with the exception of the Comptroller and the Attorney General.

Now, we must vote according to our consciences. We are not bound—no legislative body is bound legally by a platform. But, Mr. Chairman, if there is faith in parties, if there is ever to be a party platform put out again, to which a man can subscribe or for which he can vote without a sense of futility, without a sense of being engaged in a confidence game; if all the declarations of principle by political parties are not to be regarded as false pretense, as humbug, as a parcel of lies, we must stand by the principles upon which we were all elected to this Convention. There is one thing, and, in so far as I know, only one thing, that the vast majority of us have assured the people who elected us we would do in this Convention, and that is that we would stand by the position of Hughes and Wadsworth. I, for one, am going to do it. If I form a correct judgment of the self-respecting men of this Convention, it will be with a great company that I do it.

But, Mr. Chairman, don't let us rest on that. Why was it that these conventions, one after another, four of them, declared to the people that they were for the principle of this bill? In the first place, our knowledge of human nature shows us that the thousands of experienced men in these conventions and meetings had come to the conclusion that that principle met with the approval of the people of the State. It is all very well for Mr. Quigg to tell us what the men he met in Columbia county said, for Mr. Green to write letters to his friends in Binghamton, but nine hundred and seventy men in that mass meeting on the fifth of December told you what their observation was, that they would commend their party to the people of this State by declaring this principle. A thousand and odd men in the Republican conventions of 1912, 1913 and 1914 have given proof conclusive of what their observation of public opinion was. A thousand and odd men in the Democratic convention of 1914 have given proof conclusive of what their observation of public opinion was. Conventions don't put planks in platforms to drive away votes.

Again I ask, why was it that they thought that these principles would commend their tickets to the people of the State? Why was it that the people of the State had given evidence to these thousands of experienced men in the politics of the State that those principles would be popular? Well, of course, you cannot escape the conclusion that it was because the people of the State found something wrong about the government of the State. My friend, Mr. Brackett, sees nothing wrong about it.

He has been for fifteen years in the Senate; I suppose he could have stayed there as long as he wanted to. He is honored and respected and has his own way in Saratoga county. Why should he see anything wrong? My friend, Mr. Green, is comfortably settled in the Excise Department, and he sees nothing wrong. Mr. Chairman, there never was a reform in administration in this world which did not have to make its way against the strong feeling of good, honest men, concerned in existing methods of administration, and who saw nothing wrong. Never! It is no impeachment to a man's honesty, his integrity, that he thinks the methods that he is familiar with and in which he is engaged are all right. But you cannot make any improvement in this world without overriding the satisfaction that men have in the things as they are, and of which they are a contented and successful part. I say that the growth, extension, general acceptance of this principle shows that all these experienced politicians and citizens in all these Conventions felt that the people of the State saw something wrong in our State government, and we are here charged with a duty, not of closing our eyes, but of opening them, and seeing, if we can, what it was that was wrong. Anybody can see that all these one hundred and fifty-two outlying agencies, big and little, lying around loose, accountable to nobody, spending all the money they could get, violate every principle of economy, of efficiency, of the proper transaction of business. Everyone can see that all around us are political organizations carrying on the business of government, that have learned their lesson from the great business organizations which have been so phenomenally successful in recent years.

The governments of our cities: Why, twenty years ago, when James Bryce wrote his "American Commonwealth," the government of American cities was a byword and a shame for Americans all over the world. Heaven be thanked, the government of our cities has now gone far toward redeeming itself and us from that disgrace, and the government of American cities to-day is in the main far superior to the government of American States. I challenge contradiction to that statement. How has it been reached? How have our cities been lifted up from the low grade of incompetency and corruption on which they

stood when the "American Commonwealth" was written? It
has been done by applying the principles of this bill to city government, by giving power to the men elected by the people to
do the things for which they were elected. So I say it is quite
plain that that is not all. It is not all.

I am going to discuss a subject now that goes back to the beginning of the political life of the oldest man in this Convention, and one to which we cannot close our eyes, if we keep the
obligations of our oath. We talk about the government of the
Constitution. We have spent many days in discussing the powers of this and that and the other officer. What is the government of this State? What has it been during the forty years
of my acquaintance with it? The government of the constitution? Oh, no; not half the time, nor half way. When I asked
what do the people find wrong in our State government, my
mind goes back to those periodic fits of public rage in which the
people rouse up and tear down the political leader, first of one
party and then of the other party. It goes on to the public
feeling of resentment against the control of party organizations,
of both parties and of all parties. Now, I treat this subject in
my own mind not as a personal question to any man. I am
talking about the system. From the days of Fenton, and Conkling, and Arthur and Cornell, and Platt, from the days of David
B. Hill, down to the present time, the government of the State
has presented two different lines of activity, one of the constitutional and statutory officers of the State, and the other of the
party leaders—they call them party bosses. They call the system—I don't coin the phrase; I adopt it because it carries its
own meaning—they call it "invisible government." For I don't
remember how many years, Mr. Conkling was the supreme ruler in this State; the Governor did not count, the Legislatures
did not count; comptrollers and secretaries of state and what
not, did not count. It was what Mr. Conkling said; and in a
great outburst of public rage he was pulled down.

Then Mr. Platt ruled the State; for nigh upon twenty years
he ruled it. It was not the Governor; it was not the Legislature; it was not any elected officers; it was Mr. Platt. And
the capitol was not here; it was at 49 Broadway; Mr. Platt
and his lieutenants. It makes no difference what name you

give, whether you call it Fenton or Conkling or Cornell or Arthur or Platt, or by the names of men now living. The ruler of the State during the greater part of the forty years of my acquaintance with the State government has not been any man authorized by the Constitution or by the law; and, sir, there is throughout the length and width of this State a deep and sullen and long-continued resentment at being governed thus by men not of the people's choosing. The party leader is elected by no one, accountable to no one, bound by no oath of office, removable by no one. Ah! My friends here have talked about this bill's creating an autocracy. The word points with admirable facility the very opposite reason for the bill. It is to destroy autocracy and restore power so far as may be to the men elected by the people, accountable to the people, removable by the people. I don't criticize the men of the invisible government. How can I? I have known them all, and among them have been some of my dearest friends. I can never forget the deep sense of indignation that I felt in the abuse that was heaped upon Chester A. Arthur, whom I honored and loved, when he was attacked because he held the position of political leader. It is all wrong. It is all wrong that a government not authorized by the people should be continued superior to the government that is authorized by the people.

How is it accomplished? How is it done? Mr. Chairman, it is done by the use of patronage, and the patronage that my friends on the other side of this question have been arguing and pleading for in this Convention is the power to continue that invisible government against that authorized by the people.

Everywhere, sir, that these two systems of government co-exist, there is a conflict day by day, and year by year, between two principles of appointment to office, two radically opposed principles. The elected officer or the appointed officer, the lawful officer who is to be held responsible for the administration of his office, desires to get men into the different positions of his office who will do their work in a way that is creditable to him and his administration. Whether it be a President appointing a judge, or a Governor appointing a superintendent of public works, whatever it may be, the officer wants to make a success, and he wants to get the man selected upon the ground of his ability to do the work. How is it about the boss? What does the boss have to do? He has to urge the appointment of a man whose appointment will consolidate his power and preserve the organization. There has been hardly a day for the last sixteen years when I have not seen those two principles come in conflict. The invisible government proceeds to build up and maintain its power by a reversal of the fundamental principle of good government, which is that men should be selected to perform the duties of the office and not for the preservation and enhancement and power of the political leader. The one, the true one, looks upon appointment to office with a view to the service that can be given to the public. The other, the false one, looks upon appointment to office with a view to what can be gotten out of it. Gentlemen of the Convention, I appeal to your knowledge of facts. Every one of you knows that what I say about the use of patronage under the system of invisible government is true. Louis Marshall told us the other day about the appointment of wardens in the Adirondacks, hotel keepers and people living there, to render no service whatever. They were appointed not for the service to the State that they were to render; they were appointed for the service that they were to render to promote the power of a political organization. Mr. Chairman, we all know that the halls of this capitol swarm with men during the session of the Legislature on pay day. A great number, seldom here, rendering no service, are put on the payrolls as a matter of patronage, not of service, but of party patronage. Both parties are alike; all parties are alike. The system extends through all. Ah, Mr. Chairman, that system finds its opportunity in the division of powers, in a six-headed executive, in which, by the natural workings of human nature, there shall be opposition and discord and the playing of one force against the other; and so, when we refuse to make one governor elected by the people the real chief executive, we make inevitable the setting up of a chief executive not selected by the people, not acting for the people's interest, but for the selfish interest of the few who control the party, whichever party it may be.

Think for a moment of what this patronage system means. How many of you are there who would be willing to do to your

private client, or customer, or any private trust, or to a friend
or neighbor, what you see being done to the State of New York
every year of your lives in the taking of money out of her
treasury without service? We can, when we are in a private
station, pass on without much attention to inveterate abuses.
We can say to ourselves, I know it is wrong, I wish it could
be set right; it cannot be set right, I will do nothing. But here,
here, we face the duty, we cannot escape it, we are bound to
do our work, face to face, in clear recognition of the truth, un-
palatable, deplorable as it may be, and the truth is that what
the unerring instinct of the democracy of our State has seen in
this government is that a different standard of morality is applied to the conduct of affairs of State than that which is applied in private affairs. I have been told forty times since this
Convention met that you cannot change it. We can try, can't
we? I deny that we cannot change it. I repel that cynical assumption which is born of the lethargy that comes from poisoned air during all these years. I assert that this perversion
of democracy, this robbing democracy of its virility, can be
changed as truly as the system under which Walpole governed
the commons of England, by bribery, as truly as the atmosphere which made the *Crédit Mobilier* scandal possible in the
Congress of the United States has been blown away by the force
of public opinion. We cannot change it in a moment, but we
can do our share. We can take this one step towards, not robbing the people of their part in government, but toward robbing
an irresponsible autocracy of its indefensible and unjust and
undemocratic control of government, and restoring it to the
people to be exercised by the men of their choice and their
control.

Mr. Chairman, this Convention is a great event in the life
of every man in this room. A body which sits but once in twenty years to deal with the fundamental law of the State deals
not only for the present but for the future, not only by its results but by its example. Opportunity knocks at the door of
every man in this assemblage, an opportunity which will never
come again to most of us. While millions of men are fighting
and dying for their countries across the ocean, while government is become serious, sober, almost alarming in its effect up-

on the happiness of the lives of all that are dearest to us, it is our inestimable privilege to do something here in moving our beloved State along the pathway towards better and purer government, a more pervasive morality and a more effective exercise of the powers of government which preserve the liberty of the people. When you go back to your homes and review the record of the summer, you will find in it cause for your children and your children's children, who will review the Convention of 1915 as we have been reviewing the work of the preceding Conventions, to say: my father, my grandfather, helped to do this work for our State.

Mr. Chairman, there is a plain old house in the hills of Oneida, overlooking the valley of the Mohawk, where truth and honor dwelt in my youth. When I go back, as I am about to go, to spend my declining years, I mean to go with the feeling that I have not failed to speak and to act in accordance with the lessons that I learned there from the God of my fathers. God grant that this opportunity for service to our country and our State may not be neglected by any of the men for whom I feel so deep a friendship in this Convention.

ELIHU ROOT

PUBLIC SERVICE BY THE BAR

Presidential Address at the Annual Meeting of the
American Bar Association, Chicago, Illinois,
August 30, 1916

[Mr. Root has been president of the following legal societies in the
United States: Association of the Bar of the City of New York, Amer-
ican Society of International Law, New York State Bar Association,
New York Law Institute, and the American Bar Association.]

One of the most striking effects of the great war is the extraordinary increase of national efficiency which has followed
the spur of necessity. All over Europe among the struggling
nations the virile and simple virtues have emerged from beneath habits of selfish indifference. Industry, inventive energy,
thrift, self-denial, acceptance of discipline, subordination of
individual preferences to the general judgment, loyalty to ideals,
devotion to country and willingness to make sacrifices for her
sake have become general. A new gospel of patriotic service
has replaced the cynicism of privilege and personal advantage.

This change relates not merely to military efficiency but to the
whole social economy and extends throughout the field of production and to all forms of consumption and waste. It carries
a sense of individual responsibility by each citizen to help
make his country strong by production and by conservation.

When the war is over we shall find ourselves in a very different world from that which witnessed the Austrian ultimatum to
Servia. It will be a world in which the greater part of the
nations return to the peaceful competition of production and
commerce with a vast increase of power to compete caused by
the training of hardship and sacrifice. Plainly, the neutral
nations who have neither endured the sufferings nor achieved
the rewards of this hard experience may not look with indifference upon these events. They should realize the increased
efficiency which they will have to meet when they enter again

upon the competition in which all civilized nations must engage. In the amazing developments of these years there are lessons for us to learn which we must not ignore. There are lessons not merely as to submarines and aeroplanes and high explosives, but as to the whole effective capacity of the nation by which it maintains its place and progress in the world in peace as in war. No human power can withhold the people of the United States from taking part in the international competition which will follow the return of peace. It is not a matter of volition. It cannot be controlled by legislation or by change of parties or by voting. The entire community of civilized nations is going through a phase of development from which no one of them can escape and continue to hold its own, and one of the necessary incidents of that development is competition in production and trade. The United States must therefore be prepared to meet competition carried on more effectively than ever before. The power of organization will be at its highest; the advantages of applied science will be greatest; the hindrances of internal misunderstanding and dissension will be at a minimum.

One of the most important features of the present European development for Americans to consider is the fact that it has been along the line of military organization and discipline. That surrender of individual liberty to superior control which is essential to the discipline and efficiency of an army has been extended to civil life and applied in governmental direction of productive industry, of transportation, and of consumption. The habits of communities accustomed to the least possible control over individual action proved wholly unfit in a sudden emergency to meet the military competition of highly disciplined masses. The question how far the abandonment of individualism and the establishment of rigid government control is to be continued or extended for purposes of efficiency in peaceful competition is of the highest interest and importance to us. This importance is quite independent of the question how far it is probable that we shall be required to defend our wealth and security against aggression by armed force.

In either view it is plainly the duty of all Americans, whatever their calling, to consider by what means they can contribute through either the increase or the conservation of power in their own fields of action, towards the permanent higher efficiency of the people of the United States.

There is no body of citizens to whom this duty should appeal more strongly than to the lawyers, because the subject vitally affects the relations between the individual and the state regulated by law and the fundamental conceptions upon which our system of government is based.

There are two relevant truths of universal application and appeal. One is, that the people of the United States need in one important respect a change of the individual attitude toward their government. Too many of us have been trying to get something out of the country and too few of us have been trying to serve it. Offices, appropriations, personal or class benefits, have been too generally the motive power that has kept the wheels of government moving. Too many of us have forgotten that a government which is to preserve liberty and do justice must have the heart and soul of the people behind it—not mere indifference. Too many of us have forgotten that not only eternal vigilance but eternal effort is the price of liberty. Our minds have been filled with the assertion of our rights and we have thought little of our duties. The chief element of strength which the nations of Europe are acquiring is the spirit of their people, who have learned a new loyalty of devotion and sacrifice for their country. In a world where that spirit prevails the United States will slip back in the race unless we, too, have a new birth of loyalty and devotion.

The second general truth is, that national strength requires the spirit of solidarity among the people of the nation. Sectional or class misunderstanding and hatred or dislike are elements of vital weakness. To be strong a nation's citizenship must be a title to friendship and kindly interest among all her citizens. In a strong nation her people will be one for all and all for one. Every part of a country grows stronger with the prosperity of every other part. National wealth and prosperity are made up of the wealth and prosperity of individuals, and we cannot pull down each other without suffering as a people. The rights and privileges, the property and liberty and life of every American, whether he be at home or in Mexico or in the Far East, on land or sea, are our concern and the concern of each of us. Prosperity to him is a benefit to us; misfortune to him is a loss to us; and it is vital to each one of us that we shall have such a country and such a government as shall put power and prestige and honor and active interest and inflexible resolution into the protection of every American whose necessities may come by circumstances to demand the performance of his nation's duty. Whenever a part of a people give themselves up to envy and jealousy of another part that may seem more prosperous, whenever a part of a people seek to equalize conditions by pulling down rather than by building up, the power of the nation begins to wane and the forces which should make the nation great and effective are impaired and wasted by internal controversy and diminished patriotism.

When we turn to the particular field occupied by our profession we cannot fail to see that our country would be made stronger if we could change some characteristics in our administration of the law.

There is great economic waste in the administration of the law viewed from the standpoint of the nation and of the states. There is unnecessary expenditure of wealth and of effective working power, in the performance of this particular function of organized society. We spend vast sums in building and maintaining court houses and public offices and in paying judges, clerks, criers, marshals, sheriffs, messengers, jurors, and all the great army of men whose service is necessary for the machinery of justice, and the product is disproportionate to the plant and the working force. There is no country in the world in which the doing of justice is burdened by such heavy overhead charges or in which so great a force is maintained for a given amount of litigation. The delays of litigation, the badly adjusted machinery, and the technicalities of procedure cause enormous waste of time on the part of witnesses and jury panels and parties. The ease with which admission to the Bar is secured in many jurisdictions and the attraction of a career which affords a living without manual labor has crowded the Bar with more lawyers than are necessary to do the business. Of the 114,000 lawyers in the United States according to the census of 1910, a very considerable part are not needed for the due administration of justice. If that business were conducted like the business of any great industrial or transportation company which is striving for the highest efficiency at the least cost in order to compete successfully with its rivals, a very considerable percentage of the 114,000 would be discharged. We at the Bar are not producers. We perform indeed a necessary service for the community; and to the extent of that necessary service we contribute towards the production of all wealth and the effectiveness of all energy in the community, and we take toll, rightly, from all the property and business in the community for the service. Superfluous lawyers, however, beyond the number necessary to do the law business of the country, are mere pensioners and drags upon the community and upon all sound economic principles ought to be set to some other useful work. There is plenty of work for them to do on the farms of the country.

Why is it that these defects exist in American administration of justice? The American people are not quarrelsome or litigious. They are good natured, practical, simple and direct in their methods of transacting their individual business, respecters of law, and honest in their dealings. Our Bar as a whole is courageous, loyal, and able. Our judges as a whole are just, high minded, and competent. Why do we transact the business of administering justice in such an unbusinesslike way? It is not difficult to point out particular laws and methods which are defective and to say that they ought to be changed; but there is still the question, how did they become defective, and why, after all our experience, do they continue defective?

I think the underlying cause of this defective administration of justice is that the Bar and the people of the country generally, proceed upon a false assumption as to their true relation to judicial proceedings. Unconsciously, we all treat the business of administering justice as something to be done for private benefit instead of treating it primarily as something to be done for the public service. The administration of law is affected by that same general attitude which I have mentioned, in which citizens think about what they are going to get out of their country instead of thinking of what they can contribute to their country. Our political system makes such an attitude on the part of the

Bar very natural and easy. With our highly developed individualism, our respect for the sanctity of individual rights, our conception of government as designed to secure those rights, it is quite natural that lawyers employed to assert the rights of individual clients and loyally devoted to their clients' interest should acquire a habit of mind in which they think chiefly of the individual view of judicial procedure, and seldom of the public view of the same procedure. It is natural that the same habit of thought should be carried into our legislatures by the lawyers who make up the greater part of those bodies; and with our governments of narrow and strictly limited powers it is natural that there should be a continual pressure in the direction of promoting individual rights and privileges and opportunities and very little pressure to maintain the community's rights against the individual and to insist upon the individual's duties to the community. There are indeed two groups of men who consider the interests of the community. They are the teachers in the principal law schools and the judges on the Bench. With loyalty and sincere devotion they defend the public right to effective service; but against them is continually pressing the tendency of the Bar and the legislatures and, in a great degree of the public, towards the exclusively individual view.

The public tendency is exhibited at the very beginning of the whole business in permitting admissions to the Bar without adequate education and training. Few ideas have been more persistent throughout this country than the idea that the prevailing consideration in determining admission to the Bar should be that every young man is entitled to his chance to be a lawyer and that all requirements of attendance in offices and law schools and for difficult examinations are so many obstacles in the way of liberty and opportunity, defenses of aristocratic privilege and derogations from democratic right. The law schools have been slowly winning their way along the lines of better training for the Bar, but the progress is very slow and the pressure for brief and easy ways to get a license to practice is continuous. Only last year the Massachusetts legislature, by statute, reduced the requirements of school attendance for admission to the Bar to two years of evening high school, following upon an agitation carried on in support of the principle, "Let every man have his chance." One of our states, and a very great state indeed, with a very high average of general cultivation, permits any one of good moral character to practice law. Correspondence schools of law flourish, proceeding upon the idea that a man can become a lawyer incidentally by reading law books in spare hours as he goes along with his ordinary occupation. The constant pressure of democratic assertion of individual rights is always towards reducing the difficulty of Bar examinations. One consequence is the excess of lawyers that I have mentioned. Another consequence is that the efficiency of our courts is reduced, their rate of progress retarded, the expense increased, their procedure muddled and involved by an appreciable proportion of untrained and incompetent practitioners; by badly drawn, confused, obscure papers difficult to understand; by interlocutory proceedings which never ought to have been taken and proceedings rightly taken in the wrong way and inadequately presented; by vague and haphazard ideas as to rights and remedies; by ignorance of the principles upon which our law of evidence is based; by ignorance of what has been decided and what is open to argument; by waste of time with worthless evidence and useless dispute in the trial of causes; by superfluous motions and arguments and appeals; and by the correction of errors caused by the blunders of attorneys and counsel. In many jurisdictions there is a considerable percentage of the Bar whose practice causes the courts double time and labor because the practitioner is not properly trained to use the machinery furnished by the public for the protection of his clients. In the meantime other litigation waits and the public pays the expense. There is another evil arising from defective education. These half-trained practitioners have had little or no opportunity to become imbued with the true spirit of the profession. That is not the spirit of mere controversy, of mere gain, or mere individual success. To the student of the law, there come from Hortensius and Cicero, and Malesherbes and De Seze, and Erskine and Adams, from all the glorious history of the profession of advocacy, great traditions and ethical ideals and lofty conceptions of the honor and dignity of the profession, of courage and loyalty for the maintenance of the law and the liberty that it guards. It is to a Bar inspired by these traditions, imbued with this spirit, not commercialized, not playing a sordid game, not cunning and subtle and technical or seeking unfair advantage—a Bar jealous of the honor of the profession and proud of its high calling for the maintenance of justice—that we must look for the effective administration of the law. The old customs under which the young law student was really guided and instructed in the law office of the established practitioner, under which the youth was impressed by the example and spirit and learning of his senior, are rapidly passing away. In the greater part of the country these customs no longer continue. The law school has taken the place of the law office except for acquiring the mere technique of practice, and the rights of the people of the United States to have an effective administration of the law require that the standards of the best law schools shall be applied to determine the right to membership in the Bar. When we compare our own method with the test of the three years' probation of the French Licentiate and the arduous four years' training of the German Refendar we may realize how little the American people have had in mind the protection and promotion of the public interest in requiring competency at the Bar.

No one can help sympathizing with the idea that every ambitious young American should have an opportunity to win fame and fortune. But that should not be the controlling consideration here. The controlling consideration should be the public service, and the right to win the rewards of the profession should be conditioned upon fitness to render the public service. No incompetent sailor is entitled to command a public ship; no incompetent engineer is entitled to construct a public work; no untrained lawyer is entitled to impair the efficiency of the great and costly machinery which the people of the country provide, not for the benefit of lawyers but for the administration of the law.

The same failure to realize that the Bar has public duties as well as privileges has affected the relations which American legislation has sought to establish between the Bar and the Bench in the conduct of the business of the courts. In the hearing and decision of causes in all their stages the judge represents the public interest; the lawyers in the case represent primarily

HICKS' SP.A.S.—30

their particular clients. It is the function of the judge to promote the will of the sovereign people that justice be done to all parties before him; to see to it that the facts are really ascertained; that the law is honestly applied; that unfair advantage is not taken; that witnesses are protected against improper treatment; that the public time is not wasted. On the other hand, it is the business of the lawyer to conduct a case so that his client will win. His relations to the case tend to give him a one-sided view of what is just and fair in that case. The ardor and stress of conflict are not favorable to abstract considerations of justice. He is concerned in exhibiting the facts which will help his client; in stating the law upon which his own side relies; in breaking down witnesses against him and strengthening witnesses in his favor. On each side counsel plays the game for all that it is worth and sometimes superiority of counsel outweighs superiority of merit. Doubtless this contention, this struggle between the opposing sides of the case, is the best possible way in the long run to reach just results. But it is plain that in all the transaction the representative of public justice is the judge on the bench and that there is necessarily between him and the counsel on each side always a certain antagonism and contention. The natural tendencies of the American people emphasize this antagonism. We are restive under authority. We do not yield readily to discipline. We are unwilling to accept defeat. In every game we exaggerate the importance of success in comparison with all the rest of life. The restiveness of the Bar under the control of the judge on the bench finds its expression very widely in our legislation regarding procedure. That legislation is of course framed by the lawyers in our legislatures, and unconsciously, doubtless, their natural attitude of antagonism has led to a great multitude of provisions designed to protect the Bar against interference from the Bench.

The most striking illustration of this tendency is presented by the provisions found in many states, and quite recently urged upon Congress, prohibiting the judge from expressing any opinion to the jury upon questions of fact. From time immemorial it has been the duty of the court to instruct juries as to the law and advise them as to the facts. Why is it that by express statutory provision the only advice, the only clarifying opinion and explanation regarding the facts which stands any possible chance to be unprejudiced and fair in the trial of a cause, is excluded from the hearing of the jury? It is to make it certain that the individual advantage gained by having the more skillful lawyer shall not be taken away. It represents the individual's right to win if he can and negatives the public right to have justice done. It is to make litigation a mere sporting contest between lawyers and to prevent the referee from interfering in the game. The fact that such provisions can be established and maintained exhibits a democracy's tendency to yield support to the human interest of the individual as against the exercise of even its own power by its own representatives and for its own highest purposes.

Under the influence of the same disposition a large part of the detailed and specific legislative provisions regulating practice are really designed to enable law business to be carried on without calling for the exercise of discretion on the part of the court, and the evil results of the absurdly technical procedure which obtains in many states really come from intolerance of judicial control over the business of the courts. A clear recognition of the old idea that the state itself has an interest in judicial procedure for the promotion of justice, and a more complete and unrestricted control by the court over its own procedure would tend greatly to make the administration of justice more prompt, inexpensive and effective; and this recognition must come from the Bar itself.

The present condition of our law presents very strong reasons why lawyers should awake to a sense of responsibility for another and still more serious service which will require a Bar made strong by the application of stringent tests for admission, and by the best work of the best law schools in its training. The vast and continually increasing mass of reported decisions which afford authorities on almost every side of almost every question admonish us that by the mere following of precedent we should soon have no system of law at all, but the rule of the Turkish cadi who is expected to do in each case what seems to him to be right; and then the door would be thrown wide open for the rule of men rather than the rule of law, and for the exercise of personal injustice as well as personal justice. We are approach-

ing a point where we shall run into confusion unless we adopt
the simple and natural course of avoiding confusion by classification, system, the understanding and application of generally
recognized and accepted legal principles. The slow development of the common law with its rich product of legal ideas and
remedies has followed the lines of legal principles; but at all
times the application of legal principles has been conditioned upon the customs from which the law has been evolved and to
which the rules established have been applied. It is no slight
task for discriminating intelligence to distinguish the principles
which have been applied from the incidents of their application,
arising from the social and industrial and political conditions
of the day, involved in the multitude of reported cases that record the progress of the common law. Yet it is continually
more important that the Bar at large shall be trained to see
through the precedents and the incidents to the controlling principles. A few men are already taking the lead in the work of
classification—some, great teachers; some, great judges; some,
great practitioners. But these few play only a small part in administering the law. Thousands of judges and tens of thousands of lawyers in all the cities and villages of this great country
are doing that, and the problem of classifying and simplifying
our law involves the need to carry to the great mass of them,
present and future, a comprehension and discriminating understanding of the legal principles which form the thread of
Ariadne for guidance through the labyrinth of decisions. How
can that be done? Not by writing text books; the book stores
swarm with them already. Not by preaching reform; nobody
listens. Not by the imposition of a system to be accepted, as
Continental Europe accepted the Roman law. No such system
would be accepted. It would be ignored. All our instincts are
against it. Some very able and public spirited lawyers have been
for some years urging the organization of a definite and specific
movement for the restatement of our law; for a new American
Corpus Juris Civilis. They are quite right. It ought to be done.
But who is to do it and how shall he be recognized as a prophet?
Can we elect him by popular vote? Can we select him upon our
own acquaintance with men of genius and self-devotion? No.
Such a man or such a group of men must be the product of

natural selection. They must be evolved by the conditions of life, and they must speak to an audience prepared to listen.

The only way to clarify and simplify our law as a whole is to reach the lawyer in the making and mold his habits of thought by adequate instruction and training so that when he comes to the Bar he will have learned to think not merely in terms of law but in terms of jurisprudence. The living principle of the case system of instruction in our law schools is that the student is required by a truly scientific method of induction to extract the principle from the decision and to continually state and restate for himself a system of law evolved from its history. He is thus preparing not merely to accept formally dogmatic statements of principles but to receive and assimilate and make his own the systematic thought and learning of the world in the science of jurisprudence. With a Bar subjected generally to that process of instruction, the more general systematic study of jurisprudence would follow naturally and inevitably, and the influence of that study would be universal; and from that condition would evolve naturally the systematic restatement of our law, by men equal to that great work. Pour sand slowly upon the level ground; the conical pile produced will have a fixed relation between the area of its base and the height of the cone. It is so with human society. We must broaden knowledge and spirit to build up and we must build up to broaden.

To deal with American law as it is, however, is but half the problem. We are in the midst of a process of rapid change in the conditions to which the principles of law are to be applied, and if we are to have a consistent system that change must be met not at haphazard but by constructive development. The industrial and social changes of our time have been too swift for slowly forming custom. Old rules, applied to new conditions never dreamed of when the rules were stated, prove inadequate too suddenly for the courts readily to overtake them with application of the principles out of which the rules grew. We have only just begun to realize the transformation in industrial and social conditions produced by the wonderful inventions and discoveries of the past century. The vast increase of wealth resulting from the increased power of production is still in the first stages of the inevitable processes of distribution. The power of organization for the application of capital and labor in the broadest sense to production and commerce has materially changed the practical effect of the system of free contract to the protection of which our law has been largely addressed. The interdependence of modern life, extending not merely to the massed city community but to the farm and mine and isolated factory, which depend for their markets and their supplies upon far distant regions and upon complicated processes of transportation and exchange, has deprived the individual largely of his power of self-protection, and has opened new avenues through which, by means unknown to the ancient law, fatal injuries may be inflicted upon his rights, his property, his health, his liberty of action, his life itself. We have not yet worked out the *formulæ* through which old principles are to be applied to these new conditions—the new forms perhaps through which the law shall continue to render its accustomed service to society. The arrival of new conditions to which the law must be adapted has its counter part in the desuetude of old customs and the disappearance of the basis for old rules. The process of change in a nation's standards of conduct in life, which has made the Blue Laws of Connecticut a familiar evidence that laws once vigorous may die a natural death without repeal, is always going on. It is a part of the method by which the common law has developed. But that process seems to have been much accelerated in recent years. Take for example the community's standard of conduct as applied to the domestic relations, the change in the customary rights and duties recognized between parents and children, masters and servants, husbands and wives, the general relation between the sexes, which apparently is about to receive a new impulse towards change from the extension of women's work in Europe owing to the war.

These rapid changes of conditions to which the law has to be adapted furnish the chief reason why we are bombarded by such a multitude of statutes, good, bad, and indifferent, seeking to accomplish changes by express prohibitions, commands, and statutory remedies. This mass of statutes proceeds from natural impulses to hasten the development of the law in its application to conditions which move too rapidly for customs to form. Many of them will be futile, many will be abandoned, many will be modified, many will prove to be valuable contributions to the development of the law, many will prove to have been steps in the wrong direction and to retard development. Taken altogether, they are themselves making customs from which the law of the future is being evolved.

Doubtless a large part of the irritation and prejudice against the courts in recent years has been due to the misunderstanding of those who in their impatience set the courts down as opposed to progress because they themselves do not realize that there has been a progressive development of our law to meet the new conditions, but that by the nature of the institution such development must follow and not precede the public conviction of its necessity.

There is one special field of law development which has manifestly become inevitable. We are entering upon the creation of a body of administrative law quite different in its machinery, its remedies, and its necessary safeguards from the old methods of regulation by specific statutes enforced by the courts. As any community passes from simple to complex conditions the only way in which government can deal with the increased burdens thrown upon it is by the delegation of power to be exercised in detail by subordinate agents, subject to the control of general directions prescribed by superior authority. The necessities of our situation have already led to an extensive employment of that method. The Interstate Commerce Commission, the state public service commissions, the Federal Trade Commission, the powers of the Federal Reserve Board, the health departments of the states, and many other supervisory offices and agencies are familiar illustrations. Before these agencies the old doctrine prohibiting the delegation of legislative power has virtually retired from the field and given up the fight. There will be no withdrawal from these experiments. We shall go on; we shall expand them, whether we approve theoretically or not, because such agencies furnish protection to rights and obstacles to wrong doing which under our new social and industrial conditions cannot be practically accomplished by the old and simple procedure of legislatures and courts as in the last generation. Yet the powers that are committed to these regulating agencies, and which they must have to do their work, carry with them great and dangerous opportunities of oppression and wrong. If we are to continue a government of limited powers these agencies of regulation must themselves be regulated. The limits of their power over the citizen must be fixed and determined. The rights of the citizen against them must be made plain. A system of administrative law must be developed, and that with us is still in its infancy, crude and imperfect.

The development of our law under the conditions which I have pointed out will be accompanied by many possibilities of injurious error. There will be danger that progress will be diverted in one direction and another from lines really responsive to the needs of the people, really growing out of their life and adapted to their character and the genius of their institutions, and will be attempted along the lines of theory devised by fertile and ingenious minds for speedy reforms. Ardent spirits, awakened by circumstances to the recognition of abuses, under the influence of praiseworthy feeling, often desire to impose upon the community their own more advanced and perfect views for the conduct of life. The rapidity of change which characterizes our time is provocative of such proposals. The tremendous power of legislation, which is exercised so freely and with little consideration in our legislative bodies, lends itself readily to the accomplishment of such purposes. Sometimes such plans are of the highest value. More frequently they are worthless and lead to wasted effort and abandonment. The test of their value is not to be found in the perfection of reason. Man is not a logical animal, and that is especially true of the people of the United States and the people of Great Britain, from whom our methods of thought and procedure were derived. The natural course for the development of our law and institutions does not follow the line of pure reason or the demands of scientific method. It is determined by the impulses, the immediate needs, the sympathies and passions, the idealism and selfishness, of all the vast multitude who are really from day to day building up their own law. No matter what legislatures and congresses and publicists and judges may do, the people are making their own law today as truly as in the earlier periods of the growth of the common law. No statute can ever long impose a law upon them which they do not assimilate. Whether repealed or not, it will be rejected and become a dead letter. No decision that is inconsistent with their growth can long resist the pressure to distinguish and overrule. What can be done, what must be done to make true and uninterrupted progress is that those members of the democracy to whom opportunity has brought instruction in the dynamics of law and self-government, shall so lead and direct the methods of development as to respond to the noblest impulses, the highest purposes, the most practical idealism, of this great law-making multitude, so that the growth of the law shall receive its impetus from the best and not from the worst forces of the community, and be guided by the wisdom and not the folly, the virtues and not the vices, of the people.

There will always be danger of seeking lines of law development which appear upon the surface to be progress but which are really an abandonment of progress. Long continued advance in this world in any useful direction is difficult and slow. Progress in self-government requires the self-governing people to apply rules of action to their own conduct; to limit themselves by self-denying ordinances; to restrain their own impulses and cure their own faults. There must be many shortcomings in such an effort. It is a hard road to travel, and wearisome, and success must be long deferred. Human nature turns readily to any proposal of swift and easy reform which may relieve it of the burdensome task of self-control by the exercise of compulsion on some one else. That is not reform; it is surrender.. Infinite harm may be done by such attempts and long wanderings and confusion of effort may ensue; but if the people are to go on with the development of their free self-government they must ultimately come back to take up themselves the burden which they have sought to escape.

There will always be danger of developing our law along lines which will break down the carefully adjusted distribution of powers between the national and the state government. Upon the preservation of that balance, not necessarily in detail but in substance, depends, upon the one hand, the maintenance of our national power and, on the other hand, the preservation of that local self-government which in so vast a country is essential to real liberty. There is a continual tendency to restrict the exercise of national authority wherever it interferes with the local convenience or interest of a particular state or group of states; and, on the other hand, there is an equally persistent tendency to call in the exercise of national power to perform the duties of local government where states lack effectively organized power or wish to be spared expense or see an opportunity to get money out of the national treasury for local use, or where some portions of the country wish to impose their ideas on the remainder of the country. The same states that are unwilling to give the national judiciary jurisdiction to enforce the protection of aliens promised in national treaties or to permit a national force of citizen soldiery to be commanded by officers appointed by the national executive instead of militia officers appointed by the governors of the states, will urge Congress to pass sumptuary laws controlling the private life and conduct of affairs in local communities and will hand over to the national government strictly local regulations for the sake of an appropriation. Powers thus conferred under special motives and for special purposes do not revert. They are continued. And if the process goes on our local governments will grow weaker and the central government stronger in control of local affairs until local government is dominated from Washington by the votes of distant majorities indifferent to local customs and needs. When that time comes the freedom of adjustment which preserves both national power and local liberty in our system, will be destroyed and the breaking up of the union will inevitably follow.

More critical still is the danger of too great a reaction from the system of free contract upon which our government has long been developing—a reaction which will destroy the basis of individual liberty upon which our institutions rest. We are in the midst of a reaction now. It was inevitable. The individualism which was the formula of reform in the early nineteenth century was democracy's reaction against the law and custom that made the status to which men were born the controlling factor in their lives. It was an assertion of each freeman's right to order his own life according to his own pleasure and power, unrestrained by those class limitations which had long determined individual status. The instrument through which democracy was to exercise its newly asserted power was freedom of individual contract, and the method by which the world's work was to be carried on in lieu of class subjection and class domination was to be the give and take of industrial demand and supply. Now, however, the power of organization has massed both capital and labor in such vast operations that in many directions, affecting great bodies of people, the right of contract can no longer be at once individual and free. In the great massed industries the free give and take of industrial demand and supply does not apply to the individual. Nor does the right of free contract protect the individual under those conditions of complicated interdependence which make so large a part of the community dependent for their food, their clothing, their health and means of continuing life itself, upon the service of a multitude of people with whom they have no direct relations whatever, contract or otherwise. Accordingly, democracy turns again to government to furnish by law the protection which the individual can no longer secure through his freedom of contract and to compel the vast multitude on whose co-operation all of us are dependent to do their necessary part in the life of the community. Plainly, in some directions and to some extent such governmental control is necessary; but we should not forget that every increase of governmental power to control the conduct of life is to some extent a surrender of individual freedom and a step backwards towards that social condition in which men's lives are determined by status rather than by their own free will. We should be careful that in promoting the efficiency of government we do it by the just application and not by the surrender of the true principles upon which our government is founded. Let me state the case in its simplest terms: The central principle of our system of government is in the proposition that every man has a right to full and complete individual liberty, limited only by the equal liberty of every other man. From that right all others are deduced; the right to life, to property, to the pursuit of happiness, are its corollaries. Our whole system of law is in its essence only the enforcement of the reciprocal limitations of individual liberty. It is a compulsion upon me to limit my liberty by yours and upon you to limit your liberty by mine. The justification of all laws and customs which constrain human conduct is that they are necessary and appropriate for the preservation of the liberty of others. Whatever law passes beyond that limit and seeks to impose upon the individual the ideas of others as to what his conduct should be, whether to subserve the interests of others or to conform to their prejudices or to their ideas of propriety or wisdom, even though those others may constitute an overwhelming majority of the whole community, is a violation of the principles upon which our government was formed; is not the just exercise of governmental power, but is essential tyranny. The test is difficult of application. The incidence and the ultimate effect of law are often indirect and obscure. They depend upon a multitude of conditions imperfectly known and subject to controversy. The highest intelligence and the broadest knowledge are needed for the application of the test; but upon a sincere and unremitting effort that it shall be applied in every step of the development of our law depends the question whether that development shall destroy or shall deepen and strengthen the foundations of our free government.

What part is the Bar to play in this great work of the coming years? Can we satisfy our patriotism and be content with our service to our country by devoting all our learning and experience and knowledge of the working of the law and of our institutions solely to the benefit of individual clients in particular cases? During all our mature lives, in many courts and upon many occasions we have been asserting rights, protecting property, preserving liberty, by appeals to the law, to the great rules of right conduct written into our constitutions; protesting against the abuse of official power, extolling justice, pleading for loyalty to our free institutions. Haven't we meant it? Has it all been mere talk for the purpose of winning cases? Have we never really cared about law and justice except as available instruments to get particular clients out of trouble? Is the Bar doing its duty and playing its part in the development of the law? As a rule the leaders of the Bar devote themselves to their individual practice. As a rule the younger and least experienced lawyers make up the state legislatures. There are exceptions, but that is the rule. Even in the National Congress, although the average of ability and strength is much higher than the public seems to suppose, comparatively few lawyers of the first order make their appearance. The questions involved in the development of the law are seldom adapted to interest an audience in political discussion. The real consideration and discussion and the mature conclusions worthy to be followed must be among the practitioners, the judges, the teachers of the law. The fitness of a people for self-government is measured by their capacity to set up and maintain institutions through which government can be carried on effectively, and responsibly. That rule applies to all large bodies of free agents having a common purpose. It applies to the 114,000 lawyers of the United States. We must have institutions through which our duty can be done if it is to be done. In response to that necessity came the associations of the Bar—the six hundred local and state associations and this great national organization. Here is at hand an institution for the public service of the profession of the law. To enlarge its membership, to improve its procedure, to increase its scope and efficacy, to strengthen its authority and its appeal in the real life of our time—these are steps by which the lawyers of all the states may rise to the high level of patriotic duty and a dignity of service worthy of a true American Bar.

WOODROW WILSON

WARFARE AGAINST MANKIND

Address to Congress in Joint Session, April 2, 1917, Advising that Germany's Course be Declared War against the United States

[Woodrow Wilson was born in Staunton, Virginia, on December 28, 1856. He attended Davidson College, North Carolina, from 1874 to 1875, was graduated from Princeton University in 1879, and from the law department of the University of Virginia in 1881, was admitted to the bar, and practiced law in Atlanta, Georgia, for two years. He received the degree of Doctor of Philosophy from Johns Hopkins University in 1886, and subsequently received honorary degrees from ten institutions. He was Associate Professor in Bryn Mawr College from 1885 to 1888, Professor in Wesleyan University from 1888 to 1890, Professor of Jurisprudence in Princeton University from 1890 to 1910, and President of the University from 1902 to October 20, 1910. He began his political career as Governor of New Jersey, serving from January 17, 1911, to March 1, 1913, when he resigned. He was President of the United States from 1913 to 1921. He headed the American Commission to negotiate the Peace of Paris, sailing for Europe on December 4, 1918, and returning the second time on July 8, 1919. The Peace Treaty was signed on June 28, 1919. He died in Washington, D. C., on February 3, 1924.

The address printed below, although a Presidential message, was delivered in person, according to his practice, before a joint session of Congress. It was delivered on the evening of April 2; the war resolution was adopted by the Senate on April 4, and by the House on the morning of April 6; and on the same day President Wilson attached his signature.]

Gentlemen of the Congress:

I have called the Congress into extraordinary session because there are serious, very serious, choices of policy to be made, and made immediately, which it was neither right nor constitutionally permissible that I should assume the responsibility of making.

On the third of February last I officially laid before you the extraordinary announcement of the Imperial German Government that on and after the first day of February it was its purpose to put aside all restraints of law or of humanity and use its submarines to sink every vessel that sought to approach either the ports of Great Britain and Ireland or the western coasts of Europe or any of the ports controlled by the enemies of Germany within the Mediterranean. That had seemed to be the object of the German submarine warfare earlier in the war, but since April of last year the Imperial Government had somewhat restrained the commanders of its undersea craft in conformity with its promise then given to us that passenger boats should not be sunk and that due warning would be given to all other vessels which its submarines might seek to destroy, when no resistance was offered or escape attempted, and care taken that their crews were given at least a fair chance to save their lives in their open boats. The precautions taken were meagre and haphazard enough, as was proved in distressing instance after instance in the progress of the cruel and unmanly business, but a certain degree of restraint was observed. The new policy has swept every restriction aside. Vessels of every kind, whatever their flag, their character, their cargo, their destination, their errand, have been ruthlessly sent to the bottom without warning and without thought of help or mercy for those on board, the vessels of friendly neutrals along with those of belligerents. Even hospital ships and ships carrying relief to the sorely bereaved and stricken people of Belgium, though the latter were provided with safe conduct through the proscribed areas by the German Government itself and were distinguished by unmistakable marks of identity, have been sunk with the same reckless lack of compassion or of principle.

I was for a little while unable to believe that such things would in fact be done by any government that had hitherto subscribed to the humane practices of civilized nations. International law had its origin in the attempt to set up some law which would be respected and observed upon the seas, where no nation had right of dominion and where lay the free highways of the world. By painful stage after stage has that law been built up, with meagre enough results, indeed, after all was accomplished that could be accomplished, but always with a clear view, at least, of what the heart and conscience of mankind demanded. This minimum of right the German Government has swept aside under the plea of retaliation and necessity and because it had no weapons which it could use at sea except these which it is impossible to employ as it is employing them without throwing to the winds all scruples of humanity or of respect for the understandings that were supposed to underlie the intercourse of the world. I am not now thinking of the loss of property involved, immense and serious as that is, but only of the wanton and wholesale destruction of the lives of non-combatants, men, women, and children, engaged in pursuits which have always, even in the darkest periods of modern history, been deemed innocent and legitimate. Property can be paid for; the lives of peaceful and innocent people cannot be. The present German submarine warfare against commerce is a warfare against mankind.

It is a war against all nations. American ships have been sunk, American lives taken, in ways which it has stirred us very deeply to learn of, but the ships and people of other neutral and friendly nations have been sunk and overwhelmed in the waters in the same way. There has been no discrimination. The challenge is to all mankind. Each nation must decide for itself how it will meet it. The choice we make for ourselves must be made with a moderation of counsel and a temperateness of judgment befitting our character and our motives as a nation. We must put excited feeling away. Our motive will not be revenge or the victorious assertion of the physical might of the nation, but only the vindication of right, of human right, of which we are only a single champion.

When I addressed the Congress on the twenty-sixth of February last I thought that it would suffice to assert our neutral rights with arms, our right to use the seas against unlawful interference, our right to keep our people safe against unlawful violence. But armed neutrality, it now appears, is impracticable. Because submarines are in effect outlaws when used as the German submarines have been used against merchant shipping, it is impossible to defend ships against their attacks as the law of nations has assumed that merchantmen would defend themselves against privateers or cruisers, visible craft giving chase upon the open sea. It is common prudence in such circumstances, grim necessity indeed, to endeavour to destroy them before they have shown their own intention. They must be dealt with upon sight, if dealt with at all. The German Government denies the right of neutrals to use arms at all within the areas of the sea which it has proscribed, even in the defense of rights which no modern publicist has ever before questioned their right to defend. The intimation is conveyed that the armed guards which we have placed on our merchant ships will be treated as beyond the pale of law and subject to be dealt with as pirates would be. Armed neutrality is ineffectual enough at best; in such circumstances and in the face of such pretensions it is worse than ineffectual; it is likely only to produce what it was meant to prevent; it is practically certain to draw us into the war without either the rights or the effectiveness of belligerents. There is one choice we cannot make, we are incapable of making: we will not choose the path of submission and suffer the most sacred rights of our nation and our people to be ignored or violated. The wrongs against which we now array ourselves are no common wrongs: they cut to the very roots of human life.

With a profound sense of the solemn and even tragical character of the step I am taking and of the grave responsibilities which it involves, but in unhesitating obedience to what I deem my constitutional duty, I advise that the Congress declare the recent course of the Imperial German Government to be in fact nothing less than war against the government and people of the United States; that it formally accept the status of belligerent which has thus been thrust upon it; and that it take immediate steps not only to put the country in a more thorough state of defense but also to exert all its power and employ all its resources to bring the Government of the German Empire to terms and end the war.

What this will involve is clear. It will involve the utmost practicable co-operation in counsel and action with the governments now at war with Germany, and, as incident to that, the extension to those governments of the most liberal financial credits, in order that our resources may so far as possible be added to theirs. It will involve the organization and mobilization of all the material resources of the country to supply the

HICKS' SP.A.S.—31

materials of war and serve the incidental needs of the nation in the most abundant and yet the most economical and efficient way possible. It will involve the immediate full equipment of the navy in all respects but particularly in supplying it with the best means of dealing with the enemy's submarines. It will involve the immediate addition to the armed forces of the United States already provided for by law in case of war at least five hundred thousand men, who should, in my opinion, be chosen upon the principle of universal liability to service, and also the authorization of subsequent additional increments of equal force so soon as they may be needed and can be handled in training. It will involve also, of course, the granting of adequate credits to the Government, sustained, I hope, so far as they can equitably be sustained by the present generation, by well conceived taxation.

I say sustained so far as may be equitable by taxation because it seems to me that it would be most unwise to base the credits which will now be necessary entirely on money borrowed. It is our duty, I most respectfully urge, to protect our people so far as we may against the very serious hardships and evils which would be likely to arise out of the inflation which would be produced by vast loans.

In carrying out the measures by which these things are to be accomplished we should keep constantly in mind the wisdom of interfering as little as possible in our own preparation and in the equipment of our own military forces with the duty—for it will be a very practical duty—of supplying the nations already at war with Germany with the materials which they can obtain only from us or by our assistance. They are in the field and we should help them in every way to be effective there.

I shall take the liberty of suggesting, through the several executive departments of the Government, for the consideration of your committees, measures for the accomplishment of the several objects I have mentioned. I hope that it will be your pleasure to deal with them as having been framed after very careful thought by the branch of the Government upon which the responsibility of conducting the war and safeguarding the nation will most directly fall.

While we do these things, these deeply momentous things, let us be very clear, and make very clear to all the world what our motives and our objects are. My own thought has not been driven from its habitual and normal course by the unhappy events of the last two months, and I do not believe that the thought of the nation has been altered or clouded by them. I have exactly the same things in mind now that I had in mind when I addressed the Senate on the twenty-second of January last; the same that I had in mind when I addressed the Congress on the third of February and on the twenty-sixth of February. Our object now, as then, is to vindicate the principles of peace and justice in the life of the world as against selfish and autocratic power and to set up amongst the really free and self-governed peoples of the world such a concert of purpose and of action as will henceforth ensure the observance of those principles. Neutrality is no longer feasible or desirable where the peace of the world is involved and the freedom of its peoples, and the menace to that peace and freedom lies in the existence of autocratic governments backed by organized force which is controlled wholly by their will, not by the will of their people. We have seen the last of neutrality in such circumstances. We are at the beginning of an age in which it will be insisted that the same standards of conduct and responsibility for wrong done shall be observed among nations and their governments that are observed among the individual citizens of civilized states.

We have no quarrel with the German people. We have no feeling towards them but one of sympathy and friendship. It was not upon their impulse that their government acted in entering this war. It was not with their previous knowledge or approval. It was a war determined upon as wars used to be determined upon in the old, unhappy days when peoples were nowhere consulted by their rulers and wars were provoked and waged in the interest of dynasties or of little groups of ambitious men who were accustomed to use their fellow men as pawns and tools. Self-governed nations do not fill their neighbour states with spies or set the course of intrigue to bring about some critical posture of affairs which will give them an opportunity to strike and make conquest. Such designs can be successfully worked out only under cover and where no one has the right to ask questions. Cunningly contrived plans of deception or aggression, carried, it may be, from generation to generation, can be worked out and kept from the light only within the privacy of courts or behind the carefully guarded confidences of a narrow and privileged class. They are happily impossible where public opinion commands and insists upon full information concerning all the nation's affairs.

A steadfast concert for peace can never be maintained except by a partnership of democratic nations. No autocratic government could be trusted to keep faith within it or observe its covenants. It must be a league of honour, a partnership of opinion. Intrigue would eat its vitals away; the plottings of inner circles who could plan what they would and render account to no one would be a corruption seated at its very heart. Only free peoples can hold their purpose and their honour steady to a common end and prefer the interests of mankind to any narrow interest of their own.

Does not every American feel that assurance has been added to our hope for the future peace of the world by the wonderful and heartening things that have been happening within the last few weeks in Russia? Russia was known by those who knew it best to have been always in fact democratic at heart, in all the vital habits of her thought, in all the intimate relationships of her people that spoke their natural instinct, their habitual attitude towards life. The autocracy that crowned the summit of her political structure, long as it had stood and terrible as was the reality of its power, was not in fact Russian in origin, character, or purpose; and now it has been shaken off and the great, generous Russian people have been added in all their naive majesty and might to the forces that are fighting for freedom in the world, for justice, and for peace. Here is a fit partner for a League of Honour.

One of the things that has served to convince us that the Prussian autocracy was not and could never be our friend is that from the very outset of the present war it has filled our unsuspecting communities and even our offices of government with spies and set criminal intrigues everywhere afoot against our national unity of counsel, our peace within and without, our industries and our commerce. Indeed it is now evident that its spies were here even before the war began; and it is unhappily not a matter of conjecture but a fact proved in our courts of justice that the intrigues which have more than once come perilously near to disturbing the peace and dislocating the industries of the country have been carried on at the instigation, with the support, and even under the personal direction of official agents of the Imperial Government accredited to the Government of the United States. Even in checking these things and trying to extirpate them we have sought to put the most generous interpretation possible upon them because we knew that their source lay, not in any hostile feeling or purpose of the German people towards us (who were, no doubt, as ignorant of them as we ourselves were), but only in the selfish designs of a Government that did what it pleased and told its people nothing. But they have played their part in serving to convince us at last that that Government entertains no real friendship for us and means to act against our peace and security at its convenience. That it means to stir up enemies against us at our very doors the intercepted note to the German Minister at Mexico City is eloquent evidence.

We are accepting this challenge of hostile purpose because we know that in such a government, following such methods, we can never have a friend; and that in the presence of its organized power, always lying in wait to accomplish we know not what purpose, there can be no assured security for the democratic governments of the world. We are now about to accept gauge of battle with this natural foe to liberty and shall, if necessary, spend the whole force of the nation to check and nullify its pretensions and its power. We are glad, now that we see the facts with no veil of false pretence about them, to fight thus for the ultimate peace of the world and for the liberation of its peoples, the German peoples included: for the rights of nations great and small and the privilege of men everywhere to choose their way of life and of obedience. The world must be made safe for democracy. Its peace must be planted upon the tested foundations of political liberty. We have no selfish ends to serve. We desire no conquest, no dominion. We seek no indemnities for ourselves, no material compensation for the sacrifices we shall freely make. We are but one of the champions of the rights of mankind. We shall be satisfied when those rights have been made as secure as the faith and the freedom of nations can make them.

Just because we fight without rancour and without selfish object, seeking nothing for ourselves but what we shall wish to share with all free peoples, we shall, I feel confident, conduct our operations as belligerents without passion and ourselves observe with proud punctilio the principles of right and of fair play we profess to be fighting for.

I have said nothing of the governments allied with the Imperial Government of Germany because they have not made war upon us or challenged us to defend our right and our honour. The Austro-Hungarian Government has, indeed, avowed its unqualified endorsement and acceptance of the reckless and lawless submarine warfare adopted now without disguise by the Imperial German Government, and it has therefore not been possible for this Government to receive Count Tarnowski, the Ambassador recently accredited to this Government by the Imperial and Royal Government of Austria-Hungary; but that Government has not actually engaged in warfare against citizens of the United States on the seas, and I take the liberty, for the present at least, of postponing a discussion of our relations with the authorities at Vienna. We enter this war only where we are clearly forced into it because there are no other means of defending our rights.

It will be all the easier for us to conduct ourselves as belligerents in a high spirit of right and fairness because we act without animus, not in enmity towards a people or with the desire to bring any injury or disadvantage upon them, but only in armed opposition to an irresponsible government which has thrown aside all considerations of humanity and of right and is running amuck. We are, let me say again, the sincere friends of the German people, and shall desire nothing so much as the early re-establishment of intimate relations of mutual advantage between us—however hard it may be for them, for the time being, to believe that this is spoken from our hearts. We have borne with their present government through all these bitter months because of that friendship—exercising a patience and forbearance which would otherwise have been impossible. We shall, happily, still have an opportunity to prove that friendship in our daily attitude and actions towards the millions of men and women of German birth and native sympathy who live amongst us and share our life, and we shall be proud to prove it towards all who are in fact loyal to their neighbours and to the Government in the hour of test. They are, most of them, as true and loyal Americans as if they had never known any other fealty or allegiance. They will be prompt to stand with us in rebuking and restraining the few who may be of a different mind and purpose. If there should be disloyalty, it will be dealt with with a firm hand of stern repression; but, if it lifts its head at all, it will lift it only here and there and without countenance except from a lawless and malignant few.

It is a distressing and oppressive duty, Gentlemen of the Congress, which I have performed in thus addressing you. There are, it may be, many months of fiery trial and sacrifice ahead of us. It is a fearful thing to lead this great peaceful people into war, into the most terrible and disastrous of all wars, civilization itself seeming to be in the balance. But the right is more precious than peace, and we shall fight for the things which we have always carried nearest our hearts, for democracy, for the right of those who submit to authority to have a voice in their own governments, for the rights and liberties of small nations, for a universal dominion of right by such a concert of free peoples as shall bring peace and safety to all nations and make the world itself at last free. To such a task we can dedicate our lives and our fortunes, everything that we are and everything that we have, with the pride of those who know that the day has come when America is privileged to spend her blood and her might for the principles that gave her birth and happiness and the peace which she has treasured. God helping her, she can do no other.

ROBERT M. LA FOLLETTE

FREE SPEECH AND THE RIGHT OF CONGRESS TO DECLARE THE OBJECTS OF THE WAR

SPEECH IN THE UNITED STATES SENATE, OCTOBER 6, 1917, ON
A QUESTION OF PERSONAL PRIVILEGE

[Robert Marion La Follette was born in Primrose, Dane county, Wisconsin, on June 14, 1855. He was graduated from the University of Wisconsin in 1879, was admitted to the bar in 1880, began the practice of law in Madison, Wisconsin, and from 1880 to 1884 was District Attorney of Dane county. He was a Republican member of Congress from 1885 to 1891, and took a prominent part in framing the McKinley Tariff bill. From 1901 to 1905 he was Governor of Wisconsin, and from 1906 to 1925, United States Senator. In 1924 he was an unsuccessful third party candidate for President of the United States. He died in Washington, D. C., on June 18, 1925.

Throughout his political career Mr. La Follette was a progressive, independent thinker, who by effective public speaking impressed his views upon the country. He was opposed to the arming of American merchant vessels in the European War zone, and voted against the resolution of April 4, 1917, declaring war on Germany. The speech printed below, delivered six months after the United States had entered the European War, expressed his deep-seated convictions, had a dramatic effect upon the Senate, and is a representative example of his style of oratory.]

Mr. President, I rise to a question of personal privilege.

I have no intention of taking the time of the Senate with a review of the events which led to our entrance into the war except in so far as they bear upon the question of personal privilege to which I am addressing myself.

Six Members of the Senate and fifty Members of the House voted against the declaration of war. Immediately there was let loose upon those Senators and Representatives a flood of invective and abuse from newspapers and individuals who had been clamoring for war, unequaled, I believe, in the history of civilized society.

Prior to the declaration of war every man who had ventured to oppose our entrance into it had been condemned as a coward or worse, and even the President had by no means been immune from these attacks.

Since the declaration of war the triumphant war press has pursued those Senators and Representatives who voted against war with malicious falsehood and recklessly libelous attacks, going to the extreme limit of charging them with treason against their country.

This campaign of libel and character assassination directed against the Members of Congress who opposed our entrance into the war has been continued down to the present hour, and I have upon my desk newspaper clippings, some of them libels upon me alone, some directed as well against other Senators who voted in opposition to the declaration of war.

One of these newspaper reports most widely circulated represents a Federal judge in the State of Texas as saying, in a charge to a grand jury—I read the article as it appeared in the newspaper and the headline with which it is introduced:

"District Judge Would Like to Take Shot at Traitors in Congress.

"[By Associated Press leased wire.]

"Houston, Tex., October 1, 1917.

"Judge Waller T. Burns, of the United States district court, in charging a Federal grand jury at the beginning of the October term to-day, after calling by name Senators Stone of Missouri, Hardwick of Georgia, Vardaman of Mississippi, Gronna of North Dakota, Gore of Oklahoma, and La Follette of Wisconsin, said:

"If I had a wish, I would wish that you men had jurisdiction to return bills of indictment against these men. They ought to be tried promptly and fairly, and I believe this court could administer the law fairly; but I have a conviction, as strong as life, that this country should stand them up against an adobe wall to-morrow and give them what they deserve. If any man deserves death, it is a traitor. I wish that I could pay for the ammunition. I would like to attend the execution, and if I were in the firing squad I would not want to be the marksman who had the blank shell."

The above clipping, Mr. President, was sent to me by another Federal judge, who wrote upon the margin of the clipping that it occurred to him that the conduct of this judge might very properly be the subject of investigation. He inclosed with the clipping a letter, from which I quote the following:

"I have been greatly depressed by the brutal and unjust attacks that great business interests have organized against you. It is a time when all the spirits of evil are turned loose. The Kaisers of high finance, who have been developing hatred of you for a generation because you have fought against them and for the common good, see this opportunity to turn the war patriotism into an engine of attack. They are using it everywhere, and it is a day when lovers of democracy, not only in the world, but here in the United States, need to go apart on the mountain and spend the night in fasting and prayer. I still have faith that the forces of good on this earth will be found to be greater than the forces of evil, but we all need resolution. I hope you will have the grace to keep your center of gravity on the inside of you and to keep a spirit that is unclouded by hatred. It is a time for the words, 'with malice toward none and charity for all.' It is the office of great service to be a shield to the good man's character against malice. Before this fight is over you will have a new revelation that such a shield is yours."

If this newspaper clipping were a single or exceptional instance of lawless defamation, I should not trouble the Senate with a reference to it. But, Mr. President, it is not.

In this mass of newspaper clippings which I have here upon my desk, and which I shall not trouble the Senate to read unless it is desired, and which represent but a small part of the accumulation clipped from the daily press of the country in the last three months, I find other Senators, as well as myself, accused of the highest crimes of which any man can be guilty— treason and disloyalty—and, sir, accused not only with no evidence to support the accusation, but without the suggestion that such evidence anywhere exists. It is not claimed that Senators who opposed the declaration of war have since that time acted with any concerted purpose either regarding war measures or any others. They have voted according to their individual opinions, have often been opposed to each other on bills which have come before the Senate since the declaration of war, and, according to my recollection, have never all voted together since that time upon any single proposition upon which the Senate has been divided.

I am aware, Mr. President, that in pursuance of this general campaign of villification and attempted intimidation, requests from various individuals and certain organizations have been submitted to the Senate for my expulsion from this body, and that such requests have been referred to and considered by one of the committees of the Senate.

If I alone had been made the victim of these attacks, I should not take one moment of the Senate's time for their consideration, and I believe that other Senators who have been unjustly and unfairly assailed, as I have been, hold the same attitude upon this that I do. *Neither the clamor of the mob nor the voice of power will ever turn me by the breadth of a hair from the course I mark out for myself, guided by such knowledge as I can obtain and controlled and directed by a solemn conviction of right and duty.*

But, sir, it is not alone Members of Congress that the war party in this country has sought to intimidate. The mandate seems to have gone forth to the sovereign people of this country that they must be silent while those things are being done by their Government which most vitally concern their well-being, their happiness, and their lives. To-day and for weeks past honest and law-abiding citizens of this country are being terrorized and outraged in their rights by those sworn to uphold the laws and protect the rights of the people. I have in my possession numerous affidavits establishing the fact that people are being unlawfully arrested, thrown into jail, held incommunicado for days, only to be eventually discharged without ever having been taken into court, because they have committed no crime. Private residences are being invaded, loyal citizens of undoubted integrity and probity arrested, cross-examined, and the most sacred constitutional rights guaranteed to every American citizen are being violated.

It appears to be the purpose of those conducting this campaign to throw the country into a state of terror, to coerce public opinion, to stifle criticism, and suppress discussion of the great issues involved in this war.

I think all men recognize that in time of war the citizen must surrender some rights for the common good which he is entitled to enjoy in time of peace. *But, sir, the right to control their own Government according to constitutional forms is not one of the rights that the citizens of this country are called upon to surrender in time of war.*

Rather in time of war the citizen must be more alert to the preservation of his right to control his Government. He must be most watchful of the encroachment of the military upon the civil power. He must beware of those precedents in support of arbitrary action by administrative officials, which excused on the plea of necessity in war time, become the fixed rule when the necessity has passed and normal conditions have been restored.

More than all, the citizen and his representative in Congress in time of war must maintain his right of free speech. More than in times of peace it is necessary that the channels for free public discussion of governmental policies shall be open and unclogged. I believe, Mr. President, that I am now touching upon the most important question in this country to-day—and that is the right of the citizens of this country and their representatives in Congress to discuss in an orderly way frankly and publicly and without fear, from the platform and through the press, every important phase of this war; its causes, the manner in which it should be conducted, and the terms upon which peace should be made. The belief which is becoming widespread in this land that this most fundamental right is being denied to the citizens of this country is a fact the tremendous significance of which, those in authority have not yet begun to appreciate. I am contending, Mr. President, for the great fundamental right of the sovereign people of this country to make their voice heard and have that voice heeded upon the great questions arising out of this war, including not only how the war shall be prosecuted but the conditions upon which it may be terminated with a due regard for the rights and the honor of this Nation and the interests of humanity.

I am contending for this right because the exercise of it is necessary to the welfare, to the existence, of this Government, to the successful conduct of this war, and to a peace which shall be enduring and for the best interest of this country.

Suppose success attends the attempt to stifle all discussion of the issues of this war, all discussion of the terms upon which it should be concluded, all discussion of the objects and purposes to be accomplished by it, and concede the demand of the war-mad press and war extremists that they monopolize the right of public utterance upon these questions unchallenged, what think you would be the consequences to this country not only during the war but after the war?

Mr. President, our Government, above all others, is founded on the right of the people freely to discuss all matters pertaining to their Government, in war not less than in peace, for in this Government the people are the rulers in war no less than in peace. It is true, sir, that Members of the House of Representatives are elected for two years, the President for four years, and the Members of the Senate for six years, and during their temporary official terms these officers constitute what is called the Government. But back of them always is the controlling sovereign power of the people, and when the people can make their will known, the faithful officer will obey that will. Though the right of the people to express their will by ballot is suspended during the term of office of the elected official, nevertheless the duty of the official to obey the popular will continues throughout his entire term of office. How can that popular will express itself between elections except by meetings, by speeches, by publications, by petitions, and by addresses to the representatives of the people? Any man who seeks to set a limit upon those rights, whether in war or peace, aims a blow at the most vital part of our Government. And then as the time for election approaches and the official is called to account for his stewardship—not a day, not a week, not a month, before the election, but a year or more before it, if the people choose— they must have the right to the freest possible discussion of every question upon which their representative has acted, of the merits of every measure he has supported or opposed, of every vote he has cast and every speech that he has made. And before this great fundamental right every other must, if necessary, give way, for in no other manner can representative government be preserved.

Mr. President, what I am saying has been exemplified in the lives and public discussion of the ablest statesmen of this country, whose memories we most revere and whose deeds we most justly commemorate. I shall presently ask the attention of the Senate to the views of some of these men upon the subject we are now considering.

Closely related to this subject of the right of the citizen to discuss war is that of the constitutional power and duty of the Congress to declare the purposes and objects of any war in which our country may be engaged. The authorities which I shall cite cover both the right of the people to discuss the war in all its phases and the right and the duty of the people's representatives in Congress to declare the purposes and objects of the war. For the sake of brevity, I shall present these quotations together at this point instead of submitting them separately.

Henry Clay, in a memorable address at Lexington, Ky., on the 13th day of November, 1847, during the Mexican War, took a strong position in behalf of the right of the people to freely discuss every question relating to the war, even though the discussion involved a strong condemnation of the war policy of the Executive. He also declared it to be not only the right but the duty of the Congress to declare the objects of the war. As a part of that address he presented certain resolutions embodying his views on these subjects. These resolutions were adopted at that meeting by the people present, and were adopted at many other mass meetings throughout the country during the continuance of the Mexican War.

For introducing in this body some time ago a resolution asserting the right of Congress to declare the purposes of the present war, I have, as the newspaper clippings here will show, been denounced as a traitor and my conduct characterized as treasonable.

As bearing directly upon the conduct for which I have been so criticized and condemned, I invite your attention to the language of Henry Clay in the address I have mentioned.

He said:

"But the havoc of war is in progress and the no less deplorable havoc of an inhospitable and pestilential climate. Without indulging in an unnecessary retrospect and useless reproaches on the past, all hearts and heads should unite in the patriotic endeavor to bring it to a satisfactory close. Is there no way that this can be done? Must we blindly continue the conflict without any visible object or any prospect of a definite termination? This is the important subject upon which I desire to consult and to commune with you. Who in this free Government is to decide upon the objects of a war at its commencement or at any time during its existence? Does the power belong to collective wisdom of the Nation in Congress assembled, or is it vested solely in a single functionary of the Government?

"A declaration of war is the highest and most awful exercise of sovereignty. The convention which framed our Federal Constitution had learned from the pages of history that it had been often and greatly abused. It had seen that war had often been commenced upon the most trifling pretexts; that it had been frequently waged to establish or exclude a dynasty; to snatch a crown from the head of one potentate and place it upon the head of another; that it had often been prosecuted to promote alien and other interests than those of the nation whose chief had proclaimed it, as in the case of English wars for Hanoverian interests; and, in short, that such a vast and tremendous power ought not to be confided to the perilous exercise of one single man. The convention therefore resolved to guard the war-making power against those great abuses, of which, in the hands of a monarch, it was so susceptible. And the security against those abuses which its wisdom devised was to vest the war-making power in the Congress of the United States, being the immediate representatives of the people and the States. So apprehensive and jealous was the convention of its abuse in any other hands that it interdicted the exercise of the power to any State in the Union without the consent of Congress.

Congress, then, in our system of government, is the sole depository of that tremendous power."

Mr. President, it is impossible for me to quote as extensively from this address as I should like to do and still keep within the compass of the time that I have set down for myself; but the whole of the address is accessible to every Senator here, together with all of the discussion which followed it over the country, and in these times it would seem to me worthy of the review of Senators and of newspaper editors and of those who have duties to discharge in connection with this great crisis that is upon the world.

I quote further:

"The Constitution provides that Congress shall have power to declare war and grant letters of marque and reprisal, to make rules concerning captures on land and water, to raise and support armies, and provide and maintain a navy, and to make rules for the government of the land and naval forces. Thus we perceive that the principal power, in regard to war, with all its auxiliary attendants, is granted to Congress. Whenever called upon to determine upon the solemn question of peace or war, Congress must consider and deliberate and decide upon the motives, objects, and causes of the war."

If that be true, is it treason for a Senator upon this floor to offer a resolution dealing with that question?

I quote further from Mr. Clay:

"And, if a war be commenced without any previous declaration of its objects, as in the case of the existing war with Mexico, Congress must necessarily possess the authority, at any time, to declare for what purposes it shall be further prosecuted. If we suppose Congress does not possess the controlling authority attributed to it, if it be contended that a war having been once commenced, the President of the United States may direct it to the accomplishment of any object he pleases, without consulting and without any regard to the will of Congress, the convention will have utterly failed in guarding the Nation against the abuses and ambition of a single individual. Either Congress or the President must have the right of determining upon the objects for which a war shall be prosecuted. There is no other alternative. If the President possess it and may prosecute it for objects against the will of Congress, where is the difference between our free Government and that of any other nation which may be governed by an absolute Czar, Emperor, or King?

In closing his address Mr. Clay said:

"I conclude, therefore, Mr. President and fellow citizens, with entire confidence, that Congress has the right, either at the beginning or during the prosecution of any war, to decide the objects and purposes for which it was proclaimed or for which it ought to be continued. And I think it is the duty of Congress, by some deliberate and authentic act, to declare for what objects the present war shall be longer prosecuted. I suppose the President would not hesitate to regulate his conduct by the pronounced will of Congress and to employ the force and the diplomatic power of the Nation to execute that will. But if the President should decline or refuse to do so and, in contempt of the supreme authority of Congress, should persevere in waging the war for other objects than those proclaimed by Congress, then it would be the imperative duty of that body to vindicate its authority by the most stringent and effectual and appropriate measures. And if, on the contrary, the enemy should refuse to conclude a treaty containing stipulations securing the objects designated by Congress, it would become the duty of the whole Government to prosecute the war with all the national energy until those objects were attained by a treaty of peace. There can be no insuperable difficulty in Congress making such an authoritative declaration. Let it resolve, simply, that the war shall or shall not be a war of conquest; and, if a war of conquest, what is to be conquered. Should a resolution pass disclaiming the design of conquest, peace would follow in less than 60 days, if the President would conform to his constitutional duty."

Mr. Clay as a part of that speech presented certain resolutions which were unanimously adopted by the meeting and which declared that the power to determine the purposes of the war rested with Congress, and then proceeded clearly to state the purposes, and the only purposes, for which the war should be prosecuted.

HICKS' SP.A.S.—32

The last one of these resolutions is so pertinent to the present discussion that I invite your attention to it at this time. It is as follows:

"*Resolved,* That we invite our fellow citizens of the United States who are anxious for the restoration of the blessings of peace, or, if the existing war shall continue to be prosecuted, are desirous that its purposes and objects shall be defined and known, who are anxious to avert present and future perils and dangers, with which it may be fraught, and who are also anxious to produce contentment and satisfaction at home, and to elevate the national character abroad, to assemble together in their respective communities, and to express their views, feelings, and opinions."

Abraham Lincoln was a Member of Congress at the time of the Mexican War. He strongly opposed the war while it was in progress and severely criticized President Polk on the floor of the House because he did not state in his message when peace might be expected.

In the course of his speech Lincoln said:

"At its beginning, Gen. Scott was by this same President driven into disfavor, if not disgrace, for intimating that peace could not be conquered in less than three or four months. But now, at the end of 20 months * * * this same President gives a long message, without showing us that as to the end he himself has even an imaginary conception. As I have said, he knows not where he is. He is a bewildered, confounded, and miserably perplexed man. God grant he may be able to show there is not something about his conscience more painful than his mental perplexity."

Writing to a friend who had objected to his opposition to Polk in relation to this power of the President in war, Lincoln said:

"The provision of the Constitution giving the war-making power to Congress was dictated, as I understand it, by the following reasons: Kings had always been involving and impoverishing their people in wars, pretending generally, if not always, that the good of the people was the object. This our convention understood to be the most oppressive of all kingly oppressions, and they resolved to so frame the Constitution that no man should hold the power of bringing this oppression upon us. But your view destroys the whole matter and places our President where kings have always stood."

I now quote from the speech of Charles Sumner, delivered at Tremont Temple, Boston, November 5, 1846.

John A. Andrew, who was the great war governor of Massachusetts, as I remember, presided at this public meeting, which was in support of the independent nomination of Dr. I. G. Howe as Representative in Congress. Mr. Sumner was followed by Hon. Charles Francis Adams, who also delivered an address at this meeting.

This is the view of Mr. Sumner on the Mexican War, which was then in progress, as expressed by him on this occasion:

"The Mexican War is an enormity born of slavery. * * * Base in object, atrocious in beginning, immoral in all its influences, vainly prodigal of treasure and life, it is a war of infamy, which must blot the pages of our history."

In closing his eloquent and powerful address, he said:

"Even if we seem to fail in this election we shall not fail in reality. The influence of this effort will help to awaken and organize that powerful public opinion by which this war will at last be arrested. Hang out, fellow citizens, the white banner of peace; let the citizens of Boston rally about it; and may it be borne forward by an enlightened, conscientious people, aroused to condemnation of this murderous war, until Mexico, now wet with blood unjustly shed, shall repose undisturbed beneath its folds."

Contrast this position taken by Charles Sumner at Tremont Temple with that of the Secretary of the Treasury, Mr. McAdoo. He is now touring the country with all the prestige of his great financial mission and the authority of his high place in the administration. I quote the language of the authorized report of his speech before the Bankers' Association of West Virginia, September 21, 1917. According to daily press reports he is making substantially the same denunciation in all his addresses:

"America intends that those well-meaning but misguided people who talk inopportunely of peace when there can be no peace until the cancer which has rotted civilization in Europe is extinguished and destroyed forever shall be silenced. I want to say here and now and with due deliberation that every pacifist speech in this country made at this inopportune and improper time is in effect traitorous."

In these times we had better turn the marble bust of Charles Sumner to the wall. It ill becomes those who tamely surrender the right of free speech to look upon that strong, noble, patriotic face.

Mr. President, Daniel Webster, then in the zenith of his power, and with the experience and knowledge of his long life and great public service in many capacities to add weight to his words, spoke at Faneuil Hall, November 6, 1846, in opposition to the Mexican War. He said:

"Mr. Chairman, I wish to speak with all soberness in this respect, and I would say nothing here to-night which I would not say in my place in Congress or before the whole world. The question now is, *For what purposes and to what ends is this present war to be prosecuted?*"

What will you say to the stature of the statesmanship that imputes treason to his country to a Member of this body who introduces a resolution having no other import than that?

Webster saw no reason why the purposes of the war in which his country was engaged should not be discussed in Congress or out of Congress by the people's representatives or by the people themselves.

After referring to Mexico as a weak and distracted country he proceeded:

"*It is time for us to know what are the objects and designs of our Government.*

It is not the habit of the American people, nor natural to their character, to consider the expense of a war which they deem just and necessary"—not only just, but necessary—"but it is their habit and belongs to their character to inquire into the justice and necessity of a war in which it is proposed to involve them."

Mr. Webster discussed the Mexican War at Springfield, Mass., September 29, 1847, and again, while the war was in progress, he did not hesitate to express his disapproval in plain language.

Many battles had been fought and won, and our victorious armies were in the field, on foreign soil.

Sir, free speech had not been suppressed. The right of the people to assemble and to state their grievances was still an attribute of American freedom. Mr. Webster said:

"We are, in my opinion, in a most unnecessary and therefore a most unjustifiable war."

Whoever expects to whip men, free men, in this country into a position where they are to be denied the right to exercise the same freedom of speech and discussion that Webster exercised in that speech little understand the value which the average citizen of this country places upon the liberty guaranteed to him by the Constitution. Sir, until the sacrifices of every battle field consecrated to the establishment of representative government and of constitutional freedom shall be obliterated from the pages of history and forgotten of men, the plain citizenship of this country will jealously guard that liberty and that freedom and will not surrender it.

To return to my text. Mr. Webster said:

"We are, in my opinion, in a most unnecessary and therefore a most unjustifiable war. I hope we are nearing the close of it. I attend carefully and anxiously to every rumor and every breeze that brings to us any report that the effusion of blood, caused, in my judgment, by a rash and unjustifiable proceeding on the part of the Government, may cease."

He makes the charge that the war was begun under false pretexts, as follows:

"Now, sir, the law of nations instructs us that there are wars of pretexts. The history of the world proves that there have been, and we are not now without proof that there are, wars waged on pretexts; that is, on pretenses, where the cause assigned is not the true cause. That I believe on my conscience is the true character of the war now waged against Mexico. I believe it to be a war of pretexts; a war in which the true motive is not distinctly avowed, but in which pretenses, afterthoughts, evasions, and other methods are employed to put a case before the community which is not the true case."

Think you Mr. Webster was not within his constitutional rights in thus criticizing the character of the war, its origin, and the reasons which were given from time to time in justification of it?

Mr. Webster discusses at length what he considers some of the false pretexts of the war. Later on he says:

"Sir, men there are whom we see, and whom we hear speak of the duty of extending our free institutions over the whole world if possible. We owe it to benevolence, they think, to confer the blessings we enjoy on every other people. But while I trust that liberty and free civil institutions, as we have experienced them, may ultimately spread over the globe, I am by no means sure that all people are fit for them: nor am I desirous of imposing, or forcing, our peculiar forms upon any nation that does not wish to embrace them."

Taking up the subject that war does now exist, Mr. Webster asks:

"What is our duty? I say for one, that I suppose it to be true—I hope it to be true—that a majority of the next House of Representatives will be Whigs; will be opposed to the war. I think we have heard from the East and the West, the North and the South, some things that make that pretty clear. Suppose it to be so. What then? Well, sir, I say for one, and at once, that unless the President of the United States shall make out a case which shall show to Congress that the aim and object for which the war is now prosecuted is no purpose not connected with the safety of the Union and the just rights of the American people, then Congress ought to pass resolutions against the prosecution of the war, and grant no further supplies. I would speak here with caution and all just limitation. It must be admitted to be the clear intent of the Constitution that no foreign war should exist without the assent of Congress. This was meant as a restraint on the Executive power. But, if, when a war has once begun, the President may continue it as long as he pleases, free of all control of Congress, then it is clear that the war power is substantially in his own single hand. Nothing will be done by a wise Congress hastily or rashly, nothing that partakes of the nature of violence or recklessness; a high and delicate regard must, of course, be had for the honor and credit of the Nation; but, after all, if the war should become odious to the people, if they shall disapprove the objects for which it ap-

pears to be prosecuted, then it will be the bounden duty of their
Representatives in Congress to demand of the President a full
statement of his objects and purposes. And if these purposes
shall appear to them not to be founded in the public good, or not
consistent with the honor and character of the country, then it
will be their duty to put an end to it by the exercise of their constitutional authority. If this be not so, then the whole balance
of the Constitution is overthrown, and all just restraint on the
Executive power, in a matter of the highest concern to the peace
and happiness of the country, entirely destroyed. If we do not
maintain this doctrine; if it is not so—if Congress, in whom
the war-making power is expressly made to reside, is to have no
voice in the declaration or continuance of war; if it is not to
judge of the propriety of beginning or carrying it on—then we
depart at once, and broadly, from the Constitution."

Mr. Webster concluded his speech in these memorable words:
"We may be tossed upon an ocean where we can see no land
—nor, perhaps, the sun or stars. But there is a chart and a compass for us to study, to consult, and to obey. That chart is the
Constitution of the country. That compass is an honest, single-
eyed purpose to preserve the institutions and the liberty with
which God has blessed us."

In 1847 Senator Tom Corwin made a memorable speech in
the Senate on the Mexican War. It was one of the ablest addresses made by that very able statesman, and one of the great
contributions to the discussion of the subject we are now considering. At the time of Senator Corwin's address the majority
in Congress were supporting the President. The people up to
that time had had no chance to express their views at an election. After referring to the doctrine then preached by the dominant faction of the Senate, that after war is declared it must
be prosecuted to the bitter end as the President may direct, until one side or the other is hopelessly beaten and devastated by
the conflict, with one man—the President—in sole command of
the destinies of the Nation, Mr. Corwin said:

"With these doctrines for our guide, I will thank any Senator
to furnish me with any means of escaping from the prosecution
of this or any other war, for an hundred years to come, if it
please the President who shall be, to continue it so long. Tell

me, ye who contend that, being in war, duty demands of Congress for its prosecution all the money and every able-bodied man in America to carry it on if need be, who also contend that it is the right of the President, without the control of Congress, to march your embodied hosts to Monterey, to Yucatan, to Mexico, to Panama, to China, and that under penalty of death to the officer who disobeys him—tell me, I demand it of you—tell me, tell the American people, tell the nations of Christendom, what is the difference between your democracy and the most odious, most hateful despotism, that a merciful God has ever allowed a nation to be afflicted with since government on earth began? You may call this free government, but it is such freedom, and no other, as of old was established at Babylon, at Susa, at Bactrina, or Persepolis. Its parallel is scarcely to be found when thus falsely understood, in any, even the worst, forms of civil polity in modern times. Sir, it is not so; such is not your Constitution; it is something else, something other and better than this."

Lincoln, Webster, Clay, Sumner—what a galaxy of names in American history! They all believed and asserted and advocated in the midst of war that it was the right—the constitutional right—and the patriotic duty of American citizens, after the declaration of war and while the war was in progress, to discuss the issues of the war and to criticize the policies employed in its prosecution and to work for the election of representatives opposed to prolonging war.

The right of Lincoln, Webster, Clay, Sumner to oppose the Mexican War, criticize its conduct, advocate its conclusion on a just basis, is exactly the same right and privilege as that possessed by every Representative in Congress and by each and every American citizen in our land to-day in respect to the war in which we are now engaged. Their arguments as to the power of Congress to shape the war policy and their opposition to what they believed to be the usurpation of power on the part of the Executive are potent so long as the Constitution remains the law of the land.

English history, like our own, shows that it has ever been the right of the citizen to criticize and, when he thought necessary, to condemn the war policy of his Government.

John Bright consistently fought the Crimean War with all the power of his great personality and noble mind; he fought it inch by inch and step by step from the floor of the English Parliament. After his death Gladstone, although he had been a part of the ministry that Bright had opposed because of the Crimean War, selected this as the theme for his eulogy of the great statesman, as best portraying his high character and great service to the English people.

Lloyd-George aggressively opposed the Boer War. Speaking in the House of Commons July 25, 1900, in reply to the prime minister, he said:

"He has led us into two blunders. The first was the war. But worse than the war is the change that has been effected in the purpose for which we are prosecuting the war. We went into the war for equal rights; we are prosecuting it for annexation. * * * You entered into these two Republics for philanthropic purposes and remained to commit burglary. * * * A war of annexation, however, against a proud people must be a war of extermination, and that is, unfortunately, what it seems we are now committing ourselves to—burning homesteads and turning men and women out of their homes."

I am citing this language, Mr. President, as showing the length to which statesmen have gone in opposing wars which have been conducted by their governments and the latitude that has been accorded them.

"* * * The right honorable gentleman has made up his mind that this war shall produce electioneering capital to his own side. He is in a great hurry to go to the country before the facts are known. He wants to have the judgment of the people in the very height and excitement of the fever. He wants a verdict before the pleadings are closed and before "discovery" has been obtained. He does not want the documents to come, but he wants to have the judgment of the country upon censured news, suppressed dispatches, and unpaid bills."

In a speech delivered October 23, 1901, Lloyd-George charged that the English Army had burned villages, blown up farmhouses, swept away the cattle, burned thousands of tons of grain, destroyed all agricultural implements, all the mills, the irrigation works, and left the territory "a blackened devastated wilderness." He said:

"In June the death rate among the children in the Orange River Colony camps was at the rate of 192 per thousand per annum, and in Transvaal 233 per thousand per annum. In July the figures were 220 and 336 per thousand per annum, respectively. In August they had risen to 250 and 468, and in September to 442 in Orange River Colony and to 457 in the Transvaal. These are truly appalling figures. It means that at that rate in two years' time there would not be a little child left in the whole of these two new territories. The worst of it is that I can not resist the conclusion that their lives could have been saved had it not been that these camps had been deliberately chosen for military purposes. In the few camps near the coast there is hardly any mortality at all"—observe that here is a criticism of the military policies of his government—"and if the children had been removed from the Orange River Colony and the Transvaal to the seacoasts, where they could have been easily fed and clothed and cared for, their lives might be saved; but as long as they were kept up in the north there was a terrible inducement offered to the Boer commandoes not to attack the lines of communication. * * * If I were to despair for the future of this country it would not be because of trade competition from either America or Germany, or the ineffectiveness of its army, or anything that might happen to its ships; but rather because it used its great, hulking strength to torture a little child. Had it not been that his ministry had shown distinct symptoms of softening of the brain, I would call the torpor and indifference they are showing in face of all this, criminal. It is a maddening horror, and it will haunt the Empire to its dying hour. What wonder is it that Europe should mock and hiss at us? Let any honest Britisher fearlessly search his heart and answer this question: Is there any ground for the reproach flung at us by the civilized world that, having failed to crush the men, we have now taken to killing babes?"

Mr. President, while we were struggling for our independence the Duke of Grafton, in the House of Lords, October 26, 1775, speaking against voting thanks to British officers and soldiers, after the battles of Lexington and Bunker Hill, declared:

"I pledge myself to your lordships and my country that if necessity should require it and my health otherwise permit it, I mean to come down to this House in a litter in order to express my full and hearty disapproval of the measures now pursued, and, as I understand from the noble lords in office, meant to be pursued."

On the same occasion, Mr. Fox said:

"I could not consent to the bloody consequences of so silly a contest, about so silly an object, conducted in the silliest manner that history or observation had ever furnished an instance of, and from which we are likely to derive poverty, misery, disgrace, defeat, and ruin."

In the House of Commons, May 14, 1777, Mr. Burke is reported in the parliamentary debates against the war on the American Colonies, as saying he was, and ever would be, ready to support a just war, whether against subjects or alien enemies, but where justice or color of justice was wanting he would ever be the first to oppose it.

Lord Chatham, November 18, 1777, spoke as follows regarding the war between England and the American Colonies:

"I would sell my shirt off my back to assist in proper measures, properly and wisely conducted, but I would not part with a single shilling to the present ministers. Their plans are founded in destruction and disgrace. It is, my lords, a ruinous and destructive war; it is full of danger; it teems with disgrace and must end in ruin. * * * If I were an American, as I am an Englishman, while a foreign troop was landed in my country I never would lay down my arms! Never! Never! Never!"

Mr. President, I have made these quotations from some of the leading statesmen of England to show that the principle of free speech was no new doctrine born of the Constitution of the United States. Our Constitution merely declared the principle. It did not create it. It is a heritage of English-speaking peoples, which has been won by incalculable sacrifice, and which they must preserve so long as they hope to live as free men. I say without fear of contradiction that there has never been a time for more than a century and a half when the right of free speech and free press and the right of the people to peaceably assemble for public discussion have been so violated among English-speaking people as they are violated to-day throughout the United States. To-day, in the land we have been wont to call the free United States, governors, mayors, and policemen are preventing or breaking up peaceable meetings called to discuss the questions growing out of this war, and judges and courts, with some notable and worthy exceptions, are failing to protect the citizens in their rights.

It is no answer to say that when the war is over the citizen may once more resume his rights and feel some security in his liberty and his person. As I have already tried to point out, now is precisely the time when the country needs the counsel of all its citizens. In time of war even more than in time of peace, whether citizens happen to agree with the ruling administration or not, these precious fundamental personal rights— free speech, free press, and right of assemblage so explicitly and emphatically guaranteed by the Constitution should be maintained inviolable. There is no rebellion in the land, no martial law, no courts are closed, no legal processes suspended, and there is no threat even of invasion.

But more than this, if every preparation for war can be made the excuse for destroying free speech and a free press and the right of the people to assemble together for peaceful discussion, then we may well despair of ever again finding ourselves for a long period in a state of peace. With the possessions we already have in remote parts of the world, with the obligations we seem almost certain to assume as a result of the present war, a war can be made any time overnight and the destruction of personal rights now occurring will be pointed to then as precedents for a still further invasion of the rights of the citizen. This is the road which all free governments have heretofore traveled to their destruction, and how far we have progressed along it is shown when we compare the standard of liberty of Lincoln, Clay, and Webster with the standard of the present day.

This leads me, Mr. President, to the next thought to which I desire to invite the attention of the Senate, and that is the power of Congress to declare the purpose and objects of the war, and the failure of Congress to exercise that power in the present crisis.

For the mere assertion of that right, in the form of a resolution to be considered and discussed—which I introduced August 11, 1917—I have been denounced throughout this broad land as a traitor to my country.

Mr. President, we are in a war the awful consequences of which no man can foresee, which, in my judgment, could have been avoided if the Congress had exercised its constitutional power to influence and direct the foreign policy of this country.

On the 8th day of February, 1915, I introduced in the Senate a resolution authorizing the President to invite the representatives of the neutral nations of the world to assemble and consider, among other things, whether it would not be possible to lay out lanes of travel upon the high seas and through proper negotiation with the belligerent powers have those lanes recognized as neutral territory, through which the commerce of neutral nations might pass. This, together with other provisions, constituted a resolution, as I shall always regard it, of most vital and supreme importance in the world crisis, and one that should have been considered and acted upon by Congress.

I believe, sir, that had some such action been taken the history of the world would not be written at this hour in the blood of more than one-half of the nations of the earth, with the remaining nations in danger of becoming involved.

I believe that had Congress exercised the power in this respect, which I contend it possesses, we could and probably would have avoided the present war.

Mr. President, I believe that if we are to extricate ourselves from this war and restore this country to an honorable and lasting peace, the Congress must exercise in full the war powers intrusted to it by the Constitution. I have already called your attention sufficiently, no doubt, to the opinions upon this subject expressed by some of the greatest lawyers and statesmen of the country, and I now venture to ask your attention to a little closer examination of the subject viewed in the light of distinctly legal authorities and principles.

Section 8, Article I, of the Constitution provides:

"The Congress shall have power to lay and collect taxes, duties, imposts, and excises to pay the debts and provide for the common defense and general welfare of the United States."

In this first sentence we find that no war can be prosecuted without the consent of the Congress. No war can be prosecuted without money. There is no power to raise the money for war except the power of Congress. From this provision alone it must follow absolutely and without qualification that the duty of determining whether a war shall be prosecuted or not, whether the people's money shall be expended for the purpose of war or not rests upon the Congress, and with that power goes necessarily the power to determine the purposes of the war, for if the Congress does not approve the purposes of the war, it may refuse to lay the tax upon the people to prosecute it.

Again, section 8 further provides that Congress shall have power—

"To declare war, grant letters of marque and reprisal, and make rules concerning captures on land and water;

"To raise and support armies, but no appropriation of money to that use shall be for a longer term than two years;

"To provide and maintain a Navy;

"To make rules for the government and regulation of the land and naval forces;

"To provide for calling forth the militia to execute the laws of the Union, suppress insurrection, and repel invasion;

"To provide for organizing, arming, and disciplining the militia, and for governing such part of them as may be employed in the service of the United States, reserving to the States, respectively, the appointment of the officers and the authority of training the militia according to the discipline prescribed by Congress."

In the foregoing grants of power, which are as complete as language can make them, there is no mention of the President. Nothing is omitted from the powers conferred upon the Congress. Even the power to make the rules for the government and the regulation of all the national forces, both on land and on the sea, is vested in the Congress.

Then, not content with this, to make certain that no question could possibly arise, the framers of the Constitution declared that Congress shall have power—

"To make all laws which shall be necessary and proper for carrying into execution the foregoing powers, and all other powers vested by this Constitution in the Government of the United States, or in any department or officer thereof."

We all know from the debates which took place in the constitutional convention why it was that the Constitution was so framed as to vest in the Congress the entire war-making power. The framers of the Constitution knew that to give to one man that power meant danger to the rights and liberties of the people. They knew that it mattered not whether you call the man king or emperor, czar or president, to put into his hands the power of making war or peace meant despotism. It meant that the people would be called upon to wage wars in which they had no interest or to which they might even be opposed. It meant secret diplomacy and secret treaties. It meant that in those things, most vital to the lives and welfare of the people, they would have nothing to say. The framers of the Constitution believed that they had guarded against this in the language I have quoted. They placed the entire control of this subject in the hands of the Congress. And it was assumed that debate would be free and open, that many men representing all the sections of the country would freely, frankly, and calmly exchange their views, unafraid of the power of the Executive, uninfluenced by anything except their own convictions, and a desire to obey the will of the people expressed in a constitutional manner.

Another reason for giving this power to the Congress was that the Congress, particularly the House of Representatives, was assumed to be directly responsible to the people and would most nearly represent their views. The term of office for a Representative was fixed at only two years. One-third of the Senate would be elected each two years. It was believed that this close relation to the people would insure a fair representation of the popular will in the action which the Congress might take. Moreover, if the Congress for any reason was unfaithful to its trust and declared a war which the people did not desire to support or to continue, they could in two years at most retire from office their unfaithful Representatives and return others who would terminate the war. It is true that within two years much harm could be done by an unwise declaration of war, especially a war of aggression, where men were sent abroad. The framers of the Constitution made no provision for such a condition, for they apparently never contemplated that such a condition would arise.

Moreover, under the system of voluntary enlistment, which was the only system of raising an army for use outside the country of which the framers of the Constitution had any idea, the people could force a settlement of any war to which they were opposed by the simple means of not volunteering to fight it.

The only power relating to war with which the Executive was entrusted was that of acting as Commander in Chief of the Army and Navy and of the militia when called into actual service. This provision is found in section 2 of Article II, and is as follows:

"The President shall be Commander in Chief of the Army and Navy of the United States and of the militia of the several States when called into the actual service of the United States."

Here is found the sum total of the President's war powers. After the Army is raised he becomes the General in Command. His function is purely military. He is the General in Command of the entire Army, just as there is a general in command of a certain field of operation. The authority of each is confined strictly to the field of military service. The Congress must raise and support and equip and maintain the Army which the President is to command. Until the Army is raised the President has no military authority over any of the persons that may compose it. He can not enlist a man, or provide a uniform, or a single gun, or pound of powder. The country may be invaded from all sides and except for the command of the Regular Army, the President, as Commander in Chief of the Army, is as powerless as any citizen to stem the tide of the invasion. In such case his only resort would be to the militia, as provided in the Constitution. Thus completely did the fathers of the Constitution strip the Executive of military power.

It may be said that the duty of the President to enforce the laws of the country carries with it by implication control over the military forces for that purpose, and that the decision as to when the laws are violated, and the manner in which they should be redressed, rests with the President. This whole matter was considered in the famous case of Ex parte Milligan, 4 Wall. 2, 18 L. Ed. 281. The question of enforcing the laws of the United States, however, does not arise in the present discussion. *The laws of the United States have no effect outside the territory of the United States.* Our Army in France or our Navy on the high seas may be engaged in worthy enterprises, but they are not enforcing the laws of the United States, and the President derives from his constitutional obligation to enforce the laws of the country no power to determine the purposes of the present war.

The only remaining provision of the Constitution to be considered on the subject is that provision of Article II, section 2, which provides that the President "shall have power by and with the consent of the Senate to make treaties, *providing two-thirds of the Senate present concur.*"

This is the same section of the Constitution which provides that the President "shall nominate, and by and with the advice and consent of the Senate, shall appoint ambassadors, other public ministers, consuls, judges of the Supreme Court," and so forth.

Observe, the President under this constitutional provision gets no authority to declare the purposes and objects of any war in which the country may be engaged. It is true that a treaty of peace can not be executed except the President and the Senate concur in its execution. If a President should refuse to agree to terms of peace which were proposed, for instance, by a resolution of Congress, and accepted by the parliament of an enemy nation against the will, we will say, of an emperor, the war would simply stop, if the two parliaments agreed and exercised their powers respectively to withhold supplies; and the formal execution of a treaty of peace would be postponed until the people could select another President. It is devoutly to be hoped that such a situation will never arise, and it is hardly conceiv-

able that it should arise with both an Executive and a Senate
anxious, respectively, to discharge the constitutional duties of
their office. But if it should arise, under the Constitution, the
final authority and the power to ultimately control is vested by
the Constitution in the Congress. The President can no more
make a treaty of peace without the approval not only of the
Senate but of two-thirds of the Senators present than he can
appoint a judge of the Supreme Court without the concurrence
of the Senate. A decent regard for the duties of the President,
as well as the duties of the Senators, and the consideration of
the interests of the people, whose servants both the Senators
and the President are, requires that the negotiations which lead
up to the making of peace should be participated in equally by
the Senators and by the President. For Senators to take any
other position is to shirk a plain duty; is to avoid an obligation
imposed upon them by the spirit and letter of the Constitution
and by the solemn oath of office each has taken.

As might be expected from the plain language of the Constitution, the precedents and authorities are all one way. I
shall not attempt to present them all here, but only refer to those
which have peculiar application to the present situation.

Watson, in his work on the Constitution, Volume II, page
915, says:

"The authority of the President over the Army and Navy to
command and control is only subject to the restrictions of Congress to make rules for the government and regulation of the
land and naval forces. * * * Neither can impair or invade the authority of the other. * * * The powers of the
President (under the war clause) are only those which may be
called 'military.'"

The same author on the same and succeeding page points out
that the President as Commander in Chief of the Army may
direct the military force in such a way as to most effectively injure the enemy. He may even direct an invasion of enemy territory. But, says the author, this can be done "temporarily,
however, only until Congress has defined what the permanent
policy of the country is to be."

How, then, can the President declare the purposes of the war
to be, to extend permanently the territory of an ally or secure

for an ally damages either in the form of money or new territory?

Mr. King. Mr. President, will the Senator yield for a question?

Mr. La Follette. I prefer not to yield, if the Senator will
permit me to continue. I can hardly get through within the
time allotted, and I am certain to be diverted if I begin to yield.

Mr. King. I just wanted to ask the Senator whether he
thinks the President of the United States has contravened any
constitutional powers conferred upon him thus far in the prosecution of the war?

Mr. La Follette. Well, sir, I am discussing the constitutional question here, and Senators must make their own application.

Pomeroy, in his "Introduction to the Constitutional Law of
the United States" (9th edition, 1886, p. 373), says:

"The organic law nowhere prescribes or limits the causes for
which hostilities may be waged against a foreign country. *The
causes of war it leaves to the discretion and judgment of the
legislature.*"

In other words, it is for Congress to determine what we are
fighting for. The President, as Commander in Chief of the
Army, is to determine the best method of carrying on the fight.
But since the purposes of the war must determine what are the
best methods of conducting it, the primary duty at all times
rests upon Congress to declare either in the declaration of war
or subsequently what the objects are which it is expected to
accomplish by the war.

In Elliot's Debates (supplement 2d edition, 1866, p. 439, vol.
5) it is said:

"There is a material difference between the cases of making
war and making *peace.* It should be more easy to get out of war
than into it."

In the same volume, at page 140, we find:

"Mr. Sherman said he considered the executive magistracy
as nothing more than an institution for carrying the will of the
legislature into effect."

Story, in his work on the Constitution (5th edition, 1891, p.
92), says:

"The history of republics has but too fatally proved that they are too ambitious of military fame and conquest and too easily devoted to the interests of demagogues, who flatter their pride and *betray their interests*. It should, therefore, be difficult in a republic *to declare war, but not to make peace*. The representatives of the people are to lay the taxes to support a war, and therefore have a right to be consulted as to its propriety and necessity."

I commend this language to those gentlemen, both in and out of public office, who condemn as treasonable all efforts, either by the people or by their representatives in Congress, to discuss terms of peace or who even venture to suggest that a peace is not desirable until such time as the President, acting solely on his own responsibility, shall declare for peace. It is a strange doctrine we hear these days that the mass of the people, who pay in money, misery, and blood all the costs of this war, out of which a favored few profit so largely, may not freely and publicly discuss terms of peace. I believe that I have shown that such an odious and tyrannical doctrine has never been held by the men who have stood for liberty and representative government in this country.

Ordronaux, in his work on Constitutional Legislation, says: "This power (the war-making power) the Constitution has lodged in Congress, as the political department of the Government, and more immediate representative of the will of the people. (Page 495.)"

On page 496, the same author points out that "the general power to declare war, and the consequent right to conduct it as long as the public interests may seem to require" is vested in Congress.

The right to determine when and upon what terms the public interests require that war shall cease must therefore necessarily vest in Congress.

I have already referred to the fact that Lincoln, Webster, Clay, Sumner, Corwin, and others, all contended and declared in the midst of war that it was the right—the constitutional right—and the patriotic duty of American citizens, after the declaration of war, as well as before the declaration of war, and while the war was in progress, to discuss the issues of the war, to criticize the policies employed in its prosecution, and to work for the election of representatives pledged to carry out the will of the people respecting the war.

Let me call your attention to what James Madison, who became the fourth President of the United States, said on the subject in a speech at the constitutional convention, June 29, 1787:

"A standing military force, with an overgrown Executive, will not long be safe companions to liberty. The means of defense against foreign dangers have always been the instrument of tyranny at home. Among the Romans it was a standing maxim to excite war whenever a revolt was apprehended. Throughout all Europe the armies kept up under the pretense of defending have enslaved the people. It is perhaps questionable whether the best concerted system of absolute power in Europe could maintain itself in a situation where no alarms of external danger could tame the people to the domestic yoke."

I now invite your attention to some of the precedents established by Congress showing that it has exercised almost from the time of the first Congress substantially the powers I am urging it should assert now.

Many of the precedents to which I shall now briefly refer will be found in Hinds' Precedents, volume 2, chapter 49. My authority for the others are the records of Congress itself as contained in the Congressional Globe and Congressional Record.

In 1811 the House originated and the Senate agreed to a resolution as follows:

"Taking into view the present state of the world, the peculiar situation of Spain and of her American Provinces, and the intimate relations of the territory eastward of the River Perdido, adjoining the United States, to their security and tranquillity: Therefore

"*Resolved, etc.,* That the United States can not see with indifference any part of the Spanish Provinces adjoining the said States eastward of the River Perdido pass from the hands of Spain into those of any other foreign power."

In 1821 Mr. Clay introduced the following resolution, which passed the House:

"*Resolved,* That the House of Representatives participates with the people of the United States in the deep interest which they feel for the success of the Spanish Provinces of South America, which are struggling to establish their liberty and independence, and that it will give its constitutional support to the President of the United States whenever he may deem it expedient to recognize the sovereignty and independence of any of the said Provinces."

In 1825 there was a long debate in the House relating to an unconditional appropriation for the expenses of the ministers to the Panama Congress. According to Mr. Hinds's summary of this debate, the opposition to the amendment, led by Mr. Webster, was that—

"While the House had an undoubted right to express its general opinion in regard to questions of foreign policy, in this case it was proposed to decide what should be discussed by the particular ministers already appointed. If such instructions might be furnished by the House in this case they might be furnished in all, thus usurping the power of the Executive."

James Buchanan and John Forsythe, who argued in favor of the amendment, "contended that it did not amount to an instruction to diplomatic agents, but was a proper expression of opinion by the House. The House had always exercised the right of expressing its opinion on great questions, either foreign or domestic, and such expressions were never thought to be an improper interference with the Executive."

In April, 1864, the House originated and passed a resolution declaring that—

"It did not accord with the policy of the United States to acknowledge a monarchical government erected on the ruins of any republican government in America under the auspices of any European power."

On May 23 the House passed a resolution requesting the President to communicate any explanation given by the Government of the United States to France respecting the sense and bearing of the joint resolution relative to Mexico.

The President transmitted the correspondence to the House.

The correspondence disclosed that Secretary Seward had transmitted a copy of the resolution to our minister to France, with the explanation that—

"This is a practical and purely executive question, and the decision of its constitutionality belongs not to the House of Representatives or even to Congress but to the President of the United States."

After a protracted struggle, evidently accompanied with much feeling, the House of Representatives adopted the following resolution, which had been reported by Mr. Henry Winter Davis from the Committee on Foreign Affairs:

"*Resolved,* That Congress has a constitutional right to an authoritative voice in declaring and prescribing the foreign policy of the United States as well in the recognition of new powers as in other matters, and it is the constitutional duty of the President to respect that policy, no less in diplomatic negotiations than *in the use of the national force when authorized by law.*"

It will be observed from the language last read that it was assumed as a matter of course that Congress had an authoritative voice as to the use of the national forces to be made in time of war, and that it was the constitutional duty of the President to respect the policy of the Congress in that regard, and Mr. Davis in the resolution just read argued that it was the duty of the President to respect the authority of Congress in diplomatic negotiations even as he must respect it when the Congress determined the policy of the Government in the use of the national forces. The portion of the resolution I have just read was adopted by a vote of 119 to 8. The balance of the resolution was adopted by a smaller majority, and was as follows:

"And the propriety of any declaration of foreign policy by Congress is sufficiently proved by the vote which pronounces it, and such proposition, while pending and undetermined, is not a fit topic of diplomatic explanation with any foreign power."

The joint resolution of 1898 declaring the intervention of the United States to remedy conditions existing in the island of Cuba is recent history and familiar to all. This resolution embodied a clear declaration of foreign policy regarding Cuba as well as a declaration of war. It passed both branches of Congress and was signed by the President.

After reciting the abhorrent conditions existing in Cuba it reads as follows:

"*Resolved, etc.,* First.   That the people of the island of Cuba are, and of right ought to be, free and independent.

"Second.   That it is the duty of the United States to demand, and the Government of the United States does hereby demand, that the Government of Spain at once relinquish its authority and government in the island of Cuba and withdraw its land and naval forces from Cuba and Cuban waters.

"Third.   That the President of the United States be, and he hereby is, directed and empowered to use the entire land and naval forces of the United States, and to call into the actual service of the United States the militia of the several States, to such extent as may be necessary to carry these resolutions into effect.

"Fourth.   That the United States hereby disclaims any disposition or intention to exercise sovereignty, jurisdiction, or control over said island except for the pacification thereof, and asserts its determination, when that is accomplished, to leave the government and control of the island to its people."

On April 28, 1904, a joint resolution was passed by both Houses of Congress in the following terms:

"That it is the sense of the Congress of the United States that it is desirable in the interests of uniformity of action by maritime States in time of war, that the President endeavor to bring about an understanding among the principal maritime powers, with a view to incorporating into the permanent law of civilized nations the principle of the exemption of all private property at sea, not contraband of war, from capture or destruction by belligerents."

Here it will be observed that the Congress proposed by resolution to direct the President as to the policy of exempting from capture private property at sea, not contraband of war, in not only one war merely but in all wars, providing that other maritime powers could be brought to adopt the same policy.   So far as I am aware, there is an unbroken line of precedents by Congress upon this subject down to the time of the present administration.   It is true that in 1846 President Polk, without consulting Congress, assumed to send the Army of the United

States into territory the title of which was in dispute between the United States and Mexico, thereby precipitating bloodshed and the Mexican War. But it is also true that this act was condemned as unconstitutional by the great constitutional lawyers of the country, and Abraham Lincoln, when he became a Member of the next Congress, voted for and supported the resolution, called the Ashmun amendment, which passed the House of Representatives, declaring that the Mexican War had been "unnecessarily and unconstitutionally begun by the President of the United States." (See Schouler's History of the United States, vol. 5, p. 83. See also Lincoln's speech in the House of Representatives, Jan. 12, 1848.)

That the full significance of this resolution was appreciated by the House of Representatives is shown by the speech of Mr. Venable, Representative from North Carolina, and a warm supporter of President Polk, made in the House, January 12, 1848, where referring to this resolution he says:.

"Eighty-five Members of this House sustained that amendment (referring to the Ashmun amendment) and it now constitutes one of our recorded acts. I will not here stop to inquire as to the moral effect upon the Mexican people and the Mexican Government which will result to us from such a vote in the midst of a war. I suppose gentlemen have fully weighed this matter. Neither will I now inquire how much such a vote will strengthen our credit or facilitate the Government in furnishing the necessary supply of troops. * * *

"They (referring to his fellow Members in the House of Representatives) have said by their votes that the President has violated the Constitution in the most flagrant manner; that every drop of blood which has been shed, every bone which now whitens the plains of Mexico, every heart-wringing agony which has been produced must be placed to his account who has so flagitiously violated the Constitution and involved the Nation in the horrors of war. This the majority of this House have declared on oath. The grand inquest of the Nation have asserted the fact and fixed it on their records, and I here demand of them to impeach the President."

That Mr. Lincoln was in no manner deterred from the discharge of his duty as he saw it is evidenced by the fact that on the day following the speech of Representative Venable, Lincoln replied with one of the ablest speeches of his career, the opening sentences of which I desire to quote. He said:

"Some, if not all, the gentlemen of the other side of the House, who have addressed the committee within the last two days, have spoken rather complainingly, if I have rightly understood them, of the vote given a week or 10 days ago, declaring that the War with Mexico was unnecessarily and unconstitutionally commenced by the President. I admit that such a vote should not be given in mere party wantonness and that the one given is justly censurable, if it have no other or better foundation. I am one of those who joined in that vote; and I did so under my best impression of the truth of the case."

Lincoln then proceeded to demonstrate the truth of the charge as he regarded it. Evidently he did not think that patriotism in war more than in peace required the suppression of the truth respecting anything pertaining to the conduct of the war.

And yet to-day, Mr. President, for merely suggesting a possible disagreement with the administration on any measure submitted, or the offering of amendments to increase the tax upon incomes, or on war profits, is "treason to our country and an effort to serve the enemy."

Since the Constitution vests in Congress the supreme power to determine when and for what purpose the country will engage in war and the objects to attain which the war will be prosecuted, it seems to me to be an evasion of a solemn duty on the part of the Congress not to exercise that power at this critical time in the Nation's affairs. The Congress can no more avoid its responsibility in this matter than it can in any other. As the Nation's purposes in conducting this war are of supreme importance to the country, it is the supreme duty of Congress to exercise the function conferred upon it by the Constitution of guiding the foreign policy of the Nation in the present crisis.

A minor duty may be evaded by Congress, a minor responsibility avoided without disaster resulting, but on this momentous question there can be no evasion, no shirking of duty of the Congress, without subverting our form of government. If our Constitution is to be changed so as to give the President the power to determine the purposes for which this Nation will engage in war, and the conditions on which it will make peace, then let that change be made deliberately by an amendment to the Constitution proposed and adopted in a constitutional manner. It would be bad enough if the Constitution clothed the President with any such power, but to exercise such power without constitutional authority can not long be tolerated if even the forms of free government are to remain. We all know that no amendment to the Constitution giving the President the powers suggested would be adopted by the people. We know that if such an amendment were to be proposed it would be overwhelmingly defeated.

The universal conviction of those who yet believe in the rights of the people is that the first step toward the prevention of war and the establishment of peace, permanent peace, is to give the people who must bear the brunt of war's awful burden more to say about it. The masses will understand that it was the evil of a one-man power exercised in a half dozen nations through the malevolent influences of a system of secret diplomacy that plunged the helpless peoples of Europe into the awful war that has been raging with increasing horror and fury ever since it began and that now threatens to engulf the world before it stops.

No conviction is stronger with the people to-day than that there should be no future wars except in case of actual invasion, unless supported by a referendum, a plebiscite, a vote of ratification upon the declaration of war before it shall become effective.

And because there is no clearness of understanding, no unity of opinion in this country on the part of the people as to the conditions upon which we are prosecuting this war or what the specific objects are upon the attainment of which the present administration would be willing to conclude a peace, it becomes still more imperative each day that Congress should assert its constitutional power to define and declare the objects of this war which will afford the basis for a conference and for the establishment of permanent peace. The President has asked the German people to speak for themselves on this great world issue; why should not the American people voice their convictions through their chosen representatives in Congress?

Ever since new Russia appeared upon the map she has been holding out her hands to free America to come to her support in declaring for a clear understanding of the objects to be attained to secure peace. Shall we let this most remarkable revolution the world has ever witnessed appeal to us in vain?

We have been six months at war. We have incurred financial obligations and made expenditures of money in amounts already so large that the human mind can not comprehend them. The Government has drafted from the peaceful occupations of civil life a million of our finest young men—and more will be taken if necessary—to be transported 4,000 miles over the sea, with their equipment and supplies, to the trenches of Europe.

The first chill winds of autumn remind us that another winter is at hand. The imagination is paralyzed at the thought of the human misery, the indescribable suffering, which the winter months, with their cold and sleet and ice and snow, must bring to the war-swept lands, not alone to the soldiers at the front but to the noncombatants at home.

To such excesses of cruelty has this war descended that each nation is now, as a part of its strategy, planning to starve the women and children of the enemy countries. Each warring nation is carrying out the unspeakable plan of starving noncombatants. Each nurses the hope that it may break the spirit of the men of the enemy country at the front by starving the wives and babes at home, and woe be it that we have become partners in this awful business and are even cutting off food shipments from neutral countries in order to force them to help starve women and children of the country against whom we have declared war.

There may be some necessity overpowering enough to justify these things, but the people of America should demand to know what results are expected to satisfy the sacrifice of all that civilization holds dear upon the bloody altar of a conflict which employs such desperate methods of warfare.

The question is, Are we to sacrifice millions of our young men—the very promise of the land—and spend billions and more billions, and pile up the cost of living until we starve—and for what? Shall the fearfully overburdened people of this country continue to bear the brunt of a prolonged war for any objects not openly stated and defined?

The answer, sir, rests, in my judgment, with the Congress, whose duty it is to declare our specific purposes in the present war and to state the objects upon the attainment of which we will make peace.

And, sir, this is the ground on which I stand. I maintain that Congress has the right and the duty to declare the objects of the war and the people have the right and the obligation to discuss it.

American citizens may hold all shades of opinion as to the war; one citizen may glory in it, another may deplore it, each has the same right to voice his judgment. An American citizen may think and say that we are not justified in prosecuting this war for the purpose of dictating the form of government which shall be maintained by our enemy or our ally, and not be subject to punishment at law. He may pray aloud that our boys shall not be sent to fight and die on European battlefields for the annexation of territory or the maintenance of trade agreements and be within his legal rights. He may express the hope that an early peace may be secured on the terms set forth by the new Russia and by President Wilson in his speech of January 22, 1917, and he can not lawfully be sent to jail for the expression of his convictions.

It is the citizen's duty to obey the law until it is repealed or declared unconstitutional. But he has the inalienable right to fight what he deems an obnoxious law or a wrong policy in the courts and at the ballot box.

It is the suppressed emotion of the masses that breeds revolution.

If the American people are to carry on this great war, if public opinion is to be enlightened and intelligent, there must be free discussion.

Congress, as well as the people of the United States, entered the war in great confusion of mind and under feverish excitement. The President's leadership was followed in the faith that he had some big, unrevealed plan by which a peace that would exalt him before all the world would soon be achieved.

Gradually, reluctantly, Congress and the country are beginning to perceive that we are in this terrific world conflict, not only to *right* our wrongs, not only to *aid* the allies, not only to *share* its awful death toll and its fearful tax burden, but, perhaps, to *bear the brunt* of the war.

And so I say, if we are to forestall the danger of being drawn into years of war, perhaps finally to maintain imperialism and exploitation, the people must unite in a campaign along constitutional lines for free discussion of the policy of the war and its conclusion on a just basis.

Permit me, sir, this word in conclusion. It is said by many persons for whose opinions I have profound respect and whose motives I know to be sincere that "we are in this war and must go through to the end." That is true. But it is not true that we must go through to the end to *accomplish an undisclosed purpose, or to reach an unknown goal.*

I believe that whatever there is of honest difference of opinion concerning this war, arises precisely at this point.

There is, and of course can be, no real difference of opinion concerning the duty of the citizen to discharge to the last limit whatever obligation the war lays upon him.

Our young men are being taken by the hundreds of thousands for the purpose of waging this war on the Continent of Europe, possibly Asia or Africa, or anywhere else that they may be ordered. Nothing must be left undone for their protection. They must have the best army, ammunition, and equipment that money can buy. They must have the best training and the best officers which this great country can provide. The dependents and relatives they leave at home must be provided for, not meagerly, but generously so far as money can provide for them.

I have done some of the hardest work of my life during the last few weeks on the revenue bill to raise the largest possible amount of money from surplus incomes and war profits for this war and upon other measures to provide for the protection of the soldiers and their families. That I was not able to accomplish more along this line is a great disappointment to me. I did all that I could, and I shall continue to fight with all the power at my command until wealth is made to bear more of the burden of this war than has been laid upon it by the present Congress. Concerning these matters there can be no difference of opinion. We have not yet been able to muster the forces to conscript wealth, as we have conscripted men, but no one has ever been able to advance even a plausible argument for not doing so.

No, Mr. President; it is on the other point suggested where honest differences of opinion may arise. Shall we ask the people of this country to shut their eyes and take the entire war program on faith? There are no doubt many honest and well-meaning persons who are willing to answer that question in the affirmative rather than risk the dissensions which they fear may follow a free discussion of the issues of this war. With that position I do not—I can not agree. Have the people no intelligent contribution to make to the solution of the problems of this war? I believe that they have, and that in this matter, as in so many others, they may be wiser than their leaders, and that if left free to discuss the issues of the war they will find the correct settlement of these issues.

But it is said that Germany will fight with greater determination if her people believe that we are not in perfect agreement. Mr. President, that is the same worn-out pretext which has been used for three years to keep the plain people of Europe engaged in killing each other in this war. And, sir, as applied to this country, at least, it is a pretext with nothing to support it.

The way to paralyze the German arm, to weaken the German military force, in my opinion, is to declare our objects in this war, and show by that declaration to the German people that we are not seeking to dictate a form of government to Germany or to render more secure England's domination of the seas.

A declaration of our purposes in this war, so far from strengthening our enemy, I believe would immeasurably weaken her, for it would no longer be possible to misrepresent our purposes to the German people. Such a course on our part, so far from endangering the life of a single one of our boys, I believe would result in saving the lives of hundreds of thousands of them by bringing about an earlier and more lasting peace by intelligent negotiation, instead of securing a peace by the complete exhaustion of one or the other of the belligerents.

Such a course would also immeasurably, I believe, strengthen our military force in this country, because when the objects of this war are clearly stated and the people approve of those objects they will give to the war a popular support it will never otherwise receive.

Then again, honest dealing with the entente allies, as well as with our own people, requires a clear statement of our objects in this war. If we do not expect to support the entente allies in the dreams of conquest we know some of them entertain, then in all fairness to them that fact should be stated now. If we do expect to support them in their plans for conquest and aggrandizement, then our people are entitled to know that vitally important fact before this war proceeds further. Common honesty and fair dealing with the people of this country and with the nations by whose side we are fighting, as well as a sound military policy at home, requires the fullest and freest discussion before the people of every issue involved in this great war and that a plain and specific declaration of our purposes in the war be speedily made by the Congress of the United States.

NEWTON D. BAKER

THE CHALLENGE TO AMERICA

ADDRESS AT A MASS MEETING IN THE HIPPODROME, CLEVE-
LAND, OHIO, OCTOBER 17, 1917 *

[Newton Diehl Baker was born in Martinsburg, West Virginia, on
December 3, 1871. He was graduated from Johns Hopkins University
in 1892, and from the law department of Washington and Lee University in 1894. He was private secretary to Postmaster General Wilson
from 1896 to 1897, began the practice of law in Martinsburg, and
moved to Cleveland, Ohio, where he was City Solicitor from 1902 to
1912. He was Mayor of Cleveland from 1912 to 1916, and was appointed Secretary of War by President Wilson, serving from March 7, 1916,
to March 4, 1921. Since that time he has been practicing law in Cleveland. On May 20, 1929, he was appointed by President Hoover a
member of the National Commission on Law Enforcement.

The address printed below, delivered while Mr. Baker was Secretary of War, six months after the United States entered the European
War, is a restrained but moving appeal for public support in the conduct of the war.]

Everybody in this audience will realize my feelings in attempting to make a speech on this lot and under this tent. I
look back over nearly twenty years and remember how often
this tent has been filled with the people of Cleveland as they
discussed among themselves, sometimes in the words of the
speaker on the platform, sometimes of the questioner in the
audience, but always in a lively way, matters of domestic concern. It has also been used in national campaign discussions.
But to-night, I think, is the first time, surely the first time within my knowledge, when the tent has been used by somebody
who came from Washington to tell the people of Cleveland
something about a war in which our great country is engaged.

It is no small task to turn the attention of the people of the
United States away from the opportunities which they have
enjoyed and cultivated in peace to the sterner demands of war.

---

* Reprinted from *Frontiers of Freedom*, published by the George H.
Doran Company, copyright, 1918.

I have no doubt that each one of you in your various business occupations has found that this war has somewhat changed the relations which you sustain to other people, and that your business sustains to other people; but in Washington every eye and every ear and every heart is devoted all the time to a task larger beyond any comparison than any task this nation has yet undertaken, and I want to describe to you, if I can, in very brief phrase, something of the size and character and purpose and hope of that task.

When I went away from Cleveland to Washington, you may recall, peace reigned in the United States, though war raged abroad. Washington, a city of very great beauty, was a quiet and reposeful place, and yet the very night that I left Cleveland to go to Washington a disturbance broke out on the Mexican border which required us to summon a military force to patrol that border and protect the lives and property of our people in the States of Texas, Arizona and New Mexico. And for some months we were raising soldiers, the National Guard, and mobilizing our army on that border until, finally, we had an adequate force there to preserve order between the turbulent forces of the Republic of Mexico and ourselves. We had a small army. A small army was enough. Then the Mexican situation seemed to pass away, and our relation to this struggle across the water became more and more serious and more and more difficult. We began to be drawn into that struggle. It did not matter what our own motives and desires were; it did not matter that we were following a policy of neutrality and friendship to all the belligerents in that contest; it did not matter that we were a peace-loving people; that we had devoted ourselves for sevenscore years to the building up of a civilization which would do away with the necessity of war and establish among men processes for the working out of international difficulties which would not need war as a means of arbitrament—all that made no difference. Inevitably, as though some powerful magnet were drawing at the very heart and vitals of this country, each day seemed to bring us closer to this terrible thing that was going on on the other side. No man in America wished to go to war. From the President down to the humblest citizen in all this republic our only purpose, our only hope, our only prayer was that we might be permitted to be a strong and powerful friend to all of those belligerents and when the war was over, help to reconstruct and adjust our civilization with a fairer hope and promise for men everywhere. We entertained that view, as you all know, and yet, day by day, the situation became more difficult.

Now, just what was the situation? We found that our rights were being trespassed upon. We found that our present adversary—I shall refer to it always as the German Government, and I draw a sharp distinction between any government and its people where that government is an autocracy. If you speak of a government which is a democracy, you include its people, because there the people is the government; but when you refer to a government which is an autocracy, then you draw a sharp line between the government and the people, because the form of government gives the governing function to a few or a class. We found that our present adversary, the German Government, was enlarging the scope of its activities by pressing its lawless conduct upon the shoulders of neutrals, friend and foe alike, and we found that the rights of the United States were being more and more seriously menaced. We still hoped for peace. Our President wrote notes of protest; he wrote notes of pleading protest, many people believed, and up to the very last hour he looked with a deep devotion upon the ideal of peace and the hope that we could remain, as I have said, a peaceful and powerful friend of all these people.

International law is a system of agreements among nations made for the purpose of abating the horrors of warfare, and the progress of civilization consists, so far as nations and their rights are concerned, in constant improvement in international law, and in constant amelioration or betterment of the horrors and rigors of war. The progress of mankind is marked by the extent to which nations agree to allow the horrors to be visited upon the combatants alone and to protect the lives and property of innocent and noncombatant members, either of a belligerent country or a neutral country.

When men started out to fight it was the practice of a successful tribe of savages to kill all the men, women and children in the hostile tribe; but after a while that was found to be wrong. The moral sentiments rebelled against that practice, and gradually, step by step, new rules came into existence, and those rules finally, at the outbreak of this European War, made it very plain and very clear—it was written in all the books—that the struggle of war should be limited to the actual armies; that it was fair and in accordance with the laws of war for one army to attempt to disable another army, but a civilian population, not armed and not taking part in the contest, should not be subject to attack, and neutral people, people who were not in the war, were also free from danger and free from peril. The difference between civilized people and savage people consisted in the extent to which people recognized those rules. When we came to apply the established rules of international law to the conduct of the German Government, we found that at the very outset, in order to get a momentary advantage over their surprised and unprepared adversaries, the German Government had ordered the German army to march across the frontiers of Luxemburg and Belgium and to invade two peaceful neutral countries which were not involved in the war and had no part or parcel in the dispute.

Now, I shall not undertake to arouse your feelings about what happened in Belgium, and yet I think that this is a fair thing to say: Since the days of savage warfare by wholly untrained and barbarous peoples—nay, since the days of warfare by cannibals—I think there is no parallel to some of the things that were done in some of the cities of Belgium. That little country, once so bright and beautiful, so gay and carefree—for Belgium, you know, was a little France, and Brussels was in Belgium a kind of little Paris—too small to have any aggressive intentions upon any other nation; too civilized to have any sort of ambition to attack anybody else; a little, beautiful nation, made up of a fine and cultured people that gave itself to the arts and crafts and beauties of life and to rich manufactures —that little state of Belgium, apparently so secure from disaster of any kind, and chiefly from the disaster of war, has been converted, by the invasion of the German army, in many of its places, to heaps of smoldering ruins. Not military places only, but the churches that used to be filled with the congregations that went on Sundays to worship, are now simply

smoked walls and ruins. The sacred pictures and other beautiful works of art that decorated those churches are all defaced,
wrecked, as a result of artillery fire. The people of Belgium—
and I ask you to remember that they were innocent of offense,
just as innocent as you and I—the people of Belgium had placed
over them a military government. Thousands of them were
taken out and lined up against walls and shot, whole villages,
cities, were set on fire; soldiers invaded the houses and drove
out, not men with guns in hand, but all the occupants, men,
women and children, while other soldiers outside slew them
with the sword or with the gun, until of three cities it is true
to say that not one soul was left. The destruction reminds us
of those stories in ancient history when a savage adversary
leveled the city to the ground and sowed the place where it once
stood with salt in order to show that no future civilization was
to be built there. And these were innocent people! These
were people who had done nothing except to live in a country
standing, by the accident of fate, between the autocratic government of Germany and its surprise attack upon Paris. Then,
after a little while, we heard that men in Belgium were separated from their families and taken into involuntary servitude
in Germany, so that of the men who were left alive, the able-
bodied ones have been taken away from their families, away
from their homes, and their church, and have been carried off
in trainloads into the interior of Germany to work in German
munition factories and aid the German army.

Now, I do not complain, I would not complain if the German
Government were drafting its own man-power, or drafting the
man-power of an adversary whom it had conquered in war, but
I am trying to picture to you the character of our adversary's
military operations; and, in order to have you clearly understand it, I want you to realize that the Belgian people were
wholly without offense; that they have been accused of no offense by anybody, and yet, in spite of that, such was the character of war imposed by the German Government that these
slaughters and burnings, these sums of money exacted by way
of tribute, these depredations, and this involuntary servitude
were visited upon them. But the story is told, and it comes
from excellent sources, that so stout is the heart of the Belgian,

so patriotic is he, so keenly does he resent the things that have been visited upon him, that, although the German Government has taken away thousands of them in trains and put them into workshops in Germany, it has had to bring them back, starved, to die at home rather than keep them in Germany when they refused to work under an unjust government that had tyrannized in so despotic a fashion over them. Belgium really presents a wonderful picture. It is a story of patriotism that we might well imitate; a patriotism exemplified best in its noble king; exemplified in its courageous prelate, Cardinal Mercier, who, although held in prison, as it were, by the captors of his country, has never hesitated for a moment to tell his captors of the iniquity of their occupation.

We saw what went on there, and then we saw what went on in Servia; we saw what went on in Poland; we saw great stretches of this world of ours so laid waste that a year ago there was not in many parts of what used to be Poland a single child still living under the age of five years. Babies all gone! The heel of this kind of war—this ruthless war, as it had come to be called—trod upon that land until all the child life was stamped out, and men and women who were able to get away from the advancing power of the conqueror fled to the woods and lived on roots and leaves of trees and herbs, or starved to death, and over Europe now there are places tens of thousands of miles in area and extent where the bleached bones of men lie who in their lives were guilty of no wrong, no aggression, who were not partners in this conflict, who had done nothing to bring it on, and whose very nations were not engaged in the war!

Well, all of that went on, and we watched it with amazement and with horror, and yet we said to ourselves: "We are separated from it all by an ocean three thousand miles wide." The great founder of our country, George Washington, said to us that we must refrain from entangling alliances. The founders of this republic taught us that our destiny was here and not there; and so there still seemed to be a lack of personal occasion in all this to us. Then we began to consider the aggressions upon our own rights. Is there anybody in this audience who has forgotten how he felt on the day when the *Lusitania* was sunk—the fairest ship in the world, filled with passengers going abroad on their own business, protected by every line of international law? Germany herself afterwards admitted that the destruction of that ship was against and in contravention of the Law of Nations. Not merely international law written by England or France or America, but their own book on international law, written by a German authority, protected the innocent travelers upon that ship. Yet, as she sailed across the sea, carrying this precious freight of men, women and children, she was suddenly and stealthily set upon by a submarine, sunk in an hour, and on the bottom of the sea where so many secrets lie, there lie some things that are not secrets! There are the bones of your fellow-citizens, men, women and children, who lie there, eloquent forever against a nation which, in order to carry out an unrighteous cause, recks not of the lives of the innocent, but is willing to slay and to slaughter in order that it may emerge in bloody triumph to an unholy end.

Not very long ago I heard Consul Frost, who was our consul, as you may remember, at Queenstown, describe his duties when the *Lusitania* sank. The word came to his office that the great ship had gone to the bottom and that the work of rescue was on. He went down to the shore and spent days and nights there, caring for such persons as could be rescued, and he formed a corps to watch by the seaside and gather up the bodies of those who were washed ashore. For some four or five days they were kept busy and each wave that came up brought its toll with it, until, finally, there were no morgues, nor hospitals, left in which to put the bodies. And as the Atlantic, which ordinarily carried the peaceful commerce of our country with England kept rolling in, those days and those nights, carrying the bodies of American and English and French dead, all they could do was to take them out and pile them like cord-wood on the dock, until there was a pile of human cord-wood some hundred feet long and nine or ten layers high to show the savagery of that slaying. And yet, what did we say about it? All we said was: "It is not possible that anybody wanted to do that. There must have been some mistake. It must have been some misunderstood order. It is not human." We said to the German Government: "We protest against the sinking of the *Lusitania*. We call your attention to the provisions of international law which prescribe that no merchant ship, no unarmed ship, can be sunk, no matter whom she belongs to, without giving her crew and her passengers time and opportunity to escape to a safe place." And the German Government sent us word, "Yes; we recognize that principle," and in solemn phrase Von Bethmann-Hollweg, the German Chancellor, under the direction, doubtless, of his imperial master, gave Germany's pledge that it would not repeat that deed, that unarmed ships would not be sunk, unless they either resisted or tried to get away, until the ordinary visitation, search and opportunity of escape to the crew and the passengers had been afforded. That seemed a great victory for us. People everywhere said that the President of the United States had won a diplomatic victory and had rescued for civilization a great domain in international law. Yet how delusive and how deceitful our fancied security was. Six weeks after we got the solemn promise of the German Government on that subject another ship was sunk, and some nine or ten Americans were sunk with it. And then one ship and another was sunk. When the first one went down the German Government sent us word: "Yes; we disavow that act, and we will rebuke the commander of the U-boat who did it;" and yet every now and then another went down. You remember the *Sussex,* the Channel ship, that was sunk in the same way. We protested, and they promised.

And then, finally, in February, 1917, this perfectly incredible thing happened: The German Government sent us word that from then on it intended to wage ruthless warfare by U-boats; that it had marked out on the space of the great deep certain areas in which it would not permit any ship to go; that there were certain lanes of the seas into which we could send our ships and they would not attack them, and that we might send one ship a week to England if it followed a prescribed course and was painted like a barber's pole. And the German Chancellor, Von Bethmann-Hollweg, made this statement in the Reichstag: That he had resisted the establishment of ruthless warfare because he did not believe Germany was ready for it, but that he now believed Germany was ready for it, and, therefore, he was in favor of it. In other words, a solemn promise—

not a promise to give anything.; not a promise that appealed to
our greed or our pride, but a promise made in the interest of
humanity and of human life, and of the protection of the innocent, and of the observance of law—that promise was given to
us, not because it was intended to be kept, but merely in order
that the men who intended to slaughter might have time to manufacture and sharpen more instruments of execution.   There
was only one thing to do—or two, perhaps: We could yield, or
we could fight! And in all likelihood yielding would simply
postpone the fight.   Can anybody imagine what would have happened in this world if Germany, the German Government, had
been able to beat the Allies and had at its command the armies
of Europe and the fleet of England?   Just place yourself, now,
in the position of the Kaiser. It is an unpleasant invitation.
I think he must have dreams at night.

I do not love war. I look forward to the day when war will
be a reminiscence of an evil day and of a half-progressed civilization.   Surely this earth that yields so bountifully its riches
was meant for the children of men to enjoy, as an opportunity
of improvement to us, and not a place of a mutual slaughter.
I do not enjoy the idea of war, and yet there are some things
dearer than life. Our fathers fought from 1776 to 1783 to establish freedom.   Would we call back the Continental Army?
Would we send Lafayette back to France—and Rochambeau?
Would we take Washington's sword out of his hand and break
it over our knee, and say: "Don't do that. We would rather
live forever slaves to a tyrannous government than have a fight
about it?" Would we call back any of the true wars that have
been fought for principle and for the establishment of right in
this world? No! And to-night, when we are in this war, there
isn't a man in America who has inherited any of the spirit of
the founders of this government, or caught any of the inspiration of liberty and freedom; there isn't a man who loves his
children and wants them to have a chance, who does not believe
that this war must be fought to a finish; by that I do not mean
fought to an end, but fought to a finish, and that finish must
be an absolute victory over any power existing in the world that
can visit another such catastrophe upon the human race.

God didn't make many cowards when he made America. I
don't know where to find any. I have gone from one end of
this country to another. I have visited the boys in the camps.
I have seen their mothers visiting them, and I have seen those
heroic and spartan American mothers looking with pride and
love and affection upon their uniformed soldier boys, turning
aside now and then to wipe away a tear, but never saying "Turn
back." I have seen our manufacturers changed from one occupation to another in order that the great material resources of
this country might be mobilized to sustain our boys at the front.
I have seen our government at Washington co-operating with
the representatives of Labor and of Capital, both of them filled
with patriotism, in order that the sweetness of our national
life might be preserved and the full mobilization of all of its
forces brought about. I have seen consideration given to the
lives of women and children in workshops and factories, the
hours of labor of men in certain occupations shortened—all
to the end that we might build up a strong and virile people
here at home while this war is going on to strengthen our boys
at the front. And it is highly important that that should be,
for, while our boys are making the world abroad safe for democracy, we must make at home democracy safe for the world.

They are forming everywhere, a million strong! They are
going across the sea to fight your fight and my fight. They are
not going over to conquer anybody else's country. They are
not going over to impose an indemnity on anybody. They are
not going over to slaughter women and children. They are not
going over to bring back a long list of captives to put into our
workshops and factories. They are going over to rewrite the
Declaration of Independence! They are going over to carry
into effect the message of freedom which America has already
disseminated throughout the world! And they ask us, you and
me, to do our share as they do their share. They do not, all
of them, perhaps, understand the intricacies of this philosophical conflict. They may not know the details of the atrocities
which the German Government has performed or the fearful
injuries it has inflicted upon civilization. They may not know
what Thomas Jefferson said about Democracy, or what Nietz-

sche said about Power, but they were born in this country, or have acquired citizenship here, and they have caught the subtle effluvium of patriotism and of freedom. They are going over to enter the mouth of hell! They are going over to go through the gates of death! They are going over where the very worst that science can do for human destruction has been perfected. Long, sleepless, watchful nights in the trenches are ahead of them—death ahead of some of them. They are going over to give all they have in order that you and I and those who come after us and men everywhere may live in a land of opportunity and under a reign of justice! Oh, my fellow citizens, suppose a soldier came in here and said to you: "Good people, I have been selected to go off and hazard my life for you. I would like to have a coat, and shoes, and a hat, and a gun; I would like to have a gas mask; I would like to have equipment to make my task as safe as possible." Every one in this audience would empty his pockets and pour all that he had into the hat in order that the soldier might have everything that he needed for his comfort and safety. Women would take their jewels and the men their money to decorate him as a hero.

Instead of coming, he is training at Chillicothe and Montgomery and at all the camps in this country. He is marching by the moonlight and getting ready to fight your fight—and I am coming in his place. Just for a moment I represent him as an advocate to you. I am coming to ask you to clothe him and feed him, to pay his railroad fare, to carry him across the ocean, and to put a gun in his hand. I am asking you to give him a chance to live, to come back to us with victory in his hand—victory for justice and right in the world. And he will do it! When this campaign is over I want the German Emperor to have a message from the people of the United States, not written in a bank, nor written in some special select room here and there, but written by the lamp light in the humble homes of the people of the United States, and I want that word to read: "Sir Emperor, we have sent over to you, by special messenger, this message: that the American people are marching a million strong to join your adversaries and to put an end to your unjust warfare. They have come at our bidding to res-

cue the human race from your aggression, and we are back of
them with our hands, with our hearts, with our money. We
are piling up mountains of dollars in order that they may use
them to get at you and your army until you finally yield the
palm to justice and are willing to live in this world, as everybody else ought to live: with a just and due regard to the rights
of others and without a willingness to sacrifice the innocent to
an unholy ambition."

WOODROW WILSON

THE FOURTEEN POINTS

ADDRESS TO CONGRESS IN JOINT SESSION, JANUARY 8, 1918,
STATING THE WAR AIMS AND PEACE TERMS
OF THE UNITED STATES

[On March 3, following this speech, the Brest-Litovsk peace treaty
between Russia and the Teutonic Allies was signed, and on November
11, 1918, the general armistice was signed at Senlis, France. The
famous Fourteen Points laid the basis for the whole plan of the
Peace of Paris, 1919, including the League of Nations.]

Gentlemen of the Congress:

Once more, as repeatedly before, the spokesmen of the Central Empires have indicated their desire to discuss the objects
of the war and the possible basis of a general peace. Parleys
have been in progress at Brest-Litovsk between Russian representatives and representatives of the Central Powers to which
the attention of all the belligerents has been invited for the
purpose of ascertaining whether it may be possible to extend
these parleys into a general conference with regard to terms of
peace and settlement.

The Russian representatives presented not only a perfectly
definite statement of the principles upon which they would be
willing to conclude peace but also an equally definite program
of the concrete application of those principles. The representatives of the Central Powers, on their part, presented an outline
of settlement which, if much less definite, seemed susceptible
of liberal interpretation until their specific program of practical
terms was added. That program proposed no concessions at
all either to the sovereignty of Russia or to the preferences of
the populations with whose fortunes it dealt, but meant, in a
word, that the Central Empires were to keep every foot of territory their armed forces had occupied—every province, every
city, every point of vantage—as a permanent addition to their
territories and their power.

It is a reasonable conjecture that the general principles of settlement which they at first suggested originated with the more liberal statesmen of Germany and Austria, the men who have begun to feel the force of their own people's thought and purpose, while the concrete terms of actual settlement came from the military leaders who have no thought but to keep what they have got. The negotiations have been broken off. The Russian representatives were sincere and in earnest. They cannot entertain such proposals of conquest and domination.

The whole incident is full of significance. It is also full of perplexity. With whom are the Russian representatives dealing? For whom are the representatives of the Central Empires speaking? Are they speaking for the majorities of their respective parliaments or for the minority parties, that military and imperialistic minority which has so far dominated their whole policy and controlled the affairs of Turkey and of the Balkan states which have felt obliged to become their associates in this war?

The Russian representatives have insisted, very justly, very wisely, and in the true spirit of modern democracy, that the conferences they have been holding with the Teutonic and Turkish statesmen should be held within open, not closed, doors, and all the world has been audience, as was desired. To whom have we been listening, then? To those who speak the spirit and intention of the resolutions of the German Reichstag of the 9th of July last, the spirit and intention of the Liberal leaders and parties of Germany, or to those who resist and defy that spirit and intention and insist upon conquest and subjugation? Or are we listening, in fact, to both, unreconciled and in open and hopeless contradiction? These are very serious and pregnant questions. Upon the answer to them depends the peace of the world.

But, whatever the results of the parleys at Brest-Litovsk, whatever the confusions of counsel and of purpose in the utterances of the spokesmen of the Central Empires, they have again attempted to acquaint the world with their objects in the war and have again challenged their adversaries to say what their objects are and what sort of settlement they would deem just and satisfactory. There is no good reason why that challenge should not be responded to, and responded to with the utmost candor. We did not wait for it. Not once, but again and again, we have laid our whole thought and purpose before the world, not in general terms only, but each time with sufficient definition to make it clear what sort of definite terms of settlement must necessarily spring out of them. Within the last week Mr. Lloyd George has spoken with admirable candor and in admirable spirit for the people and Government of Great Britain.

There is no confusion of counsel among the adversaries of the Central Powers, no uncertainty of principle, no vagueness of detail. The only secrecy of counsel, the only lack of fearless frankness, the only failure to make definite statement of the objects of the war, lies with Germany and her allies. The issues of life and death hang upon these definitions. No statesman who has the least conception of his responsibility ought for a moment to permit himself to continue this tragical and appalling outpouring of blood and treasure unless he is sure beyond a peradventure that the objects of the vital sacrifice are part and parcel of the very life of Society and that the people for whom he speaks think them right and imperative as he does.

There is, moreover, a voice calling for these definitions of principle and of purpose which is, it seems to me, more thrilling and more compelling than any of the many moving voices with which the troubled air of the world is filled. It is the voice of the Russian people. They are prostrate and all but helpless, it would seem, before the grim power of Germany, which has hitherto known no relenting and no pity. Their power, apparently, is shattered. And yet their soul is not subservient. They will not yield either in principle or in action. Their conception of what is right, of what is humane and honorable for them to accept, has been stated with a frankness, a largeness of view, a generosity of spirit, and a universal human sympathy which must challenge the admiration of every friend of mankind; and they have refused to compound their ideals or desert others that they themselves may be safe.

They call to us to say what it is that we desire, in what, if in anything, our purpose and our spirit differ from theirs; and I believe that the people of the United States would wish me to respond, with utter simplicity and frankness. Whether their present leaders believe it or not, it is our heartfelt desire and hope that some way may be opened whereby we may be privileged to assist the people of Russia to attain their utmost hope of liberty and ordered peace.

It will be our wish and purpose that the processes of peace, when they are begun, shall be absolutely open and that they shall involve and permit henceforth no secret understandings of any kind. The day of conquest and aggrandizement is gone by; so is also the day of secret covenants entered into in the interest of particular governments and likely at some unlooked-for moment to upset the peace of the world. It is this happy fact, now clear to the view of every public man whose thoughts do not still linger in an age that is dead and gone, which makes it possible for every nation whose purposes are consistent with justice and the peace of the world to avow now or at any other time the objects it has in view.

We entered this war because violations of right had occurred which touched us to the quick and made the life of our own people impossible unless they were corrected and the world secure once for all against their recurrence.

What we demand in this war, therefore, is nothing peculiar to ourselves. It is that the world be made fit and safe to live in; and particularly that it be made safe for every peace-loving nation which, like our own, wishes to live its own life, determine its own institutions, be assured of justice and fair dealing by the other peoples of the world as against force and selfish aggression.

All the peoples of the world are in effect partners in this interest, and for our own part we see very clearly that unless justice be done to others it will not be done to us. The program of the world's peace, therefore, is our program; and that program, the only possible program, as we see it, is this:

1. Open covenants of peace, openly arrived at, after which there shall be no private international understandings of any kind but diplomacy shall proceed always frankly and in the public view.

2. Absolute freedom of navigation upon the seas, outside territorial waters, alike in peace and in war, except as the seas may be closed in whole or in part by international action for the enforcement of international covenants.

3. The removal, so far as possible, of all economic barriers and the establishment of an equality of trade conditions among all the nations consenting to the peace and associating themselves for its maintenance.

4. Adequate guarantees given and taken that national armaments will be reduced to the lowest points consistent with domestic safety.

5. A free, open-minded, and absolutely impartial adjustment of all colonial claims, based upon a strict observance of the principle that in determining all such questions of sovereignty the interests of the populations concerned must have equal weight with the equitable claims of the government whose title is to be determined.

6. The evacuation of all Russian territory and such a settlement of all questions affecting Russia as will secure the best and freest co-operation of the other nations of the world in obtaining for her an unhampered and unembarrassed opportunity for the independent determination of her own political development and national policy and assure her of a sincere welcome into the society of free nations under institutions of her own choosing; and, more than a welcome, assistance also of every kind that she may need and may herself desire. The treatment accorded Russia by her sister nations in the months to come will be the acid test of their good will, of their comprehension of her needs as distinguished from their own interests, and of their intelligent and unselfish sympathy.

7. Belgium, the whole world will agree, must be evacuated and restored, without any attempt to limit the sovereignty which she enjoys in common with all other free nations. No other single act will serve as this will serve to restore confidence among the nations in the laws which they have themselves set and determined for the government of their relations with one another. Without this healing act the whole structure and validity of international law is forever impaired.

8. All French territory should be freed and the invaded portions restored, and the wrong done to France by Prussia in 1871 in the matter of Alsace-Lorraine, which has unsettled the peace

HICKS' SP.A.S.—35

of the world for nearly fifty years, should be righted, in order that peace may once more be made secure in the interest of all.

9. A readjustment of the frontiers of Italy should be effected along clearly recognizable lines of nationality.

10. The peoples of Austria-Hungary, whose place among the nations we wish to see safeguarded and assured, should be accorded the freest opportunity of autonomous development.

11. Rumania, Serbia, and Montenegro should be evacuated; occupied territories restored; Serbia accorded free and secure access to the sea; and the relations of the several Balkan states to one another determined by friendly counsel along historically established lines of allegiance and nationality; and international guarantees of the political and economic independence and territorial integrity of the several Balkan states should be entered into.

12. The Turkish portions of the present Ottoman Empire should be assured a secure sovereignty, but the other nationalities which are now under Turkish rule should be assured an undoubted security of life and an absolutely unmolested opportunity of autonomous development, and the Dardanelles should be permanently opened as a free passage to the ships and commerce of all nations under international guarantees.

13. An independent Polish state should be erected which should include the territories inhabited by indisputably Polish populations, which should be assured a free and secure access to the sea, and whose political and economic independence and territorial integrity should be guaranteed by international covenant.

14. A general association of nations must be formed under specific covenants for the purpose of affording mutual guarantees of political independence and territorial integrity to great and small states alike.

In regard to these essential rectifications of wrong and assertions of right we feel ourselves to be intimate partners of all the governments and peoples associated together against the imperialists. We cannot be separated in interest or divided in purpose. We stand together until the end.

For such arrangements and covenants we are willing to fight and to continue to fight until they are achieved; but only because we wish the right to prevail and desire a just and stable peace such as can be secured only by removing the chief provocations to war, which this program does remove.

We have no jealousy of German greatness, and there is nothing in this program that impairs it. We grudge her no achievement or distinction of learning or of pacific enterprise such as have made her record very bright and very enviable. We do not wish to injure her or to block in any way her legitimate influence or power. We do not wish to fight her either with arms or with hostile arrangements of trade if she is willing to associate herself with us and the other peace-loving nations of the world in covenants of justice and law and fair dealing.

We wish her only to accept a place of equality among the peoples of the world—the new world in which we now live—instead of a place of mastery.

Neither do we presume to suggest to her any alteration or modification of her institutions. But it is necessary, we must frankly say, and necessary as a preliminary to any intelligent dealings with her on our part, that we should know whom her spokesmen speak for when they speak to us, whether for the Reichstag majority or for the military party and the men whose creed is imperial domination.

We have spoken now, surely, in terms too concrete to admit of any further doubt or question. An evident principle runs through the whole program I have outlined. It is the principle of justice to all peoples and nationalities, and their right to live on equal terms of liberty and safety with one another, whether they be strong or weak.

Unless this principle be made its foundation no part of the structure of international justice can stand. The people of the United States could act upon no other principle; and to the vindication of this principle they are ready to devote their lives, their honor, and everything that they possess. The moral climax of this the culminating and final war for human liberty has come, and they are ready to put their own strength, their own highest purpose, their own integrity and devotion to the test.

JAMES HAMILTON LEWIS

THE LEAGUE OF NATIONS

Speech in the United States Senate, February 24, 1919, on the Proposed Constitution of a League of Nations, Replying to Addresses by Senators Borah, Reed, and Lodge

[James Hamilton Lewis was born in Danville, Pittsylvania county, Virginia, on May 18, 1863. In 1866 he moved with his parents to Augusta, Georgia, where he attended Houghton College, going later to the University of Virginia at Charlottesville. He studied law in Savannah, Georgia, and has received honorary degrees from two universities. After being admitted to the bar in 1882 he moved to the Territory of Washington, where he served as a member of the Territorial Senate. In 1892 he was an unsuccessful candidate for Governor, and in 1894 was defeated as a candidate for United States Senate; but in 1896 he was elected Congressman at large from Washington, and served until 1899. During the Spanish-American war he served as Inspector General on the staff of General F. D. Grant. In 1903 he was attached to the Joint High Commission on the Canadian and Alaskan Boundary, and in that year moved to Chicago, where he resumed the practice of law and served as Corporation Counsel from 1905 to 1907. In 1908 he was defeated as Democratic candidate for Governor of Illinois, but in 1912 was elected United States Senator and served from 1913 to 1919. He was assigned to special service in Europe during the World War and was knighted by Belgium and Greece. He is now head of the firm of Lewis, Folsom & Murdock in Chicago.

The speech printed below was delivered on the same day that President Wilson reached Boston on the return from his first trip to Europe as head of the American delegation to the Peace Conference of Paris. Neither the Treaty of Peace nor the proposed Covenant of the League of Nations had been laid before the Senate. An unofficial copy of the Covenant had, however, been received and it was understood that it would be an integral part of the Peace Treaty. The project was immediately vigorously opposed in the Senate. Senator Lewis, by this speech, made himself the champion of the League, and his effort, by direction of President Wilson, was distributed widely throughout the United States.]

Mr. President, We have at this time entered upon a discussion of the document termed the constitution of the league of nations.

Sir, at the outset one would think that at a time like this any man in America could advance to a discussion of that grave question in a spirit qualifying him impartially to judge the thing as it is and to refrain from coloring it with personal animosity or political prejudice. But, sir, I deplore to have to confess that had there been a stranger from another world whose spirit in spectral form in the gallery of this Senate could have heard the attacks made on the project, he could have believed that he had returned to the Roman forum, to the senate of that imperial country, and that some Cataline by the name of Taft or Wilson was being arraigned by a Cicero on the charge of betraying his country to its enemies and for delivery of his native land to its foreign foes.

What, sir, is the thing of which we speak? It is, as we understand it, the presentation of a plan that has for its professed object the devising of some system of universal peace to mankind. Does that suggest an offense against civilization? Has there ever been a time when that holy dream has not been the consummation prayed for by all mankind? Was there ever a theme nobler or one note in the music of patriotism more sublime? Can we not chant the joyful refrain:

> "Long have I sought this day,
> And prayed to know the way,
> To take calm peace by the hand
> And lead it to a bleeding land."

If, sir, by any fair method the result may be had, shall we spurn it because the path to the mansion is not paved as we would have chosen? Let us concede that neither the steps leading to the result, nor the final work can appeal to all men alike nor find favor in every mind. Also let it be understood that the supposed weakness or error in a design may not be due to any inherent vice in the proposal, nor, sir, owing to any frailty in the completed proposition. Differences presenting themselves against any proposal can be due to the varying attitude of each human mind as it presents a standard to itself of a specific remedy which it sees most appropriate for that particular felt evil. Each devised solution, though appearing just to its authors, may be most unfit to the situation. Our individual view is as likely to be wrong by the standard of another mind as the joint proposal before us is to any mind.

Therefore, sir, let us at the outset dismiss the feeling that because we may differ from the wisdom of a document that this difference in itself establishes that the document must be wrong, and we unquestionably must be right.

The question before us ever repeats itself—what is the thing sought to be done? What is it all for? Sir, we have seen in the panorama of present time the greatest war that civilization has recorded in all its annals. To the horror of the contemplation there arises the startling fact that 7,000,000 of earth's men have been sent to their graves by the shot and stroke of mortal brother, and 14,000,000 more hobble through life but a shattered part of their former selves, while those who depend upon them for bread and sustenance lean now upon a broken staff, and that sinking to earth hopeless. All through the world now will be seen these miserable victims dragging their way on life's road, their legless bodies leaning painfully on crutch or staff, and their pitied fellows just beyond who now are to catch at life's existence by their armless sleeves. Then to the horror of our sight we behold those whose blindness will forever gaze darkened to the skies; those sightless ones who will have to feel with trickling fingers the faces of their beloved to know their own. This legion of dying, helpless, useless, and suffering millions are to be a charge on Christianity and Charity for generations yet unborn.

Does not this in itself suggest the justice and the morality of some effort on the part of mankind for a remedy that such curse and desolation may not ever be repeated again?

If we advert to the material losses, to the money waste, then, sir, know that there are $180,000,000,000 of the earnings of ten generations of mankind gone to ashes in the nowhere. All melted in the fires lighted by men for the consuming of their fellows—in the name of war!

We need not pause to moralize from the standard of war upon the right or wrong of the issues which justify these unholy sacrifices. We speak of the condition. We are now told by proclamation that this present horror is at an end; that the war of devastation of lands and destruction of humanity has been halted, and that we are to make peace.

Mr. President, the great Webster, when beholding his country moving to secession of States, seeing the deluge of blood that was to gush from the bleeding wounds of the sons of the States and reflecting upon what the flag of the Union meant in all the sacrifices made to establish it and hold it up as an ensign of freedom and justice, exclaimed his prayer to God that no future children of the Union should ever be brought to where they would ask the miserable interrogatory, "What is it all for?"

Yet here in this assembly each man of Christian belief, urged by humane emotion, or the throb of brotherly kindness, must, as he broods on the horrors and destructions of world war, ask in the name of all we speak of as God, "What is it all for?" Where has civilization been benefited or improved, where mankind elevated or advanced, justice vindicated in her temple, or the laws of God or the creeds of Christ fulfilled in this bloody inheritance?

Sir, if there are those who be moved to overcome such monster evil, shall they be held here or elsewhere as offensive to the wisdom of man or statesmanship of country? "The head and front of their offending" is but that they seek the fulfillment of the celestial proclamation of the Master, "Peace on earth, good will to men."

Mr. President, in different forms at different times the compacts we speak of as treaties for peace have been undertaken by those who sincerely sought some avenue through which there could be an escape from holocausts which all of us have lately beheld and no tongue can adequately describe. These efforts have produced no peace nor brought us deliverance from wars.

Each age has but added increased machinery for dealing death and multiplied inventions for destruction of communities. This proclamation before us is to offer relief—to at last pledge men to preserve mankind from murder done in the name of civilization and liberty. We have listened, sir, to many speeches upon this floor on the contents of the document, particularly since the proclamation of the so-called constitution. Despite the desire of the President that debate be deferred for reasons of his own, eminent Senators felt they owed obligations to their constituencies and to themselves to express their opposition. This they did with expressions of ridicule and condemnation. Such naturally justified others in bringing forth reply. I am one of those who, to do justice to the truth of the situation, speak of the thing as I see it, and this in opposition to the views of many.

These Senators who have assumed, sir, to oppose this proposition have invariably placed their opposition upon the ground that this remedy proposed as the league for peace would involve us in the affairs of Europe; also entangle us with nations of the Asiatic world, and thus withdraw from us forever the integral sovereignty of our independent Republic. Sir, I appreciate the meaning of the Republic of the United States. It has been the pride of its fathers and remains the glory of its sons.

I heard my distinguished friend, the eminent Senator from Missouri [Mr. Reed], in a speech yesterday, to be referred to by his friends with admiration and by his opponents with confusion, speak opposing this design. In the long line and progression of matter presented by him he recited fifty and more of the European wars which have transpired since the foundation of this country. At the conclusion of each description the able Senator would exclaim, "And not an American in it." I ask, has it come in this era of life that there exists a man who could contemplate the loss of all those lives, the devastation of all those lands, the demolishment of all their homes, the widowing of all those wives, the bereaved mothers without children, and not feel that the "dam'd manner of their taking off" is not of concern to civilization and feel that if we could lay our hands against it ever being repeated we owe to do so not only unto ourselves but unto the thing we profess and call religion? Surely these slaughtered are our fellow mankind. In their death and agony they are our brothers in misery and war.

Mr. President and my fellow Senators, you will recall where Victor Hugo in *Les Miserables,* tracing the movement of Jean Valjean, locates him as he seeks refuge in a little church from the pursuing Inspector Javert.

The little worship house is hidden in the brushes. Nothing can be seen but the gleam of the altar light upon the sacred place where this little curé counts his rosary in the shadowed precincts. Jean Valjean is seen as he crouches behind a pew in the rear. The holy man, beholding him, says: "Come up. Come in." Jean, shrinking, replies: "You say for me to come up and come in your house, not knowing me nor how wretched is my condition?" Then the holy man of God says: "This is not my house; this is the house of Christ, and, besides, before you spoke, I knew you." "Knew me?" asked Jean. "Yes," replies the priest; "when I saw that you were wretched I knew you were my brother."

And shall we in America—

> Light again the fires of hell to weld anew the chain
> On that red anvil where each blow is pain.

Sir, we must feel the misery of these of every land in such wretchedness as we would feel the agonies of our brothers. I say to my eminent friend from Missouri that these agonizing brutalities and this unmeasured weight of misery to Europe has brought to this our land two things—their fleeing descendants who sought refuge with us as an asylum, and the misery of their poor forcing them to be dependents upon us. For that if there were not another reason, it can be seen how their interest is ours, and for the cause which they suffer we may speak.

Mr. President, because every effort in the form of an individual treaty for peace with separate countries has failed, there has been resort to an association of ideas, and in this resort some formation of a plan designated "a league of nations." It is this constitution for a league that is at this time presented. It is this that is assailed, condemned, abhorred—indeed, sir, as though it were a compact for the dissolution of the Union and a decree for the ostracism of its men and the death of its children.

Mr. President, we must pause to note that this constitution was not the work of Woodrow Wilson individually. If there be a man who fancies that for partisan reasons or personal perversity mere opposition to it is justified because it was from the hand of Woodrow Wilson, let him recall that this work appears to have been the work of representatives of fourteen great countries. That there were fourteen represented in the deliberations and that when the result came forth it carried that which is not borne by many documents of the whole world—the unanimous vote and acclaimed decision of all the convention of delegates.

Now, sir, the judgment of these men that some of us impeach by our opposition may be wrong, but we flatter our vanity and lay proud unction to our soul when we conclude that any individual here is superior in wisdom or higher in patriotism than all those combined who there were the representatives of the political intelligence of the earth.

Then, sir, we move at once to the specific objection urged by the eminent Senators opposing the policy expressed in the constitution of the league. Meaning, of course, no invidious distinction as against others who have spoken, I choose the eminent Senator from Idaho [Mr. Borah] and the equally eminent Senator from Missouri [Mr. Reed] as pronouncing more fully the viewpoints of the objectors and as comprehensively sufficient so that we may allude to them as the representatives of the attack, particularly with regard to the fundamental objections urged.

It is first contended that the constitution, so called, and the doctrine on which it is based, violates the fundamental theory of the fathers of our Government. To sustain that contention the Senators bring forth the declarations of George Washington. On Saturday, a most appropriate and sacred day, the memorial of George Washington, February 22, the Senator from Missouri, voicing that which was also spoken with great capacity by the Senator from Idaho, took refuge for his attack in the provisions of that great message known as Washington's Farewell. From this he assumed a justification for his condemnation of the plan now before the Senate.

Time and time again there has been presented to this body all that Washington has said on the point urged. Equally often it has been pointed out what he meant, each contending side differing from the other in the construction claimed.

We need not pause to remark the difference in time and condition of the then and the now, nor observe on how isolated we were, how separate we were, how weakened was our State. We can, however, note that the admonition of Washington was against an arrangement with foreign lands that would be political—relation by which the identity of our country at home would be merged in the political relations and obligations of the land abroad.

He likewise, sir, inveighed against coalitions by our country with some one country in Europe. This, if done, could awaken the animosities of the other countries of Europe and turn them against us for that we had combined against them by joining some one either as an exhibition of our favoritism to one country of Europe or as our expression of our enmity to the other. But there never is any expression from the Nation's first master of Government against this Nation taking any course anywhere for the peace of itself or of the world, nor for both. To the contrary, he specifically invited his countrymen to contemplate those relations that would produce the "harmony of intercourse of the world."

Former Secretary of State Richard Olney, in the *Atlantic Monthly* for May, 1898, produced a letter of Washington to his friend defining his own meaning of the clause in his Farewell Address. Says Mr. Olney in his article entitled "International Isolation of the United States":

"That Washington was of the opinion that the regimen suited to the struggling infancy of a nation would be adapted to its lusty manhood is unsupported by a particle of evidence. On the contrary, there is authority of the highest character for the statement that he entertained an exactly opposite view, and 'thought that a time might come when, our institutions being firmly consolidated and working with complete success, we might safely and perhaps beneficially take part in the consultation held by foreign States for the common advantage of the nations.'"

Mr. President, then Thomas Jefferson is resorted to, Jefferson, who is the author of the expression "entangling alliances," which frequently is imputed to Washington. We are constantly advised that Jefferson admonished us against alliances which were entangling. This is true, and if such, sir, were contemplated in the plan before us, in the spirit that Jefferson and Washington opposed, there would be no man of any political party on this floor advocating this measure.

I respectfully assert that the eminent Senators have in many instances in their condemnation been wrong in their premises. In other instances wrong in the conclusions they drew from right premises. I charge that in other instances, where their premises were correctly stated from the documents, the conclusions they drew were violent and unjustified by any just judgment that should follow the expression and definition of terms in the instrument. I make bold, first, to declare the situation and position of both Washington and Jefferson on the fundamentals of our Government involved in the construction of the document.

Mr. President, I ask your consideration a moment as to what Washington and Jefferson really meant and what each would have done under conditions like these controlling us. If the eminent Senators, Mr. Borah and Mr. Reed—for whom we have so great a respect that we hesitate to differ from them and so great an affection that we find it painful at any time to oppose them—shall really seek to know what Washington or Jefferson would have done, in order that they may follow at this time their guidance, I beseech their attention and that of their allies in this body.

I invite consideration to expressions of Thomas Jefferson, that all may see that he was not encrusted against advance. I am anxious that all may know that this apostle of democracy was not a worshiper of a fetish in the doctrine of *non movere*. He was for change upon changed conditions. I assert it never could have been the idea of Thomas Jefferson that the country would not develop, or that in its advancing conditions new remedies would not be found for new arising evils. I deny that he was such a slave of the ancients that he would have denied the progress of the modern.

No man respects the fathers, I hope, more than I. I recall the admonition of the prophet in the Holy Scripture proclaiming, "Remove not the ancient landmarks thy fathers have set." But I condemn the thought there shall ever be decreed that we must ever be "ruled by the ashes from their sceptered urns." I speak for the Government of the sons as well as for the creed of the fathers. I demand advanced government for advanced people. I call down condemnation on those who put tombstones and sepulchers as blocks in the path of growing progress. Hear what Mr. Jefferson said in writing to Eldridge Gerry, January 26, 1799:

"I am not for raising hue and cry against progress—to go backward instead of forward, to look for no improvement, to believe that government, religion, morality, and every other science were in the highest perfection in ages of the darkest ignorance, and that nothing can ever be devised more perfect than what was established by our forefathers."

Apropos, sir, of the change of our institutions, says the same philosopher, writing to Samuel Kerchinal July 12, 1916:

"Some men look at constitutions with sanctimonious reverence and deem them, like the Ark of the Covenant, too sacred to be touched. They ascribe to the men of the preceding age a wisdom more than human and suppose what they did to be beyond amendment. I knew that age well. I belonged to it and labored with it. It deserved well of its country. It was very like the present, but without the experience of the present, and 40 years of experience in government is worth a century of book reading, and this they would say themselves were they to rise from the dead. I am certainly not an advocate for frequent and untried changes in laws and constitutions. I think moderate imperfections had better be borne with, because, when once known, we accommodate ourselves to them and find practical means of correcting their ill effects. But I know also that laws and institutions must go hand in hand with the progress of the human mind."

Now, sir, I have asserted, and I wish to vindicate my assertion, that neither of these eminent fathers would have been opposed to a policy that would have made for peace—not even to an alliance to secure such blessing—and I dare say, and offer here my thought, that neither would have been against the proposition such as that now brought before this body under the conditions surrounding us.

I call attention to Prof. Latané's view of what Washington said in his Farewell Message on alliances:

"It will be observed that Washington warned his countrymen against permanent alliances. He expressly said that we might 'safely trust to temporary alliances for extraordinary emergencies.' Further than this, many of those who are continually quoting Washington's warning against alliances not only fail to note the limitations under which the advice was given, but they also overlook the reasons assigned. In a succeeding paragraph of the Farewell Address he said:

"With me a predominant motive has been to endeavor to gain time to our country to settle and mature its yet recent institutions, and to progress without interruption to that degree of strength and consistency which is necessary to give it, humanly speaking, the command of its own fortunes."

When, Mr. President, in the order of any evolution of government has a land ever reached where it was in the "command of its own fortunes" so supremely, so sublimely, as this land of Washington's, this our United States of to-day!

The eminent Senator from Missouri drew an inspiring picture by an epic of oratory in his peroration of Saturday describing the glory with which this country had endowed itself in the service it had done to other countries. He recited how it was our American soldiers and marines that saved England and rescued France when those lands were at the mercy of the German invader. Sir, there never could be greater proof of what command she has of herself, the thing that Washington sought to acquire, than that she could contribute such force of salvation to save the wreck of the Old World. That our Republic in her own strength crossed 3,000 miles of sea carrying her soldiers and equipment, and with these sons of the New World saved the fathers of the Old World to their children and gave to civilization a democracy for their future preservation.

Then, Mr. President, we pause to see what would the Washington and Jefferson of the olden day have done in this day? Sir, during the brief interval of peace following the treaty of Amiens in 1801, Napoleon undertook the establishment of French power in San Domingo. Fortunately for America the expedition failed. It was Mr. Jefferson who then said:

"The day that France takes possession of New Orleans fixes the sentence which is to restrain her forever within her low-water mark. It seals the union of two nations, who in conjunction can maintain exclusive possession of the ocean."

What two nations, I ask, does the writer then mean? Says Mr. Jefferson:

"From that moment we must marry ourselves to the British fleet and Nation."

Surely, if there were an entangling alliance to make an arrangement for peace, Jefferson could never have been the first to suggest such an "alliance" and such a "marriage with England," with her navy, and this for the preservation of this our new America. Yet he continues:

"We must turn all our attentions to a maritime force, for which our resources place us on very high grounds."

Then, sir, when Monroe was later sent to Paris to support Livingston, he was instructed by Jefferson, "in case there was no prospect of a favorable termination of the negotiations," to avoid a rupture [with France] until the spring, and "in the meantime enter into conferences with the British Government, through their ambassador at Paris, to fix principles of alliance and leave us in peace until Congress meets." Jefferson had already informed the British minister at Washington that if France should, by closing the mouth of the Mississippi, force the United States to war, "they would throw away the scabbard." Monroe and Livingston were now instructed, in case they should become convinced that France meditated hostilities against the United States, "to negotiate an alliance with England and to stipulate that neither party should make peace or truce without the consent of the other." Thus, notwithstanding his French proclivities and his warning against "entangling alliances," the author of the immortal Declaration of Independence was ready and willing in this emergency to form an alliance with England.

We well know that "the unexpected cession of the entire Province of Louisiana to the United States" was the only thing that avoided the culmination of that project.

I do not bring these things to the attention of eminent Senators, on the theory that it is all new to them, or can now be first information. I do so to invite their attention to the fact that in cases like the one we have before us, the exceptional condition which is now ours and commands or calls for the action we contemplate, would have been the rule of action with them. I ask, sir, that you note that the rule which we see that they would have had in their day for peace, is but the rule we now in our day invoke. Then, I ask the able Senators who call up the spirits of Washington and Jefferson, does the present plan proposed by Wilson run counter to the theory which the fathers would have had, under the same circumstances? We must answer, no; not at all, sir.

Where, now, I ask the Senators, do they find their justification for their very first contention that there is in this league a violation of the Monroe doctrine? What do they mean when they present this theory as being one which Mr. Jefferson approved in the conduct of Mr. Monroe, but which would be violated by the proposal of President Wilson?

Stated in terse terms, the doctrine known as the Monroe doctrine—much misunderstood generally, but, of course, in a body like this, with much information upon the subject, perfectly comprehended—had no further or other purpose than to say to the European monarchies, "You shall not establish your governments upon the Western Continent." Let thoughtful men dismiss from their minds that this was a solicitude only for the people of South and Central America. If, sir, we find a fire lighted in these galleries above and surrounding us and we know the chance is that it may be readily extinguished, it may be that we will have no concern for the fate of those who will sit here below. But if we know it will leap its barriers and consume these walls and lick up this parquet, we turn at once to extinguish it by any means at our hand. Sir, it was out of fear for this Government of the United States that if monarchical governments were established to the south of us, supported by imperial armies and navies, they soon could move their batteries upon us, to the extinguishment of the Republic we had founded here.

Secretary Hamilton Fish, in a report to President Grant, as to a European nation taking Cuba, said that the United States "opposes the creation of European dominion on American soil, or its transfer to other European powers." It is unnecessary to multiply examples, for all are applications of the foundation principle of the Monroe doctrine, that we must provide for our peace and safety. "It is doubtless true," said Mr. Webster in his speech on the Panama mission, in April, 1826, "that this declaration must be considered as founded on our rights, and to spring mainly from a regard to their preservation."

The theory was that we should do everything to prevent these kingly forces from establishing their form of government upon this continent, which had been dedicated to the experiment of free republics. The Holy Alliance of Prussia, Austria, and Russia then threatened its domination in the South American lands. It was then that Britain, through George Canning, her premier, in his interposition with Rush, our United States minister, proposed the possible peril and got the declaration of opposition. The danger was forced upon the attention of our own President. Then the doctrine was promulgated as one for our own self-preservation, which we call the Monroe doctrine, after the name of our then President—*nomen venerabile et gentibus clarum.*

Mr. President, we pause here to reflect, Why should we, the democracy, wish to abandon the Monroe doctrine? What in the world has the United States to gain by surrendering this doctrine? Why should the present Democratic administration wish to do so? Sir, it has been the theme of our discourse in speech; it has been the delight of our praise in platform; it was the creature of our doctrines; it has been the charge and trust of our keeping. Under Polk and Lincoln we advanced to its maintenance with the lives of our sons; under Cleveland we asserted it successfully as against Britain; and from Wilson there will not be found a declaration that was opposed to it. All to the contrary. What purpose would Wilson have to violate it? The man who would voluntarily destroy the principle of it and establish the privilege of monarchies to slay Republics, kill liberty, and overthrow freedom would go down to such ignominy and odium that no tongue could describe, no charity palliate. Sir, there are those who impute to this man Wilson a pride of conduct and a conceit of personality so overweening that he will neither hear advice nor listen to counsel. Surely these will not then regard him such a fool as to visit upon himself a fate so far removed from what they say he harbors—of being renowned in the esteem and perpetuated in the hearts of his countrymen— as to do the thing that strikes his political death knell. Will he do such a thing? Should he be accused of it? His reply must

HICKS' SP.A.S.—36

be, in the words of the prophet to the Lord, "Is thy servant a
dog, that he should do such a thing?"

We turn to see, sir, what Wilson said, and we find his address
to this body on January 22, 1917, at which time, it will be recalled, he suggested the propositions that have now culminated
in a peace treaty. Then said the President:

"I am proposing, as it were, that the nations should with one
accord adopt the doctrine of President Monroe as the doctrine
of the world; that no nation should seek to extend its polity
over any other nation or people, but that every people should be
left free to determine its own polity, its own way of development,
unhindered, unthreatened, unafraid, the little along with the
great and powerful.

"I am proposing that all nations henceforth avoid entangling
alliances which would draw them into competitions of power,
catch them in a net of intrigue and selfish rivalry, and disturb
their own affairs with influences intruded from without."

Continuing, he said to the Senate:

"There is no entangling alliance in a concert of power."

This seems the view Mr. Jefferson held when he proposed a
concert of powers—for peace. Now, then, Mr. President, we
can understand what is meant by article ten of this convention
for a league of peace; sir, if I mistake not, we can summon
from our now directed thought the spirit that penned it. It
reads:

Article 10.

"The high contracting parties undertake to respect and preserve as against external aggression the territorial integrity and
existing political independence of all States members of the
league. In case of any such aggression, or in case of any threat
or danger of such aggression, the executive council shall advise upon the means by which the obligation shall be fulfilled."

Will eminent men whose profession has been the comparison
of statutes and decisions fail to observe that almost the exact
language of the distinguished President to the Senate on January 22, 1917, is incorporated in article 10? And I ask any Senator who shall with reflection read these articles if he will not

see that that article has the object of the Monroe doctrine as its care and solicitude?

Now, how stand we? Heretofore, Senators, our country alone has constituted the sponsor of the doctrine, pledging its honor, and time and time again tendering its power to enforce it—against whom? Against those who now have agreed to become parties by literal word to its enforcement. Instead now, sir, of having America alone as the sponsor of the doctrine we call the Monroe doctrine, by the genius of the mind that directed our affairs, we have the world as a guarantor of the Monroe doctrine.

Mr. President, let me ask the able Senators, for their contemplation—would this question, Senators, have been left open? Do you fancy, Senators, that Britain would have left it open, or even in doubt, and this even were we to concede that our own land had not protected it with the safeguard prohibiting external aggression? Would Britain have allowed the nations of the earth to possess the balance of power in commerce and in colonies in the Western Hemisphere through seizing any part of Central or South America? It was Canning, her minister, who delighted to exclaim that he "called in the New World to balance the old"; he, the British premier, took credit to himself as being one of the authors of the system. What object would Britain have, sir, in not preserving the Monroe doctrine, when, were she to open the gates to its violation, every rival of hers in Europe would colonize their people and governments in South America to her loss, which she must pay?

I propound to you the next query—the corollary to the first: Would Spain and Italy and France, with the children of their hearts' blood and bone and life of their nations making up the nationalities of these South and Central American lands, sitting at this council table, be content to surrender them to the inroads and invasion of their commercial rivals—once their military conquerors? Ah, what profit, Senators, can you conceive that any nation in council at the European peace table could have for yielding the Monroe doctrine? Sir, I am unable to contemplate a theme upon which such a thought could be predicated. Let us dismiss it as "a thing of which dreams are made."

Then, Mr. President, we turn to treat the form of this document—the form so violently denounced or so satirically ridiculed. Having referred to the fundamentals upon which the eminent Senators made their arguments opposing the principle of this constitution, I now, sir, turn to note the comments on the composition.

I know that here and there we hear that this was a product of General Smuts, of South Africa, or Lord Cecil of England. Mr. President, I only mention this that I may parenthetically advert to one thought. We observe that Britain is so proud of this document that she delights to have it advertised that one of her sons was one of its creators. Along comes Italy and professes that Cavour, in his first fulmination for a united Italy, is really the sponsor of much of the phrase that brings these nations together in some harmonious compact. Still more interesting it is to find that Germany steps up and claims, in behalf of her fathers of the revolution of 1848, the theory as one born in the compact for the confederation of the South German States. It is only here in America that we note the absence of a spirit willing to give credit to its own for the spendor of his contribution. I know not what motives animate the heart of the man that can be content to discredit his own countryman, that he may give the credit elsewhere, merely that it might tend, sir, in some way to detract from the greatness the world accords to one of his own public servants. I only know I can not envy his standard or praise his envy.

But I heard the eminent Senator from Idaho [Mr. Borah], as he closed his general comment, condemn the whole document. "Among other things," said the able Senator, "it savors of the odor of Trotzky"—Trotzky, the contemptible, because of the means he has adopted for government, of murder and destruction. The eminent Senator would have us know that it to his mind produced a suggestion of internationalism. He read a treatise of Trotzky that approved a plan of this spirit. Because of that the Senator would have us believe the document unworthy; two features being sufficient to the Senator from Idaho. One was the enforced peace; the other was the combination with the world to enforce it. These were malodorous because approved in principle by Trotzky, as the Senator affirms.

Senators, hear me. I trust the senior Senator from Massachusetts [Mr. Lodge] pays me now particular audience. If my eminent friend from Idaho shall tender Trotzky and his low standing to make contemptible any of the elements of this compact, I tender the senior Senator from Massachusetts, Hon. Henry Cabot Lodge, and his high standing, to give it respectability. I read the speech of Hon. Henry Cabot Lodge, the Senator from Massachusetts, now leader of the opposition, on this compact very early in its age. Indeed, it is when it was literally in its chrysalis, before it took its full shape and wings of life. I beseech you to hear me. I read the speech of Senator Lodge, delivered in the city of Washington on May 16, 1916.

I quote from the proceedings of the League to Enforce Peace, a gathering at the Capital.

Said the Senator:

"It is well, in understanding any great work—and the work of this league is a very great work, indeed—to know precisely where we stand, and I have been glad to learn that the league has laid down as a principle that it is not engaged in attempting to bring the war in Europe to an end; that its work lies beyond that war, for I have a somewhat deep impression that when the peace we all hope for comes it will not be brought about by expeditions from the United States nor by mass meetings and resolutions, no matter how admirable such resolutions may be. The United States has led the world in the matter of arbitration. From the day of the Jay treaty of 1794 and the Pinckney treaty of 1795 down to 1912, 84 arbitration treaties had been negotiated by the Executive of the United States, 83 had been ratified by the Senate, and only 1, the treaty of 1897 with England, rejected. I think that is a remarkable record. We have carried the principle of voluntary arbitration to its limit, and it is well to recognize that it has a limit, because when we undertake to put into treaties for voluntary arbitration questions which no nation, when the stress comes, will submit to arbitration, we do not advance the cause of peace, but quite the reverse, for we do vast mischief by making treaties which we know in our hearts we are not prepared to carry out when the time comes.

"The limit of voluntary arbitration has, I think, been reached. Much has been achieved by it. It has taken out of the range of arms a large mass of questions which once were causes, frequently of war, constantly of reprisals, and by the general consent of civilized mankind has put them before a tribunal and had them there decided. If we have reached the limit of voluntary arbitration, what is the next step? I think the next step is that which this league proposes, and that is to put force behind international peace.

"We may not solve it in that way, but if we can not solve it in that way, it can be solved in no other.

*   *   *   *   *   *   *   *   *

"I trust that we have entered on the path that will lead us to the upbuilding of our national defense both in the Army and in the Navy. I hope this is not only to make our peace secure, but because we as a Nation shall find it very difficult to induce others to put force behind peace if we have not force to put behind our own peace. I know—and no one, I think, can know better than one who has served long in the Senate, which is charged with an important share of the ratification and confirmation of all treaties—no one can, I think, feel more deeply than I do the difficulties which confront us in the work which this league undertakes. But the difficulties can not be overcome unless we try to overcome them. I believe much can be done. Probably it will be impossible to stop all wars, but it certainly will be possible to stop some wars and thus diminish their number. The way in which this problem is to be worked out must be left to this league and to those who are giving this great question the study which it deserves. I know the obstacles. I know how quickly we shall be met with the statement that this is a dangerous question which you are putting into your agreement; that no nation can submit to the judgment of other nations"— one would imagine that were one of the orations of the last week, Mr. President—"and we must be careful at the beginning not to attempt too much. I know the difficulties which arise when we speak of anything which seems to involve an alliance. But I do not believe that when Washington warned us against entangling alliances he meant for one moment that we should not join with the other civilized nations of the world if a method could be found to diminish war and encourage peace."

Continuing, said the Senator:

"It was a year ago that in delivering the chancellor's address at Union College I made an argument on this theory: That if we were to promote international peace at the close of the present terrible war, if we were to restore international law as it must be restored, we must find some way in which the united forces of the nations could be put behind the cause of peace and law. I said then that my hearers might think that I was picturing a Utopia, but it is in the search for Utopias that great discoveries have been made. 'Not failure, but low aim, is the crime.'

"This league certainly has the highest of all aims for the benefit of humanity, and because the pathway is sown with difficulties is no reason that we should turn from it."

I say, "Plato, thou reasonest well."

Mr. President, it is an interesting thing at this time, to find in a speech of the very able Senator from Massachusetts as complete a defense of this constitution of the league as could be given by anyone, anywhere. So, sir, from his eminent intellectuality we can draw much confidence and great consolation. Every objection which has been put forth by eminent Senators opposing it—that it would be an alliance which violates the precept of Washington—is denied by the eminent and learned Senator who now opposes it. Every objection upon the ground of using force to establish peace is opposed and controverted by the able Senator. Every opposition to our lending ourselves to other nations to enforce peace for all the world is met by the Senator and overcome, while he advocates the co-operation of force as a thing wholly just. Finally, the theory of the league of nations is the acme of his splendid oration so late as 1916; and to the youth of the great college which had honored him, and which he honored by his learning, teaching them of the lessons of government; he there proposed, as the *ultima thule* of human aspirations for peace and happiness, this league of nations. Therefore, Mr. President, I am not moved seriously by the mere fact that there may be something in it which my eminent friend, the Senator from Idaho, thinks meets the approval of Trotzky. I appeal from Trotzky to Lodge!

Mr. President, this brings us to the detailed objections; and only a few of them will I take up. Only those of large pretension—those on which Senators opposing say the document can not stand and by which it must fall. I fancy that the President of the United States will set forth with great clearness the reasons for many of the provisions. None are perfect. None can be. That there will be many emendations, many changes from the composite and individual minds which will assemble around the conference table, we must expect. The Constitution of the United States came forth finally—as Gladstone said, "the greatest work struck off at one time by the mind of men"—but seven years elapsed before it reached the point that the country would take it as acceptable, and then but by a real minority, instead of a majority, of its countrymen, and the meaning of its terms have been disputed over ever since.

Yet we know how it was brought about and finally how it was accepted. It will not be presumed that a document such as this before us—with its importance, its significance—could have come forth in a state of absolute perfection, and thus be the exception to every rule of human conduct of a similar kind that has prevailed since life wrote its records.

But we take first the position, made much of and with great force by the Senators and lately advanced by the eminent Senator from Missouri, referring to the voting strength.

The Senator from Missouri laid his hand upon what he felt was a defenseless weakness in the document—one which, according to his heart's conviction, involves us in surrender and destruction. The Senator called attention to the fact that the executive council is made up of five, and that in this council of five the United States has but one vote.

Mr. President, if this executive council had for its authority the privileges of the league, and it could pass wholly and com-

pletely upon the destinies of the United States so far as she will
have them ventured in this arrangement, I, too, would pause to
consider what would be the effect of the numerical majority.
The eminent Senator from Missouri says this clause puts us in
the 'peril of the power of kings. That we would be under the
dictate of kings—kings!—and that these emperors and monarchs, with all of their natural aversion to our institutions,
would be inimical to our welfare, and enemies to our interests,
and for the baleful power of kings we must be on guard and
beware their edict in this league.

Kings, sir? I pause. Where are they? Yonder in Britain
the thing called the Crown is as impotent as the picture of it
upon the sands, sir, that is washed by a receding and incoming
tide. As little voice has the king to his people in direction as
the smallest infirm mayor of a city in our land. The royal prerogative which was once a thing before which we quailed, and
finally disdained, has ceased of its existence. More of democracy, in justice let it be admitted, than is found in the land of
Britain, we know not of in America!

Italy? So impotent was her King that when he dared utter
a voice against a mere commanding general of the army marching against the German Emperor a revolution surrounded his
gates. For an hour it seemed as if his life would be hazarded to
the fury of the mob, and there were not found any of his people
who would lift an arm to preserve the King at such a moment.

In Greece a humble citizen from a small island, called Vene-
zilos, overthrew the royal power and blocked its mouth to silence; while in Russia we have beheld what has happened to
one called the Czar. Truly we can exclaim as to monarchs
Shakespeare's apostrophe to the rose—

> What's in a name;
> A rose by any other name would smell as sweet.

A king by any other name would be as useless.

Kings! How we glorify our spirit of proud democracy of
republican America, from whence came the edict that hurled
kings at the feet of the peasant and melted their scepter before
the eyes of their countrymen, who beheld it with joy, and re-
joiced over it in praise!

We remember Richard II, replying to the question asking "Where is the Duke with his power?" saying:

> For God's sake let's sit upon the ground
>   And tell sad stories of the death of Kings—
> How some have been deposed,
>   Some poisoned by their wives—some sleeping killed.
>   All murdered.
>
> *   *   *   *   *   *   *
>
> Cover your heads—and mock not flesh and blood
>   With solemn reverence—throw away respect,
> Tradition form and ceremonious duty—
>   For you have but mistook me all this while.

Why, sir, we would not wish them dead as men but as kings; and I wish my eminent friends to contemplate for a moment how impotent they are. We heard the able Senator from Missouri in one of his characteristic and magnificent outbursts in this body a short time ago, contending against the plan of the league, offer the fact that every monarch was cousin by blood; another an uncle by relation; others bearing so close affinity that we could never hope for them to be otherwise than in conjunction with each other, as against republics and our country. Yet in the face of that, he saw one uncle topple another from the throne, another uncle turn his batteries upon his relation, and how five went down to nothingness; how, as against their own blood, not the kings spoke, but their people against and over them. Then the people's war overthrew crowns, toppled emperors, and by their will, their voice, their decree, drove royalty to hiding, as refuge from death or salvation from the fury of revolution. Democracy, like justice, is at last abroad in the land. It is from the United States it speaks its warning and extends its power.

Oh, sir, we need not fear the name of a king; we need not be affrighted. The mere suggestion of a scepter need not alarm the soul of the quiet. And the American in the presence of kings is now the tranquil monarch.

Then, Mr. President, we pause to reflect, that if the able Senator from Missouri be correct in assuming that there is a disposition on the part of those who make up this council to be inimical to the welfare of the United States and its justice, or that they wait in the end to execute some vengeance which the Senator fears lurks within them and could all be executed within the power granted in this particular clause, then, sir, I say we are undone now. For if these nations are in this disposition and mettle for our destruction, we destroyed our land when we entered into conclave with them in the allied council of war with only one vote to their five. Or we are now trembling in the balance of destruction when we sit in the allied council of peace with the same proportion—of voice and authority.

Surely, it must be apparent to all that if their attitude of heart be such as the eminent Senator feels then there is nothing we can do or undo that could avoid the vengeance which their hearts brood against us and now hangs like a fate to descend upon our head. It does not require a voting trust to give them the disposition, and no lack of it would relieve them of their inclination. They have the power jointly there to outvote us in everything now, and had it while the war proceeded, under the allied control. If their actions have not invited confidence or do not justify it, let us cease all intercourse with them as being unworthy and dangerous.

Mr. President, I ask the able Senators who have assailed this document to contemplate this thought: If the Senator from Missouri and the Senator from Idaho be correct in their construction, what think they of France and of Italy and the other nations sitting down and adopting a system which as against each of them in its voting proportions could be equally as destructive in operation as the Senators assume could operate against us? As this is plainly true, would these trained diplomats have put themselves in such a trap? Would they have adopted it? Would they have entered into it? Therefore you must see that the construction is not a probable one. That the danger summoned up as possible for us must be impossible for any.

I now ask you who is it has a right to vote? The able Senators are correct when they use the expression taken from the definition of those who are to be represented in the council— "self-governing countries," colonies, dominions. What is the meaning of the word? Evidently Britain had in mind India as a colony; Canada is known by the name "Dominion"; and Britain herself designated as "country." But our able friend, the Senator from Idaho, reads in this document that every country or colony which merely governs itself would have a right to cast its individual vote. The Senator from Missouri, complimenting the Senator from Idaho—and rightfully well he might —paid tribute to the alacrity of his genius in bringing forth an article from the *London Times,* in which article it is assumed that it is the contention of Britain that each of these little independencies is to be treated as a country, and as such have the right of a vote. Of course were this true the majority of voting powers would appear to be with Britain. I beg to say to the Senator from Idaho that he misread the article. If he will but look at it, he will see that neither his own construction nor that of the Senator from Missouri is at all justified. Let me invite him to his correction. Says the *London Times*:

"It is again a source of legitimate pride to Englishmen that article 19 in the covenant might almost be taken as an exposition of the principle animating the relations of Great Britain with India and the Dominions."

Then, says the Senator from Idaho, seeking to accent this provision, "Listen to this language: 'That the dominions are in this document recognized as nations before the world is also a fact of profound significance in the history of these relations.'"

My able friend, in the haste of his investigation, or possessed so completely by his opposition to the document in general, neglected to note what article 19 is, referred to by the *Times.* Article 19, which the Senator from Missouri and the Senator from Idaho would have you believe conveyed this separate vote as "nations" to these colonies of Britain, has nothing whatever to do with votes, nor, indeed with the lands to be included in the league. Article 19 refers to those countries from the enemy, not from the allies, those who are not in the league now. We see what article 19 means when we read it:

Article 19.

"To those colonies and territories which as a consequence of the war have ceased to be under the sovereignty of the States which formerly governed them and which are inhabited by peoples not yet able to stand by themselves under the strenuous conditions of the modern world there should be applied the principle that the well-being and development of such peoples form a sacred trust of civilization and that securities for the performance of this trust should be embodied in the constitution of the league."

Surely, Mr. President, I hope there will be applied some principle to these colonies that will recognize them as self-governing when it can be done; and to their people the right of human beings deserving of the care and the charity of mankind. But it must be quite apparent, sir, that the fear both eminent Senators had that the expressions of the *London Times* meant to give a construction to this document to mean that those who are to have individual votes which would, as Senators assumed, have given a majority of votes against the United States in every possibility is all based on a wrong assumption of premises. It is now seen that the reading by both Senators and construction was the result of a complete misapprehension.

Sir, who are those who really have the vote? I come to the position taken by the Senator from Missouri—most effective, if true; most alarming, if right; most convincing, if just. It is that in the final vote of the league this Nation would stand in from the beginning in the minority, and, as such, would be impotent. I will pass the phase of the preliminary construction of the league. I now assume for basis of argument that the league is formed. Will it be assumed that the United States of America will ever tolerate this league to be formed without also incorporating in it the countries—the "self-governing countries"—of South America? Will it be possibly assumed that we could ever think of having them omitted? Is it not obvious that as we protect them under the Monroe doctrine we would as a first step in the course of that guaranty place them where by their voice and vote they could protect themselves? Would not this be our first act as a benefit to them and service to ourselves? Even were we indifferent to them being in, they would come in on their own situation under the constitution of the league as "self-governing countries," within the definition of "countries, dominions, and colonies." This is plainly without a doubt. Sir, is there an American who would assume that our President could even concede in thought, far less by vote, that such a possibility of their being omitted ever could exist? We need only answer by recalling his pledges to them made in his Mobile (Ala.) speech.

Yet, I will accept the view expressed by both eminent Senators—Mr. Borah from Idaho and Mr. Reed of Missouri—wrong, as I think I am able to manifest them, in this reading of the constitution, to be—I will accept it as though the reading were correct. I will assume that Britain voted each of the nations in the council, or if not, then each of her colonies; yet there stands the United States of America, and the eleven countries upon her own continent, with all of their destinies wrapped and intertwined with the fate of this American Hemisphere—I ask where would their vote be, sir? With everything that Britain could command in the main council, we would, with these countries of our Hemisphere, having nine to five on every European policy. The United States, Argentina, Brazil, Bolivia, Chile, Peru, Uruguay, Paraguay, Cuba, against Britain, France, Italy, Spain, Japan, or against Britain, India, Canada, Australia, and South Africa, or as against all in any unit against the Western Hemisphere—they 10 to the United States, South and Central America, 15.

Mr. Reed. Where from?

Mr. Lewis. The South American countries. I assume, sir, it would not be possible to bar them from admittance to the league.

Mr. Reed. They are not in the league now.

Mr. Lewis. Ah, sir, I call the able Senator's attention to the fact that it is not the council, as he has assumed in all his arguments, that sits upon these admissions and destinies of countries. They are the mere board of directors, now arranging for the first stockholders of the concern. After that primary organization the company as formed is to admit the applying members. The eminent Senators made their error of conclusion in assuming that it was the council who settled the destinies and the fates of admission or rejection of States. I reply, read the document; it provides that it is the league which votes the policies, not the committee on first membership—the executive council. It is only the league, as we shall see in a moment. I will not concede for a moment that our country would sit in the council or the league and, admitting members of the league, omit the

South American countries, "self-governing," under the very stable standard they have prescribed, of allowing "any self-governing State to the league by two-thirds vote of the league members." Therefore it must be apparent, sir, that we need only consider the Western Hemisphere as being true to itself, for us to know that every vote of such country will be for its own preservation; certainly never for its destruction.

It is the old royalties of Europe that have threatened to over-run these lands. It was these old kingdom lands that tried to capture and conquer South America. Shall it be ever presumed that these countries would now vote to surrender themselves to their ever ancient foes? Certainly impossible. When this, then, brings us justly to contemplate their number—eleven—and then the number of the colonies which Great Britain could bring in under the definition—six—there is not one instance where the majority would not be so great and overwhelmingly in our be-half that there could not be a possibility of the danger of our being ever outvoted by the British Empire on any question of our prime concern that the Senators from Missouri and Idaho so deeply fear.

Now, sir, we take the second test proposed by the contend-ing Senators. The Senator from Missouri and the Senator from Idaho say, "Now, here sits Japan, here is the policy of the United States of Japanese exclusion as against Japanese immigration. These countries of the league council—England, France, Italy, and Spain—say the Senators, could vote with Japan, could vote out the policy of exclusion by the United States.

Why, Mr. President, apart from the interest that the conti-nents of the Western Hemisphere, including all South and Cen-tral American lands, would have in protecting themselves against the invasion of the Asiatic millions, behold the colonies of Great Britain, which opposing Senators say will vote as units in the league. There are the four Australias, South Africa, British Columbia—all by their laws have declared for the same policy of exclusion as that prevailing in the United States. All these, as "in all beseeming ranks march one way." Sir, will these be found voting against the laws and policies they have passed and which to-day are the preservation of their existence, the policy of their sovereignty? Will their mother, Britain, be found voting against her children on so vital a necessity and drive them to a severance from the Empire and in commercial union with America? It would hardly be conceived that such a mad course can be presumed. Only by indulging these phantoms of imagination, so far from possible realities, can we entertain the fears of the alarmed Senators. And now I turn for a moment to another theme of great anxiety to the opposing Senators.

The able Senators say, in the voice of the Senator from Missouri [Mr. Reed]: "These nationalities, who can not speak our tongue, will sit in judgment as to the size of our Navy and our Army." "The Constitution provides such privilege," says the Senator, and on this charge calls down perfidious damnation on its presumed operation. Where is the evidence for such verdict; where the fact for such judgment? Why, the prescription is that the armaments are to be reduced or are to be established according, sir, to the necessity of each State, as that State shall manifest such—I prefer to read the exact words:

"The high contracting parties recognize the principle that the maintenance of peace will require the reduction of national armaments," first, "to the lowest point consistent with national safety."

Sir, who determines that? The country itself knows what is consistent with its own national safety. It is the sole and only judge. We would be the sole and supreme judge of what was consistent with our national safety, and the voice to express and assert it.

And second, "to the enforcement, by common action, of international obligations, having special regard to the geographical situation and circumstances of each State."

The State itself is the judge of its special "geographical situation" and of its particular circumstances. Only when each State has determined this status for itself does the action of the league begin. First, the State's own people must approve, or, as the constitution says, "when adopted." That is, when the limitation suggested is adopted by the country to which the limitation is proposed, and the adoption only follows the fullest home consideration and decision. Then, only then, can the league enforce the decision of each State made with each other. This reciprocal and interdependent relation brings each to a common point of reduction proportionate to each other and to the necessity of each.

Now, I propound to the Senators this query for their contemplation: If I am not right, Britain has given her navy up to the other four countries of the executive council to limit and control. This you know she would never do. These lands have been her ancient foes; may be again. If I am not right, America can destroy the British Navy with the votes of South America alone, or with six votes in addition to her own. If the Senators be right in their contention, that Britain and France and Italy and Japan, could sit alone in their sovereign judgment and decide on our Navy and our Army, then Spain, with a memory of the days of Wellington; Italy, with the history of her conflict with England; France, with the specter of Napoleon and Waterloo and lately Fashoda—these Governments, with our one vote, could destroy the British Navy by reducing it by their votes as against hers, to such a minimum as to make it useless to her necessities. All this could never be, and could never be thought in the mind of any. That is why you find in this expression the specific language that I have very little doubt, Mr. President, was the word of Britain. If I may assume to use the colloquial yet very expressive term of the Senator from Missouri, this was where Britain was "on the job." The apt words of the Senator apply here, I fancy, more than to any other phrase found in this whole document, for we read—

"Having special regard to the geographical situation and circumstances of each State."

Then, sir, you will see that each State is, under this document, specifically its own judge as to its circumstances and peculiar situation, and only by that construction, will Britain be able to have the navy of such supremacy that she feels necessary to her welfare. The construction of the able Senators who have opposed this document, if well taken, would mean the death of the navy of any one of the countries of the executive council at the vote of the other four. Can any of us think that the trained diplomats of the Old World would have allowed language, far less provisions of agreement, that could be construed to do such a thing? Do you think the United States, with her late experiences, would have tolerated a document of that kind, or a construction that was possible of that nature? The United States is not represented by men who would commit national murder of their land and political suicide of themselves. So the able Senators must see that the charge they have made and the danger they express—that this league, by the specific votes of this council, could dictate our Army and Navy by their voice, without ours—was without foundation in the document itself; is without reason in any declaration of words or paragraph of authority. To these fears we cry "Avaunt."

Now, sir, say the Senators, there is the feature of arbitration, which, as they charge, compels us to arbitrate those things to which a sense of honor and a sense of right ought never to yield. I beseech the Senators to recall that the specific words of arbitration are very much after the form of words which have been debated here on this floor in connection with arbitration treaties tendered in the administration of President Taft. We find, Mr. President, that arbitrable questions are wholly left as follows:

"The high contracting parties agree that whenever any dispute or difficulty shall arise between them which they recognize to be suitable for submission to arbitration and which can not be satisfactorily settled by diplomacy."

Reserving, sir, that thing which has been discussed, and which the eminent Senator from Pennsylvania who listens to me [Mr. Knox], as the late great Secretary of State, has so often had occasion to recur to here in his arguments, because of his own experience. That question that was discussed on the floor of the Senate so often, and no doubt was in the mind of the writer of this document, that there were certain questions of national honor or sovereign policy which could not be arbitrated. Others which should only be submitted to arbitration by the voluntary will of certain nations of the world. Therefore, sir, instead of the fear expressed by the eminent Senator, that this arbitration of our difficulties will be left perforce to our common enemies, and those of antagonism to dictate to us, the fact appears clearly upon the document that it is left by the words, by the terms of the bond, to the honor and the sense of the Nation itself as to whether it shall choose the method of arbitration or some other disposition for that particular grievance or dispute. It is a voluntary arrangement, except as to matters that could bring on war. As to the latter the league offers solution to prevent war, by prescribing a court for the solution of the dispute.

Mr. President, it must be plain that the eminent Senators have read this document in a mystifying light that has greatly confused them.

The able Senator from Missouri strikes a responsive chord and makes a severe impress by his emphasis on the charge that he would have you accept, that into this league, under the terms of this document, could enter with its power and interfere in local contests. He cites two possible illustrations most commanding at the present time to the attention of two very kindly great people of our own land. One, the Pole who was striving for liberty for his country; the other, the noble, patriotic Irishman that has dreamed of an Irish republic since the foundation of his generation. Sir, the able Senator asserts that under this document, lands such as these, Poland and Ireland, in their struggle for political equality, could be set upon, overreached, overrun by the league forces on the charge of internal disputes, and be made the victims of force; that by such power of the league these little lands could be throttled to silence against their revolt. If this charge is apparently justified I confess the evil, and one to be a cause of veto of the league. If there is in all the document one clause, yea, one word, to summon this accusation I will surrender my defense. I now ask the able Senators to reflect that the specific words in the document are "external aggression." Only under external aggression can the league have any jurisdiction. Does any man of reflection pause for a moment to ask himself why the word "external" was added? If every form of aggression without or within was to be within the jurisdiction of this league the word "aggression" alone would have been there. It would have covered all. The word "external" was added to make it impossible that there should ever arise, in the mind of any living man, the apprehension that the internal conflicts of a people however aggressive should ever be subject to the jurisdiction of these powers.

And, Mr. President, in the paragraph that the Senator from Missouri attacked so fiercely, reading that any matter that gave promise of war was a "subject of concern to the league," in which he saw evils, I invite the lawyers to the consideration of the construction. When it came to that the league reserves no power at all, no privilege of active conduct. They say to themselves that it is a matter of concern upon which they assume to offer counsel. This, as we in the United States have done time and time again to any land on the Western Continent and to many lands in Europe, yet in so doing we never have assumed to intrude our force in order to execute our friendly counsel, and we can readily appreciate what effect the counsel of this body would have with its suggestions. Let us reflect on them and their operations in the course of human action among nations. It suggests the possibility of friendships with the interceding friend or the commercial or political opposition of the interceder. The expression or reservation that war is a matter of concern to it, the league, and that it would seek to ameliorate and avoid it by accessible means, is as natural as that we would seek to extinguish a light conflagration advancing toward us, which might mean, sir, ultimately a fire of universal destruction. But the fear expressed by the able Senator that it meant that these great nations would forcibly seize these little ones and literally throttle their life and suppress their existence by the despotism of their power, I respectfully urge, has no foundation in any line or letter of the document now before this assemblage. "Beware of the wraith sent to the stage to frighten the players."

Now, Mr. President, I offer proof of my construction. I offer proof that my learned friend from Missouri will have to accept as conclusive. I commend the test I present to the Senator from Idaho, and call up his historical information, to say nothing of his acumen, to justify the illustration I tender. I say that if it be true that anything in this document—anything in the paragraph read—would allow any land—America, France, or Britain—or any combination of lands to suppress the internal dissensions in Ireland or Poland or elsewhere, then by the same authority, Britain would have realized that such power also would have meant the privilege of Russia or Japan to enter into India and interfere in her internal revolts, and summon all the forces of the league,—that France, long with her eye "avaricious with hope" in the dream of Eastern possession, would have had the privilege to enter into England's colony of Egypt. Do you fancy that Britain ever would have accepted a document that would have allowed any outside nations to enter into any colony of hers for the purpose of suppressing revolts and lending themselves to the dispute one way or the other—on the ground of maintaining order? This she knows might mean the destruction of her sovereignty over them. For the new intruder could by its presence convert them to itself and appropriate them to its own uses, as England did with Egypt, under privilege of "restoring order," France in Algiers, the United States in the Philippines. The answer springs to our lips—never!

Well, sir, as it would not be allowed to apply to colonies of Britain against her, it can not apply to any country, by Britain or France, against us. It does not give to any the power to do that with any land which Britain could not do in our land, and which Britain would not allow from us or any other in her land. So let us have done with this invented terror. Sir, common logic and common sense advise us of its impossibility. In the document not a line or a sentence can be read by the flicker of imagination to justify the accusation.

Mr. President, I must move on. I know that this long analysis of the charter is burdening, but of that I must take the responsibility. The necessity is that two industrious, able assailants in two days' occupation thundered against its walls. I must expose how invincible it is even after assault.

Mr. President, in the concluding features of this analysis I have but this following thought to offer on this section: It is to say that it must have been in the minds of those who framed this provision of this document that wherever it was apparent to those directing or about to threaten an unjust war that they would bring upon themselves the collective forces of those who would suppress their unjust attacks; these would restrain themselves nor dare proceed further upon it. Let me ask, Does anybody imagine that Germany would have entered upon the war—unholy invasion—she did, had she known that these forces that finally overcame her were ready to combine to vanquish her if she ventured upon the course of universal destruction? The hasty yielding by her when she felt the unconquerable power of their combination answers the question. This applies to explain the provision. It is the text of Job, saying—

"How forcible are right words."

Mr. President, after all it is public opinion. Public opinion, stimulated by public conscience, will guide the construction of the document. Public opinion, inspired by public virtue, will sustain this league in what it shall undertake, or it will over-throw and defeat it in any attempt against the equities of men or the rights of countries. It will appeal to public opinion before ever it assumes to execute any policy, and on this judgment it will advance or withdraw.

You will remember, Senators, that Joseph Alison, writing in 1840 from Possel House, Glasgow, dilating upon Guizot and his history of European civilization, says:

"The one great error of Napoleon was in assuming that government could be conducted by prescription, forgetful after all that it is the opinion of mankind—first through the intellectual man and then by restraining the thoughtless or defiant man, which, after all, is the director of all actions on earth—that makes for the true advance of men."

So here, too, sirs, as to this, as to all other great tasks, it will be the public opinion of mankind by which all of this will be construed and executed, or judged and defeated. On this rock must we build our house, if the storm is not to destroy it.

Mr. President, I now advert to the text advanced by the Senator from Idaho [Mr. Borah], which I regard of such great significance that I can not permit it to remain in the state he left it. The able Senator from Idaho concluded his masterly oration by creating the issue of "nationalism." He would have left the country to understand that there was now an issue against the democracy, of "nationalism" created by those who oppose this covenant, and that those who espouse it in the spirit of democracy were opposed to home nationalism. Of course, the Senator knew that no issue can be so fascinating to the creator of ideals, or so fitting to popular appeal, as one's own country. We still refrain:

> Breathes there a man with soul so dead,
> Who never to himself hath said,
> This is my own, my native land.·

Mr. President, I will draw no political party line here in this discussion. Yet, sir, I can not allow my eminent friend, the Senator from Idaho, to leave that discussion where it opposed "internationalism," or world citizenship, against nationalism or home citizenship. Yet if there is to be such a distinction, democracy shall not be charged with being guilty of home abandonment. I must remind the Senator that it was not democracy that hurled this country into Asia and in the name of "world duty" and "trustee for civilization" took possession of the Philippine Islands and established an American government there, and thus gave Asia the right to demand reciprocity to come into America with her citizens for that we had gone into Asia with our people. It was not democracy that went into China and put its army at the demand of a foreign nation there for their protection, having our Americans killed by murderous Chinese. Then later assumed jurisdiction over the railroads of China to divide them among American and English financiers under the name of the "open door," more justly designated as the "dollar diplomacy," and thus arousing the hatred of China against the United States and creating the suspicions of Japan against anything American. It was not democracy that plunged the United States into the affairs of Europe at Algeciras in the European convention of 1905 and for the first time in our career as a Nation brought the United States to the hazard of war with Spain, France, and Germany—for the vanity of the United States, establishing the "balances of the Old World," and the right of kings to filch the little land of Morocco. Sir, we, the democracy endured it. We raised no voice against our Government in matters with foreign nations after the acts were done. Like patriots our theory again was that of Decatur, "My country, may you be right; but right or wrong, my country." The democracy, in common with all our land, is now paying the price of these violations in billions of lost money and in the death of thousands of her children.

Let not the able Senator from Idaho fancy he can delude the public mind in drawing that issue against the spirit of democracy. The people remember—and ever will they be reminded "Lest we forget." Still, sir, less justified was the eminent Senator in the effort to conjure up by the name of Roosevelt the issue "nationalism." I invite my learned friend to recall his history. I rejoice in the exquisite apostrophe he paid to the man—the distinguished ex-President. Its language was of beauty which will not be excelled, and in tribute, let none desecrate by denying its deserts. But I will not allow him to summon Roosevelt dead and raise up his valiant spirit in this historic shade as a justification of the doctrine of nationalism, nor to cast him upon a pedestal as the apostle statue that stood for America only, and by that make the issue of homeland only— as creed of Republican Roosevelt as against "world citizenship" —to be charged as the aspiration of a democracy. I dare assert that the returning spirit of Theodore Roosevelt would exclaim, as he would have in life—in the words of the human to the royal artist—"paint me as I am."

I recall to every one that it was Theodore Roosevelt who demanded in behalf of his country and to the ear of the whole world that our United States, merely because the neutrality of Belgium was violated, and before a citizen of this land was ever assailed or a dollar of property attacked, should send our armies in millions and our navies in squadrons and rush ourselves, unprepared as we were, into the war of Europe, that we might avenge what he denounced as the brutalizing of Belgium.

Nationalism—the issue for Roosevelt? Let it not be forgotten that the character of his life, as extending itself into world affairs, and ever summoning the United States as avenging angel in behalf of Christianity and justice for mankind everywhere, was voiced by his historian in the exquisite eulogy of Senator Lodge upon the dead patriot when he closed his epitome in behalf of that distinguished scholar, soldier, and statesman—patriot and President—saying—

"In all his last days the thoughts which filled his mind were to secure a peace which should render Germany forever harmless and advance the cause of ordered freedom in every land and among every race."

See what it was that the ex-President gave as his view, his hope, his demand, as to a league of peace of the world. On that great project he spoke and wrote more than once with no uncertain sound. On the 1st of January, 1915, he published a book entitled *America and the World War*. He had been thinking closely and carefully over the problems created by the war, and he presented the results of his reflection for the serious consideration of his fellow countrymen. In the chapter significantly headed "An International Posse Comitatus," he says, at page 123:

"I earnestly hope that we shall ourselves become one of the joint guarantors of world peace under such a plan as that I in this book outline, and that we shall hold ourselves ready and willing to act as a member of the international comitatus to enforce the peace of righteousness as against any offender, big or small. This would mean a great practical stride toward relief from the burden of excessive military preparation. It would mean that a long step had been taken toward at least minimizing and restricting the area and extent of possible warfare. It would mean that all liberty-loving and enlightened peoples, great and small, would be free from the haunting nightmare of terror which now besets them when they think of the possible conquest of their land."

Again, in the same volume, in his chapter on "Preparedness Against War," while denouncing Mr. Bryan's peace treaties with fierce emphasis and almost "a damnable reiteration," he proceeds to say, at page 202, that "international peace will only come when the nations of the world form some kind of league which provides for an international tribunal to decide on international matters, which decrees that treaties and international agreements are never to be entered into recklessly and foolishly, and when once entered into are to be observed with entire good faith, and which puts the collective force of civilization behind such treaties and agreements and court decisions, and against any wrong-doing or recalcitrant nation."

In the chapter headed "Utopia or Hell?" he concedes that the project of a league of nations may for a time be a Utopian vision, but suggests the hopeful possibility that "after the war has come to an end the European contestants will be sufficiently sobered to be willing to consider some such proposal, and that the United States will abandon the folly of the pacifists and be willing to co-operate in some practical effort for the only kind of peace worth having, the peace of justice and righteousness."

"My proposal" he says, "is that the efficient civilized nations, those that are efficient in war as well as in peace, shall join in a world league for the peace of righteousness. This means that they shall by solemn covenant agree as to their respective rights which shall not be questioned, that they shall agree that all other questions arising between them shall be submitted to a court of arbitration, and that they shall also agree— and here comes the vital and essential point of the whole system —to act with the combined military strength of all of them against any recalcitrant nation, against any nation which transgresses at the expense of any other nation the rights which it is agreed shall not be questioned, or which on arbitrable matters refuses to submit to the decree of the arbitral court."

In his final chapter, summing up the argument, at page 253, he says:

"It is because I believe our attitude should be one of sincere good will toward all nations that I so strongly feel that we should endeavor to work for a league of peace among all nations rather than trust to alliances with any particular group. * * * The prime necessity is that all the great nations should agree in good faith to use their combined warlike strength to coerce any nation, whichever one it may be, that declines to abide the decision of some competent international tribunal. Our business is to create the beginnings of international order out of the world of nations as these nations actually exist. We do not have to deal with a world of pacifists, and therefore we must proceed on the assumption that treaties will never acquire sanctity until nations are ready to seal them with their blood."

More than a year after the publication of this volume the ex-President produced another, taking his title from a phrase used by the heroine in George Borrow's *Lavengro,* "Fear God and take your own part." At page 410 of this book he reproduces the following passages from his address before the Nobel Prize Committee, May 5, 1910:

"Something should be done as soon as possible to check the growth of armaments, especially naval armaments, by international agreement. No one power could or should act by itself, for it is eminently undesirable from the standpoint of the peace of righteousness that a power which really does believe in peace should place itself at the mercy of some rival which may at bottom have no such belief, and no intention of acting on it.

"Finally, it would be a master stroke if those great powers honestly bent on peace would form a league of peace, not only to keep the peace among themselves, but to prevent, by force if necessary, its being broken by others.

"The supreme difficulty in connection with developing the peace work of The Hague arises from the lack of any executive power, of any police power to enforce the decrees of the court. Each nation must keep well prepared to defend itself until the establishment of some form of international police power competent and willing to prevent violence as between nations. As things are now, such power to command peace throughout the world could only be assured by some combination between those great nations which sincerely desire peace and have no thought themselves of committing aggressions. * * * The combination might at first be only to secure peace within certain definite limits and certain definite conditions, but the ruler or statesman who should bring about such a combination would have earned his place in history for all time and his title to the gratitude of all mankind."

This volume was published in February, 1916.

Here, sir, we have the creed of the Republican masters—of Roosevelt as he spoke—and as he spake he will be judged.

Mr. President, I have done with this analysis. Feebly have I performed the task assigned me. Yet I have assumed to point out the particular peaks upon which Senators mounted and the promontories upon which they stood from which they proclaimed to the valleys below the desolation and destruction of their land. I have assumed to show that their foundation was not mountain tops of truth, but hills of false echo.

I dare assume that I have demonstrated, if not to the conversion of men about me, then to the satisfaction of public conscience how infinitely wrong the able Senators were in their construction. In their premises wrong when right in conclusions, and wrong in the conclusions when right in premises. On that false foundation all their baleful philosophy of opposition was built.

Mr. President, the Senator from Idaho demands that the people be given the opportunity to decide. I answer yes, it will be so; the people shall decide. This document will not be approved nor brought here in any form for verdict without the voice of the people being heard upon it. I will have the eminent Senator from Idaho understand that it never can be permitted by me, that through his great force the impression shall go abroad, that the democracy intended this as a secret charter to be forced in a star-chamber proceeding. It will be before the Senate. Before then it will receive the consideration and audience of the people. The people will pass on the merits of this project for peace as they pass on every similar document of its purport heretofore presented in the form of a treaty. This will be through and by their Senators speaking on this floor the voice of their constituents. But, sir, this undertaking and covenant will have that superior advantage of the voice of the distinguished champion of its birth who will do as he has done in every other measure he has found in his heart to advocate for the welfare of his countrymen. He will go to his people with the proofs of his sincerity, with the truth of his cause, with the result that has ever followed his appeal to his fellow citizens —the approval of his undertaking, as they have ever approved whenever he has gone to them with that which he has demanded in the name of humanity for mankind and justice for country.

> Knowing that He cometh as one
> To serve the broken—they ever cry:
> "Make way for the friend, He cometh
> For the cause of truth and the righteousness of men."

Senators, it is now for our country to make her decision. It is to the white paths of peace or the black plains of war. And when my country comes to the final judgment, let her not come blindfolded with the scarf of delusion. Let her behold herself in her now new relation to the world. The to-morrows greet her as the accepted friend to each or as the enemy of all. This, my beloved land, with her brow crowned with the glory of her unparalleled achievement, her body radiant with the blaze of fame's immortal star, is now never again to be the separated land from all the world's conflicts. This America is now an island with the Bering Sea at the north, with maddened Russia frenzied in hatred of us threatening at its icy doors. The Atlantic on the east, whose tides boom the summons to every ancient European grudge or national rivalry to sate itself at first advantage. On the Pacific the mysterious lands of the mystic East brood in silent meditation as to their course in retaliation for the long affront against their people and indignity of years against their nation. At the south the Panama Canal and the Gulf that widens to a sea, echo in their every singing wave the doubt and suspicions of South and Central America against the professed friendships of the United States.

Mr. President, our to-morrows approach heavily upon us with the burdens of uncertainty. Let us not be deceived in the security that we are exempt from the inheritances which from the dawn of time have befallen those who march in rivalry to overcome by superiority their rival nations. For us there is but one of two fates decreed. It is to be victor or victim. We will live in the brotherhood of peace, tranquil in the family fraternity of nations through interchange of benefits and blessings; or we will live the life of one threatened by the powerful, hated by those who fear us, and the object of hoped-for destruction by those who long for the day of power to execute their hidden vengeance. Sir, Japan and China can be one in common grievance on the east, while the new Russia and the Germanic lands may be a union of purpose with a kindred hatred waiting revived strength to avenge it upon us. In Europe abide those commercial rivalries that can leave our former battle field allies indifferent to the results that our avowed enemies may attempt upon us. Our America is now more imperiled in her future than has been her lot since her Republic sprung to life. Only to herself can she look with sure confidence. Only within herself can she find complete security. She must choose to trust herself wholly and abide in her own strength without aid and without friends, or trust herself wholly to abide in the friendships of Christian people and in the protecting love of godly nations.

If, sir, we are to be wholly alone and separate from the earth's companionships, then our country must prepare for armies and navies of a volume that shall make us supreme against any land and every foe. But these shall swell the debt of the nation to where it will exhaust the rich and beggar the poor, and awaken a discontent to burst forth in internal daily dissensions, provoking in the end civil revolutions. We must dwell on our new changed conditions; we must measure with the fleets of the sea knitting us to every shore of every land; the air woven into a canopy of death or in curtains of life by the shuttle weavings of the aeroplane. We must reckon with the depths of the sea knotted into traps of destruction by the gyrating maneuvers of the submarine, and sight with new vision the engines of destruction encompassing us about from every hidden vantage. From all this we must see that the peace our country seeks of the earth for mankind is not for others only. It is also for ourselves.

Let our country behold itself as the light of truth reveals us—in danger! True, we can overcome it all and be victors through all. We can prepare now to empty every home of its first born; we can smite the tears from every mother's heart and wring with agony the soul of every wife. More, we can consign every boy to the fate of a cripple—and many to the horrors of sightless eyes and a hopeless life. We can empty the treasuries of the cities and make barren the farms. We can leave our country a graveyard for her dead children—stricken by her own hand—and turn our churches of God into the mourning houses where the wails of the desolate will cry unto Heaven to consign the creators of their desolation to the depths of hell. All this we can have, that we may boast of military glory and the vanquishing by world murder of every foe.

Or, sirs, we can salute the regenerated earth in the new spirit with which our children reincarnated it with their sacred bodies, still sanctifying the soil that is their distant grave. We can join in friendship that surrenders no right nor yields one privilege of a just people. We can proclaim that so long as mankind will be true to us we can covenant to be just and fair to it. That we submit every national grievance to the adjustment of a Christian spirit by the balances of right and wrong among honest people. That we will join all who equally join us in casting aside the iron instruments of death which murder men and pauperize lands—and in their place put the pulpits of Christ and the world courts of justice. Then we can declare, by the sacred memory of the dead who fell that their loved ones should live, that war and death shall end and love of man and the life of the world begin—all consecrated anew to justice on earth and God in heaven.

Which shall it be? The holy voice again proclaims to mankind in the morn of the twentieth century as it cried out in the night of the first, "Choose ye this day whom ye will serve." We reply, "For us and our house we serve the Lord." So, sir, when we are gladdened by the sight of the new army bearing banners streaming with the ensign, "Peace on earth and good will to men," our hearts will be quickened to joy and our lips break in praise that the first evangel to bring the glory of the newborn age and lead the rejoicing processions of the redeemed earth was our United States of America—thank God!

HENRY CABOT LODGE

TREATY OF PEACE WITH GERMANY

Speech in the United States Senate, August 12, 1919, in
Opposition to the Resolution of Ratification
of the Versailles Peace Treaty

[Henry Cabot Lodge was born in Boston, Massachusetts, on May
12, 1850. He was graduated from Harvard College in 1871, from the
Harvard Law School in 1875, and was admitted to the bar in 1876.
He was editor of the *North American Review*, 1873 to 1876; lecturer
in American history at Harvard University, 1876 to 1879; editor of
the *International Review*, 1879 to 1881; and lecturer at Lowell Institute, Boston, in 1880. He was an accomplished writer of essays
and historical works. He began his political career as a member of
the Massachusetts House of Representatives, 1880 to 1881; was a
Republican member of Congress, 1887 to 1893; and served as United
States Senator from 1893 to 1924. He was a member of the Alaskan
Boundary Commission in 1903; a member of the United States Immigration Commission, 1907 to 1910; and represented the United
States at the Conference on Limitation of Armaments in 1921. He
died on November 9, 1924, in Cambridge, Massachusetts.

At the time when he delivered the speech printed below, he was
Republican floor leader in the Senate and Chairman of the Committee
on Foreign Relations. He became an implacable opponent of the
League of Nations Covenant, and it was largely due to his efforts that
the resolution of ratification of the Treaty was defeated.]

Mr. President, In the *Essays of Elia,* one of the most delightful is that entitled "Popular Fallacies." There is one very popular fallacy, however, which Lamb did not include in his list,
and that is the common saying that history repeats itself. Universal negatives are always dangerous, but if there is anything
which is fairly certain, it is that history never exactly repeats
itself. Popular fallacies, nevertheless, generally have some
basis, and this saying springs from the undoubted truth that
mankind from generation to generation is constantly repeating
itself. We have an excellent illustration of this fact in the proposed experiment now before us, of making arrangements to
secure the permanent peace of the world. To assure the peace

[592]

of the world by a combination of the nations is no new idea. Leaving out the leagues of antiquity and of mediæval times and going back no further than the treaty of Utrecht, at the beginning of the eighteenth century, we find that at that period a project of a treaty to establish perpetual peace was brought forward in 1713 by the Abbé de Saint-Pierre. The treaty of Utrecht was to be the basis of an international system. A European league or Christian republic was to be set up, under which the members were to renounce the right of making war against each other and submit their disputes for arbitration to a central tribunal of the allies, the decisions of which were to be enforced by a common armament. I need not point out the resemblance between this theory and that which underlies the present league of nations. It was widely discussed during the eighteenth century, receiving much support in public opinion; and Voltaire said that the nations of Europe, united by ties of religion, institutions, and culture, were really but a single family. The idea remained in an academic condition until 1791, when under the pressure of the French Revolution Count Kaunitz sent out a circular letter in the name of Leopold, of Austria, urging that it was the duty of all the powers to make common cause for the purpose of "preserving public peace, tranquillity of States, the inviolability of possession, and the faith of treaties," which has a very familiar sound. Napoleon had a scheme of his own for consolidating the Great European peoples and establishing a central assembly, but the Napoleonic idea differed from that of the eighteenth century, as one would expect. A single great personality dominated and hovered over all. In 1804 the Emperor Alexander took up the question and urged a general treaty for the formation of a European confederation. "Why could one not submit to it," the Emperor asked, "the positive rights of nations, assure the privilege of neutrality, insert the obligation of never beginning war until all the resources which the mediation of a third party could offer have been exhausted, until the grievances have by this means been brought to light, and an effort to remove them has been made? On principles such as these one could proceed to a general pacification, and give birth to a league of which the stipu-

lations would form, so to speak, a new code of the law of nations, while those who should try to infringe it would risk
bringing upon themselves the forces of the new union."

The Emperor, moved by more immediately alluring visions,
put aside this scheme at the treaty of Tilsit and then decided
that peace could best be restored to the world by having two all-
powerful emperors, one of the east and one of the west. After
the Moscow campaign, however, he returned to his early dream.
Under the influence of the Baroness von Krudener he became a
devotee of a certain mystic pietism which for some time guided
his public acts, and I think it may be fairly said that his liberal
and popular ideas of that period, however vague and uncertain,
were sufficiently genuine. Based upon the treaties of alliance
against France, those of Chaumont and of Vienna, was the final
treaty of Paris, of November 20, 1815. In the preamble the
signatories, who were Great Britain, Austria, Russia, and Prussia, stated that it is the purpose of the ensuing treaty and their
desire "to employ all their means to prevent the general tranquillity—the object of the wishes of mankind and the constant
end of their efforts—from being again disturbed; desirous,
moreover, to draw closer the ties which unite them for the common interests of their people, have resolved to give to the principles solemnly laid down in the treaties of Chaumont of March
1, 1814, and of Vienna of March 25, 1815, the application the
most analogous to the present state of affairs, and to fix beforehand by a solemn treaty the principles which they propose to
follow, in order to guarantee Europe from dangers by which
she may still be menaced."

Then follow five articles which are devoted to an agreement
to hold France in control and checks, based largely on other
more detailed agreements. But in article 6 it is said:

"To facilitate and to secure the execution of the present
treaty, and to consolidate the connections which at the present
moment so closely unite the four sovereigns for the happiness
of the world, the high contracting parties have agreed to renew
their meeting at fixed periods, either under the immediate auspices of the sovereigns themselves, or by their respective ministers, for the purpose of consulting upon their common interests,
and for the consideration of the measures which at each of those

periods shall be considered the most salutary for the repose and prosperity of nations and for the maintenance of the peace of Europe."

Certainly nothing could be more ingenuous or more praiseworthy than the purposes of the alliance then formed, and yet it was this very combination of powers which was destined to grow into what has been known, and we might add cursed, throughout history as the Holy Alliance.

As early as 1818 it had become apparent that upon this innocent statement might be built an alliance which was to be used to suppress the rights of nationalities and every attempt of any oppressed people to secure their freedom. Lord Castlereagh was a Tory of the Tories, but at that time, only three years after the treaty of Paris, when the representatives of the alliance met at Aix-la-Chapelle, he began to suspect that this new European system was wholly inconsistent with the liberties to which Englishmen of all types were devoted. At the succeeding meetings, at Troppau and Laibach, his suspicion was confirmed, and England began to draw away from her partners. He had indeed determined to break with the alliance before the Congress of Verona, but his death threw the question into the hands of George Canning, who stands forth as the man who separated Great Britain from the combination of the continental powers. The attitude of England, which was defined in a memorandum where it was said that nothing could be more injurious to the idea of government generally than the belief that their force was collectively to be prostituted to the support of an established power without any consideration of the extent to which it was to be abused, led to a compromise in 1818 in which it was declared that it was the intention of the five powers, France being invited to adhere, "to maintain the intimate union, strengthened by the ties of Christian brotherhood, contracted by the sovereigns; to pronounce the object of this union to be the preservation of peace on the basis of respect for treaties." Admirable and gentle words these, setting forth purposes which all men must approve.

In 1820 the British Government stated that they were prepared to fulfill all treaty obligations, but that if it was desired "to extend the alliance, so as to include all objects, present and future, foreseen and unforeseen, it would change its character to such an extent and carry us so far that we should see in it an additional motive for adhering to our course at the risk of seeing the alliance move away from us, without our having quitted it." The Czar Alexander abandoned his Liberal theories and threw himself into the arms of Metternich, as mean a tyrant as history can show, whose sinister designs probably caused as much misery and oppression in the years which followed as have ever been evolved by one man of second-rate abilities. The three powers, Russia, Austria, and Prussia, then put out a famous protocol in which it was said that the "States which have undergone a change of government due to revolution, the results of which threaten other States, *ipso facto* cease to be members of the European alliance and remain excluded from it until their situation gives guaranties for legal order and stability. If, owing to such alterations, immediate danger threatens other States, the powers bind themselves, by peaceful means, or, if need be, by arms, to bring back the guilty State into the bosom of the great alliance." To this point had the innocent and laudable declaration of the treaty of Paris already developed. In 1822 England broke away, and Canning made no secret of his pleasure at the breach. In a letter to the British minister at St. Petersburg he said:

"So things are getting back to a wholesome state again. Every nation for itself, and God for us all. The time for Areopagus, and the like of that, is gone by."

He also said, in the same year, 1823:

"What is the influence we have had in the counsels of the alliance, and which Prince Metternich exhorts us to be so careful not to throw away? We protested at Laibach; we remonstrated at Verona. Our protest was treated as waste paper; our remonstrances mingled with the air. Our influence, if it is to be maintained abroad, must be secured in the source of strength at home; and the sources of that strength are in sympathy between the people and the Government; in the union of the public sentiment with the public counsels; in the reciprocal confidence and co-operation of the House of Commons and the Crown."

These words of Canning are as applicable and as weighty now as when they were uttered and as worthy of consideration. The Holy Alliance, thus developed by the three continental powers and accepted by France under the Bourbons, proceeded to restore the inquisition in Spain, to establish the Neapolitan Bourbons, who for 40 years were to subject the people of southern Italy to one of the most detestable tyrannies ever known, and proposed further to interfere against the colonies in South America which had revolted from Spain and to have their case submitted to a congress of the powers. It was then that Canning made his famous statement, "We have called a new world into existence to redress the balance of the old." It was at this point also that the United States intervened. The famous message of Monroe, sent to Congress on December 2, 1823, put an end to any danger of European influence in the American Continents. A distinguished English historian, Mr. William Alison Phillips, says:

"The attitude of the United States effectually prevented the attempt to extend the dictatorship of the alliance beyond the bounds of Europe, in itself a great service to mankind."

In 1825 Great Britain recognized the South American Republics. So far as the New World was concerned the Holy Alliance had failed. It was deprived of the support of France by the revolution of 1830, but it continued to exist under the guidance of Metternich and its last exploit was in 1839, when the Emperor Nicholas sent a Russian army into Hungary to crush out the struggle of Kossuth for freedom and independence.

I have taken the trouble to trace in the merest outline the development of the Holy Alliance, so hostile and dangerous to human freedom, because I think it carries with it a lesson for us at the present moment, showing as it does what may come from general propositions and declarations of purposes in which all the world agrees. Turn to the preamble of the covenant of the league of nations now before us, which states the object of the league. It is formed "in order to promote international co-operation and to achieve international peace and security by the acceptance of obligations not to resort to war, by the prescription of open, just, and honorable relations between nations, by the firm establishment of the understandings of international law as the actual rule of conduct among governments and by the maintenance of justice and a scrupulous respect for all treaty obligations in the dealings of organized peoples with one another."

No one would contest the loftiness or the benevolence of these purposes. Brave words, indeed! They do not differ essentially from the preamble of the treaty of Paris, from which sprang the Holy Alliance. But the covenant of this league contains a provision which I do not find in the treaty of Paris, and which is as follows:

"The assembly may deal at its meetings with any matter within the sphere of action of the league or affecting the peace of the world."

There is no such sweeping or far-reaching provision as that in the treaty of Paris, and yet able men developed from that treaty the Holy Alliance, which England, and later France were forced to abandon and which, for 35 years, was an unmitigated curse to the world. England broke from the Holy Alliance and the breach began three years after it was formed, because English statesmen saw that it was intended to turn the alliance—and this league is an alliance—into a means of repressing internal revolutions or insurrections. There was nothing in the treaty of Paris which warranted such action, but in this covenant of the league of nations the authority is clearly given in the third paragraph of article 3, where it is said:

"The assembly may deal at its meetings with any matter within the sphere of action of the league or affecting the peace of the world."

No revolutionary movement, no internal conflict of any magnitude can fail to affect the peace of the world. The French Revolution, which was wholly internal at the beginning, affected the peace of the world to such an extent that it brought on a world war which lasted some 25 years. Can anyone say that our Civil War did not affect the peace of the world? At this very moment, who would deny that the condition of Russia, with internal conflicts raging in all parts of that great Empire, does not affect the peace of the world and therefore come properly within the jurisdiction of the league. "Any matter affecting the peace of the world" is a very broad statement which

could be made to justify almost any interference on the part
of the league with the internal affairs of other countries. That
this fair and obvious interpretation is the one given to it abroad
is made perfectly apparent in the direct and vigorous statement
of M. Clemenceau in his letter to Mr. Paderewski, in which he
takes the ground in behalf of the Jews and other nationalities
in Poland that they should be protected, and where he says that
the associated powers would feel themselves bound to secure
guaranties in Poland "of certain essential rights which will afford to the inhabitants the necessary protection, whatever changes may take place in the internal constitution of the Polish Republic." He contemplates and defends interference with the
internal affairs of Poland—among other things—in behalf of a
complete religious freedom, a purpose with which we all deeply
sympathize. These promises of the French prime minister are
embodied in effective clauses in the treaties with Germany and
with Poland and deal with the internal affairs of nations, and
their execution is intrusted to the "principal allied and associated powers"; that is, to the United States, Great Britain, France,
Italy, and Japan. This is a practical demonstration of what can
be done under article 3 and under article 11 of the league covenant, and the authority which permits interference in behalf of
religious freedom, an admirable object, is easily extended to the
repression of internal disturbances which may well prove a less
admirable purpose. If Europe desires such an alliance or
league with a power of this kind, so be it. I have no objection,
provided they do not interfere with the American Continents or
force us against our will but bound by a moral obligation into
all the quarrels of Europe. If England, abandoning the policy
of Canning, desires to be a member of a league which has such
powers as this, I have not a word to say. But I object in the
strongest possible way to having the United States agree, directly or indirectly, to be controlled by a league which may at
any time, and perfectly lawfully and in accordance with the
terms of the covenant, be drawn in to deal with internal conflicts in other countries, no matter what those conflicts may be.
We should never permit the United States to be involved in any
internal conflict in another country, except by the will of her
people expressed through the Congress which represents them.

With regard to wars of external aggression on a member of the league the case is perfectly clear. There can be no genuine dispute whatever about the meaning of the first clause of article 10. In the first place, it differs from every other obligation in being individual and placed upon each nation without the intervention of the league. Each nation for itself promises to respect and preserve as against external aggression the boundaries and the political independence of every member of the league. Of the right of the United States to give such a guaranty I have never had the slightest doubt, and the elaborate arguments which have been made here and the learning which has been displayed about our treaty with Granada, now Colombia, and with Panama, were not necessary for me, because, I repeat, there can be no doubt of our right to give a guaranty to another nation that we will protect its boundaries and independence. The point I wish to make is that the pledge is an individual pledge. We have, for example, given guaranties to Panama and for obvious and sufficient reasons. The application of that guaranty would not be in the slightest degree affected by 10 or 20 other nations giving the same pledge if Panama, when in danger, appealed to us to fulfill our obligation. We should be bound to do so without the slightest reference to the other guarantors. In article 10 the United States is bound on the appeal of any member of the league not only to respect but to preserve its independence and its boundaries, and that pledge if we give it, must be fulfilled.

There is to me no distinction whatever in a treaty between what some persons are pleased to call legal and moral obligations. A treaty rests and must rest, except where it is imposed under duress and securities and hostages are taken for its fulfillment, upon moral obligations. No doubt a great power impossible of coercion can cast aside a moral obligation if it sees fit and escape from the performance of the duty which it promises. The pathway of dishonor is always open. I, for one, however, can not conceive of voting for a clause of which I disapprove because I know it can be escaped in that way. Whatever the United States agrees to, by that agreement she must abide. Nothing could so surely destroy all prospects of the world's peace as to have any powerful nation refuse to carry out an obligation, direct or indirect, because it rests only on moral grounds. Whatever we promise we must carry out to the full, "without mental reservation or purpose of evasion." To me any other attitude is inconceivable. Without the most absolute and minute good faith in carrying out a treaty to which we have agreed, without ever resorting to doubtful interpretations or to the plea that it is only a moral obligation, treaties are worthless. The greatest foundation of peace is the scrupulous observance of every promise, express or implied, of every pledge, whether it can be described as legal or moral. No vote should be given to any clause in any treaty or to any treaty except in this spirit and with this understanding.

I return, then, to the first clause of article 10. It is, I repeat, an individual obligation. It requires no action on the part of the league, except that in the second sentence the authorities of the league are to have the power to advise as to the means to be employed in order to fulfill the purpose of the first sentence. But that is a detail of execution, and I consider that we are morally and in honor bound to accept and act upon that advice. The broad fact remains that if any member of the league suffering from external aggression should appeal directly to the United States for support the United States would be bound to give that support in its own capacity and without reference to the action of other powers because the United States itself is bound, and I hope the day will never come when the United States will not carry out its promises. If that day should come, and the United States or any other great country should refuse, no matter how specious the reasons, to fulfill both in letter and spirit every obligation in this covenant, the United States would be dishonored and the league would crumble into dust, leaving behind it a legacy of wars. If China should rise up and attack Japan in an effort to undo the great wrong of the cession of the control of Shantung to that power, we should be bound under the terms of article 10 to sustain Japan against China, and a guaranty of that sort is never involved except when the question has passed beyond the stage of negotiation and has become a question for the application of force. I do not like the prospect. It shall not come into existence by any vote of mine.

Article 11 carries this danger still further, for it says:

"Any war or threat of war, whether immediately affecting any of the members of the league or not, is hereby declared a matter of concern to the whole league, and the league shall take any action that shall be deemed wise and effectual to safeguard the peace of nations."

"Any war or threat of war"—that means both external aggression and internal disturbance, as I have already pointed out in dealing with article 3. "Any action" covers military action, because it covers action of any sort or kind. Let me take an example, not an imaginary case, but one which may have been overlooked because most people have not the slightest idea where or what a King of the Hedjaz is. The following dispatch appeared recently in the newspapers:

Hedjaz Against Bedouins.

"The forces of Emir Abdullah recently suffered a grave defeat, the Wahabis attacking and capturing Kurma, east of Mecca. Ibn Savond is believed to be working in harmony with the Wahabis. A squadron of the royal air force was ordered recently to go to the assistance of King Hussein."

Hussein I take to be the Sultan of Hedjaz. He is being attacked by the Bedouins, as they are known to us, although I fancy the general knowledge about the Wahabis and Ibn Savond and Emir Abdullah is slight and the names mean but little to the American people. Nevertheless, here is a case of a member of the league—for the King of Hedjaz is such a member in good and regular standing and signed the treaty by his representatives, Mr. Rustem Haidar and Mr. Abdul Havi Aouni.

Under article 10, if King Hussein appealed to us for aid and protection against external aggression affecting his independence and the boundaries of his Kingdom, we should be bound to give that aid and protection and to send American soldiers to Arabia. It is not relevant to say that this is unlikely to occur; that Great Britain is quite able to take care of King Hussein, who is her fair creation, reminding one a little of the Mosquito King, a monarch once developed by Great Britain on the Mosquito Coast of Central America. The fact that we should not be called upon does not alter the right which the King of Hedjaz possesses to demand the sending of American troops to Arabia in order to preserve his independence against the assaults of the Wahabis or Bedouins. I am unwilling to give that right to King Hussein, and this illustrates the point which is to me the most objectionable in the league as it stands; the right of other powers to call out American troops and American ships to go to any part of the world, an obligation we are bound to fulfill under the terms of this treaty. I know the answer well—that of course they could not be sent without action by Congress. Congress would have no choice if acting in good faith, and if under article 10 any member of the league summoned us, or if under article 11 the league itself summoned us, we should be bound in honor and morally to obey. There would be no escape except by a breach of faith, and legislation by Congress under those circumstances would be a mockery of independent action. Is it too much to ask that provision should be made that American troops and American ships should never be sent anywhere or ordered to take part in any conflict except after the deliberate action of the American people, expressed according to the Constitution through their chosen representatives in Congress?

Let me now briefly point out the insuperable difficulty which I find in article 15. It begins: "If there should arise between members of the league any dispute likely to lead to a rupture." "Any dispute" covers every possible dispute. It therefore covers a dispute over tariff duties and over immigration. Suppose we have a dispute with Japan or with some European country as to immigration. I put aside tariff duties as less important than immigration. This is not an imaginary case. Of late years there has probably been more international discussion and negotiation about questions growing out of immigration laws than any other one subject. It comes within the definition of "any dispute" at the beginning of article 15. In the eighth paragraph of that article it is said that "if the dispute between the parties is claimed by one of them, and is found by the council to arise out of a matter which, by international law, is solely within the domestic jurisdiction of that party, the council shall so report and shall make no recommendation as to its settlement." That is one of the statements, of which there are several in this treaty, where words are used which it is difficult to believe their authors could have written down in seriousness. They seem to have been put in for the same purpose as what is known in natural history as protective coloring. Protective coloring is intended so to merge the animal, the bird, or the insect in its background that it will be indistinguishable from its surroundings and difficult, if not impossible, to find the elusive and hidden bird, animal, or insect. Protective coloring here is used in the form of words to give an impression that we are perfectly safe upon immigration and tariffs, for example, because questions which international law holds to be solely within domestic jurisdiction are not to have any recommendation from the council, but the dangers are there just the same, like the cunningly colored insect on the tree or the young bird crouching motionless upon the sand. The words and the coloring are alike intended to deceive. I wish somebody would point out to me those provisions of international law which make a list of questions which are hard and fast within the domestic jurisdiction. No such distinction can be applied to tariff duties or immigration, nor indeed finally and conclusively to any subject. Have we not seen the school laws of California, most domestic of subjects, rise to the dignity of a grave international dispute? No doubt both import duties and immigration are primarily domestic questions, but they both constantly involve and will continue to involve international effects. Like the protective coloration, this paragraph is wholly worthless unless it is successful in screening from the observer the existence of the animal, insect, or bird which it is desired to conceal. It fails to do so and the real object is detected. But even if this bit of deception was omitted—and so far as the question of immigration or tariff questions are concerned it might as well be—the ninth paragraph brings the important point clearly to the front. Immigration, which is the example I took, cannot escape the action of the league by any claim of domestic jurisdiction; it has too many international aspects.

Paragraph 9 says:

"The council may, in any case under this article, refer the dispute to the assembly."

We have our dispute as to immigration with Japan or with one of the Balkan States, let us say. The council has the power to refer the dispute to the assembly. Moreover the dispute shall be so referred at the request of either party to the dispute, provided that such request be made within 14 days after the submission of the dispute to the council. So that Japan or the Balkan States, for example, with which we may easily have the dispute, ask that it be referred to the assembly and the immigration question between the United States and Jugoslavia or Japan as the case may be, goes to the assembly. The United States and Japan or Jugoslavia are excluded from voting and the provision of article 12, relating to the action and powers of the council apply to the action and powers of the assembly provided, as set forth in article 15, that a report made by the assembly "if concurred in by the representatives of those members of the league represented on the council and of a majority of the other members of the league, exclusive in each case of the representatives of the parties to the dispute, shall have the same force as a report by the council concurred in by all the members thereof other than the representatives of one or more of the parties to the dispute." This course of procedure having been pursued, we find the question of immigration between the United States and Japan is before the assembly for decision. The representatives of the council, except the delegates of the United States and of Japan or Jugoslavia, must all vote unanimously upon it as I understand it, but a majority of the entire assembly, where the council will have only seven votes, will decide. Can anyone say beforehand what the decision of that assembly will be, in which the United States and Jugoslavia or Japan will have no vote? The question in one case may affect immigration from every country in Europe, although the dispute exists only for one, and in the other the whole matter of Asiatic immigration is involved. Is it too fanciful to think that it might be decided against us? For my purpose it matters not whether it is decided for or against us. An immigration dispute or a dispute over tariff duties, met by the procedure set forth in article 15, comes before the assembly of delegates for a decision by what is practically a majority vote of the entire assembly. That is something to which I do not find myself able to give my assent. So far as immigration is concerned, and also so far as tariff duties, although less important, are concerned, I deny the jurisdiction. There should be no possibility of other nations deciding who shall come into the United States, or under what conditions they shall enter. The right to say who shall come into a country is one of the very highest attributes of sovereignty. If a nation cannot say without appeal who shall come within its gates and become a part of its citizenship it has ceased to be a sovereign nation. It has become a tributary and a subject nation, and it makes no difference whether it is subject to a league or to a conqueror.

If other nations are willing to subject themselves to such a domination, the United States, to which many immigrants have come and many more will come, ought never to submit to it for a moment. They tell us that so far as Asiatic emigration is concerned there is not the slightest danger that that will ever be forced upon us by the league, because Australia and Canada and New Zealand are equally opposed to it. I think it highly improbable that it would be forced upon us under those conditions, but it is by no means impossible. It is true the United States has one vote and that England, if you count the King of the Hedjaz, has seven—in all eight—votes; yet it might not be impossible for Japan and China and Siam to rally enough other votes to defeat us; but whether we are protected in that way or not does not matter. The very offering of that explanation accepts the jurisdiction of the league, and personally, I cannot consent to putting the protection of my country and of her workingmen against undesirable immigration, out of our own hands. We and we alone must say who shall come into the United States and become citizens of this Republic, and no one else should have any power to utter one word in regard to it.

Article 21 says:

"Nothing in this covenant shall be deemed to affect the validity of international engagements, such as treaties of arbitration or regional understandings like the Monroe doctrine, for securing the maintenance of peace."

The provision did not appear in the first draft of the covenant, and when the President explained the second draft of the convention in the peace conference he said:

"Article 21 is new."

And that was all he said. No one can question the truth of the remark, but I trust I shall not be considered disrespectful if

I say that it was not an illuminating statement. The article was new, but the fact of its novelty, which the President declared, was known to everyone who had taken the trouble to read the two documents. We were not left, however, without a fitting explanation. The British delegation took it upon themselves to explain article 21 at some length, and this is what they said:

"Article 21 makes it clear that the covenant is not intended to abrogate or weaken any other agreements, so long as they are consistent with its own terms, into which members of the league may have entered or may hereafter enter for the assurance of peace. Such agreements would include special treaties for compulsory arbitration and military conventions that are genuinely defensive.

"The Monroe doctrine and similar understandings are put in the same category. They have shown themselves in history to be not instruments of national ambition, but guarantees of peace. The origin of the Monroe doctrine is well known. It was proclaimed in 1823 to prevent America from becoming a theater for intrigues of European absolutism. At first a principle of American foreign policy, it has become an international understanding, and it is not illegitimate for the people of the United States to say that the covenant should recognize that fact.

"In its essence it is consistent with the spirit of the covenant, and, indeed, the principles of the league, as expressed in article 10, represent the extension to the whole world of the principles of the doctrine, while, should any dispute as to the meaning of the latter ever arise between the American and European powers, the league is there to settle it."

The explanation of Great Britain received the assent of France.

"It seems to me monumentally paradoxical and a trifle infantile," says M. Lausanne, editor of the *Matin* and a chief spokesman for M. Clemenceau, "to pretend the contrary.

"When the executive council of the league of nations fixes the 'reasonable limits of the armament of Peru'; when it shall demand information concerning the naval program of Brazil (art. 7 of the covenant); when it shall tell Argentina what shall be the measure of the 'contribution to the armed forces to protect the signature of the social covenant' (art. 16); when it shall demand the immediate registration of the treaty between the United States and Canada at the seat of the league, it will control, whether it wills or not, the destinies of America.

"And when the American States shall be obliged to take a hand in every war or menace of war in Europe (art. 11) they will necessarily fall afoul of the fundamental principle laid down by Monroe.

" * * * If the league takes in the world, then Europe must mix in the affairs of America; if only Europe is included, then America will violate of necessity her own doctrine by intermixing in the affairs of Europe."

It has seemed to me that the British delegation traveled a little out of the precincts of the peace conference when they undertook to explain the Monroe doctrine and tell the United States what it was and what it was not proposed to do with it under the new article. That, however, is merely a matter of taste and judgment. Their statement that the Monroe doctrine under this article, if any question arose in regard to it, would be passed upon and interpreted by the league of nations is absolutely correct. There is no doubt that this is what the article means. Great Britain so stated it, and no American authority, whether friendly or unfriendly to the league, has dared to question it. I have wondered a little why it was left to the British delegation to explain that article, which so nearly concerns the United States, but that was merely a fugitive thought upon which I will not dwell. The statement of M. Lausanne is equally explicit and truthful, but he makes one mistake. He says, in substance, that if we are to meddle in Europe, Europe cannot be excluded from the Americas. He overlooks the fact that the Monroe doctrine also says:

"Our policy in regard to Europe, which was adopted at an early stage of the wars which have so long agitated that quarter of the globe, nevertheless remains the same, which is not to interfere in the internal concerns of any of the powers."

The Monroe doctrine was the corollary of Washington's neutrality policy and of his injunction against permanent alliances. It reiterates and reaffirms the principle. We do not seek to meddle in the affairs of Europe and keep Europe out of the Americas. It is as important to keep the United States out of

European affairs as to keep Europe out of the American Continents. Let us maintain the Monroe doctrine, then, in its entirety, and not only preserve our own safety, but in this way best promote the real peace of the world. Whenever the preservation of freedom and civilization and the overthrow of a menacing world conqueror summon us we shall respond fully and nobly, as we did in 1917. He who doubts that we could do so has little faith in America. But let it be our own act and not done reluctantly by the coercion of other nations, at the bidding or by the permission of other countries.

Let me now deal with the article itself. We have here some protective coloration again. The Monroe doctrine is described as a "regional understanding" whatever that may mean. The boundaries between the States of the Union, I suppose, are "regional understandings," if anyone chooses to apply to them that somewhat swollen phraseology. But the Monroe doctrine is no more a regional understanding than it is an "international engagement." The Monroe doctrine was a policy declared by President Monroe. Its immediate purpose was to shut out Europe from interfering with the South American Republics, which the Holy Alliance designed to do. It was stated broadly, however, as we all know, and went much further than that. It was, as I have just said, the corollary of Washington's declaration against our interfering in European questions. It was so regarded by Jefferson at the time and by John Quincy Adams, who formulated it, and by President Monroe, who declared it. It rested firmly on the great law of self-preservation, which is the basic principle of every independent State.

It is not necessary to trace its history or to point out the extensions which it has received or its universal acceptance by all American statesmen without regard to party. All Americans have always been for it. They may not have known its details or read all the many discussions in regard to it, but they knew that it was an American doctrine and that, broadly stated, it meant the exclusion of Europe from interference with American affairs and from any attempt to colonize or set up new States within the boundaries of the American Continent. I repeat it was purely an American doctrine, a purely American policy, designed and wisely designed for our defense. It has never been an "international engagement." No nation has ever formally recognized it. It has been the subject of reservation at international conventions by American delegates. It has never been a "regional understanding" or an understanding of any kind with anybody. It was the declaration of the United States of America, in their own behalf, supported by their own power. They brought it into being, and its life was predicated on the force which the United States could place behind it. Unless the United States could sustain it it would die. The United States has supported it. It has lived—strong, efficient, respected. It is now proposed to kill it by a provision in a treaty for a league of nations.

The instant that the United States, who declared, interpreted, and sustained the doctrine, ceases to be the sole judge of what it means, that instant the Monroe doctrine ceases and disappears from history and from the face of the earth. I think it is just as undesirable to have Europe interfere in American affairs now as Mr. Monroe thought it was in 1823, and equally undesirable that we should be compelled to involve ourselves in all the wars and brawls of Europe. The Monroe doctrine has made for peace. Without the Monroe doctrine we should have had many a struggle with European powers to save ourselves from possible assault and certainly from the necessity of becoming a great military power, always under arms and always ready to resist invasion from States in our near neighborhood. In the interests of the peace of the world it is now proposed to wipe away this American policy, which has been a bulwark and a barrier for peace. With one exception it has always been successful, and then success was only delayed. When we were torn by civil war France saw fit to enter Mexico and endeavored to establish an empire there. When our hands were once free the empire perished, and with it the unhappy tool of the third Napoleon. If the United States had not been rent by civil war no such attempt would have been made, and nothing better illustrates the value to the cause of peace of the Monroe doctrine. Why, in the name of peace, should we extinguish it? Why, in the name of peace, should we be called upon to leave the interpretation of the Monroe doctrine to other nations? It is an American policy. It is our own. It has guarded us well, and I, for one, can never find consent in my heart to destroy it by a clause in a treaty and hand over its body for dissection to the nations of Europe. If we need authority to demonstrate what the Monroe doctrine has meant to the United States we cannot do better than quote the words of Grover Cleveland, who directed Mr. Olney to notify the world that "to-day the United States is practically sovereign on this continent, and its fiat is law to which it confines its interposition." Theodore Roosevelt, in the last article written before his death, warned us, his countrymen, that we are "in honor bound to keep ourselves so prepared that the Monroe doctrine shall be accepted as immutable international law." Grover Cleveland was a Democrat and Theodore Roosevelt was a Republican, but they were both Americans, and it is the American spirit which has carried this country always to victory and which should govern us to-day, and not the international spirit which would in the name of peace hand the United States over bound hand and foot to obey the fiat of other powers.

Another point in this covenant where change must be made in order to protect the safety of the United States in the future is in article 1, where withdrawal is provided for. This provision was an attempt to meet the very general objection to the first draft of the league, that there was no means of getting out of it without denouncing the treaty; that is, there was no arrangement for the withdrawal of any nation. As it now stands it reads that—

"Any member of the league may, after two years' notice of its intention to do so, withdraw from the league, provided that all its international obligations, and all its obligations under this covenant shall have been fulfilled at the time of its withdrawal."

The right of withdrawal is given by this clause, although the time for notice, two years, is altogether too long. Six months or a year would be found, I think, in most treaties to be the normal period fixed for notice of withdrawal. But whatever virtue there may be in the right thus conferred is completely nullified by the proviso. The right of withdrawal cannot be exercised until all the international obligations and all the obligations of the withdrawing nations have been fulfilled. The league alone can decide whether "all international obligations and all obligations under this covenant" have been fulfilled, and this would require, under the provisions of the league, a unanimous vote so that any nation desiring to withdraw could not do so, even on the two years' notice, if one nation voted that the obligations had not been fulfilled. Remember that this gives the league not only power to review all our obligations under the covenant but all our treaties with all nations for every one of those is an "international obligation."

Are we deliberately to put ourselves in fetters and be examined by the league of nations as to whether we have kept faith with Cuba or Panama before we can be permitted to leave the league? This seems to me humiliating to say the least. The right of withdrawal, if it is to be of any value whatever, must be absolute, because otherwise a nation desiring to withdraw could be held in the league by objections from other nations until the very act which induces the nation to withdraw had been completed; until the withdrawing nation had been forced to send troops to take part in a war with which it had no concern and upon which it did not desire to enter. It seems to me vital to the safety of the United States not only that this provision should be eliminated and the right to withdraw made absolute but that the period of withdrawal should be much reduced. As it stands it is practically no better in this respect than the first league draft which contained no provision for withdrawal at all, because the proviso here inserted so incumbers it that every nation to all intents and purposes must remain a member of the league indefinitely unless all the other members are willing that it should retire. Such a provision as this, ostensibly framed to meet the objection, has the defect which other similar gestures to give an impression of meeting objections have, that it apparently keeps the promise to the ear but most certainly breaks it to the hope.

I have dwelt only upon those points which seem to me most dangerous. There are, of course, many others, but these points, in the interest not only of the safety of the United States but of the maintenance of the treaty and the peace of the world, should be dealt with here before it is too late. Once in the league the chance of amendment is so slight that it is not worth

considering. Any analysis of the provisions of this league covenant, however, brings out in startling relief one great fact.
Whatever may be said, it is not a league of peace; it is an alliance, dominated at the present moment by five great powers,
really by three, and it has all the marks of an alliance. The
development of international law is neglected. The court which
is to decide disputes brought before it fills but a small place.
The conditions for which this league really provides with the
utmost care are political conditions, not judicial questions, to
be reached by the executive council and the assembly, purely
political bodies without any trace of a judicial character about
them. Such being its machinery, the control being in the hands
of political appointees whose votes will be controlled by interest and expedience, it exhibits that most marked characteristic
of an alliance—that its decisions are to be carried out by force.
Those articles upon which the whole structure rests are articles which provide for the use of force; that is, for war. This
league to enforce peace does a great deal for enforcement and
very little for peace. It makes more essential provisions looking to war than to peace, for the settlement of disputes.

Article 10 I have already discussed. There is no question
that the preservation of a State against external aggression can
contemplate nothing but war. In article 11, again, the league
is authorized to take any action which may be necessary to
safeguard the peace of the world. "Any action" includes war.
We also have specific provisions for a boycott, which is a form
of economic warfare. The use of troops might be avoided but
the enforcement of a boycott would require blockades in all
probability, and certainly a boycott in its essence is simply an
effort to starve a people into submission, to ruin their trade,
and, in the case of nations which are not self-supporting, to
cut off their food supply. The misery and suffering caused by
such a measure as this may easily rival that caused by actual
war. Article 16 embodies the boycott and also, in the last paragraph, provides explicitly for war. We are told that the word
"recommends" has no binding force; it constitutes a moral
obligation, that is all. But it means that if we, for example,
should refuse to accept the recommendation, we should nullify
the operation of article 16 and, to that extent, of the league. It

seems to me that to attempt to relieve us of clearly imposed duties by saying that the word "recommend" is not binding is an escape of which no nation regarding the sanctity of treaties and its own honor would care to avail itself. The provisions of article 16 are extended to States outside the league who refuse to obey its command to come in and submit themselves to its jurisdiction; another provision for war.

Taken altogether, these provisions for war present what to my mind is the gravest objection to this league in its present form. We are told that of course nothing will be done in the way of warlike acts without the assent of Congress. If that is true, let us say so in the covenant. But as it stands there is no doubt whatever in my mind that American troops and American ships may be ordered to any part of the world by nations other than the United States, and that is a proposition to which I for one can never assent. It must be made perfectly clear that no American soldiers, not even a corporal's guard, that no American sailors, not even the crew of a submarine, can ever be engaged in war or ordered anywhere except by the constitutional authorities of the United States. To Congress is granted by the Constitution the right to declare war, and nothing that would take the troops out of the country at the bidding or demand of other nations should ever be permitted except through congressional action. The lives of Americans must never be sacrificed except by the will of the American people expressed through their chosen Representatives in Congress. This is a point upon which no doubt can be permitted. American soldiers and American sailors have never failed the country when the country called upon them. They went in their hundreds of thousands into the war just closed. They went to die for the great cause of freedom and of civilization. They went at their country's bidding and because their country summoned them to service. We were late in entering the war. We made no preparation as we ought to have done, for the ordeal which was clearly coming upon us; but we went and we turned the wavering scale. It was done by the American soldier, the American sailor, and the spirit and energy of the American people. They overrode all obstacles and all shortcomings on the part of the administration or of Congress, and gave to their country a great place in the great victory. It was the first time we had been called upon to rescue the civilized world. Did we fail? On the contrary, we succeeded, we succeeded largely and nobly, and we did it without any command from any league of nations. When the emergency came we met it and we were able to meet it because we had built up on this continent the greatest and most powerful nation in the world, built it up under our own policies, in our own way, and one great element of our strength was the fact that we had held aloof and had not thrust ourselves into European quarrels; that we had no selfish interest to serve. We made great sacrifices. We have done splendid work. I believe that we do not require to be told by foreign nations when we shall do work which freedom and civilization require. I think we can move to victory much better under our own command than under the command of others. Let us unite with the world to promote the peaceable settlement of all international disputes. Let us try to develop international law. Let us associate ourselves with the other nations for these purposes. But let us retain in our own hands and in our own control the lives of the youth of the land. Let no American be sent into battle except by the constituted authorities of his own country and by the will of the people of the United States.

Those of us, Mr. President, who are either wholly opposed to the league or who are trying to preserve the independence and the safety of the United States by changing the terms of the league and who are endeavoring to make the league, if we are to be a member of it, less certain to promote war instead of peace, have been reproached with selfishness in our outlook and with a desire to keep our country in a state of isolation. So far as the question of isolation goes, it is impossible to isolate the United States. I well remember the time, 20 years ago, when eminent Senators and other distinguished gentlemen who were opposing the Philippines and shrieking about imperialism, sneered at the statement made by some of us, that the United States had become a world power. I think no one now would question that the Spanish War marked the entrance of the United States into world affairs to a degree which had never obtained before. It was both an inevitable and an irrevocable step, and our entrance into the war with Germany certainly showed once and for all that the United States was not unmindful of its world responsibilities. We may set aside all this empty talk about isolation. Nobody expects to isolate the United States or to make it a hermit Nation, which is a sheer absurdity. But there is a wide difference between taking a suitable part and bearing a due responsibility in world affairs and plunging the United States into every controversy and conflict on the face of the globe. By meddling in all the differences which may arise among any portion or fragment of humankind we simply fritter away our influence and injure ourselves to no good purpose. We shall be of far more value to the world and its peace by occupying, so far as possible, the situation which we have occupied for the last 20 years and by adhering to the policy of Washington and Hamilton, of Jefferson and Monroe, under which we have risen to our present greatness and prosperity. The fact that we have been separated by our geographical situation and by our consistent policy from the broils of Europe has made us more than any one thing capable of performing the great work which we performed in the war against Germany, and our disinterestedness is of far more value to the world than our eternal meddling in every possible dispute could ever be.

Now, as to our selfishness. I have no desire to boast that we are better than our neighbors, but the fact remains that this Nation in making peace with Germany had not a single selfish or individual interest to serve. All we asked was that Germany should be rendered incapable of again breaking forth, with all the horrors incident to German warfare, upon an unoffending world, and that demand was shared by every free nation and indeed by humanity itself. For ourselves we asked absolutely nothing. We have not asked any government or governments to guarantee our boundaries or our political independence. We have no fear in regard to either. We have sought no territory, no privileges, no advantages, for ourselves. That is the fact. It is apparent on the face of the treaty. I do not mean to reflect upon a single one of the powers with which we have been associated in the war against Germany, but there is not one of them which has not sought individual advantages for their own national benefit. I do not criticize their desires at all. The services and sacrifices of England and France and Belgium and Italy are beyond estimate and beyond praise. I am glad they should have what they desire for their own welfare and safety. But they all receive under the peace territorial and commercial benefits. We are asked to give, and we in no way seek to take. Surely it is not too much to insist that when we are offered nothing but the opportunity to give and to aid others we should have the right to say what sacrifices we shall make and what the magnitude of our gifts shall be. In the prosecution of the war we gave unstintedly American lives and American treasure. When the war closed we had 3,000,000 men under arms. We were turning the country into a vast workshop for war. We advanced ten billions to our allies. We refused no assistance that we could possibly render. All the great energy and power of the Republic were put at the service of the good cause. We have not been ungenerous. We have been devoted to the cause of freedom, humanity, and civilization everywhere. Now we are asked, in the making of peace, to sacrifice our sovereignty in important respects, to involve ourselves almost without limit in the affairs of other nations, and to yield up policies and rights which we have maintained throughout our history. We are asked to incur liabilities to an unlimited extent and furnish assets at the same time which no man can measure. I think it is not only our right but our duty to determine how far we shall go. Not only must we look carefully to see where we are being led into endless disputes and entanglements, but we must not forget that we have in this country millions of people of foreign birth and parentage.

Our one great object is to make all these people Americans so that we may call on them to place America first and serve America as they have done in the war just closed. We cannot Americanize them if we are continually thrusting them back into the quarrels and difficulties of the countries from which they came to us. We shall fill this land with political disputes about the troubles and quarrels of other countries. We shall have a large portion of our people voting not on American questions and not on what concerns the United States but dividing on issues which concern foreign countries alone. That is an unwholesome and perilous condition to force upon this country. We must avoid it. We ought to reduce to the lowest possible point the foreign questions in which we involve ourselves. Never forget that this league is primarily—I might say overwhelmingly—a political organization, and I object strongly to having the politics of the United States turn upon disputes where deep feeling is aroused but in which we have no direct interest. It will all tend to delay the Americanization of our great population, and it is more important not only to the United States but to the peace of the world to make all these people good Americans than it is to determine that some piece of territory should belong to one European country rather than to another. For this reason I wish to limit strictly our interference in the affairs of Europe and of Africa. We have interests of our own in Asia and in the Pacific which we must guard upon our own account, but the less we undertake to play the part of umpire and thrust ourselves into European conflicts the better for the United States and for the world.

It has been reiterated here on this floor, and reiterated to the point of weariness, that in every treaty there is some sacrifice of sovereignty. That is not a universal truth by any means, but it is true of some treaties and it is a platitude which does not require reiteration. The question and the only question before us here is how much of our sovereignty we are justified in sacrificing. In what I have already said about other nations putting us into war I have covered one point of sovereignty which ought never to be yielded, the power to send American soldiers and sailors everywhere, which ought never to be taken from the American people or impaired in the slightest degree. Let us beware how we palter with our independence. We have not reached the great position from which we were able to come down into the field of battle and help to save the world from tyranny by being guided by others. Our vast power has all been built up and gathered together by ourselves alone. We forced our way upward from the days of the Revolution, through a world often hostile and always indifferent. We owe no debt to anyone except to France in that Revolution, and those policies and those rights on which our power has been founded should never be lessened or weakened. It will be no service to the world to do so and it will be of intolerable injury to the United States. We will do our share. We are ready and anxious to help in all ways to preserve the world's peace. But we can do it best by not crippling ourselves.

I am as anxious as any human being can be to have the United States render every possible service to the civilization and the peace of mankind, but I am certain we can do it best by not putting ourselves in leading strings or subjecting our policies and our sovereignty to other nations. The independence of the United States is not only more precious to ourselves but to the world than any single possession. Look at the United States to-day. We have made mistakes in the past. We have had shortcomings. We shall make mistakes in the future and fall short of our own best hopes. But none the less is there any country to-day on the face of the earth which can compare with this in ordered liberty, in peace, and in the largest freedom? I feel that I can say this without being accused of undue boastfulness, for it is the simple fact, and in making this treaty and taking on these obligations all that we do is in a spirit of unselfishness and in a desire for the good of mankind. But it is well to remember that we are dealing with nations every one of which has a direct individual interest to serve and there is grave danger in an unshared idealism. Contrast the United States with any country on the face of the earth to-day and ask yourself whether the situation of the United States is not the best to be found. I will go as far as anyone in world service, but the first step to world service is the maintenance of the United States. You may call me selfish if you will, conservative or reactionary, or use any other harsh adjective you see fit to apply, but an American I was born, an American I have remained all my life. I can never be anything else but an American, and I must think of the United States first, and when I think of the United States first in an arrangement like this I am thinking of what is best for the world, for if the United States fails the best hopes of mankind fail with it. I have never had but one allegiance—I cannot divide it now. I have loved but one flag and I cannot share that devotion and give affection to the mongrel banner invented for a league. Internationalism, illustrated by the Bolshevik and by the men to whom all countries are alike provided they can make money out of them, is to me repulsive. National I must remain, and in that way I, like all other Americans, can render the amplest service to the world. The United States is the world's best hope, but if you fetter her in the interests and quarrels of other nations, if you tangle her in the intrigues of Europe, you will destroy her power for good and endanger her very existence. Leave her to march freely through the centuries to come as in the years that have gone. Strong, generous, and confident, she has nobly served mankind. Beware how you trifle with your marvelous inheritance, this great land of ordered liberty, for if we stumble and fall, freedom and civilization everywhere will go down in ruin.

We are told that we shall "break the heart of the world" if we do not take this league just as it stands. I fear that the hearts of the vast majority of mankind would beat on strongly and steadily and without any quickening if the league were to perish altogether. If it should be effectively and beneficently changed the people who would lie awake in sorrow for a single night could be easily gathered in one not very large room, but those who would draw a long breath of relief would reach to millions.

We hear much of visions and I trust we shall continue to have visions and dream dreams of a fairer future for the race. But visions are one thing and visionaries are another, and the mechanical appliances of the rhetorician designed to give a picture of a present which does not exist and of a future which no man can predict are as unreal and shortlived as the steam or canvas clouds, the angels suspended on wires, and the artificial lights of the stage. They pass with the moment of effect and are shabby and tawdry in the daylight. Let us at least be real. Washington's entire honesty of mind and his fearless look into the face of all facts are qualities which can never go out of fashion and which we should all do well to imitate.

Ideals have been thrust upon us as an argument for the league until the healthy mind, which rejects cant, revolts from them. Are ideals confined to this deformed experiment upon a noble purpose, tainted as it is with bargains, and tied to a peace treaty which might have been disposed of long ago to the great benefit of the world if it had not been compelled to carry this rider on its back? *Post equitem sedet atra cura,* Horace tells us, but no blacker care ever sat behind any rider than we shall find in this covenant of doubtful and disputed interpretation as it now perches upon the treaty of peace.

No doubt many excellent and patriotic people see a coming fulfillment of noble ideals in the words "league for peace." We all respect and share these aspirations and desires, but some of us see no hope, but rather defeat, for them in this murky covenant. For we, too, have our ideals, even if we differ from those who have tried to establish a monopoly of idealism. Our first ideal is our country, and we see her in the future, as in the past, giving service to all her people and to the world. Our ideal of the future is that she should continue to render that service of her own free will. She has great problems of her own to solve, very grim and perilous problems, and a right solution, if we can attain to it, would largely benefit mankind. We would have our country strong to resist a peril from the West, as she has flung back the German menace from the East. We would not have our politics distracted and embittered by the dissensions of other lands. We would not have our country's vigor exhausted or her moral force abated by everlasting meddling and muddling in every quarrel, great and small, which afflicts the world. Our ideal is to make her ever stronger and better and finer, because in that way alone, as we believe, can she be of the greatest service to the world's peace and to the welfare of mankind.

ELBERT H. GARY

RECONSTRUCTION AND READJUSTMENT

Address at the Annual Meeting of the American Bar
Association, Boston, Massachusetts,
September 4, 1919

[Elbert Henry Gary was born near Wheaton, Illinois, on October 8, 1846. He attended Wheaton College and the University of Chicago, from which he received his law degree in 1867. He was engaged in the general practice of law in Chicago for twenty-five years, was at one time a Judge of Dupage county, and was President of the Chicago Bar Association from 1893 to 1894. In 1899 he was general counsel and a director of the Illinois Steel Company, and when the United States Steel Corporation was organized, in 1901, he gave up his law practice to become Chairman of its Executive Committee. Later he became Chairman of the Board of Directors, Chairman of the Finance Committee, and Chief Executive Officer of the Corporation, positions which he held until his death. In 1917 he was a member of the International High Commission appointed to assist the Allies in the prosecution of the war. He died in New York City on August 15, 1927.

Judge Gary's remarkable success in developing the United States Steel Corporation, and his practice at annual meetings of the corporation of delivering an address on the economic condition of the country, earned for him the title of business statesman. The speech printed below, delivered before the Versailles Peace Treaty was signed, and while plans for rehabilitating the world were still unformed, was a noteworthy and significant pronouncement.]

It is not astonishing that, in consequence of the events of the last five years, world affairs have become disrupted, disjointed or disarranged. There is demand for reconstruction and readjustment. These words are not synonymous but are akin, and are usually grouped in discussion. There is universal inquiry as to what can be done towards ascertaining and establishing an equilibrium which shall be generally acceptable and prove to be permanent. The questions involved are national and international, domestic and foreign. They are moral, social, political and economic. Practically speaking, the last is of first consideration in the minds of the vast majority, for it involves life, health and comfort. Until one is first provided with food, clothing and shelter, other matters receive scant attention.

The eyes of the peoples of the entire world, since August 1st, 1914, and probably before, have been continuously focused on the United States of America. It is not boasting to say that, all in all, we are the greatest of nations. This is susceptible of demonstration by facts and figures. Geographical location, climate, wealth, resources, temperament and fundamental rules of conduct, have furnished to the inhabitants of this country the widest field for progress, prosperity and influence; and with this there is a corresponding responsibility, which we must recognize.

Many of the immediate international questions growing out of the war have, in the main, been settled, or methods for their settlement have been approved by the Peace Council at Paris. It will for the present be assumed that the work of that Council, in substance, will be ratified even though there may be some additions, explanations or reservations to the original draft, not materially affecting the main plan and structure. The major part of the people of this country love peace and abhor war, and therefore favor the Peace Treaty and League of Nations as a material aid in preventing future prolonged wars. They believe that, under the most difficult and complicated circumstances, the President, as their properly constituted leader and representative, secured the best terms and conditions practicable and that the same should be approved.

Of signal importance there is to be considered by the people of the United States their attitude towards other countries. We have been provoked to feelings of anger and hostility towards the Central Powers and their associates in the war. We are convinced they have disregarded the laws of God and man, and should make restitution and suffer penalties; and this has been provided for. What shall be our attitude toward them? We would not benefit ourselves or others by indulging sentiments of hate or revenge. It is not necessary to forget or to forgive, certainly unless there is repentence on the part of those who are guilty of moral turpitude, but we should at least be sufficiently wise to consider the ultimate effect upon our own interests of unnecessary antagonisms.

From an economic standpoint, considering of paramount significance the question of benefit to ourselves, we ought to resume business relations with Germany and Austria at once. They are capable of producing many articles of commerce which we need and desire, and which are not produced elsewhere in like quality, much as it may be regretted. Like grades of leather and leather goods, woolen cloths and cutlery of various kinds, drugs, chemicals and toilet articles and other things too numerous to mention, we have not been able to obtain during the war as we did previously.

There are at least two good reasons why we should liberally resume the buying of German and Austrian goods. We desire them to supply our own wants, and besides the purchases will have a decided influence in re-establishing the rates of international exchange. We should seek and fully reciprocate the friendship of all other nations whenever it is compatible with principle. We should, if practicable, be neutral as between all other countries if we are to have their respect and confidence. Our position should be uniformly honest, dignified, kind, impartial, and in all respects above reproach. This is right and it will be profitable. It is a time for the exercise of patience and wisdom and the application of the highest ideals of propriety and virtue in dealing with world affairs. No man liveth to himself alone, and no nation liveth to itself alone. These are truths of daily illustration.

The subject of international exchange, with its present dislocations and discrepancies, is troubling the minds of the great bankers and they must solve the problems pertaining to it. However, it is a part of common economic discussion. The existing irregularities and inequalities cannot be corrected by mere dictum or desire. The shipment of gold is not a cure or a considerable palliative. Agreements for readjustments will not suffice. It would seem to the ordinary observer that in some way we must get back to the original basis of determining relative exchange rates, namely, one of respective credits. If one in New York were desirous of paying a debt in London, and another in the latter city at the same time desired to pay the same amount in the former there would be no difficulty in establishing a fair rate of exchange; and if this equality of credit and debit could be maintained the whole problem would be solved. The practical application of what has been remarked to the international situation is that the United States, so far as possible, should finance other deserving countries less fortunate in rehabilitating their productive capacity and resources, and that we should purchase their products up to the limits of our requirements and ability. Also, that our investing capitalists, through bankers and otherwise, should buy the securities of foreign concerns, the payment of which might be guaranteed by their respective Governments. Thus will we evince our friendship for others and at the same time advance our own interests in many ways. The point is emphasized that, as a rule, we help ourselves when we help others, and injure ourselves when we injure others. Better a thousand times if Germany had appreciated this fact in the unfortunate days preceding the precipitation of the war. Better for us if we apply this principle at the present time, not only towards our associates in the war, and all neutral countries as well, but also towards those who were our enemies, and the large majority, at least, of whose peoples we hope, will hereafter be our friends and our coadjutors in striving to uphold the peace and prosperity of the world.

The early adoption of the American dollar as a basis or standard of currency and values is worthy of universal consideration. Much could be said in favor of the suggestion.

Of great consequence to all countries is the opportunity to import and export supplies of all kinds in exchange for other commodities or money, unrestricted as to location or by discriminatory legal provisions, established rules of business or practices of any kind, so that all shall be on the same basis of privilege. Discussions relating to the open sea, or command over or control of the sea, have frequently been confusing. Interpretation of language has been unnecessarily literal and misleading. A fleet of ships, largest in capacity and fastest in movement, may exercise a predominant influence in international trade, but every nation may provide itself with the best, limited only by its financial ability or policy, and there can be no reasonable objection to the success which follows enterprise and expenditure. The underlying principle is that all the navigable waters and all the ports of entry and shipment connected with these waters, should in times of peace, be free and open to every one on equal terms and conditions; and that there should be continued in force laws and rules to insure these advantages.

Hereafter every nation and every individual must have full opportunity to prosper according to merit. This Americans demand and this they concede. In this statement of principles, there is not intended to be included matters relating to domestic protection, production or safety. It is doubtful that in practice and method the high seas and sea-ports heretofore have been as open and free as commonly supposed; but we have entered upon a new era. We are reconstructing, reorganizing and rebuilding, and must start right. There must be straight thinking and action. There must be equal protection to all, coercion imposed upon none, no waivers of legitimate and fundamental claims insisted upon. When the League of Nations is in full force and effect its provisions must be ample and must be scrupulously observed by all who are parties to it.

Another international question of moment pertains to race or color. By some it is considered delicate, but to the average person in the United States and in other lands, it appears to be of practical import, calling for frank and fair discussion. It is social and economic, and has no proper place in partisan politics. There are various viewpoints. If we were to pass only upon questions relating to international right, comity or friendship, it is difficult to perceive why the United States should permit to locate here the citizens of many different countries, which might be mentioned, and who have been allowed to immigrate without restriction as to numbers, and at the same time deny the right to others simply on account of their race or color. It is possible that if comparisons as to intelligence and general merit were to be made between those who are permitted to immigrate to the United States and those who are denied that privilege, the advantage would be found to be in favor of the latter. If we were deciding the inquiry as to pecuniary profit to this country to be derived from the largest production and further development of enterprise, then in that case, unquestionably, all restrictions concerning immigration, based on color or race, should be removed. But if the paramount reason for limitations is found in a just and reasonable claim that to admit them would be to encourage, and indeed make certain, the residence here of an overwhelming multitude of certain foreigners with resulting effects that would be inimical to the best interests of the whole or major part of the American people, then there might be a reasonable restriction as to numbers, determined by our domestic laws applicable to all nationalities. Doubtless all nations, through their duly constituted representatives, would agree to this. It would seem to be appropriate for the League of Nations, when completed and adopted, to pass upon these matters by unanimous vote, without unnecessary delay, after a full hearing upon the merits, taking into account all the circumstances and conditions which have a bearing.

Henceforth there should be maintained in practice the principle of international co-operation as distinguished from hostility, or selfish, secret isolation. Fair, honest, friendly, and persistent competition between nations is desirable and necessary to the highest progress and prosperity, but mean, tricky, overbearing and destructive competition is unwholesome, unhealthful and disadvantageous to all who are affected. In practice the Peace Treaties and League of Nations as finally established should be accepted by every one. As remarked by the President, its full value depends upon the disposition and effort of the people in this regard. If, in good faith, individuals do their respective parts, the League will be an instrument for the preservation of peace and tranquillity. In economic matters there should be demonstrated a desire to live and to let live, to assist and encourage others, to bear in mind the rights of every one, to maintain on the heights of progress the emblem of justice bearing the motto: "Might depends upon Right."

And now, having barely suggested what it is believed will be the temper of the people of the United States towards those of other lands, it is appropriate to discuss questions especially economic and applicable to our own domestic affairs. It may be remarked that, as a separate nation, we did not suffer pecuniary loss and damage to the extent inflicted upon others; nor were there destroyed or maimed as many persons, though the number of brave and fine men who were killed in battle, or who died from disease or accident, or were seriously crippled, is appalling; and, sad to say, there were included a considerable number of splendid women. The names of all these are indelibly placed on the lists of glory, and their deeds will be remembered by a grateful people.

Without any intention on our part, this country, at the end of a horrible and destructive war, was left richer than it was at the commencement. Our wealth, in money and other property, our income, our productive resources, our population, our advantages, our prospects and our opportunities were augmented. We do not boast of this situation; nor are we called upon to deplore it. We have become what we are in the natural course of events. We must beware of the dangers of wealth, but we are entitled to its blessings and benefits, provided we do not fail to appreciate the obligations which are incident. What we see in this respect others of foreign lands perceive at a distance with even clearer vision. The man who supposes he deceives others generally deceives only himself; the same is true of nations.

The inhabitants of other lands are looking towards us with various emotions; some with envy or jealousy, some with distrust, perhaps some with bitterness, and some with covetousness; but, it is believed, the large majority with friendliness, confidence and hope. However this may be, when it comes to economic considerations there is little doubt that the peoples of every country are at present endeavoring to ascertain how they can most readily improve their pecuniary standing by reconstruction and readjustment; to secure their full share, or more. of the wealth of the world; and foreigners are gazing upon this country as the most fertile field of adventure and exploitation. They will carry their endeavor into the markets of non-producing countries. By every known plan of operation, producers in Great Britain, France, Germany and other lands will seek to control or excel in the overseas trade. Long before the war was ended committees were formed and studies commenced by them with the idea of entering a post-war commercial strife for the world's business. These committees have personally, or through representatives, visited and for months remained within the limits of other countries making examination of properties, manufactories, terminals and transportation facilities, learning the various situations, and making reports on the same. They have been preparing for the most stubborn contest in economic warfare. Evidences of this disposition and intention have been seen on every hand. Besides this, the men occupying high official positions abroad are talking of these matters, lending encouragement and making promises of assistance by Governmental action or otherwise. The credit of different Governments will be furnished to private enterprise and management. It is reported that attempts have already been made by individuals, on their own account, to secure control of some of the most valuable and necessary raw products located in foreign lands, and the scheme will no doubt embrace the most desirable seaports for loading and delivery, and also the most advantageous coaling stations. Considerable success has already resulted. Arrangements, by contract or otherwise, have been or will be made for obtaining preference as to time and terms in the loading and unloading of goods, and also in the sale of materials and the obtaining of supplies. In short, everything practicable within the limits of law and opportunity will be done by foreign Governments and their merchants to extend trade and to promote their own financial interests, even to the extent of proceeding within the natural spheres of others. The contest for commercial position and progress will be fiercer than ever before, with the difference, it is hoped, that there will hereafter be an international tribunal which will exercise supervision over the conduct of individual nations and will restrict all of them within the limits of law, reason, propriety and justice. Heretofore, wars have generally resulted from economic rivalries; from the struggle for commercial supremacy; and the late wars, in the opinion of many of us, were no exception.

The attitude of other nations and their alertness to reach the largest success in the race for economic position is not attacked or complained of. It is their right and their national duty. The fullest opportunity to every one to succeed by every lawful means within the confines of moral principles and in consonance with the rules and regulations of the League of Nations, is what we advocate. Moreover, the vigor and vitality of trade all over the world is what is needed for the greatest universal prosperity. As already observed, if one is properly enriched others will be benefited. Surely from the viewpoint of this country we wish to see others prosperous and progressive.

In justice to ourselves, we must be diligent and aggressive. We must conserve our strength and our resources. We must view the world situation from the point of experience, caution and wisdom. We should profit by the deliberations, discussions and conclusions of others. As of vital consequence there should be the most consistent and intense spirit of co-operation between all our people, between capital and labor, employers and employés, between the State and private interests, between the various groups of individuals or collection of individuals, between producers and consumers, between professionals and non-professionals. Good-natured rivalry, sharp competition, aggressive effort for legitimate success, faithful administration and observance of the laws, loyalty to country—all these must be encouraged and required; and everything that destroys or obstructs or interferes with legitimate enterprise, or limits prosperity, or that tends to minimize the motive for attempting to accelerate and sustain orderly progress in business, should be discouraged. This country cannot afford to restrict opportunity to utilize all its resources for increasing its wealth or of maintaining its financial, commercial and industrial position. Economic progress and success are a source of protection and peace, and a bulwark against outside unjustifiable attack of any kind. It is the basis for happiness and contentment.

As a guaranty of the fullest reasonable economic success, including domestic and export business, we must have a merchant marine equal in every particular to the best, with all advantages and no disadvantages in comparison with others, unhampered by laws, rules or regulations which might interfere with practical and successful business operation. We must be prepared to deliver the surplus of everything we produce at the doors of non-producing countries in packages and on terms satisfactory to those who desire to purchase. Our merchant ships must never again be compelled to haul down the American flag, or to occupy an inferior position in the international struggle for economic excellence and advancement. Americans, if given an equal chance with all others, will furnish business to comfortably support a merchant marine surpassed by none. If the League of Nations shall remain in effective force, it is hoped a large navy for the enforcement of legitimate civil rights may not be necessary; but, still, the United States should maintain a navy of sufficient strength to protect her commerce in every part of the world in times of exigency. Heretofore it has not always been absolutely independent and safe, notwithstanding what may have been said or written to the contrary. Our merchant marine and our navy should be, by comparison with others, in proportion to the volume of our part in the world's business affairs. Besides, an adequate navy and auxiliary merchant marine will be needed in order to properly perform our share of duty in preserving the principles and executing the obligations prescribed by the constitution and rules of the League of Nations.

The labor question at present is of commanding interest, first because labor is essential to economic growth and virility, and secondly because it is persistently sought by self-appointed leaders to enlist the sympathy and support of workmen in agitation for the substitution of the rule of force for the rule of law and reason. It is commonly designated as Bolshevism. These agitators will not succeed in the United States. I have heretofore spoken on this subject and will not repeat. However, it may be observed that the antidote for this poison is plenty of work at reasonable rates of compensation when compared with the cost of living; healthful, safe and agreeable working conditions; opportunity for workmen to advance in positions according to merit; and a chance to invest their savings in the business with which they are connected. The employers must not and will not give the employés good ground for complaint, and intelligent public sentiment will exercise a controlling influence in preventing a return to barbarism. Employers and employés are under equal responsibility to the general public, of which they are an important part, to assist in maintaining industrial peace and prosperity.

The problem of readjustment is perhaps of the first moment. There are many things out of proper alignment. For instance, the cost of living, within a comparatively short time, has more than doubled, while the fixed salaries of life positions have remained stationary. Incomes, perhaps inherited or provided by investment in long time, safe 5% bonds, are not increased, but are, in fact, reduced by one-half, for their purchasing power is thus decreased. This is essentially wrong and must be corrected whenever and however possible. With respect to the salaries to which allusion has been made, they can and ought promptly to be increased. Incomes limited by rates of interest are more difficult of readjustment. Prices of commodities are too large in many cases; and the average, designated general level, is too high. They are not regular and are not relative. Some have advanced 50%, others 200%. Many small articles, bringing immense sums in the aggregate, have been advanced beyond all reason because the facts escape exposure and public criticism on account of the smallness of the items. The middle-man is charged perhaps 50% advance, adds this increase to his previous selling price, and then insists upon and secures 100% advance on the whole. Besides, in many cases, he cuts in two the previous package or portion. This is not assumption, it is an ordinary, every day occurrence. The seller of spirits of camphor, cologne or alcohol, pours into the bottle 50 or 75% of water and then doubles the selling price of the whole quantity. All of us have noticed during the last few years that the liquids used as lotions, such as alcohol, cologne, etc., seem to be very hard. This is because of the quantity of lime in the water used. These examples appear insignificant, but they are illustrative and represent conditions which involve millions. The irregularities can be overcome by law if properly and systematically enforced; and they would, in part at least, be cured by increases in the sale in this country of a better quality of goods manufactured in foreign places.

The term "level of prices" has been used to denote those which obtained prior to the war. Though frequently used, it is not accurate as applied to the period intervening between then and the present. There has been no level, but rather a changing, irregular range of prices. The producer of an article of food increases the selling price to a purchaser who is a manufacturer of an article of clothing; the latter increases his price to the producer who has fuel for sale; this one increases his selling price to the builder of a dwelling house; then an increase by the owner is passed on to the tenant, who is a laboring man working for the seller of food, the point where the illustration commenced; the workman then increases his rates for compensation accordingly. On and on all have been going, some at a faster pace than others, and, of course, there results confusion, inequalities, unreasonable prices and economic disturbances. A scientific readjustment should be attempted. We ought to commence somewhere to go back and downward in this whirl of augmentation by lowering one price after another with the intention of getting back to a level founded on a just and relative basis. How could it be accomplished?

The Industrial Board appointed by the Department of Commerce, made an attempt to do this, but failed because there were differences of opinion, and perhaps some modification of opinion, by members of the Government official family. It was proposed by the Government to invite the leaders of various lines of industry to co-operate in making reductions of selling prices and to reform them on a basis which should be equitable as between producers and as between them and consumers. One of the industries, at least, accepted such an invitation promptly and agreed upon substantial decreases in selling prices and evinced a willingness to co-operate in perfecting and carrying out the general plan. The immediate effect upon business generally was good and the outlook appeared to be promising when the activities of the Board were interrupted and the members resigned. No better plan as yet has been proposed.

If and when we adopt the methods of some of the European countries in regard to quality and condition of articles sold for consumption, and require rigid public inspection, together with reasonable and systematic control of the necessities of life, we shall witness great improvement in health and material reductions in the cost of living. We are making some effort in this direction.

Sound economy admittedly is proper and necessary at this particular time. There should be no actual waste. Other countries will economize, some to the point of unhealthful privation. We need not and should not go so far. Our Government expenditures made during the war amounted to millions upon millions. The annual interest charges will be enormous. To provide these amounts and the extraordinary increases in Governmental expenses, burdensome taxes will be imposed. They are now very large and are increasing. It is pertinent to say that strict economy should be practiced by our Government. Every department should pay particular attention to this subject, and the chief should personally give instructions in detail upon the subject and see that they are carried out. Unnecessary rules of practice, resulting in duplications of work, inconsequential and ineffective forms, should be eliminated. Government affairs ought always to be managed with the same efficiency and economy that the best governed private interests practice. A part of the money that is being spent for investigations, compilations and, in some instances, prosecutions, might better be expended towards the development of trade in South America; and some of the money paid for high fees to special attorneys and their assistants ought to be used in payment of increased salaries to regular officials. It is not easy to draw the line between waste and proper expenditure. The liberal spending of money by individuals who can afford it, for distribution among those who will properly conserve or use it, is not waste nor should be objected to; but if one eats only half of the meal served and throws into the fire or the sewer the other half it is waste. If there is an unnecessary outlay for food or clothing or anything else, by reason of miscalculation or otherwise, the surplus should, in some way, be properly utilized. One may be extravagant if one can afford it and is not profligate, but none of us is excusable for being wasteful, especially at this time. We might readjust ourselves to changed conditions even more than during the war. Many denied themselves not only luxuries, but comforts, during the last few years and donated an equivalent for war purposes. This was highly commendable, and it is to be hoped we shall not return to the ante-war wasteful practices, for the country will need, during the transitional period, long or short, all that properly may be conserved. History relates that heretofore more than one nation has been overcome or fallen into decay by reason of extravagance and waste.

On the assumption that all the natural resources and facilities of the United States, in peace times as well as during war conditions, ought to be used to the best advantage, it is believed a fundamental question to be discussed, considered and decided at present, is the treatment of accumulated capital, or wealth in the hands of private individuals or private corporations. The experience of the eighteen months preceding and ending November 11th, 1918, should be of enlightening value, for the lessons learned by practical demonstration are always superior to untried or unsatisfactory theories.

Probably it will be generally conceded that during the war, when the greatest production of war material was demanded by our Government for the military necessities of itself and associates in the war, the large and integrated concerns with highly perfected organizations and abundance of working capital, saved the situation. Except for them such necessities could not have been adequately supplied. What would have happened without their facilities no one could, with a feeling of certainty, express an opinion. The representatives of our Government in every department connected with the war, as well as those who represented our associates abroad, were constantly calling for more and more war materials, and at the same time expressing opinions of doubt and alarm concerning failure to provide them. However, with no harmful interruption or delay, all demands were met; and knowledge of this fact no doubt had a decided influence upon the German mind when the truth was ascertained.

But now the question occupying the thoughts of men, to a large degree, is what, if anything, can properly be done to conserve these means of economic stability and progress when war is not upon us and, let us hope, not threatening our future safety. The general public, including labor, which receives 85 to 90 per cent. of the cost of production, is vitally interested in this subject.

It is useful, while discussing a problem in contemplation of future action or inaction, to illustrate by negative reference what ought not to be done.

Government, state or municipal control or management, is frequently suggested and stubbornly urged by public speakers and publicists. The reasons given ordinarily relate to the protection of the public against imposition or inefficiency, which is desirable. Here again experience, especially during the war, is illuminating. The Government took over the possession and management of certain *quasi* public concerns, and, with the assistance of a large part of the previously formed organizations, realized some success in operation; but, as a total result, the experiment was a failure. Every day that passes furnishes evidence to justify this assertion. The properties and businesses taken over have been or will be returned to the owners for the real reason, if not admitted, that the undertakings were too big and complicated for new and inexperienced chiefs to manage. What the results of this experiment will be as to the future values of the properties no one can, with accuracy, predict. It cannot be entirely satisfactory to the owners or, for some years at least, to the general public.

There are reasons why governmental management will not be successful. To reach the highest efficiency in the development and operation of any enterprise there must be personal, pecuniary incentive to succeed. There must be individual attention, thought and decision which ponders over the difficult and complicated problems by day and night and then solves them with a view of securing personal benefits for self or principals represented. Whatever is everyone's business is no one's business—a common expression, but applicable. There must be a motive for economy in administration; for perfecting and maintaining a complete organization, skilled, honest and faithful; for such treatment of employés as will tend to secure loyalty and efficiency in service; for everything that makes for success; and for discarding or rejecting whatever is calculated to impede, obstruct, or minimize it. This means, in great measure, pecuniary profit to those who assume the risks of business, though the assertion is ventured that the private individual in general charge of a large concern, if right minded, is as much interested in and as faithful and loyal to the public welfare as a duly elected public official. Again, there is always danger that partisan politics, if brought into the control or management of business, will have an adverse effect upon the results.

During the war the Government seriously contemplated taking over the management of additional large business lines, but after full investigation, discussion and consideration, concluded it would be unwise, although there were persistent and able advocates who favored the proposed action. The results fully justified the determination arrived at. It was believed by many that the Government assumed the management of many departments of business activity other than those actually included in the Government list. This was because there was co-operation between Governmental agencies, such as the War Industries Board, and aggregations of private interests, represented by small committees, whereby voluntary arrangement was made for allocations of burdens or distributions of products. The control of operations, from the raw products to the finished materials was continued in the hands of the owners. There was clearly demonstrated during the war the value and practical benefit of private management as compared with public management. If it be said that Government conduct of business has sometimes been successful the answer is that the same business in the hands of private, responsible individuals, with capital and success at stake, would have resulted more favorably.

The ideal plan merely for the extension of enterprise, development of resources and the certainty of greatest production, with resulting increases to the public treasuries through taxation, assessment of dues, etc., and a corresponding benefit to the large numbers of workmen, would be to leave the matter entirely and independently in the hands of the private individuals who furnish the necessary capital and who would be inspired by the desire to reap pecuniary advantages. However, it is a patent fact that the ability of capital to accomplish desirable results also involves opportunity to do harm; that uncontrolled concentration of capital, with unbridled license in operations, may be injurious to the welfare of others, including the general public. All fair-minded, well-intentioned men, will admit that the public interests must always be of primary importance; that there should be a curb upon the cupidity of human nature. Of course, from every standpoint, including selfish desire to continuously and permanently prosper, as well as the instinct to secure and retain the respect and confidence of the community, every intelligent person should be prompted to use capital in such manner as to be of benefit to all others and of no intentional harm to anyone; but, unfortunately, such is not the case. The human element interferes. Greed and avarice have a powerful influence upon the mind, and the concentrated power of the public is often necessary to protect one against oneself.

In view and by reason of these conceded facts and considerations there has been attempted to establish by law a preventive against wrong and, in numerous instances, it has been invoked. However, it provides for the punishment of offenders and for the destruction in whole or in part of the property and business involved. This seems remarkable and irrational, especially after the experiences of the last few years, and on the eve of the greatest struggle for economic progress the world has ever witnessed. If the Legal Department of the Government, basing action on its interpretation of the law, had been upheld in its contention, unlimited by the rule of reason, as applied by the Courts to the industries of this great country, property and business in an alarming proportion would have been destroyed and its benefits to the general population eliminated in the effort to prevent future harmful practices.

Proceeding on the assumption that large capital is desirable and necessary for the safety and legitimate progress of the nation, and yet that it must be controlled against possible harm, we are confronted with what has appeared to many to be a difficult problem. It should be met and solved now if we are going to conserve our vitality and strength; if we are not to weaken or neutralize it at this juncture in world affairs when we are called upon to pay enormous debts, to finance our own necessities and to assist our neighbors across the seas, to maintain a state of preparedness against possible, though not probable, future wanton attacks, and to aid in maintaining the peace of the world to the extent of using force, if and when necessary, all of which will require billions of money. Can we hold our position, and are we to be included in clear thinking, wisely concluding peoples? Shall we profit by the experience of the past and by the example of others?

Is there any solution of these problems? I am talking to men who are more competent than I to answer. Still, the general proposition is ventured that whenever it is practicable and effective, resort should be made to the prevention of threatened or possible harm, without destroying the property or business in question, and which can, if preserved, be of substantial benefit to the community and to the nation. This principle has sometimes been invoked by the courts so far as it was believed the provisions of the law permitted. Why not have the law so framed and administered as to allow the courts to cover the whole subject by injunction, rather than by the destruction of property or business? If capital is proceeding or threatens to proceed improperly, it can be restrained by injunction and the order enforced in the regular way. A court of equity should have, if necessary, enlarged powers of preventive remedy, unlimited by statutory provisions. If there is to be punishment inflicted it should be upon the individuals who are reprehensible, and not upon the owners, as stockholders or otherwise, of the properties involved, who are in no respect responsible for misconduct.

If it be said that preventive measures by injunction are too late after there has been established unreasonable concentration of capital, which naturally and necessarily includes the power to do harm, or that in the administration of affairs pertaining to organization or management there is involved too much detail or complication for practical hearing and determination by a court, then it might be answered that there should be no objection to the whole matter of previous assemblage of capital by corporations, form of organization, or management of affairs being subjected to the consideration and decision of a competent non-partisan tribunal, consisting of men selected for their peculiar qualification defined by the creative law, having adequate jurisdiction and powers, subject, however, to appeal and a final determination by a Federal Court concerning certain defined and vital questions pertaining to monopoly and restraint of trade. A law for Federal incorporation or license could embody provisions for the control or regulation suggested. This might satisfactorily solve the problems relating to concentrated wealth in control of corporations.

It is to be remarked that with reference to this whole subject and all other matters mentioned for future determination, full publicity and knowledge of all the facts and conditions in detail, will furnish the most effective remedy for defects, inconsistencies or wrongs.

These matters are not political. They are of universal interest. On their proper disposition depends the greatest legitimate advancement in economic affairs. Those in general charge of large business units are quite willing to meet these questions in a spirit of fairness, justice and loyalty to the public. The present conditions are not satisfactory. During the war, when greater production, larger and more costly extensions and more rapid deliveries were required, it was deemed by the Government proper and necessary to relax or at least liberally interpret the supposed inhibitions of existing laws and rules in order to meet the military demands. The departments of the Government in control of war matters were then more potential than the Department of Justice, whose hands were partially bound by statutory provisions. If this Governmental attitude was appropriate and necessary during war the same is true, if to a less extent, in times of peace, for the object to be obtained in both cases is the largest production and development.

Prudent, open-minded and thoughtful persons endeavor to conceive and consider both or all sides of every question presented, to be fair in conclusion and to be frank in expression if called upon to give utterance. We must admit the war, with all its horrors and results, has abnormalized the minds of men throughout the earth. The period in many aspects is serious, in some particulars it is critical. There are difficulties, perhaps dangers, in the pathway of progress. Vision is liable to be twisted and decision illogical and unjust. Selfishness, cupidity and hate improperly influence the action of men even beyond their own perception. Various factions in their antagonisms go to extremes that are essentially wrong. The worst of all movements of the present grow out of propaganda and agitation calculated to obtain something for nothing, to forcibly take from those who have been successful the property which has been honestly acquired and to distribute the same amongst others less prosperous. The idea is not confined to any individual, community, class or race, though it may be exaggerated more in some than in others. It is supported on the theory that might is right; that power is supreme.

But we have reason to hope that, in this country at least, all classes will be treated impartially and justly; that all laws will be upheld and wisely administered; that person and property will be protected; that co-operation, to the full limit of propriety, will be adopted and practiced; that there will be established and maintained a basis for continuing international peace, a practical method of sustaining international banking credits and facilities, friendly connections which will secure the rights and interests of all countries to the undue prejudice of none, open and uninterrupted avenues of commerce throughout the world, a consistent and persistent policy of reconstruction and readjustment which shall readily restore a normal and proper relationship concerning the pecuniary affairs of the people of this country, a spirit of sincere co-operation between labor and capital, calculated to preserve the rights of each, faithful effort on the part of both to render full justice to the general public, and a fixed national program which will encourage full development and conservation of the economic strength of the United States. Capital and labor both will be fully employed on a basis that will be fair to each and also to all others, and on a scale of returns that will provide an incentive for investment, development and exertion, and this will insure the largest production at lowest reasonable cost. This will tend to decrease living expenses, increase the comfort and contentment of the people and add to the riches of the nation, which relies on the prosperity of its citizens for the standing and influence among nations to which it is entitled. There will be no necessity, time or desire on the part of the vast majority for listening to the vicious doctrines of self-appointed agitators. The extension of education, art, science and moral growth will follow in due proportion. We shall set a good example to all the world. Anarchy and brutality will give way to reason and justice. This is not the worst period of our history; it is the best, for it looks forward to a future that is bright and glorious if we but rise to the heights of practical advantage. In briefing the situation, in forming an opinion that shall be sound and in conducting the case before the bar of public sentiment the members of the American Bar Association have great responsibility.

HICKS' SP.A.S.—41

WILLIAM E. BORAH

THE LEAGUE OF NATIONS

Speech in the United States Senate, November 19, 1919, in Opposition to the Resolution of Ratification of the Versailles Peace Treaty

[William Edgar Borah was born near Fairfield, Illinois, on June 29, 1865. He attended the Southern Illinois Academy and the University of Kansas, was admitted to the bar in 1889, and in 1890 began the practice of law in Lyons, Kansas. The next year he moved to Boise, Idaho, where he won distinction as a lawyer by his conduct of cases of national interest. Since 1907, he has been a Republican member of the United States Senate, and is now Chairman of the Senate Committee on Foreign Relations.

Although he had never before held public office when he entered the Senate, he immediately took rank as a leader. His position of influence in the Senate has been compared to that of Webster in his day, and this prominence has been attributed largely to the magnetism and persuasiveness of his oratory. The speech printed below was delivered on the day on which the Senate first rejected the resolution of ratification of the Peace Treaty. It has been said that he "had more than any other man to do with defeating the Versailles Treaty."]

Mr. President, After Mr. Lincoln had been elected President before he assumed the duties of the office and at a time when all indications were to the effect that we would soon be in the midst of civil strife, a friend from the city of Washington wrote him for instructions. Mr. Lincoln wrote back in a single line, "Entertain no compromise; have none of it." That states the position I occupy at this time and which I have, in an humble way, occupied from the first contention in regard to this proposal.

My objections to the league have not been met by the reservations. I desire to state wherein my objections have not been met. Let us see what our attitude will be toward Europe and what our position will be with reference to the other nations of the world after we shall have entered the league with the present reservations written therein. With all due respect to those who think that they have accomplished a different thing and challenging no man's intellectual integrity or patriotism, I do not believe the reservations have met the fundamental propositions which are involved in this contest.

When the league shall have been formed, we shall be a member of what is known as the council of the league. Our accredited representative will sit in judgment with the accredited representatives of the other members of the league to pass upon the concerns not only of our country but of all Europe and all Asia and the entire world. Our accredited representatives will be members of the assembly. They will sit there to represent the judgment of these 110,000,000 of people, just as we are accredited here to represent our constituencies. We can not send our representatives to sit in council with the representatives of the other great nations of the world with mental reservations as to what we shall do in case their judgment shall not be satisfactory to us. If we go to the council or to the assembly with any other purpose than that of complying in good faith and in absolute integrity with all upon which the council or the assembly may pass, we shall soon return to our country with our self-respect forfeited and the public opinion of the world condemnatory.

Why need you gentlemen across the aisle worry about a reservation here or there, when we are sitting in the council and in the assembly and bound by every obligation in morals, which the President said was supreme above that of law, to comply with the judgment which our representative and the other representatives finally form? Shall we go there, to sit in judgment, and in case that judgment works for peace join with our allies, but in case it works for war withdraw our co-operation? How long would we stand as we now stand, a great Republic commanding the respect and holding the leadership of the world, if we should adopt any such course?

So, sir, we not only sit in the council and in the assembly with our accredited representatives, but bear in mind that article 11 is untouched by any reservation which has been offered here; and with article 11 untouched, and its integrity complete, article 10 is perfectly superfluous. If any war or threat of war shall be a matter of consideration for the league, and the league shall take such action as it deems wise to deal with it, what is the necessity of article 10? Will not external aggression be regarded as a war or threat of war? If the political independence of some nation in Europe is assailed will it be regarded as a war or threat of war? Is there anything in article 10 that is not completely covered by article 11?

It remains complete, and with our representatives sitting in the council and the assembly, and with article 11 complete, and with the assembly and the council having jurisdiction of all matters touching the peace of the world, what more do you need to bind the United States if you assume that the United States is a Nation of honor?

We have said that we would not send our troops abroad without the consent of Congress. Pass by now for a moment the legal proposition. If we create executive functions, the Executive will perform those functions without the authority of Congress. Pass that question by and go to the other question. Our members of the council are there. Our members of the assembly are there. Article 11 is complete, and it authorizes the league, a member of which is our representative, to deal with matters of peace and war, and the league through its council and its assembly deals with the matter, and our accredited representative joins with the others in deciding upon a certain course, which involves a question of sending troops. What will the Congress of the United States do? What right will it have left, except the bare technical right to refuse, which as a moral proposition it will not dare to exercise? Have we not been told day by day for the last nine months that the Senate of the United States, a co-ordinate part of the treaty-making power, should accept this league as it was written because the wise men sitting at Versailles had so written it, and has not every possible influence and every source of power in public opinion been organized and directed against the Senate to compel it to do that thing? How much stronger will be the moral compulsion upon the Congress of the United States when we ourselves have indorsed the proposition of sending our accredited representatives there to vote for us?

Ah, but you say that there must be unanimous consent, and that there is vast protection in unanimous consent.

I do not wish to speak disparagingly; but has not every division and dismemberment of every nation which has suffered dismemberment taken place by unanimous consent for the last three hundred years? Did not Prussia and Austria and Russia by unanimous consent divide Poland? Did not the United States and Great Britain and Japan and Italy and France divide China, and give Shantung to Japan? Was that not a unanimous decision? Close the doors upon the diplomats of Europe, let them sit in secret, give them the material to trade on, and there always will be unanimous consent.

How did Japan get unanimous consent? I want to say here, in my parting words upon this proposition, that I have no doubt the outrage upon China was quite as distasteful to the President of the United States as it is to me. But Japan said: "I will not sign your treaty unless you turn over to me Shantung, to be turned back at my discretion," and you know how Japan's discretion operates with reference to such things. And so, when we are in the league, and our accredited representatives are sitting at Geneva, and a question of great moment arises, Japan, or Russia, or Germany, or Great Britain will say, "Unless this matter is adjusted in this way I will depart from your league." It is the same thing, operating in the same way, only under a different date and under a little different circumstances.

If you have enough territory, if you have enough material, if you have enough subject peoples to trade upon and divide, there will be no difficulty about unanimous consent.

Do our Democratic friends ever expect any man to sit as a member of the council or as a member of the assembly equal in intellectual power and in standing before the world with that of our representative at Versailles? Do you expect a man to sit in the council who will have made more pledges, and I shall assume made them in sincerety, for self-determination and for the rights of small peoples, than had been made by our accredited representative? And yet, what became of it? The unanimous consent was obtained nevertheless.

But take another view of it. We are sending to the council one man. That one man represents 110,000,000 people.

Here, sitting in the Senate, we have two from every State in the Union, and over in the other House we have Representatives in accordance with population, and the responsibility is spread out in accordance with our obligations to our constituency. But now we are transferring to one man the stupendous power of representing the sentiment and convictions of 110,-000,000 people in tremendous questions which may involve the peace or may involve the war of the world.

However you view the question of unanimous consent, it does not protect us.

What is the result of all this? We are in the midst of all of the affairs of Europe. We have entangled ourselves with all European concerns. We have joined in alliance with all the European nations which have thus far joined the league, and all nations which may be admitted to the league. We are sitting there dabbling in their affairs and intermeddling in their concerns. In other words—and this comes to the question which is fundamental with me—we have forfeited and surrendered, once and for all, the great policy of "no entangling alliances" upon which the strength of this Republic has been founded for one hundred and fifty years.

My friends of reservations, tell me where is the reservation in these articles which protects us against entangling alliances with Europe?

Those who are differing over reservations, tell me what one of them protects the doctrine laid down by the Father of our Country. That fundamental proposition is surrendered, and we are a part of the European turmoils and conflicts from the time we enter this league.

Let us not underestimate that. There has never been an hour since the Venezuelan difficulty that there has not been operating in this country, fed by domestic and foreign sources, a powerful propaganda for the destruction of the doctrine of no entangling alliances.

Lloyd-George is reported to have said just a few days before the conference met at Versailles that Great Britain could give up much, and would be willing to sacrifice much, to have America withdraw from that policy. That was one of the great objects of the entire conference at Versailles, so far as the foreign representatives were concerned. Clemenceau and Lloyd-George and others like them were willing to make any reasonable sacrifice which would draw America away from her isolation and into the internal affairs and concerns of Europe. This league of nations, with or without reservations, whatever else it does or does not do, does surrender and sacrifice that policy; and once having surrendered and become a part of the European concerns, where, my friends, are you going to stop?

You have put in here a reservation upon the Monroe doctrine. I think that, in so far as language could protect the Monroe doctrine, it has been protected. But as a practical proposition, as a working proposition, tell me candidly, as men familiar with the history of your country and of other countries, do you think that you can intermeddle in European affairs and keep Europe from intermeddling in your affairs?

When Mr. Monroe wrote to Jefferson, he asked him his view upon the Monroe doctrine, and Mr. Jefferson said, in substance, our first and primary obligation should be never to interfere in European affairs; and, secondly, never permit Europe to interfere in our affairs.

He understood, as every wise and practical man understands, that if we intermeddle in her affairs, if we help to adjust her conditions, inevitably and remorselessly Europe then will be carried into our affairs, in spite of anything you can write upon paper.

We can not protect the Monroe doctrine unless we protect the basic principle upon which it rests, and that is the Washington policy. I do not care how earnestly you may endeavor to do so, as a practical working proposition, your league will come to the United States. Will you permit me to digress long enough to read a paragraph from a great French editor upon this particular phase of the matter, Mr. Stephen Lausanne, editor of *Le Matin,* of Paris:

"When the executive council of the league of nations fixes 'the reasonable limits of the armament of Peru'; when it shall demand information concerning the naval program of Brazil; when it shall tell Argentina what shall be the measure of the 'contribution to the armed forces to protect the signatures of the social covenant'; when it shall demand the immediate registration of the treaty between the United States and Canada at the seat of the league, it will control, whether it will or no, the destiny of America. And when the American States shall be obliged to take a hand in every war or menace of war in Europe (art. 11), they will necessarily fall afoul of the fundamental principle laid down by Monroe, which was that Americans should never take part in a European war.

"If the league takes in the world, then Europe must mix in the affairs of America; if only Europe is included, then America will violate of necessity her own doctrine by intermixing in the affairs of Europe."

If the league includes the affairs of the world, does it not include the affairs of all the world? Is there any limitation of the jurisdiction of the council or of the assembly upon the question of peace or war? Does it not have now, under the reservations, the same as it had before, the power to deal with all matters of peace or war throughout the entire world? How shall you keep from meddling in the affairs of Europe or keep Europe from meddling in the affairs of America?

There is another and even a more commanding reason why I shall record my vote against this treaty. It imperils what I conceive to be the underlying, the very first principles of this Republic. It is in conflict with the right of our people to govern themselves free from all restraint, legal or moral, of foreign powers. It challenges every tenet of my political faith. If this faith were one of my own contriving, if I stood here to assert principles of government of my own evolving, I might well be charged with intolerable presumption, for we all recognize the ability of those who urge a different course. But I offer in justification of my course nothing of my own—save the deep and abiding reverence I have for those whose policies I humbly but most ardently support. I claim no merit save fidelity to American principles and devotion to American ideals as they were wrought out from time to time by those who built the Republic and as they have been extended and maintained throughout these years. In opposing the treaty I do nothing more than decline to renounce and tear out of my life the sacred traditions which through fifty years have been translated into my whole intellectual and moral being. I will not, I can not, give up my belief that America must, not alone for the happiness of her own people, but for the moral guidance and greater contentment of the world, be permitted to live her own life.

Next to the tie which binds a man to his God is the tie which binds a man to his country, and all schemes, all plans, however ambitious and fascinating they seem in their proposal, but which would embarrass or entangle and impede or shackle her sovereign will, which would compromise her freedom of action I unhesitatingly put behind me.

Sir, since the debate opened months ago those of us who have stood against this proposition have been taunted many times with being little Americans. Leave us the word American, keep that in your presumptuous impeachment, and no taunt can disturb us, no gibe discompose our purposes. Call us little Americans if you will, but leave us the consolation and the pride which the term American, however modified, still imparts. Take away that term and though you should coin in telling phrase your highest eulogy we would hurl it back as common slander. We have been ridiculed because, forsooth, of our limited vision. Possibly that charge may be true. Who is there here that can read the future? Time, and time alone, unerring and remorseless, will give us each our proper place in the affections of our countrymen and in the esteem and commendation of those who are to come after us. We neither fear nor court her favor. But if our vision has been circumscribed it has at all times within its compass been clear and steady. We have sought nothing save the tranquillity of our own people and the honor and independence of our own Republic. No foreign flattery, no possible world glory and power have disturbed our poise or come between us and our devotion to the traditions which have made us a people, or the policies which have made us a Nation, unselfish and commanding. If we have erred we have erred out of too much love for those things which from childhood you and we together have been taught to revere—yes, to defend even at the cost of limb and life. If we have erred it is because we have placed too high an estimate upon the wisdom of Washington and Jefferson, too exalted an opinion upon the patriotism of the sainted Lincoln. And blame us not therefore if we have, in our limited vision, seemed sometimes bitter and at all times uncompromising, for the things for which we have spoken, feebly spoken, the things which we have endeavored to defend have been the things for which your fathers and our fathers were willing to die.

Senators, even in an hour so big with expectancy we should not close our eyes to the fact that democracy is something more, vastly more, than a mere form of government by which society is restrained into free and orderly life. It is a moral entity, a spiritual force as well. And these are things which live only and alone in the atmosphere of liberty. The foundation upon which democracy rests is faith in the moral instincts of the people. Its ballot boxes, the franchise, its laws, and constitutions are but the outward manifestations of the deeper and more essential thing—a continuing trust in the moral purposes of the average man and woman. When this is lost or forfeited your outward forms, however democratic in terms are a mockery. Force may find expression through institutions democratic in structure equally with the simple and more direct processes of a single supreme ruler. These distinguishing virtues of a real republic you can not commingle with the discordant and destructive forces of the Old World and still preserve them. You can not yoke a government whose fundamental maxim is that of liberty to a government whose first law is that of force and hope to preserve the former. These things are in eternal war, and one must ultimately destroy the other. You may still keep for a time the outward form, you may still delude yourself, as others have done in the past, with appearances and symbols, but when you shall have committed this Republic to a scheme of world control based upon force, upon the combined military force of the four great nations of the world, you will have soon destroyed the atmosphere of freedom, of confidence in the self-governing capacity of the masses, in which alone a democracy may thrive. We may become one of the four dictators of the world, but we shall no longer be master of our own spirit. And what shall it profit us as a Nation if we shall go forth to the dominion of the earth and share with others the glory of world control and lose that fine sense of confidence in the people, the soul of democracy.

Look upon the scene as it is now presented. Behold the task we are to assume, and then contemplate the method by which we are to deal with this task. Is the method such as to address itself to a Government "conceived in liberty and dedicated to the proposition that all men are created equal"? When this league, this combination, is formed four great powers representing the dominant people will rule one-half of the inhabitants of the globe as subject peoples—rule by force, and we shall be a party to the rule of force. There is no other way by which you can keep people in subjection. You must either give them independence, recognize their rights as nations to live their own life and to set up their own form of government, or you must deny them these things by force. That is the scheme, the method proposed by the league. It proposes no other. We will in time become inured to its inhuman precepts and its soulless methods, strange as this doctrine now seems to a free people. If we stay with our contract, we will come in time to declare with our associates that force—force, the creed of the Prussian military oligarchy—is after all the true foundation upon which must rest all stable governments. Korea, despoiled and bleeding at every pore; India, sweltering in ignorance and burdened with inhuman taxes after more than a hundred years of dominant rule; Egypt, trapped and robbed of her birthright; Ireland, with 700 years of sacrifice for independence—this is the task, this is the atmosphere, and this is the creed in and under which we are to keep alive our belief in the moral purposes and self-governing capacity of the people, a belief without which the Republic must disintegrate and die. The maxim of liberty will soon give way to the rule of blood and iron. We have been pleading here for our Constitution. Conform this league, it has been said, to the technical terms of our charter and all will be well. But I declare to you that we must go further and conform to those sentiments and passions for justice and freedom which are essential to the existence of democracy. You must respect not territorial boundaries, not territorial integrity, but you must respect and preserve the sentiments and passions for justice and for freedom which God in his infinite wisdom has planted so deep in the human heart that no form of tyranny however brutal, no persecution however prolonged can wholly uproot and kill. Respect nationality, respect justice, respect freedom, and you may have some hope of peace, but not so if you make your standard the standard of tyrants and despots, the protection of real estate regardless of how it is obtained.

Sir, we are told that this treaty means peace. Even so, I would not pay the price. Would you purchase peace at the cost of any part of our independence? We could have had peace in 1776—the price was high, but we could have had it. James Otis, Sam Adams, Hancock, and Warren were surrounded by those who urged peace and British rule. All through that long and trying struggle, particularly when the clouds of adversity lowered upon the cause there was a cry of peace—let us have peace. We could have had peace in 1860; Lincoln was counseled by men of great influence and accredited wisdom to let our brothers—and, thank heaven, they are brothers—depart in peace. But the tender, loving Lincoln, bending under the fearful weight of impending civil war, an apostle of peace, refused to pay the price, and a reunited country will praise his name forevermore—bless it because he refused peace at the price of national honor and national integrity. Peace upon any other basis than national independence, peace purchased at the cost of any part of our national integrity, is fit only for slaves, and even when purchased at such a price it is a delusion, for it can not last.

But your treaty does not mean peace—far, very far, from it. If we are to judge the future by the past it means war. Is there any guaranty of peace other than the guaranty which comes of the control of the war-making power by the people? Yet what great rule of democracy does the treaty leave unassailed? The people in whose keeping alone you can safely lodge the power of peace or war, nowhere, at no time and in no place, have any voice in this scheme for world peace. Autocracy which has bathed the world in blood for centuries reigns supreme. Democracy is everywhere excluded. This, you say, means peace.

Can you hope for peace when love of country is disregarded in your scheme, when the spirit of nationality is rejected, even scoffed at? Yet what law of that moving and mysterious force does your treaty not deny? With a ruthlessness unparalleled your treaty in a dozen instances runs counter to the divine law of nationality. Peoples who speak the same language, kneel at the same ancestral tombs, moved by the same traditions, animated by a common hope, are torn asunder, broken in pieces,

divided, and parceled out to antagonistic nations. And this
you call justice. This, you cry, means peace. Peoples who
have dreamed of independence, struggled and been patient,
sacrificed and been hopeful, peoples who were told that through
this peace conference they should realize the aspirations of
centuries, have again had their hopes dashed to earth. One of
the most striking and commanding figures in this war, soldier
and statesman, turned away from the peace table at Versailles
declaring to the world, "The promise of the new life, the victory of the great humane ideals for which the peoples have shed
their blood and their treasure without stint, the fulfillment of
their aspirations toward a new international order and a fairer
and better world are not written into the treaty." No; your
treaty means injustice. It means slavery. It means war. And
to all this you ask this Republic to become a party. You ask it
to abandon the creed under which it has grown to power and
accept the creed of autocracy, the creed of repression and force.

I turn from this scheme based upon force to another scheme,
planned one hundred and forty-three years ago in old Independence Hall, in the city of Philadelphia, based upon liberty.
I like it better. I have become so accustomed to believe in it
that it is difficult for me to reject it out of hand. I have difficulty in subscribing to the new creed of oppression, the creed
of dominant and subject peoples. I feel a reluctance to give
up the belief that all men are created equal—the eternal principle in government that all governments derive their just powers from the consent of the governed. I can not get my consent to exchange the doctrine of George Washington for the
doctrine of Frederick the Great translated into mendacious
phrases of peace. I go back to that serene and masterful soul
who pointed the way to power and glory for the new and then
weak Republic, and whose teachings and admonitions even in
our majesty and dominance we dare not disregard.

I know well the answer to my contention. It has been piped
about of late from a thousand sources—venal sources, disloyal
sources, sinister sources—that Washington's wisdom was of
his day only and that his teachings are out of fashion—things
long since sent to the scrap heap of history—that while he was
great in character and noble in soul he was untrained in the

arts of statecraft and unlearned in the science of government. The puny demagogue, the barren editor, the sterile professor now vie with each other in apologizing for the temporary and commonplace expedients which the Father of our Country felt constrained to adopt in building a republic!

What is the test of statesmanship? Is it the formation of theories, the utterance of abstract and incontrovertible truths, or is it the capacity and the power to give to a people that concrete thing called liberty, that vital and indispensable thing in human happiness called free institutions and to establish over all and above all the blessed and eternal reign of order and law? If this be the test, where shall we find another whose name is entitled to be written beside the name of Washington? His judgment and poise in the hour of turmoil and peril, his courage and vision in times of adversity, his firm grasp of fundamental principles, his almost inspired power to penetrate the future and read there the result, the effect of policies, have never been excelled, if equalled, by any of the world's commonwealth builders. Peter the Great, William the Silent, and Cromwell the Protector, these and these alone perhaps are to be associated with his name as the builders of States and the founders of governments. But in exaltation of moral purpose, in the unselfish character of his work, in the durability of his policies, in the permanency of the institutions which he more than anyone else called into effect, his service to mankind stands out separate and apart in a class by itself. The works of these other great builders, where are they now? But the work of Washington is still the most potent influence for the advancement of civilization and the freedom of the race.

Reflect for a moment over his achievements. He led the Revolutionary Army to victory. He was the very first to suggest a union instead of a confederacy. He presided over and counseled with great wisdom the convention which framed the Constitution. He guided the Government through its first perilous years. He gave dignity and stability and honor to that which was looked upon by the world as a passing experiment, and finally, my friends, as his own peculiar and particular contribution to the happiness of his countrymen and to the cause of the Republic, he gave us his great foreign policy under which we have lived and prospered and strengthened for nearly a century and a half. This policy is the most sublime confirmation of his genius as a statesman. It was then, and it now is an indispensable part of our whole scheme of government. It is to-day a vital, indispensable element in our entire plan, purpose, and mission as a nation. To abandon it is nothing less than a betrayal of the American people. I say betrayal deliberately, in view of the suffering and the sacrifice which will follow in the wake of such a course.

But under the stress and strain of these extraordinary days, when strong men are being swept down by the onrushing forces of disorder and change, when the most sacred things of life, the most cherished hopes of a Christian world seem to yield to the mad forces of discontent—just such days as Washington passed through when the mobs of Paris, wild with new liberty and drunk with power, challenged the established institutions of all the world, but his steadfast soul was unshaken—under these conditions come again, we are about to abandon this policy so essential to our happiness and tranquillity as a people and our stability as a Government. No leader with his commanding influence and his unquailing courage stands forth to stem the current. But what no leader can or will do, experience, bitter experience, and the people of this country in whose keeping, after all, thank God, is the Republic, will ultimately do. If we abandon his leadership and teachings, we will go back. We will return to this policy. Americanism shall not, can not die. We may go back in sackcloth and ashes, but we will return to the faith of the fathers. America will live her own life. The independence of this Republic will have its defenders. Thousands have suffered and died for it, and their sons and daughters are not of the breed who will be betrayed into the hands of foreigners. The noble face of the Father of his Country, so familiar to every boy and girl, looking out from the walls of the Capitol in stern reproach, will call those who come here for public service to a reckoning. The people of our beloved country will finally speak, and we will return to the policy which we now abandon. America disenthralled and free in spite of all these things will continue her mission in the cause of peace, of freedom, and of civilization.

FRANCIS P. GARVAN

CHEMICAL WARFARE

ADDRESS DELIVERED BEFORE THE JOINT SESSION OF THE
SOCIETY OF CHEMICAL INDUSTRY AND THE AMERICAN
CHEMICAL SOCIETY, COLUMBIA UNIVERSITY, SEPTEMBER 7,
1921

[Francis Patrick Garvan was born in East Hartford, Connecticut,
on June 13, 1875. He was graduated from Yale College in 1897, and
from the New York Law School in 1899. He was Assistant District
Attorney of New York county from 1900 to 1910, and as such participated in the conduct of the Thaw murder trial. He has been Dean
of the Fordham Law School, and Assistant United States Attorney
General. From 1917 to 1919 he was manager of the New York office
of the Alien Property Custodian and Director of the Bureau of Investigation. From March 4, 1919 to 1921, he was Alien Property Custodian, after which time he became President of the Chemical Foundation formed to purchase and administer the German-owned chemical
patents which had been taken over by the Alien Property Custodian.
He and his wife have been indefatigable in promoting research and
in the popularization of knowledge concerning chemistry. In recognition of their work, the American Institute of Chemists, on May 4,
1929, conferred upon them a medal for "signal contributions to the
forwarding of chemical research and industry."]

"Nothing can be more certain than that the character and
rapidity of our national development in all matters which relate to *industry, agriculture, public health* and the *preservation
of the physical framework of our civilization* will be dependent
upon the quantity and quality of sound research which is carried on. The truth of this assertion becomes even more apparent when one recognizes the fact that every modern nation
stands in a relation of industrial and commercial competition
with other nations. In the measure in which this is true, to fall
behind the others in scientific development, is to *precipitate* a
trend of events which spells national depression and disaster.
In other words, the price of a sound, comprehensive national
life is, in these times, widespread and intelligent scientific re-

search." These are the words of Prof. Angell, the new president of Yale University. But President Angell stopped halfway.

Pasteur thought it through when he said:

"In our century science is the soul of the prosperity of nations and the living source of all progress. Undoubtedly, the tiring daily discussions of politics seem to be our guide—empty appearances—what really leads us forward are a few scientific discoveries and their application."

But sound and comprehensive scientific research and a practical development of the application of the results and discoveries of such research is impossible in any country, without an appreciative understanding of the truth of these two quotations by the peoples of that country, reflected in their educational system, their business development, their governmental guidance and, if necessary, control and supervision.

These two quotations express, in my opinion, the truest appreciation of the cause of the war and point out to us its chief lesson. But more than that, they throw upon your shoulders as chemists the great responsibility of seeing to it that that lesson is learned and applied by your respective states.

The reputation for honesty and disinterested truthfulness of the chemists of the three nations joined here today is so well established and recognized that only from your lips will the peoples of our different countries accept the truth of these propositions.

Economists like Hauser, Lord Moulton or Angell may thunder these truths. Historians, cold or imaginative, like Balfour, Wells, Irwin or Symons, may present in startling form their conclusions or prophecies, but a war weary world hesitates to adopt their conclusions.

You and you only do they trust, and progress and safety place the heavy responsibility upon you of making chemistry, its aims and possibilities, understood by public schools, high schools, universities and post-graduate schools, by industry and agriculture, and by the representatives of the people in municipality, state and nation.

The people of the United States are ninety-nine per cent. right at heart and appreciative; so are the people of England

and of Canada. Their appreciation of chemistry must no longer be defined in the terminology of the propaganda of foreign hostile interests seeking only their destruction.

Your work must never again be allowed to cease in the laboratory.

The discovery and its application which today is only the latest proof of the truth of Pasteur and Angell occurred in 1856. In that year, your fellow Englishman, William Henry Perkin, aged eighteen, while engaged in scientific research in a laboratory in London, having for its object the artificial production of quinine, obtained a muddy, dark precipitate which, washed in alcohol, proved to be the dye we call mauve.

This discovery, with its principles, has been the basis for all the subsequent development of the coal-tar industry and practically of all organic chemistry.

His efforts met English industries without understanding; met a public and a government without appreciation, and fellow chemists without a realization of the responsibilities of directing and enlightening English thought.

The German Hoffman put the discovery in his bag and took it back to Germany. Almost instantly, he, and he typifies his chemical successors, was able to make German industry, German universities and the German Government realize the importance of the contents of that bag.

Immediate success led to a greater appreciation of an ever closer alliance of science and industry, and an ever closer alliance between science, industry and the militaristic state. This triple alliance changed Germany from an agricultural nation into the second industrial nation of the world, but in that change, it brought about a succession of periods of over-production, each one in turn overcome by greater consolidation, by ever increasing corruption in methods of bribery, espionage, dumping, et cetera, and by ever intensified state aid and direction.

In 1914, we find the German people demanding the control of the markets of the world. We find their hearts corrupted by the methods which they had felt it necessary to adopt to overcome their successive periods of over-production. We find them swollen with pride at their successes and ready to

inspire or acquiesce in the hazard of battle. This triple alliance
of industry, science and the militaristic state—and the evidence
is overwhelming that each was equally guilty—considered that
it would be quicker and cheaper to attempt to gain this end by
victory on the field of battle, rather than to find increased markets for a surplus production by further intensified methods of
peaceful penetration.

The same chemical research with its well-served industry
had in turn well served the militaristic state. As chemical
progress indexed commercial progress, so explosives had kept
pace with dyes and pharmaceuticals, the ammunition factories
of her peaceful penetration were the arsenals of her munitions
preparation.

In the fall of 1913, the chemical application of Perkin's discovery was able to notify the war lord that Germany was ready;
that she controlled 95 per cent. of the organic chemistry of the
world upon which industry and the production of explosives
were dependent; that she had crushed out every incipient effort toward the development of the Perkin discoveries by every
other nation and was able to deal the dependent industries of
those nations tremendous blows, and that now by the final
triumph in the development of the Haber processes of making
nitrates from the air, her agricultural production and munition
production were safe from the menace of any blockade.

You know the rest.

All this German chemists accomplished not alone in their
laboratories but in the forum of public opinion. They had
educated and moulded thought in Germany until every man
of whatever rank, in or out of industry, education or governmental service, realized the importance of chemistry in his life
and in the life of his country.

They knew that the alliance of science and industry had
increased the wealth of the world a thousand-fold in the past
hundred years.

They knew that it was the life-blood of industry; they knew
it was the safety of their state and the only sure foundation
upon which to base the hope of the health of their children and
their children's children, and they had impressed upon the
world the discouraging and withering idea that the Germans

and the Germans alone were mentally equipped to lead in this great age of chemistry.

You may answer me that I reproach you with results which could not have been foreseen, but I tell you that for three years I have been reading the records and the correspondence and the private papers of German chemists, German business men and German Imperial representatives, and I have been forced to realize that every result had been foreseen, realized, appreciated and worked for by every chemist in the German nation.

Just one or two instances: Prior to 1908, German patent laws contained the so-called working clause, by which your inventions, if patented in Germany, must be worked there within a certain period of time or they were thrown open to the German manufacturers and developers. Agitation was rife in this country that we should protect our future in like manner.

But by 1908 Germany had decided that she had so far advanced in science that she no longer needed that clause to protect herself and that if enacted by the United States it would threaten her control of organic chemistry in the world and destroy the purposes upon which she was bent.

The president of the Bayer Chemical Company, at that time the head representative of this march for world control in America, although on paper an American citizen, acting under instructions from the consolidated government of chemical industries of Berlin, went to Commissioner Moore at the Patent Office in Washington. It was the beginning of one of Washington's hot summers. With fulsome praise of his outstanding position in the patent world and the great inventive genius of this country needing protection, he reproached him for not representing the United States at the International Patent Conference about to be held in Stockholm. Mr. Moore responded that the unenlightened Congress had not given him any funds with which to go. Mr. Moore then went on his vacation. Mr. Muurling, the predecessor of Schweitzer and Metz as the American voice of Germany's chemical interests, went to Robert Bacon, then Acting Secretary of State, drew the picture of the United States unrepresented at that great Conference, pointed out to him that he had a fund which he could apply to any purpose which he deemed for the best interests of the country in its foreign relations, with the result that Mr. Moore was recalled from his vacation and sent abroad; but with him went a letter to the German chemists, telling them that the American representative of the German dream had done his part and that they must now do theirs.

The result was that Moore was induced to go from Stockholm to Berlin, where he was fêted and dined by the Kaiser himself and returned to negotiate the Treaty of 1909 with Germany, by which Germany was released from ever working her chemical patents in this country and by which the last hope of development of organic chemistry in this country was crushed.

No more loyal Americans ever lived than Robert Bacon and Commissioner Moore, but they were unconscious tools in the hands of the German chemists, the handmaidens of the German dream of world control. And you were to blame, because you had not instructed your Government officials up to a realization of the importance of chemistry and its guidance and protection by the state.

When the war broke out in 1914, four billion dollars of annual industry in this country, to say nothing of our physicians and hospitals, were dependent upon the will of the German Emperor as exercised through six importing firms and about four mere assembling plants. At the Kaiser's nod he summoned their assistance.

Listen! April 25, 1915, Boy-Ed writes to Albert:

"Very Honorable Privy Counsellor:

"Today's *World* prints the enclosed short article on the alleged erection of dye factories in New Jersey by Germans. In case you are not able to take any steps to prevent an undertaking of this kind, I am requesting you to indicate to whose attention I could call the matter.

"With greetings, etc.,   (Signed) Boy-Ed."

Albert answers, April 28, 1915:

"With regard to dyes, I got in touch with local experts in order to determine what truth there is in the news. According to my knowledge of things, the matter is a fake, inasmuch as our factories have bound themselves orally and by word of honor to do nothing in the present situation which might help the United States."

As a result, Bernstorff was able to cable his country that they had in their possession the weapon by which four million men in this country could be instantly thrown out of work, as an argument why America should attempt to force England to lift the blockade.

As a result, the German Government did issue an order, only to be met by a final realization of your own intrinsic ability. As a result, Germany was able to shut off as a further threat the supply of salvarsan and luminal from this country, which in her heartlessness she did, leaving thousands of epileptics and ten million syphilitics without any relief from the ravages of that plague and consequently menacing the other ninety millions of our people.

I could go on pointing out the results, but it is not necessary.

But why dwell upon the errors of yesterday?

The situation is as acute today as it was in 1908, in 1910, in 1914, or in 1916 and 1917.

Yes, the war is over, but the situation is the same.

This was an industrial war, brought on by industrial Germany in her lust-mad haste to capture the markets of the world. Industrial Germany, in her arrogance and pride, preferred the formidable hazard of battle to the progressive and sure infiltration which within ten or twenty years might well have given her the whole domination she sought from complacent and unthinking people.

Her ambitions are the same today as they were in 1914. Her methods are the same in peace and war.

Through the most extraordinary coalition of Science, Industry and Government that the world ever saw, Germany in the past leaped leagues ahead of rival nations, and as she ran she found means to clog the feet of her competitors.

Rapidly recovering from the debilitation of war losses, Germany is once more driving ahead in this special and all-important field. Once more she plans to deceive her rivals as to the importance of this special key industry of chemical production. Again she tries to clog the feet of competitors.

Once more she sends her spies and agents to this country and reinspires Germans, camouflaged as Americans, to poison the well from which America should draw her full strength for peace or war. Can that be done successfully here and in England and France, Germany will be a menace to world peace within a decade.

It is our people, our statesmen she seeks to lull and benumb. Let her gain her end and she will have developed within ten years, from her experience in the Great War and through the magic of her doctors of chemical research, through her tremendous and closely welded chemical industry under government protection, from her intensified alliance of Science, Industry and Government, peace weapons and war weapons of potency unforeseeable.

We have in our grasp today the means to make the United States forever independent in peace and war. In our grasp are the essentials for the control of disease, for the vast increase of food production, for the immense development of domestic and foreign industries, for secure national defense. We have universities ready to supply us with the personnel to put us in the forefront in this chemical age.

Are we so unconcerned, so dully perceptionless, so stupidly asleep that we will permit German intrigue to stifle this priceless acquisition, which has cost us millions of dollars and 27 per cent. of our war casualties?

Do we think that we are at peace because our Government has formulated a set of words declaring that peace exists, and because our President has put his signature to the document? Fatal assumption!

With the German people, dominated by their ineradicable mania of superiority, the war has passed into another stage merely. But it is the same war, waged with new weapons.

All the defeats and punishment suffered by Germany from 1914 to 1918 were invaluable discipline and experience for continuing the indecisive struggle.

Germany was not conquered. She was merely stopped, thrown back for a time. She did not experience the agonies of invasion. Her people did not groan under the horrors that fell upon Belgium, France, Roumania and Russia. Never forget that the German people greeted the baffled German armies as the Romans were accustomed to salute the legions of victorious Cæsar.

The retiring hordes, flowing back into the Fatherland, were garlanded with flowers. The incidents of roadway and city square as the gray-green warriors fell back before the menace of Foch, Haig and Pershing cry with shouting tongues to thoughtful men. A subdued people, a people conscious of defeat, do not crown their unsuccessful legionaries with laurel and jasmine.

Their attitude shouts aloud the set purpose of the German mind to begin anew, patiently, devotedly, in the silence of their laboratories, their task of dominating a world so ridiculously inferior to themselves.

If this were mere speculation, I would waste neither your time nor my own; but my assertions are buttressed by timbers of hard fact.

In Germany today industrial reorganization for world domination first in the peaceful arts and then in war is proceeding mightily under the sympathetic eye and fostering care of a government which differs in no important particular, so far as the world outside of Germany is concerned, from the government of the Hohenzollerns. The German purpose stands forth as clearly as a mountain in the sunlight: First, reconquer in industry and commerce, then we Germans will see.

Their secret documents prove it. The heart of the news that comes out of Germany proves it. They prove it out of their own mouths.

Moles in the darkness, German agents in America are once more plotting against our security, our prosperity and against the health of our very children. The German design to render the United States impotent is being prosecuted today with more subtle viciousness than marked the intrigue of Von Bernstorff, Dr. Albert and Hugo Schweitzer in the years before we entered the war.

The times are too tense with danger for passive tactics. On one side we have the same old crowd of German agents masquerading as good Americans. On another side we perceive American citizens supporting the German intrigues. In Congress we hear and stand aghast at the ignorant and malicious outbursts of certain legislators, unmindful of their country's welfare. Folly drips from their mouths. Stupid suspicion of the motives of honest men and appalling ignorance of the times mark their astounding incapacity. There are some who, like Jacob of old, have set themselves to steal the birthright of chemical independence from the American nation. They may disguise for a time the hairy hands of the German dye monopoly that controls them, but in the end the people will know them for what they are.

Their voices are the voices of elected Representatives and Senators in the American Congress, but the hands that manipulate them are the hands of the German Dye Trust, the most powerful monopoly ever formed by man, the Interessen Gemeinschaft, the "I. G."

Joseph Frederick Naumann, German economist, editor and member of the Reichstag, in the most successful and probably the ablest book that has appeared in Germany since the beginning of the war, *Central Europe,* frankly admits this charge.

"The war," he says, "was really only a continuation of our previous life with other tools but based on the same methods. In this, indeed, lies the secret of success * * * if our opponents like to label this intrinsic connection between war and peace 'German militarism,' we can only regard this as reasonable, for Prussian military discipline influences us all in actual fact, from the captain of industry to the maker of earthworks. * * * Happen what will, the German spirit has received its baptism of fire; the national genius was and is a reality. Both to ourselves and to the outside world we have shown ourselves as in essence a single unit. Now it is our concern to carry through to its goal this essential German character, proved in the most sinister of wars. This will and must be set on foot directly peace is concluded."

And a little further along:

"We shall enjoy our golden age as other conquering nations in other ages and with other abilities and excellence have done before us. Our epoch dawns when English capitalism has reached and overstepped its highest point, and we have been educated for this epoch by Frederich II, Kant, Scharnhorst, Siemens, Krupp, Bismarck, Bebel, Legien, Kirdorf and Ballin.

Our dead have fallen on the field for the sake of our fatherland, Germany, foremost in the world."

Because the peculiar circumstances of my service to the United States gave me a most effective perspective of the German purpose of advancing German power while weakening American strength, I am driven to speak out. With the hope that this truth will stick fast in the national consciousness, I have the temerity to awake the lessons of the war and urge you to do your part toward awakening the American people before it is too late.

If, in the reaction of war and in the general distaste for discussing matters pertaining to war, we permit ourselves again to be lulled and numbed by German propaganda; if we look on indifferently while a few demagogues in Congress and a few shortsighted, selfish men in business life play the German game; if we allow Germany to stifle American industry that would within a very few years make the United States absolutely safe, then, I say, it will have been through your neglect and temerity and failure to realize that it is your responsibility not only to search the truth, but to preach it.

Your responsibility today is the same as it was during all these years of neglect, only intensified as it must be by your consciousness of the results of that neglect.

You alone in your town or village can see to it that these truths are realized by public school and high school; you alone in your state can see to it that these truths are realized by universities and state legislators in control of education.

You alone can see to it that in the National Government, your representatives in Patent Office, in Bureau of Education, in State Department and in Congress are kept abreast with your development and needs, in order that every insidious attack may be exposed and refuted.

You must be mindful of the fact that most of our school heads, our great editors, our government officials, both administrative and legislative, have been educated in what one of your English compatriots has called "Museums of Ancient Learning" and that the war has for the first time and but partially, opened their minds to a realization of the scientific progress of the last century and its true relation to national progress.

Are you awake? I do not think so, with the exception of a few. You have listened without apparent protest, contenting yourselves with resolutions and telegrams both good but not sufficient to controvert the German lie that there was a "Dye Monopoly" in this country, or that such a monopoly would result from the enactment of a selective embargo, when you knew that the development of a dye industry is synonymous with the development of education in organic chemistry and that no monopoly in education is possible without the compulsory partnership of industry, university and government, such as exists in Germany. (A monopoly which never worries those tools of German propaganda.)

You knew that Senator Frelinghuysen spoke the truth when he pledged his honor on the floor of the Senate that there were already forty-six independent dye concerns in his own state, and the Senators from this Empire State, when they find their voice, can stand up and say that there are twenty-nine more here.

I say you have heard it called a "dye fight," when you knew it was a fight of organic chemistry; when you knew that "dyes as dyes" do not in normal times constitute a gross business of more than $40,000,000 a year, not as much as our children spend in toy balloons or our five and ten cent stores take in in a month.

You heard without audible resentment the German lie that the chemical foundation was another monopoly and had purchased for less than their value, patents belonging to the innocent men of Germany. You knew that no stockholder, trustee or president ever has or ever can make a penny out of the chemical foundation; that it was formed to represent the American people in their purchase of their freedom from the clutch of the hands seeking to misuse the beneficence of their laws to choke our industrial development, our means of defense, and our hope of the preservation and conservation of the health of our manhood and womanhood.

You know that the U. S. Constitution gave Congress power to issue patents in order to offer inducement to the publication of each successive discovery in science, in order that it may be made the stepping stone for future progress, and you know that practically all German patents were taken out with the intent to conceal and suppress advance in scientific information and what the foundation bought was useless, unless American business spent millions of dollars to find out the necessary information which the patents concealed.

You knew that the attack on the foundation was a German attempt to diminish the usefulness of the organization which they know will never quit until every man, woman and child in this land knows the whole hideous past chemical story and has a vision of the wondrous future of chemistry in the idealistic hands of the Anglo-Saxon race.

It was only freedom from blackmail and the consequences of imbibed German propaganda intended for our destruction that the foundation bought. All other nations accomplished the same result without any compensation to Germany.

What would they? Should the American Government give back to the Germany, which in 1915 attempted by the use of her patents to throw four million American citizens out of work, in order to blackmail our Government, the right to do so now for the purposes of her peace-time conquest of the world's markets?

Would you have the American Government hand back the patents covering the only weapon with which we can fight the dread scourge syphilis, to the country which once shut off our supply while we were at peace with her, to further her wartime purposes, without assurance greater than her word, greater than her scrap of paper assurance, that an attempt to use the same power would not again be made to accomplish some one of her aims?

Did it not bring to your minds the lessons of the war when you saw the importing representative of the German "I. G." stand on the floor of the House of Representatives, flanked by fifteen of the seventeen Congressmen who voted against the declaration of war, leading the cheering when the first great unsuccessful test came as to whether American chemists should be given a chance to catch up their neglect of forty years and atone for it by leading this country through the development of organic chemistry into the realms of intensified national industrial progress, sweet security to home and child and blessed advance in the medical service of humanity? Do you not feel that the voices of two German importing firms were louder in protest and more persistent in their appeal for Germany than the voices of your fifteen thousand members for America's lessons of the war.

Again I repeat, Herman A. Metz stood upon the floor of the House as that vote was announced and shouted to a gallery of American citizens "I've got you licked." And when he screamed in triumph, he meant "I, the representative of the Interessen Gemeinschaft, the 'I. G.,' the combination of German Government and German chemical industries; I've licked the advice of your General Pershing; I've licked the advice of your Secretary of War; I've licked the advice of your Secretary of Navy; I've licked your President; I've licked your Administration; I've licked your thirty million dollars investment in your colleges; I've licked your chemistry in your high schools and your public schools; I've licked your research institutions and the future development of medicine in America."

Motives of politicians are questioned, interests in industries are antagonistic, but your heritage, the purity and spotlessness of your great white plume, insure you attention and burden you with the responsibility. Each in your own community must tell the story of chemistry to the Boy Scouts and the Rotary Clubs, the school boards and the public and high school teachers, the local editors, clergymen and physicians. You can point out how chemistry can serve each of your local industries, the agriculture of your community and the public health of your city; and more than all, you can meet and refute not only the false ideas which have been inculcated in the past by German propaganda but each new lie which her system puts forth. The universities have already harkened to you. The study of man, his emotions and the tongues and learning of the dead past, last sanctuaries of lost causes, are already being forced into their proportionate place in the curricula, and the understanding by man of the world in which he lives and his relation to it is being given its proper importance. In this country, during the past year, over thirty millions of dollars have been appropriated by the different universities to the promotion of the study of chemistry. For instance, Yale has appropriated three and one-half millions to build the finest laboratory in the world, and has also established chairs of research, whose occupants will be free from the labor of teaching. Harvard and Princeton are about to follow suit; Cornell has appropriated five hundred thousand dollars; so it is right straight across the country. I need only mention that great research institutions are springing up, such as the endowment in Leland Stanford, for research studies in the chemistry of foods and a great, as yet unnamed, philanthropist, is establishing a wonderful institution to insure in this country the proper research into the chemistry of plant life. This phase of the situation is most encouraging.

But most of our representatives in the executive and legislative branches of our States and of our nation are graduates of universities of the past, and their experience, as my experience, with chemistry and science in general, is as yet a closed book to them, and it is for you to supply to them the true information, to enable them not only to safeguard our progress by encouraging and fostering legislation, but also to prevent them from being influenced by information at the hands of your enemies.

You can tell them and they will believe you, at least ninety-nine out of one hundred, for they are honest men, that your science is the life-blood of industry, eliminating waste and purifying the products of the soil, of the mine and of the factory. You can tell them that there has come into the world a realization that the empirical system of medicine has reached its limit, and that chemistry is ready to join hands with medicine and physics, in eliminating the waste of disease and in intensifying the vigor and strength of our people, and then you can talk to them about war.

They will not believe the imagination of a Wells or the prophecy of Will Irwin, but you know and can tell them that with twenty years of progress, if progress there is to be, by great and small nations of the world in the study and development of chemistry, *war will be unthinkable.*

The thrilling picture painted by Wells of the appalling destructive persistency of radio-active elements and of the awful hopelessness of defense against such forces, is as definitely prophetic as Jules Verne's vision of the submarine or Rudyard Kipling's description of the swooping flight of the night mail flyer from London to Quebec. Inspiration of men of letters raised high above the weights of fear and superstition and dull habits that clog trammeled imagination lifts them to regions where they are fired by whispers of hidden things.

The creative chemist today is their blood brother in unappeasable imaginative effort. The world of his dreams is the scarcely touched source of natural force, and the goal of achievement to which he has set his face as he toils against the heartbreaking road that all must tread who dream of benefitting the race, is the absolute mastery of man over nature. Wittingly they weave their webs and wittingly they set the snare that will some day catch the sun, as Wells puts it.

Our research chemists know as certainly as they comprehend the relationship of the molecules they take apart and put together, that human beings will not cease fighting each other and killing each other until the game is made too frightful for imagination to contemplate.

They do not believe that war can be stricken from the list of man's evil practices by appeals to his better nature or by reasoning with his intellect. For men have been slaying each other from anger or self interest since the time when the first hairy males hated the animal scent of each other, or coveted each others' females, or quarreled to a deadly finish over the raw flesh of a mammoth trapped in asphalt bogs. Even in that remote time, there must have been a few gentle souls, among the very old; among the few that had caught a gleam of the glory of life, who pleaded in strange, guttural eagerness for milder and more tolerant ways. Such doubtless were clubbed to death by their incensed sons, or driven from the fire to perish in exile. The clucking first men peace advocates of 20,000 years ago scarce daring to raise rude gutturals of protest against the murder and rapine done by their brutelike sons, were few and fearful creatures we surmise; but their kind has increased marvelously since mankind has learned through suffering of his own making to think more clearly than the brutes around him, and today there are millions of protestants against war where one dared to speak out a few centuries ago. The idea that war is a crime instead of a glorious sport has taken hold of peoples according to the degree of their experience and their intelligence.

The comprehension that it is nothing but an appalling wastage of the toil of generations, that it is altogether brutalizing without a single compensatory side, is surely penetrating our thick minds. Bitter experience that the wastage and destruction of war is not confined to a period of warring but that they persist through miserable after years, is getting home to our understanding. The vast majority of human beings alive today would give thanks to the variously named Supreme Being, if they could but know that the legalized, wholesale murder called war was done for, finished. We are perfectly sure that this is so. Why, then, does not man end it once and for all? Why, knowing the better, does he continue to practice the worse in double guilt?

Perhaps we find an answer to this speculation in the tracery of the development of the peace idea. Put it squarely; peace advocates have multiplied and the peace idea has spread in singular relationship to the killing, searing, burning, mangling, poisoning, mass-destroying development of war weapons. As warfare has slowly grown more terrible, so men have turned slowly but in greater and greater numbers to peace hopes and peace plans.

As struggles between nations became more destructive, not only in actual warfare but in the paralyzing blows delivered to peace-time industry, more and more came to kneel at the altar of peace. When war science learned how to destroy thousands at a stroke, to ruin whole cities in the space of a breath drawn in the middle of the night, peace seemed more and more desirable.

As the researchers in the sciences contributed in ever-increasing frightfulness to the power and long distance application of war weapons, destroying all the romance of industrial combat and nullifying individual courage, men began to see increasing merit in the dreams of those who would abolish war utterly and who would police the evil doers of the earth as such are policed in our cities.

When the creative chemist showed military commanders how an opposing host could be stricken from life on the wings of the wind, laid horribly in death by a vapor as noiseless as the pinions of Azrael; how life could be expelled from great cities by a death dew of acids sprinkled from invisible airplanes, peace became a boon to be prayed for in utter sincerity. Hypocrisy smiling at gunpowder blanched before phosgene gas.

Peace is much more popular now that men know how to destroy each other with cotton in the form of nitrocellulose drawn from the air, than when they abolished each other with cellulose in the form of a club.

I do not say that the spread of education and gradual refinement of the spiritual side of man has not played a part in the growth of the ideal, nor that the operation of pure reason has not contributed to the vitality of the desire.

I do maintain with history at my back that successive inventions of horribly destructive weapons and successive demonstrations of the magnified and unpreventable ruin and misery wrought by one new weapon after another, have been successive shocks to man's long-time notions about the indispensability of war.

There was a time when he said that war could not be prevented. Then he began to say that it was disagreeable on the whole, that it ought to be prevented. Now he is beginning to see that it is so frightful that it *must* be prevented.

Until a day in April six years ago his dislike for war was never so intense as to make him pause to think deliberately before he plunged into it. Until April, 1915, his fears for his personal safety and for the safety of those he left at home was never so overpowering as to make him say "I dare not begin." Great guns and high explosives were terrible weapons but familiar ones. He knew something about them.

Fighting was a series of such small dangers, limited, instantaneous, each complete in itself, with no continuing or overhanging peril. Moreover, his own tremors were eased by the assurance that his loved ones were not in the same danger that he risked. His home was secure. He had something to go back to.

HICKS' SP.A.S.—43

In other words, the element of safety in all wars previous to the great war closed in November, 1918, safety not only of combatant forces relatively, but of civilian populations actually, was large enough to reinforce the self-interest which prompted him to go to war in the first place. Always that self-interest, that determination to get by force what he had been unable to win in peaceful competition, overcame the constantly growing suggestion that war was a foolish, stupid business, entirely unworthy of his experience and his intelligence. He got hard knocks for several thousand years but these scarcely jarred his imagination.

All this time he had been fighting with understandable weapons, hurting his enemies with these familiar weapons or getting hurt by them. There was nothing mysterious about it, nothing to daunt his imagination, stun all thought, fill the soul with dread or unthinkable disaster.

As rapidly as his enemies found a new weapon he matched the invention with a similar one of his own or a better one. David's sling was the answer to the challenge of the club of the giant of Gath. The blunderbuss was the answer to the cross-bow, even as the Arabalest had overmatched the challenge of the Longbow. As time went on the long-barrelled rifle answered the blunderbuss, the highpower magazine rifle answered the muzzle loader and the machine gun took up the challenge of the magazine rifle.

Cannon that carries a high explosive shell 75 miles replied to the crude ordnance that was the last word in the gunnery of the Spanish-American war. Nitroglycerin and T. N. T. displaced gunpowder. The superdreadnaught of steel crowded from the sea the wooden frigate. Steadily warfare became more perilous, more unendurable, more impressive to imagination, but until the past few years, whatever its killing improvements, the sight and use of man-killing tools did not inspire us with horror.

Old-fashioned war weapons could be felt and seen and heard. They did not drop death upon us from four miles overhead or steal upon us to rob us of life while we slept. They did not freight the wind with danger. When they struck us or burst near us, that was the end of the blow or of the explosion.

They did not turn corners to search us out with lung-searing poison or sink treacherously into holes and bide their time for days and weeks to set fire to our lungs or blind us. They were not invisible, inaudible. They were of the known world, changed a good deal from what our great-grandfathers and their great-grandfathers knew, but still recognizable as the traditional tools of war.

Then the creative chemist, taking a big step forward and making more intelligent use of atomic force, introduced into warfare weapons that could not be seen or heard, that impressed ordinary imagination as things not of this earth at all but of the pit itself.

He showed armies how to use poison gas to kill each other and more often to blind or burn or stupefy each other. He introduced poison into the winds of the heavens and cunningly employed the winds to sweep destruction across wide areas. This new method of making war was the biggest jar ever suffered by our tradition-clinging minds. It was a method which struck at the mind in assaulting the body. Terror unfathomable was locked in it.

Inheritors of subconscious fears 200 centuries old, curious weaknesses of the spirit that 200 centuries have not been able altogether to eradicate. Fear of the dark, fear of the unknown, man stood appalled by this new weapon which worked frightful casualties without betraying itself by form or shape or color, without making a sound personal to itself.

It made him think of the future when the inept, unhappy gas contrivances would be so perfected, simplified, concentrated and increased in number and in destructive power, as to make the gas weapons of the Great War as clumsy by comparison as were the smooth-bore rifles of the Revolutionary War compared with the latest Thompson gun.

These things hit at the heart of imagination, surveying what creative chemistry has already done in war in its first few experimental steps. We stand back impressed as never before in the whole history of war tools. We are bound by sheer intelligence to comprehend that chemical science "has only begun to fight." It has learned how to utilize, not very skillfully, a few gasses. It has not done anything beyond small scale experimenting with radio active forces. But the lessons of the Great War were a tremendous impulse to the research chemist.

The creative chemist is searching out among rare elements, such as radium, arguments against warfare that can no more be refuted than pigmy man can oppose the tornado or the earthquake or contend with Vesuvius. The strange stuff that illuminates the dials of our watches may be the very medium that will eventually produce the resistless force that will make fighting intolerable.

Chemists are seeking through forces as yet imperfectly comprehended to turn man toward sanity. They are aiming at his imagination. Who will dare say they are pursuing a fruitless quest after the experience of the Great War which began as a war of great steel projectiles and ended as a war of invisible energy.

Hard headed military men, usually slow to convince that weapons other than the traditional arms of their service must be learned and relied upon, join nowadays with chemists in an appeal to the public understanding which is little short of the striking appeal made by the imaginative story of Mr. Wells, for they realize that chemistry is merely on the brink of great things, and none see so clearly as they that chemistry aims to abolish war by making it desperately perilous to great nations as well as small, to governments as well as to the led peoples; to vainglorious politicians as well as to the obedient servants in uniform.

Gentlemen, I have tried to tell you that I believe that the Perkin discoveries of 1856 and their profane application in the hands of the Germans, precipitated the trend of events which spelled our late great disaster, and the disaster will recur again in some other form, unless we learn and preach the great lesson to be learned therefrom.

There is one incident which to my mind illustrates every phase of the disconnected thought which I have so poorly expressed to you. In 1906, Sir William Henry Perkin, after England had knighted him for the discovery, the application of which she had so sadly neglected and out of which her enemy was even then forging the weapons of her attempted destruction, came to this country to be present at our celebration of the fiftieth anniversary of his discovery. Medals, banquets, and honorary degrees were presented to him, and in response he said: "You have been so good to honor me by having this jubilee in remembrance of the part I have taken in connection with this coal-tar industry, and while I am thankful that I had to do with its foundation and early development, yet I feel that the part I have taken is indeed small when compared with the labors of the army of scientific men and others, both inside and outside the color works, who have advanced it to the present condition.

"However, it is very gratifying to me to receive all the general and kindly expressions of feeling you are manifesting, and I thank you very heartily. But, what have I that I have not received? It is not, therefore, for me to boast. I can only say in reference to the successes that have attended my efforts: 'Not unto me, O Lord, not unto me, but unto Thy great name be all the praise.'"

On that occasion—the shame of it as we look back on it now—the representative of the development of America's grasp of this discovery who addressed Dr. Perkin and presented the testimonials which brought forth the answer I have quoted, was Dr. Hugo Schweitzer, a chemist, scientist and researcher, a German spy, secret service number 963,192,637, head of the German Secret Service in America, head of the system by which every effort to develop the organic chemical industry in this country was crushed out, head of the system of dye salesmen by which every fact and circumstance of the four million dollars a year American dependent industries was reported to Berlin, carded and charted there, taken into the great industrial establishment at Grosser Lichterfeld, outside of Berlin, and there placed at the disposal of competing German industry; the inventor of the idea of the purchase of the New York *Evening Mail* to corrupt our information; the inventor of the idea of the German Publication Society, formed to publish, for our delectation, the literature of German Kultur; head of the Chemical Exchange, by which all available phenol supply in America was turned away or made inaccessible to the Allies.

Dr. Albert, in praising him, said: "The breadth of high-mindedness with which you at that time (meaning the beginning of the war) immediately entered into the plan, has borne fruit as follows: One and a half million pounds of carbolic acid have been kept from the Allies. Out of this one and a half million pounds of carbolic acid, four and one-half million pounds of picric acid can be produced.

"This tremendous quantity of explosive stuffs has been withheld from the Allies by your contract. In order to give one an idea of this enormous quantity, the following figures are of interest: Four million five hundred thousand pounds equals two thousand two hundred and fifty tons of explosives. A railroad freight car is loaded with twenty tons of explosives, the two thousand two hundred and fifty tons would, therefore, fill one hundred and twelve railway cars. A freight train with explosives consists chiefly of forty freight cars, so that the four million five hundred thousand pounds of explosives would fill three railroad trains with forty cars each.

"Now one should picture to himself what a military coup would be accomplished by an army leader if he should succeed in destroying three railroad trains of forty cars, containing four and a half million pounds of explosives. Of still greater and more beneficial effect is the support which you have afforded to the purchase of bromine. We have a well-founded hope that we shall be in a position to buy up the total production of the country.

"Bromine, together with chloral, is used in making nitric gases, which are of such great importance in trench warfare. Without bromine these nitric gases are of slight effect; in connection with bromine, they are of terrible effect. Bromine is produced only in the United States and Germany."

This in the neutral country of the United States might well have cost the war and civilization. Thank God, Perkin died before he could see what civilization had done with his discovery.

Gentlemen, personal responsibility is a thing that cannot be escaped. Thinking so we may go to our graves, but there will come forth from the unforeseeable transmutations of destiny or from the Divine will, some reaction of our unconsidered acts or of our deliberate evasion of the moral law that may cause misery to a multitude.

Two years ago there leaned against a lamppost on the Bowery a stranger, with only his landlady's borrowed quarter in his pocket, only hate in his heart and wrong thinking in his head. Today, this man, Trotzky, controls the destinies and happiness of three hundred millions of Russian men, women and children. He, the mouthpiece of false ideas, seized upon the ignorant and desperate masses in the hour of their agony, and has proved their destruction.

Contrast his unwholesome and blasphemous career with that of Joan of Arc, who has always seemed so human, so natural, so close to all of us. Her sweet, simple girlish figure, sublime in her faith, sustained in her virtue and mighty in the power of her dominant will and the justice of her cause. She has been with us now for hundreds of years and never more so than during this war when she staunched the heart of France and led her brave as of old. As it is with these two individuals of humble origin, so it is with the richest.

Contrast the Emperor of Germany, in whom self-love and ambition had crushed out all spirituality, leading his people and forcing them on in the conquest which has brought such unspeakable misery and suffering to untold millions of men, women and children.

Contrast him, I say, with that magnificent figure, Cardinal Mercier, that soul of resistance to injustice and falsehood, whose memory constitutes a solace, stored up for the distressed people of all future times.

As it is with the lowly peasant man or woman, as it is with the emperor on his throne, or a prince of the church, so it is with the scientist or the researcher. Contrast the influences intended by Perkin, who at the end of his life received his richly earned honors with bowed head and in humble voice, "What have I that I have not received? Not unto me, O Lord, not unto me, but unto Thy great name be all the praise."

Contrast him, I say, with Schweitzer, the scientist and researcher, representative of the profane application of his science in peace and war, and in the shadow of that contrast, and in the humility and in the shame which we should feel, let us look forward to the day when the English and American chemists can meet again, with the evidence about us of our atonement for our neglect, evidence of permanent peace in all the world, of a higher and more equal standard of living for all our peoples and of a great marching forward in our battle against disease. Until that day, let no man write his epitaph.

CHARLES E. HUGHES

THE PATHWAY OF PEACE

ADDRESS DELIVERED BEFORE THE CANADIAN BAR ASSOCIA-
TION, MONTREAL, CANADA, SEPTEMBER 4, 1923

[Charles Evans Hughes was born in Glens Falls, New York, on
April 11, 1862. He attended Colgate University from 1876 to 1878,
was graduated from Brown University in 1881, and from Columbia
University Law School in 1884. He practiced law in New York City
from 1884 to 1891, was Professor of Law in the Cornell Law School
from 1891 to 1893, and then returned to New York City, where except
while in the service of the public he has since maintained an office.
He was President of the American Bar Association from 1924 to 1925,
and is an Honorary Bencher of the Middle Temple, London. He was
Governor of New York state from 1907 to 1910; Associate Justice of
the United States Supreme Court from 1910 to 1916; was the unsuccessful Republican candidate for the Presidency of the United States
in November, 1916; was United States Secretary of State from 1921
to 1925; has been a member of the Permanent Court of Arbitration
at The Hague since September 30, 1926; was Chairman of the United
States Delegation to the Sixth Pan-American Conference at Havana,
Cuba, in 1928; and in 1929 was elected a member of the Permanent
Court of International Justice at The Hague.

The speech printed below was delivered while he was Secretary of
State.]

"War," said Sir Henry Maine, "appears to be as old as mankind, but peace is a modern invention." It is hardly that; it
would seem to be an occasional experience, rather than an
achievement. To one who reviews the history of strife from
"the universal belligerency of primitive mankind," peace appears merely as the lull between inevitable storms always gathering in some quarter with the fateful recurrence of the operations of nature. Nineteen centuries of Christian faith, with its
evangel of peace on earth and good will to men, with its sweet
reasonableness and constant appeals through myriad activities
to man's highest hopes, have erected no effective barrier to
war. It maintains hospitals, it cares for the wounded and
soothes the dying; it shines resplendent in countless lives of supreme self-sacrifice; but it leaves untouched the fields of car-

nage and unimpaired the justification of noble and generous spirits in the use of the most ruthless instrumentalities of destruction. The economic satisfactions proffered by an advancing civilization and dependent upon peace, the enticements of soft living, the hopes of families, the tenderest attachments are all futile to oppose the summons to arms. The resources of science, all inventive skill, the long discipline of the organization of trade and industry, everything that can be commanded in thought and action, in accumulated stores and capacity of production, are under pledge to the god of war.

We may gain something in our quest for peace if we recognize at once that war is not an abnormality. In the truest sense, it is not the mere play of brute force. It is the expression of the insistent human will, inflexible in its purpose. The culture of civilization has strengthened, not enfeebled it. It is the old human spirit with the latest equipment. As Winston Churchill has said of the "valiant spirit of man in the late war": "Son of the Stone Age, vanquisher of nature with all her trials and monsters, he met the awful and self-inflicted agony with new reserves of fortitude. * * * His nervous system was found in the twentieth century capable of enduring physical and moral stresses before which the simpler natures of primeval times would have collapsed. Again and again to the hideous bombardment, again and again from the hospital to the front, again and again to the hungry submarines, he strode unflinching. And withal, as an individual, preserved through these torments the glories of a reasonable and compassionate mind." It was with this equipment, spiritual as well as material, at a time when peace was lavishly bestowing the choicest rewards of human effort, that the nations that had most to lose plunged into the most ruinous and horrible conflict known to history.

When we consider that the inability to maintain a just peace attests the failure of civilization itself, we may be less confident of the success of any artificial contrivances to prevent war. We must recognize that we are dealing with the very woof and warp of human nature. The war to end war has left its curse of hate, its lasting injuries, its breeding grounds of strife, and to secure an abiding peace appears to be more difficult than ever. There is no advantage in shutting our eyes to the facts;

nor should we turn in disgust of panaceas to the counsel of despair. The pathway of peace is the longest and most beset with obstacles the human race has to tread; the goal may be distant, but we must press on.

It is not surprising that many should be captivated by the proposal, with its delusive simplicity and adequacy, for the outlawry of war. War should be made a crime, and those who instigate it should be punished as criminals. The suggestion, however futile in itself, has at least the merit of bringing us to the core of the problem. Even among its sponsors appear at once the qualifications which reflect the old distinction, so elaborately argued by Grotius, between just and unjust wars. "The grounds of war," said he, "are as numerous as those of judicial actions. For where the power of law ceases, there war begins." He found the justifiable causes generally assigned for war to be three—defense, indemnity, and punishment. War is self-help, and the right to make war has been recognized as the corollary of independence, the permitted means by which injured nations protect their territory and maintain their rights. International law leaves aggrieved states who cannot obtain redress for their wrongs by peaceful means to exact it by force. If war is outlawed, other means of redress of injuries must be provided. Moreover, few, if any, intend to outlaw self-defense, a right still accorded to individuals under all systems of law. To meet this difficulty, the usual formula is limited to wars of aggression. But justification for war, as recently demonstrated, is ready at hand for those who desire to make war, and there is rarely a case of admitted aggression, or where on each side the cause is not believed to be just by the peoples who support the war.

There is a further difficulty that lies deeper. There is no law-giver for independent states. There is no legislature to impose its will by majority vote, no executive to give effect even to accepted rules. The outlawry of war necessarily implies a self-imposed restraint, and free peoples, jealous of their national safety, of their freedom of opportunity, of the rights and privileges they deem essential to their well-being, will not forego the only sanction at their command in extreme exigencies. The restraints they may be willing to place upon themselves will always be subject to such conditions as will leave them able to afford self-protection by force, and in this freedom there is abundant room for strife sought to be justified by deep-seated convictions of national interests, by long-standing grievances, by the apprehension of aggression to be forestalled. The outlawry of war, by appropriate rule of law making war a crime, requires the common accord needed to establish and maintain a rule of international law, the common consent to abandon war; and the suggested remedy thus implies a state of mind in which no cure is needed. As the restraint is self-imposed, it will prove to be of avail only while there is a will to peace.

It is this difficulty which constantly suggests recourse to force to maintain peace. Peoples who would engage in war, it is said, must be compelled to be peaceful; there should be an international force adequate to prevent aggression and to redress wrongs. The analogy of domestic peace is pressed; the force of the state—that is, of all the people—maintains the authority of the municipal law and compels public order. The analogy has held good in the case of great empires and within the range of their imperial power. The earliest empires, established through conquest and the greed of dominion, doubtless diminished wars among the subject peoples while the imperial authority continued, and the centuries of the *pax Romana* were made possible by the unchallengeable sway of Rome. It is unfortunately true that it is self-determination which makes for war and places obstacles in the way of all plans for keeping the peace. Thirty-five years ago the most distinguished of publicists found some promise of peace in the alliance of the three emperors and in the consequent isolation and agreement for peaceful adjustment of a limited group of questions which otherwise might lead to conflict. But time has shown how illusory are alliances of great powers so far as the maintenance of peace is concerned.

In considering the use of international force to secure peace, we are again brought to the fundamental necessity of common accord. If the feasibility of such a force be conceded for the purpose of maintaining adjudications of legal right, this is only because such an adjudication would proceed upon principles commonly accepted, and thus forming part of international law, and upon the common agreement to respect the decision of an impartial tribunal in the application of such principles. This is a limited field where force is rarely needed and where the sanctions of public opinion and the demands of national honor are generally quite sufficient to bring about acquiescence in judicial awards. But in the field of conflicting national policies, and what are deemed to be essential interests, when the smoldering fires of old grievances have been fanned into a flame by a passionate sense of immediate injury, or the imagination of peoples is dominated by apprehension of present danger to national safety, or by what is believed to be an assault upon national honor, what force is to control the outbreak? Great powers agreeing among themselves may indeed hold small powers in check. But who will hold great powers in check when great powers disagree? The trust in force must in truth be trust in common agreement behind the force. And we are thus brought back to the sentiment of peoples, to the common accord which makes peace possible. The application of force when there is disagreement means war, not peace; and then the basis of confidence, if found at all, is merely in the disparity of arms.

All contrivances for maintaining peace by economic pressure, as well as by military force, depend upon the sentiment which will apply the pressure and direct the force when the test comes. Such arrangements are likely to fail when they are most needed, because national interests are diverse and unanimity of action under stress of crises involving conflicts of opinion is well-nigh impossible. The independence and equality of states is the postulate of international relations. There is no path to peace except as the will of peoples may open it. The way to peace is through agreement, not through force. The question then is not of any ambitious general scheme to prevent war, but simply of the constant effort, which is the highest task of statesmanship in relation to every possible cause of strife, to diminish among peoples the disposition to resort to force and to find a just and reasonable basis for accord. If the energy, ability, and sagacity equal to that now devoted to preparation for war could be concentrated upon such efforts aided by the urgent demands of intelligent public opinion, addressed not to impossibilities but to the removal or adjustment of actual differences, we should make sure approach to our goal.

Over against the arbitrament of war we put the reign of law. But the reign of law is limited by the content of the law and by the processes of its development. International law consists of those principles and rules of conduct which civilized states regard as obligatory upon them, and hence are generally observed in their relations with each other. They are deduced by reason and exemplified by practice, and, resting on general consent, can be modified or added to only by consent. Lord Mansfield described the law of nations as "founded upon justice, equity, convenience, the reason of the thing, and confirmed by long usage." Lacking in definite sanction other than public opinion, it is in constant danger of being supplanted by considerations of expediency whenever the exigency is so severe, or the immediate advantages so great, or opinion so divided, as to warrant the risk. There was abundant illustration of this in the recent war, which began in "repudiation of every element of fundamental right upon which the law of nations rests" and was prosecuted with but slight regard to any obligatory principle which was thought to stand in the way of success. If we are to live in a world of order and of peace the foundations of international law must be secured, its postulates must be reasserted, and there must be expert attention to its development in dealing with the unsettled questions of a legal nature which have arisen in international intercourse.

It has been said that if the founders of international law did not create a sanction, they did create a law-abiding sentiment. This is in truth the most important sanction, and to-day there is need that this law-abiding sentiment should be re-created and that the tendency, increased by nine years of war and the confusion and unrest following war, to rely on force should be checked. It is not that the field of law is broad; it is necessarily a narrow one, limited, as has been said, to those principles and rules of general application which have found general acceptance. But the spirit which maintains the law within that field, which recognizes its restraints although self-imposed, which safeguards the independence, the equality, and the proper jurisdiction and privileges of the members of the family of na-

tions and assures the sanctity of international engagements—
this upholding of correlative rights and obligations—is of vital
importance not simply with respect to these rights and obligations in themselves but in producing the will to peace. However narrow may be the field in which the principles of law obtain, there will be no peace in the world if the spirit of men
permit these principles to be trampled upon as self-interest may
prompt.

It is, therefore, most desirable that all discussion of international relations should not revolve about questions of policy
and expediency, however important these may be, but that
along with this necessary discussion there should be the determination to re-establish the law, to quicken the sense of the obligation of states under the law. As soon as possible the codification of international law should be undertaken, not merely
to give formal definiteness to accepted principles, but to height-
en the respect for these postulates and rules by fresh discussion
and restatement. And with this enterprise, attention should be
given to the resolution of all the manifold uncertainties and di-
versities of opinion as to matters which properly belong within
the domain of law, and to the provision of new rules needed to
meet new situations. It would be difficult to conceive a process
requiring more deliberation and patience. For at every step the
general consent of nations must be had, and at every step, except in the simplest matters, the opposing policy and objections
of some nation will be encountered. The difficulty must be met
by conference, and by conferences which have the sole object
of promoting the codification and development of law. It must
be met by the aroused and insistent purpose of the members of
the bar, who by their unremitting and organized endeavor may
produce among their peoples the profound conviction that there
will be no continuing peace unless conscience and a dominant
sense of justice demand and insure the supremacy of law.

As legal principles and rules are supported by general acceptance, we may look with confidence for the general support
of opinion in their application and vindication through impartial tribunals. The difficulty here is not the acceptance of the
theory of judicial settlement, but in establishing entire confidence in the impartiality of tribunals and their freedom from

political influence. It must also be recognized that questions arise which, although requiring for their solution the application of principles of law or the interpretation of treaties, touch so closely the vital interests or the pride and honor of states that they are unwilling to allow the settlement to pass into other hands. And beyond all questions of law there lie the most difficult situations, where there are no determining principles, where national policies and ambitions conflict, where nations seek expansion and opportunities of trade by spheres of political and economic influence among weaker peoples, where rivalries are embittered by mutual distrust and ever-present fear, where intrigue is the busy servant of the lust of power, where compelled adjustments have left deep wounds and a passionate desire for a redress of injuries inflicted by force and sought to be redressed by force. As against these causes of strife, creating the disposition to look for pretexts for the use of force, efforts to maintain a permanent peace have thus far proved to be futile. Plans for commissions of inquiry, for periods of cooling off, for the use of good offices, are all important and may be efficacious to a gratifying extent. But these measures deal with cases already aggravated, and it may well be doubted whether in grave crises they would avail. Great powers, well armed and having a vivid sense of opportunity, supported by popular clamor for the vindication of national interests, are disposed to seize what they believe to be within their grasp. Resistance by force means war. Fear of opposing force may stay the hand, but this does not mean peace—rather, renewed preparation and a waiting for the day. There is only one way to make peace secure and that is the difficult but necessary effort to translate particular controversies into voluntary reasonable agreements. To this purpose, of a definite, concrete sort, rather than to fanciful programs, the intelligence of peoples should be devoted.

We have to take account of both the advantages and disadvantages of democratization. It is generally thought that democracies are disposed to peace, but this is yet to be demonstrated where there is deep feeling and a national sense of injury. Great wars, involving vast populations, cannot be fought without public support, but the most serious causes of war are precisely those which carry popular appeal. The peoples of the warring nations were never so united as during the last war, and this was equally true of both sides. A sense of injury is easily created and confused with the sense of justice. A despot may be as indisposed to war as any people, and democracies never lack leaders to inflame popular passion. While we should expect peoples to be slow to war in minor exigencies, the test comes when national sentiment is deeply aggrieved.

Apart from this, it is necessary to reckon with the special difficulties inherent in the democratic organization of government with respect to the endeavor to maintain peace by concluding international agreements which end controversies closely affecting national interests. There are, indeed, governments with an essentially democratic basis where the executive power is still able to conclude many important international agreements without reference to the legislature; but this is due to the persistence of special traditions. Usually in democracies there is a final or co-ordinate authority which rests with the parliament or legislature. The negotiations of so-called plenipotentiaries, the engagements of foreign offices, the conclusions of conferees, are thus merely preliminary. The more important the agreements, as insuring peace by settling bitter disputes, the more certain it is that they will involve mutual concessions. Thus in each country it is likely to be insisted that the other has gained at its expense, and this gives exceptional opportunity to critics who assume the most extreme positions on patriotic grounds. In the case of the Webster-Ashburton treaty, Daniel Webster was accused of taking upon himself to act for the British envoy and of making twelve important sacrifices of the interests of his country, while Lord Palmerston asserted that the treaty was a capitulation, the result of the incompetence and weakness of Lord Ashburton. Since the recent Washington conference those who are dissatisfied with the naval treaty in Great Britain, Japan, and the United States have sought to make it appear in each of these countries that its particular interests were sacrificed to the others; of course these critics cannot all be right, and I am happy to say that the manifest result of their conflicting contentions is to put even in a clearer light the essential fairness of the arrangement.

Aside from honest criticism, modern negotiations between democracies furnish rare opportunities for the ready tongues of demagogues. There are today serious questions between peoples which ought to be taken up and settled in order to heal festering sores. But those in charge of foreign affairs do not dare to undertake to negotiate agreements because they know that in the presence of attack inspired by political or partisan motives the necessary adjustment could not receive approval of the legislative branch and would evoke such an acrimonious controversy on both sides that matters would be made worse instead of better. The discussion of international agreements naturally and properly engages the attention of the public press, but that also not only gives opportunity for reasonable criticism, but for the pseudopatriots to seize a point of vantage against the government they desire to attack. Conferences are often treated as though they provided an actual solution of all difficulties, but for most countries they accomplish nothing unless the conclusions are ratified by a popular assembly. Democracies may be loath to go to war, but they are extremely difficult agencies of international compromises in the interest of peace.

In this task of promoting peaceful settlements diplomacy is indispensable. Conferences are simply an extension of its method where a number of states are parties to the negotiations. No one can fail to realize the importance of having the public deeply interested and well informed upon policies, interests, and undertakings in order to maintain a check upon improper aims and a wholesome attitude toward foreign relations, but there is a necessary distinction to be observed with respect to the conduct of negotiations. While intrigues and secret understandings, breeding suspicion and leading to counter intrigues and secret arrangements, are the appropriate instruments of the injurious rivalries and ambitious schemings which make for war, premature publicity is a serious handicap to the honorable negotiations which seek to end dangerous disputes. Concessions will not be made and fair compromises are rendered almost impossible in the presence of the keen, efficient, and indefatigable news gatherers who naturally regard it as a primary obligation to let nothing escape their ken or their pen. It is inevitable that fragments of information should be picked up, that the pieces of the puzzle should be inaccurately joined, and that the interests of peaceful adjustments should be in constant danger of being sacrificed to "scoops."

It is suggested that all would be easy if negotiators would simply tell the public everything that they are doing. But the trouble is that in every negotiation, as all business men know, there are preliminary positions to be taken, tentative plans to be discussed, arguments to be presented and demolished and nothing can be accomplished if every suggestion, every advance and every retreat must be publicly made. Negotiators under such restriction would inevitably take their positions not to promote a settlement, but to win public approval by the firmness and vigor of their partisanship. Eager as democracies may be for peace in the abstract, it is easy to excite a public clamor for "no compromise" in the concrete. But the point is not that the negotiators of democratic governments will be disposed to conduct their proceedings in public. The difficulty is that in the midst of their work when patience and reticence, and an equable public temper are needed, misleading statements, misapprehensions and unfounded rumors are likely to become current and perhaps also make necessary, in order to avoid greater difficulties, disclosures which it would be in the interest of successful prosecution of the negotiations to withhold for the time being. Open diplomacy is openness of results; the absence of secret agreements and understandings, not the immediate publication of all intermediate steps. When we consider the self-imposed restraints that are necessary in the interest of peace, is it too much to hope that to a much greater degree there will be embraced in these, as a matter of public interest, the self-imposed restraint upon publicity before disclosures in relation to negotiations are properly authorized? If we are to have peace, we must develop a public sentiment which will aid in conserving the opportunities to work for peace by facilitating the practical arrangements that make for the adjustments of peace.

Perhaps the most troublesome sources of irritation are to be found in the subjects which states properly decline to regard as international in the legal sense. Every state, jealous of its sovereign rights, refuses to permit the intrusion of other nations into its domestic concerns. In every plan for the arbitration of international controversies, domestic questions are perforce excluded. But in these days of intimate relations, of economic stress, and of intense desire to protect national interests and advance national opportunity, the treatment of questions which from a legal standpoint are domestic often seriously affects international relations. The principle, each nation for itself to the full extent of its power, is the principle of war, not of peace. Let it be recognized that force is the inevitable resort of unrestrained selfishness; that peace is to be reconciled with national aims only as an enlightened self-interest permits the reasonable restraint that is consistent with the fair opportunity of others—in a world where we must either fight or "live and let live" in a decent regard for the welfare of others as well as our own.

But how are we to take proper cognizance of the just interests of other states in the turmoil of politics and amid the contests of local ambitions appealing exclusively to some supposed immediate national interest? No state could be asked, or for a moment would consider, submitting its treatment of domestic interests to any sort of international arbitrament. It will decide for itself the questions within its own jurisdiction; that is the essence of sovereignty. But the case is not hopeless. What could be regarded as more essentially a matter of its own concern than the provision a state should make for its own defense, the arms it should provide, the number and armament of its battleships. Yet we have recently seen the great naval powers, obedient at last to the desire to end a ruinous competitive struggle in arms, voluntarily agree to reduce their fighting ships to agreed proportions. I believe that we shall be able at no distant day to keep within reasonable limits some of our pressing economic rivalries by fair international agreements in which the self-interest of rivals will submit to mutual restrictions in the furtherance of friendly accord.

All things are possible if nations are willing to be just to each other. The fact that in the class of matters now under consideration there may be no possibility of arbitrament does not imply that we do not have any means at hand which are compatible with the recognition of sovereign rights. We have not only the possibilities of negotiating international agreements, but also of advising the legislatures of states as to the interests of other states affected by national legislation. A joint commission is a familiar agency which is distinct from that of arbitration for the reason that the states concerned in their creation have each an equal representation. In relation to domestic questions which have an international bearing, it would be quite possible to make more frequent use of this method, not to decide but to inform, not to arbitrate but to investigate, to find the facts and to report to the governments of the states represented the effect of measures and where injury would lie. We have at this time, under our treaty of 1909 relating to boundary waters and questions arising along the boundary between Canada and the United States, an International Joint Commission with powers of investigation and report within the scope of the treaty.

While I do not undertake to speak officially upon this subject, I may take the liberty of stating as my personal view that we should do much to foster our friendly relations and to remove sources of misunderstanding and possible irritation, if we were to have a permanent body of our most distinguished citizens acting as a commission, with equal representation of both the United States and Canada, to which automatically there would be referred, for examination and report as to the facts, questions arising as to the bearing of action by either government upon the interests of the other, to the end that each reasonably protecting its own interests would be so advised that it would avoid action inflicting unnecessary injury upon its neighbor. We rejoice in our long friendship and in permanent peace, and it would be a short-sighted view that either of us has any real interest which is to be promoted without regard to the well-being of the other and the considerate treatment which conditions good will. I am saying this personal word as much to the people of the United States as to the people of Canada; it breathes neither complaint nor criticism, but a keen desire for the co-operation of the closest friends, each secure in independence and in the assurance of amity.

I recur to the main point, that the only real progress to abiding peace is found in the friendly disposition of peoples and that facilities for maintaining peace are useful only to the extent that this friendly disposition exists and finds expression. The means of waging war in its most horrible form are now apparently within the reach of all and are more easily contrived and concealed than ever. War is not only possible, but probable, where mistrust and hatred and desire for revenge are the dominant motives. Our first duty is at home with our own opinion, by education and unceasing effort to bring to naught the mischievous exhortations of chauvinists; our next is to aid in every practicable way in promoting a better feeling among other peoples, the healing of wounds, and the just settlement of differences.

Our own relations furnish the happiest illustration and strengthen our faith. It is not that we began in friendship or had the advantage of a tradition of brotherly love. Quite the contrary. Our 100 years and more of peace were preceded by long periods of bitterness and of savage strife; the new world received as an unfortunate heritage the warring ambitions of the old. It is not that since the close of that era we have been without serious controversies. The peace of Ghent left us many questions of difficulty which apparently defied amicable settlement. But we now recall the serious disputes of the nineteenth century with mutual gratification at the conquests of peace and the arduous achievements of self-restraint. It is not that we have been lacking in national pride, in courage, or martial spirit. The long record of fortitude, of heroism, and military ardor and capacity in the Great War has no more inspiring chapter than that written by the sons of Canada who with eager swiftness rushed to the support of the motherland in the struggle to maintain the very essentials of liberty, and to the final success of that struggle the Dominion pledged all her resources of material and spiritual power. It was the privilege of our own people in that war, convinced of the vital character of the issue, to take our place at your side, and the friendship which had grown out of the unlikely soil, sown with the seeds of early differences, came to glorious fruition in the common sacrifices on the fields of France. It is pleasant to recall that it was Alexander Hamilton, the apostle both of national strength and of international peace, who first suggested, in his recommendation to President Washington in 1794, the limitation of armament on the Great

Lakes, and our undefended line of over 5,000 miles is at once a memorial and a prophecy—a memorial of the past triumphs of reasonableness and a prophecy that all future problems will be solved without breach of amity.

The reason for this happy condition points to the solution the world needs. We have formed the habit of peace; we think in terms of peace. Differences arise, but our confidence in each other's sense of justice and peaceful intent remains unshaken and dominates our purposes and plans. The only pathway of peace is that in which our peoples are walking together. In the depth of our grief at the loss of the great leader, whose every thought, whose constant endeavor, were directed to the establishment of peace, it is a precious memory that almost his last words were spoken on the soil of your country testifying to our abiding friendship, our mutual interests, our common aims. Let these words of the late President ever remain as the expression and assurance of abiding peace: "Our protection is in our fraternity, our armor is our faith; the tie that binds more firmly year by year is ever-increasing acquaintance and comradeship through interchange of citizens; and the compact is not of perishable parchment, but of fair and honorable dealing which, God grant, shall continue for all time."

DAVID HUNTER MILLER
WOODROW WILSON

MEMORIAL ADDRESS DELIVERED IN THE MADISON AVENUE
PRESBYTERIAN CHURCH, NEW YORK CITY,
FEBRUARY 10, 1924

[David Hunter Miller was born in New York City on January 2, 1875. He served as Lieutenant in the Spanish-American War, attended the New York Law School from which he was graduated in 1910, was admitted to the bar in 1911, and has since practiced law in New York City. In June, 1917, he was appointed Special Assistant in the Department of State, Washington, D. C., and subsequently became a member of the Inquiry headed by Colonel House to prepare data for the Paris Peace Conference. In October, 1918, he became legal adviser to the Mission of Colonel House to Paris, and later was legal adviser to the American Commission to Negotiate Peace. With Sir Cecil Hurst, he drew up the first draft of the Covenant of the League of Nations. In 1921 he was counsel to the German Government on the Upper Silesian question before the League of Nations. He is the author of many books and articles on international affairs. The speech printed below was delivered seven days after the death of President Wilson.]

It is said in the Scripture, "Blessed are the peacemakers; for they shall be called the children of God."

Those were the words that came to my soul when I was asked to speak here on this Sabbath in memory of Woodrow Wilson; for of all the ages, he was foremost among those whom Jesus blessed, he was verily a child of God.

For a moment, but only for a moment, let us think of the man himself, of the human side of him. Others, many others, could here speak better and more worthily than I; for my knowledge of Woodrow Wilson rests not on long intimacy of personal friendship, not on decades of association, but rather on that revelation which comes during labors together in a common cause, that sensing of verities at crucial moments, when the inner soul of a man is bright as day to see.

If in a phrase I had to sum up that personal side, I should think of him as I knew him in Paris, as a Christian gentleman.

At the height of his triumphs, when the cheers of the scores of thousands in the streets were echoed by admiring millions the world over, he issued his orders in the form of requests; he gave his thanks for services that were his due; and when his subordinates came to see him at his house, they had the precedence one shows to a guest.

Of course, you may say that these are little things, signs perhaps of nothing more than a kindly thoughtfulness of others even amidst the pressure of great duties; but I have mentioned one or two of these little things lest you might think that Woodrow Wilson sometimes forgot them; he never did.

But while these memories may mean something to me, there are others that will mean more to you; let us think of them a little.

The fame of this great man will rest primarily, I think, on his ideals; and foremost even among those, on his ideals of peace. For ideals are so much more powerful and even so much more real than realities themselves. Things as they ought to be are always more vital than things as they are. For things as they are together make up only this fleeting instant that we call the present as it is lost behind us; but things as they ought to be look forward to the eternal distances of God himself.

It is in the perspective of those distances that we must view the ideals of peace of Woodrow Wilson. Wonderful when we think of it. It was he who led this country into the greatest war of history. It was he who insisted on the use of every ounce of force, force to the utmost, righteous force, as he called it, to win that war. It was he who made a fact of one impossibility after another; the miracle of the draft, the miracle of the four million men, the miracle of the two millions in Europe, the miracle of thirty billions of money; and through it all and despite the incredible burden of it all, the supreme miracle of winning the war by the irresistible force of those war papers and speeches which were acclaimed by all humanity, even by millions of the hostile forces themselves; we saw it, we lived through it, we were part of it, and so we cannot even dream what a marvel it was.

And yet, despite all this and while doing the work of ten strong men, with the genius of a thousand, he was thinking

most of all of those ideals of peace. They were not put aside
to be brought out at a more convenient season; rather were
they kept burning in his soul. In the summer of 1918, while
the struggle was at its supreme crisis of terror, even then he
was planning his covenants of peace, he was taking counsel
with others, he was writing in its first form his greatest paper.

Woodrow Wilson, remaining steadfast and true to his ideals
through all the horror and hate of the conflict, is a sublime
figure.

Let me turn now for a moment to a darker picture. We
must remember with shame that when the Armistice let loose
the frightened dogs of envy and of malice, there were found
among Americans and in the American press those who urged
that Woodrow Wilson should abandon his ideals, break his
solemn word, betray the honor of his country and leave the
ruins of the war to smoulder in hate instead of building them
into a monument of peace. Of course, to him such words
meant nothing; but they were the aid to all who lacked his vision and the comfort of all who went about to do evil.

We must blush, too, to remember that during that year Woodrow Wilson shared the fate of other great Americans, in being
vilified and maligned by some of his own people. Some of
the things then printed and said by public men about Woodrow
Wilson and his work, bring to mind the bitter newspaper attacks on George Washington in 1794 and the venomous Civil
War pamphlets against Abraham Lincoln.

But, unswerved by calumny, Woodrow Wilson remained
steadfast to the end. When he was told in the summer of 1919,
as he started, worn out, on his last speaking trip, that it would
kill him, he answered, "Well, I am perfectly willing to die for
the League of Nations." He never wavered, never faltered.

No doubt, you have been told that in making the Peace Treaties at Paris he compromised with his principles. I assert with
every confidence of knowledge that he did not. Of course, he
agreed to things which others did not approve, but that was inevitable in any event. That is no test. The test of moral character in such a case is this—Does a man bargain away something
he himself thinks is vital? If not, he has to his own self been
true; and that Woodrow Wilson ever was.

As Americans we can mourn proudly for Woodrow Wilson. A great man, surely, more than a great man, I think; for I believe that history will write him down as the greatest of all. Perhaps it is too soon to know the final verdict, but at least we can say that of all he was certainly the most famous. We have had great leaders of our nation, but never before did we have a leader who was at the same time the leader of the world.

His speeches were read by scores of millions of people in almost every known language. In the remote fastnesses of Africa, surrounded by miles of desert, live the tribes of the Senussi. Their chief told a friend of mine that he had read all the works of Woodrow Wilson. In Paris, I saw the cheering thousands greet him with a delirium of welcome never given to any one else; and the posters which were put up in that capital on his arrival, acclaimed him, not only as the leader of this country, but of all countries.

Truly when Woodrow Wilson spoke, his voice was heard around the world.

Nothing like it was ever before known. There have been men whose teachings in the course of generations or perhaps of centuries have swayed as much of mankind as did Woodrow Wilson within two years; and there have been men who in a short time were supreme at home or in a limited field; but this man almost overnight became the master of the soul of the civilized world; and from that time in 1917 until the day when the shadow of the Angel of Death first fell athwart his path, he was the leader and the ruler of all living, able to change and changing with a word, the destinies of mankind.

We think of the power of a President of the United States as very great, and we know that in war time it is of necessity enormously increased; but even that authority was only a fraction of the dominion of Woodrow Wilson.

And the character of that authority, the moral leadership that was the vital part of it, has made its influence and its effects permanent. The principles of national freedom and of liberty that Woodrow Wilson laid down, are now written in the constitutions of many countries; they have become part of the public law of the world and, doubtless most important, they are guarded as precious treasures in the bosoms of millions of mankind.

Think, Americans, of the height to which Woodrow Wilson raised our country. First of all, he showed the world that this was the mightiest nation of the globe, that there was nothing that its strength might not achieve, no force that could prevail against it; and yet, with that giant's strength disclosed, America, under Woodrow Wilson, was not feared, but only loved. Our word was law, our fiat was supreme; it was accepted without question, but not because it was announced as the decree of a dictator, but because it was revered as righteous, it was known as fair, it was lauded as unselfish, a stream from the very fountain of divine justice.

Never has the flag of any nation been raised to such a peak of glory as was the flag of America by Woodrow Wilson.

And yet you hear some say that he failed—if such be failure, God grant me some small share of it as my success. Did he fail because he passed beyond before all that he dreamed and planned had come to pass? That is a fate common to us all; the supreme beauty of our task below is that it is always to be attempted, never to be finished, but only to be passed on to other workers, our successors in the unceasing and ever changing current of humanity.

It would ill become me, if in these few and feeble words of tribute, I said nothing of the League of Nations, that monument of Woodrow Wilson that will never die; for I sat at his hand while the Covenant was framed, I worked with him, I tried to help him; no memory in life or death could be as precious.

I saw him toil with all his wonderful vision, with all the energy of that marvelous intellect, with all the strength of that great mind, to make that document true and righteous; and I say to you that in that paper there is no thought unworthy, no word ignoble, no purpose selfish.

And when I say that that monument of Woodrow Wilson is imperishable, I leave aside those petty questions of form which have been so much debated by little minds. The Covenant is human; all things human must change and be made better; only the divine work is perfect; but the principles of the League of Nations, that conferences must take the place of war, that justice must prevail and not aggression, that law must rule and not mere might, are principles that will remain forever in the international structure, because they are divine principles of eternal truth.

But again some say that he failed, because, they say, there was a vote against that eternal charter of human peace, that sublime work of Woodrow Wilson, that Covenant of the League; well, this is no time for disputation, here is no place for argument or I might say something about that vote.

But there is a question that I want to put to you about it—a question I have never heard asked; and for such a question I know of no time more appropriate than this day, and I know of no place more appropriate than this house of God.

The question that I put to you is this—

How would Christ vote on the League of Nations?

I say to you that until that question is answered, and until it is answered rightly, we need not think of other things.

"If this counsel or this work be of men, it will come to naught; but if it be of God, ye cannot overthrow it; lest haply ye be found even to fight against God."

The noblest statesman known to history has gone to his rest. His life will be an eternal memory of honor to his country that he loved so well and served so truly, and his work will be an eternal benefit to humanity.

Woodrow Wilson was a friend of all the world; and those who knew him best loved him most.

EDWIN A. ALDERMAN

WOODROW WILSON

MEMORIAL ADDRESS DELIVERED BEFORE A JOINT SESSION
OF THE TWO HOUSES OF CONGRESS, DECEMBER 15, 1924

[Edwin Anderson Alderman was born in Wilmington, North Carolina, on May 15, 1861. He was graduated from the University of
North Carolina in 1882, and has received honorary degrees from eleven
institutions. He was Professor of History in the North Carolina State
Normal School in 1892; was Professor of Education in the University
of North Carolina from 1893 to 1896, and its President from 1896 to
1900; President of Tulane University, from 1900 to 1904; and since
June 14, 1904, has been President of the University of Virginia. He
is an effective public speaker and was invited by both Houses of
Congress to deliver the address printed below.]

In his oration in memory of the first Athenians who fell in the
Peloponnesian War, Pericles commended the fitness of the
Athenian public funeral, but doubted the wisdom of any speech,
declaring that where men's deeds have been great they should be
honored in deed only, and that the reputation of many should
never depend upon the judgment or want of it of one, and their
virtue exalted or not, as he spoke, well or ill. I can, in some
faint measure, comprehend what was passing in the mind of
the great Athenian as I stand here to-day, in this Chamber
which has often resounded with his own lucid eloquence, to
seek to make clear in brief speech the character and achievements of Woodrow Wilson, the twenty-eighth President of the
United States.

In the case of a statesman, all experience warns us not to
attempt to fix his final place in history until the generation that
knew him and loved him, or hated him, shall have passed away
and a new generation, to whom he was not a familiar figure,
shall have come upon the stage, capable of beholding him with
eyes undimmed by emotion and judging him with minds unclould-
ed by prejudice or by passion. Loyalty and duty and reverence
none the less urge us to set down, while memory is clear and
events are fresh, what we know of men upon whom their

fellow men placed great burdens of power, to whom whole races and nations turned in moments of peril and disaster, and upon whose decisions, from time to time, rested the courses of history. Woodrow Wilson was such a man; and, in such a spirit, I undertake to discover the sources of his power and to perceive the bases of his far-shining fame, more widespread about the earth in his lifetime than the fame of any of his predecessors in office, and more interwoven into the fabric of civilization than any of those who have gone before him, save Washington, the founder of the Republic, Jefferson, the fountain of its idealism, and Lincoln, the exemplar of its magnanimity and the preserver of its internal unity.

The presidential office constitutes one of the glories of the framers of our Government and the presidential succession a miracle of good fortune in the hazard of democratic politics and a constant tribute to the sober instincts of popular judgment. The makers of the Constitution apparently forgot their fear of tyranny when they created the Presidency and seemed to proceed on the principle that if you place immense authority in a man's hands you kill his greed for usurpation and awake in him a magic capacity and a solemn purpose to transform his weaknesses into strength and his unworthiness into worthiness.

Some American Presidents have been commonplace men, but none of them has ever betrayed his trust or stained his honor; and from George Washington to the present hour the line of American Presidents have surpassed in character, ability, and devotion any line of kings and prime ministers known to me in modern history. They have not always been scholars. Indeed, few of them have been scholars, but when chosen, and the method of their choice sometimes bewilders the reflective and grieves the judicious, they have dug out of their latent forces and brought to bear upon their awful tasks such common sense, strong wills, noble industry, uprightness of purpose, that the great office still wears a more than imperial quality to enrich the imagination and to enlist the faith of mankind.

It would have been wiser to intrust this task of interpretation to one closer to Woodrow Wilson when he was the head of the state and his will shaped the destinies of men. Such was not my privilege. My qualifications are of a simpler and a more unpretentious nature. I studied the shorter catechism, a drastic, bracing, moral tonic, with him in the Presbyterian Church of which his father, Joseph R. Wilson, was pastor, in the old city of Wilmington, N. C., my birthplace, where from time to time Thomas Woodrow Wilson would appear at home from college, to my younger eyes a tall, slender youth of curious homeliness, detachment, and distinction.

As a child sitting in the pew of my father, who was an officer in that church, and looking into the finely molded face of Joseph R. Wilson and listening to the words he spoke, I had my first perception that beauty and music and power to move even young hearts lay in the English tongue when fitly joined to substantial thought and serious eloquence; and he has remained to me, as he did to his famous son, through the discipline of a generation of sermons, a standard of good preaching to which it is a delight and a comfort now and again to repair. The world owes a great debt to Joseph R. Wilson; for, though the son studied under many masters, none influenced him so strongly as his father, who bred in him an impatience of dullness and diffuse thinking, a precise sense of word values, a scorn of priggishness and formal piety, the power to proceed straight to the core of a subject under discussion and to utter measured thoughts with a vigor and beauty that in later days and on a grander stage were destined to awaken the pride of his countrymen and to command the attention of the world.

I do the day's work at the University of Virginia, where Woodrow Wilson "learned the law and the reason thereof." It came to pass that we were associated in the task of training American youth, and I became his friend by reason of the ties that bind men together in such endeavor; and further, because I thought I saw in him, in a new era in the evolution of American democracy, a promise of liberal leadership and of sympathy that never slept for the disadvantaged men who bear the burdens of the world. The sturdiest romantic tradition of American public life has been the rise into power and fame of the youth who struggled up to his heights from humble and unlovely beginnings. The career of Woodrow Wilson is no part of such tradition, for his racial inheritances and cultural opportunities were about as strong and fine as an American youth can have. His forbears for eight generations belonged to the Scotch race, perhaps the most active of the intellectual aristocracies which govern the United States, modified in the direction of a kindling imagination and a quickened joy of life and battle by Celtic admixture and residence. His parents, his ancestors on both sides, and his associates on all sides were religious men and women of Presbyterian faith.

He was the son, as I have said, of a Presbyterian minister of such distinction that it was in his house that the Southern Presbyterian Church was organized when the Civil War came to rend even the religious life of the Nation. His mother was the daughter of a Presbyterian minister, in Carlisle, England. He married, in his young manhood, the daughter of a Presbyterian minister. His grandfather, Thomas Woodrow, for whom he was named, was a learned, doughty servant of God, and his uncle, James Woodrow, was a modern-minded Presbyterian minister, who, in his day, upheld stoutly against the allegation of heresy itself the banner of liberal thought and religious tolerance. His elementary and undergraduate education was under Presbyterian influences and in Presbyterian colleges—Davidson College, North Carolina, and Princeton, the college of New Jersey. Later, at the University of Virginia, in the study of law, and at Johns Hopkins University, in the study of politics and jurisprudence, he was to broaden his training and to establish a just claim as the most carefully educated man whom the people of this democracy, somewhat wary of learning and fearful lest intellectual subtlety dull the edge of common understanding, ever dared to place at the head of the Government.

Chester A. Arthur, Grover Cleveland, and Woodrow Wilson, alone, of our long presidential line, issued out of the preacher's home into public life. Cleveland and Wilson may be called the direct contribuions of the Presbyterian manse to the Nation's service; and it is not without significance that the only two great successes, since 1860, of the Democratic Party, in which they now rank as titular saints, were achieved under their leadership. They were quite dissimilar in background and qualities, as a curious fate which opposed them to each other, face to face, in dour antagonism in later life made very clear, but alike in the firmness of their wills, the fixity of their conclusions, and the sensitiveness of their consciences. Surely, the great religious faith that sent forth these two American Presidents is justified of its children.

Woodrow Wilson was born in Virginia in the year 1856, in the middle period of the nineteenth century, and, with the exception of his undergraduate years at Princeton, the first twenty-nine years of his life were passed in five Southern States, in the study of literature, history, and jurisprudence. He did not obtain at any of the colleges in which he studied a high reputation as a technical scholar. There surrounds his college career a legend of mature culture, an impression of pursuing a steadfast aim in realms of thought not included in the curriculum, an air of self-reliance untouched by eccentricity or exclusiveness; for he could be gay and charming with the choicest of his fellows and bold and assertive enough in the rough and tumble of college affairs. He had a way, even in youth, of moving amid the things of the mind and of demeaning himself in the society of books as if they had always been friends of his and he knew where he was going with them. The habit of respecting his mind and using it sternly and reverently clung to him throughout life. The sum of the college tradition about him is that he was a high-minded, proud-spirited, reflective, ambitious youth, never sturdy of body, eager to learn about men and affairs, and intent upon putting learning to use in action. The era in which he grew to manhood and the mood of the society in which his formative years were passed did much to fashion his ideals and to determine his ambitions.

The echoes of the great debate over the nature of the Union filled the air, and the towering figures of Calhoun and Webster yet dominated the imagination of opposing political schools. His early youth was passed away from, yet in the midst of, the tumult of the war which lay inherent in the logic of that debate. I am loath to praise any war, for all war is the collapse of human reason; but no sincerer war than this has occurred in human history. It was a war of ideals, of principles, of loyalty to ancient axioms of freedom, held dearer than life by both sides. The influence of the Civil War upon the youth of the man who was destined to be the Commander in Chief of all the forces of the undivided Republic in the greatest war of all time illustrates alike the calmness of his own mind and the sincerity of the mighty struggle itself. His people, post-revolutionary in American origin, had become southern in sentiment. He records, with deep feeling, how the passing sight of the grave face and regnant figure of Robert E. Lee, long after the war, stirred the emotions of his young heart; but there was developed in him no fierce passion of sectionalism, but rather a stern and cool will to comprehend the historic forces at play within American life, and to direct those forces toward the fulfillment of the longings of democratic society.

He was of the group of young southern-born men who knew the contributions of the South to American history, who had no apologies to offer for its part in the great struggle, ennobled by so much valor and self-sacrifice, but who felt that the South must again become whole-heartedly a part of the Federal Union it had done so much to establish. He saw about his hearthstone the faces of grim men who were subjected to such a test of manhood as our poor human nature has seldom been forced to endure. They were not men of the broadest social imagination, but they were men of intense and romantic loyalties to causes, and of an elevation of thought about the State as something to love and serve and not something to batten on or to profit by. War did not unfold to him in his far southern home any of its marching splendors and waving banners. He saw only the filthy backwash of war, its ruin and its bitterness, cities in ashes, ignoramuses in power, revenge in action, and great leaders led away to imprisonment and obloquy.

It is true that he had heard the civil struggle ended upon a sweet, clear note of "charity to all and malice to none"; and nothing in his life shows the balance of his mind better than his quiet perception of the fact that to his youth a challenge had come to help complete unfinished social and moral tasks, unpoisoned by hate and unwasted by vengeance. It might well have been within the Almighty's inscrutable purpose to give such a man such a preparation and such a social background for a supreme far-off test, when a distraught world would have sore need of the man of faith and will who would see clearly and reason accurately, and who would not falter or turn back when once he had set his feet upon a path.

Woodrow Wilson was 29 years old when he quit the formal life of a college student. One may treat as negligible the single year he spent vainly seeking to use a mind absorbed in the philosophy of law and its application to government, in the gainful practice of that profession. The span of his life was yet to stretch over 37 years, and he was to spend 25 of those years in teaching American youth politics and government in four different institutions of learning—Bryn Mawr College, Wesleyan College, Johns Hopkins University, Princeton University. Thus the man who was to be intrusted with the most stupendous administrative task in American history, spent three-fourths of his life as student, teacher, educational administrator, and writer of books. It was not the training adapted to equip for his work a prophet of force or a master of political intrigue; Ulysses would not have prescribed it for Telemachus nor Machiavelli for his prince, but I fancy that all of us who hold the democratic faith will one day be grateful for these studious, reflective years in the life of Woodrow Wilson, when he pondered over the comparative merit of forms of government and modes of culture, when his practical mind, with its adventurous and romantic passion for action received unfolding for a mighty purpose.

It was in the still air of these laborious days that he reflected how to get things done after the fashion of his dreaming; when he nurtured enthusiasm for men and saw himself as their servant, when looking deep into the life of the social organism, he saw that not ideas, but ideals, conquered men's souls; when he learned calmness from Wordsworth, concentration of energy from Walter Bagehot, and with Edmund Burke discovered the real difference between a statesman and a pretender in the circumstance that one lives by the way and acts on expediency, the other lives on principles and acts for immortality; when he came to see faith as life's most substantial heroism and finally, pursuing a lonely road gained a wide, luminous view of this world, as a world ordered of God, moved by the tides of His spirit, and thus laid the basis of a fame, which one day

> Full high advanced
> Shone like a meteor streaming to the wind.

Woodrow Wilson was the first professional teacher to pass almost directly from the classroom to the White House. Thousands of Americans to-day recall with gratitude his high gifts as a teacher; and as a fellow teacher, I would care to commemorate that element of his enduring service to his countrymen. To me and to the hosts of those who teach in this land, those quiet, busy years at Princeton, as a teacher, characterized by great personal happiness in a home of culture, of intense charm, energy and growing insight, seem to constitute his real golden age. Large classes flocked to his lecture hall to applaud his varied knowledge, and to gain from him new phases of life and truth. There was beauty in the cadences of his voice and power to arouse and persuade the intellect in the clarity and orderliness of his talk, brightened by bland humor and tingling wit. When he entered upon the presidency of Princeton, a new aspect of his qualities appeared. It was clear that he had thought deeply of the meaning of education and of universities, as molding forces in a democracy. The problem of education was to him the problem of enriching the Nation's life with minds of maturity, integrity of character, and social sympathy. "What a man ought never to forget with regard to a college," he once said at Swarthmore, "is that it is a nursery of honor and principle." He inaugurated new principles of educational contact, which now lie at the core of the development, not alone of his own university, but of all institutions of liberal culture in his country.

A dramatic struggle, marked by unusual phases of bitterness and ill will, characterized his administrative career at Princeton. Universities are little worlds in themselves, and, like the greater world about them, have a way of refusing to be reformed and of preferring to be let alone, or to be reborn into new aims and processes only under tremendous pressure and the passage of slow time. The total effect on him of all this academic warfare was the hardening of his resolution, the acquisition of formidable political skill to gain his ends, the arousing of his passion for democracy, and the fixing of his purpose to rescue universities from material control. He was born to fight for the goodness which is at the heart of things, and this ideal quickly grew into an objective of freedom which caught the eye of the Nation at the precise moment when a great tide of liberal hope and opinion was flowing in and over a generation of self-satisfaction and contentment with things as they are. Unlike most cultivated Southerners of his generation, Woodrow Wilson had the impulse to write as well as to talk and became a writer of eminence fit to claim a place in the literature of his country along with Jefferson, Madison, Lincoln, and Roosevelt.

At 29 he published his first book, *Congressional Government,* a postgraduate thesis, revealing the actual operations of our Government and outlining with a touch of genius his theory of the wisest and most efficient relation of the Executive to Congress. This book contained a definite system of political philosophy which he put into practice and to which he clung to the end of his career. In this respect a likeness to Thomas Jefferson appears, for each of them had developed, before he entered office, a definite theory of government and applied its doctrines to the solution of national problems. A series of seven volumes on political and historical subjects—*Congressional Government—a Study in American Politics, The State—Elements of Historical and Practical Politics, Division and Reunion, George Washington, A History of the American People, Constitutional Government in the United States,* and four volumes of literary and social studies—*An Old Master and Other Political Essays, Mere Literature and Other Essays, Free Life, The New Freedom, When a Man Comes to Himself*—came from his pen in these days. It is impossible to read these books without concluding that the guiding motive of all his studies pointed toward political life and the goal of political office.

The opportunity to enter politics seemed worlds away to the man who was writing "mere literature" of this quality in 1895— "There is more of a nation's politics to be got out of its poetry than out of all its systematic writers upon public affairs and constitutions. Epics are better mirrors of manners than chronicles; dramas oftentimes let you into the secrets of statutes; orations stirred by a deep energy of emotion or resolution, passionate pamphlets that survive their mission because of the direct action of their style along permanent lines of thought, contain more history than parliamentary journals. It is not knowledge that moves the world, but ideals, convictions, the opinions or fancies that have been held or followed; and who-ever studies humanity ought to study it alive, practice the vivi-section of reading literature, and acquaint himself with some-thing more than anatomies which are no longer in use by spirits."

In the year 1910 Woodrow Wilson withdrew from university direction and entered active politics. His last service to educa-tion was an effort, far from successful, to give to American universities what he considered a democratic regeneration in spirit, and to bring it about that the "voices of common men should murmur in their corridors." His first political declara-tion was an avowal that the time had come to reconceive the lib-erties of America, to break the dominance of cliques and ma-chine, to confer on candidates for high office power and responsibility for leadership, to secure for all men a fairer ad-justment of human relationships; and, further, that he was entering the field of politics in a new era, with no pledges to bind him and no promises to hinder him. Upon such a platform he was elected Governor of New Jersey, and in that office, and through his policies and principles, set forth in public speeches, this historian of his country, this southern-born Scotch-Irish Presbyterian teacher, an awkward circumlocution but a deadly definition of stubborn idealism, became, in 1912, the nominee of the Democratic Party for President, received a great majority in the Electoral College, and became President of the United States on March 4, 1913.

In 1916 he was renominated and re-elected in the very midst of the greatest crisis in the secular history of mankind. I am conscious that I am summing up, in bald sentences, revolution-ary transformations in the career and fortunes of an American citizen such as have seldom happened to any man in our annals, and never before to the teacher or scholar—the nearest approach in breathless action being the transfer of Abraham Lincoln from a main-street, second-story law office to unimagined burdens of authority. Both stories will forever enrich and adorn the epic of democracy.

Woodrow Wilson once said that the true teacher or the true artist or historian must always work for the whole impression. Working in this spirit, I can not, at this time and place, attempt even to enumerate the legislative measures which, under his leadership, went forward in the Sixty-third Congress; but I venture to claim that no such well thought out program of financial, social, and industrial reform, no such inspiring spectacle of governmental efficiency and concentrated energy, no such display of fearless devotion to public interests, moving high above the plane of partisan advantage or of private gain, has been spread before the eyes of this generation as is afforded by the list of enduring enactments which crowned the accession to power of Woodrow Wilson; and I set up the further claim that a President had come upon the great scene at a time of one of those strange failures of government to redress public grievances, who had not only the will and purpose to change the note of industrial life in the Nation, and to halt the domination of American politics by its privileged financial interests, but also the sense of direction and skill to carry to some sort of fulfillment a policy of practical emancipation from materialism, and the restoration of equality of opportunity. The Congress that furnished the teamwork in this memorable period of legislative energy was admirable and intelligent; but leadership lay in the President, not by use of patronage or by social amenities, but by the steady drive of intellectual force which his opponents within and without his party could not resist.

The new President concluded his first inaugural with these words: "The Nation has been deeply stirred; stirred by a solemn passion, stirred by the knowledge of wrong, of ideals lost, of government too often debauched and made an instrument of evil. The feelings with which we face this new age of right and opportunity sweep across our heartstrings like some air out of God's own presence, where justice and mercy are reconciled and the judge and the brother are one. We know our task to be no mere task of politics, but a task which shall search us through and through, whether we be able to understand our time and the need of our people, whether we be indeed their spokesman and interpreter, whether we have the pure heart to comprehend and the rectified will to choose our high course of action. This is not a day of triumph; it is a day of dedication. I summon all honest men, all patriotic, all forward-looking men, to my side. God helping me, I will not fail them, if they will but counsel and sustain me!"

Passionate sincerity shines out of these moving words. It was a spiritual moment in our history. Men were looking at life with kinder and juster eyes. A new spokesman of humanity had appeared in our politics, with a will and a purpose and a program. An eager and a nipping air seemed to blow away the atmosphere of materialism which had in varying degree hung over the Capital since Lincoln's day. Not since Jefferson had a leader with such a program dwelt at Washington. If in 17 months a world war had not come to turn the thoughts of mankind to the defense of civilization itself, it is not immoderate to believe that the great reforms already inaugurated would have been followed by others equally vital, and the domestic policy of the Nation ordered in accordance with the best liberal thought of modern, self-governing communities.

But war came, apparently falling out of the blue, like some tragic drama of the high gods, upon a busy and peaceful people, bent upon working out here in a favored land some scheme of life by which every man should have liberty, without hindrance, to be what God made him. In reality, there had arrived the moment of explosion of confined passions and forces long gathering through the ages, the awful fruitage of centuries of human greed and incompetence, of malignant nationalistic ambitions, of scientific progress diverted from high ends to purposes of destruction, of vain and feeble puppets in places of power, of a European polity based on fear and balance of power, rather than reason and concert of action. In the twinkling of an eye, our gain-getting age became a brawling age of terror and revolution, to be thought of hereafter as the end of an old epoch and the beginning of a new epoch in human annals.

It has been often predicted that this greatest drama in history must needs be one day really written as a drama by some Aeschylus who will paint the darkening sky, the rushing of the wind, the tension of the time, as catastrophe leapt to catastrophe, the movements of the bewildered antagonists amid the muttering of the storm and the lightning. In such a drama alone could one hope to find a just portrait of the peace-loving figure of the American scholar President, as he lifts his shoulders to the burdens, seeks to readjust his mind and nature, absorbed in purposes of new freedom for common men, to the tasks of the dreadful hour, and with tragic loneliness and patience grapples with events.

I saw President Wilson for the last time in the fullness of his strength on the evening of April 2, 1917. He was standing at this desk, speaking the momentous words which were to lead this democracy into war, and to teach to all free peoples, then bewildered and depressed, the meaning of the conflict, and to lift up their hearts. All mankind was his audience. The air of this hall was tense with emotion, and the dullest sensed the historic significance of the great scene. There were then etched into my mind, in lines never to be erased, the face and form and manner of Woodrow Wilson—the lithe figure, the bony structure of the forehead, the lean, long visage as of a covenanter, somber with fixed purpose. The culture of generations was in his tones, the scholar's artistry in his words, the inheritance of a gentleman's breeding in his manner, and calm courage in his discerning eyes. I was somehow reminded of the unbending lineaments and figure of Andrew Jackson, whom Woodrow Wilson resembled physically; and, in the very soul of him, morally exhibiting the same grim resolution, as of a stranger to the fear that weaklings feel.

The direction of American affairs, as the Republic swept into the current of the Great War, was in the hands of a liberal statesman, bred of democracy, firm of will, jealous of his country's honor, gifted with power to argue with cogency, capable of seeing far ahead the movements of social progress, incapable of fear, unmoved by passion or greed of conquest, intent upon justice, dreaming of peace and the righting of immemorial wrongs. I do not intend a résumé of the events of the two years and eight months intervening between the onset of war and the entrance of America into the struggle, but rather an analysis of what Prof. L. P. Jacks, a thoughtful English scholar to whom I am indebted for a better understanding of Woodrow Wilson, once called the "war mind" of Woodrow Wilson. To have taken any other primary step than the issuance of a declaration of neutrality in August, 1914, would have been the act of a madman or a superman, and Mr. Wilson was merely the trustee of the most powerful country on earth hitherto dedicated to the tradition of its own non-intervention in foreign affairs and the non-interference of European nations in cisatlantic problems.

The country was unfamiliar with European complications and unaware of the new international position decided for them, in Theodore Roosevelt's words, by fate and the march of events. Even the intellectuals who grasped the truth that the war was a conflict between two opposing schools of civilization would have been shocked by any other initial policy than the policy of neutrality. Military glory as an end in itself held no lure for President Wilson and no power to confuse his judgment, as his course in Mexico and his Mobile declaration had shown. I have little doubt as to where lay his sympathies from the first hour of the conflict, but he was not the man in a position of vast responsibility to be swayed by sympathy or prejudice or self-interest. Rather, he was the man, careless of fleeting judgments, to seek the position of moral responsibility imposed upon the United States and to so place its power at the service of mankind that other ages would hold it in grateful remembrance. I have read the speeches of President Wilson from the beginning of the war to its end, and I find in them an amazing strength and unity. I am not troubled by the inconsistency of his early advocacy of peace and his later proclamation of "force to the limit," for there is no inconsistency.

As Lincoln with supreme wisdom planted his policy not on slavery but on union, Woodrow Wilson with a similar greatness tied his policy to the idea that the United States, the most powerful of all States, should be a servant, a minister, a friend, not a master among the nations. Never before in the history of mankind has a statesman of the first order made the humble doctrine of service to humanity a cardinal and guiding principle of world politics. As long as he thought this principle was best served by neutrality, we kept out of the war. The long series of diplomatic papers, the patience that endured the barbarism of the *Lusitania* and bore without flinching the contumely of foes and the misgivings of friends may justly be thought of as mere incidents in the evolution of this great idea. When at last the insolent brutality of the renewal of submarine warfare taught him that force alone could advance his doctrine, he took us into war. His much derided Notes to the Imperial German

Government deserve rank among the enduring documents of international history, and constitute one of the most decisive arguments ever addressed to the conscience of civilization, to illustrate the solemn hesitation that ought to mark the course of rulers who carry nations into war, to give proof that in such a collapse of civilization, at least one nation should retain its poise, and to unite his countrymen while he taught the world.

When on March 5, 1914, before the war, in discussing the Panama tolls, he said "We are too big, too powerful, too self-respecting a Nation to interpret with too strained or refined a reading the words of our own promises, just because we have power enough to give us leave to read them as we please," he made clear all that subsequently possessed his mind. When a year later he said "We do not want anything that does not belong to us. Is not a Nation in that position free to serve other nations?" he revealed the heart of his policy; and so when, on the memorable night of April 2, he asked Congress to acknowledge a state of war it was to a crusade, not to a war, that his statesmanlike policy had brought his countrymen; and they could not doubt that the diplomatic victory was his, the moral victory was his, that a mighty people were behind him, that the leadership of mankind rested where democracy on a continental scale had begun, in the American Republic.

In December, 1916, the President had sought through a statement by each side of its war aims to discover if any basis of peace might be found. This inquiry exhibited diplomatic genius of the first order, for it enraged the Germans and aided the Allies to consolidate their moral position before the world. The great achievement was obscured for a moment by a storm of obloquy from superheated patriots who misread the grim humor and misinterpreted his precise language when he declared that all sides, according to their own general statement to their own people, had the same aims.

Again, on January 22, 1917, Mr. Wilson for the last time sought mediation in a speech in which he defined the fundamental conditions of a permanent peace. No greater state paper than this exists in the records of modern states. The result of this masterstroke was to bring us nearer war, but also nearer to lasting peace, to establish him still more closely as the one dispassionate voice of mankind, and again to bring upon him an outburst of condemnation for his noblest pre-war utterance in which he used, but explained none too skillfully, the phrase "peace without victory," by which he meant that only a reconciled Europe could be a tranquil and stable Europe, and that community of power must succeed balance of power.

Still preoccupied with the thought of lasting peace, Mr. Wilson appeared before the Congress in the early winter of 1918, at the darkest moment of the allied fortunes and formulated fourteen points of peace. These generalizations were almost revolutionary in their scope and idealism and ultimately formed the general basis of the peace to be drafted; but they carried, too, a political adroitness aiming directly at putting an end to the fighting. They planted new seeds of aspiration and new hopes of justice between nations in the minds of men; and it is not easy to ostracize such ideas. Its timeliness, as well as its strength, gives to this document a place among the great charters which have marked the progress of mankind. Our other great papers, the Declaration, the Farewell Address, Virginia Bill of Rights, the Constitution, were local or continental in their application. This paper, and the complementary addresses following it, aimed at nothing less than to endow the broken and weary nations with a new order and a new life. Desperate peoples for an hour looked into the shining face of Hope, and had sight of an old heaven and a new earth arising out of horror but ennobled by the self-sacrifice of millions. In Burke's vivid phrase, he was now the Lord of the Ascendant; his speeches had the strength of battalions along the front of battle; his voice was the voice of free peoples; and all over the earth, in the great capitals, among the tribes of the desert, in the islands of the sea, men felt the molding of his thought and sensed the grandeur of his aims.

The conversion of American energies into war energies, the transformation of the American spirit and philosophy of life into war spirit and war philosophy, the actual throwing into the furnace of modern war, across 3,000 miles of sea, the resources of men and money and resolution of the American people, takes rank among the greatest practical enterprises of mankind. It may well be conceded that mistakes were made and that judgments went wrong; but "it is the grim silence of facts that counts." Military experts impartially chosen, not political generals, commanded armies in this war. No congressional committees, as in former wars, directed its strategy and confused its processes. No serious bickerings or scandals or conflicts marred the unity of its course. Far-seeing fiscal and economic legislation gave steadiness to the Nation in the vast undertaking. Men and materials flowed to the armies in the field. The genius of the Army and Navy displayed itself in war. The genius of the President struck down the enemy morale and laid the foundations of peace. No democracy in history and few autocracies have ever given such an exhibition of efficient cooperation or earned such triumphant success.

The logic of events, to which Wilson's matchless skill in exhortation and argument had contributed so much, now decreed that in 10 months ancient dynasties would abdicate and flee, and that under American leadership the mighty war would come to an end, an armistice would be declared, and a peace conference come into being. Long generations hence we shall warm our hearts at the fire of the glory that then shone about this Republic, won for it by the steadfast mind of its President, the unity of its people, the disinterestedness of its purposes, and the valor of its youth unafraid to die.

On December 12 the *George Washington,* steaming through long lines of gray battleships over a gray sea amid the roar of guns and shoutings, dropped anchor at Brest, and an American President, for the first time, appeared in Europe to take part in a parliament of nations assembled to determine for years to come the course of history. Whether he should have gone at all, or only once, or by whom he should have been accompanied is a sea of fascinating but futile conjecture, upon which I shall not embark. Woodrow Wilson was not a master of manipulating men or of dramatizing himself, but a master and in some sense a slave of ideas and ideals. It seemed to him that it was his moral responsibility, under God, to go to Europe, heedless of the rocks ahead of him and the whirlpools behind him. It was a fearful responsibility to assume, for all the peace congresses of civilization, from Westphalia and Vienna to Paris, had satisfied nobody and had generally broken their creators.

This congress was the gigantic legatee of the failures of all past congresses, and in none of these congresses of the past did any one man ever occupy a position of such terrible greatness.

I am sure Aristotle's fine summary of tragedy must often have visited his mind as his ship wended her way across the seas—"Tragedy, in its pure idea, shows us a mortal will engaged in an unequal struggle with destiny, whether that destiny be represented by the forces within or without the mind. The conflict reaches its tragic issue when the individual perishes; but, through his ruin, the disturbed order of the world is restored and the moral forces reassert their sway." Three underlying ideas and purposes, all born of American daring and American experience, guided his mind and drove him on. The first was faith in the whole kindling length and logic of democracy itself; faith in men, faith in the supremacy of spiritual force, given new sacredness by what he saw about him of suffering and death. The second was the essential democratic idea of the right of men everywhere to determine their own affairs. The third was the idea of co-operation of peoples, the partnership of opinion among democratic nations, which once had welded discordant States in a new world into a Federal Union, and might again weld discordant peoples in an old world into a parliament of man.

For six months, at the Congress of Paris, in an alien air surcharged with cynicism and suspicion, almost single handed he fought for these principles, buoyed and sustained in the first period of his struggle by high tides of hope and faith that surged up to him out of the bruised hearts of peoples who trusted him to lead them over the failure of brute force into God's peace, and in the second period buffeted by the ebb tides of fading enthusiasm, of disintegrating unity, of selfish dominion, and ancient fears.

He had gone to Paris with the "fourteen points of peace," accepted alike by his Allies and by the Central Powers as the basis for the coming settlement. The "fourteen points" lived in his mind as a doctrine of international justice and the League of Nations was an integral part thereof, conceived as the medium to interpret and administer those principles of justice, and to introduce into the relations of modern states the idea of organic international co-operation based on reason. No man could have achieved this program in its entirety or secured a perfect peace of justice at Paris. Statesmanship of the most transcendent form could not have diagnosed, much less healed, that tremendous ailment of the world. The Versailles treaty, though a huge advance over any one of the five great treaties since Westphalia in sympathy and counsel with the peoples concerned, in the redress of bitter wrongs, in consideration for the weak and thought of the future, proved to be not God's peace. It was a peace shot through with the fear and resentment of suffering and ill-used men; a settlement corrupted by previous bargains among the allied powers made under the lure of traditional policies and the stern necessities of war and inconsistent with the high purpose of the charter which Wilson had presented for the guidance of the congress.

When the odium of nations and races began to beat upon him because he could not perform a task beyond mortal achievement, Wilson saw himself confronted with the alternative of world-wide chaos and disintegration or an imperfect peace with the League of Nations. He could not, with his vast sense of political and social institutions, postpone by headstrong and willful conduct the normal and peaceful ordering of men's lives.

Woodrow Wilson was not a revolutionist. Political reform by "red ruin and the breaking up of laws" was not in his blood. He chose the League of Nations, surrendering, in the anguish of compromise, such portions of his doctrine of international justice as he could not get. I am of those who believe that he gained more than he sacrificed at Versailles, and I know that he alone among mortal men could have salvaged out of that sea of passion the League of Nations, the bravest and most reasonable effort to rationalize national relations in political history. The statement sometimes made that he fell beaten down by the superior adroitness and intelligence of his European colleagues is a piece of analysis entitling its author to a high place in any hierarchy of inferior minds. What was liberal in the Versailles treaty Wilson's faith and courage helped to put there. What was reactionary he fought against to the limit of his strength and accepted only to gain an instrument which he believed had in it power to purge and correct.

He had the heart to match the moral hopes of mankind against their passions. He sought to give the twentieth century a faith to inspire it and to justify the sacrifice of millions of lives; and if there was failure in Jan Smut's words, it was humanity's failure. To make him, the one undaunted advocate of those hopes, the scape-goat of a world collapse is to visit upon him injustice so cruel that it must perish of its own unreason. Therefore I do not envisage Woodrow Wilson as a failure as he came back to these shores bearing in his hands the covenant of the league and the imperfect treaty itself. I envisage him rather as a victor and conqueror as he returned to America, untouched by sordidness or dishonor, unsurpassed in moral devotion, and offering to his country leadership in the broadest and worthiest cause in all the story of human struggle for a better life. What statesman in the history of world adjustment in defense of a code of shining, if unattainable, idealism had ever borne himself more stoutly or battled with such foes or achieved with so little support at home or abroad, so astounding a result?

When President Wilson first sailed for Europe in December, 1918, American sentiment, irrespective of party, generally approved his declared purpose to incorporate in the treaty of peace some sort of league covenant. The heart of the time was then in tune with the age-old dream. The President of the United States had a right to assume that the American people were behind him on the issue of the League of Nations, notwithstanding the adverse verdict of the electorate on his general policies. Eight years before, in 1910, in his Nobel lecture, Theodore Roosevelt himself said:

"It would be a master stroke if those great powers honestly bent on peace would form a league of peace not only to keep the peace among themselves but to prevent, by force if necessary, its being broken by others. The man or statesman who should bring about such a condition would have earned his place in history for all time and his title to the gratitude of all mankind."

HICKS' SP.A.S.—46

A list of eminent Americans of all parties then in line with that pronouncement in 1918 would be an illuminating contribution to the higher impulses of that era.

When he returned a different spectacle met his eyes. The great cause for which he had even then given his life had become confused with a group of political policies given by his enemies the generic name of Wilsonism, and about this raged the wrath, despair, and hatred of the overstrained time. The tired warrior of the common good, who had kept the faith, fought the fight, and won a victory, instead of hearing the acclaim of his own people, "Well done, thou good and faithful servant," saw himself ringed about with foes of mind to rend and destroy him.

I can not give time here to determining whether Wilson himself was to blame, in tactical judgment alone, or how much he was to blame for the change in American opinion; nor do I deny that honest men opposed the league and the treaty; nor do I undertake the task of apportioning with nice justice the responsibility for the caldron of heat and "swelter'd venom" of deadlock and indecision, of partisanship and passion, in which for weary months this largest question of modern times boiled and bubbled. Other ages will make that solemn appraisement. I may be permitted the reflection that something less of malice in the hearts of his enemies, and something more of compromise in his own heart, and something more of political genius and firm purpose in the hearts of those who held the faith, and there might have been another world!

I have lately been reading, and I wish all of his countrymen might one day quietly read, the 30 speeches made by the President on that fateful western tour which he undertook in September, 1919, in order to secure from the American people the stamp of approval which he desired for his work in Europe, and which the American Senate was unwilling to give. There is no series of political speeches, made under circumstances of such strain, in our annals attaining a higher level of oratory and exposition. He was forwarned, as he fared forth, that his life might be the forfeit of his enterprise. He replied, "I would forfeit my life to attain the end I seek," and he meant it; for he was incapable of melodramatic pose, and the consecration of that statement runs like a thread of gold through the sustained appeal.

Undeterred by the stabbing of physical pain and failing strength Woodrow Wilson here reveals the scope and depth of his conviction that national isolation for America or any country is forever ended; that the outlawry of war is democracy's next great task; that suicide hovers over civilization in the present system of the relation of states and the present potentialities of destructive warfare; that the hour has struck for the creation of an instrument to gather behind it the organized manhood of the world, bent upon evolving a clearer international conscience, a firmer international law substituting reason for passion in human affairs, and that the covenant of the League of Nations is such an instrument if mankind will but adapt it to its uses. This is the Wilsonism that the quiet justice of humanity will remember throughout the ages. But all this force and eloquence and martyrdom were to avail nothing. Woodrow Wilson fell stricken as if in battle at Pueblo, Colorado, on September 25, 1919, and came home shorn of his unmatched strength to persuade and move the hearts of his countrymen.

The American Senate, in the plain discharge of its constitutional duty, discussed the treaty for a period of eight months, during five months of which period the President struggled against mortal illness, rejected it on March 20, and elected to remain outside the first organized scheme of international cooperation in modern history.

The last words spoken to the people at Pueblo by the President were these: "Now that the mists of this great question have cleared away, I believe that men will see the truth, eye to eye and face to face. There is one thing that the American people always rise to and extend their hand to, and that is the truth of justice, liberty, and peace. We have accepted that truth, and it is going to lead us, and through us the world out into pastures of quietness and peace such as this world never dreamed of before." The prophecy of the stricken advocate of reason has not yet come true. There are those who hope and believe that it will never come true. It is not seemly that I should here attempt any controversial discussion; but I should lack the courage of the man I seek to interpret if I did not, as an American citizen, cry out, even in this Chamber, God grant that it may come true and gain new authority to protect mankind against its imminent dangers.

It is commonly said that the historic rank of Woodrow Wilson is wrapped up in the destiny of the covenant; that if it fails, his rank will be merely that of one more radiant spirit whose reach exceeded his grasp, and if it succeeds, his apotheosis in history is secure. I find the formula too glib and automatic for the forces and ideas it presumes to envelop. Apotheosis and immortality are weighty words that ill fit our poor flesh, so foredoomed to the iniquity of earthly oblivion; but surely the fame of Woodrow Wilson does not rest upon an instrument the orderly growth of which into final usefulness may so change its structure and modify its form as to cause it to become another and an even better instrument. It depends upon an unconquerable idea, so greatly conceived and set forth that it must continue to grow and is now growing into new and finer form, and his fame must grow with it into whatever bright renown it may attain.

Posterity will be eager to have knowledge of the personality and the salient qualities of a statesman set apart to play such a rôle in the world's affairs. I shall picture him as I knew him —not the Wilson whom mankind will remember as the stern war leader of a mighty nation; but another Wilson, known to me—a Wilson of sprightliness and humor and handsome courtesy, of kindly countenance and fascinating conversation with power to "beguile you into being informed beyond your worth, and wise beyond your birthright." The sensitive shyness and reserve that clings to men who can not capitalize their personal advantages to win friends clung to him. Intimacies were sacred relations to his spirit, but these intimacies could not overflow into inveterate amiability. He did not wear his heart on his sleeve for daws to peck at; but tenderness governed his demeanor with those he trusted; and he wore about him a quiet grace of dignity.

Woodrow Wilson was a deeply religious man. Men who do not understand the religious spirit need not even try to understand him. No man in supreme power in any nation's life, since Gladstone, was so profoundly penetrated by the Christian faith. He was sturdily and mystically Christian. He took God Almighty in earnest as the Supreme Reality, and he carried Him into his home and saw His immanence and guidance in private and public life. He had the habit of prayer, and he read and reread the English Bible. Through all his speeches flamed the glory of an insistent belief that morality and politics should march hand in hand. Many of his tendencies, perhaps the most of them that occasioned debate and censure, sprang from his pragmatic belief in God. There was actually such a thing as God's will to this man; and when he thought he had divined that will, he knew the right, the absolute right, and he was prepared to stand on that, if friends deserted him or he parted company with friends, if applause came or if the blow fell. "Interest divides men; what unites them is the common pursuit of right," was one of his great utterances, and not unlike the stout-hearted old medieval bishops, he stood ready to wield sword or bludgeon if the foe showed his face. "God save us from compromise," "Let's stop being merely practical, and find out what's right," were phrases often on his lips.

It was the Christian philosophy at work in his spirit that placed him almost instinctively on the side of the common man and against the privileged and the powerful. Wilson could be, and sometimes was, aloof and unrelenting to this or that friend or foe; but mankind, in the mass, never failed to soften his spirit and awaken his emotions. He would have gone to the stake to protect mankind, as a whole, from tyranny and injustice; but the ambitions of any individual man, even a friend, stirred him slightly. His greatest defect as a leader of men was this shrinking from human contacts at close range. When he had proved the rightness of his case and stated it boldly, a strange, moral fastidiousness and loyalty to the overlordship of reason prevented him from seeking to win men to his side by talking it over in whispers or by sweet and soothing persuasiveness. As Augustine Birrell said of Carlyle, "It seemed to him to be his duty to teach, not to tickle mankind." This inhibition left him a master of ideas, but not a master of using men, and substituted admiration and respect for love and enthusiasm in the nature of the mass of his followers.

Wilson evoked no such popular devotion as did Henry Clay or James G. Blaine or Theodore Roosevelt. Men of his prophetic quality rarely do. Edmund Burke once said of Charles James Fox, with a deep sigh, "He was made to be loved." That sigh often, no doubt, stirred in Woodrow Wilson's heart. He was a selfless man in so far as personal glory or profit was concerned. It was "perfection, not renown" that allured him. It was God's praise, not men's praise that gave him strength. The ambition which drove him to pre-eminence was the ambition to create new ideals or to reillumine old, neglected ones. Intellectually he does not belong with Kant or Burke or Hamilton or John Marshall; but he had a brain of high order, functioning in a different atmosphere and a broader field, a brain which worked straight and quick; and he suffered ill, fools and those of untidy minds. I should call his greatest mental gifts the power to look into the future, to assemble facts, to marshal his propositions in due order, to generalize fairly and to state his interpretations with such terseness and soundness, that they sank into minds that listened.

As an Executive, he was not an incarnation of action like Napoleon or Roosevelt. The lightning decision was not after his manner; but his industry was tireless, his judgment of men sound, and his mind did its own thinking, and men could not frighten or deceive or cajole him. The possession of a tenacious memory enabled him to keep the whole before him, to dispense with threshing around, and to dread irrelevance and bombast. No dogmatism or abruptness controlled his relations to men who approached his problem from the same angle. He gave his entire trust to those who worked with him, defended them against injustice, and upheld them against slander or misrepresentation.

The world used to be full of people busy in discerning, imagining, and cataloguing the faults of Woodrow Wilson. Dogmatist and hermit, rhetorician and pacifist, egocentric and ingrate, dreamer and drifter were some of the milder coinages of his more civil and restrained enemies. Well, he had his faults. I am not here to portray or to defend his faults. Some of them were protective devices to conserve physical strength, and others lay buried deep in the impulses in his blood; but inhibitions born of pride and courage and high ambition are such as nations learn to forget and to forgive, and even to love and cherish. Posterity is incurious about the minor faults of its heroes. England does not concern itself with the flaws of Nelson and William Pitt. Men do not remember Andrew Jackson's stubbornness and prejudice. They recall only the fury and fire of his purpose to preserve the Federal Union.

His countrymen will not forever remember the volubility and histrionic arts of Theodore Roosevelt, but they will never let die the memory of the valiant force of him penetrating the Nation's spirit, increasing the sum of its energies, awakening youth to high adventure, and stridently proclaiming the glory of upright living. They do not tattle about Washington's blazing profanity at Monmouth, but see his stately figure riding into the storm of battle beneath the tattered flag of a new nation he would fain bring into the world. They do not whisper about Lincoln's choice of companions or his taste in anecdotes or his cunning in politics; but they read incised on white marble walls the sacred poems which his literary genius has left to posterity, behold him in the night watches correcting his mistakes and using even his humility as a sword with which to carve out the victory of his cause. And so it will be with Woodrow Wilson in the long perspective of the years. The destiny in his blood decided that he should possess—

> The unconquerable will * * *
> And courage never to submit or yield,
> And what is else not to be overcome.

His ambition to serve his country was as intense as Cromwell's. It was not easy for him to forget or to forgive. The pride of righteousness sometimes froze the more genial currents of his soul, but he was willing to die, and did die, to guarantee to humble men a fairer chance in a juster world, and therefore the savage assaults of his enemies will shrivel into the insignificance of Horace Greeley's editorials against Lincoln's policies, or the futility of the early century pamphleteers against Thomas Jefferson as iconoclast and anti-christ, and his mere detractors will themselves either attain a repellant fame

as detractors of greatness or else they will pass out of memory
and no one will ask

> Who or what they have been
> More than he asks what waves
> Of the midmost ocean have swelled,
> Foamed for a moment and gone.

The four closing years in the life of Woodrow Wilson were
harsh, unheroic, uninspiring years in public affairs, such as
generally follow the emotional climaxes of war, and it is a commonplace to describe them as years of personal tragedy to him.
A vast disillusionment, a chaos miscalled peace, a kind of shame-
facedness and cynicism in the recollection of its dreams and
faith in the triumph of moral ideals, seemed to hold the Nation and the world in its grasp. As far as Woodrow Wilson
himself was concerned, it is well perhaps not to confuse the
bodily pain, the palsied side, and all the cold malignities of the
time with the essential meaning of those years. Adversity had
been wanting in his career, and now it was come upon him, and
he was to have acquaintance with its sublime refinement, and
the country was to gain knowledge of its power to smite the
hearts of just men with love for the baffled fighter who had
known none too much of popular affection in his career of self-
reliant conquest.

He carried his head high in the dying days of his public service, omitting no duty his strength could bear, meeting the gracious courtesy of his successor at the end with an equal courtesy, as they rode away from the White House, so deeply associated in American history with memories of sorrow and pain,
as well as pomp and power, while unseen of human eyes to
each of them alike "tragedy with sceptered pall comes sweeping by."

In the days left to him as the first private citizen of the Republic, unlike Burke, he did not waste his strength in windy
opposition or factious controversy. He wrote no memoirs.
"With my historical sense, how could I be my own biographer,"
he said. He exploited in no way his wide fame, uttered no complaint, suffered no pity, displayed no vain glory. It was as if
a great gentleman, "weary of the weight of this unintelligible
world," sought his peace at last in a quiet home luminous with

love and perfect care, and shut out at last from the noises and the storm. From this sanctuary, day by day, it was given him to behold the processes of his own immortality, as simple men and women gathered about his home and perceived in his wan image the poignant symbol of their great days and the historic link forever binding them to noble enthusiasms.

The very depth and dignity of his silence won through to the imagination of men, and when he spoke, the world stood at attention heartened to have knowledge that his high hopes for mankind were undimmed, and that there was no faltering in that firm faith of his that liberty guided by reason and not by force was the contribution of his century to human advancement. I doubt not that regrets visited his mind for lost opportunities that might have been better used, as he reviewed the pageant of his life in these long sequestered days; but a durable satisfaction must needs have fortified his soul, that even the devil's advocate must bear witness that—

> He had loved no darkness,
> Sophisticated no truth,
> Allowed no fear.

A grace which his heart craved came in the exaltation and excitement of the vision of a valiant new generation on the march, intent to light its torches at the still burning fire of his purpose to substitute for the arbitrament of war and death the reign of law, to restore to the land of his love and his loyalty its surrendered ascendancy, and to guarantee to the principles he had fought for eternal validity. The puzzle and complex of his dual nature seemed at last to fall into a mold of simplicity and consistency. "We die but once, and we die without distinction if we are not willing to die the death of sacrifice. Honor and distinction come only as rewards for service to mankind." Thus Woodrow Wilson had spoken in the days of his strength to high-hearted American youth, and now he could of right claim the supreme distinction as his very own! And so even as death enfolded him in its shadows, men paused in their busy lives and came to comprehend that a man of great faith had lived in their era, akin in heart and blood to John Milton and John Hampden, Mazzini, and Luther, that a prophet had guided their country and stirred the heart of mankind in an hour of destiny, and that an incorruptible liberal aflame with will to advance the slow ascent of man had joined those whom men call immortal and stood among that high fellowship,

> Constant as the Northern Star
> Of whose true, fixed, and lasting quality,
> There is no fellow in the firmament.

HARRY EMERSON FOSDICK

A CHRISTIAN CONSCIENCE ABOUT WAR

Sermon Delivered at the League of Nations Assembly Service in the Cathedral at Geneva, Switzerland, September 13, 1925

[Harry Emerson Fosdick was born in Buffalo, New York, on May 24, 1878. He was graduated from Colgate University in 1900, and from the Union Theological Seminary, New York City, in 1904. He has received honorary degrees from ten institutions. He was pastor of the First Church, Montclair, New Jersey, from 1904 to 1915, and is now pastor of the Park Avenue Baptist Church, New York City. He was Instructor in Homiletics from 1908 to 1915, and since then has been Professor of Practical Theology, in the Union Theological Seminary. He has published thirteen books on modern Christianity, is a preacher and lecturer of great power, and is an outstanding figure of statesmanlike stature in the American pulpit.]

"All they that take the sword shall perish with the sword." —
Matthew 26:52.

One ought to read with awe these words spoken nearly two thousand years ago and only now beginning to seem obviously true. Reliance on violence is suicidal, said Jesus. "All they that take the sword shall perish with the sword."

When the Master said that, it could not possibly have seemed to be true. Then it seemed evident that those who took the sword and knew how to use it could rule the world. Reliance on violence did not seem suicidal but necessary, salutary, and rich in its rewards. In these words of Jesus we have one of those surprising insights where, far ahead of the event, a seer perceives an obscure truth which only long afterward will emerge clear, unmistakable, imperative, so that all men must believe it.

Pythagoras in the sixth century B. C. had such a flare of insight when he guessed that the sun did not go about the earth but that the earth circled about a central fire. It was a surprising leap of intuition. No one believed it. Long centuries had to pass before Copernicus and Galileo came and people in general were convinced of what Pythagoras with his inner eye had seen. So when the Master said that the sword would destroy those who used it, that seemed incredible. War suicidal! The world did not even note this strange thing that He said, and ever since men have tried to explain it away or laugh it off as idealism too lofty for this earth. But today that insight of the Master comes to its own. Once more the seer is justified of his vision. Reliance on violence is self-defeating; war is suicidal; civilization itself cannot survive it. That fact has been written in fire across the world until not seers alone, but multitudes of plain people of every tongue, tribe, and nation under heaven are beginning to see the truth once so incredible—"If mankind does not end war, war will end mankind."

Today my plea is simple and direct. Of all the people on earth who ought to take in earnest this unforeseeable confirmation of the Master's insight, Christians come first. This question of war and its denial of the method and spirit of Jesus is peculiarly their business. Speaking from this historic Christian pulpit to Christians of many races and nations gathered here, one finds himself inevitably concerned with that matter—addressing, as it were, the conscience of Christendom about war. The destinies of humankind depend upon the arousing of that conscience. Here in Geneva you once more are setting your minds to the high task of working out the technique of international co-operation. In this sanctuary we set ourselves this morning to consider the dynamic without which all technique will fail—the conscience of Christians about war.

Doubtless we represent here many different kinds of Christianity. We belong to different Churches, hold various theories about ecclesiastical polity, subscribe to diverse creeds. But one thing does unite us all. We all start with and include the Master Himself. To all of us He is the Lord and His way is the way of life. At the fountainhead of our Christianity is Jesus Christ. His life with the Father, His faith in the moral possibilities of man, His devotion to the Kingdom of Heaven on earth, His Good Samaritan, His Golden Rule, His Sermon on the Mount, His law of finding life by losing it, His insight into the self-defeating nature of violence, and His substitution of the way of love—all this is included in any special kind of

Christianity we severally may profess. How, then, can any of us avoid the conviction that this colossal and ominous question of war, upon the answer to which the future of man depends, is in particular a crucial affair for Christianity? It has been said again and again that if another war befalls us and shakes civilization to its foundations, as it surely would, the Christians of the world will be to blame. Surely that is true. The continuance of war will advertise that the 576,000,000 professed Christians on earth have not had an earnest conscience about their Master's view of life; it will bear evidence that while they have called Him, "Lord, Lord," they have not been willing to do what He said.

Let us dwell, then, on some elements that ought to enter into the operation of the conscience of Christians about war.

For one thing, there is plainly the futility of war to achieve any of the purposes that Christianity is meant to serve. Indeed, there is modern war's futility to achieve any good purposes whatever. Once it was possible really to win a war. Once victors and vanquished stood in such opposite categories at a war's conclusion that there was no possibility of mistaking the prestige, prosperity, increased power and happiness of the one and the dismal annihilation of the other, but one shocking revelation of the last war was the indiscriminate ruin in which war plunged victor, vanquished, and neutrals alike, the ferocious and untamable way in which war, once let loose, tore at the garments of civilization as a whole so that, regardless of who won it, half the world found itself unclad and shivering when the storm was over.

In the history of war we have one more example of a mode of social action possibly possessing at the beginning more of good than evil, which has outgrown its good, accentuated its evil, and become at last an intolerable thing.

That was true of slavery. Men at first reduced to slavery those whom else they would have slaughtered after battle. Slavery was a substitute for massacre, profitable, doubtless, but also merciful. It was a forward step from brutal murder to enforced labor. But slavery did not retain its philanthropic good. In the end it outgrew all its benefit and became an intolerable curse. In an evolutionary world ethics and modes of social action evolve also.

So there may have been times when war could serve good ends, when armed conflict was a means of social progress. Of this war or that it may be claimed that the sword won benefactions lacking which mankind would be the poorer. At least, there is little use in arguing the contrary. For the conviction now growing strong in this generation's mind is that whatever may have been true about war in times past, modern war is futile to achieve any good or Christian thing.

To fight with the gigantic paraphernalia of modern science; to make war in our intimately interrelated and delicately balanced modern world, where our most indispensable means of existence already have become international; to fight, not with armies against armies as of old, but with entire populations massed against entire populations so that bombs rain indiscriminate destruction on whole cities and blockades mean indiscriminate starvation to millions of families; to make war now, when an average five hours of fighting, as in the last war, burns up the endowment of a great university; to fight, knowing that, agreements or no agreements to limit the weapons of war, demonic forces like gas and bacteria are certain to be used —that is obviously futile to achieve any good thing for which a Christian man might wish or pray.

The old appeals for war in the name of a good cause fall coldly now on the instructed ear and cease to carry conviction to thoughtful minds. "Would you not go to war to protect the weak?" men ask. The answer seems obvious. A modern war to protect the weak—that is a grim jest. See how modern war protects the weak: 10,000,000 known dead soldiers; 3,000,000 presumed dead soldiers; 13,000,000 dead civilians; 20,000,000 wounded; 3,000,000 prisoners; 9,000,000 war orphans; 5,-000,000 war widows; 10,000,000 refugees. What can we mean —modern war protecting the weak? The conviction grows clear in increasing multitudes of minds that modern war is no way to protect the weak.

A World Court would protect the weak. A League of Nations would protect the weak. An international mind, backed by a Christian conscience, that would stop the race for armaments, provide co-operative substitutes for violence, forbid the nations to resort to force, and finally outlaw war altogether— that would protect the weak. But this is clear: war will not do it. It is the weak by millions who perish in every modern war.

As for Christianity, the dilemma which it faces in all this seems unmistakable. The war system as a recognized method of international action is one thing; Christianity with all its purposes and hopes is another; and not all the dialectic of the apologists can make the two lie down in peace together. We may have one or we may have the other, but we cannot permanently have both.

Another stake which Christianity has in this task of overpassing war and providing international substitutes for it lies in the new and ominous developments of nationalism. In our modern world nationalism, with its attendant patriotic emotions and loyalties, has increasingly taken a form which threatens to be the chief rival of Christianity. To be sure, passionate love of country is nothing modern or new. Its roots are deep in man's instincts and man's history. We here today are patriots. We intend to be patriots. We should think less of each other if we were not patriots. Love of fatherland is one of the oldest, deepest, most instinctive and most noble sentiments of man.

But within the last four hundred years nationalism has taken a new and startling form in our Western world. With the England of Elizabeth, the France of Louis XI, the Russia of Peter the Great, the development began which more and more has nationalized both the inner and the outer life of all of us. Our politics have become nationalized until the aggrandizement of one's own country in the competitive struggle with other nationalities has been the supreme aim of statesmanship. Our economic life has become nationalized; the powerful financial interests of each nation have wielded so enormous an influence over its statecraft that government, with its army and navy to back it, has frequently been a docile instrument for the furtherance of the country's economic aims. Our education has become nationalized; our children have been taught from infancy history all out of perspective, with national egoism for its organizing center and with hatred of other nations masquerading as patriotic training of the young. Even our religion has been nationalized; with state churches or without them, the center of loyalty in the religious life of the people has increasingly become the nation. Let Protestantism acknowledge its large responsibility for this in Western Christendom! In our fight for liberty we broke up the inclusive mother church into national churches; we reorganized the worship of the people around nationalistic ideals; we helped to identify religion and patriotism. And so far has that identification gone that now, when war breaks, the one God of all humanity, whom Christ came to reveal, is split up into little tribal deities, and before these pagan idols even Christians pray for the blood of their enemies.

Never before has human life, its statecraft, its economics, its education, its religion, on so large a scale been organized on a nationalistic basis, and the issue is obvious. The supreme object of devotion for multitudes is the nation. In practical action they know no higher God. They really worship Caesar. That is the limit of their loyalty. What once was said of the king is said now of the nation: it can do no wrong. And such sheer paganism is sometimes openly flaunted, at least in my country, and I presume in yours, as, "Our country! * * * may she always be in the right; but our country, right or wrong."

Nevertheless, at the same time that this nationalistic process has been going on, another movement has been gathering headway. The enlarging fellowship of human life upon this planet, which began with the clan and tribe and has moved out through ever widening circles of communication and contact, has now become explicitly and overwhelmingly international, and it never can be crowded back again. Moreover, within this unescapable internationalism of modern life, not yet adequately recognized in government, mankind has been learning one great lesson from his social experiments. In area after area he has succeeded in getting what he wanted, not by violence, but by overpassing violence and substituting co-operation. That is. what social progress consists in. All social progress can be defined as carrying over one more realm of human life from the regime of force to the regime of co-operation. Wherever we have civilized any social group, the essential thing which has happened is that in that group, not force, but co-operation has become the arbiter.

That is true of the family. A household where men captured their wives, exposed their children in infancy, relied for obedience on the power of life and death over their offspring, would be recognizably uncivilized. A civilized family, with all its faults, enters into marriage by mutual consent, relies on reasonableness, not on force, for its coherence, and from the beginning welcomes children into the democracy of the household. At least we have learned that violence is no way to bring up a good family. That same path of progress we have traveled in education. Once violence ruled our schools. It was said of an old pedagogue, Rev. James Boyer, that "it was lucky the cherubim who took him to heaven were nothing but wings and faces or he infallibly would have flogged them by the way." But now our schools at their best would be ashamed to rely on violence since reasonableness and co-operation so plainly offer, not only a more ideal, but a more effective substitute. In religion also, being civilized means traveling that road from violence to co-operation. Once force was used to compel faith. If a man wished to be a Christian he could be a Christian, but if he did not wish to be a Christian he had to be a Christian, and the centuries are sad with the horrors of religious persecution. But social progress has largely left all that behind and what compelled its supersession was not sentimentality but the insight that violence is self-defeating, that force is no way to get religion. So, too, has government been carried over from violence to co-operation. The process is lamentably incomplete, but, so far as it has gone, it has furnished the indispensable background for all the civilization we possess. Still upon our Western clothes we wear the buttons, now decorative only, on which once our fathers' swordbelts hung. How impossible it would have seemed to them that the time would ever come when the common carrying of private weapons would be unnecessary because co-operative and peaceful government had provided a substitute! In one realm after another the Master's insight has proved true. Violence defeats itself. It is no way to achieve family life or education or religion or stable government. Those who rely on it as their mainstay and effective instrument are sure to miss

what they are seeking to achieve. Always progress has consisted in carrying over human life from violence to co-operation.

And now we face the next great step, the most momentous
step in human history. Can we achieve a like result with our
international relationships? Can we carry them over from brutality and organized slaughter. to reasonableness and co-operation? How the best thinking and praying of our time center
around that hope of superseding belligerent nationalism with
co-operative international substitutes for war!

Here, then, we face one of the most crucial and dramatic
conflicts of loyalty that men ever dealt with. On the one side,
our life has been organized as never before in history on a nationalistic basis. On the other hand, the one hope of humanity
today, if it is to escape devastating ruin, lies in rising above and
beyond this nationalism and organizing the world for peace. On
the one side is a narrow patriotism saying, "My country against
yours," on the other, a wider patriotism saying, "My country
with yours for the peace of mankind." Is there any question
where real Christianity must stand in that conflict? Is there
any question that if she does not stand there she faces the most
tragic and colossal moral failure of her history? One would
like to cry so that all Christians should hear: Followers of
Christ, so often straining out the gnat and swallowing the camel,
tithing mint, anise, and cummin, and neglecting the weightier
matters of the law, what do all the minutiæ of creed and institution that distinguish us amount to in the presence of this
gigantic problem in which one of the central meanings of Christ
for the world is involved? A narrow belligerent nationalism is
today the most explicit and thoroughgoing denial of Christianity,
its thought of God and its love of man, that there is on earth.

How evident this central problem is when we try to discuss
the real issues of the world today! Some still see those issues
in terms of one nation against another. That is the level on
which their thinking runs. America versus Japan or France
versus Germany—so in a long list of nation against nation they
see the world's affairs. How desperately real the problems are
on that level no one needs to be told, but, after all, those are
not the deepest issues. A clear conviction grows in the best
thinking of today that mankind's realest conflict of interest is

not between this nation and that, but between the forward-looking, progressive, open-minded people of all nations, who have caught a vision of humanity organized for peace, and the backward-looking, reactionary, militaristic people of the same nations. The deepest line of conflict does not run vertically between the nations; it runs horizontally through all the nations. The salvation of humanity from self-destruction depends on which side of that conflict wins.

What has happened thus to make a local, national patriotism, however sacred and beautiful in many of its forms, inadequate to meet our present need is clear. In unforgettable words the world has been told by a great patriot: "Patriotism is not enough." Why is it not enough? Well, patriotism once took men of little, local loyalties and expanded their outlook and allegiance. They had been citizens of a shire; patriotism made them citizens of a nation. Patriotism once called men to the widest imaginable outreach of their devotion; it broke down local provincialisms; it stretched human horizons; it demanded unaccustomed breadth of vision and unselfishness of life. To be a patriot for the nation meant a large loyalty as against the meanness and parochialism of a local mind. But the world has moved. Life has expanded and become international. Now it is possible for patriotism to fall from its high estate. Instead of calling men to wider horizons, it can keep them within narrow ones. Once the issue was patriotism versus a small parochialism; now the question may become patriotism versus a large care for humanity. Once patriotism was the great enemy of provincialism; now it can be made to mean provincialism and to sanctify the narrow mind.

This conflict of loyalties creates your difficult problems here in Geneva. You know how tenacious the adhesions of nationalism are, how difficult to entwine the thoughts and affections of men around new ideals and new methods of world peace. But this inner struggle between two loyalties goes deeper than the realm of statesmanship; it runs far down into the souls of men where the destinies of religion lie. How can a man be a follower of Jesus Christ and still be a belligerent nationalist, when once this better hope of a world organized for peace has dawned upon his view? Whatever else Christianity may be-

lieve in, it must believe in God, Father of all men; it must believe in men of every tribe, tongue, people, and nation, as God's
children; it must believe in the Kingdom of God on earth. The
spirit of Christianity is not narrowly nationalistic, but universally inclusive. When the world, therefore, organizes itself on
the basis of belligerent nationalism the very genius of the Christian Gospel is at stake. Once more we can have our old war
systems with their appalling modern developments, or we can
have Christianity, but we cannot permanently have both. They
worship irreconcilable gods.

I need not, and I must not, press the analysis further. Two
generations ago one of our great statesmen, Charles Sumner,
said, "Not that I love country less, but Humanity more, do I
now and here plead the cause of a higher and truer patriotism.
I cannot forget that we are men by a more sacred bond than
we are citizens—that we are children of a common Father
more than we are Americans." Shall not each one of us here
pray for his own country, as I pray earnestly for mine, that
that spirit may come into the ascendency? Christianity essentially involves it.

The first Christians saw this. "The early Christian Church,"
says a recent writer, "was the first peace society." Then came
Christianity's growing power—the days when Christians, no
longer outcast, were stronger than their adversaries, until at
last the imperial household of Constantine himself accepted
Christianity. Then Christianity, joined with the state, forgot
its earlier attitudes, bowed to the necessities of imperial action,
became sponsor for war, blesser of war, cause of war, fighter of
war. Since then the Church has come down through history too
often trying to carry the cross of Jesus in one hand and a drip-
ping sword in the other, until now when Christians look out
upon the consequence of it all, this abysmal disgrace of Christendom making mockery of the Gospel, the conviction rises that
we would better go back to our first traditions, our early purity,
and see whether those first disciples of the Lord were not
nearer right than we have been.

We cannot reconcile Jesus Christ and war—that is the essence of the matter. That is the challenge which today should
stir the conscience of Christendom. War is the most colossal

and ruinous social sin that afflicts mankind; it is utterly and irremediably unchristian; in its total method and effect it means everything that Jesus did not mean and it means nothing that He did mean; it is a more blatant denial of every Christian doctrine about God and man than all the theoretical atheists on earth ever could devise. It would be worth while, would it not, to see the Christian Church claim as her own this greatest moral issue of our time, to see her lift once more, as in our fathers' days, a clear standard against the paganism of this present world and, refusing to hold her conscience at the beck and call of belligerent states, put the Kingdom of God above nationalism and call the world to peace? That would not be the denial of patriotism but its apotheosis.

Here today, as an American, under this high and hospitable roof, I cannot speak for my government, but both as an American and as a Christian I do speak for millions of my fellow citizens in wishing your great work, in which we believe, for which we pray, our absence from which we painfully regret, the eminent success which it deserves. We work in many ways for the same end—a world organized for peace. Never was an end better worth working for. The alternative is the most appalling catastrophe mankind has ever faced. Like gravitation in the physical realm, the law of the Lord in the moral realm bends for no man and no nation: "All they that take the sword shall perish with the sword."

JAMES M. BECK

THE FUTURE OF DEMOCRATIC INSTITUTIONS

Address Delivered at a Meeting of the American Bar Association, Denver, Colorado, July 14, 1926

[James Montgomery Beck was born in Philadelphia, on July 9, 1861. He was graduated from Moravian College, Bethlehem, Pennsylvania, in 1880, and has received honorary degrees from six institutions. He is an honorary bencher of Gray's Inn, London, a member of many learned societies, an author, and a speaker of great skill, popularity, and force. He was admitted to the Philadelphia bar in 1884. From 1896 to 1900 he was United States Attorney for the Eastern District of Pennsylvania; from 1900 to 1903, he was Assistant United States Attorney General; from 1903 to 1921, he practiced law in New York City; from 1921 to 1925, he was Solicitor General of the United States; and since 1927 he has been a Republican Member of Congress from the First Pennsylvania District.]

We hold our annual meeting at an auspicious time. It is an anniversary period of great and heroic memories. Ten days ago the Republic, with the joyous *io triomphe* of a great people, celebrated the one hundred and fiftieth anniversary of the adoption of the Declaration of Independence.

Today we can recall another great memory, which is inseparably connected with the great Declaration. Tonight, one hundred and thirty-seven years ago, the Duke de Liancourt obtained access to the bedroom of Louis the XVI and told that ill-fated monarch of the seizure and destruction that day of the Bastile by a long-oppressed and outraged people. The startled King said: "Why, it is a revolt!" and Liancourt prophetically exclaimed "No, Sire; it is a revolution."

It would be strange, indeed, if The American Bar Association did not take note of these anniversaries and it is this consideration that has prompted the selection of my subject, "The Future of Democratic Institutions," in response to your gracious invitation to address you. No class can take a more peculiar interest, or feel a greater sense of pride, in these world-shaking events than our profession. Of the fifty-five signers

[742]

of the Declaration of Independence, twenty-six were lawyers, and of the five hundred and fifty members of the French National Convention, three hundred and seventy were also members of our profession. Moreover, the author of the great Declaration was a young Virginia lawyer, then only in his thirty-third year.

Our deliberations would seem wanting if we did not take note in this sesqui-centennial year of the great epic of 1776, when the Fathers created a new nation and dedicated it forever to the cause of human freedom. The flame then lit on that little altar in Independence Hall still illuminates the world. To countless millions it has been as a pillar of cloud by day and a pillar of fire by night. Tom Paine was a true prophet when he said a few months before the adoption of the Declaration, in his stirring appeal, "Common Sense," that "the birthday of a new world is at hand," but he could not have realized the full truth of his prediction. Little did he or any of the Fathers appreciate that they had "lifted the gates of empires off their hinges and turned the stream of the centuries into a new channel."

We can now see, in the perspective of history, that the greatest revolution in human thought and social conditions that the world has ever known and of which both the American and the French Revolutions were but incidents, was then in progress. It had begun long before 1776.

The Declaration did not create us a people. We were potentially a great people before it was adopted. Declarations, constitutions and governments do not create peoples, but peoples create governments and ordain constitutions.

France did not begin its great career with the Fall of the Bastile, and the attempt of the French Convention to revise chronology by declaring the date of its constitution the year "One" proved abortive. Similarly, the American Commonwealth antedated the United Colonies and the United States of America. It began with the landing of the first English pioneers upon the coasts of Virginia.

As such, the American Commonwealth is the noble child of that great revolution in human thought, the Renaissance. It came into being through the same great impulse that gave to the world Frobisher and Raleigh, Drake and Spenser, Sidney and

Coke, Bacon and Shakespeare. Never did human imagination rise to greater heights than in those "spacious days of Queen Elizabeth," and its finest flower was the birth of democracy in the new world, of which the American Revolution was but a single, although a very noble, result. Of Plymouth Rock, which shares the glory with the shores of Virginia of the great adventure a New England poet has well said:

> "Here on this rock, and on this sterile soil,
>   Began the kingdom, not of kings, but men;
>   Began the making of the world again.
>   Here centuries sank, and from the hither brink,
>   A new world reached and raised an old world link,
>   When English hands, by wider vision taught,
>   And here revived, in spite of sword and stake,
>   Their ancient freedom of the Wapentake.
>   Here struck the seed—the Pilgrims' roofless town,
>   Where equal rights and equal bonds were set;
>   Where all the people, equal-franchised, met;
>   Where doom was writ of privilege and crown;
>   Where human breath blew all the idols down;
>   Where crests were naught, where vulture flags were furled,
>   And common men began to own the world!"

In the Eighteenth Century, humanity was in labor, and of that mighty travail a twin birth resulted. One was industrial and the other was spiritual; one, the birth of the machine and the other, the birth of democracy. Twin children are not more inseparably united. While heroic souls in England, France and America were valorously fighting for greater freedom for the masses, Watt was developing his steam engine and Ramsey and Fitch were applying it to transportation. The dynamic power of man was about to be increased a thousand-fold. The day was coming when he would out-fly the eagle in the air, out-swim the fish beneath the surface of the waters, and speak with the rapidity of light itself. Like Prometheus, man was about to storm the hitherto inaccessible ramparts of divine power, and, measured by dynamic strength, he was about to become a superman.

It was inevitable that such an infinite expansion of physical power should be accompanied by a struggle for greater freedom. No two facts in all history are of more tremendous and inestimable importance, or of more pregnant consequence to the future, for good and ill, than the seemingly indefinite expansion of man's dynamic power, and his invincible demand for the full right to pursue his own true and substantial happiness. The democracy of the hand and the democracy of the soul are, in the last analysis, but one manifestation of the same unconquerable spirit, whose ultimate claim is that man shall be in truth, as well as in theory, "master of his soul and captain of his fate."

De Tocqueville, that extraordinarily keen and prophetic intellect, well said, nearly a century ago:

"The gradual development of the principle of equality is a providential fact. It has all the chief characteristics of such a fact; it is universal, it is durable, it constantly eludes all human interference, and all events as well as all men contribute to its progress."

I have said that the Declaration of Independence did not constitute us a people; it is equally true that it did not constitute us a nation. Sovereignty as a nation began with the first shots of the "embattled farmers" at Concord Bridge. Months before the Declaration of Independence, the colonies had, to a greater or less extent, become independent and assumed sovereignty. The Declaration of Independence simply recognized an accomplished fact, and its purpose was not to create a new nation, but to justify its existence to the world.

This does not lessen either its dignity or nobility. On the contrary, its dominant purpose, when rightly conceived, ennobles the great Declaration and has given it its due place as one of the noblest documents in the annals of statecraft. The American nation could have contented itself either with facts that spoke more eloquently than words, or, at least, with the formal proposal of Richard Henry Lee, which had been adopted on July 2d and which declared "That these United Colonies are, and of a right ought to be, free and independent states." This resolution had been proposed as early as June 7th by Richard Henry Lee, under instructions from the mother commonwealth of Virginia, and its passage was then so certain that on June 9th a Committee of Five was appointed to draft a declaration to the world of both the existing fact and its moral justification. This committee consisted of Thomas Jefferson, John Adams,

Benjamin Franklin, Roger Sherman and Robert R. Livingston. To Jefferson was assigned the immortal honor of drafting the Declaration, and it is to his undying glory that that Declaration, with a few changes by Franklin and John Adams, was his inspiration.

What then was the purpose of the Declaration of Independence? As clearly set forth in its noble Preamble, it was an appeal to the conscience of the world in support of the moral justification of the Revolution. It commences, "When in the course of human events, it becomes necessary for one people to dissolve the political bands which have connected them with another . . . . *a decent respect to the opinions of mankind requires that they should declare the causes which impel them to the separation.*"

Few state papers ever contained a nobler sentiment than this. It believed that there was a great human conscience, which, rising higher than the selfish interests and prejudices of nations and races, would approve that which was right and condemn that which was wrong. It constituted mankind a judge between contending nations, and, lest its judgment should temporarily err, it established posterity as a court of last resort. It placed the tie of humanity above that of nationality. It solemnly argued the righteousness of the separation at the bar of history, solemnly prefixing its statement of grievances with the words: "To prove this, let facts be submitted to a candid world"; and finally concluded its appeal from the judgment of the moment to that of eternity, in the words: "Appealing to the Supreme Judge of the world for the rectitude of our intentions."

The great Declaration was more than an eloquent plea for the favorable judgment of the world. Another great purpose was to give to man new title papers to liberty. For thousands of years, man had lived under conditions, which justly provoked the cynical remark of Rousseau, with which he began his immortal book, "man is born free and is everywhere in chains." Prior to the middle of the Eighteenth Century, the conception of the sovereignty of the people was almost unknown. Even in France, where the ideas of liberty were then germinating, the people had so little conception of their own rightful sovereignty that, thirteen years after the Declaration of Independence and at the beginning of the French Revolution, the only claim that the French people made was that they should share equally with the clergy and the nobility in the constitution of the legislative body. In 1789 that body had not been convened for over one hundred and fifty years and there was thus no novelty in Louis XIV's arrogant boast, *"L'état, c'est moi."* The state was conceived as a sacred institution, which existed apart from the people, and had its sanction, not in their will but in some inherent claim. In nearly every nation, the fountain-head of all power and justice was an hereditary monarch, whose power was absolute, except as he graciously gave immunities to the people, which were called "liberties." Even in those nations, where the soil had been broken and the seeds of liberty implanted, the utmost claim of the masses was for some participation, by the grace of the king, in the legislative councils of the nation. A few inspired spirits, like Locke, Burlamaqui, Montesquieu and Rousseau, were suggesting the then wholly revolutionary idea that, in the origin of human society, sovereignty had rested with the people and that it was only by their consent, given by a mythical social contract, that the state, as a separate entity, had been created and its sovereign power vested in an hereditary king. The mighty shadow of the greatest of the Cæsars still rested upon the earth.

Even the men of the Revolution, at its beginning, fully accepted this theory of government. Until the Declaration of Independence, the foremost spirits of the Revolution insistently claimed that they had no quarrel with the King, to whose intervention in their behalf they appealed as suppliants, but solely with the Parliament. It is noteworthy that the Declaration says nothing about the Parliament and even refrains from mentioning it by name, and that this terrific indictment was preferred against a stupid and obstinate King.

If the Declaration today gives us a quickened pulse, it is not because of the counts of the indictment against the misrule of George the Third, but because Jefferson, at heart an idealist and with all the enthusiasm of youth, challenged this universal conception as to the nature of government and asserted in eloquent phrase the sovereignty of the people.

He drew for all mankind, without distinction to race, condition or creed, a title deed to liberty, so broad and comprehensive that "time cannot wither nor custom stale" its eternal verity. As with the blast of a mighty trumpet, the Declaration asserts that all men are created equal; that they have a right as the gift of God, and independent of government, to life, liberty, and the pursuit of happiness; that governments derive their just powers from the consent of the governed; that the people have the inherent right to alter or abolish their government when it has ceased to answer their necessities, thus constituting the people the first and only estate. These far-reaching principles satisfy the highest ideals of liberty.

By the much quoted and much misunderstood axiom, that "all men are created equal," Mr. Jefferson did not mean either a natural equality or even an equality of natural opportunity, for either would contradict the common observation of men. He was simply defining the province of government, and he was contending that all men were *politically* equal and that the government, therefore, should not give to any man an artificial and law-made advantage over another. His target was hereditary privilege. "Equal and exact justice to all men, special privileges to none." When asked fifty years later and nine days before his death to write a sentiment for the forthcoming fiftieth anniversary of the Declaration—the day of jubilee on which, by a singular coincidence, he was destined to die—he wrote:

"The eyes of men are opened and opening to the rights of man. * * * The mass of men are not born with saddles on their backs nor a favored few booted and spurred, ready to ride them legitimately by the grace of God."

In the noble preamble Jefferson was not attempting to discuss a *form* of government. The Declaration of Independence is no more a treatise on the science of government than the book of Genesis is of natural science. Jefferson's only purpose was to hold up to the imagination of men the great ideals of liberty. He was not appealing to the cold reason of men, as much as to their imagination. Many of the eloquent phrases in the preamble can be as little reconciled with existing realities as some of the Beatitudes with practical Christianity. It can be said of equality, as George Eliot, in the great Climax to *Romola,* finely said of justice, that it "is not without us as a fact, but only within us as a great yearning."

Shortly before his death, Jefferson said:

"This was the object of the Declaration of Independence. Not to find out new principles, or new arguments, never before thought of, not merely to say things which had never been said before; but to place before mankind the common sense of the subject, in terms so plain and firm as to command their assent, and to justify ourselves in the independent stand we are compelled to take. Neither aiming at originality of principle or sentiment, nor yet copied from any particular or previous writing, it was intended to be an expression of the American mind, and to give to that expression the proper tone and spirit called for by the occasion."

Due to this fact, few, if any, political documents have more profoundly influenced the struggling masses throughout the world. It remains the classic definition of democracy, if not of liberty, and its noblest echo was the speech of Abraham Lincoln over the new-made graves at Gettysburg, when, inspired by Jefferson, he solemnly said that "government of the people, by the people and for the people shall not perish from the earth."

It is no mean event, therefore, in the annals of mankind that bids us today to recall in grateful memory the great Declaration of a century and a half ago.

It would be interesting to contrast what the Declaration of Independence would have been, if Franklin, Hamilton or Marshall, instead of Jefferson, had been its draughtsman. Franklin would have restricted it to a utilitarian discussion of the practical advantage to foreign nations of assisting in the creation of a new government and thus weakening the power of the British Empire. He would have invested it with a touch of humor which would have caused the whole world to laugh. Hamilton or Marshall would have confined the Declaration to an analytical and dry-as-dust statement of the constitutional principle involved in taxing the colonies without the consent of the local legislatures. Jefferson, although a lawyer, threw away his law books and with a flaming imagination wrote the gospel of liberty.

An ardent soul, his was also a great intellect. No one of his time, with the exception of Franklin, ever gave so much of a life to intellectual pursuits. From early boyhood until his latest hours, he remained the unwearying and zealous student of the great subjects, which challenge the attention of the human intellect. A valued correspondent of four great colleges, the successor of Franklin as President of the American Philosophical Society, he crowned his most useful life by founding the ancient and honorable University of Virginia upon lines so broad and catholic as to anticipate many of today's most valued improvements in education. Art, music, literature, history, politics, science, agriculture, philosophy, religion, all engaged his thoughts, and when his great library, which in the days of his poverty he was compelled to sell to the government, was transported to Washington, it required sixteen wagons, and it was found that they were written in many languages and comprised in their sweep nearly every department of intellectual activity. Here was a man who could supervise a farm, draw the plans for a mansion or public building with the detail of a capable architect, study nature like a scientist, make useful inventions, play a Mozart minuet on the violin, ride after the hounds, write a brief or manage an intricate law case, draft state papers of exceptional importance, and conduct correspondence with distinguished men in many languages upon questions of history, law, ethics, politics, science, literature and the fine arts.

How did he, the student and recluse, become, in the apt language of one of his contemporaries, "the most delightful destroyer of dust and cobwebs that his time has ever known." I find that secret primarily in his sturdy optimism, in the fact that he believed in the work which he attempted to do, in his own ability to do it, in its significance in the predestined advancement of humanity, and in the ability and disposition of his fellow men to follow a true leader. He believed passionately in the people. In that lay his great strength.

It would be flattery of the dead to claim that Jefferson was the "Father of Democracy." "There were great men before Agamemnon" and there were great democrats long before Thomas Jefferson. The Elizabethan dramatist, Dekker, said of Christ that He was "the first of gentlemen," and it could be added that the gentle Teacher of Nazareth, Who loved the plain people and sympathized with their sorrows, was the first and greatest of democrats. I prefer to liken Jefferson to that noble idealist of Rostand's fancy, Chanticleer. While his clarion voice, of which the great Declaration was the noblest note, did not cause the Sun of Democracy to rise, it did proclaim more truly than any other human note, the "reddening morn" of the present democratic era.

I am tempted, if only briefly, to discuss the more interesting question as to the present and future state of democratic institutions.

Let me disclaim any intention or ability to answer the great interrogatory that is implied in the subject of my address. Political institutions are never static, but are always in a state of flux, and who can say whither the great current is flowing?

> "These changing tides which sometimes seem
> In wayward, endless course to tend,
> Are but the eddys of a mighty stream
> Which moves to its appointed end."

Let us first ask what is the present state of democratic institutions. When the greatest war of history had ended, and the roar of the last gun on the long battle line had died away in distant echoes, it seemed indeed that Jefferson's political faith had received its most impressive vindication, that "government of the people, for the people, and by the people" had been vindicated and the world had been made "safe for democracy." Not in a thousand years had there been such a dissolution of ancient forms. Crowns had fallen "thick as autumn leaves that strew the brooks of Vallambrosa." Hohenzollern had followed the Hapsburgs and Romanoffs into the night of exile. Ancient dynasties perished; kingdoms fell and empires of a thousand years vanished into thin air. Indeed, as President Wilson passed through Europe and the masses arose to acclaim him with vociferous enthusiasm, it seemed as if the existing governments of even the victorious nations were crumbling.

And then a mighty change came over the world's dream of democracy. Russia, Turkey, China, Italy, Poland, Portugal, Spain and even Greece, which gave us the very word "democracy," accepted the rule of dictators. A reaction, swift and terrible, against parliamentary government, through which alone institutional democracy can function, swept over the world like the shadow of a huge eclipse. Today's dispatches tell us that only yesterday Belgium temporarily constituted King Albert a Dictator, and that France on Thursday will consider a like delegation of dictatorial powers in fiscal matters.

It is a curious paradox that this does not necessarily mean a revolt against democracy in its ultimate meaning, for a government can be democratic, if it is *of* the people, even though it is not *by* the people. Mallock, in his book, *The Limits of Democracy,* accuses Lincoln of tautology in speaking of government "of" and "by" the people, but such is not the fact. A people may themselves authorize a dictatorship and, if so, it as truly represents democracy *in its sanction* as a parliamentary majority, which too often represents the minority.

The great fact today is that while democracy as a form of government is at low ebb, as a social spirit it is at high tide. Let us not be discouraged if there is a temporary reaction against democratic parliamentary institutions. Human progress moves in a constant series of ascending and descending curves, or, to change the metaphor, its forces are at times centripetal and at times centrifugal. Man has, throughout all history, passed through a ceaseless cycle of integration and disintegration. Every age, marked by the concentration of power in the hands of a few, has been followed by a redistribution of that power among the many and, in turn, every democratic movement, when it has spent its force, has been succeeded by a period of integration.

Take English history. The autocracy of William the Conqueror was followed by the comparative democracy of Magna Charta, and that was, in turn, succeeded by the absolutism of Edward the First, only, in turn, to be supplanted by the democracy of the Peasants' Revolt. When that had spent its force, there came the absolutism of the Tudors, only to be followed by the execution of Charles the First and the democratic Commonwealth. Cromwell then became a dictator and this was followed by the Restoration and later the absolutism of the Georges, only to be followed by the Chartist movement, in turn succeeded by the early Victorian reaction towards absolutism. In our time democracy in England has triumphed in the virtual destruction of the political power of the Crown and the House of Lords. No country is more responsively democratic and yet last May it was on the edge of an abyss, and it seemed as if the power of the people would again be integrated into that of a class.

No present fact is more significant than the reaction in many nations against parliamentary democracy and in favor of one-man power. It matters not whether the one man be called a czar, emperor, king or dictator—the essential fact is his power. The revolt is not against democracy as a social ideal, but against the inefficiency and venality of parliamentary institutions.

At no time within the memory of living man has Lincoln's ideal of a government of and by and for the people been more openly denied and flouted.

There have not been wanting prophets who could see only the ultimate downfall of democratic institutions. Nowhere in the world has the great experiment of democracy been tried with greater promise of success than in our own favored land, and yet two of the greatest political philosophers of the nineteenth century predicted its failure even in America. Thus Carlyle said:

"America's battle is yet to fight; and we, sorrowful though nothing doubting, will wish her strength for it. New Spiritual Pythons, plenty of them; enormous Megatherions, as ugly as were ever born of mud, loom huge and hideous out of the twilight Future of America; and she will have her own agony, and her own victory, but on other terms than she is yet quite aware of."

He shared the view of Macaulay that our fate was only deferred by the purely physical cause that we still had an abundance of cheap land, which, as long as it was available, would prevent that discontent which has hitherto proved the grave of democracies.

Macaulay, in his well-known prophecy, went further and it is well to remember who the prophet was. He was not a Tory, but a Whig. Possibly he was the most scholarly student of history of our English-speaking race. Thackeray likened his brain to the dome of the British Museum Library. Lord Melbourne once said that he wished he could be as sure of any one thing as

Macaulay was of everything. He had an unrivaled experience as one of the great administrators and legislators of the British Empire. His prediction was made at the end of a life which had been rich in study and experience. His deliberate judgment was that "institutions purely democratic must, sooner or later, destroy liberty or civilization, or both." Speaking to Americans, he added:

"As long as you have a boundless extent of fertile and unoccupied land, your laboring population will be far more at ease than the laboring population of the old world, and, while that is the case, the Jefferson politics may continue to exist without causing any fatal calamity."

But he added that the destruction of our country would come when "North America has two hundred inhabitants to the square mile."

Nearly seventy years have passed since Macaulay made this prediction, and the Republic still endures. But America has not yet reached the growth which Macaulay had in mind, and he could further justify his prophecy by the fact that within a few years after his prediction our Republic nearly perished in a civil war.

It cannot be questioned that democratic institutions are continuously becoming more unworkable. The giant growth of our nation has put an undue strain upon its governmental machinery, and an ever-widening suffrage has made the problem of a qualified electorate ever more difficult. Even our attempted reforms, conceived in good faith, as, for example, the direct primary, have made government "of the people" and "by the people" more hazardous. The representative system is increasingly losing its strength. The complexity of our problems makes it increasingly difficult for the people to determine national policies by the simple expedient of voting for either John Doe or Richard Roe.

An even greater danger to representative government is found in the present tendency to substitute direct referendums for the deliberate action of a legislature. Let it once become the habit of the American people to refer questions of national policy to the people themselves by a referendum and democracy will break down, for referendums are impracticable for the simple reason that Lord Bacon once suggested, in another connection, that the average man is more apt to give an affirmative than a negative to any proposition. Above all, the indifference of the people to their government and their absorption in materialism and pleasure lead many thoughtful men to wonder how long a people, which finds more delight in the cinema and the stadium than in the duties of citizenship, will be worthy of a democratic form of government.

If there be any who believe that the Eighteenth Amendment has contributed to the political honesty of the people, or otherwise made the problem of self-government more practicable, I envy him his faith. No one can question that democratic institutions in the government of our cities have been generally a failure and the fact that our population is increasingly concentrating in the cities therefore gives little encouragement to the optimist.

A still more serious menace to the perpetuity of democratic institutions arises from the increased disintegration of the party system. If the present chaos in Europe, which in some countries approaches anarchy, reveals any one fact, it is that a democracy can only function through two, or at most three, political parties. Wherever there are more parties, a minority, which holds the balance of power, can impose its will, and thus the rule of the majority, which is democracy, ceases, and the rule of the minority, which means an oligarchy, begins. Germany has at least six well defined parties, and it was recently almost impossible to form a ministry. For the same reason, the procession of successive ministries in France has almost had the speed of a cinema. Briand alone has formed ten ministries within a few years, and France has had thirty-five ministries in twenty-one years. In England a few years ago the Labor Party, although in a minority at the polls, constituted the Government.

Unquestionably, democracy everywhere is threatened by the bloc system in politics and, unfortunately, the party system cannot be insured by any form of government, but only by the political sagacity of the people. Even in America, the tendency to disintegrate into groups, or blocs, is of sinister importance.

Let us hope that the old-time political sagacity of the American people will recognize that, if their form of government is to endure, the integrity of the party system, through which alone it is possible to define measurably the general will, shall be restored in all its former vigor. What would have been the history of the United States in the last century and a half if we had had a half dozen parties instead of the two great historic parties?

The World War revealed, as in a vast illumination, the fact that democracy as a governmental institution is not workable, unless there be a people, who are politically capable of self-government. The founders of our nation recognized this. Washington, Franklin and Hamilton all said that the success of popular government depended less upon its form than upon the moral and intellectual capacity of the people. If they fail to take an intelligent interest in their government, and if they are unprepared to show the spirit of self-restraint, which in my recent book on the Constitution I have called "constitutional morality," there can be no successful democracy.

Let us not lay the "flattering unction to our souls" that we have finally and completely solved the great problem of popular government. It is still, to use the words of Lincoln, "an unfinished task," and to it the living, from generation to generation, must still dedicate themselves, for "eternal vigilance is the price of liberty."

In this connection, it must always be remembered that a democratic government, as any form of government, is but a means to an end and not, in itself, an end. It must be judged by its fruits. It is not necessarily a final truth, but may prove to be only an inspiring prophecy. President Wilson's eloquent call to arms that "the world must be made safe for democracy," while most effective for its immediate purpose, incorrectly assumed that democracy was an end, of which the world was simply the means; whereas, in truth, the welfare of the world is the end and democracy is but the presently accepted means. Even as the greatest of all teachers said that the governmental institution of the "Sabbath was made for man and not man for the Sabbath," we can say that democracy is made for man and not man for democracy.

Our political philosophy has changed the divine right of a king to the divine right of King Demos, and one theory is as untenable as the other. The right of a majority, often mistaken, to impose its will upon the minority, who are only too often in the right, is not by divine ordinance, but is only based upon the purely utilitarian consideration that the common welfare requires a temporary subordination of the minority to the majority in the interests of peace. Law is only the reasoned adjustment of human relations and its authority consists only in its reasonableness and service to the common weal. A democracy slowly realizes this. When a majority imposes upon a minority some oppressive law, which transcends the fair province of government, the minority—if they have the spirit of freemen —protest as they would against the tyrannous edict of a king. The idea that any law is sacrosanct is preposterous. The laws do not stereotype society. If democratic institutions should prove more prejudicial to the common welfare than other forms of government, to it will come the stern challenge of the great Woodman, "Why cumbereth it the ground?"

Moreover, all forms of government must depend upon the character, or as Aristotle expressed it, the *"ethos"* of the people. It was well said by Lord Morley, one of the most scholarly publicists of our day, that "the forms of government are much less important than the force behind them. Forms are only important as they leave liberty and law to awaken and control the energies of the individual man."

I fear that the founders of the Republic recognized this more clearly than we of this later generation. Even after the adoption of the Constitution, the best form of government that the wit of man has yet devised, Washington, on February 7, 1788, wrote that it would only be effective "as long as there shall remain any virtue in the body of the people," and on the last day of the Convention, Franklin said:

"There is no form of government but what may be a blessing to the people, if well administered for a course of years, and can only end in despotism, as other forms have done before it, when the people shall become so corrupted as to need despotic government, being incapable of any other."

Were Franklin alive to-day, he would see an extraordinary verification of his prophecy in current European developments, where great, historic peoples, who are also liberty-loving, have willingly acquiesced in the despotism of a dictator rather than endure further the incapacity of parliamentary government that will not function.

In weighing the political institutions of a democracy in the scales of a candid judgment, care must also be taken to distinguish between the ponderables and the imponderables. Judged simply on the ponderables, the judgment on democracy, as a form of government after a century and a half, would not be wholly favorable. Its inefficiency, wastefulness and venality shock the judgment. The believer in democracy is only comforted by the reflection that undemocratic governments have also been wasteful, inefficient and dishonest, and have added tyranny to these vices. Possibly the most repellant feature of democratic institutions is the coarse flattery of the mob. By degrading manhood, it tends to destroy true leadership. With the destruction of the representative principle, the average politician becomes a mere flatterer of the many and, sometimes, even of the minority, who, under the party system, hold the balance of power. A democratic age abhors the spectacle of that Gallery of Mirrors in the Palace of Versailles, where three thousand courtiers would crowd upon the so-called "Sun King" to crave the servile honor of handing His Majesty his napkin at dinner. But in a democracy three hundred thousand politicians equally become the obsequious flatterers of King Demos. To flatter the many is no more creditable than to flatter a king.

When, however, the imponderables are taken into consideration, it is easier to defend democracy, for its theory satisfies the noblest aspirations of men. It not only educates them, but gives them hope. In this age of education a democracy is the only form of government that is consistent with self-respect. To it there is no thinkable alternative with which a proud and intelligent people will be lastingly satisfied. Hence my belief, that the present dominance of dictators is only a passing phase.

Referring to that great democrat, Abraham Lincoln, Lowell finely said in his classic address on democracy:

"Democracies have likewise their finer instincts. I have seen the wisest statesman and most pregnant speaker of our generation, a man of humble birth and ungainly manners, of little culture beyond what his own genius supplied, become more absolute in power than any monarch of modern times through the reverence of his countrymen for his honesty, his wisdom, his sincerity, his faith in God and man, and the noble humane simplicity of his character."

Again, Mr. Lowell, himself an intellectual aristocrat, but a democrat by instinct, well said:

"The democratic theory is that those constitutions are likely to prove steadiest which have the broadest base, that the right to vote makes a safety-valve of every voter, and that the best way of teaching a man how to vote is to give him the chance of practice. For the question is no longer the academic one, 'Is it wise to give every man the ballot?' but rather the practical one, 'Is it prudent to deprive whole classes of it any longer?' It may be conjectured that it is cheaper in the long run to lift men up than to hold them down, and that the ballot in their hands is less dangerous to society than a sense of wrong in their heads."

Let us also remember that democracy is something more than a form of government—it is a great spirit. Whatever may be said in this temporary ebb-tide of democracy, as to the fate of parliamentary institutions, democracy as a social ideal is as dominating and beneficent to-day as it has ever been. The equality of man, properly interpreted, is still our ideal, but we mean thereby not an enforced equality, which would standardize man to the level of mediocrity, but, in its last analysis, his right to inequality. In other words, the inalienable right of man to pursue his own true and substantial happiness, as proclaimed in the great Declaration, means his right to be unequal, for there can be no career open to talent, or any natural justice, if each man is not entitled to the fair fruits of his superior skill and industry. Social democracy asserts the right of every man to make the best of his life, and wars eternally against any form, whether it be of hereditary privilege or class legislation, that would handicap a man in the competition of life. This great conception of a "career open to talent," as Napoleon expressed it, or of "the square deal," to use Theodore Roosevelt's effective expression, remains the most dominant and vitalizing influence in life to-day.

To it we owe the greatness of the Republic. The ideal that every man has a right, free from governmental interference, to make of his dead self the stepping stone to a higher destiny gives to the masses that hope which has made us the most virile nation that the world has ever known. In many other lands, a man is forever identified with his class or caste. Once a coalminer, he and his children and his children's children can never hope to be anything else. Thus lacking an incentive to achievement, he sullenly identifies himself with his class and is deaf to the calls of social justice.

In America the democratic spirit gives to every man the hope of rising. To this we owe our illimitable energy and our inexhaustible strength. It is the great imponderable of the subject, and while there is much in democratic institutions to-day which, judged by the ponderables, would cause our faith to waver and our minds to be clouded with despair, yet, judged by this great imponderable, we know that the march of man, wherever democracy has led him, is steadily forward. He may, at times, sink into a "slough of despond" or a morass of difficulty, but that eternal hope, which the spirit of democracy has planted in his breast, gives him the strength to struggle out of the morass and march resolutely forward to the "Delectable Mountains." Such was the spirit of Washington, Jefferson, Franklin and Lincoln and it is this invincible faith, triumphing over fear, that has made them the great leaders of the American people. As long as democracy can produce such leaders, it vindicates itself.

I fear I have detained you far too long, but I cannot refrain, before concluding, from recognizing the fact that democracy has hitherto had its most effective and noblest expression in the Constitution of the United States. It is true that that great charter is not in method wholly democratic. On the contrary, it marked a salutary reaction against the extreme claims of democracy. Its essential spirit was finely expressed by Edmund Burke, when he said:

"Liberty, to be enjoyed, must be limited by law, for law ends where tyranny begins, and the tyranny is the same, be it the tyranny of a monarch, or of a multitude—nay, the tyranny of the multitude may be the greater, since it is multiplied tyranny."

While the Constitution does set limits to the power of the majority and, to this extent, negatives the extreme claims of democracy, yet, as it was adopted by the American people and has now been maintained by them for over one hundred and forty years, it is broad-based upon the more permanent general will of the American people and is, therefore, in the final sense of the word, democratic.

It is significant that, in all the violent changes of this changing world, our form of government has been most stable. It has been in the past, and will increasingly be in the future, the model for democratic governments, and upon its maintenance and perpetuity the future of democratic institutions may depend.

Let us hope, pray and work that the proud prophecy of John Bright, one of the noblest democrats of our time, may yet be verified:

"I see from the East unto the West, from the rising of the sun to the going down thereof, in spite of what misled, prejudiced, unjust and wicked men may do, the cause of freedom still moving onward; and it is not in human power to arrest its progress."

CALVIN COOLIDGE

THE STATESMANSHIP OF PEACE

ADDRESS AT THE DEDICATION OF THE LIBERTY MEMORIAL IN
KANSAS CITY, MISSOURI, ON ARMISTICE DAY,
NOVEMBER 11, 1926

[Calvin Coolidge was born in Plymouth, Vermont, on July 4, 1872.
He was graduated from Amherst College in 1895, studied law, and
began practice in Northampton, Massachusetts. He has been Coun-
cilman, City Solicitor, and Mayor of Northampton; was a member
of the General Court of Massachusetts from 1907 to 1908; State
Senator from 1912 to 1915; Lieutenant Governor from 1916 to 1918;
and Governor from 1919 to 1921. He was elected Vice President of
the United States and served from 1921 to August 3, 1923, when, on
the death of President Harding, he became President. He was elected
to succeed himself in 1925, and served until March 3, 1929, having
declined to be a candidate for re-election.]

Fellow Countrymen:

It is with a mingling of sentiments that we come to dedicate
this memorial. Erected in memory of those who defended their
homes and their freedom in the world war, it stands for service
and all that service implies. Reverence for our dead, respect
for our living, loyalty to our country, devotion to humanity,
consecration to religion, all of these and much more is represented in this towering monument and its massive supports. It
has not been raised to commemorate war and victory, but rather the results of war and victory which are embodied in peace
and liberty. In its impressive symbolism it pictures the story
of that one increasing purpose declared by the poet to mark all
the forces of the past which finally converge in the spirit of
America in order that our country as "the heir of all the ages,
in the foremost files of time" may forever hold aloft the glowing
hope of progress and peace to all humanity.

Five years ago it was my fortune to take part in a public service held on this very site, when Gen. Pershing, Admiral Beatty,
Marshal Foch, Gen. Diaz and Gen. Jacques, representing several of the allied countries in the war, in the presence of the

American Legion convention, assisted in a formal beginning of this work, which is now reaching its completion. To-day I return at the special request of the distinguished Senators from Missouri and Kansas, and on the invitation of your committee on arrangements, in order that I may place the official sanction of the National Government upon one of the most elaborate and impressive memorials that adorn our country. It comes as a fitting observance of this eighth anniversary of the signing of the armistice on November 11, 1918. In each recurring year this day will be set aside to revive memories and renew ideals. While it did not mark the end of the war, for the end is not yet, it marked a general subsidence of the armed conflict, which for more than four years shook the very foundations of western civilization.

We have little need to inquire how that war began. Its day of carnage is done. Nothing is to be gained from criminations and recriminations. We are attempting to restore the world to a state of better understanding and amity. We can even leave to others the discussion of who won the war. It is enough for us to know that the side on which we fought was victorious. But we should never forget that we were asserting our rights and maintaining our ideals. That, at least, we shall demand as our place in history.

The energy and success with which our country conducted its military operations after it had once entered the war has now become a closed record of fame. The experience of this thriving city and these two adjoining States was representative of that of the country. Soon came the marshaling of the National Guard. From its existing units in Missouri and Kansas the foundation of the Thirty-fifth Division was laid. The Eighty-ninth Division was raised almost entirely in these two States. A portion of the Forty-second, known as the Rainbow Division, came from this city. The whole martial spirit of this neighborhood, which within a radius of 200 miles had furnished the famous Regiment of Missouri Volunteers, commanded by Col. John W. Doniphan, when he made one of the most celebrated of marches to the conquest of Chihuahua in the Mexican War, reasserted itself as it had done in '61 and '98. While these divisions were serving with so much distinction on the battlefields of France their fellow citizens were supporting them with scarcely less distinction in patriotic efforts at home. They were furnishing money for Liberty loans, subscribing to the relief associations headed by the Red Cross, turning out munitions from the factories and rations from the fields. The whole community was inspired with a devotion to the cause of liberty. Returning at the end of the war, these divisions have increased their distinction by being represented in high places in civil life. From the Eighty-ninth came the great administrator and colonial governor, Major-Gen. Leonard Wood, and from the Thirty-fifth Division came a distinguished son of Missouri, the present Secretary of War, Col. Dwight F. Davis.

Under no other flag are those who have served their country held in such high appreciation. It is, of course, impossible for the eyes of the Government to detect all individual cases of veterans requiring relief in every part of our land. But the Veterans' Bureau is organized into departments and subdivisions, so that if any worthy person escapes their observation it is because the utmost care and attention could do no more. In the last eight years about $3,500,000,000 have been expended by the National Government for restoration, education, and relief. Nearly $3,200,000,000 have been pledged to accrue in future benefits to all veterans. Whenever they may be suffering from illness, whatever may be its cause, the doors of our hospitals are open to them without charge until they are restored to health. This is an indication of praise and reward which our country bestows upon its veterans. Our admiration is boundless. It is no mere idle form; it is no shadow without reality, but a solid and substantial effort rising into the dignity of a sacrifice made by all the people that they might in some degree recognize and recompense those who have served in time of national peril. All veterans should know this and appreciate it, and they do. All citizens should know it and be proud of it, and they are.

Considering the inspiring record of your soldiers in the field and the general attitude of appreciation which has been constantly reiterated by the whole nation, it would be but natural to suppose that this mid-Western country would give appropriate expression to the honor and devotion in which it holds those who served their country and the ideals for which they were contending. But the magnitude of this memorial and the broad base of popular support on which it rests can scarcely fail to excite national wonder and admiration. More than one person out of four in the entire population of this city responded to an appeal for funds, which gave pledges in excess of $2,000,000. It represents the high aspirations of this locality for ideals expressed in forms of beauty. We cannot look upon it without seeing a reflection of all the freshness and vigor that marks the life of the broad expanse of the open country and the love of the sciences and the arts and the graces as expressed in the life of her growing towns. These results are not achieved without real sacrifice. They supply their own overpowering answer to those who charge our countrymen with a lack of appreciation for the finer things of life. Those who have observed such criticism cannot fail to discover that it results in large part from misunderstanding. But assuming it to be correct, I am of the firm conviction that there is more hope for the progress of true ideals in the modern world even from a nation newly rich than there is from a nation of chronically poor. Honest poverty is one thing, but lack of industry and character is quite another. While we do not need to boast of our prosperity or vaunt our ability to accumulate wealth, I see no occasion to apologize for it. It is the expression of a commendable American spirit to live a life not merely devoted to luxurious ease, but to practical accomplishment. Nowhere is this better exemplified than in our great midcontinental basin. It is the spirit which dares, which has faith and which succeeds. It is not confined to materialism, but lays hold on a higher life.

No one can doubt that our country was exalted and inspired by its war experience. It attained a conscious national unity which it never before possessed. That unity ought always to be cherished as one of our choicest possessions. In this broad land of ours there is enough for everybody. We ought not to regret our diversification, but rather rejoice in it. The seashore should not be distressed because it is not the inlands, and the fertile plains ought not to be distracted because they are not the mountain tops. These differences which seem to separate us are not real. The products of the shore, the inlands, the plain and the mountain reach into every home. This is all one country. It all belongs to us. It is all our America.

We had revealed to us in our time of peril not only the geographical unity of our country, but, what was of even more importance, the unity of the spirit of our people. They might speak with different tongues, come from most divergent quarters of the globe, but in the essentials of the hour they were moved by a common purpose, devoted to a common cause and loyal to a common country. We should not permit that spirit which was such a source of strength in our time of trial to be dissipated in the more easy days of peace. We needed it then and we need it now. But we ought to maintain it, not so much because it is to our advantage as because it is just and human and right.

Our population is a composite of many different racial strains. All of them have their points of weakness; all of them have their points of strength. We shall not make the most progress by undertaking to rely upon the sufficiency of any one of them, but rather by using the combination of the power which can be derived from all of them. The policy which was adopted during the war of selective service through the compulsory Government intervention is the same policy which we should carry out in peace through voluntary personal action. Our armies could not be said to partake of any distinct racial characteristic, many of our soldiers were foreigners by birth, but they were all Americans in the defense of our common interests. There was ample opportunity for every nationality and every talent. The same condition should prevail in our peace time social and economic organization. We recognize no artificial distinctions, no hereditary titles, but leave each individual free to assume and enjoy the rank to which his own services to society entitle him. This great lesson in democracy, this great example of equality which came to us as the experience of the war ought never to be forgotten. It was a resurgence of the true American spirit which combined our people through a common purpose into one harmonious whole. When Armistice Day came in 1918 America had reached a higher and truer national spirit than it ever before possessed. We at last realized in a new vision that we were all one people.

Our country has never sought to be a military Power. It cherishes no imperialistic designs, it is not infatuated with any vision of empire. It is content within its own territory, to prosper through the development of its own resources. But we realize thoroughly that no one will protect us unless we protect ourselves. Domestic peace and international security are among the first objects to be sought by any government. Without order under the protection of law there could be no liberty. To insure these necessary conditions we maintain a very moderate military establishment in proportion to our numbers and extent of territory. It is a menace to no one except the evil-doer. It is a notice to everybody that the authority of our Government will be maintained and that we recognize that it is the first duty of Americans to look after America and maintain the supremacy of American rights. To adopt any other policy would be to invite disorder and aggression which must either be borne with humiliating submission or result in a declaration of war.

While of course our Government is thoroughly committed to a policy of permanent international peace and has made and will continue to make every reasonable effort in that direction, it is therefore also committed to a policy of adequate national defense. Like every thing that has any value, the army and navy cost something. In the last half dozen years we have appropriated for their support about $4,000,000,000. Taken as a whole, there is no better navy than our own in the world. If our army is not as large as that of some other countries, it is not outmatched by any other like number of troops. Our entire military and naval forces represent a strength of about 550,- 000 men, altogether the largest which we have ever maintained in time of peace. We have recently laid out a five year program for improving our aviation service. It is a mistake to suppose that our country is lagging behind in this modern art. Both in the excellence and speed of its planes it holds high records, while in number of miles covered in commercial and postal aviation it exceeds that of any other country.

Although I have spoken of our national defenses somewhat in relation to other countries, I have done so entirely for the purpose of measurement and not for comparison, for our Government stands also thoroughly committed to the policy of avoiding competition in armaments. We expect to provide ourselves with reasonable protection, but we do not desire to enter into competition with any other country in the maintenance of land or sea forces. Such a course is always productive of suspicion and distrust, which usually results in inflicting upon the people an unnecessary burden of expense, and when carried to its logical conclusion ends in armed conflict. We have at last entered into treaties with the great Powers eliminating to a large degree competition in naval armaments. We are engaged in negotiations to broaden and extend this humane and enlightened policy and are willing to make reasonable sacrifices to secure its further adoption.

It is doubtful if in the present circumstances of our country the subject of economy and the reduction of the war debt has ever been given sufficient prominence in considering the problem of national defense. For the conduct of military operations either by land or sea three elements are necessary. One is a question of personnel. We have a population which surpasses that of any of the great Powers. Not only that, it is of a vigorous and prolific type, intelligent and courageous, capable of supplying many millions of men for active duty. Another relates to supplies. In our agriculture and our industry we could be not only well-nigh self-sustaining, but our production could be stimulated to reach an enormous amount. The last requirement, which is also of supreme importance, is a supply of money. It is difficult to estimate in figures the entire resources of our country and impossible to comprehend them. It is estimated to be approaching in value $400,000,000,000. No one could say in advance how large a sum could be secured from a system of war taxation, but everyone knows it would be insufficient to meet the cost of war. It would be necessary for the Treasury to resort to the use of the national credit. Great as that might be, it is not limitless. To carry on the last conflict we borrowed in excess of $26,000,000,000. This great debt has been reduced to about $19,000,000,000. So long as that is unpaid it stands as a tremendous impediment against the ability of America to defend itself by military operations. Until this obligation is discharged it is the one insuperable obstacle to the possibility of developing our full national strength. Every time a Liberty bond is retired preparedness is advanced.

It is more and more becoming the conviction of students of adequate defense that in time of national peril the Government should be clothed with authority to call into service all of its man power and all of its property under such terms and conditions that it may completely avoid making a sacrifice of one and a profiteer of another. To expose some men to the perils of the battle field while others are left to reap large gains from the distress of their country is not in harmony with our ideal of equality. Any future policy of conscription should be all inclusive, applicable in its terms to the entire personnel and the entire wealth of the whole nation.

It is often said that we profited from the world war. We did not profit from it, but lost from it in common with all countries engaged in it. Some individuals made gains, but the nation suffered great losses. Merely in the matter of our national debt, it will require heavy sacrifices extended over a period of about thirty years to recoup those losses. What we suffered indirectly in the diminution of our commerce and through the deflation which occurred when we had to terminate the expenditure of our capital and begin to live on our income is a vast sum which can never be estimated. The war left us with debts and mortgages, without counting our obligations to our veterans, which it will take a generation to discharge. High taxes, insolvent banks, ruined industry, distressed agriculture, all followed in its train. While the period of liquidation appears to have been passed, long years of laborious toil on the part of the people will be necessary to repair our loss. It was not because our resources had not been impaired, but because they were so great that we could meantime finance these losses while they are being restored, that we have been able so early to revive our prosperity. But the money which we are making to-day has to be used in part to replace that which we expended during the war.

In time this damage can be repaired, but there are irreparable losses which will go on forever. We see them in the vacant home, in the orphaned children, in the widowed women, in the bereaved parents. To the thousands of the youth who are gone forever must be added other thousands of maimed and disabled. It is these things that bring to us more emphatically than anything else the bitterness, the suffering, and the devastation of armed conflict.

It is not only because of these enormous losses suffered alike by ourselves and the rest of the world that we desire peace, but because we look to the arts of peace rather than war as the means by which mankind will finally develop its greatest spiritual power. We know that discipline comes only from effort and sacrifice. We know that character can result only from toil and suffering. We recognize the courage, the loyalty, and the devotion that are displayed in war, and we realize that we must hold many things more precious than life itself.

> 'Tis man's perdition to be safe
> When for the truth he ought to die.

But it can not be that the final development of all these fine qualities is dependent upon slaughter and carnage and death. There must be a better, purer, process within the realm of peace where humanity can discipline itself, develop its courage, replenish its faith, and perfect its character. In the true service of that ideal, which is even more difficult to maintain than our present standards, it can not be that there would be any lack of opportunity for the revelation of the highest form of spiritual life.

We shall not be able to cultivate the arts of peace by constant appeal to primal instincts. To the people of the jungle, the stranger was always the enemy. As the race grew up through the family, the tribe, the clan and the nation, this sentiment always survived. The foreigner was a subject of suspicion without rights and without friends. This spirit prevailed even under the Roman Empire. It would not have been sufficient for St. Paul to claim protection because he was a human being, or even an inhabitant of a peaceful province. It was only when he asserted that he was a Roman citizen that he could claim any rights or the protection of any laws. We do not easily emancipate ourselves from these age old traditions. When we come in contact with people differing from ourselves in dress and appearance, in speech and accent, the inherited habits of our physical being naturally react unfavorably. Nothing is easier than an appeal to suspicion and distrust. It is always certain that the unthinking will respond to such efforts. But such reaction is of the flesh, not of the spirit. It represents the opportunist, not the idealist. It serves the imperialistic cause of conquest, but it is not found in the lesson of the Sermon on the Mount. It may flourish as the impulse of the day, but it is not the standard which will finally prevail in the world. It is necessary that the statesmanship of peace should lead in some other direction.

If we are to have peace, therefore, we are to live in accordance with the dictates of a higher life. We shall avoid any national spirit of suspicion, distrust, and hatred toward other nations. The Old World has for generations indulged itself in this form of luxury. The results have been ruinous. It is not for us who are more fortunately circumstanced to pass judgment upon those who are less favored. In their place we might have done worse. But it is our duty to be warned by their example and to take full advantage of our own position. We want understanding, good will, and friendly relations between ourselves and all other people. The first requisite for this purpose is a friendly attitude on our own part. They tell us that we are not liked in Europe. Such reports are undoubtedly exaggerated and can be given altogether too much importance. We are a creditor nation. We are more prosperous than some others. This means that our interests have come within the European circle, where distrust and suspicion, if nothing more, have been altogether too common. To turn such attention to us indicates at least that we are not ignored.

While we can assume no responsibility for the opinions of others, we are responsible for our own sentiments. We ought to be wise enough to know that in the sober and informed thought of other countries we probably hold the place of a favored nation. We ought not to fail to appreciate the trials and difficulties, the suffering and the sacrifices of the people of our sister nations, and to extend to them at all times our patience, our sympathy, and such help as we believe will enable them to be restored to a sound and prosperous condition. I want to be sure that the attitude and acts of the American Government are right. I am willing to intrust to others the full responsibility for the results of their own behavior.

Our Government has steadily maintained the policy of the recognition and sanctity of international obligations and the performance of international covenants. It has not believed that the world, economically, financially, or morally, could rest upon any other secure foundation. But such a policy does not include extortion or oppression. Moderation is a mutual international obligation. We have therefore undertaken to deal with other countries in accordance with these principles, believing that their application is for the welfare of the world and the advancement of civilization.

In our prosperity and financial resources we have seen not only our own advantage but an increasing advantage to other people who have needed our assistance. The fact that our position is strong, our finances stable, our trade large, has steadied and supported the economic condition of the whole world. Those who need credit ought not to complain, but rather rejoice that there is a bank able to serve their needs. We have maintained our detached and independent position in order that we might be better prepared, in our own way, to serve those who need our help. We have not desired or sought to intrude, but to give our counsel and our assistance when it has been asked. Our influence is none the less valuable because we have insisted that it should not be used by one country against another, but for the fair and disinterested service of all. We have signified our willingness to co-operate with other countries to secure a method for the settlement of disputes according to the dictates of reason.

Justice is an ideal, whether it be applied between man and man or between nation and nation. Ideals are not secured without corresponding sacrifice. Justice can not be secured without the maintenance and support of institutions for its administration. We have provided courts through which it might be administered in the case of our individual citizens. A Permanent Court of International Justice has been established to which nations may voluntarily resort for an adjudication of their differences. It has been subject to much misrepresentation, which has resulted in much misconception of its principles and objects among our people. I have advocated adherence to such a court by this nation on condition that the statute or treaty creating it be amended to meet our views. The Senate has adopted a resolution for that purpose.

While the Nations involved can not yet be said to have made a final determination, and from most of them no answer has been received, many of them have indicated that they are unwilling to concur in the conditions adopted by the resolution of the Senate. While no final decision can be made by our Government until final answers are received, the situation has been sufficiently developed so that I feel warranted in saying that I do not intend to ask the Senate to modify its position. I do not believe the Senate would take favorable action on any such proposal, and unless the requirements of the Senate resolution are met by the other interested nations I can see no prospect of this country adhering to the court.

While we recognize the obligations arising from the war and the common dictates of humanity, which ever bind us to a friendly consideration for other people, our main responsibility is for America. In the present state of the world that responsibility is more grave than it ever was at any other time. We have to face the facts. The margin of safety in human affairs is never very broad, as we have seen from the experience of the last dozen years. If the American spirit fails, what hope has the world? In the hour of our triumph and power we can not escape the need for sober thought and consecrated action. These dead, whom we here commemorate, have placed their trust in us. Their living comrades have made their sacrifice in the belief that we would not fail. In the consciousness of that trust and that belief this memorial stands as our pledge to their faith, a holy testament that our country will continue to do its duty under the guidance of a Divine Providence.

HUGH S. GIBSON

REDUCTION OF NAVAL ARMAMENTS

ADDRESS DELIVERED AT A MEETING OF THE PREPARATORY
COMMISSION FOR THE DISARMAMENT CONFERENCE,
GENEVA, SWITZERLAND, APRIL 22, 1929

[Hugh S. Gibson was born in Los Angeles, California, on August 16, 1883. In 1907 he was graduated from l'École Libre des Sciences Politiques, Paris, and in 1908 was appointed United States Secretary of Legation at Tegucigalpa, Honduras. His other diplomatic posts are the following: Second Secretary of the American Embassy, London, 1909 to 1910; Secretary of Legation, Havana, Cuba, 1911 to 1913; Secretary of Legation, Brussels, 1914 to 1916; First Secretary of the American Embassy, Paris, 1918; Minister to Poland, 1919 to 1924; Minister to Switzerland, 1924 to 1927; and Ambassador to Belgium since 1927. In 1925 he was Vice Chairman of the American Delegation to the Geneva Conference for the Control of the Traffic in Arms; in 1926–1927 he was Chairman of the American Delegation to the Preparatory Disarmament Conference; in 1927 he was a delegate to the International Conference on Private Manufacture of Arms and Chairman of the American Delegation to the Conference for Limitation of Naval Armament. His speech, printed below, which was delivered at the Preparatory Disarmament Conference of 1929, is said to have come, after the long technical discussions of the previous days of the Conference, "like a breath of fresh air into a stuffy room." In its style and frankness it is reminiscent of the speeches made by Joseph H. Choate at the Second Hague Conference.]

Mr. Chairman: I have sought your permission to make a general statement of the views of my government in regard to the question of disarmament and have felt warranted in doing so at this stage of the proceedings because, while we have not entered upon a second reading of the draft convention, we are bringing up for reconsideration various questions which have been previously discussed. It is felt, therefore, that in view of certain changed conditions it may facilitate the approach to these questions if I am permitted to take this occasion for stating my government's views as to the means best calculated to promote an early agreement.

During the first reading of the draft convention it was the

duty of each one of us to put forward the views of his government on the various problems before the commission and endeavor to persuade his colleagues that those views should be adopted. It was only in this way that we were able to throw full light upon the complicated questions the solution of which we seek. When we come to the second reading, a renewal of the old discussions is no longer in order. Our first duty is for each one of us to examine all phases of the problem before us with a view to discovering what measures of concession can be offered by each delegation. Agreement upon a single text can be achieved only by a maximum of such concession.

For the purposes of my presentation the disarmament problem may be divided into two parts, land and naval armaments. As regards land armaments, the American delegation will be able when we reach this question in discussion to defer to the countries primarily interested in land armaments with such measure of concession as I trust will materially facilitate agreement among them.

My country's defense is primarily a naval problem. The American Government has found no reason for modifying its view that the simplest, fairest and most practical method is that of limitation by tonnage by categories—a method which has been given practical and satisfactory application in the Washington Treaty. While it is realized that this does not constitute an exact and scientific gauge of strategic strength, we have nevertheless found that it constitutes a method which has the advantage of simplicity and of affording to each power the freedom to utilize its tonnage within the limitation of each category according to its special needs.

The American delegation has urged this view throughout the first reading, but, in view of the inacceptability to some other delegations of our unmodified thesis, my government has sought in the various methods presented some solution which might offer the possibility of compromise and general acceptance. During the third session of the Preparatory Commission the French delegation brought forward a method which was an attempt to combine its original total tonnage proposals with the method of tonnage by categories. Under this method a total tonnage was assigned to each nation and this total divided among categories of ships by specified tonnages. If I am not mistaken, certain modifications were suggested in informal discussions, so as to provide that the tonnage allocated to any given category might be increased by a certain percentage to be agreed upon, such increase to be transferred from any other category or categories not already fixed by existing treaty.

In the hope of facilitating general agreement as to naval armaments, my government is disposed to accept the French proposal as a basis of discussion. It is, of course, the understanding of my government that this involves an agreement upon the method alone and not upon any quantitative tonnages or the actual percentages to be transferred from one category to another. All quantitative proposals of any kind should properly be reserved for discussion by a final conference.

My government is disposed to give full and friendly consideration to any supplementary methods of limitation which may be calculated to make our proposals, the French thesis, or any other acceptable to other powers, and, if such a course appears desirable, my government will be prepared to give consideration to a method of estimating equivalent naval values which takes account of other factors than displacement tonnage alone. In order to arrive at a basis of comparison in the case of categories in which there are marked variations as to unit characteristics, it might be desirable in arriving at a formula for estimating equivalent tonnage to consider certain factors which produce these variations, such as age, unit displacement and calibre of guns. My government has given careful consideration to various methods of comparison and the American delegation will be in a position to discuss the subject whenever it comes before the commission.

In alluding briefly to these possible methods I desire to lay special emphasis on the fact that for us the essential thing is the achievement of substantial results. Methods are of secondary importance.

I feel that we are able to deal to best advantage with the specific questions on our agenda only if we bear clearly in mind the recent important changes in world conditions.

Since our last meeting the nations of the world have bound

themselves by solemn undertaking to renounce war as an instrument of national policy. We believe (and we hope that our belief is shared by the other nations) that this agreement affirming humanity's will to peace will advance the cause of disarmament by removing doubts and fears which in the past have constituted our principal obstacle. It has recently been my privilege to discuss the general problem of disarmament at considerable length with President Hoover, who has always been an ardent advocate of peace and good understanding. I am in a position to realize, perhaps as well as any one, how earnestly he feels that the Pact for the Renunciation of War opens to us an unprecedented opportunity for advancing the cause of disarmament, an opportunity which admits of no postponement.

Any approach to the disarmament problem on purely technical grounds is bound to be inconclusive. The technical justification of armaments is based upon the experience of past wars and upon the anticipation of future wars. So long as the approach to the problem is based upon old fears and old suspicions there is little hope of disarmament. The lessons of the old strategies must be unlearned. If we are honest, if our solemn promise in the Pact means anything, there is no justification for the continuation of a war-taxed peace. Great armaments are but the relic of another age, but they will remain a necessary relic until the present deadlock is broken, and that can be accomplished only by the decision of the powers possessing the greatest armaments to initiate measures of reduction.

In the opening statement at the Three-Power Naval Conference in 1927 I took occasion, in suggesting certain tonnage levels as a basis of discussion, to say that the United States is prepared to agree to a plan for limitation at still lower levels which maintain the relative status of existing treaties with respect to the powers represented at that conference. This is still the attitude of my government, and I am authorized to state that on this basis we are willing to agree to any reduction, however drastic, of naval tonnage which leaves no type of war vessel unrestricted.

A large part of the suggestions for limitation hitherto made seems to have been of such a nature as to sanction existing armaments or even to set higher levels, with tacit encouragement to increase existing establishments. This is only a timid expedient, and an agreement on the basis of existing world armaments (or at higher levels) can never be justified before enlightened public opinion as a positive achievement. At best it is purely negative Fundamentally, our purpose should be to release large numbers of men from military service to productive effort, and, second, to reduce the heavy burden of taxation. So long as the nations are burdened with increasing taxation for the maintenance of armaments it is idle to pretend that the world is really advancing toward the goal of disarmament. In recent years the word "limitation" has come to be used chiefly in describing agreements at existing levels or still higher levels, and is generally looked upon as having nothing to do with actual reduction. It is useless to attempt to correct this impression by explaining that limitation may be at any level lower or higher than those existing. As a practical matter it would seem to be best to accept the general public understanding of these terms. Let us therefore take the bold course and begin by scrapping the term "limitation" in order to concentrate upon a general reduction of armaments.

My government believes that there can be no complete and effective limitation of armament unless all classes of war vessels, including cruisers, destroyers and submarines, are limited. It could not agree to any method which would result in leaving any class of combatant vessels unrestricted. In its reply, under date of Sept. 28, 1928, to communications from the British and French Governments concerning an understanding reached between them as to a basis of naval limitation, my government pointed out that this understanding applied to only one type of cruiser and one type of submarine, and would leave totally unlimited a large class of effective fighting units. This note also called attention to the American position at the Geneva Naval Conference and the fact that a proposal for general reduction was urged by the American delegation.

The willingness of my government, I may even say its eagerness, to go to low levels is based upon the fundamental belief that naval needs are relative, namely, that what we may require for our defense depends chiefly upon the size of the navies maintained by others. Aside from the signatories of the Washington Treaty there is no conceivable combination of naval powers which could threaten the safety of any of the principal naval powers. What justification can there be for the powers which lead in the respective classes of naval vessels to sanction further building programs in those classes? In the case of the United States we have already expressed our willingness to agree on a basis that would mean a substantial reduction of our present destroyer and submarine types. In the case of cruisers, it is only possession by others of greatly superior strength in this class which has led to the adoption of the present building program.

My government cannot find any justification for the building and maintenance of large naval establishments save on the ground that no power can reduce except as a result of general reduction. Let us ask ourselves honestly what these establishments are for. As regards the relations of the maritime powers among themselves, there is no such need. Even if the danger of war is admitted, it could be guarded against just as well by the maintenance of relative strength at lower levels as at higher levels. The principal naval powers have nothing to fear from the naval strength of the countries non-signatory to the Washington Treaty. There is no conceivable combination of naval strength among the non-signatory powers which need give concern. As an example, the cruiser strength of all the non-signatory countries in the world does not attain to one-half of the cruiser tonnage of the greatest single fleet.

The people of every country are crying out against the burdens of taxation and demanding the suppression of unnecessary expenditure. My government is convinced that expenditure for disproportionate naval establishments is indefensible in that it can be avoided by a sensible agreement among the naval powers. And we must recognize that the people who pay taxes are bound to feel well-founded resentment against any policy which commits them to needless taxation through failure to reach rational agreements.

My government believes firmly in its idea that naval needs are relative and that radical general reduction is possible only on the theory of relative needs. I trust that these views may commend themselves to other governments and that it may be possible to agree upon such reductions. If, however, it is impossible to agree on this thesis, it is obvious that there will remain only the thesis of absolute naval needs. This would mean that all thought of reduction is abandoned, that each country retains a free hand in building, with an inevitable tendency toward competition. Surely we can hardly envisage such a sequel to our solemn understanding to keep the peace.

My government has always felt that we need no exact balance of ships and guns, which can be based only upon the idea of conflict. What is really wanted is a common-sense agreement, based on the idea that we are going to be friends and settle our problems by peaceful means. My government has never believed that an effective approach to the problem of disarmament could be made by methods of reduction of armaments alone. It feels that genuine disarmament will follow only from a change of attitude toward the use of force in the settlement of international disputes. It is for that reason that I venture to make this appeal that the countries here represented examine the whole problem afresh in the hope that they will find in general world conditions and in the solemn obligation they have taken among themselves a reassurance as to their security, and that they will find in this the confidence to enable them to dispense with the armaments which hitherto have seemed so essential.

CLAUDE G. BOWERS

PRIVILEGE AND PILLAGE

SPEECH OF THE TEMPORARY CHAIRMAN OF THE DEMOCRATIC
NATIONAL CONVENTION, HOUSTON, TEXAS,
JUNE 26, 1928

[Claude Gernade Bowers was born in Hamilton county, Indiana, on
November 20, 1878. He was educated in the public schools and by
private tutors, and is an honorary Master of Arts of Tufts College.
From 1901 to 1906 he was engaged in newspaper work in Indiana. He
was a member of the Board of Public Improvements of Terre Haute,
Indiana, from 1906 to 1911, was a delegate to the Democratic National Convention in 1908, and Secretary to United States Senator
John W. Kern from 1911 to 1917. From 1917 to 1923 he was editor
of the Ft. Wayne, Indiana, *Journal Gazette*, and since 1923 he has
been on the editorial staff of the New York *World*. In 1925 he published a work entitled *Jefferson and Hamilton—The Struggle for
Democracy in America*, in recognition of which, on July 4, 1926, he
received the Jefferson medal at Monticello. He made the "key-note
speech" at the Indiana Democratic Convention in 1920, and in the
speech printed below performed a similar service at the Democratic
National Convention of 1928.]

The American Democracy has mobilized today to wage a war
of extermination against privilege and pillage. We prime our
guns against autocracy and bureaucracy. We march against
that centralization which threatens the liberties of the people.
We fight for the Republic of the fathers, and for the recovery
of the covenant from the keeping of a caste and class. We battle for the honor of the nation, besmirched and bedraggled by
the most brazen and shameless carnival of corruption that ever
blackened the reputation of a decent and self-respecting people.

We stand for the spirit of the preamble of the Declaration
that is made a mockery; for the Bill of Rights that is ignored;
for the social and economic justice which is refused; for the
sovereign rights of States that are denied; and for a return to
the old-fashioned civic integrity of a Jackson, a Tilden, a Cleveland and a Wilson. We stand for the restoration of the government to the people who built it by their bravery and cemented
it with their blood.

[781]

We do not underestimate the enemy. The little gilded group that now owns and controls the Government can pour a golden stream into the slush fund and make no impression on the fortunes they have legislated into their coffers. The enemy enters the campaign unembarrassed by a debt—Harry Sinclair has paid that off. It enters the campaign with his money in its pocket and his blessing on its head.

For forty years the party in power has conjured with the name of Lincoln while following the leadership of Hamilton; and now, after eight years of successful privilege and pillage, it throws off the Lincolnian mask. It could hardly keep the Lincoln mask on its face and Sinclair's money in its chest.

Thus at Kansas City, where they dramatized the issue, it was not Lincoln, but Hamilton, who rode at the head of the procession.

Thus they frankly base their policies on the political principles of Hamilton, and we go forth to battle for the principles of Thomas Jefferson. The issues are as fundamental as they were when Jefferson and Hamilton crossed swords more than a century ago. To understand the conflicting views of these two men on the functions of government is to grasp the deep significance of this campaign.

Now Hamilton believed in the rule of an aristocracy of money, and Jefferson in a democracy of men.

Hamilton believed that Governments are created for the domination of the masses, and Jefferson that they are created for the service of the people.

Hamilton wrote to Morris that Governments are strong in proportion as they are made profitable to the powerful, and Jefferson knew that no Government is fit to live that does not conserve the interest of the average man.

Hamilton proposed a scheme for binding the wealthy to the Government by making government a source of revenue to the wealthy, and Jefferson unfurled his banner of equal rights.

Hamilton wanted to wipe out the boundary lines of States, and Jefferson was the champion of their sovereign powers.

Hamilton would have concentrated authority remote from the people, and Jefferson would have diffused it among them.

Hamilton would have injected governmental activities into all the affairs of men, and Jefferson laid it down as an axiom of freedom that "that government is best which governs least."

Just put a pin in this: There is not a major evil of which the American people are complaining now that is not due to the triumph of the Hamiltonian conception of the State. And the tribute to Hamilton at Kansas City was an expression of fealty to him who thought that Governments are strong in proportion as they are made profitable to the powerful; who proposed the plan for binding the wealthy to the Government by making government a source of revenue to the wealthy; who devised the scheme to tax the farm to pay the factory; and whose purpose was to make democracy in America a mockery and a sham.

Thus we are challenged once more to a conflict on the fundamentals; and a clear call comes to us to-day to fight anew under the Jeffersonian banner, with the Jacksonian sword, and in the Wilsonian spirit, and, crashing the gates of privilege, make Jeffersonian democracy a living force again in the lives and homes of men.

The friendly enemy at Kansas City has rendered a clarifying service by proclaiming Hamilton as its father and beau ideal. This ought to awaken the Lincolnians among Republicans to a realization of what are the fundamentals of their party's faith. It was Lincoln who said that "the principles of Jefferson are the definitions and the axioms of a free society." What a comment on the confusion of the public mind on the elements of American politics when a great party is able to claim a joint parenthood in Abraham Lincoln and Alexander Hamilton!

Why, you cannot believe with Lincoln in democracy and with Hamilton against it.

You cannot believe with Lincoln that "God loved the common people or he would not have made so many of them," and with Hamilton that the people are "a great beast."

You cannot believe with Lincoln that the principles of Jefferson are "the definitions and the axioms of a free society," and with Hamilton that they are the definitions of anarchy.

You cannot believe with Lincoln in a government "of the people, by the people and for the people," and with Hamilton in a government of the wealthy, by the influential and for the powerful.

There are Lincoln Republicans and Hamilton Republicans, but never the twain shall meet, not even at Kansas City, until you find some way to ride two horses going in opposite directions at the same time. We here propose to take our stand so uncompromisingly on the elemental principles of Jeffersonian democracy that liberal and progressives may fraternize with us in a common fight against the common foe in the common interest of the average man and woman.

We enter the campaign no strangers to the public. The brilliant record of our eight years of power is as a splotch of glorious sunshine against the smutty background of eight years of privilege and crime. In those eight years we wrote more progressive and constructive measures into law than has been written by the opposition in forty years of power.

One thing those eight years did—they buried beyond the reach of resurrection the ancient slander that the party of Wilson is incapable of constructive statesmanship.

They did one thing more—they destroyed the falsehood that Democracy means hard times.

They did another thing—they demolished the fallacy that the party that gave the Federal Reserve system to the nation is an enemy of business.

And those eight years did one thing more—they gave another immortal to the skies.

What a majestic figure was he who led us in those fruitful years! The cold, even light of his superb intellect played upon the most intricate problems of the times and they seemed to solve themselves. He lifted the people to such heights of moral grandeur as they had never known before; and his name and purpose made hearts beat faster in lowly places where his praise was sung in every language in the world. And when at length, his body broken, but his spirit soaring still, he fell stricken while still battling for his faith, there passed to time and to eternity and to all mankind the everlasting keeping of the immortal memory of Woodrow Wilson.

We submit that a party that stands for that democracy which is inseparable from the liberties of men, and has given a Jefferson, a Jackson and a Wilson to the service of mankind, has earned the right in times like these to the co-operation of independents and progressives in the struggle for the preservation of popular government and the purging of the nation of that corruption which has made America a by-word and a hissing in the very alleys of the world.

Sixteen years ago the late Senator Beveridge warned us of the "invisible government." That invisible government now feels strong enough to take on visibility. From the moment of the election of 1920, there was a mobilization of the Black Horse Cavalry of privilege and pillage, and it cantered down Pennsylvania Avenue, up and down from one end to the other. Strange creatures new to the capital, put in an appearance. Desk room was found for one of these in the Department of Justice. The best minds established a temple of the new patriotism in the Little Green House on K Street. Men who were the very symbols of privilege, whose fortunes had been made on the favors of the Government, were put in possession of the instrumentalities of the State. Acting on the Hamiltonian theory that governments are strong in proportion as they are made profitable to the powerful, the foremost of these was placed in a strategic public station that he might personally supervise the delivery of the goods. The representatives of special interest hastened to the Capital with their receipts for campaign contributions, to be given a key to the Treasury and a guest card at the patriotic club on K Street where "there was a sound of revelry by night." Within five months the conditions in Washington had become a scandal and a stench. The reign of privilege and pillage had begun.

The moment the bell rang these men set to the task of undoing the work of Woodrow Wilson and to the commercialization of the Government. In the midst of the usual scandal they hurried a tariff law upon the statutes at a cost of from three to four billions a year to the consumers.

They found the Tariff Commission we created an embarrassment—they ignored it. It was not facts they sought. They had promises to keep. When a little later they found it convenient to have a complacent commission to find the facts they sought— they packed it. From that moment the acoustics of the commission have been bad. The cries of the millions for relief cannot be heard, but the dulcet whisper of the pig-iron industry is enough to bring a 50 per cent. increase in its loot.

They found the Federal Trade Commission in the way—they packed it. They took the weapons we provided for the protection of the people against exploitation and turned them over to the powers of pillage.

Thus Privilege was speedily entrenched in every department of the Government; and Privilege moved into the office of the Attorney-General to spike the guns of Justice; and Privilege took possession of the strategic points in all the departments and commissions; and when the machinery of this potential plutocracy had been completed, there, at the control, sat the very personification of the erstwhile invisible government, looking after the interest of his flock.

It is a tragic thing to find a Government mortgaged to a little group that could be crowded into the directors' rooms of the Aluminum Company of America. Under the rule of this regime the average man has had no more stake in the Government for which he may be called upon to die than if he had never touched our soil.

For example, what stake in Government has the farmer of to-day? From the moment of the realization of the Hamiltonian State under the banner of the bloody shirt in the brutal days of Reconstruction the American farmer has been but a hewer of wood and a drawer of water. During the sixty years of Jeffersonian supremacy the farmer was on an equality with every other industry, and it is no mere coincidence that his decline and degradation began with the triumph of the Hamiltonian State. In the Jeffersonian concept of society the farmer had a position of paramount importance; but in all the political writings of Hamilton the only reference to the farmer is a promise that in compensation for his submission to taxation in the interest of others he may put his wife and children to work in the mills.

Thus while the little group represented by Mr. Mellon has found fine plucking in the vineyard of the State, there have been nothing but thorns and thistles for the tillers of the soil. And the result is a condition of ruination that is a disgrace to our civilization. Millions of farms have been abandoned. Two million men have been driven from the paternal acres by economic necessity within the year. The hammer of the auctioneer knocking down farmlands has sounded like the continuous bombardment of a major battle in the West. Does the ruling caste want figures? Then take this—in five years of this Administration there has been a depreciation in the value of farm lands and equipment of thirty billion dollars!

And what does the ruling caste say to this? It calls it "temporary depression." And what does it propose? It proposes that the farmers shall become better business men.

Now when it suits the pleasure of the privileged to legislate money into its coffers it is applauded by the claquers as patriotic statesmanship; but when the farmer demands his share in the unhappy game of paternalism, they denounce him as a radical. and a crank.

One day the head of the State by a scratch of the pen increased the tariff loot of the pig-iron industry by 50 per cent.; and the next day he delivered a homily to the farmers on the wickedness of expecting profit from a governmental act.

One day Mr. Mellon offered an argument against a farm relief bill; and the next day a Republican Senator by substituting "tariff" for "farm relief," and "duties" for "equalization fee" converted the Mellon argument into a devastating denunciation of the very processes through which much of the Mellon fortune has been made.

One month ago the President bitterly denounced with contemptuous phrasing the revolving fund of a farm relief bill; and the next day he heartily approved the revolving fund for the favored shipping interest.

And then, with millions of producers on the verge of bankruptcy and despair, they contemptuously kicked their case from court and adjourned the Congress with a cheer. Thus for eight long years they have stood in the midst of the wreckage of the farms and have done nothing—nothing to decrease the cost of transporting the farmer's produce to the marts; nothing to rehabilitate his lost markets across the sea; but they have added a billion a year to the cost of the things the farmer has to buy.

Now we do not ask paternalistic privilege for the farmer, but we do demand that the hand of privilege shall be taken out of the farmer's pockets and off the farmer's throat. We propose

to tear down the system of privilege and put the farmer on an
absolute equality with every other industry—that is Jeffersonian
democracy. We do not propose that the most basic of all our
industries shall longer be a door-mat for all the others to wipe
their feet upon as they enter the Temple of Privilege.

Ah, but when we protest against the commercialization of
government they say we are enemies of business. Well, history
refutes them. Thomas Jefferson was not an enemy of business.
He merely objected to the use of the instrumentalities of the
State to make it possible for a few men to pick the pockets of
their fellow-men under the protection of the police.

Andrew Jackson was not an enemy of business. He discriminated between business and brigandage; and he was so much
the friend of honest business that he fought to make it free.

Woodrow Wilson was not an enemy of business. In the eight
years of his Administrations we gave more intelligent legislative service to honest business than had been given it in a generation before.

We defy them to name a Democratic President who was an
enemy of business.

But we differ from those to whom Mr. Mellon is sacrosanct
in our definition of a business man. In every tax reduction
measure of the last eight years the Democratic minority in Congress has fought the battle of 95 per cent. of the American business men against his 5 per cent.

We hold that the owner of a little shop, the proprietor of a
store in an average town, is as much a business man as the barons of iron and steel. The man who owns and operates a ranch
in Texas or Montana is as much of a business man as the bank-
er in New York. The men who till the soil and feed the nation
are better business men to the Jeffersonian than the most successful speculator in stocks and bonds. We cannot understand
the régime in power for we are interested in the Babbitts, and
they in the bulls and the bears.

We wage no war on big business if it be honest business; we
find no fault with fortunes, however large, provided they are
not accumulated through the misuse of governmental power.
But we do wage war upon the commercialization of government
that makes for corruption and crime.

Privilege and pillage are the Gold Dust Twins of normalcy. The Wilson Administration is a green spot bounded on one side by the Mulhall mess and on the other by an oil tanker flying a pirate's flag.

The last seven and a half years have been putrid beyond precedent. We make no charge—we follow the official record.

We have seen a governmental department designed for the legal protection of the people converted into a rendezvous for the barters of illegal permits.

We have seen the agents of the Department of Justice sent forth at the nation's cost and with the Administration's sanction on the infamous mission of "framing" a United States Senator who had dared to expose the criminality of its proceedings. Nothing more disgraceful blackened the days of Federalist Sedition law. A baser and more dastardly prostitution of the judicial processes has not shamed the story of a civilized nation since the unspeakable Jeffreys sat upon the bench. And he died, deservedly, like a miserable felon in the Tower.

We have seen the money appropriated for the care of the sick and wounded soldiers squandered on the pleasures of a drunken libertine. We have seen the nation's oil reserves, set aside by the prescience of Roosevelt, and sacredly guarded by the honesty and wisdom of Wilson and Daniels, bartered away by a member of the Cabinet for a bribe in a little black bag.

Shameful as these things are, more shameful far has been the cynical silence and indifference of the high functionaries of the State to whom the people had a right to look for the protection of the nation's property and the nation's honor. We submit in no spirit political of flubdubbery that it is a shocking thing that we have waited vainly for seven years for one word, one syllable, one whisper of the mildest criticism of these criminals and crimes from a single representative of the Administration.

They heard La Follette's denunciation of Teapot Dome—and were silent. They saw the various processes in the alienation of the nation's property—and were silent. They heard the gossip of the capital that buzzed for weeks and months—and were silent. There was not a man among them with enough will power, or lung power, to blow a police whistle.

Nay, more; when a warning of the impending crime was sent to a member of the Cabinet, but recently knighted by the golden wand, he sent the letter to Albert B. Fall with this notation: "I should be glad to convey to this gentleman any reply you may suggest."

I sometimes think that the virtues of silence may be overdone. Sometimes silence is golden—for the thief.

Some years ago a corruptionist de luxe phrased the shibboleth of the powers of pillage in these words—"Addition, division—and silence." When the pillagers got their loot, there was addition; when the faithless public servants got their share, there was division; and from the men sent by the people in the watchtower to guard their treasurers, there has been the invaluable contribution of silence.

Imagine Andrew Jackson silent in the midst of such crimes; imagine Tilden; imagine Cleveland; imagine Wilson! Why, they would have thundered their denunciations from the loftiest station in the world and have scourged the rascals forth with scorpion whips tipped with consuming flame.

Do they tell us that all these things have been exposed and something has been done? This is our answer: If an Attorney General of odorous memory no longer sits at the council table of the nation's chief, it is because a Democratic Senator so exposed the crimes of his régime that that public sentiment lashed him out; and if he was permitted to go without rebuke, and to march out with all the honors of war, it was not with the consent of the party of Thomas Jefferson.

And this is our answer: If the nation's oil reserves have been restored it is because the inquisitorial genius of Walsh of Montana exposed the crime and forced the proceedings that brought the restitution of the nation's stolen goods.

And why the silence in the watchtower? Because the organization of the party of the men stationed there was a beneficiary of the crime. Not only did it know of the crime and maintain silence—it knew of the division of the spoils and knew that a goodly part was being used to pay the party debt.

What a picture for American history! We see the erstwhile Chairman of the National Committee of the régime in power laying aside his duties as an elder of the Church to slink into the office of Sinclair to get the tainted bonds. We see him sneaking about like a receiver of stolen goods to men of means to persuade them dishonestly to contribute these to the party fund under cover. We see him sending a portion of these bonds to the dictator of the Administration, affectionately known as "Andy," and thus we know that the high functionaries of the State knew that the party was to be a beneficiary of the crime. And the revered head of the Treasury made no protest against the party taking its share out of the pot filled by the pillaging of the nation's property. Silence was golden—for the party chest.

And thus the campaign debts of the régime in power have been paid by Harry Sinclair and now with pious platitudes it enters another campaign free from debt—because there was a Teapot Dome.

And why this strange insensibility to the common instincts of honor? Keep in mind the Hamiltonian theory that governments are strong in proportion as they are made profitable to the powerful. There is no moral difference between selling legislation in advance for campaign funds and selling oil reserves, and it is not remarkable that he who practices the one may condone the other. Or that he who thinks that giving money to a slush fund is "just like giving money to a church" should play the silence end in the tale of the tainted bonds in the game of "Addition, division and silence."

And so we go forth to recover the Government from those who pillage by law as well as those who steal by stealth. Even as a minority we dragged those loathsome crimes to light. We exposed the stealing, the perjury, the silences of the sacrosanct. We forced the restitution of the nation's stolen goods. We compelled the expulsion of Daugherty and the prosecution of Fall. Put us in possession of the Government and we will turn the light on every crack and crevice and cleanse the Augean stables from mow to manger.

We have no legislation to put upon the auction block. No Harry Sinclair has paid our party debt. We are free. We unfurl the Jeffersonian banner bearing Jefferson's device: "A good government is an honest government," and we invite all enemies of corruption to fight with us beneath its folds for the redemption of the violated honor of the Republic.

Now they hope to drug the conscience of the nation with the doped soothing syrup of a fake prosperity; and we want to know what prosperity they mean. They point to a few powerful corporations enjoying the pap of paternalistic privilege, and our answer is that you cannot judge the prosperity of a people by the earnings of a privileged monopoly.

Many years ago Thomas Jefferson advised a friend, impressed with the evidence of prosperity in the homes of the nobility in Paris and Versailles, to go out into the country and look into the pots in the fireplaces of the peasants. That is our answer now.

Four million jobless men is not prosperity; a million abandoned farms is not prosperity; the utter ruin of the basic industry of America is not prosperity; the failure of 4,000 banks in the seven years of normalcy is not prosperity; the failure of 23,146 commercial houses in 1927 is not prosperity; and if this year's record is foreshadowed by the first four months there will be 28,000 commercial failures in 1928.

The difference between the prosperity of the Hamiltonian "nation" that they mean, and the Jeffersonian nation that we know, is this: they could crowd their "nation" into one corner of this vast hall, and the nation that we know includes cities and towns and the countryside, and 118,000,000 people in the homes of men. Their prosperity is a spotted thing—an evidence of disease; and we want to spread it like a healthy glow over every element and section of our population.

Do they offer us their claim of the payment of eight billions of the public debt up to July of last year? Our answer is that six and a third billion of this amount was paid with the money or the cash assets of the Wilson Administration.

Do they offer us their record of economy? Our answer is that with the elimination of the interest on war debts, the last three years of this régime has cost the people more than four and a quarter billion more than the last three peace years of the Wilson Administration.

Mythical prosperity, mythical economy, mythical facts, mythical figures, and mythical men, the last eight years may well be treated by the historian of the far future as the mythical age of American history.

And mythical, too, their virile foreign policy that was promised. We hear about it but we see it not. It is an anemic outcast stumbling blindly in the darkness of No Man's Land. They dare not face the world made over by the war and meet new duties called for by new occasions. They found us enjoying the moral leadership of all mankind, and they have made us the most distrusted and unpopular nation on the globe.

Thus through the stupidity of their dollar diplomacy we have stumbled into a petty war with Nicaragua that is taking its daily toll of American lives. Just why we have the war no one seems to know; just how we came to have the war no one cares to tell. Do they tell us that we are there to guarantee an honest election? Why, not long ago we were unable to guarantee an honest election in the City of Philadelphia. Do they say that we are there to prevent rioting in the election? Why, at the time we were sending the marines to Nicaragua we were campaigning with bombs in the City of Chicago.

Now we propose to end dollar diplomacy in Latin America in the interest of justice; but we propose it, too, in the interest of American business. We do not propose to sacrifice the future markets of our manufacturers and merchants to serve the interest of little groups of financiers and concessionaires. There, within a generation, loom our richest markets; and we are sowing the seed from which our rivals across the sea will reap the harvest in trade. We cannot submit a bill of lading at the point of a bayonet and make the Latin-Americans take it. We cannot write a bill of sale with a mailed fist. We cannot match a marine with a musket against a British or German salesman with a smile. We can serve the ultimate ends of business better through the noble spirit of the Mobile speech of Woodrow Wilson than they have done with their dollar diplomacy, backed by the muskets of the marines who are dying needlessly today in the swamps of Nicaragua.

Never in a century has there been such a call to us to battle for the faith of our fathers as there is today; and never has the control of Government been so completely concentrated in the hands of a ruling caste as now. The dreams of the Hamiltonians have literally come true while the people slept. They wanted organized wealth in possession of the Government—and we have it. They wanted the sovereign rights of States denied—and we have it. They wanted bureaucratic agents swarming over the land like the locusts of Egypt—and we have it. They wanted Government made profitable to the powerful—and we have it. They wanted, through administration, to make a mockery of democracy—and we have it. The Hamiltonian State is necessarily a temple of gold resting on the bowed backs of peasants in other people's fields—and we almost have that now. They would deify dollars and minimize men, limit self-government and centralize power, cripple democracy, empower bureaucracy, welcome plutocracy—and we will soon have that, too.

Give the plunderbund but eight years more of such governmental co-operation and a combination of power companies will put a few men in control of the public utilities of a mighty empire. Make no mistake about it—that is the great Jacksonian struggle of tomorrow. And with that sinister possibility upon us, the people must determine whether they will entrust their interest to those who believe that governments are strong in proportion as they are made profitable to the powerful, or to the Jeffersonians who believe that governments are created for the service of mankind. Once in possession and entrenched, the plunderbund of the power monopoly cannot be dislodged by the fighting force of a dozen Andrew Jacksons.

And so we are going back—back to the old landmarks of liberty and justice in this campaign. Let me suggest a text for people grown cynical and confused. "Saith the Lord, stand ye in the ways and see, and ask for the old paths, which is the good way, and walk therein, and ye shall find rest for your souls."

We are mobilized to lead the people back to the old paths of constitutional liberty, and to the good way. We are going back —back to the old landmarks of liberty and equality, when ordinary men had rights that even power respected; when justice, not privilege, was the watchword of the State; when the preamble of the Declaration and the Bill of Rights had meaning; when the nation embraced every section and every class; and before the Pittsburgh Bratianu had decided to make Rumanian peasants of American farmers to fill the coffers of a purse-proud caste.

Our principles have been written in the triumphs of the people and baptized in the blood of our bravest and our best. Jefferson phrased them, Jackson vitalized them, Wilson applied them, and we go forth to battle for them now.

We face a foe grown arrogant with success. It were infamy to permit the enemy to divide us, or divert us, on the eve of such a battle. Issues are involved that go to the determination of the future of our institutions and our children. The call that comes to us is as sacred as the cause of humanity itself. From the grave at the Hermitage comes the solemn warning that no party ever won or deserved to win that did not organize and fight unitedly for victory—and we shall thus organize and fight. This is a unique campaign. The very precinct committeemen and the district captains become minute men of liberty in the reassertion of the principles of freedom.

And we shall win because our cause is just. The predatory forces before us seek a triumph for the sake of the sacking. Their shock troops are the Black Horse Cavalry whose hoof-beats have made hideous music on Pennsylvania Avenue during the last eight years. They are led by money-mad cynics and scoffers—and we go forth to battle for the cause of man. In the presence of such a foe "he who dallies is a dastard and he who doubts is damned." In this convention we close debate and grasp the sword. The time has come. The battle hour has struck. Then to your tents, O, Israel!

FRANKLIN D. ROOSEVELT

THE HAPPY WARRIOR

SPEECH AT THE DEMOCRATIC NATIONAL CONVENTION, HOUS-
TON, TEXAS, JUNE 27, 1928, NOMINATING ALFRED E.
SMITH AS A CANDIDATE FOR THE PRESIDENCY

[Franklin Delano Roosevelt was born in Hyde Park, New York, on
January 30, 1882. He was graduated from Harvard College in 1904,
from the Columbia University Law School in 1907, was admitted to
the bar of New York City, and has since been in practice there except
when in public service. From 1910 to March 17, 1913, he was a member of the New York Senate, and from 1913 to 1920 he was Assistant
Secretary of the Navy. In that capacity he had charge of inspecting
the United States naval forces in European waters from July to September, 1918, and in 1919 of the demobilization in Europe. In 1920
he was the unsuccessful Democratic candidate for Vice President of
the United States. On November 6, 1928, he was elected Governor of
New York State.]

I come for the third time to urge upon a convention of my
party the nomination of the Governor of the State of New
York. The faith which I held I still hold. It has been justified in the achievement. The whole country now has learned
the measure of his greatness.

During another four years his every act has been under the
searchlight of friend and foe and he has not been found wanting. Slowly, surely, the proper understanding of this man has
spread from coast to coast, from North to South. Most noteworthy is this fact, that the understanding of his stature has
been spread by no paid propaganda, by no effort on his part,
to do other than devote his time, his head and his heart to the
duties of his high office and the welfare of the state.

It is, however, not my belief that I should urge popularity
as the criterion in making our choice. A higher obligation falls
upon us. We must, first of all, make sure that our nominee
possesses the unusual qualifications called for by the high office of President of these United States. Mere party expediency must be subservient to national good. We are Americans
even before we are Democrats.

What sort of President do we need to-day? A man, I take it, who has four great characteristics, every one of them an essential to the office. First of all leadership, articulate, virile, willing to bear responsibility, needing no official spokesman to interpret the oracle.

Next, experience, that does not guess, but knows from long practice, the science of governing, which is a very different thing from mere technical bureau organizing. Then honesty— the honesty that hates hypocrisy and cannot live with concealment and deceit.

Last, and in this time most vital, that rare ability to make popular government function as it was intended to by the Fathers, to reverse the present trend toward apathy and arouse in the citizenship an active interest—a willingness to reassume its share of responsibility for the nation's progress. So only can we have once more a government, not just for the people, but by the people also.

History gives us confident assurance that a man who has displayed these qualities as a great Governor of a state has invariably carried them with him to become a great President. Look back over our list of Presidents since the war between the states, when our rapid growth made our nation's business an expert's task. Who stand out as our great Presidents? New York gave us Grover Cleveland, teaching in Albany that public office is a public trust; Theodore Roosevelt, preaching the square deal for all; Virginia and New Jersey gave to us that pioneer of fellowship between nations, our great leader, Woodrow Wilson.

Let us measure our present Governor by those standards. Personal leadership is a fundamental of successful government. I do not mean the leadership of the band of good fellows and good schemers who followed President Harding, nor the purely perfunctory party loyalty which has part of the time in part of the country sustained the present Chief Executive. I mean that leadership which by sheer force of mind, by chain of unanswerable logic, has brought friends and foes alike to enact vitally needed measures of government reform.

His stanchest political adversaries concede the Governor's unique and unparalleled record of constructive achievement in the total reorganization of the machinery of government, in the business-like management of state finance, in the enactment of a legislative program for the protection of men, women and children engaged in industry, in the improvement of the public health, and in the attainment of the finest standard of public service in the interest of humanity.

This he has accomplished by a personality of vibrant, many-sided appeal, which has swept along with it a Legislature of different political faith.

During the last month alone, the Republican controlled Congress of the United States repeatedly passed important bills over the veto of a Republican President. During eight years at Albany the wisdom of every veto by a Democratic Governor has been sustained by a Republican Legislature. In the same way the fitness of his appointments has been recognized and confirmed without exception by a hostile Republican State Senate, whereas a friendly Federal Senate has on occasion after occasion rejected the nominations sent in by its titular party leader.

The second great need is experience. By this I refer not merely to length of time in office—I mean that practical understanding which comes from the long and thoughtful study of the daily dealings with the basic principles involved in the science of taxation, of social welfare, of industrial legislation, of governmental budgets and administration, of penology, of legislative procedure and practice, of constitutional law.

In all these matters the Governor of New York has developed himself into an expert, recognized and consulted by men and women of all parties. In any conference of scholars on these subjects he takes his place naturally as a trained and efficient specialist. He also possesses that most unusual quality of selecting appointees not only skilled in the theoretical side of their work, but able to give the highest administrative success to their task.

The high standard of the appointees of the Governor, their integrity, their ability, has made strong appeal to the citizens of his state, urban and rural, regardless of party. I add "rural" advisedly, for each succeeding gubernatorial election has shown for him even greater proportional gains in the agricultural sections than in the large communities.

As one who served his state in the Legislature of which this Governor was then also a member, and who later for nearly eight years held an administrative post under President Wilson at Washington, I can bear witness that the problems which confront the Governor of New York and those national problems which confront the President at Washington differ chiefly in geographic extent and not in the fundamental of political principle.

The Governor's study of the needs of his own state has given him deep insight into similar problems of other states and also of their application to the machinery and the needs of the Federal government. In the last analysis a matter of administrative reform, of industrial betterment, of the regulation of public carriers, of the development of natural resources, of the retention of the ownership of primary water power in the people, of the improvement of the lot of the farmer differs little, whether the problem occur in Albany, in Spokane, in Atlanta, or in Washington.

How well the people of his state understood and approved the wise solution of these questions is best shown by the fact that he has been elected and re-elected, and re-elected, and again elected Governor by huge majorities—in the hundreds of thousands—in a normally Republican state.

Now as to the requisite of honesty, I do not mean an honesty that merely keeps a man out of jail, or an honesty that, while avoiding personal smirch, hides the corruption of others. I speak of that honesty that lets a man sleep well of nights, fearing no Senatorial investigation, that honesty that demands faithfulness to the public trust in every public servant, that honesty which takes immediate action to correct abuse.

The whole story of his constant and persistent efforts to insure the practice of the spirit as well as the letter of official and private probity in public places is so well understood by the voters of his state that more and more Republicans vote for him every time he is attacked. This is a topic which need not be enlarged upon. The voting public of the nation is fully wise

enough to compare the ethical standards of official Albany with
those of official Washington.

And now last of all, and where the Governor excels over all
the political leaders of this day, comes the ability to interest the
people in the mechanics of their governmental machinery, to
take the engine apart and show the function of each wheel.

Power to impart knowledge of and create interest in, government is the crying need of our time. The soul of our country,
lulled by mere material prosperity, has passed through eight
gray years.

Our people must not acquiesce in the easy thought of being
mere passengers so long as the drivers and mechanics do not
disturb our comfort. We must be concerned over our destination, not merely satisfied that the passing scenery is pleasant to
the eye. We must be interested in whether the national destination is heaven or hell, and not content that the man at the
wheel has assured us that we shall there find a full bank account and a soft bed.

In an era of the ready-made we must not accept ready-made
government; in a day of high-powered advertising we must
not fall for the false statements of the most highly organized
propaganda ever developed by the owners of the Republican
party. We do not want to change these united sovereign states
of America into the "United States, Incorporated," with a limited and self-perpetuating board of directors and no voting
power in the common stockholders.

This is a time of national danger unless America can be
roused again to wakefulness. I say this in no spirit of the
demagogue, in no wish to attack the legitimate course of the
life or business of our citizens. I see only one hope of a return to that participation by the people in their government
which hitherto marked us out as the great outstanding success
among democratic republics.

That hope lies in the personality of the new man at the wheel,
and especially in his purpose to arouse the spirit of interest and
the desire to participate.

The Governor of the State of New York stands out to-day
as having that purpose, as having proved during these same

eight years not only his desire but his power to make the people as interested in their government as he is himself.

I have described so far qualities entirely of the mind—the mental and moral equipment without which no President can successfully meet the administrative and material problems of his office.

It is possible with only these qualities for a man to be a reasonably efficient President, but there is one thing more needed to make him a great President. It is that quality of soul which makes a man loved by little children, by dumb animals, that quality of soul which makes him a strong help to all those in sorrow or in trouble, that quality which makes him not merely admired, but loved by all the people—the quality of sympathetic understanding of the human heart, or real interest in one's fellow men. Instinctively he senses the popular need because he himself has lived through the hardship, the labor and the sacrifice which must be endured by every man of heroic mold who struggles up to eminence from obscurity and low estate. Between him and the people is that subtle bond which makes him their champion and makes them enthusiastically trust him with their loyalty and their love.

Our two greatest Presidents of modern times possessed this quality to an unusual degree. It was, indeed, what above all made them great. It was Lincoln's human heart and Woodrow Wilson's passionate desire to bring about the happiness of the whole world which will be the best remembered by the historians of a hundred years from now. It is what is so conspicuously lacking in our present Administration, a lack which has been at the bottom of the growing dislike and even hatred of the other nations toward us. For without this love and understanding of his fellow men no Chief Executive can win for his land that international friendship which is alone the sure foundation of lasting peace.

Because of his power of leadership, because of his unequaled knowledge of the science of government, because of his uncompromising honesty, because of his ability to bring the government home to the people, there is no doubt that our Governor will make an "efficient" President; but it is because he also possesses, to a superlative degree, this rare faculty of sympathetic understanding I prophesy that he will also make a great President, and because of this I further prophesy that he will again place us among the nations of the world as a country which values its ideals as much as its material prosperity—a land that has no selfish designs on any weaker power, a land the ideal and inspiration of all those who dream of a kinder, happier civilization in the days to come.

If the vision of real world peace, of the abolishment of war, ever comes true, it will not be through the mere mathematical calculations of a reduction of armament program nor the platitudes of multilateral treaties piously deprecating armed conflict. It will be because this nation will select as its head a leader who understands the human side of life, who has the force of character and the keenness of brain to take, instinctively, the right course and the real course toward a prosperity that will be more than material, a leader also who grasps and understands not only large affairs of business and government, but in an equal degree the aspirations and the needs of the individual, the farmer, the wage-earner—the great mass of average citizens who make up the backbone of our nation.

America needs not only an administrator, but a leader—a pathfinder, a blazer of the trail to the high road that will avoid the bottomless morass of crass materialism that has engulfed so many of the great civilizations of the past. It is the privilege of democracy not only to offer such a man, but to offer him as the surest leader to victory. To stand upon the ramparts and die for our principles is heroic. To sally forth to battle and win for our principles is something more than heroic. We offer one who has the will to win—who not only deserves success, but commands it. Victory is his habit—the happy warrior—Alfred E. Smith.

HARLAN F. STONE

FIFTY YEARS' WORK OF THE UNITED STATES SUPREME COURT

ADDRESS DELIVERED AT THE SEMICENTENNIAL MEETING OF THE AMERICAN BAR ASSOCIATION, SEATTLE, WASHINGTON, JULY 26, 1928

[Harlan Fiske Stone was born in Chesterfield, New Hampshire, on October 11, 1872. He was graduated from Amherst College in 1894, and from Columbia University Law School in 1898. In the interval between college and law school he taught physics and chemistry in Putnam High School, Newburyport, Massachusetts, and while in law school he taught history in Adelphi Academy, Brooklyn. He was admitted to the bar in 1898, began practice in New York City, and maintained an office there until 1924. In the Columbia University Law School he was lecturer from 1899 to 1902, Professor of Law from 1902 to 1905, and Dean from 1910 to 1924. During the European war, he was a member of the Federal Board on Conscientious Objectors. When called to be Attorney General of the United States in 1924, he was a member of the firm of Sullivan & Cromwell. He relinquished the Attorney Generalship on March 2, 1925, to become Associate Justice of the United States Supreme Court.]

When, in an amiable and unguarded moment, I accepted Mr. Strawn's invitation to speak here this evening, I fear I did not appreciate how difficult it is for a judge to make an address not wholly devoid of human interest, and at the same time avoid making it an arsenal from which counsel may, to his utter confusion and undoing, draw ammunition for future conflicts at the bar.

In younger and more innocent days, with no premonitions of the future, I took the time from busy days at the bar to write occasional articles in the law journals on matters of scientific and technical interest, only to experience, in a repentant old age, the unhappy fate of hearing them on occasion cited to me in court in support of both sides of the same question. However much the judge may become accustomed and reconciled to such startling agility of counsel, it requires a larger judicial experience than mine to prepare one to face with equanimity the varying implications which may be drawn by diligent counsel from his own innocent remarks. So if what I am about to say should prove to be more dull and uninteresting than even judicial pronouncements are wont to be, I should like to persuade myself that you would attribute it to a newly developed instinct of self-preservation, cautiously applied with an eye to the future.

In the realm of law it is not the old and settled but the new and unsettled questions which stir the interest and invite discussion; but from all such allurements I turn aside to examine in retrospect some phases of the work of the great court of which I chance to be the youngest and least experienced member.

And it is altogether appropriate that on the conclusion of the first 50 years of the association's existence we should recall some of the more significant developments in the history of the court during the same period. It is worthy of note that the last and in many respects the most striking phase of its history coincides with the life of this association. The first phase embraces that early period when it became established as a court, and by recourse to those methods and processes with which lawyers have been familiar for centuries for the first time in history made all the agencies of a government subject to the supremacy of a constitution. That period ended with the death of the great Chief Justice in 1835.

During the next 40 years the drama of the slavery struggle, the Civil War, and reconstruction occupied the stage of American history. Out of the varying phases of that struggle came the great questions with which the court in that period was called on to deal. Of lesser public interest, but still of vital importance to the progress of the law and to the future of the expanding Nation, were the development by the court during those years of the beginnings of public and private law affecting business corporations and the first steps toward the nationalistic interpretation of the commerce clause of the Constitution.

In 1878, just 50 years ago, a change in the character of the questions to which the court was addressing itself was apparent. Following the initial stages of Civil War reconstruction came the era of railway building, the rise of the business corporation as an instrumentality of business and commerce, and the beginning of the great industrial and commercial expansion of the

Nation. This expansion, which was well under way in the early eighties, has continued with accelerated speed and broadening scope down to the present day. In it have originated most of the great questions which have engaged the attention of the court during the last 50 years, and it has furnished the fact material out of which have come the significant developments both of the constitutional and the private law applied by the court during the last phase of its history.

The changing personnel of the court during this, as in earlier periods, gives a note of human interest to an institution which from the beginning has seemed singularly impersonal. Fifty years ago this year the court was presided over by Chief Justice Waite, whom President Grant had appointed to that office two years before. Among the eight Associate Justices were Justice Bradley, Field, Harlan, and Miller, who now, after half a century, still stand out among the great figures of the court. Since then three Chief Justices and twenty-nine Associate Justices have been appointed. Chief Justice Fuller was appointed by President Cleveland in 1888, Chief Justice White by President Taft in 1910, and Ex-President Taft himself became Chief Justice in 1921. The terms of seven Chief Justices, the last, our present Chief Justice, still actively carrying on the duties of his office, have thus spanned the 127 years since the appointment of Chief Justice Marshall, and during the entire history of the court 10 chief justices and 65 associates have sat upon its bench. In 1897, Mr. Justice Field, then 83 years of age, retired from the bench, after a service of 34 years, exceeding by a few months that of Chief Justice Marshall, and exceeding that of Chief Justice Taney, whose death in 1864, in his eighty-eighth year, had closed a service of 28 years. And to-day Mr. Justice Holmes, in his eighty-eighth year, with youthful spirit unabated, is still actively carrying on his work as a Justice of the court, after 26 years of service, and a total judicial service in the Supreme Court of the United States, and the Supreme Judicial Court of Massachusetts, of which he was formerly chief justice, of more than 46 years.

The last 50 years of the work of the court is represented by the series of official reports extending from the ninety-seventh volume to the two hundred and seventy-sixth volume, now in the press, making 179 volumes in all, a monument to the scholarship, skill, and patient industry of the judges. In these volumes will be found opinions of far-reaching importance which have profoundly influenced the course of development of the American system of constitutional government, and in them we discern those trends of the law which are of especial interest and importance in any attempt to review the progress of the work of the court during the last half century.

Of outstanding importance are the decisions of the court under the commerce clause and the great judgments giving definition and application to the provisions of the fourteenth amendment. Of relatively less moment, but still of the highest importance in any consideration of the development of the law in the last half century, are cases in numerous other widely varying fields of law which during that period have been extended and intensively tilled by the court.

To them, with the time at my command, only brief reference can be made. By the decision two years ago in Myers v. United States, 272 U. S. 52, 47 S. Ct. 21, 71 L. Ed. 160, after more than 137 years of public debate both in and out of Congress, it was settled that the executive power vested in the President by the Constitution included the power to remove an inferior officer appointed by him, and was not subject to limitation by Congress. Of lesser significance, because of the final outcome, but nevertheless attracting wide attention at the time, was the battle over the constitutionality of the Federal income tax, finally settled by the adoption of the sixteenth amendment.

During the last 30 years we have witnessed the striking extension of Federal police power effected not directly by court action, but by acts of Congress in the exercise of powers incidental to the constitutional power to tax, to regulate commerce, to make treaties, and finally the power to prohibit trafficking in intoxicating liquors conferred by the eighteenth amendment. The progressive occupation and expansion of this field have enlarged enormously the Federal power and increased correspondingly the number and variety of questions brought to the court for solution. Of great juristic interest also, although not necessarily involving constitutional questions, were the legal battles under the Sherman Act, with their far-reaching consequences to business and industry, the increasing resort to the original jurisdiction of the court in suits between States, and the extension of the equity jurisdiction of the Federal courts for the appointment of receivers for insolvent corporations.

Turning points in the application of the Sherman Act were the Trans-Missouri Freight Association Case, 166 U. S. 290, 17 S. Ct. 540, 41 L. Ed. 1007, the Northern Securities Case, 193 U. S. 197, 24 S. Ct. 436, 48 L. Ed. 679, the Standard Oil and Tobacco Cases, 221 U. S. 1, 31 S. Ct. 502, 55 L. Ed. 619, 34 L. R. A. (N. S.) 834, Ann. Cas. 1912D, 734, and 221 U. S. 106, 31 S. Ct. 632, 55 L. Ed. 663, in which the court declared that only unreasonable restraints were prohibited; United States v. Trenton Potteries Co., 273 U. S. 392, 47 S. Ct. 377, 71 L. Ed. 700, 50 A.L.R. 989, in which the court held specifically what had been implied in earlier decisions, that agreements fixing the prices of commodities sold in interstate commerce are in themselves unreasonable and illegal restraints, regardless of the reasonableness of the price agreed upon. In the Maple Flooring & Cement Manufacturers' Association Cases, 268 U. S. 563, 45 S. Ct. 578, 592, 69 L. Ed. 1093, and 268 U. S. 588, 45 S. Ct. 586, 592, 69 L. Ed. 1104, it was held that the mere gathering and dissemination by trade associations of information as to the economic status of a trade or business, even though by the operation of economic laws they might indirectly affect prices, were not a violation of the statute when there was no agreement, express or implied, to fix prices or otherwise restrain commerce. The court entered a new field in the enforcement of the act in the Duplex Printing Co. Case, 254 U. S. 443, 41 S. Ct. 172, 65 L. Ed. 349, 16 A. L. R. 196, and the Bedford Stone Case, 274 U. S. 37, 47 S. Ct. 522, 71 L. Ed. 916, 54 A. L. R. 791, in which the rule was stated broadly that strikes by labor unions in one State against the use of material prepared by nonunion labor in another were restraints of interstate commerce in such materials and violations of the act.

In the exercise of original jurisdiction in suits between States, in boundary disputes, in suits involving the disposition of public waters, in suits concerning nuisances maintained in one State to the detriment of citizens of another, the court has found it necessary to build up its own system of common law, defining these rights which one State may assert against another.

The development of the doctrine of equity receiverships in cases where there is diversity of citizenship, has added an important field to the jurisdiction of the Federal courts, and afforded to suitors a more complete remedy than it is possible for State courts to give. For only in the Federal courts is it possible to secure a uniform administration of the assets of insolvent corporations where their property is located in different States and by making bills for foreclosure, ancillary to the bill to appoint equity receivers, in insolvency proceedings, it has become possible to secure a uniform foreclosure of mortgages of railroad systems and other corporate properties extending into many States.

But it is the decisions of the court under the commerce clause and the fourteenth amendment to which we must recur as representing the most significant developments in the constitutional field. Before 1860 the court had rendered only 20 decisions under the commerce clause, dealing principally with navigation, immigration, slavery, and the liquor traffic. After the Civil War, with the era of railroad building and business depression and the multiplication of business corporations carrying on their business across State lines, there arose the inevitable conflict of interest between local regulation and taxation and the power to regulate reserved to the Federal Government by the commerce clause. By 1870 there had been in all only 30 decisions of the court under this clause, but keeping pace with the rising tide of business enterprise, the decisions numbered 77 by 1880, and 148 by 1890. During these periods, for the first time, cases affecting railroads, telegraph lines, sales of goods across State lines, and taxation affecting commerce predominated.

Great as is the practical wisdom exhibited in all the provisions of the Constitution, and important as were the character and influence of those who secured its adoption, it will, I believe, be the judgment of history that the commerce clause and the wise interpretation of it, perhaps more than any other contributing element, have united to bind the several States into a nation.

Beginning soon after the appointment of Chief Justice Waite and continuing down to the present time, there has come from the court the series of decisions defining the powers of the national Government over commerce. They present an impressive record of the application of constitutional principles to the growing needs and interests of the expanding nation. Here, as elsewhere in the application of the Constitution, the problem has been to maintain the national interest and at the same time bring it into an effective harmony with local interests and the principles of local government.

On the whole, essentially local interests have been preserved both in the field of regulation and in that of taxation, but whatever has vitally concerned the free flow of the very lifeblood of the Nation in its commerce has been dealt with on broadly nationalistic lines and step by step brought completely within the power of the Federal Government. This development of the Constitution, culminated perhaps in Wabash, St. Louis & Pacific Railway v. Illinois, 118 U. S. 557, 7 S. Ct. 4, 30 L. Ed. 244, holding a State without power to regulate rates within its borders where the commerce was interstate, and in the Minnesota Rate Case, 230 U. S. 352, 33 S. Ct. 729, 57 L. Ed. 1511, 48 L. R. A. (N. S.) 1151, Ann. Cas. 1916A, 18, upholding the Federal power to fix intrastate rates for interstate carriers. Again it was carried to its logical conclusion where the path of the fifth amendment, paralleling the fourteenth, converged with that of the commerce clause when the court held in Interstate Commerce Commission v. Brimson, 154 U. S. 447, 14 S. Ct. 1125, 38 L. Ed. 1047, that these clauses permit regulation of the rates of interstate carriers by the Interstate Commerce Commission; and in the Second Employers' Liability Cases, 223 U. S. 1, 32 S. Ct. 169, 56 L. Ed. 327, 38 L. R. A. (N. S.) 44, holding that Congress has power to enact employers' liability acts applicable to carriers in interstate commerce and varying the common-law rules of employers' liability.

With the advent of the automobile, for the first time since the court was organized, there has developed a nation-wide volume of interstate carriage not confined to waterways or to the rails or rights of way of the carriers, but carried on over public highways which are under State or municipal control. This new type of commerce has thus presented to the court for determination an entirely new class of questions, involving the extent of the power of a State in the regulation of its own highways and in taxation for their upkeep to affect this new type of interstate traffic. The improvement of the airplane and growth of interstate carriage by that vehicle of commerce and the use of the radio as an instrumentality of commerce will likewise present questions differing in many respects from those which have heretofore engaged the attention of the court.

In these fields, as in others where interstate commerce is concerned, it seems clear that the function of the court must continue to be, as in the past, to prevent discrimination and the erection of barriers against interstate commerce, but upon careful scrutiny of every relevant fact and circumstance, to save to the States the regulation and control of all interests peculiarly local which do not infringe the national interest in maintaining untrammeled the freedom of commerce across State lines.

Another group of cases having an important bearing on the business and commercial expansion of the Nation has arisen under the fourteenth amendment, with respect to the power of the several States over foreign corporations. In Paul v. Virginia, 8 Wall. 168, 19 L. Ed. 357, the court, speaking by Mr. Justice Field, followed the pronouncement of Chief Justice Taney in Bank of Augusta v. Earle, 13 Pet. 519, 10 L. Ed. 274, that corporations are not citizens within the meaning of section 2, Article IV, of the Constitution, which guarantees to the citizens of each State "the privileges and immunities of citizens in the several States." From these decisions it followed that a State might exclude a foreign corporation not engaged in interstate commerce from carrying on business within its territory. In Doyle v. Continental Insurance Co., 94 U. S. 535, 24 L. Ed. 148, it was held that the power to exclude included the power to impose onerous conditions upon the privilege of transacting business within the State. It seemed that under the application of this doctrine all the protection of the fourteenth amendment might be withdrawn from a foreign corporation seeking access to a State and not engaged in interstate commerce. But later cases have followed the line of argument advanced in the dissent of Mr. Justice Bradley in Doyle v. Continental Insurance Co., by holding that the power to exclude does not embrace the power to impose unconstitutional conditions upon the admission of a corporation to do business within a State. These decisions have given a different trend to the rule announced in Doyle v. Continental Insurance Co., which it was thought might seriously curtail commerce among the States.

But the great battle ground of the Constitution during the last half century has been the fourteenth amendment. Because of the nature of the rights and immunities secured by it and the character of the social and economic development of the Nation, this amendment so far as can now be discerned, will continue to be the principal field of constitutional controversy for many years to come. The amendment was adopted in 1866. The first of the decisions handed down under it was that in the Slaughter House Cases, 16 Wall. 36, 21 L. Ed. 394. Although decided something more than 50 years ago, they may appropriately be considered here, because they are more identified with the development of constitutional law in the last than in the earlier period. They were the first of the long series of cases brought to the court under the new amendment, and marked the turn of the tide which, with the strong nationalistic spirit engendered by the Civil War, had set in against the emphasis of State rights.

The opinion of the court declared that, notwithstanding its broad language, the amendment had not transferred the security and protection of the civil rights of citizens of the States from the States to the special care of the Federal Government, but had merely created in addition to State citizenship a new citizenship of the United States. This new citizenship it had clothed with new privileges and immunities of limited character peculiar to it, and these alone were protected by that clause of the amendment which prohibited a State from abridging the privileges and immunities of citizens of the United States.

In view of the later judicial history of the amendment it is a noteworthy fact that in upholding, as the court did in that case, a statute of Louisiana granting exclusive monopolistic powers for the maintenance of stockyards and slaughterhouses, it made only passing reference to the due process and equal protection clauses of the amendment which, under later decisions, have become the chief guaranties of civil liberty of the individual as against State action.

It was within the 50-year period with which we are immediately concerned that the decisions of the court have given to the fourteenth amendment its real character as a guaranty against the encroachments of the States upon the liberty of the individual. Due process was held to mean not merely due legal procedure which, in the historic words of Webster in the Dartmouth College Case "hears before it condemns, proceeds upon inquiry, and renders judgment only after trial." But in Davidson v. New Orleans, 96 U. S. 97, 24 L. Ed. 616, Mr. Justice Miller, speaking for the court, pointed out that the protection of the clause extended beyond injustices which might be inflicted by an arbitrary procedure to all those which might be imposed by any arbitrary exercise of the power of a State, whatever the form of procedure adopted. Continuing the famous passage from Webster's argument in the Dartmouth College case, which anticipated by a half century the comprehensive interpretation of the due-process clause, "The meaning is that every citizen shall hold his life, liberty, property, and immunities under the protection of the general duties which govern society. Everything which may pass under the form of an enactment is not, therefore, to be considered the law of the land. If this were so, acts of attainder, bills of pains and penalties, acts of confiscation, acts reversing judgments, and acts directly transferring one man's estate to another, legislative judgments, decrees, and forfeitures, in all possible forms, would be the law of the land."

It was in Davidson v. New Orleans also that Mr. Justice Miller pointed out the future course of judicial definition and application of the phrase "due process of law." In the absence of a more precise definition in the Constitution itself there was wisdom, he said, "in the ascertaining of the intent and application of such an important phrase of the Federal Constitution, by the gradual process of judicial inclusion and exclusion, as the cases presented for decision shall require, with the reasoning on which such decisions may be founded." Noteworthy monuments marking the boundary drawn by this process of exclusion and inclusion, as it has been plotted by the court, are the opinions of Mr. Justice Matthews and Mr. Justice Moody in Hurtado v. California, 110 U. S. 516, 4 S. Ct. 111, 292, 28 L. Ed.

232, and in Twining v. New Jersey, 211 U. S. 78, 29 S. Ct. 14, 53 L. Ed. 97, holding that due process was not limited to the due process of the settled usage of the past, but might include new methods of procedure unknown to the common law, provided only that they be in harmony with the accepted underlying principles of such procedure according to the traditions of the common law; that is, that they should be orderly and provide for reasonable notice and opportunity to be heard.

It was thus determined that the constitutional requirement of due process did not bind us rigidly to any rule of the past and that the limitations of the amendment were consistent with the enlightened progress of the law.

A notable step was taken under the fourteenth amendment in Munn v. Illinois, 94 U. S. 113, 24 L. Ed. 77, in upholding the legislative power to regulate rates of a business said to be "affected with a public use," and resulted finally in the confirmation of the now firmly established legislative power to regulate the rates of all public utilities. An important limitation on the doctrine was that announced in Smyth v. Ames, 169 U. S. 466, 18 S. Ct. 418, 42 L. Ed. 819, that the fourteenth amendment forbids a rate which is confiscatory. The court has thus been called on to solve one of the most difficult and perplexing of economic questions, What is the minimum limit of the rate of return to which the capital invested in a public utility may be restricted before the point of confiscation is reached, and how shall that capital investment be ascertained?

In that and later cases it was pointed out that the value of invested capital could not be computed on the basis of unregulated earnings. To say what the investment value is and to separate it from considerations of an unregulated earning capacity and from the elements of business advantage and opportunity conferred upon it by the franchise of the utility itself, constitute the great problem of constitutional rate making, the correct solution of which is of incalculable importance to the future economic development of the Nation.

The interests of the individual guaranteed by the fourteenth amendment are subject, within certain limitations, incapable of a complete or comprehensive definition, to the power of the State government to protect the interests of its society as a whole.

For want of a better generalization, we call this power to protect the social or community interest the police power. It is the course of marking out step by step the line which separates the boundary of the immunity of the individual from this controlling interest of the State by the process of inclusion and exclusion which has given rise to the most perplexing questions and to wide differences of opinion. These questions are none the less perplexing and differences emphatic, because with the social and economic changes which take place from generation to generation that boundary line necessarily becomes a shifting one.

All those restraints on the individual which have been found necessary in order to enable modern men to get on together in civilized life or to conserve the health, morals, and stability of modern communities involve some impairment of the individual interest in liberty or property. The extent of that restraint necessarily varies in time and in space. Restraints upon those rights which in primitive and sparsely settled communities might well be regarded as arbitrary and unreasonable, may be indispensable to the safety and orderly life of the modern city.

The past 50 years have wrought extensive changes in the daily life of the individual and in the character of his contacts with his fellows. From a people devoted to agriculture, living for the most part in thinly settled communities, we have developed into a great business and industrial civilization. In the course of this transformation there has been a shift of population from country to city, giving rise to a new type of social and economic problem. Mass production in industry, new methods of transportation, and transmission of intelligence have raised problems quite unknown a generation ago. Crowded traffic, congestion in cities, the necessity of restricting the use of the highways, abuses in particular classes of business, or in particular types of community which may be remedied by regulation are only examples of an infinite number of new situations which present almost daily to the court the question, Where does individual right to liberty and property end and the community interest begin?

As civilization becomes more complex and the tension of life in organized society increases, it is inevitable that such new problems should continue to arise and that with changing conditions affecting community life there should be both in point of time and in space some shifting of the line which sets off the valid exercise of the police power from the immunity of the individual. Mr. Justice Sutherland, in speaking for the court, when in Village of Euclid v. Ambler Realty Co., 272 U. S. 365, 47 S. Ct. 114, 71 L. Ed. 303, 54 A. L. R. 1016, it recently upheld a city-zoning ordinance, said (page 336):

"Building zone laws are of modern origin. They began in this country about 25 years ago. Until recent years urban life was comparatively simple, but with the great increase and concentration of population, problems have developed, and constantly are developing, which require, and will continue to require, additional restrictions in respect of the use and occupation of private lands in urban communities. Regulations, the wisdom, necessity, and validity of which, as applied to existing conditions, are so apparent that they are now uniformly sustained, a century ago, or even half a century ago, probably would have been rejected as arbitrary and oppressive. Such regulations are sustained, under the complex conditions of our day, for reasons analogous to those which justify traffic regulations, which, before the advent of automobiles and rapid-transit street railways, would have been condemned as fatally arbitrary and unreasonable. And in this there is no inconsistency, for while the meaning of constitutional guarantees never varies, the scope of their application must expand or contract to meet the new and different conditions which are constantly coming within the field of their operation. In a changing world it is impossible that it should be otherwise. But, although a degree of elasticity is thus imparted, not to the meaning but to the application of constitutional principles, statutes and ordinances, which, after giving due weight to the new conditions, are found clearly not to conform to the Constitution, of course, must fall. * * *

"A regulatory zoning ordinance, which would be clearly valid as applied to great cities, might be clearly invalid as applied to rural communities. * * * Thus the question whether the power exists to forbid the erection of a building of a particular kind or for a particular use, like the question whether a particular thing is a nuisance, is to be determined, not by an abstract consideration of the building or of the thing considered apart,

but by considering it in connection with the circumstances and
the locality. * * * If the validity of the legislative classification for zoning purposes be fairly debatable, the legislative
judgment must be allowed to control."

It was to be expected that the application of a constitutional
limitation so vaguely defined, to state action affecting all the
varying situations which may arise in our present-day civilization, would give rise to strong differences of opinion, often resulting in decisions by a divided court. These differences usually result, not from any disagreement as to the nature of the
formulas which have been developed by the court in the application of the fourteenth amendment, but to differences in the
appreciation and appraisement of social and economic conditions
and of the relation to them of legislative action to which those
formulas are to be applied. There is general agreement that
arbitrary and unreasonable legislative action is forbidden; that
businesses "affected with a public use" may be regulated, and
so on. Differences arise in determining whether particular legislation operates arbitrarily and unreasonably when applied to
particular situations, or whether a particular business is so affected with a public use as to be the subject of regulation.

The character of these differences suggests the great importance, in applying the fourteenth amendment to cases as they
arise, of the court's being fully informed as to all phases of the
particular social conditions affected, the evils supposed to originate in them, and the appropriateness of the particular remedy
sought to be applied. Unfortunately, in briefing questions of
this character it has been the disposition of the bar very generally to be content with the elaboration of legal formulas and
the citation of authorities, without a painstaking examination
of the fact situation which has given rise to the constitutional
question.

Lawyers who in the presentation of a negligence case would
prove with meticulous care every fact surrounding the accident
and injury, in this field too often go little beyond the challenged
statute and the citation of authorities in supposedly analogous
cases. The court is thus often left to speculate as to the nature
and extent of the social problems giving rise to the legislative
problem or to discover them by its own researches. Intimate

acquaintance with every aspect of the conditions which have given rise to the regulatory problems are infinitely more important to the court than are the citation of authorities or the recital of bare formulas.

The extent to which a particular abuse has been the subject of legislative investigation and legislative action in other States or communities than the one immediately concerned, while not decisive of the constitutional question, are often of great importance in determining the nature of the question with which the legislature had to deal and in determining what are appropriate methods of dealing with it. Often the court has brought before it legislation of more or less local application, dealing with what are peculiarly local problems, or, again, new questions growing out of entirely new situations without any adequate presentation of the legislative history or analysis or explanation of the actual situation which produced it.

It is true that the court has often said that every presumption must be indulged in favor of the constitutionality of the legislative action. As is the case with other legal formulas, this presumption may prove to be a prop which will save the plaintiff's case from collapse, but there is no safe or satisfactory reason for his discarding any available data which support presumption.

These differences of opinion as to the scope of the police power in its application to particular social problems have revived in the last 25 years the discussion of earlier days, of the power of the court to declare laws of the States and of Congress unconstitutional. While the exercise of this power has been strongly challenged as judicial usurpation, the history of the judicial function before the adoption of the Constitution, the language of the Constitution itself in Article VI, and the long course of judicial decision, leave that question no longer debatable. Hence, much of the discussion has been addressed to the question, whether the power should be limited and to suggested ways and means of limiting it.

Whatever views one may cherish as to the methods by which constitutional government may be attained in those countries which are homogeneous with respect to their local interests and local government, he can not long reflect upon our own situation and our own history without realizing how impossible it would be to preserve the rights and autonomy of our governments, both State and national, free from encroachment, each upon the other, without resort to the mediation of some impartial body.

When it comes to limiting the power of the court to declare laws unconstitutional, it is important to bear in mind that whatever limitations have been proposed upon the exercise of this power in the protection of the individual from the encroachments of government under the fifth and the fourteenth amendments, must likewise restrict the power of the court to draw the line which marks the separation of the constitutional powers of the States from each other and from the powers of the Federal Government.

The last 50 years of our constitutional history have shown a steadily increasing number of contacts between the operations of State governments and those of the National Government on the one hand and the activities of the several State governments on the other. One finds examples of the first in the exercise of the powers, both State and National, over commerce, intrastate and interstate; in the expansion of the Federal police power within the territorial limits of the States; in the field of taxation wherever either government attempts to extend its taxing power so as to affect the instrumentalities of the other or enter the exclusive field of taxation of the other. We have seen, with increasing frequency, examples of these contacts between State governments in original suits, in which one State seeks the vindication of its sovereign rights as against the other in the only court competent to adjudicate them. Wherever these contacts between the two governments occur, it is inevitable that there should result from time to time real or apparent conflicts of interest which give rise to conflicting views of the constitutional rights and powers of the governments concerned. Governmental action often taken through the agency of statutes may also be taken by the acts of officers whose powers and duties are defined by statutes. It follows that when conflicting claims of governmental right of power are brought to the Supreme Court for adjudication, they must of necessity be resolved in the great number of cases by passing on the constitutionality of some statute, State or Federal.

During the entire history of the court and chiefly during the last 50 years we have seen it at work, sitting as the impartial umpire to settle these controversies between sovereign governments, and it has settled them sometimes by holding that the State, by passing a particular statute, has exceeded its power, and sometimes by holding that Congress, in its legislation, has exceeded the powers delegated to the National Government. Without this method for the peaceable settlement of these controversies upon their merits there could be recourse only to the uncertainties of diplomatic negotiations between the governments concerned or to force.

It is a fact worthy of some comment that in the discussion of the powers of the court to declare statutes unconstitutional, we have been disposed to leave entirely out of account this indispensable function of the court as the arbiter between sovereign governments, and we have taken little thought of the effect on its exercise of that function, of the proposals which have been made for limiting its authority to declare statutes unconstitutional. Whether that power should be limited is a political question which I do not discuss, but in a gathering of lawyers it is entirely appropriate that some consideration should be given to the effect of the particular methods of limitation which have been suggested.

The devices proposed for setting limits upon the exercise of this power have been aimed at giving to statutes a weight which they would otherwise not possess in their competitive struggle with the provisions of the Constitution. They have been of two kinds. It has been suggested that a statute might be made to prevail over constitutional objections if it were passed by the legislative body twice. It has also been suggested that if a statute whose constitutionality was contested were upheld by the vote of a minority of two or three of the members of the court, it should become law despite all constitutional objections.

When any such device is applied to the function which the court exercises as the arbiter between the rival claims of governments or the separate branches of the National Government, the question at once arises, Shall it be applied equally to statutes passed by Congress and to statutes passed by State legislatures, or shall it be applied to only one, the acts of Congress? If applicable only to one, it is apparent that the sovereign State and the National Government no longer stand on a plane of equality in matters of constitutional right or immunity, but the way is opened for the gradual curtailment of the constitutional powers granted to or reserved by one through the enactment of statutes by the other, which, whenever their constitutionality is assailed, have greater weight before the court than the Constitution itself.

But if the device of the weighted statute were to be applied both to the acts of Congress and to State statutes in the field of the conflict of powers of government under our dual system, then each would be given the opportunity to extend its own constitutional power in particular fields at the expense of the other by the enactment of statutes which, before the Supreme Court, must be given a weight greater than is given to other forms of governmental actions or to the provisions of the Constitution itself.

But governments do not always exercise their sovereign powers through the enactment of statutes. Under our system they may act with equal competency through the executive or the judicial power, and such action when it is supported by the Constitution is as authoritative as if the Government spoke through legislation alone. The consequence of these proposals therefore would be to give a weight and effect to the legislative action which would not attach to other forms of governmental action when it is asserted that both are sanctioned by the Constitution.

In a controversy between States, founded upon diverse claims of constitutional right, greater weight must needs be given to the statute of one than to the executive action of the other, merely because governmental action in one case has found expression in a statute rather than through some other equally competent agency.

The same inequality between the different types of responsible governmental action would occur with respect to the three branches of the National Government. Under such a scheme the executive action of the President or the judicial action of courts, each founded upon a claim of constitutional right, would have less weight than the action of the legislative branch. In practice the device of the weighted statutes could only operate to effect a gradual transfer of constitutional powers from the executive and judicial branches of the Government to the legislative.

These are but illustrations in somewhat elementary fashion of the truth that under our system of the distribution of constitutional powers, the power vested in one branch or agency of the Government can not be subtracted from one litigant without adding to that of the other, and that giving artificial weight to one form of governmental action wherever it comes into conflict with the other forms, or with the Constitution itself, can only result in an inevitable shifting of governmental powers as they have been distributed by the Constitution. And that redistribution of power would take place, not as the result of judicial action based on the provisions of the great document itself but by increasing the power of one at the expense of the other by resort to its own legislative action.

The progress of the court to its present position as the acknowledged arbiter between conflicting claims of governmental power is in itself an interesting chapter of constitutional history. That it has attained to that position is not due alone to the fact that its great powers were conferred upon it by a written constitution. It is due quite as much to the position which it early assumed and has always maintained of independence from every external influence, and to thoroughness and fidelity in the performance of its judicial labors.

When the court was organized it would have been easy for it to have fallen into a condition of dependence on the other great branches of the Government. That such was not its fate is due to its adherence to the tradition of independence of English and American courts and the complete realization of the fact that irrespective of whether it deals with the right of private litigants or the rights and powers of governments, a court is not truly a court unless it acts with complete independence.

If time would permit, it would be interesting to refer to the repeated decisions of the court in the past 50 years, where, as in earlier periods, its action has shown the complete detachment of its judges from all external influences. Where the court

has divided the divisions have not been along party or political
lines, but have rested on more fundamental differences of legal
and political philosophy. And so it may be said, with the support of its entire history, that the position of the court as the
controlling influence which holds each of the governments in
our system and each branch of the National Government moving within its own orbit, with general acquiescence in the fairness and justice of its judgments, has been due more to its steadfast adherence to the best traditions of judicial independence
than to any other cause.

But if throughout its history judicial independence has been
the pole star by which the court has shaped its course, a prodigious industry and the exhaustive scrutiny of the facts and law
of each case have been the motive power behind its judgment.
It is only since the Civil War that its docket has become crowded
with cases and that the growth of the country and expansion
of all governmental activities, both State and National, have
steadily increased the pressure of work upon the judges.

Very remote seem the days when the court adjourned for
lack of business, and when the first Chief Justice resigned in
order that he might find more active occupation as Governor
of New York. The jurisdictional act of May, 1925, limiting appeals and writs of error and enlarging the discretionary jurisdiction of the court, was passed in the hope of relieving the pressure on the court and enabling it to catch up with its docket.
Since its enactment steady progress has been made. For the
first time in many years there has been a progressive reduction
in the number of cases awaiting action by the court. In the
October term of 1927, which came to its close in June, 1,049
cases were placed on the docket, of which 17 were original
causes. Of this total number, 859 were disposed of during the
term. Of those 365 cases were on the merits and 492 were on
petition for certiorari—about 100 of which you may be surprised to learn were granted. In addition to the cases regularly
appearing on the docket a large number of motions were heard
and disposed of by the court as made. At the close of the term
there were only 190 cases on the docket instead of 295, as at the
close of 1926 term, and of these 44 were applications for certiorari, so that when the court adjourned in June there were

only 126 cases on the docket awaiting the disposition of the court on their merits. There is now reasonable ground for the expectation that by the end of another term the court may be able to hear cases on their merits as soon after they are docketed as counsel are prepared to present them.

This is greatly to be desired, not that the court may be relieved of a heavy burden of labor, but that it may be able to make better disposition of its time. Time, which has hitherto been given to relatively unimportant matters, it is hoped may now be devoted to cases of far-reaching public importance. We ought not to be completely absorbed in the technique of the law. Who could listen to those inspiring addresses which we heard yesterday and for a moment suppose that law could exist and function separate and apart from science or from adequate understanding and appreciation of the significant facts of modern life which affect social right? The questions which come to us are rooted in history and in the social and economic development of the Nation. To grasp their significance our study must be extended beyond the examination of precedents and legal formulas, by reading and research in fields extralegal, which, nevertheless, have an intimate relation to the genesis of the legal rules which we pronounce. If we attain that much to the desired end, it will be through the aid of the jurisdictional act of May, 1925, and by more faithful observance by lawyers of the rules regulating arguments and the preparation of briefs, and especially the preparation of applications for certiorari, which I commend to your thoughtful consideration.

It may be of interest, and in some measure reassuring to members of the bar, if I devote a few moments to describing how this grist of legal work is ground out week by week during the term. There has been no change in the method of work in the past 50 years, and so far as I have been able to learn the court's habits of work have undergone little or no change from the beginning. I betray no secrets in describing them. In 1874 Mr. Justice Campbell, in his eulogy of Justice Curtain, and more recently former Justice Hughes, have described the daily work of the court.

Every Saturday the court sits in conference, meeting at noon, just when the call for golf is most alluring. At the sessions of the court during the week the judges have heard arguments in cases on the merits. The time of arguments, as you know, is limited so as to make impracticable decision from the bench in most cases. During the spacious hours of leisure before the court sits at 12, and after it adjourns at half past four, the judges have had opportunity to examine the records in the argued and submitted cases, and to examine the petitions and briefs upon current applications for certiorari. They have also received and examined the papers in the miscellaneous motions affecting the cases which have been docketed. On the day before the conference each judge receives a list giving the cases which will be taken up at the conference and the order in which they will be considered. This list usually includes every cause which is ready for final disposition, including the cases argued the day before the conference, and all pending motions and applications for certiorari.

At conference each case is presented for discussion by the Chief Justice, usually by a brief statement of the facts, the questions of law involved, and with such suggestions for their disposition as he may think appropriate. No cases have been assigned to any particular judge in advance of the conference. Each justice is prepared to discuss the case at length and to give his views as to the proper solution of the questions presented. In Mr. Justice Holmes' pungent phrase, each must be ready to "recite" on the case. Each judge is requested by the Chief Justice, in the order of seniority, to give his views and the conclusions which he has reached. The discussion is of the freest character and at its end, after full opportunity has been given for each member of the court to be heard and for the asking and answering of questions, the vote is taken and recorded in the reverse order of the discussion, the youngest in point of service voting first.

On the same evening, after the conclusion of the conference, each member of the court receives at his home a memorandum from the Chief Justice advising him of the assignment of cases for opinions. Opinions are written for the most part in recess, and as they are written they are printed and circulated among the justices, who make suggestions for their correction and revision. At the next succeeding conference these suggestions are brought before the full conference and accepted or rejected, as the case may be. On the following Monday the opinion is announced by the writer as the opinion of the court.

In the preparation of opinions it has been from the beginning the practice to state the case fully in the opinion. This practice gives a clarity and focus to the opinion not otherwise attainable, and has added in no small degree to the prestige and influence of the court. In recent years there has been a trend toward brevity and directness in the judicial style which without sacrifice of the essentials of the opinions has, I believe, enhanced their value as expositions of legal science.

In the first reported opinion of the court, Georgia v. Brailsford, 2 Dall. 402, 415, 1 L. Ed. 433, a dissenting opinion was written, a practice which has been continued from time to time throughout the history of the court. In the last 50 years there have been some notable instances of the dissenting opinion ultimately becoming the prevailing opinion of the court. Notwithstanding the ideal of certainty in the law, the dissenting opinion is not without its value even though it never secures the adherence of a majority. One can not trace the path of the law without becoming convinced that its course is very different from what it would have been if uninfluenced by the considered and powerful dissents of able judges.

An interesting, and I am inclined to believe, important feature of the court's method of doing its work is that every decision, even of a motion, is a nine-judge decision. No one knows in advance of the vote and the assignment of the case by the Chief Justice who will write the opinion. No judge, more than another, is expected to advise his associates with respect to any case.

The method of dealing with motions and applications for certiorari is in nowise different. The popular impression that the work of examining these applications is divided up among the judges is not true. Every motion and every petition, with papers supporting it, is examined by every judge of the nine and he comes to conference with a memorandum, often written out in his own hand, embodying the results of his investigation of each application.

Petitions for certiorari are granted on the affirmative vote of four of the nine judges. This part of the court's work is very laborious. At the opening of the last term there were awaiting disposition 228 applications for certiorari, which had accumulated during the summer vacation. At the end of the first seven weeks of the term these applications had been taken up and disposed of in addition to the current work of hearing and disposing of argued and submitted cases and the preparation of opinion.

Of course, so heavy a burden of work could not have been disposed of in so brief a time if all the judges had not spent some of the summer in examining the accumulations of applications for certiorari. Nor would such a continuous burden of work as I have described be supportable were it not for the very great skill of the more experienced judges in reading records and getting quickly to the essential points in each case, nor, indeed, if it were not for the extraordinary and abiding interest which attends it.

He would indeed be a rash prophet who would venture to predict the course of judicial decision in the next 50 years. Could we have a vision of the future social and economic development of America, it would perhaps be possible to indicate with reasonable certainty the line along which it must proceed. But that vision is denied to us except dimly. From the history of the court we know that firm adherence to its established traditions of judicial independence and of performance of judicial duty with painstaking thoroughness and fidelity are the strongest assurance that it will meet and sustain the responsibility of the future. Often unjustly and unreasoningly attacked, those attacks have left no scar. The faithful performance of the great work of the court day by day and year by year has won to it deserved confidence in its disinterestedness and stability as an institution, and brought it to an undisputable triumph over hasty criticism and the dissatisfaction of the moment. Those who bear its responsibilities now and in the future will do well to ponder this significant fact and to recall as well that in the course of its long history the only wounds from which it has suffered have been those which, in the words of former Justice Hughes, were "self-inflicted."

MABEL WALKER WILLEBRANDT

PROHIBITION ENTERS POLITICS

SPEECH DELIVERED AT THE OHIO CONFERENCE OF
METHODIST EPISCOPAL MINISTERS, SPRINGFIELD,
SEPTEMBER 7, 1928

[Mrs. Mabel Walker Willebrandt was born in Woodsdale, Kansas,
on May 23, 1889. She was graduated from the Tempe, Arizona, Normal School in 1911; taught school and was for three years principal
of the Lincoln Park School in Pasadena, California; was graduated
from the law department of the University of Southern California in
1916; and has received honorary degrees from four institutions. In
1915, she was admitted to the California bar and began practice in
Los Angeles. From September 27, 1921, to May 28, 1929, when she
resigned, she was Assistant Attorney General of the United States in
charge of the Bureau of Federal Prisons, and of cases under prohibition laws and tax laws. She is now Washington counsel of the Avia-
tion Corporation.

The speech printed below was one of the most widely discussed of
those delivered during the presidential campaign of 1928. Mrs. Willebrandt was designated by the Republican National Committee, at the
request of Bishop Henderson, to address the Ohio Conference on the
relation of prohibition to the presidential campaign, and her address,
afterwards bitterly attacked, was approved in advance by counsel of
the Republican National Committee.]

I acknowledge with gratitude the invitation of this body representing so many leaders of the Methodist Church.

There is in Washington a statue of Francis Asbury, your first
bishop. It is an equestrian figure standing in the city where
many generals mounted upon charging war horses also stand.
But there is this difference—Asbury does not carry a sword;
he carries a Bible. His horse does not prance. He rather
droops as if content to save his energy for getting on rather
than expend it in style. So was Asbury's leadership; so have
been his followers. The Word for a sword, quiet perseverance
rather than prancing dress parade. But Asbury was a soldier;
and you, his followers, are soldiers as truly as were Cromwell's
Ironsides. There is as great need for courage, steadfastness

of purpose, clearness of vision, to-day as when Asbury led your ancestors to the worship of God.

Your church has always been interested in conditions that make for the welfare of mankind. You and your congregations prayed and fought, argued and voted to bring prohibition, first in your communities and then in the states, and nation at large. You worked first to develop through the leaven of religious teaching a *state of mind* that should value the welfare of the community above dangerous liberties of the individual. After you got that state of mind in enough people, it was not so hard to make your town or your county dry. Working for the state of mind was your hardest task. We know that was achieved very generally before the Eighteenth Amendment was ever proposed or passed, since out of 2,540 counties of the United States all but 305 had declared themselves dry. But nurturing the prohibition state of mind, which is essentially a spirit of social unselfishness, is still the hardest task.

The Eighteenth Amendment was passed not only by the required three-fourths of the states, but by every one in the Union except three. Spotted throughout the nation, however, were many willful sections where much of the local sentiment was against change in the Constitution. The worst of these spots was in New York City. The Empire State as a whole achieved the "will to unselfishness" which ratification of the Eighteenth Amendment typifies. But Manhattan is ruled by Tammany, an organization that for underworld connections and political efficiency is matched no place else in America.

Scattered over the United States were numbers of the intelligentsia who organized the Association Against the Prohibition Amendment. They worked along more or less futilely through 1921, 1922, and 1923. In 1924 at the Democratic convention in Madison Square Garden, Tammany tried to capture the Democratic party.

Tammany didn't then realize that it could not sweep that party off its feet by typical Tammany methods. Screaming whistles and brass bands failed to win Southern leaders. Tammany's candidate was the man who had just abandoned the policy of co-operation between state and national government, provided for in the concurrent clause of the Eighteenth Amendment. He was the one Governor in all the American States who, notwithstanding his oath to support the Constitution of the United States, pulled down one of the 46 pillars the people had erected for its support. New York had ratified the Amendment. That ratification was a pledge to concurrent effort. But the audacious Governor was unconvinced by such reasoning. Tammany wanted the least possible prohibition. Tammany had reared him; gave him his power. Tammany's desires were his convictions.

Certain leaders in the Association Against the Prohibition Amendment saw the importance of securing as spokesman of their cause so powerful a leader as the Governor of New York. Thus the wealthy groups of Anti-prohibitionists and Tammany —symbol of predatory politics—and Governor Smith were found in early alliance.

They have prepared well for this critical hour. Newspapers in rural and Southern communities were bought by New York money and have switched from a long-settled dry policy to preaching the doctrine of "it can't be enforced." At the same time there have been insinuated into strategic positions in dry enforcement men who were members of the Association Against the Prohibition Amendment. They have left office proclaiming from the lecture platform and through the press one general chorus that "Prohibition can never be enforced."

Others announce that its enforcement will invade every man's home, will drag him unwillingly to testify, and will unduly harass even the law-abiding. Thus has there been created a state of mind of irritation with and confusion over all the government's efforts at prohibition, however orderly and regular they may be.

Anti-prohibitionists have never won against *united drys*. It is clever strategy, therefore, to divide their forces. That is what is attempted in making prohibition a party issue. Thousands of organizations committed to prohibition, but tabooing political discussions from their platforms, now face the necessity of defending prohibition in the field of partisan politics. Your organization is such a one. You and thousands of others fought for and secured this national policy. You did not make it a political issue. Your adroit Tammany foe has done so.

You can do nothing else but follow wherever defense of the Eighteenth Amendment leads.

It is not abandoning your non-partisan policy of not discussing politics or letting your organization be torn by political dissensions to take a stand against the Democratic nominee and for the Republican National ticket this year. In fact, there is no choice. The Republican party platform and both its candidates are, by declaration and record, committed to the principle and the enforcement of prohibition. Whereas the governor of New York, with characteristic Tammany ruthlessness, after his nomination was quite safe, repudiated the dry plank in his party's platform.

He proposes that the Eighteenth Amendment to the Constitution shall be altered so as to "give each individual state the right wholly within its borders to import, manufacture or cause to be manufactured, and sell alcoholic beverages, the sale to be made only by the state itself and not for consumption in any public place." He makes this astonishing concession to lawbreakers in the name of "a great moral issue involving the righteousness of our national conduct and the protection of our children's morals."

It is a curious thing that during the entire history of this nation down to the adoption of the Eighteenth Amendment, when any state might have done so, just one state tried the experiment of selling whisky. It was South Carolina. In 1892 the then Governor Ben Tillman—afterwards United States Senator—proposed such a scheme. It was adopted and continued with varying modifications down to 1915, when it was abandoned and state-wide prohibition substituted.

The scheme was a failure. There was corruption. There was drunkenness. There was not a saloon, it is true. There were dispensaries where people bought whisky by the bottle— the original package—and took it into the back alleys to drink. In this faster age they would take it into automobiles.

Democratic apologists insist that electing a wet President would make no difference in the United States. It is true that he would not have power to accomplish the plan that has been proposed. A dry Congress would prevent that. He could not give liquor to this Nation legally; but under him liquor would be easier to get illegally. The inevitable result of his leadership would be increased disregard for law, evasion of responsibility of enforcement, and enlarged avenues of nullification of the Constitution. No dry Congress could prevent that, and honest anti-prohibitionists don't want liquor at that price.

But it is pointed out that he promises to enforce the prohibition laws vigorously so long as they remain unchanged. That promise, however well intentioned, is itself a ridiculous impossibility. When were battles ever won by appointing as commander-in-chief a man denouncing the very cause for which the war is being waged and openly denouncing the tactics of war? If we learned nothing else out of the great war, we learned the value of morale. Nowhere is it more apparent than in this huge but delicate organization of the Federal Government. Every one admits—Republican and Democrat alike—the splendid effect of the conscientious practices of obedience to law by President Coolidge. Likewise the election of a president openly disavowing his belief in the prohibition law and openly announcing the use of his leadership to change the Constitution in such a way as to permit the distribution of liquors would shatter the courage and morale of the agencies of enforcement.

What prohibition agents would risk their lives in enforcing the Eighteenth Amendment for such a national leader? Over 750 prohibition agents have been killed or maimed in line of duty by gangsters furnishing liquor to the socially selfish who insist upon having it at any cost.

The President selects and appoints a vast army of officers whose state of mind is of chief importance in securing enforcement of the prohibition laws. He appoints two cabinet officers directly and personally responsible for it—the Secretary of the Treasury and the Attorney General of the United States. He appoints at least four assistant cabinet officers who share these responsibilities. He appoints ninety-one United States district attorneys to supervise the prosecution of prohibition laws in the Federal courts, and they each appoint from five to fifty assistants. Would these men brave ridicule from the wet papers and make political enemies to enforce vigorously a law that their commander-in-chief was actively working to remove? In

the loss of morale of United States attorneys and their assistants, prohibition enforcement could be wholly defeated by
letting cases die before they ever reach the courts. And dry
members of Congress could not prevent that. The President
appoints ninety-one United States marshals, who, with dozens
of deputies, serve papers and make the arrests. The possibility of tip-offs and evasions of duty is very great, even when
the highest morale is preserved; enforcement is almost completely checkmated when the morale of the United States marshal's office drops. The President appoints all Federal judges.
The Federal judge who disbelieves in the law and who uses the
prestige of his office to express his private opinions freely on
the demerits of the law that he is enforcing contributes greatly
to lawlessness in his community. We have had a few Federal
judges who harangue agents in open court, and who yield to
their temptation to express disgust and impatience when improperly prepared cases are brought before them. The tendency to do all these things which give such aid and comfort
to the bootlegger, and spread the spirit of lawlessness, would
be bound to be increased if the Chief Executive was himself engaged in public criticism of the law and the Constitution.

The President recommends appropriations to Congress for
enforcement of prohibition, and it would be unnatural for a
President opposed to the law to sign large appropriation bills
to carry it into effect. Finally, and most important of all, the
President can place responsibility upon all agencies of the Federal Government for doing their share and intercorrelating their
efforts to discharge the responsibility of this difficult task of
enforcement. The natural tendency of all of them is to do as
little as possible within the boxed-up limits of their respective
assignments. A President leading the legal revolt against the
law could not get very far in securing harmony of effort between antagonistic units and instilling a spirit of co-operation in
enforcing this law.

It is reasonable to assume that the Governor's oath promising
to "support the Constitution of the United States" binds him
to assist in the letter and spirit of enforcement of the Federal
Constitution. But New York, since through Governor Smith's
leadership the enforcement act of the State was repealed, has

become the center, not only of lawlessness and disregard for the Constitution of the United States and free and open distribution of liquor, but it has also become the center of the dissemination of the false doctrine that the law can't be enforced. That statement could be received with more conviction if it emanated from a State where Federal Government and State had joined hands and worked valiantly to do the job. In New York State there are between 2,000 and 3,000 state police; there are more than 16,000 city police; there are 113 Supreme Court state judges; and sixty-two county prosecutors. All of these agencies might be enlisted to reduce the crime and lawlessness that is alleged to flow from disregard of the prohibition law, but they are now and have been inactive as to prohibition since New York State repealed its enforcement act. As a consequence, bootlegging has vastly increased; liquor-running over the Canadian border has multiplied; "blind pigs" that used to operate secretly and with some degree of shame operate openly with bars and brass rails; hundreds of night clubs in Manhattan are just a new form of the old-fashioned saloons that Tammany used to protect. These night clubs have open bars, and yet they can exist only so long as they can get licenses from the city administration. Of course the law is not being enforced in New York; it is being evaded and nullified; a few hundred Federal agents and thirteen Federal judges with four United States attorneys, cannot alone cope successfully with so much lawlessness. But that does not prove that the Eighteenth Amendment should be abandoned. The Governor, under whom nullification and evasion has become the state policy, can hardly make such an argument convincingly.

If President Lincoln were here to-day, he would answer Governor Smith, who has paralyzed his own State agencies from assisting the Federal Government in enforcing the Constitution, just as he answered the adroit political argument of Douglas in their famous debate at Jonesboro, Illinois, September 15, 1858, saying:

"What do you understand by supporting the Constitution of a State or of the United States? Is it not to give such constitutional helps to the rights established by that Constitution as may be *practically needed?* There can be nothing in the words 'support the Constitution' if you may run counter to it by refusing support to any right established under the Constitution."

What would Governor Smith say in answer to Abraham Lincoln's searching question addressed to Douglas October 13, 1858, at Quincy, Illinois:

"If you *withhold* that necessary legislation for the support of the Constitution and constitutional rights, do you not commit perjury? I ask every sensible man if that is not so? That is undoubtedly just so, say what you please."

Any citizen has an absolute legal right to work for the repeal of the Eighteenth Amendment. Any group of citizens has the unquestioned right to band together and spend money in a union of effort to accomplish that end. It is, however, a matter of grave doubt whether it be proper under our Constitution for the President of the United States to become the champion of any one faction for the change of the Constitution. It is significant that when our Constitution was drawn, the oath which the President is obliged to take was made different and broader than the oath exacted of other Federal and State officers. The President must swear to "preserve, protect and defend" the Constitution. Other officers only swear to "support" the Constitution. "Preserve, protect and defend" are strong words to outline the presidential duty. It would seem that, if he chooses to be President of the United States, that oath makes him take the Constitution the way it is when he enters into office. He becomes the champion of that document and all it means. He is to resist any effort to change it by other than constitutional methods. Groups of citizens have a right to work for its change, but the President is like the chairman of a meeting. He is to remain neutral, not the champion and the spokesman of a minority group working for an amendment.

Another reason that it would appear that the President of the United States during his term of office is to remain the champion of the Constitution as he takes it rather than the advocate of a change is that in defining his duties the Constitution gives him no part or influence in the various steps of amending the Constitution. The President is obliged from time to time to recommend to Congress "measures" that seem to him necessary for the welfare of the country. A constitutional change is not a measure; it starts by resolution which when passed is referred to the sovereign States, and when three-fourths of them have ratified the proposed constitutional amendment it becomes effective. Unlike a measure or a law, the President does not sign it and is powerless to oppose it. It is therefore doubtful if a President can, without violating the very spirit of his oath established by the founders of the Constitution itself, engage in using the force and power of his office while he is President of the United States, to effect a constitutional change.

Prohibition can be enforced. Not by left-handed efforts. Not by tinkering with the Constitution. Not by wasting time juggling percentages in the Volstead Act. But by intelligent, courageous, systematic, consecrated leadership from the chief executive of the nation. You can have such leadership from Herbert Hoover. He believes in the Constitution. He obeys it. No bootlegger has access to his pantry or his councils. He is not a bigot. He is intolerant only of intolerance. He concedes all men the right of different convictions. But he concedes no man the right of evasion or nullification of either the letter or spirit of the Constitution or our laws. He is an engineer. He believes in constructive effort and success. He never compromises with "the impossible." He meets and conquers it. Enforcement of the Eighteenth Amendment is a vast job in legal and human engineering. There are forty-eight states, forty-five of which have adopted it, thereby pledging concurrent exercise of their police power to accomplish its observance. The machinery for enforcement of each must be inventoried and brought into gear with the Federal Government. Waste and false motion in the latter can be eliminated. No more money is needed. There is plenty of man power. Six separate investigation units of the Treasury Department, one in the Post Office, one in the Immigration, and one in the Department of Justice can be co-ordinated and intercorrelated. Prosecutors in State and Federal governments can be brought into closer relationship. Careful training of agents and wise and early legal guidance will prevent the escape of law-breakers through technical errors, and save the community the annoyance of an untrained agent's blunders.

State by State the causes of crime, sources of supply of liquor and places of greatest lawlessness must be surveyed; results analyzed and remedial steps fearlessly applied. It is fundamentally a question of leadership and developing a will to win. No citadel ever was taken by a general who said it could not be done. The enforcement of this act must be in the hands of those who believe in it—wish it to succeed—who will work vigorously and constructively to that end—that means the hands of Hoover.

Preach that message. Rouse your communities. The issue is bigger than party lines. Hoover is a partisan, but far more, too. Having touched far horizons with healing hands, he has become a citizen of the world. He lives spiritual consecration in public office.

There are 2,000 pastors here. You have in your churches more than 600,000 members of the Methodist Church in Ohio alone. That is enough to swing the election. The 600,000 have friends in other States. Write to them. Every day and every ounce of your energy are needed to rouse the friends of prohibition to register and vote.

The Eighteenth Amendment is now in politics. You did not put it there. The Republican party did not put it there. Neither did the rank and file of the loyal constitutional Democrats. Neither did the National Democratic Convention put it there. It was put there by its enemies; and Governor Smith by a formal act as ruthless as was ever recorded in American politics became their leader. You whose labors and whose prayers accomplished it as the constitutional policy of this nation, will follow it to the political arena where Tammany has dragged it. The forces against prohibition have never been able to prevail against the united strength of Republican and Democratic drys. They cannot do so now, for you will not only remain united, but recruit your ranks by thousands who are now voters or those who, under the normal issues of the average election would not come out to vote. You have a chance to defeat the anti-prohibition forces so decisively that the question of repeal will be laid to rest forever. You have a chance to prove to the politician that he can no longer gamble with this issue, that he must accept the Amendment as an obligation. You have a chance to prove by electing Herbert Hoover that obedience to law can be secured and that America does not retreat before organized crime.

ALFRED E. SMITH

RELIGION AND POLITICS

CAMPAIGN SPEECH MADE AT OKLAHOMA CITY, OKLAHOMA,
SEPTEMBER 20, 1928

[Alfred Emanuel Smith was born in New York City on December 30,
1873. His political career is set forth in detail in the speech printed
below, which was delivered during his campaign as Democratic candidate for President of the United States, in which he was defeated by
President Hoover. The speech has a direct connection with the one
made by Mrs. Willebrandt on September 7, 1928, printed in this volume, and deals with a question which, once before in connection with
his career, while he was a candidate for the Democratic Presidential
nomination in 1924, had engaged the attention of the country. It is a
remarkable speech, because, although intensely personal and charged
with restrained emotion, it remains dignified, even without the aid of
the occasion of its delivery or the voice and personality of the speaker.]

Our country has achieved its great growth and become a
model for the nations of the world under a system of party
government. It would be difficult to predict what might be the
evil consequences if that system were changed. If it is to survive, campaigns for the presidency must be fought out on issues really affecting the welfare and well-being and future
growth of the country. In a presidential campaign there should
be but two considerations before the electorate: The platform
of the party, and the ability of the candidate to make it effective.

In this campaign an effort has been made to distract the attention of the electorate from these two considerations and to
fasten it on malicious and un-American propaganda.

I shall to-night discuss and denounce that wicked attempt.
I shall speak openly on the things about which people have been
whispering to you.

A former Senator from your own State, a member of my
own party, has deserted the party which honored him, upon
the pretense, as he states it, that because I am a member of
Tammany Hall I am not entitled to your support for the high
office to which I have been nominated. Here to-night I challenge both the truth and the sincerity of that pretense. I brand

it as false in fact. I denounce it as a subterfuge to cover treason to the fundamentals of Jeffersonian Democracy and of American liberty.

What Mr. Owen personally thinks is of no account in this campaign. He has, however, raised an issue with respect to my record with which I shall deal to-night without mincing words. I know what lies behind this pretense of Senator Owen and his kind and I shall take that up later.

What he says, however, has been seized upon by the enemies of the Democratic Party and the foes of progressive government. They have thus made my record an issue in this campaign. I do not hesitate to meet that issue. My record is one of which I am justly proud and it needs no defense. It is one upon which I am justified in asking your support.

For the present, let us examine the record upon which has beaten the light of pitiless publicity for a quarter of a century. I am willing to submit it to you and to the people of this country with complete confidence.

Twenty-five years ago I began my active public career. I was then elected to the Assembly, representing the neighborhood in New York City where I was born, where my wife was born, where my five children were born and where my father and mother were born. I represented that district continuously for twelve years, until 1915, when I was elected Sheriff of New York county.

Two years later I was elected to the position of President of the Board of Aldermen, which is really that of Vice-Mayor of the City of New York.

In 1918 I was selected by the delegates to the State convention as the candidate of the Democratic Party for Governor and was elected.

Running for re-election in 1920, I was defeated in the Harding landslide. However, while Mr. Harding carried the State of New York by more than 1,100,000 plurality, I was defeated only by some 70,000 votes.

After this defeat I returned to private life, keeping up my interest in public affairs, and accepted appointment to an important State body at the hands of the man who had defeated me.

In 1922 the Democratic Convention, by unanimous vote, re-nominated me for the third time for Governor. I was elected by the record plurality of 387,000, and this in a State which had been normally Republican.

In 1924, at the earnest solicitation of the Democratic presidential candidate, I accepted renomination. The State of New York was carried by President Coolidge by close to 700,000 plurality, but I was elected Governor. On the morning after election I found myself the only Democrat elected on the State ticket, with both houses of the Legislature overwhelmingly Republican.

Renominated by the unanimous vote of the convention of 1926, I made my fifth State-wide run for the governorship and was again elected the Democratic Governor of a normally Republican State.

Consequently, I am in a position to come before you to-night as the Governor of New York finishing out his fourth term.

The record of accomplishment under my four administrations recommended me to the Democratic Party in the nation, and I was nominated for the presidency at the Houston convention on the first ballot.

To put the picture before you completely, it is necessary for me to refer briefly to this record of accomplishment.

In the face of bitter Republican opposition, I succeeded in bringing about a reorganization of the government of the State of New York, consolidating eighty or more scattered boards, bureaus and commissions into nineteen major departments and bringing about efficiency, economy and thoroughgoing co-ordination of all the State's activities.

Under it was set up for the first time the Cabinet of the Governor.

A drastic reform was secured in the manner and method of appropriating the public money, commonly referred to as the executive budget.

During my legislative career, as well as during my governorship, I sponsored and secured the enactment of the most forward-looking, progressive, humanitarian legislation in the interests of women and children ever passed in the history of the

State. I appointed the first Commission on Child Welfare, while Speaker of the Assembly, as far back as 1913.

I had a large part in the enactment of the Workmen's Compensation Law and the rewriting of the factory code, which went as far as government possibly could to promote the welfare, the health and the comfort of the workers in the industrial establishment of our State.

I have stood behind the Department of Education with all the force and all the strength I could bring to my command.

The present Commissioner of Education is a Republican. Any one in Oklahoma, or in any part of the United States, may write to Frank P. Graves, Department of Education, Albany, N. Y., and ask him the blunt question, "what Governor of that State rendered the greatest service to the cause of public education?" and I am confident he will write back a letter with my name in it.

Figures sometimes speak louder than words. In 1919, my first year in office, the State appropriated to the localities for the promotion of public education $11,500,000. Last year, for the same purpose, I signed bills totalling $86,000,000, an increase in appropriations for public education of $74,500,000 during the period of my governorship.

I have given of my time, my energy and my labor without stint to placing the Department of Public Health upon the highest level of efficiency and usefulness, to bettering the condition of the unfortunate wards of the State hospitals and institutions for the poor, the sick and the afflicted and to the development, over the opposition of a hostile Legislature, of a comprehensive, unified park system, having in mind not only present requirements but the needs and the welfare of the generations to come.

For ten years I battled against bitter Republican opposition to retain for the people of the State of New York the control of their water power, their greatest God-given resources, and have prevented their alienation and preserved them for our people and for our posterity.

I sponsored legislation which brought about reform of the ballot, on the passage of direct primary laws and provisions against corrupt practices in elections.

The first bill for a bonus by the State of New York to the World War veterans was signed during my administration.

Although a city man, I can say to you without fear of contradiction that I did more for agriculture and for its promotion in the State of New York than any Governor in recent history. Co-operative marketing was encouraged. New impetus was given to the construction of the State highways. State aid was furnished to towns and counties to bring the farm nearer to the city and, during my terms of office, there was appropriated in excess of $15,000,000 for the eradication of bovine tuberculosis.

The business of the State of New York was handled in a strictly business way. The number of public place holders was cut down. Appointments and promotions were made on a strictly merit basis. In consequence, there was effected a reduction in taxes to the farmer and the small home owner, from 1923 to 1928, of from two mills to one-half mill of the State's levy upon real property, together with a substantial reduction in the income tax.

Public improvements in the State, long neglected under Republican rule, are being carried out at a rate unprecedented in all its history.

Bear in mind that all this was accomplished without the co-operation of the Legislature, because during my entire career as Governor both branches of the Legislature have been Republican, except for a period of two years when one branch—the Senate—was Democratic. It was brought about because I took the issues to the people directly and brought the force of public opinion, regardless of party affiliation, to the support of these constructive measures.

During my governorship I have made appointment of scores of men to public office requiring the confirmation of the Senate, and while the Senate was in control of my party in only two out of the eight years I have been Governor, not a single appointment of mine was ever rejected.

The reason for this was that I made my appointments to public office in the State of New York without regard to politics, religion or any other consideration except the ability, the integrity and the fitness of the appointee and his capacity properly to serve the State.

Contrast this with the rejection of major appointments made by the President of the United States by a Senate of his own party.

I read in the press only recently that a Republican Congress passed four bills over the veto of the Republican President in one single day. During my entire eight years, the Legislature, hostile to me, never passed a single bill over my veto.

Has there been one flaw in my record, or one scandal of any kind connected with my administration that gives any meaning to this cry of Tammany rule, a cry which thousands of independent and Republican citizens of my own State treat with ridicule and contempt?

The Republican Party will leave no stone unturned to defeat me. I have reduced their organization in the State of New York to an empty shell. At the present time, $60,000,000 of public improvements are in progress in my State. If there was anything wrong or out of the way, does it not strike you, as men and women of common sense, that the Republican Party in New York would leave no stone unturned to bring it to light?

The fact is, they have searched, and searched in vain, for the slightest evidence of improper partisanship or conduct. They found no such thing; they could find no such thing; it did not exist. And in the face of this, Senator Owen and his kind have the nerve and the effrontery not to charge, but merely to insinuate, some evil which they are pleased to call Tammany rule.

One scandal connected with my administration would do more to help out the Republican National Committee in its campaign against me than all the millions of dollars now being spent by them in malicious propaganda. Unfortunately for them, they cannot find it, because the truth is it is not there. I challenge Senator Owen and all his kind to point to one single flaw upon which they can rest their case. But they won't find it. They won't try to find it, because I know what lies behind all this, and I will tell you before I sit down to-night.

I confess I take a just pride in this record. It represents years of earnest labor, conscientious effort and complete self-sacrifice to the public good in some endeavor to show my appreciation and gratitude to the people who have so signally honored me.

Don't you think that I am entitled to ask the people of this country to believe that I would carry into the service of the nation this same devotion and energy and sacrifice which I have given in service to the State? Don't you think that my party is entitled to make this argument to the American people, because it is not only the record itself that speaks in unmistakable language for me, it is the expressed approval of the leading fellow citizens of my State, who have never had the slightest affiliation with Tammany Hall, and many of whom have been its political opponents.

My election to the governorship four times has not been accomplished merely by Democratic votes, because New York is a normally Republican State. I have been elected by the votes of the Democrats, together with the votes of tens of thousands of patriotic, intelligent citizens of all forms of political belief who have placed the welfare of the State above party consideration.

Take the statement of a man who has not supported me for the governorship, Charles Evans Hughes; a statement not made for political purposes, but in presenting me to the Bar Association of New York City. He described me as "one who represents to us the expert in government and, I might say, a master in the science of politics."

He said of me, "the title that he holds is the proudest title that any American can hold, because it is a title to the esteem and affection of his fellow citizens."

Nicholas Murray Butler, President of Columbia University, in conferring upon me an honorary degree, stated that I was "alert, effective, public spirited and courageous, constantly speaking the true voice of the people."

The Very Rev. Howard Robbins, Dean of the Episcopal Cathedral of St. John the Divine, stated that I had shown myself "a singularly well-balanced, capable and forceful executive." He added: "He has been independent and fearless. He has had the interest of all the people of the State at heart and his sincerity and courage have won for him a nationwide recognition."

Robert Lansing, Secretary of State under President Wilson, said of me: "His public career is convincing proof that he possesses the true spirit of public service, and is eminently fitted to fill with distinction and ability any office for which he might be chosen candidate."

Virginia G. Gildersleeve, Dean of Barnard College, stated that I had "made an excellent Governor and shown a knowledge of State affairs which very few of our Governors have ever possessed."

A group of distinguished educators, headed by Prof. John Dewey of Columbia University, said of my record of public education: "His whole attitude on education has been one of foresight and progress."

I could tax your patience for the rest of this evening with similar expressions from men and women who are the leaders of thought and affairs in the State of New York, independents in politics, most of them never affiliated with any political organization.

Do Senator Owen and the forces behind him know more about my record than these distinguished men and women who have watched it and studied it? But Senator Owen and his kind are not sincere. They know that this Tammany cry is an attempt to drag a red herring across the trail.

I know what lies behind all this and I shall tell you. I specifically refer to the question of my religion. Ordinarily, that word should never be used in a political campaign. The necessity for using it is forced on me by Senator Owen and his kind, and I feel that at least once in this campaign, I, as the candidate of the Democratic Party, owe it to the people of this country to discuss frankly and openly with them this attempt of Senator Owen and the forces behind him to inject bigotry, hatred, intolerance and un-American sectarian division into a campaign which should be an intelligent debate of the important issues which confront the American people.

In New York I would not have to discuss it. The people know me. But in view of the vast amount of literature anonymously circulated throughout this country, the cost of which must run into huge sums of money, I owe it to my country and my party to bring it out into the open. There is a well-founded belief that the major portion of this publication, at least, is being financed through political channels.

A recent newspaper account in the City of New York told the story of a woman who called at the Republican National headquarters in Washington, seeking some literature to distribute. She made the request that it be of a nature other than political. Those in charge of the Republican Publicity Bureau provided the lady with an automobile and she was driven to the office of a publication notorious throughout the country for its senseless, stupid, foolish attacks upon the Catholic Church and upon Catholics generally.

I can think of no greater disaster to this country than to have the voters of it divide upon religious lines. It is contrary to the spirit, not only of the Declaration of Independence, but of the Constitution itself. During all of our national life we have prided ourselves throughout the world on the declaration of the fundamental American truth that all men are created equal.

Our forefathers, in their wisdom, seeing the danger to the country of a division on religious issues, wrote into the Constitution of the United States in no uncertain words the declaration that no religious test shall ever be applied for public office, and it is a sad thing in 1928, in view of the countless billions of dollars that we have poured into the cause of public education, to see some American citizens proclaiming themselves 100 per cent. American, and in the document that makes that proclamation suggesting that I be defeated for the presidency because of my religious belief.

The Grand Dragon of the Realm of Arkansas, writing to a citizen of that State, urges my defeat because I am a Catholic, and in the letter suggests to the man, who happened to be a delegate to the Democratic convention, that by voting against me he was upholding American ideals and institutions as established by our forefathers.

The Grand Dragon that thus advised a delegate to the national convention to vote against me because of my religion is a member of an order known as the Ku Klux Klan, who have the effrontery to refer to themselves as 100 per cent. Americans.

Yet totally ignorant of the history and tradition of this country and its institutions and, in the name of Americanism, they breathe into the hearts and souls of their members hatred of millions of their fellow countrymen because of their religious belief.

Nothing could be so out of line with the spirit of America. Nothing could be so foreign to the teachings of Jefferson. Nothing could be so contradictory of our whole history. Nothing could be so false to the teachings of our Divine Lord Himself. The world knows no greater mockery than the use of the blazing cross, the cross upon which Christ died, as a symbol to install into the hearts of men a hatred of their brethren, while Christ preached and died for the love and brotherhood of man.

I fully appreciate that here and there, in a great country like ours, there are to be found misguided people and, under ordinary circumstances, it might be well to be charitable and make full and due allowance for them. But this campaign, so far advanced, discloses such activity on their part as to constitute, in my opinion, a menace not alone to the party, but to the country itself.

I would have no objection to anybody finding fault with my public record circularizing the whole United States, provided he would tell the truth. But no decent, right-minded, upstanding American citizen can for a moment countenance the shower of lying statements, with no basis in fact, that have been reduced to printed matter and sent broadcast through the mails of this country.

One lie widely circulated, particularly through the southern part of the country, is that during my governorship I appointed practically nobody to office but members of my own church.

What are the facts? On investigation I find that in the cabinet of the Governor sit fourteen men. Three of the fourteen are Catholics, ten Protestants, and one of Jewish faith. In various bureaus and divisions of the Cabinet officers, the Governor appointed twenty-six people. Twelve of them are Catholics and fourteen of them are Protestants. Various other State officials, making up boards and commissions, and appointed by the Governor, make a total of 157 appointments, of which thirty-five were Catholics, 160 were Protestants, twelve were Jewish, and four I could not find out about.

I have appointed a large number of judges of all our courts, as well as a large number of county officers, for the purpose of filling vacancies. They total in number 177, of which sixty-four were Catholics, ninety were Protestants, eleven were Jewish, and twelve of the officials I was unable to find anything about so far as their religion was concerned.

This is a complete answer to the false, misleading and, if I may be permitted the use of the harsher word, lying statements that have found their way through a large part of this country in the form of printed matter.

If the American people are willing to sit silently by and see large amounts of money secretly pour into false and misleading propaganda for political purposes, I repeat that I see in this not only a danger to the party, but a danger to the country.

To such depths has this insidious manner of campaign sunk, that the little children in our public schools are being made the vehicles for the carrying of false and misleading propaganda. At Cedar Rapids, Iowa, the public prints tell us that a number of school girls asked their parents if it were true that there would be another war if Smith was elected. When questioned by their parents as to how they came to ask such questions, one of the girls said:

We were told at school that Wilson started the war in 1917, and if Governor Smith were elected he would start another war.

As contemptible as anything could possibly be is an article on the very front page of a publication devoted to the doings of a church wherein the gospel of Christ is preached. I refer to the *Ashland Avenue Baptist,* a publication coming from Lexington, Ky., in which a bitter and cruel attack is made upon me personally and is so ridiculous that ordinarily no attention should be paid to it. It speaks of my driving an automobile down Broadway at the rate of fifty miles an hour, and specially states I was driving the car myself while intoxicated.

Everybody who knows me knows full well I do not know how to drive an automobile, that I never tried it. As for the rest of the contemptible, lying statement, it is as false as this part.

On the inside of this paper, the morning worship on the following Sunday gives as the subject, "What think ye of Christ?" The man or set of men responsible for the publication of that wicked libel, in my opinion, do not believe in Christ. If they profess to, they at least do not follow His teachings. If I were in their place I would be deeply concerned about what Christ might think of me.

A similar personal slander against me was dragged out into the open about a week ago when a woman in the southern part of the country read what purported to be a letter from a woman in my own State. Fortunately, the names of both women were secured. One of my friends interviewed the woman in New York State, and she promptly denied having written such a letter. The woman in the southern part of the country refused to talk about it and refused to produce the letter.

I single out these few incidents as typical of hundreds. I well know that I am not the first public man who has been made the object of such baseless slander. It was poured forth on Grover Cleveland and upon Theodore Roosevelt, as well as upon myself. But as to me, the wicked motive of religious intolerance has driven bigots to attempt to inject these slanders into a political campaign. I here and now drag them into the open and I denounce them as a treasonable attack upon the very foundations of American liberty.

I have been told that politically it might be expedient for me to remain silent upon this subject, but so far as I am concerned no political expediency will keep me from speaking out in an endeavor to destroy these evil attacks.

There is abundant reason for believing that Republicans high in the councils of the party have countenanced a large part of this form of campaign, if they have not actually promoted it. A sin of omission is some times as grievous as a sin of commission. They may, through official spokesmen, disclaim as much as they please responsibility for dragging into a national campaign the question of religion, something that according to our Constitution, our history and our traditions has no part in any campaign for elective public office.

Giving them the benefit of all reasonable doubt, they at least remain silent on the exhibition that Mrs. Willebrandt made of herself before the Ohio Conference of the Methodist Episcopal Church when she said:

"There are two thousand pastors here. You have in your church more than 600,000 members of the Methodist Church in Ohio alone. That is enough to swing the election. The 600,000 have friends in other states. Write to them."

This is an extract from a speech made by her in favor of a resolution offered to the effect that the conference go on record as being unalterably opposed to the election of Governor Smith and to endorse the candidacy of Herbert Hoover, the Republican candidate.

Mrs. Willebrandt holds a place of prominence in the Republican Administration in Washington; she is an Assistant Attorney-General of the United States. By silence, after such a speech, the only inference one can draw is that the administration approves such political tactics. Mrs. Willebrandt is not an irresponsible person. She was Chairman of the Committee on Credentials in the Republican National Convention at Kansas City.

What would the effect be upon these same people if a prominent official of the government of the State of New York under me suggested to a gathering of the pastors of my church that they do for me what Mrs. Willebrandt suggests be done for Hoover?

It needs no words of mine to impress that upon your minds. It is dishonest campaigning. It is un-American. It is out of line with the whole tradition and history of this government. And, to my way of thinking, is in itself sufficient to hold us up to the scorn of the thinking people of other nations.

One of the things, if not the meanest thing, in the campaign is a circular pretending to place someone of my faith in the position of seeking votes for me because of my Catholicism. Like everything of its kind, of course it is unsigned, and it would be impossible to trace its authorship. It reached me through a member of the Masonic order who, in turn, received it in the mail. It is false in its every line. It was designed on its very face to injure me with members of churches other than my own.

. I here emphatically declare that I do not wish any member of my faith in any part of the United States to vote for me on any religious grounds. I want them to vote for me only when in their hearts and consciences they become convinced that my election will promote the best interests of our country.

By the same token, I cannot refrain from saying that any person who votes against me simply because of my religion is not, to my way of thinking, a good citizen.

Let me remind the Democrats of this country that we belong to the party of that Thomas Jefferson whose proudest boast was that he was the author of the Virginia statute for religious freedom. Let me remind the citizens of every political faith that that statute of religious freedom has become a part of the sacred heritage of our land.

The constitutional guaranty that there should be no religious test for public office is not a mere form of words. It represents the most vital principle that ever was given any people.

I attack those who seek to undermine it, not only because I am a good Christian, but because I am a good American and a product of America and of American institutions. Everything I am, and everything I hope to be, I owe to those institutions.

The absolute separation of State and Church is part of the fundamental basis of our Constitution. I believe in that separation, and in all that it implies. That belief must be a part of the fundamental faith of every true American.

Let the people of this country decide this election upon the great and real issues of the campaign and upon nothing else.

For instance, you have all heard or read my Omaha speech on farm relief. Read the Democratic platform on farm relief, compare my speech and that platform plank with the platform plank of the Republican Party and the attitude of Mr. Hoover, so that you may decide for yourselves which of the two parties, or the two candidates, according to their spoken declarations, are best calculated to solve the problem that is pressing the people of this country for solution. By a study of that you will be conserving the interest of the cotton growers of this State and promoting its general prosperity.

Take my attitude on the development of our natural water power resources. Take the Democratic platform on that subject. Compare it with the Republican platform and with Mr. Hoover's attitude and record on the same subject, and find out from which of the two parties you can get, and to which of the two candidates you can look forward with any degree of hope for, the development of these resources under the control and ownership of the people themselves rather than their alienation for private profit and for private gain.

Compare the Democratic platform with the Republican platform and Mr. Hoover's attitude with mine on the all-important question of flood control and the conservation of our land and property in the valley of the Mississippi. And then take the record and find out from which party you got the greatest comfort and hope for a determination of that question.

Take the subject of the reorganization of the government in the interest of economy and a greater efficiency. Compare the platforms. Compare the speeches of acceptance, and be sure to look into the record of the Republican failure to carry out its promises along these lines during the last seven and a half years.

I declare it to be in the interest of the government, for its betterment, for the betterment and welfare of the people, the duty of every citizen to study the platforms of the two parties, to study the records of the candidates and to make his choice for the Presidency of the United States solely on the ground of what best promotes interest and welfare of our great republic and all its citizens.

If the contest is fought on these lines, as I shall insist it must be, I am confident of the outcome in November.

HERBERT HOOVER

THE SOUTH, NATIONAL PROBLEMS, AND THE AMERICAN HOME

SPEECH DELIVERED IN ELIZABETHTON, TENNESSEE, OCTO-
BER 6, 1928, AT THE CELEBRATION OF THE 158TH ANNIVERS-
ARY OF THE BATTLE OF KING'S MOUNTAIN

[Herbert Clark Hoover was born at West Branch, Iowa, on August
10, 1874. He was graduated in Engineering from Stanford University
in 1895, and has received honorary degrees from twenty-six institutions. From 1895 to 1913 he was engaged in engineering work in the
United States, Europe, Canada, Australia, South Africa, India and
China. From 1913 to 1914 he was the representative in Europe of
the Panama-Pacific International Exposition. During the European
War and immediately afterwards he was a member of many councils,
commissions, and boards, and was chairman of the following: American Relief Committee in London, 1914 to 1915; Commission for Relief in Belgium, 1915 to 1919; American·Relief Administration for
Children's Relief in Europe, 1919; and the European Relief Council,
1920. From June, 1917 to July, 1919, he was United States Food Administrator, and in 1920, he was Vice Chairman of President Wilson's
Second Industrial Conference. From 1921 to 1928, he was Secretary
of Commerce in the Cabinets of Presidents Harding and Coolidge.
In November, 1928, he was elected President of the United States.
The speech printed below is noteworthy, not primarily in connection
with its ostensible occasion, but because, delivered during the campaign for the Presidency, it was directed to the entire South, which
had been traditionally hostile to Republican doctrines.]

I am proud to have been invited as your guest in this celebration of your progress and this review of your part in national
history.

When Southerners go North or Northerners go South to deliver public addresses they seem to feel it necessary to first
launch into an explanation that all lines of sectionalism have
disappeared in the United States. I am from the West, where
our people are proud to be the melted product of both the North
and South. Our accent differs from that of the people of Alabama and Vermont, but we have the same hearts, the same kind
of homes, the same ideals and aspirations. Every morning and

evening we read the same news; every night we listen by radio
to the same voices. Our mental and physical frontiers are gone.
It happens that we need geographical divisions for statistical
and descriptive use, but otherwise we could leave this question
to orators and humorists.

Your celebration to-day raises many memories of our national beginnings. Patriotism is of many inspirations. It receives
refreshment from many springs. None are more powerful than
our traditions of service, of suffering, of accomplishment and
of heroism. The rivulets of these traditions from every part
of our country in the course of history merge into the great
stream of national memories which is the constant refreshment
of national ideals. These memories are indeed the imponderable
force which builds and cements our national life.

To the Westerner, appreciative of history and tradition, this
occasion presents a double significance. As you have shown
to-day, this locality was once the nation's frontier. Here were
enacted some of the most stirring scenes in the brilliant drama
of our pioneer era. Seven years before the Declaration of Independence there came to the banks of the Watauga—which
was then the Far West—the first permanent settlers. They
were soon followed by others from the back country of North
Carolina. In these settlements frontiersmen, remote from the
centers of civilization, freed by difficult distance from the sway
of all governmental authority, voluntarily created their own
frame of popular government. They erected what was to all
practical purposes a free and independent state, under their own
constitution.

In the articles of the Watauga Association were implanted
some of the great principles which later found permanent lodge-
ment in our fundamental law. Similar associations sprang into
being in other parts of these mountains. Historians of our
frontier agree that no more striking proof of the native capacity
of our early Americans for local self-government was ever giv-
en than by these associations. They not only created a government; the Watauga men, determined in their independence,
rallied to the improvised army during the Revolution which at
King's Mountain struck a decisive blow for the Colonial cause.

They, with their compatriots from Virginia and the Carolinas, attacked and disastrously defeated a formidable army under competent leadership, fading again into the forests as soon as their task was accomplished. No battle more dramatic or marked by courage and skill of a higher order has been fought on this continent. It was a turning point in the Revolutionary War. It compelled the retirement of General Cornwallis toward the coast, revived the flagging spirit of the discouraged Colonists and opened the way for the final victory at Yorktown. I wish to compliment you upon your pageant commemorating these achievements.

These states, in common with those to the North, began the greatest drama of all history—the spread of Americans from a feeble foothold on the Atlantic seaboard to the most powerful nation in the world in scarce two centuries. The great West was won not by the action of the government but by the individual effort of intrepid and courageous men from all these Atlantic states. They builded their own self-government. Tennessee, Kentucky and Texas were gained by pioneers under Sevier, Robertson, Clark, Boone, Houston and others. They not only won homes for themselves, but for a long time determined the course of history westward. The Mississippi River ceased to be a boundary, and year after year the powerful pulsation of westward expansion throbbed with heroism and sacrifice. They were ready to fight for the simple right of self-government. General Fremont, the pathfinder to the Pacific Coast, came from Georgia, and, true to tradition, he fought for and erected the first self-government of my own state of California.

To me it is an inspiration to be standing on this spot, for, in a sense, I have a common heritage with you. The earliest ancestor of whom I have record, Andrew Hoover, a settler in Maryland about two centuries ago, migrated to North Carolina and built his home a hundred miles from this spot. In Randolph county, of that state, he did his part in building the community, and his grave lies in the little burying ground on what was then the Uharrie River Farm. His son, my great-great-grandfather, was part of that movement which started West from your frontier.

As Secretary of Commerce I have been profoundly interested in the amazing progress of the South in this past seven and one-half years. In order that the department might assist to the fullest extent in that progress we increased our branch offices in the South from three in 1920 to twenty-nine in 1928. As a result of the contact thus established we were able to observe your increasing prosperity.

The record is impressive. There are in the South about 8,-000,000 families, and in this period they have shown increase in numbers by perhaps ten per cent. Contrasted with this, the manufacturing output has increased by over sixty per cent. The number of employees has increased by over thirty per cent. The value of crops has increased by over forty-five per cent. The shipments from Southern ports have increased by fifty per cent; the net income of your railways has grown by over 140 per cent; electrical power in use has been increased by 125 per cent. The postal receipts have grown by forty-five per cent. That this enormous increase in wealth and production has had wide distribution can be seen on every hand. It is indicated by increased wages and decreased cost of living; in twenty per cent of new homes, in a gain of 150 per cent of automobiles and thirty per cent in telephones. Life insurance in force has increased by 70 per cent and bank clearings have increased by fifty per cent. Depositors in savings banks have more than doubled. Building and loan association assets have increased 180 per cent. In nearly every case these percentages exceed the corresponding increase in the country as a whole. All this has been accomplished in seven and a half years.

In every phase of life the South is moving forward. New vistas of betterment are opening. The ability and energy of the people are constantly growing and are of more dynamic scope. They have engaged in every form of useful community effort to improve both the material and spiritual sides of life. I have had the honor to be president of the Better Homes Association. In that organization more than 2,000 towns have actively co-operated throughout the South during this last year. Fourteen out of twenty-four of the annual prizes given by this association for the most successful work during the last five years have been awarded to the Southern committees for leadership in bettering homes. Moreover, as director in various national committees devoted to increase of playgrounds and public parks, I have had occasion to note with gratification the extraordinary progress made throughout the South in the provision for wholesome recreation. You have not been negligent of education. In the last seven years the attendance in high schools has increased by ninety-one per cent and in institutions of higher learning by seventy per cent. Your moral and spiritual foundations have been strengthened.

I know that the people of the South will agree with me that these results could never have been attained but for helpful co-operation and sound policies in the national government, and that change of these policies can bring only distress and disaster.

The South possesses vast resources of raw materials and electrical power, easy access to the sea, a great reserve of labor, a wealth of soil, a moderate climate. Most of these factors have been here always. Such resources exist in many other countries, but if they are not accompanied by fine leadership, by intellect and character as well as sound policies of government, there could be no such development as we have witnessed in the South during this last seven years. That leadership has not been by immigration from the North. It has been the product of Southern men and women. The South has again proved to have in her blood that strain of leadership and fortitude which contributed so much to found our republic and so much to build our own West.

I realize that I come here as the candidate of a political party with whose policies many of you within my sight and many within the sound of my voice have often differed. I respect your views regarding that difference. Yet so closely welded in common interest are the pressing issues of our nation to-day that it should be no longer unusual for a citizen of any region to vote for a President who represents the principles which correspond to his convictions.

Our national officials are chosen in order that they may protect the political and economic health of the American people. In a contest such as this there is no place for personal bitterness. A great attribute of our political life has been the spirit of fair play with which our Presidential contests have been waged in former years and the sportsmanlike spirit in which we have accepted the result. We prove ourselves worthy of self-government and worthy of confidence as officials in proportion as we keep these contests free from abuse, free from misrepresentation and free from words and acts which carry regret. Whatever the result, we remain fellow countrymen.

No better illustration of true sportsmanship in American politics can be found than in the historic contest waged in this state between two brilliant brothers, one of whom honors us with his presence at this meeting, the beloved Alfred Taylor, of Tennessee. In the annals of chivalry no chapter portrays human nature to better advantage than your own "War of the Roses," in which Alfred Taylor, the Republican, and Robert Taylor, the Democrat, engaged in fierce political combat, attracted the attention of the whole nation and stirred this whole state from center to circumference. Yet in the heat of strife they kept in mind the advice of that good mother who had admonished her two stalwart sons never to forget the tie of brotherhood.

It is in that spirit I wish to discuss the problems that concern our country and the methods I believe necessary to obtain their solution.

Our country has entered upon an entirely new era. For fourteen years our attention in public life has been given mainly to the World War and reconstruction from it. These fourteen years have witnessed a revolution in our world relations, in many phases of our economic life, and our relations of government to them. Due to the ingenuity and hard work of our people and the sound policies in government, we have come since the war to be the greatest reservoir of the world's wealth. We have transformed ourselves from a country borrowing capital from abroad to the foremost lender of capital to foreign countries. Our people, growing in efficiency and productive power, are pressing for expansion of world markets. Competition for these markets grows keener each year. Our increasing foreign trade has penetrated into every country in the world. Political diseases arising from the war misery of foreign countries have at times disturbed us by their infection of certain of our people.

The poverty of Europe presses huge immigration toward us. We still have unsettled debts due us from the war.

For all these reasons our international relations have vastly increased. By our growth of wealth and power we have a great burden of responsibility for the peace of the world. Abolition of the liquor traffic has become a part of our fundamental law and great problems of enforcement and obedience to law have arisen from it. From the violence of the war we have inherited increase in crime. Technicalities of court procedure have been used to defeat justice and aid law violators. The invention of the gas engine has brought the automobile and the airplane. It has shortened distances, but it has brought new problems in roads and traffic. Discoveries in electricity have meant an immense expansion in power and communication, which bring also their problems of regulation to protect public rights.

The war has vastly increased the expenditures of the government. The assessment of taxes and expenditures of public moneys have come to bear a vital part in business stability. During these years we have adopted a measure of Federal control of credit. Errors in that delicate adjustment can cause us fabulous losses. The war has dislocated our transportation relations both within our country and with foreign countries. Development of inland waterways, of merchant marine and consolidation of railways are forced upon us. More acute than all are the readjustments in the world's producing and consuming power. Great expansion of agricultural production in Canada and the Southern Hemisphere, combined with increasing efficiency and larger production by our own farmers, have rendered unstable those branches of our agriculture which are dependent upon foreign markets.

These circumstances have brought a long train of difficulties to the American farmer. With fewer men needed upon the farm and with more needed in other lines of production, our great cities have, within this fourteen years, a little less than doubled in population, with resultant social problems. Increasing skill and prosperity have brought us more material comfort and greater leisure but also serious questions as to how we should use our leisure time. New inventions, including the automobile and the radio, have brought us into closer relations with our neighbors, and given us a keener knowledge of each other, a broader vision of the world and higher ambitions. This higher standard of living, this new prosperity, is dependent upon an economic system vastly more intricate and delicately adjusted than ever before. It now must be kept in perfect tune if we would not, through its dislocation, have a break-down in employment and in the standards of living of our people. From all this, new moral and spiritual as well as economic problems crowd upon us.

Our government was created in the belief that economic activities—that is, the forces of business and commerce—would translate themselves into widely distributed public welfare if left alone by the government. The government has come more and more to touch this delicate web at a thousand points. We indeed wish the government to leave it alone to the utmost degree, but yearly the relations of government to national prosperity become more and more intimate, regardless of what we wish to think. All this places a greater strain upon the flexibility of our government and should give us deep concern over every extension of its authority lest we overburden it to the breaking point.

I wish to remind you of something which may sound humble and commonplace, but it vibrates through every hope of the future. It is this—the unit of American life is the family and the home. It is the economic unit as well as the moral and spiritual unit. But it is more than this. It is the beginning of self-government. It is the throne of our highest ideals. It is the source of the spiritual energy of our people. For the perfecting of this unit of national life we must bend all of our material and scientific ingenuity. For the attainment of this end we must lend every energy of the government.

I have before emphasized that the test of our government is what it does to insure that the home is secure in material benefit and comfort; what it does to keep that home free from bureaucratic domination; what it does to open the door of opportunity to every boy and girl within it; what it does in building moral safeguards and strengthening moral and spiritual inspiration. From the homes of America must emanate that purity of inspiration only as a result of which we can succeed in self-government. I speak of this as a basic principle that should guide our national life. I speak of it as the living action of government in the building of a nation. I speak of it as the source from which government must itself rise to higher and higher standards of perfection from year to year.

I cannot within the limits of time discuss in detail the policies of our government or the solution of the multitude of issues that confront us and the attitude of my party and myself toward them. I shall mention shortly those which have more particular interest to the South.

As never before does the keeping of our economic machine in tune depend upon wise policies in the administrative side of the government. And from its stability do we assure the home against unemployment and preserve its security and comfort.

I advocate strengthening of the protective tariff as Henry Clay, of Kentucky, advocated it; not as an abstract economic theory but as a practical and definite policy of protecting the standards of living of the American family. The purpose of the tariff is not to balance the books of business corporations but to safeguard the family budget. With the increasing pressures from countries of lower standards of living it has become the fundamental safeguard of the American workman and the American farmer. I wish to see complete protection for the farmer of our home market. It is vital to the South as well as to other parts of the country. It would produce a needed further diversification in Southern agriculture. A retreat to the Underwood tariff schedules on farm produce would ruin millions of our farmers to-day.

And likewise the great manufacturing industries of the South are dependent upon it. Your vast spinning industry, your iron and steel industries are the product of it. No more beneficent exhibit of the result of the protective tariff act passed in 1922 exists than in this very city. Here factories are in course of erection and expansion whose establishment within the United States is due solely to that tariff act. Directly and indirectly they will provide an improved livelihood to more than 15,000 homes. If it were not for that protection these goods would be imported to-day as the product of foreign labor.

We must continue our endeavor to restore economic equality

to those farm families who have lagged behind in the march of progress.

In the last seven and a half years Congress has passed more than a score of constructive acts in direct aid of the farmer and the improvement of his marketing system. They have contributed greatly to strengthen the agricultural industry. Our party has undertaken to go farther than this and to still further reorganize farmers' marketing systems, placing them on a basis of greater stability and security.

I may repeat these proposals. We stand specifically pledged to create a Federal Farm Board of men sympathetic with the problem, to be clothed with powers and resources with which not only to further aid farmers' co-operatives and assist generally in solving the multitude of different farm problems which arise from all quarters of our nation, but in particular to build up with initial advances of capital from the government farmer-owned and farmer-controlled stabilization corporations which will protect the farmer from depressions and the demoralization of summer and periodic surpluses. Such an instrumentality should be able to develop as years go on the constructive measures necessary to solve the new farmers' problems that will inevitably arise. It is no proposal of subsidy or fee or tax upon the farmer. It is a proposal to assist the farmer onto his own feet, into control of his own destinies.

This is not a theoretic formula. It is a business proposition designed to make farming more profitable. No such far-reaching and specific proposal has ever been made by a political party on behalf of any industry in our history. It marks our desire for establishment of farmer's stability and at the same time maintains his independence and individuality.

I do not favor any increase in immigration. Restriction protects the American home from widespread unemployment. At the same time we must humanize the laws, but only within the present quotas.

The purpose of the Eighteenth Amendment is to protect the American home. A sacred obligation is imposed on the President to secure its honest enforcement and to eliminate the abuses which have grown up around it; I wish it to succeed.

I believe in continued development of good roads. They

bring the farmers' produce to market more cheaply, and by them we gain in neighborly contacts and uplift of spirit.

I advocate the enlarged and vigorous development of our inland waterways because they tend to diversify industry, they cheapen the transportation of farm produce and they bring larger returns to the farm home.

I rejoice at the enactment of legislation authorizing the construction of flood control works of the Mississippi and other rivers, for they give protection to thousands of homes and open the opportunity for new homes. We should complete these works with the utmost energy.

Because three million of our homes obtain their support from manufacture of articles which we import, we must continue to promote and defend our foreign trade.

We must assure a sound merchant marine to safeguard our overseas trade against foreign discrimination.

We must inexorably pursue the present policies of economy in government, for through every tax reduction we leave more income in every home.

It is vital that the government continue its effort to aid in the elimination of waste in production and distribution, through scientific research and by direct co-operation with business. By it we have made great gains in stability. From stability in business come increased consumption of farm products, regularity of employment and certainty to the family budget.

We must maintain our navy and our army in such fashion that we shall have complete defense of our homes from even the fear of foreign invasion.

Our foreign policies must ever be directed to the cause of peace, that we never again need sacrifice our sons on the field of battle.

To our veterans who gave freely of their all in times of danger we must continue to be not only just but generous in enacting and interpreting the laws for their relief.

To protect our people from violence at home we must revise our court procedure to produce swifter and surer justice, and we should begin with the Federal government.

I believe in the merit system of the civil service, and I believe further that appointive offices must be filled by those who deserve the confidence and respect of the communities they serve.

It is absolutely essential to the moral development and the enlarged opportunity of the boys and girls in every home that we increasingly strengthen our public school system and our institutions of higher learning.

All legislation, all administrative action, must stand the supreme test that it provide equal opportunity for all our citizens, not for any special group.

I do not favor any general extension of the Federal government into the operation of business in competition with its citizens. It is not the system of Lincoln or Roosevelt. It is not the American system. It not only undermines initiative but it undermines state and local self-government. It is the destruction of states' rights. Democracy, however, must be master in its own house. It can assure the conservation of our governmentally controlled natural resources in the interest of the people. It has demonstrated that by the power of regulation it can prevent abuse; it can and must control natural monopolies in full public interest. It can do so without abdicating the very principles upon which our nation has been founded and through which we have reached a standard of living and comfort unparalleled in the world. Violation of public interest by individuals or corporations should be followed by the condemnation and punishment they deserve, but this should not induce us to abandon progressive principles and substitute in their place deadly and destructive doctrines. There are local instances where the government must enter the business field as a by-product of some great major purpose such as improvement in navigation, flood control, scientific research or national defense, but they do not vitiate the general policy to which we should adhere.

The President has primarily the great task of administering the biggest business in the world—the United States government. It is a business involving an expenditure of $3,500,000,-000 a year and the employment of hundreds of thousands of people. Its honest and efficient administration touches the welfare of our people to a degree perhaps as great as the legislative and political policies. The President also has the responsibility of co-operating with Congress in the enactment of laws and securing their enforcement. In the determination of policies he is not only the leader of a party. He is more than this. He is the President of the whole people. He must interpret the conscience of America. He must guide his conduct by the idealism of our people. The Presidency is no dictatorship. It is not intended to be. Safeguards are provided to prevent it. Our fathers knew that men were not made for government, but government for men—to aid and to serve them. Our government rests solely upon the will of the people; it springs from the people; its policies must be approved by the people.

From my experience in government in the past years, both in war and peace, I have been profoundly impressed with the fact that we have increasing need to replace dictation by law to the fullest extent possible by co-operation between the administrative side of our government and the forces in the community. Scores of activities organized in these years through co-operation with voluntary bodies both on the economic and welfare side have convinced me that far more of the problem of progress can be accomplished by voluntary action assisted with co-operation by the government than has been supposed.

One test of our economic and social system is its capacity to cure its own abuses. New abuses and new relationships to the public interest will occur as long as we continue to progress. If we are to be wholly dependent upon government to cure every evil, we shall by this very method have created an enlarged and deadening abuse through the extension of bureaucracy and the clumsy and incapable handling of delicate economic forces. And much abuse has been and can be cured by inspiration and co-operation rather than by regulation of the government.

I have had the good fortune of many journeys to the South and of many warm friendships there. To me came the opportunity of service during the long months of greatest disaster which has ever come to our own country outside of war—the Mississippi flood. In that service I came to even more fully appreciate not only the character and the devotion of the Southern people, but I found proof of a phase of our American life that I had long believed existed but was difficult of demonstration. I, with other Americans, have perhaps unduly resented the stream of criticism of American life, the stature and character of our people. More particularly have I resented the sneers at Main Street. For I have known that in the cottages that lay behind the street rested the strength of our national character.

When it came to the organization necessary to meet that great catastrophe the pressure of time alone made it necessary to rely wholly upon the leadership, intelligence, the devotion, the sense of integrity and service of hundreds of towns and villages on the border of the flood. It was they who must undertake the instant work of rescue, the building of gigantic camps, the care of children, the provision of food, the protection of health of three-quarters of a million of homeless people. All that we who were in the direction could do was to outline the nature of the service that every town and village should perform, and assist them with resources.

In the face of that terrific problem that would test the stamina and quality of any people there was not a failure in a single case. This perhaps stands out larger in my mind than in that of most men because under similar conditions of great emergency I have had the duty to organize populations abroad. And in no country do there exist the intelligence, the devotion, the probity, the ability to rise to a great emergency that exist in the Main Street of the American town and village. I do not wish to disparage the usefulness of Broadway, Pennsylvania Avenue or State Street, but it is from Main Street and its countryside that the creative energies of the nation must be replenished and restored.

I rejoice with you at the wonderful development in the South not alone because of the benefits which it has brought but because it represents something more fundamental. Many of our most difficult problems in national life have come because of the extraordinary growth of our great cities. History shows that crowded cities too often breed injustices and crimes, misery and suffering. The people of the South, and of New England especially, are showing the country how to join industry with agriculture to their mutual benefit. The importance of your effort and your success cannot be overstated.

The Federal government can assist this movement of wider spread of industry by scientific research, by surveys of the resources of each region and study of its interest and adaptability of various industries. And the government can do more. It can directly assist not only the South but the whole nation in this course by the improvement of our roads, waterways and ports and by the encouragement of the spread of electrical power to factory and farm, by building up the merchant marine and expansion of the foreign markets natural to each section.

I have endeavored in this address to present to you the policies which have made and will make for prosperity of our country. They hold the hope of the final abolition of poverty. They make for better homes. They make for more individuality in life. They open the door of opportunity to boys and girls of town and country as well as of the great cities. From these accomplishments comes the lift of moral and spiritual life. From them comes an America greater and higher in purpose.

JAMES A. REED

PROHIBITION

SPEECH IN THE UNITED STATES SENATE, FEBRUARY 16 AND
18, 1929, ON A PROPOSED AMENDMENT OF THE
NATIONAL PROHIBITION ACT

[James A. Reed was born near Mansfield, in Richland county, Ohio,
on November 9, 1861. In 1864 he moved with his parents to Cedar
Rapids, Iowa, where later he attended Coe College, studied law, and
began practice. In 1887 he moved to Kansas City, Missouri, where
he has since maintained a law office. He combined political activity
with practice, was counselor of Kansas City from 1897 to 1898, Prosecuting Attorney of Jackson county from 1898 to 1900, and Mayor of
Kansas City from 1900 to 1904. He was a Democratic member of the
United States Senate from 1911 to 1929, and declined to stand for
renomination in 1928, when he was an outstanding candidate for the
Democratic Presidential nomination. He is opposed to Woman Suffrage, the League of Nations, and National Prohibition. His whole
career has been marked by courage and independence. At sixteen he
won a state oratorical contest, and has always shown such debating
and campaign abilities that he seems to win his fights by the sheer
power of his oratory. When he made the speech printed below, the
Senate had under consideration the amendments to the Volstead Act
popularly known as the Jones Act.]

Mr. President, I desire to discuss not only the pending bill
but the whole prohibition question, to marshal the facts and lay
before the country the unspeakable condition to which we have
been brought by prohibition.

On yesterday my duties as chairman of a committee compelled
me to leave the floor. During my absence unanimous consent
to limit debate was obtained. Because of that limitation I shall
only be able to present the barest outlines of a picture which
ought in all good conscience to be exposed in every detail.

I assert, Mr. President, that it will not be long until the moral
sensibilities of all thoughtful people are awakened to the truth
that the prohibitory law is the worst crime ever committed
within the borders of the United States. It will not be long

until the reign of hypocrisy, cant, chicanery, and fraud will come to an ignominious end.

I characterize the prohibitory law as a crime because it violates the principles of natural justice, has brought widespread disrespect for authority, and has become the facile instrument of graft, bribery, blackmail, and oppression.

The day will soon be here when the men who vote for prohibition that they may gain or retain office and who themselves violate the letter and the spirit of the law will be held in that contempt which justice demands should be visited upon all knavish hypocrites who wear the mask of pretended virtue. The day will soon come when judges who by brutal penalties have made malefactors of decent boys and men will sink into that obloquy which is the just reward of cruelty, oppression, and wrong. The day will soon come when organized groups shall no longer dictate policies of government. The voice of the people will again be heard, and that voice will pronounce the knell of those who surrender principle that "thrift may follow fawning."

Mr. President, I saw the original prohibitory law voted. I saw the veto of President Wilson incontinently overruled. I heard the affirmative vote of man after man who had drunk liquor all his life and who intended to keep on drinking. Time and time again I have seen prohibition bills come before Congress. I have heard roll call after roll call paralleling the one I have just described. Sir, the man who will vote to send his fellow man to jail for selling a drink of whisky and who will buy one himself is a coward—a canting and contemptible coward. I do not apply those terms to men who observe the doctrines they would force on others, but I hold in an abhorrence and contempt that can not be described in any tongue man has ever spoken the creature who to keep his place in the Senate or House of Representatives votes to make a felon of others for doing that which he himself connives at and practices.

If there were no men to drink liquor, there would be no men to make it or to sell it. Morally, if not legally, the man who buys illicit liquor aids, abets, and is fellow conspirator of the man who sells it to him. He who knowingly gets his liquor at second hand—that is, from an illegal purchaser—is morally upon the same plane as that purchaser. What a piece of knavish hypocrisy it all comes to.

Recently, at a great political convention, a number of leading prohibitionists were meeting in a room to determine their course of action. I was informed, and I have no reason for disbelief, that in the center of the table at which they sat and pondered their creed was a quart of rapidly vanishing whisky that had been liberally supplied for convention inspiration.

The Democratic convention was to meet in the driest State under the driest Government in the world. Just before it assembled there was enacted in Houston one of the Nation's periodic and regular farces. A boat, alleged to be loaded with great quantities of liquor was seized. The liquor was accommodatingly on deck where it could be easily observed and quite as easily captured. Only a plain, ordinary fool could doubt that the seizure was arranged for. The papers spread it broadcast that the Democrats were to have a convention as dry as a Sahara Desert camel. But when the delegates and visitors arrived word was passed that in particular hotel rooms and elsewhere liquors could be obtained in sufficient quantities to satisfy all appetites and appease every thirst.

There was a Republican convention held in Kansas City. Some of the leading "political prohibitionists" were paying the bell boys $7, $8, $9, and $10 a pint for a class of whisky that no respectable Missourian would ever think of drinking. The supply was just across the street. The bell boys raised the price and for a few brief days enjoyed "Republican prosperity." Then the sniveling hypocrites of the convention hilariously joined in adopting a prohibition platform.

I have sometimes been tempted to write a list of the names of the men who vote dry and drink wet. I do not know but I shall yet do so.

I repeat, for the man who believes in this thing and who lives it, I make no criticism of hypocrisy. But I do criticize, on the ground that he belongs to that class of individuals who think that because they choose to live in a certain way, they have the right to make everybody else live the same way. Paraphrasing the statement of a distinguished French savant—"they

conceive liberty to consist in depriving others of their liberty."
The proponents of the pending barbaric bill and of similar laws
could be aptly described in the verse of Robert Buchanan:

> A race that binds
> Its body in chains and calls them liberty,
> And calls each fresh link progress.

This, sir, is an immoral law. It is the worst crime ever committed within the borders of the United States of America. I make that assertion because prohibition is the breeding place and feeding ground of crime. That which produces crime is itself a crime.

The Presiding Officer (Mr. Couzens in the chair). The time of the Senator from Missouri on the bill has expired. He has 10 minutes on the pending amendment.

Mr. Bruce. Mr. President, I move that the Senator be permitted to proceed—

The Presiding Officer. The Senator from Missouri still has ten minutes on the pending amendment.

Mr. Bruce. Very well.

Mr. Reed of Missouri. Well, Mr. President, I cannot get started in that time.

Prohibition was doomed to failure because it attempted to force the habits of a part of the people—probably a minority—upon all the people. Such laws have never been enforced and never will be. A great British statesman said, "You can not indict an entire people," and I venture to say you can not force a free people.

Prohibition is a progenitor of crime, because it has driven the liquor business from the open day into the dark and secret places. Taken out of the hands of a class of people who were, for the most part, law-abiding and who were obliged to conduct their business in public places and under the constant surveillance of officers, it has been put into the hands of men who are already criminals, or who become criminals the moment they engage in the business. Operating in violation of law, it inevitably follows these men must close the eyes and stop the ears of the officers of the law. The profits are prodigious and can be split several times. Accordingly the collection of graft and the extortion of blackmail has become nation-wide.

There has never been any attempt to enforce this law as we enforce the laws against murder, arson, rape, burglary, and other heinous crimes. In the last 18 months I have traveled extensively in the United States. I have yet to enter a State, a city, a town, or a village where I was not tendered liquor and where a few minutes' conversation did not disclose the fact that illicit stills were clustered roundabout at which moonshine of the "purest ray serene" could be obtained at constantly falling prices. There may be some who do not want liquor, who never did want it, or who do not now know where to get it. But the boys all know; that is, all the boys who know much of anything.

There is not a policeman in a city of the United States who can not collect enough evidence in 24 hours to keep the courts busy for 24 months. In the cities are bars where to the stranger they sell half of 1 per cent beer. The man who is known gets the spiked article. In city after city they are selling beer spiked with ether.

Let us tell the truth, even though Bishop Cannon—who, I believe, the Senator from Virginia [Mr. Glass] in the recent campaign described as one of the three American popes—may frown, that he may hold his job and draw his salary. There is not a man with good sense who has looked about him but knows that in the city of Washington he can in an hour's time have delivered at his office or at his home enough whisky to entertain the entire senatorial or congressional body, their wives and their sweethearts, assuming that wives and sweethearts would partake, which, of course, they would not. [Laughter.]

To say that the law has ever been enforced is to stand in the face of truth and deliberately or ignorantly lie to the American people. Graft, without stint and beyond measure, is the order and routine of our day.

Recently a grand jury, sitting in Philadelphia—perhaps still sitting—investigated the bank accounts of some police officers. These men drew salaries of from $3,000 to $4,000 a year, but their bank deposits ranged from $14,000 to $195,000. The inference to be drawn is obvious. Bribery! Graft! The arrested are, for the most part, those who do not pay the graft. Occasionally a victim is dragged in for the purpose of making a record and deceiving the public into the belief that the law is being enforced. Why will Senators close their eyes to facts? Why do we not face the truth as it is? Why do we cringe like cowards and go to heel like spaniels at the lash of an organization that can influence a few votes?

Mr. President, when you pass a law that a large percentage of the people despise, violation is certain to become general. A people deliberately violating one law will easily come to violate other laws. Thus we have sown the dragon's teeth, from which has sprung a general disrespect for law.

The former Prohibition Director, General Andrews—the best man who ever held that office—testified that in 12 months' time the department had seized 172,600 stills; that prior to prohibition there had never been 500 licensed stills in the United States, and that moonshining had been inconsequential because it was unprofitable. He practically admitted that he had not captured more than 1 still in 10. Translated that means there were in existence at that time 1,726,000 stills. General Andrews estimated that, at least, five persons were attached to each still or engaged in the distribution of the liquor. That gives us the startling total of over 8,000,000 people deliberately and willfully violating the law.

(At this point Mr. Reed of Missouri was admonished by the Presiding Officer that his time had expired. Thereupon, after debate, the unanimous consent agreement limiting debate was by unanimous consent set aside so that Mr. Reed of Missouri could proceed.)

Mr. Reed of Missouri. Mr. President, I thank the Senate for its very generous attitude, and I thank the Senator from Washington [Mr. Jones] for his consideration.

I agree with the Senator from Idaho [Mr. Borah] that this question might as well be opened up and discussed. I hope that it will be. It is time to pry open the door of the "whited sepulchre" and expose the "dead men's bones" therein concealed.

When interrupted I had denounced this law as a nursery of crime and asserted that disrespect for one law naturally breeds general disrespect for law. Respect for law, respect for courts, and respect for officials of State or Nation is impaired or completely destroyed once the public is convinced that thousands of public officers are receivers of graft, that graft has become a system and bribery is ordained as a custom. The people have the right so to believe. Do they not see planted in every city of the United States hundreds of tiny drug stores, frequently so insignificant they do not employ a pharmacist? Proprietary medicines stand sparsely on the shelves, thus maintaining the mere pretense of a drug store, yet these places evidently prosper. The real source of income of most of these stores is the illicit sale of liquor. Sensible men at once ask what the policeman on that beat is doing. And then they ask what the policemen on all the beats are doing. Likewise when men know that they can go into cities as absolute strangers and in 20 minutes' time find an abundant supply of liquor they believe, as all sane men must believe, that the officers are not attempting to enforce the law. They have the right also to conclude that somebody is collecting graft. Respect for law and respect for government is thus speedily destroyed.

It is important to bear in mind that a bootlegger necessarily sells to a large number of individuals. In a little while the officers know about the bootlegger; they are bound to; and a system of collection and protection is established. Remember also that inevitably the bootleggers' operations soon or late bring him in contact with a graver class of outlaws who peddle narcotics as well as liquor. These, in turn, have their relations with the most dangerous elements of society. Shortly there is effected a general coalition which embraces all the criminal and vicious elements of the underworld.

Always there has to some extent existed among the real criminal classes a sort of community of interest, a kind of solidarity. But the distinctly criminal class has hitherto embraced a very small percentage of the people. Every honest man's hand was against them as their hands were against every honest man. But gravely consider the ghastly truth that the criminal element has now been recruited by an army of possibly millions of liquor violators, and that there has been established what may be justly described as an offensive and defensive alliance embracing a vast army of outlaws and involving many officers of the law.

What now is the effect upon the efficiency of the officer thus involved? Called upon to apprehend a man guilty of the gravest crime, he is likely to find himself in pursuit of one in whose pay he has been. He fears to perform his duty lest he be exposed and ruined. Thus the law breeds crime. The minute an officer accepts a dollar of whisky graft, his morale is broken. He ceases to be effective against any class of criminals. He becomes a cringing coward. He walks in the shadow of constant fear. Above his head hangs the sword of destruction that any criminal may at any moment cause to fall.

Mr. Bruce. Mr. President, may I interrupt the Senator just for a moment? That is exactly what Mr. Collins, the chief of police, said. He said that the criminal outrages of every sort that prevail in that city—we all know to what a fearful extent— are attributable to prohibition.

Mr. Reed of Missouri. I thank the Senator. I do not go so far as to say that all crime is to be attributed to prohibition. I heard the prohibitionists' charge that all crime was to be attributed to the saloon. They cried aloud, abolish the saloon and you will abolish crime. We were told the jails would be empty, the penitentiaries uninhabited. But the prisons are so overcrowded that arms and legs are sticking out of the windows. Farms are established on which to herd the overflow. We were told that there would be no more widows' tears nor orphans' sighs; that workhouses would be abolished and poorhouses would be no more. The demon rum was held responsible for all of human ills.

Now, the fact was and is that a percentage of human beings will drink too much; that intoxicated men will sometimes commit crime; but the whole truth is, and always was, and always will be, that there is a percentage of human beings who are natural criminals. The prohibitionists have heaped upon the head of old John Barleycorn all the sins that were and are inherent in humanity. I shall not follow that unfair example by claiming that all the crime to-day can be charged to this law. I am trying to show, however, that the law promotes and increases crime. In further support of that claim I remark that when you hang up the prize of great profits, you lure men to that prize. And prohibition made the illicit liquor trade the most profitable business on earth.

Consider also that it is particularly easy for men to violate a law when they believe they are doing nothing but disobeying the mandate of some legislative body, a large percentage of whose members were probably "full" the night before they imposed the law on others, whilst another large percentage were impelled by selfish political reasons.

On this point we should keep constantly in mind that there is a wide gulf between the prohibitory statutes and laws leveled against acts universally denounced by all civilized nations. The first is restrictive, the second protective. The first limits the enjoyment of a natural right; the second protects the enjoyment of a natural right. The distinction is recognized in the law. The phrase *malum prohibitum* refers to acts not wrong in themselves but merely illegal because forbidden by law. The second class is described in the phrase *malum in se,* which embraces acts wrong in themselves. Such crimes are nearly always accomplished by force or fraud. They are repugnant to the interests and wishes of the victim and hence meet with his determined resistance. Their general existence would speedily break down civilized society. They are abhorred of all people. The worst criminal will protest against such acts if visited upon himself. The murderer will fight to the death one who attempts to take his life. The thief will resist the stealing of his property. The highwayman will protest against the robbery of himself. The burglar will defend his own home from plunder by another rogue. All of these classes will appeal to the law for protection when their rights are violated. Frequently they will assist in the apprehension of rascals who have committed crimes against third parties. Even more certainly all good and honest men and women regard with abhorrence and will assist in the suppression of these and many other crimes.

It may therefore be justly said that for the protection of themselves all people stand for the suppression and apprehension of villains who by force or fraud accomplish their wicked designs. Against them is raised the universal voice of mankind. Their apprehension and punishment is regarded as a sacred duty.

Once more I emphasize the fact that this class of crime is committed against the will and the protest of the victim. Contrast such acts with those against which the prohibition law is leveled. It is true that law does not expressly forbid the citizen from taking a drink. Nevertheless, that is its object. It tries to cut off the supply in order that it may prevent the citizen from doing that which he desires to do.

There are two great difficulties inherent in the enforcement of the prohibitory law.

First. It seeks to prevent the man who wants to sell liquor from selling it to a man who wants to buy. There is a total absence of either force or fraud. On the contrary, both parties are in complete accord. There is a perfect and harmonious meeting of minds. The seller and buyer are doing exactly what each desires to do.

Second. They jointly engage in a transaction which each believes to be moral and to be within his natural rights. Or, at least and at the worst, each regards the transaction as desirable. They feel they are doing only that which has been done by a large proportion of men since the dawn of history.

It is indisputable that, throughout the centuries, all races of men have indulged in stimulants. Dominant and progressive nations have generally used alcohol.

Call the roll of the master builders of civilization and in the majority will be the names of those who have insisted upon the right as free men to regulate their personal conduct, even to the occasional quaffing of a toast to Bacchus. Poets, who have conjured from words the mystery and melody of music; orators, whose eloquence has aroused enslaved peoples to resist the oppression of tyranny; martyrs, who died in defense of the rights of men; artists, whose inspired visions are preserved in the glories of architecture, in canvas, in marble, and in bronze; saints, who labored amongst the lowly and consecrated their lives to the ennoblement of mankind; statesmen, who blazed the highway of human progress and guided millions from the darkness of despotism to the sunlit fields of liberty, have nearly all, in greater or less degree, used alcohol in some form.

Prior to prohibition a considerable percentage of the population took an occasional drink and only a small proportion drank to excess. The principles of self-restraint and temperance were everywhere being inculcated. The progress was remarkable and highly commendable.

Then agitation against intemperance itself became intemperate. It took the form of organized propaganda, heavily financed. It got into the hands of a little group of professionals who collected and disbursed huge sums of money. The more they agitated, the more they could alarm the people. The more the people were alarmed, the more cash was contributed. The more cash contributed, the greater the emoluments of the agitators. They went into politics; they played the game ruthlessly.

The war was on. Millions of young men were in the Army camps. Millions were beyond the sea. Weak-kneed legislators became alarmed and began to yield. Suddenly Wayne B. Wheeler loomed as the big boss. Congress was stampeded; the Eighteenth Amendment was forced through for the express purpose of coercing the will of those States which did not desire to impose prohibition upon their people. The direct intention was to take away from the several States, for all time, the right to enact their own police regulations.

The methods used to secure adoption of the Eighteenth Amendment by the several States were regarded by many as frequently obnoxious and disgraceful.

Certain it is that the amendment was submitted during the excitement of the war and ratified either during the war or in the troublous times succeeding. The conditions forbade mature consideration and deliberate action. Immediately following came the Volstead Act. It was not prepared by statesmen sitting in solemn council and desirous of producing a statute that would deal fairly and equitably with the situation. On the contrary, it was largely devised by the group of professional propagandists who had for years lived out of the profits of agitation. These enterprising gentlemen gathered from various State prohibitory statutes their extremest provisions and their grossest cruelties. The bill was forced through Congress under the lash of Wayne B. Wheeler, backed by a horde of propagandists and paid lobbyists. Congressmen were threatened with annihilation by the Anti-Saloon League and its cohorts. The most detestable kinds of bulldozing and lobbying were employed.

What wonder President Wilson vetoed the measure! What wonder that Congressmen who had proclaimed him the greatest man since the days of Christ, and who had denounced all who, in any respect, differed from him, now cringed and cowered before the threat of political annihilation by the Anti-Saloon League!

Thus was born the Volstead Act, the cruelties and enormities of which the present Jones bill proposes to magnify.

Let us consider some further circumstances, especially the assertion, constantly reiterated, that the people of the United States amended the Constitution, that the people, therefore, after due deliberation, determined upon a new national policy.

Technically, it is true that the Constitution was amended in the form laid down and that the law pursuant thereto was enacted by the Congress. Both have been sustained by the Supreme Court and are, therefore, legally binding. But that is very far from their ratification or adoption by a popular vote of the people. The people, in fact, never had an opportunity for a direct vote. The amendment was submitted by a total of 347 Senators and Representatives, all of whom had been elected, at least, 11 months before they voted for submission.

In the campaign of 1916, neither party had recommended nation-wide prohibition. The question was not at issue in that election. The people had had no opportunity, by direction or indirection, to vote upon it. Yet, the submission of an amendment is the first and one of the most important acts necessary to any change in the Constitution.

In the State legislatures an estimated liberal total of 5,000 members voted to ratify the amendment. Many of these men had been elected before the constitutional amendment was proposed, and many of these legislators in States where a popular vote had been taken voted in direct opposition to the last-expressed will of the people upon that issue. Thus it appears that a constitutional amendment to govern 48 States and 120,-000,000 people was actually submitted and adopted by a total of not more than 5,347 individuals in the State and Federal legislatures.

I do not claim that the constitutional amendment was illegally adopted, but I do emphasize the fact that both the constitutional amendment and the law were enacted by a very small number of the people without proper time for discussion, and that the voice of the people has never been directly heard. I also urge the importance of these facts in connection with the problem of enforcement, for the constitutional amendment and the laws thus adopted may be very far from expressing the will of a majority of the people.

I am confident that, with ample time for discussion and upon a popular vote a majority would have rejected the nation-wide proposition. To enforce a law, adopted under the conditions stated, which proposed to reverse the custom of the ages and to regulate the individual habits of a great people, is indeed difficult if not impossible.

Again I remark that when you undertake to enforce this law you are at once confronted by the fact that the great percentage of the people want a drink once in a while, think they have the right to a drink, and hence, regard not as a enemy, not as a criminal, but as an accommodating individual the man who comes around with a suitcase containing the desired amount of liquor.

A further difficulty arises from the fact that the prohibition of the legitimate sale of liquor has made its illicit sale highly profitable, and, as I have remarked, whenever you make a crime of a business not ordinarily regarded as wrong, men will engage in it on account of the huge profits to be realized.

At the time General Andrews appeared before the committee and gave the startling figures I have recited, he exhibited one of the stills seized. It was an ordinary copper wash boiler with a small copper contrivance attached. He stated that in that wash boiler 60 gallons of alcohol could be made in 24 hours, which could in turn be transformed into 120 gallons of whisky. At the then current price the product would have brought about $2,400.

Consider the fact that a man with an ordinary wash-boiler contrivance could, in a day's time, make so huge a profit. That mere fact makes violation certain. Add to that the fact that millions of people who had always enjoyed a drink and always proposed to have one were distributed throughout the

United States, and you have a situation making it impossible to enforce the law.

Referring to these difficulties, General Andrews testified that as soon as one source of supply was cut off another sprang into existence. When importations were reduced moonshining increased.

There is still another difficulty in the way of enforcement. Making whisky is a simpler chemical process than making bread. It can be even produced by so primitive an equipment as a teakettle and a little corn or rye meal or potatoes, or anything containing starch or sugar.

Fermentation is a natural process. Distillation consists simply in separating and condensing the alcohol produced by fermentation. With the slightest knowledge and the simplest apparatus whisky can be made in every home of the land. The number of people who have learned how to make it is one of the most prominent results of this law. To-day whisky is being made in the kitchen, in the cellar, in the garret, in the garage, and along the creeks, frequently by a class of people who are willing to take the chance of being caught. So enforcement has, at each stage, and in every State, become a farce.

If that were all, the case would not be so terrible; but running along with that condition is another and an appalling situation. Formerly when liquor could be obtained any place, the moral elements of all communities were arrayed in a general endeavor to warn people against the evils of strong drink. The pulpits thundered anathemas on almost every Sabbath day. Great temperance orators went over the country and provoked tears from the eyes of their auditors. Young men and young women were told "Here is a danger. Here lurks an enemy that may destroy you. You must build up your character, you must strengthen your own purpose, you must live without it, or, if you touch it, it must be in very moderate quantities. Here it is. If you want to be a fool, you can be a fool. If you want to destroy yourself, you can destroy yourself. But your duty to your home, your duty to your country, and to your church and to yourself is that of self-restraint." It was presented as a great question of morals, and it was dealt with by the moral forces of society, the church, the school, the home.

Now, all that is changed. There is not a man in the Senate Chamber who has heard an old-fashioned temperance lecture since the Volstead Act was passed. Instead you have heard demands for enforcement of the law and for more penalties. The whole atmosphere is different. In the old days temperance forces were all engaged in saving the drunkard. They wept over the old fellow who for 75 or 80 years had drunk his whisky or sipped his wine and was still hale and hearty. He was pictured as a terrible sot. Over him they shed cataracts of tears. They were bent upon rescuing him from "evil." How the tender hearts of the good sisters and good brethren did ache at the awful spectacle. But the modern professional prohibitionists have turned their kindly hearts to stone; their eyes are now tearless as those of a granite sphinx. They no longer sing: "Rescue the perishing"; they hiss through set teeth, "Chuck them in the penitentiary for life." Closely, indeed, does the hiss of fanaticism resemble the hiss of a serpent.

They once talked of tremendous economic loss. Now, when they lock thousands of men within penitentiary walls, eternally blast their names, herd them with brutes, curse their souls, and destroy them utterly; there creeps over the faces of these humanitarians of a later day the ravening glee of the tiger as it exults above a dying victim.

With chuckle and nudge, they bear the glad tidings: "We convicted 500 men to-day." "Five hundred more must wear the stripes." "Five hundred more are locked in jail."

A boy is driving along the highway. He has a flask of whisky in his car. He is, perhaps, an ignorant and inexperienced lad, the kind of boy that in the old days good women put their arms about and led away from the bar and into the white-ribbon hall and there prayed with and wept over and persuaded to sign the pledge. But now the boy is grabbed by an officer too corrupt or cowardly to tackle larger game, is ruthlessly rushed to the penitentiary and so is absolutely destroyed. On such a scene, the hard-eyed pack of reformers look with approval and shout: "More law, more punishment." "Another twist to the thumbscrew." "Another turn of the rack." "A little more pain, a little more agony, a little more of human wreckage— just a bit more of the lash, good executioner."

Monsters of that kind have existed in every age. They regard law as an instrument of punishment, not of redemption. They believe that the more cruel the punishment, the heavier the club, the longer the agony, the better the law. Such as they broke men upon the wheel; drew them asunder by horses, quartered them, cut out their entrails and burned them before their faces; seared their eyeballs; tore their tongues from their throats. Such as they said that was the way to stop crime; that was the way to make people observe the law and respect government.

Then came an era of humanity. We began to see that revenge was not the just purpose of the law; that punishment should be inflicted only to deter others from the commission of crime and to reform the culprit.

This prohibitory law—what a monstrous thing it is! Under the law as it stands—without fitting it with more nails to be driven into the hands and feet of its victims—for a single act penalties can be piled up that will put in the penitentiary for a long period of years an individual who has been guilty of a single trivial violation.

A boy delivers a gallon of moonshine. He can be indicted for possession; he can be indicted for transportation; he can be indicted for conspiracy to violate a Federal statute. He can also be similarly indicted under State laws, and conviction under the State code does not bar conviction under the Federal code.

I am not sure how many schemes have been worked out to pile penalty upon penalty, but I do know that the law as it now stands is as "cruel as the grave." Penalties may be imposed for the simple act of transporting a pint of liquor far greater than those for manslaughter or murder in the second degree frequently visited upon the killer.

Mr. Blease. Mr. President—

The Presiding Officer (Mr. Smith in the chair). Does the Senator from Missouri yield to the Senator from South Carolina?

Mr. Reed of Missouri. I yield.

Mr. Blease. I call the Senator's attention to the fact that they can also punish him by putting a tax on his property and then take his property, putting it on the block, and sell it.

Mr. Reed of Missouri. Yes; that is true. If I undertook to tell all that can be done it would take a very long time. I thank the Senator.

What is the act? Merely *malum prohibitum*. The act is bad because it has been prohibited. The penalties that exist to-day are altogether in disharmony with the general policy of the criminal statutes.

Mr. President, it is hard to believe that any human being would want to send a lad to the penitentiary for having possession of a pint of liquor. That is indeed hard to believe. It is hard to believe that in a civilized country we would tear a father from his family, disgrace the wife, the daughters and the sons, and brand them forever with a mark that time can not erase because that father sold a gill of wine or a bottle of beer to a man who wanted to buy.

One would naturally think that for such a violation a fine of a few dollars would be a heavy penalty. But, sir, there is no knife so sharp as that held in the hand of the bigot. It "pierces even to the dividing asunder of the soul and body, of the joints and marrow." There is no cruelty so relentless as the cruelty of fanaticism.

On an occasion the question of poisoned liquor was being discussed. It was stated that a prominent man had been made totally blind by a single drink. When some of those present expressed their sorrow and horror, a lady, naturally a kind-hearted woman, the wife of a great educator, exclaimed through her set teeth, "It serves them right; they ought to go blind if they break our law."

Mr. Bruce. I would call the Senator's attention to the fact that 187 of the essays which were handed in by contestants in the Durant prohibition competition were in favor of capital punishment or execution in some form or another for violation of the Volstead Act, and that even a Member of this body on one occasion, when I asked him whether he favored capital punishment for violation of the Volstead Act, replied that he did for some.

(At this point Mr. Reed of Missouri yielded the floor for the day.)

Monday, February 18, 1929

Mr. Reed of Missouri. Mr. President, before continuing the discussion of Saturday, I desire again to thank the Senate for abrogating the unanimous-consent agreement limiting debate in order to accommodate me. For that and many courtesies of the past I am deeply grateful. Second, I desire to remove the anxiety which seems to have been created in the minds of some by the remark I made on Saturday that I might "yet tell the names of those who do not vote as they drink." I assure all interested parties that they may compose their agitated nerves. I am not going to do it! [Laughter.] I might feel compelled to tell the names of people who commit real crimes. I should hate to have to do that. Certain it is, I would never violate the confidence or hospitality of friends by disclosing the fact that occasionally they try to introduce a bit of artificial sunshine into the dull days of life. Accordingly, all may be at ease. I have made many mistakes and done many wicked things, but I have never fallen to the level of a prohibition informer. [Laughter.] I thought at the time I had perpetrated a joke, but it appears I should have so labeled it.

Mr. President, on Saturday I made reference to the fact that one of the saddest effects of the law is that it apparently has transformed the kindly sentiments and humanitarian services of the old-time temperance worker into a spirit of persecution. Force is substituted for reason, penalties for persuasion, and cruelties for charity. I repeat that where we once sought to "rescue the perishing," we now send them to the penitentiary. We have abandoned the Bible, the prayer book, and the temperance tract for the lash, the prison, the gun, and the bludgeon.

As was stated by the distinguished Senator from Maryland [Mr. Bruce], in the recent Durant prohibition enforcement prize competition 187 contestants demanded the death penalty. The vast majority of the plans proposed to pile penalty upon penalty. But perhaps the most classic illustration of fanaticism gone mad, of love turned to hate, and charity changed to crime is found in the suggestions of two persons, one of them a woman.

One contestant urged that the liquor-law violators should be hung by the tongue from an airplane and thus carried over the

United States. The woman urged that the Government poison the liquor and distribute the deadly potion to the people through bootleggers. She humanely argued that "only a few hundred thousand persons would die and that it would be worth all the deaths to get prohibition enforced."

If these illustrations were no more than the sporadic utterances of insane persons, the matter would not be worth the mentioning, but the spirit of persecution is abroad in the land. Many people seem to have conceived the idea that whatsoever is done under the form of a statute is just and righteous; that law can sanctify any cruelty, any atrocity.

Sir, law has been the instrument of tyrants, the weapon of brutes since time began. By it despots have sought to cloak villainies that have stained the earth with blood, saturated it with tears, and filled the winds of time with the groans of the tortured and the dying. Law! What, sir, is law? It is—and I speak now of proper laws—it is a rule of conduct springing from common custom and ordained by general consent. It must be all that and more than that; it must be founded upon justice; it must express equity and right; it must be humane in its provisions. Such a law naturally commends itself to the intelligence and appeals to the soul of mankind. An unjust law, a cruel law may be as much a crime as is the act of an individual who assassinates in the dark.

Law! It is urged that a majority may dictate any kind of a law, however brutal, however unjust, however atrocious. Such was not the theory of the founders of this Republic. They declared that all just laws spring from the consent of the governed. They forbade cruel and unusual punishments. They set bounds to the authority of government itself. They created checks and balances in order to preserve the liberty of the citizen. As they unfurled the battle flags of the Revolution they asserted that all men were entitled to life, liberty, and the pursuit of happiness, and that all just governments were established to preserve these inalienable rights.

Law, I repeat, has been the instrument and cloak of every conceivable atrocity, and that no law can ever transform a villainy into a virtue. Why, sir, the Savior of mankind was crucified according to the forms of Roman law and with the sanction of Jewish law. I repeat now what I think I once before said in this presence, that the wretches who led Him to Calvary, who drove the nails into His feet and His hands, were as great criminals as though they had executed Him against the express letter of the law.

Joan of Arc was burned at the stake in strict accordance with the thing that was then called law. But the judges who signed the decree of execution and the wretch who applied the torch were murderers more foul than assassins who cut the throats of sleeping victims, for they acted in cool deliberation and imposed the cruel death by fire.

John Calvin slowly roasted Servetus, the foremost physician of the time. He acted in accordance with the provisions of the law of Geneva and pretended to act by authority and at the behest of the law of God. But Calvin branded in blood-red letters across his memory the word murderer.

The highway of the centuries is marked by gibbets, crosses, stakes, dungeons where the bravest and the best were hanged, crucified, impaled, and imprisoned according to laws proclaimed by monsters who, by force and fear, ruled an enslaved world. Their laws were nothing save general rules for the perpetration of villainies.

The British Government dragged our ancestors across the sea and put them to trial according to the laws of England, but the laws were atrocious, the penalties were cruel, and our fathers repudiated both England and her laws. For hundreds of years there was written in the laws of England death penalty after death penalty for offenses many of which involved no real or but slight moral turpitude. Thousands and thousands of small offenders were thus brutally penalized. Men could be thrown into prison for killing a rabbit or even hanged for trespassing upon the sacred domain of some titled tyrant and for stealing a deer or sheep. But the judges who pronounced sentence and the officers who dragged the victims to the gibbet were as certainly murderers as they would have been had there been no form of law observed. The "it is hereby decreed" of a despot who in his own person exercises authority and the "be it enacted" of a few men gathered together in a legislative as-

sembly are alike powerless to make wrong right or rob cruelty
of its criminality.

Let no man say because I have thus spoken that I am declaring we should defy the prohibition law. I do not so say. We
have the power of remedy in our own hands. We know full
well that general hatred and defiance of the law will undermine
the very structure of our Government. It is therefore our business to proceed by constitutional methods to remedy existing
wrongs. The right way is to repeal bad laws and to change bad
constitutions.

I have been speaking upon the theory that this is a bad law,
that it is a destructive law. I now urge that it has introduced
corrupting agencies and debased morals into the political life of
our country.

If I were to undertake to marshal all the facts at my command, we would be here until the cock would crow in the morning. I shall call attention to just a few. I have already said
that this law was enacted at the demand of an organization. At
the head of that organization was Mr. Wayne B. Wheeler. I
hold in my hand the biography of Wayne B. Wheeler written
by Justin Steuart who was formerly publicity secretary to Mr.
Wheeler. It was written within the shadows of his tomb and
I presume has that touch of charity which a work written under the circumstances should exemplify. Here is the opening
sentence:

"Wayne B. Wheeler controlled six Congresses, dictated to
two Presidents of the United States, directed legislation in
most of the States of the Union, picked the candidates for the
more important elective State and Federal offices, held the balance of power in both Republican and Democratic Parties, distributed more patronage than any dozen other men, supervised
a Federal bureau from outside without official authority"—
we know that bureau was the Prohibition Bureau—"and was
recognized by friend and foe alike as the most masterful and
powerful single individual in the United States. He achieved
this position by sheer force of personality. The story of his
rise to power, his use of that power, and his sudden death, just
when the foundations seemed crumbling under him, is without
parallel.

"Where Wheeler sat was always the head of the table. He

had an instinct for pre-eminence. A tireless opportunist, he dramatized himself as the champion of prohibition until the general public pictured him as a mighty St. George fighting single-handed against a swarm of dragons.

*   *   *   *   *   *   *   *

"He loved the limelight. Attacks pleased him nearly as much as praise. He collected the personal newspaper notices, which became voluminous in the last five years of his life. He circulated widely typed, mimeographed, or printed copies of these collections, with such titles as 'Knocks and Boosts.' * * * He urged the need of loyalty upon others, but frequently disregarded the orders of superior officers and ignored resolutions passed by the boards of the Anti-Saloon League, which were responsible for its political or legislative policy. He did not cut the cables like Dewey, but waited until boards or committees had adjourned and their members returned to widely separated parts of the Nation, and then forgot them."

*   *   *   *   *   *   *   *

"He loved power. If power could not be won, he loved the semblance of power. He never attacked the administration. Such attack might be construed as evidence that he lacked influence with the administration. His favorite text was: 'The powers that be are ordained of God.' This did not prevent his own insubordination. Because of the influence over the policy of the Prohibition Department that would be his under the Haynes régime, he supported Roy A. Haynes for Commissioner of Prohibition under the reorganization bill in the face of the objections of many of the sanest men in the league. By a political maneuver he prevented the election of the ablest man in the league to its national superintendency while he persuaded or dragooned delegates to support his own candidate."

*   *   *   *   *   *   *   *

"He was the exponent of force. From his first days as superintendent of a district in Ohio, when he assailed the courts for leniency, to the end of his life he preferred threats to persuasion. He made difficult the development of the league's policy of education on prohibition. He desired the most severe penalties, the most aggressive policies, even to calling out the Army and Navy, the most relentless prosecution. A favorite phrase was: 'We'll make them believe in punishment after death.' This, with 'red-blooded' and 'intestinal fortitude,' crept into many a speech, regardless of its theme—and so forth, and so on, *ad nauseam*.

That is the picture presented by the eulogist and former secretary to this man. He "preferred force." "He would make the people believe in hell fire." That obscene spirit has permeated our country to an extent astounding and horrible and sad beyond the expression of words. It has usurped the kindly persuasion and gentle ministrations of the temperance folks of a few years ago. Then many women with tender hands and sweet faces and noble hearts entered the saloons there to appeal to the saloonkeeper and to the lowly and fallen to lead better lives. Now the doctrine of force espoused by Wayne B. Wheeler has supplanted the spirit of charity and love taught by Jesus Christ. Formerly we sought to persuade. We now seek to compel. But, sirs, you can not compel a free people. Hence, it is solemnly admitted by prohibition Senators that eight years of pretended enforcement has been but a prolonged farce.

Returning to the Anti-Saloon League, it raised and spent over $30,000,000. In the spirit of Mr. Wheeler, it entered into the various State campaigns. It adopted his philosophy, which was that he did not care how a man drank, or what his habits were, or what his opinions were, or how he would vote on any other question; if he would only cast his vote as Mr. Wheeler dictated. That, according to Wheeler, was the sole test of a man's fitness for office.

Think of that degrading and despicable philosophy! Here is the great United States, with all its multitudinous interests, its foreign relations, its difficult problems of government. The rights and interests of millions are constantly to be guarded and conserved. Disregarding all these, a man posing as a moral leader insisted that the sole qualification for office was a pledge to him that the legislator vote on one particular question as he dictated. Moreover, he asserted his right to go into a Republican convention and nominate any scoundrel he could if that scoundrel would only vote as he demanded upon that one question; to then go into a Democratic convention and nominate any scoundrel he could if that man would vote as he demanded; to change from one party to the other, being bound neither in morals nor by the ethics of politics to support the candidate nominated by the convention into which he had voluntarily entered, and in the proceedings of which he had participated! Wheeler is dead but his mantle has fallen upon the shoulders and his soul has entered the body of the Right Rev. Bishop Cannon. The philosophy of hate survives. There is not a slum district in a city of the United States where the slum boss does not have a higher code of political morals than that. And so I say the doctrines and practices of the Anti-Saloon League have been a debasing influence in our politics.

But Mr. Wheeler was not the only protagonist of these nefarious doctrines. Another distinguished leader gives us a photograph of his own soul in his own words. I refer to that peerless knight and accomplished gentleman, "Pussyfoot" Johnson. [Laughter.] It was disclosed in hearings before a Senate committee that "Pussyfoot" Johnson had been regularly in the pay of the Anti-Saloon League from 1917 to 1922, and that he had drawn from it various sums of money. It was also shown that Mr. "Pussyfoot" Johnson had given utterance to the following exalted expressions:

"Did I ever kill anybody? It has been often said that I did. Stories of slaughter have been repeated and printed. I let them pass, for in the wild days they served a useful purpose."

It served a useful purpose to have people think he was a killer engaged in a great moral movement!

"They helped spread terror among the lawless, and that aided my work. Most of the stories of sudden death date back to a fight that I had in a pool hall in Chelsea, Indian Territory. I was cornered one night by an angry mob, but fought my way out with the butt end of a broken billiard cue. I got out with a black eye and some bruises, but three of my assailants were carried out unconscious. The newspaper dispatches carried the valuable information that I had then and there put three men to sleep. Under the reputation that Chelsea then had this was interpreted generally that I had killed the three men, which was not true. They were put to sleep all right. However, they finally woke up. I never killed anybody.

"Did I ever lie?"

Now, he denies the killing. Follow on:

"Did I ever lie to promote prohibition? Decidedly, yes. I have told enough lies for the cause to make Ananias ashamed of himself. The lies that I have told would fill a big book; but I have never lied to my associates. I have never lied to the public. I have told to sinners a thousand lies for the purpose of decoying them into telling the truth. I am not seeking to defend this, only to state the fact that my conscience does not annoy me for it and to insist that I would do it again if the occasion arose.

"Did I ever bribe anybody? Yes. In 1913 I bribed some Russian officials to give me a lot of secret information concerning Section X of their Government administration. I bribed Eurasian railway officials all over India, because that is the accepted way of getting favors in that country. In my law-enforcement work for the Government I bribed many bad men to give me information about their associates, but outside of that I have never bribed anybody."

That is the man who helped fix the moral standards of the people of the United States. From that foul and polluted fountain you draw the waters of your purity!

How did they raise this $30,000,000. In part it was subscribed by very wealthy men. One of those wealthy men has a moral record that would not look well if it were presented here on the floor of the Senate. Even now in his 10-cent stores the public regularly is supplied with glasses, corks, bottles, corkscrews, and other paraphernalia to make the preservation and consumption of booze easy, and all at cut prices.

Another distinguished contributor amassed his immense fortune by the creation of the greatest and most oppressive monopoly that ever cursed this people. By the way, I am not sure but that his son, just now riding in the chariot of another reform, is about to gain control of the single branch of the Standard Oil Co. that is not at present completely dominated by the old crowd; but that is another tale.

One way in which they raised the money was to have preachers take up collections in their churches on Sundays, and in a great many instances they divided with the preachers. I do not make that as any wholesale charge; I simply quote such evidence as we had before us. But they got the money, and they used a very large part of it in politics. For many years they violated the law by failing to report their political collections and disbursements.

They had several Congressmen and two or three Senators in their pay. Consider the situation of a Member of Congress with the money of the Anti-Saloon League in his pocket when that organization demanded his vote for one of its pet measures. To all intents and purposes his vote was bought in advance. But the moralists of the league saw nothing wrong in thus indirectly bribing Members of Congress.

I do not challenge the right of the organization to stand for its policies, but I do dispute the right of that or any organization to put money in the purses of the men who are to vote for laws to force those policies upon the country. No man ever did that who was not utterly depraved, who had not lost all sense of honor, all respect for law, all the qualities of decency.

Then, sir, this law has to be enforced by a class of men who are mostly under-cover men. What is an under-cover man? A spy. What is a spy? He is unquestionably the lowest order of animal life. Save the man who, in a great war, may bravely imperil his life to discover the position of an enemy in order that he may give information to his own army, the spy is a creature who has abandoned in advance every principle of honor.

What is it that keeps men decent in this world except a sense of honor? Destroy that, and man becomes a beast, devoid of respect for law, for decency, or for the rights of others. The man who will engage in a business knowing in advance that he must peep through keyholes, that he must draw aside the curtains of windows, that he must lurk in the shadows and creep like some vile beast upon an unwary victim; who knows that he must be prepared, like "Pussyfoot" Johnson, to lie and to deceive, to gain friendships only to betray—a man of that kind, sirs, will do anything that cowardice does not prevent. He will commit perjury, he will accept bribes, he will levy graft, he will tempt the weak, he will seduce the honest boy into crime in order that he may gain the credit and profit of a conviction.

What wonder, then, that the cold written record of the Prohibition Unit directors discloses an alarming story of rascality. Bear in mind that the record probably does not show one-tenth of the whole truth, because it deals only with dismissals for misconduct absolutely proven. It necessarily fails to show the resignations that were tendered for causes that were substantially known, but of which complete evidence was not produced.

Prohibition Director Andrews gave the list of dismissals for cause:

Employees Separated from the Prohibition Unit for Cause from the Beginning of Prohibition to February 1, 1926, Inclusive.

Cause	Prohibition enforcement officers, agents, and inspector	Prohibition agents serving as marines	Warehouse agents	Clerks	Messengers	Field supervisors	Attorneys	Chemists	Total
False statement on application ..	20	...	1	1	...	...	...	...	22
Extortion, bribery, or soliciting money	121	...	...	2	...	...	...	...	123
Falsification of expense accounts	80	....	2	...	...	...	1	...	83
Collusion and conspiracy [1]	61	....	1	8	...	...	1	...	71
Illegal disposition of liquor and other property	41	....	3	...	2	...	...	...	46
Embezzlement	1	.....	...	4	...	...	...	1	6
Dereliction of duty [2]	43	....	24	1	...	...	...	1	69
Robbery of warehouse	2	...	6	...	...	...	...	...	8
Intoxication and misconduct [3] ..	187	5	11	10	...	1	1	...	215
Violation of national prohibition act	7	...	1	...	...	...	...	...	8
Disclosing confidential information	8	1	...	4	...	...	...	...	13
Unsatisfactory service and insubordination	119	4	10	8	...	1	...	1	143
Acceptance of gratuities	7	...	...	...	...	...	...	...	7
Submission of false reports	22	...	...	...	...	...	...	...	22
Theft	6	1	2	...	2	...	...	...	11
Contempt of court	6	...	...	...	...	...	...	...	6
Assault	8	...	...	1	...	...	...	...	9
Perjury or subornation of perjury	3	...	...	...	...	...	...	...	3
Political activity	3	...	...	...	...	...	...	...	3
Misuse of firearms	3	...	...	...	...	...	...	...	3
Failure to file income-tax return	1	...	...	...	...	...	...	...	1
Former criminal record	2	...	...	...	...	...	...	...	2
False pretenses (issued worthless checks)	1	...	...	...	...	...	...	...	1
Total	752	11	61	39	4	2	3	3	875

[1] This covers such cases as conspiracy to violate the national prohibition act, to extort bribes from violators, to defraud the United States Government, etc.

[2] This classification includes failure to report violations of the national prohibition act; leaving guard duty without permission, etc.

[3] Misconduct covers such matters as immorality, assault, arrest for speeding, gambling, fighting, creating disturbance, etc.

What does that table spell? It spells this: You can not get decent men to do such abominable work, hence it goes into the hands of the offscourings of humanity, largely into the hands of men who are criminals or near criminals.

I notice that two men were discharged for having had previous criminal records. They are not so particular now. Men with known criminal records are now employed. And how do they work? The gorge rises in the stomach of decency when we contemplate the fact that prostitutes have been employed to decoy men. Agents have set their traps in hotels and by the expenditure of a lot of Federal money finally induced some poor bell boy or some waiter to bring in a little liquor to a party which he supposed was composed of decent men and women when it was in reality an assembly of official black-legs and prostitutes. All this is done beneath the white cloak of purity; all this is sanctified by the glory of the cause.

What saloon was ever baser than that? What divekeeper was more depraved? Where can you find a blacker picture in the old days of the old saloon?

What right has an officer of the law to commit a crime in order to entrap a victim? What right has he to become the procurer of a crime, the inducing cause of a breach of the law?

Mr. President, I turn now to another picture, and, as I try to paint with my poor brush, please compare the kindly expression that transfigured the countenance of the old-time temperance worker with the passion that distorts the face of the advocates of force. The old temperance forces appealed to our moral and spiritual attributes. They sought by gentle persuasion to rescue the perishing.

Then it was a glorious thing if one man who was addicted to drink could be induced to quit. They brought him to the temperance hall, they had him tell how the prayers of good women and the saving grace of God had taken away his thirst, clothed him once more in his right mind, and made him a good citizen. As they passed their pledges around they said, "This man was standing at the gates of hell, and we have pulled him back. He was lost, and has been found. A gracious God, through us, as His humble servants, has saved this soul from destruction."

It was a beautiful and glorious work. I have nothing but

flowers and crowns for all the people who did that work. No word of mine would ever speak harshly of them. They were engaged in a great labor of charity—the saving of men. Each time they could snatch a single brand from the burning their souls lightened up with a holy zeal. Properly they felt that they had accomplished much for they were rescuing men.

Now, behold their successors. Their proudest boast is the number of convictions secured. Gleefully they count the human beings they have taken from their families, from public life, from their duties as citizens, and have locked up in penitentiaries.

Let me read the figures. I have them by the courtesy of my friend the Senator from Texas [Mr. Sheppard], who recently recited them in a speech eulogizing prohibition. The Senator declared that in the year 1928 the following admirable results were obtained:

"Seventy-eight thousand arrests in the Federal courts"— 78,000 human beings upon whose shoulders the law laid its heavy hand and placed an ineradicable stain.

"Fifty-eight thousand prison sentences"—58,000 men imprisoned. This we are told is the glory of prohibition.

"Aggregate of all sentences, 5,631 years." If Adam had been put in jail when he was a boy he would have just about served out that period of time.

"Fines, $7,031,709," and in addition "652 persons convicted and placed on probation for five years." "Suspended and pardoned sentences totaled 4,627; probated sentences 2,265 years."

Stop a little and think, you rescuers of the perishing. If you could have indicted the old saloon and shown by good and true evidence that in a single year it had sent 58,000 human beings to jail and that it had caused the arrest of 78,000 human beings, you would have had a stronger case than was ever proved against the old saloon, bad as it was.

Observe that, in the opinion of the distinguished Senator, the number of prison sentences imposed is the proper yardstick by which to measure the success of prohibition. The more men sent to prison, the more beneficent is the law. Accordingly he introduced the figures for 1927. In that year the arrests totaled 51,945; convictions, 36,546; sentenced to prison, 11,818; aggregate of sentences, 4,477 years.

As the sentences for 1928 were much greater than for 1927, the Senator insists that prohibition is becoming progressively successful. That is to say, we are arresting more people every year, sending more people to prison every year, ruining more men and women every year, taking more fathers and sons and brothers from their families and from life, destroying them utterly, body and soul, branding them so that as they go down the path of time their names will be anathema upon the lips of all people—we are doing more of that every year; hence prohibition is a glorious success.

Oh, how the spirit of Christ has been killed! Whence comes this malevolent and monstrous thing to usurp his place in the temple where once we bowed at the shrine of charity?

Concluding his eulogy of prohibition, its penalties, and prisons, my good brother burst into ecstatic song. I will reproduce the verse, but beg to be permitted to adorn it with a single original line, being something of a poet myself. [Laughter.] Said my friend the Senator from Texas [Mr. Sheppard], eyes lifted heavenward and face illumined with a divine radiance:

> O beautiful! for spacious skies,
> For amber waves of grain,
> For purple mountains majesties
> Above the fruited plain—
> America! America!
> God shed His grace on thee,
> And crown Thy good with brotherhood
> From sea to shining sea!"
> As an hundred thousand prisoners look
>   through the bars at me,
> Oh, happy day!

You will observe I am almost overcome with emotion by the beauty of the sentiment and the rhythm of the words.

In two short years 125,000 to 130,000 have been jailed, an army as great as has conquered kingdoms; a mighty host of human beings, with hearts that beat, with nerves that feel, with souls to be exalted or destroyed. Into prison cells in contact with vice, with every form of horrid crime, these men were thrust, and thereby you think you serve the good and merciful God.

Turn your eyes to that picture and answer whether a law that does a thing like that to men who have only responded to an appetite, ingrained in man from the first, is not what I denounce it to be, a crime within itself.

Look again at the picture. Poor boys and impoverished mothers are sentenced to hard labor until death shall break their prison bars. And for what, pray? Because on the testimony of a sneak and informer they were convicted of having for the second or third time been caught with a little liquor in their possession, or of selling a drink to somebody who desired to buy it. Look closely at the picture. It is a shifting panorama—a tragedy running through the years—the victims are dressed in ignominious stripes. They hear the click of the lock that shuts them in forever. They are thrust into foul cells. They are forced into the parade of the lock step. They eat loathsome prison food. They speak in whispers. They are slaves toiling beneath the muzzle of rifles at hard and unrequited tasks. They are compelled to associate with the vilest of criminals. The light of hope has faded from their eyes. Despair has settled upon their souls and left its shadow upon their faces. They long for the fresh fields. Their nostrils beg for the breath of flowers. Their hearts ache for the loved ones left at home. And these victims, sirs, in the great majority of cases are not bad people. There lie within prison walls many boys who heroically sprang from the trenches and bravely faced the fire of the machine guns in France. There lie rotting within those cells many men who were useful citizens and who beyond all doubt were never guilty of a real crime.

Look once more! One hundred and thirty thousand human beings in prison stripes are marching in the lock step. The procession extends for miles. It winds in and out like the folds of a gigantic striped serpent. Leering at it from the sidelines are the hard eyes of Bishop Cannon. Truly, the dream of Wayne B. Wheeler is realized. He has made "them believe in hell." And, merciful God, this occurs beneath the American flag. But still the fanatics demand punishment and yet more punishment. The cry is that of the degenerate Roman of Rome's degenerate days, "A man for the tiger and a man for the lion this morning, O good Quirites!" To this sad estate has the Congress of the United States and the American Government come.

I have already told you that General Andrews testified to the immense number of stills in operation. Let me call another witness. Mr. Buckner, then district attorney of New York, after a careful estimate, arrived at the conclusion that every year approximately 60,000,000 gallons of denatured alcohol were diverted from industry and redistilled for beverage purposes. The Government had loaded most of this denatured alcohol with poison. Doctor Doran, the present prohibition director, has testified that in most cases where denatured alcohols are redistilled, the poisons can not be altogether removed.

It follows that these poisons are eating away the vitals of millions of people. Malt extracts that will make more beer than ever was manufactured in the United States are now sold and made use of in the homes. Anybody can buy a can of it and make 5 gallons of beer in about five days. It is advertised on billboards throughout the country. Have you not all seen the billboard pictures of the amiable-looking old German lady holding a can in her hand and saying, "This is what Louie uses, and Louie knows." [Laughter.] The alcoholic content of that kind of beer is greater than that of the old-time brewery product and the beer is more injurious. Millions of homes are thus turned into little breweries and the beer is made in the presence and frequently with the aid of the children. If there is any danger to come from it and if the children should be guarded, the home is a mighty poor place for a brewery.

According to their own estimates, the authorities seized not more than five or ten per cent of the liquor being smuggled into the country. And General Andrews declared that as importations decreased, moonshining increased. We have now progressed to the point that the "moon shines on the moonshine everywhere." [Laughter.]

When prohibition was enacted we all thought the vineyards were thereby destroyed. But the price of California wine grapes has risen from $20 a ton to about $175. The reason is that people are making wines in vast quantities.

Cider? They have now worked out a plan where one can

let his cider get hard, freeze it in a refrigerator, bore a hole
in the center where the alcohol is, and be drunk in five minutes.
Compared with that stuff old bourbon whisky was a mild tonic.
[Laughter.]

Even from the silos, where nature makes the stuff, the farm
boy is drawing a supply.

All about the country everywhere—there is no exception—
stills are running, in the mountain dells, along the banks of
creeks, in cellars, in garrets, in garages, and, upon occasion, in
the jails.

The seizures are merely farcical. A few days ago, within a
short distance of the Capitol, the police finally discovered a
still that had evidently been in operation for a very long time.
It had a capacity of 1,800 gallons per day. When the raid
was finally made, the officers found the still in full operation,
but they could not find anybody who would admit he owned it.
So they virtuously smashed the still. Thus was the majesty
of the law vindicated. The whole apparatus probably was not
worth more than a few hundred dollars. It had doubtless
turned out hundreds of thousands of gallons of liquor. This
seizure was widely advertised throughout the country. There
was a great beating of tom-toms over it. The Nation was informed that the prohibition officers had dried Washington up.
Such is the ridiculous farce being enacted and re-enacted all
over the country.

This is the age of progress and discovery. Some enterprising
genius discovered that an excellent variety of whisky could be
made from corn sugar; that, in fact, it had some advantages
over sour mash. For whereas sour mash gives off an offensive
odor liable to arouse the neighborhood gossips, whisky can be
made out of corn sugar and the occupant of the next room not
know whether they are running a still or doing the family
washing.

Behold the march of the corn-sugar business. In 1914 sales
were 175,000,000 pounds; in 1928 the sales were 968,000,000
pounds.

Everywhere in shop windows you can see whisky flasks exposed for sale. Since prohibition there have been sold more
flasks, more corks, more bottle stoppers, more corkscrews than

were carried or used by all the tribes of men who through all the ages have marched across this bank and shoal of time.

The supply of charred kegs is inexhaustible. Here is an advertisement in the *Washington Star* of February 16—just a little ad. It only mentions six things. The first three of them I will read:

"Big cut-price specials at Peoples Hardware Chain Stores.

"Bottle caps, 3 gross, 50 cents; 3-gallon charred keg, $1.59; Peoples malt sirup, 45 cents."

Six or seven places are indicated where these articles can be bought in the Capital from this one chain of stores. [Laughter.]

We may laugh or we may rave; the cold, hard fact remains that the prohibition law is not regarded and enforced and will not be regarded and enforced as are laws against real crimes.

If a Washington hardware store were to advertise "machine guns for gangsters at a reduced rate" the police would be looking after that place within the next 15 minutes.

But what avails argument and proof. Indeed, both are unnecessary in view of the high authority available. The National United Committee for Law Enforcement on February 18, 1929, put out a statement. I read excerpts, but I shall be glad to insert the entire article in the *Record*. One heading is:

The Truth About Washington

"The Capital City is seething in lawlessness and saturated with poison liquor, dispensed by bootleggers under various aliases, operating openly and sold in hundreds of places as sugar is sold in groceries.

"One does not need a card of introduction or speak the shibboleth of the underworld to obtain admission or accommodation; all that is required is a thirst and the price. Anybody's money is good for rotten rum in Death Valleys.

"Washington is a Sodom of Suds, sold openly behind false fronts and fictitious names, containing from 4 to 60 per cent of alcoholic poison and in some cases so labeled.

"We make no loose charges. We are not hiding behind 'estimates' previously made, or charges now headlining the press, or being uncorked in fluid eloquence on the floors of Congress, but after personal investigation by trained operatives.

* * * * * * * *

"Hundreds of such places, scattered all over the city, and in some cases in solid blocks, and not far removed from the Capitol itself, are found to be operating in violation of the law.

Death Valleys in Washington

"For the past month the united committee has been making an under-cover investigation into conditions in this Capital City. For this work we brought experienced and trained men from outside the city, and unknown in Washington. They report to us the places visited, the hour, the date, observations, character of premises, and purchases seen and made.

"The places include hotels, back-room bars, restaurants, lunch rooms, barber shops, tailor shops, cigar, delicatessen, and candy stores, and private houses with 'rooms to let'.

Specimen Report

"No. 247. Entered; E Street NW.; cigar store; 12.15 p. m.; purchased five drinks of gin, 25 cents per drink; sold in back room with sign 'No admittance' on door. Time, 20 minutes."

Then there is given a list of places visited and dates, following which the statement continues:

"Here are 342 places in which the law is flagrantly and openly violated and in which wine, gin, red liquor, corn, or whisky was being sold, and purchased, by the drink and bottle. In addition, there are numerous places all over the city where bottled 'bay rum' is sold to all comers, containing 60 per cent of alcohol, according to the label, and not marked for external purposes or number of Government permit given. Over 300 of these emptied bottles were left or taken from the down-and-out men in one week at the Gospel Mission."

Then the statement charges, in substance and effect, that there is graft among the police.

Here is an article from the Buffalo *Courier-Express*. It was sent to me by a former Senator. It is entitled "So this is Volsteadism":

"As an indication of the need of definite information from presidential candidates to what they mean when they pledge themselves to prohibition enforcement, Detroit's bootlegging industry may be cited. Doubtless, comparable figures could be obtained in any city situated as Detroit is, in a border or coast district, where rum runners ply their trade.

"Detroit's liquor business, including smuggling, manufacturing, and distribution, is estimated to employ 50,000 persons, with an output valued at $215,000,000. It is second, according to a story printed yesterday morning in this newspaper, only to the automobile industry. The chemical industry is a big business in Detroit, but it is a 'poor third' when compared with the bootlegging trade. Its annual production is valued at only $87,000,000, or considerably less than one-half of the estimated value of the illicit liquor business."

But, Mr. President, why should we produce figures or evidence when Prohibition Director Doran states:

"It is a matter of policy whether Congress wants to embark in the police business. If Congress wants to embark in the police business, it will take $300,000,000 and a system of United States courts covering the land."

"If the Government wants to embark in the police business." Volsteadism is from beginning to end nothing but police business. The suppressing of the manufacture, the transportation, and the sale of liquor comes within the category, "police business." So long as millions want to buy and other millions want to sell, you can not suppress that business, even if you were to do as Wheeler suggested: To call out the Army, the Navy, and the National Guard. Even if you were to do that, you would have to organize a force to watch the officers and privates to keep them sober while they were standing guard. That is the cold truth about the matter.

But, lest the evidence and authorities I have cited should be challenged, I call attention to certain admissions made during this debate by distinguished dry Senators. First, I quote the Senator from Texas [Mr. Sheppard], who in seeking to avoid the terrific effect of Doctor Doran's statement, could think of nothing better to say than this:

"I understand it to be his idea that better results could be accomplished if the Federal Government concentrated its efforts on suppressing the supply of industrial alcohol at its source."

Mr. President, alcohol does not have a source; it has 10,000 sources. It is not produced in one place where it can be watched and held down. According to the information I receive—and I state it only on information and belief—industrial alcohol is not to-day as popular as "good old moonshine" made by the boys around the town, who are getting rich at the business.

Second, I quote the Senator from Washington, who stands sponsor for this barbaric amendment. However, I do not believe he wrote it. I think it was sent here by the Department of Justice. I will ask the Senator if that is not correct?

Mr. Jones. As I understood, the bill was prepared in the Department of Justice.

Mr. Reed of Missouri. The Senator from Washington recently declared:

"The greatest trouble we have had, I think I may say, has been from the intelligence unit of the Government seeking to discredit and to have removed men who are standing by the enforcement of the law. In one or two instances I was compelled to go to the President of the United States in order to protect men who were enforcing the law and standing by its enforcement from the machinations of the intelligence unit. I am glad to say that the President of the United States stood by me on that proposition."

Lord God of Hosts!—and I say it reverently—has it come to pass that the officials of one department of the Government are working with law violators against the officials of another department who are engaged in the enforcement of the law? If so, then the contamination of this law is even worse than I have pictured it; for I did not presume that officers sworn in one department of the Government would dare to undo the work of other officers sworn to enforce this law. Here we have another illustration of the fact that when you declare that a crime which the majority of human beings do not believe is a crime, everywhere people protest, everywhere the arm of the law is paralyzed.

The Senator from Washington continued:

"I do not know what their business"—that is, the business of the intelligence unit—"has been in other States. I do know that the principal work of the intelligence unit in the State of Washington has been to discredit the prohibition enforcement officers."

The Senator nods his head, and says that is the fact. While I differ from the Senator on many, many things, I know that he is a man whose word is good everywhere.

But, sir, the story can all be epitomized in a very brief statement by the distinguished Senator from Georgia [Mr. Harris], who is the author of the proposal to increase the prohibition-enforcement appropriation by $25,000,000. We all know that if there are four sincere prohibitionists in all this world, the Senator from Georgia [Mr. Harris] is one, the Senator from Washington [Mr. Jones] is another, and the Senator from Texas [Mr. Sheppard] is the other two. [Laughter.] Standing here at the end of ten years of this thing, looking back through those years and surveying the scene, the Senator from Georgia declares:

"Every Senator, whether he is in favor of this law or not, knows that its enforcement is a farce. * * * Not only is this law violated, * * * but it is causing the people of this country to lose respect not only for this law but for all laws; and I do not know of any greater harm that is being done than for our people to lose respect for law of any kind."

To that I say, "Amen." General disrespect for all laws is the greatest harm that can befall our Nation or can curse our race, and it is the direct product of this law. It is its legitimate child. It springs from it as naturally as plant life springs from the fertile earth.

Said the Senator from Georgia:

"It has been a farce from the first"—he then added by way of apology—"because they have not had the money with which to enforce it."

How much money? How much money? We are spending this year, directly and indirectly, $59,000,000. Those are the figures given to me by the Senator from Wyoming [Mr. Warren], who is in charge of the appropriation bills. That is the amount spent by the Federal Government alone. That undoubtedly can not include many incidental expenses. How can you estimate the increased cost of courts and separate that cost from the usual expenses of litigation?

It would, it seems to me, be very difficult to do that. How much more does it cost if 100,000 men are locked up in jail and taken from useful employments? The economic loss and expense is not less than $200,000,000. How much more does it cost? The figures given, of course, do not embrace the expenses of enforcement in the 48 States. Neither do the figures I have given include imprisonments made by State officers. I do not know what may be the situation in other States, but I am sure the convictions by the State courts of Missouri far outnumber those secured by the Federal officers within that State. First and last, it seems to me it would be wholly within the limits of conservative statement if we were to say that this law costs the State and local governments at least $100,000,000 per annum. And that the economic loss is at least $200,000,000 more.

How much does it cost? The revenue which the Government might derive mounts to stupendous sums. If this business were taken over and properly managed, if the Government obtained a revenue upon the liquor that is to-day being sold, I am sure the annual interest upon the national debt could be paid, and I think the entire debt could be wiped out in 20 years of time.

How much does it cost? No man can measure its cost. No man can give an accurate estimate. This much we may be sure, the amount is appalling.

You say, "Ah, but we abolished the saloon. We eliminated the distillery."

You did not abolish the saloon. You split the saloon into a hundred parts and scattered the parts into every hamlet and village. You have made peripatetic that which was a fixture. Instead of being located in one spot, the saloon perambulates around the country in automobiles. The bar is condensed into a gripsack. The sales are by the case instead of by the glass. The saloon is still here, and more people are engaged in the business than in pre-Volstead days. You did not exterminate the brewery. You made millions of little breweries and installed them in the homes of the people.

Ah, but why need I argue the failure of prohibition when it is solemnly admitted on the floor of the Senate by distinguished dry Senators that the whole enforcement has been a farce? If the admissions do not cover the case, then no logic or assertion of mine will avail.

But, Mr. President, there is a phase of this question graver than any I have touched upon. In preliminary, let me repeat that there never has been a race of men that has not had some form of stimulant—not one. You may dig in the catacombs, you may explore the sepulchers of vanished races of men, and you find there the evidence that always, in some form, man has used stimulants. That fact betokens a natural appetite, a natural demand. The great races have been the ones most addicted to alcoholic beverages.

A condition of that kind must be dealt with in a practical way. If the appetite or desire generally exists, the fact should be recognized and so dealt with as to produce the best possible results. I will go as far as any other man will go in appeals to people to restrain themselves, in pointing out the evils of overindulgence, in doing everything that can be done by moral suasion and sensible regulation to limit the use of these stimulants. I am, however, convinced you make a tragic mistake when for the persuasions of argument you substitute legislative command, "Thou shalt not drink." By saying that you create an entirely different psychology. Like it or not, the average man says, "I don't care a snap of my fingers for that law." Like it or not, we must face the fact that men are just men, and women are just women, and that when you tell them they "shall not" do a thing which they believe they have the right to do, you plant in their minds the impulse to immediately proceed to do it. That is exactly what has occurred.

Another phase of this psychology is that liquor, once a common thing that anyone could obtain at any place has now been lifted, notwithstanding the enormous quantities of it still available, to a point where it is regarded as in the nature of a luxury. There is not a living American who does not regard almost every luxury as a prime necessity of his life.

Accordingly, at parties, at balls, at dinners, and at dances this "luxury" is dealt out. The lad who once was told that strong drink was the potion of death, that in the cup lurked the coiled serpent of destruction, now regards drinking as a good-natured escapade and a pint of whisky on the hip as the equipment of all good fellows.

Ah, this is no dream, this is no occasional thing; it exists almost everywhere among almost all classes of society. The cocktail is dispensed as a luxury and the highball follows on. Men and women who in the old days would not have served a drink in their homes now regard it as a necessary act of courtesy. Mothers, who a few years ago would have warned their daughters not to associate with boys who drank, now, all too often, will hand their daughters the liquor served at parties.

That is true. Deny it? Yes; stand up and deny it, and try a little longer to mislead the world. The fact is here, and if a man could consistently with decency do so, he could read a list of names as long as my friend Sheppard's list of jailbirds.

Girls guzzle it with boys. It is served in clubs, not by the clubs, oh, no; not by the proprietors of hotels and eating houses, oh, no. All they furnish are the glass, and the ginger ale, and all the boy does is to furnish the moonshine. Thus we are corrupting the youth of the land. I say to you prohibition friends, and I say it as solemnly as I have ever uttered anything in my life, we are corrupting a class that rarely was endangered or tainted in the past, and upon your souls and consciences the weight of the burden must rest.

There follows a tale more horrible. Whereas once people could get good beer, and a little stimulant from it, they now resort to home-brew which while it is made in the homes in vast quantities, is rather vile stuff. Or they consume gin and rum and whisky. These strong liquors are now used by millions who before prohibition never touched anything but light wines and mild beer.

Ah, if the story but ended there, it would not be as black as that which I am about to relate. Bootleggers of whisky are likely to become bootleggers of drugs. When men can not get a stimulant in the form of the kind of liquor they want, they go to something stronger than that. According to the best authorities, there are in the United States to-day more than a million drug addicts.

We never at any time had that number of habitual drunkards.

Mrs. Bonfils, a distinguished writer and a lady of great ability and unquestioned honesty, and to whom I am indebted for much of the information I am about to give, says that dope is peddled to schoolgirls. They are told: "Here is a little breath of happiness that makes you forget." In the short space of 10 days the iron grip of the drug is fastened upon their souls and bodies; they are manacled slaves the rest of their lives. Dope is also distributed and used in alarming quantities by the worst criminal classes. From it they get the inspiration of a false courage that enables them to commit crime. All too often the lady of fashion in the seclusion of her boudoir resorts to drugs to soothe her tired nerves; likewise dope is frequently the bracer of the professional gentleman who for the hour needs extra enthusiasm.

Is the dope habit growing? Oh, you people who have turned all the batteries of your wrath against a glass of beer, what say you to the fact that, running parallel with your prohibition movement, has come this horrible advance in the use of narcotics?

The secretary of the opium conference of the League of Nations declares that 786 tons of opium and 12 tons of coca leaves are more than sufficient to supply all the medical uses throughout the world.

Honorable Stephen Porter, author of the Porter bill, estimates the need of legitimate narcotics for the medical practice of the world to be 125 tons or less. John Palmer Gavit, former managing editor of the New York *Evening Post,* and one time chief of the Washington bureau of the Associated Press, discloses in his new book, *Opium,* that the world is producing between eight and ten thousand tons of raw opium every year and doing it legitimately.

United States Attorney Charles H. Tuttle, a very high-class man, states his belief that the value of drugs smuggled into the United States last year was between $25,000,000 and $50,000,-000.

What happened to the cases of ships bringing that in? The first case I cite is that of the ship *President Taft,* which came into the harbor of San Francisco on July 14, 1927, with a cargo of 830 tins of narcotics, valued at $29,300. A fine of $146,650 was levied against the company. The company appealed to Washington and the fine actually paid was $3,000.

July 1, 1926, the *President Lincoln* came into San Francisco Harbor carrying 197 tins of contraband opium; the fine levied was $32,825; the company appealed to Washington and got off with a payment of $1,000.

May 1, 1925, 388 tins of narcotics were seized on the Korean ship *Maru.* There were levied fines of $31,050; the fine actually paid was $100.

The *Rochambeau* brought $5,000,000 worth of dope into New York Harbor in December, 1928. The case against that company is still pending.

The *President Harrison* brought into New York Harbor on October 2, 1928, $1,000,000 worth of dope. These doubtless are but a few of the great number of importations and miscarriages of justice.

Notice this: The price of narcotics has fallen from $50 an ounce to $25 an ounce in the city of San Francisco. In Chicago it has fallen from $50 to $20 an ounce. In New York narcotics can be bought for $12 an ounce. That shows that the market is flooded. Besides, new varieties of dope are being created.

It is further stated that in 1922, 24 per cent. of the prisoners in the Leavenworth prison were drug addicts, and that to-day 60 per cent. are drug addicts.

What has that to do with prohibition? Everything. If people have a natural desire for some kind of a stimulant, and if they are set on satisfying that desire, then, in the name of high heaven, let us permit them to have that kind of a stimulant which does not utterly destroy them. Let us not drive them to these baser expedients.

We can not make people over. All that we can do is to restrain and help and guide and counsel. We should bear in mind that the personal habits of the individual are the business of the individual. So long as those habits do not impinge upon the rights of other people, we have no right to interfere except by persuasion. There is the line, and when we overleap it we bring disaster.

Senators, did you ever stop to think of the absurdity of this prohibition law? If the subject were not serious, its contemplation would provoke laughter. Consider this: A man approaches a bar and asks for a glass of beer. The bartender sells it to him. The transaction thus far is voluntary and perfectly amicable. Then the bartender concludes to rob the customer, and murders him in cold blood and takes his purse.

A United States marshal witnesses the sale of the beer and the murder. Under the law this ridiculous situation exists! The marshal can arrest the culprit and take him before the United States court for selling a glass of beer, but he can not take him there to be tried for the cold-blooded murder and robbery. We trust the States to try every kind of crime except violations of the prohibitory law. We trust them to protect us by the apprehension of burglars, of highwaymen, of fraud mongers, of fiends, and of thieves, criminals of every kind, no matter how desperate or vile; but we do not trust the States to regulate the sale of that which a large percentage of the people want to buy. What an absurdity! The purpose of the Eighteenth Amendment was to force prohibition upon unwilling States. So we have the spectacle of great States with millions of people, the majority of whom protest against prohibition.

There is no man of good common sense who does not know that there can be no effective enforcement of any law among any free people where the majority of the people are opposed to it. It can not be done and it ought not to be done, for freedom consists in the right to live under laws enacted by the consent of the people.

All the while that we have proceeded along this line of unreasonable restriction of mild stimulants the deadliest serpents that ever have been loosed, the serpents of opium and of narcotics, are destroying the people of the land. Drugs are not like whisky, which can be smelled on the breath, and thus bring exposure. They do not give any evidence at first. The poison is distilled gradually. It steals through the veins. The habit grows through the years, until at last from the pallid lips of the victim comes the cry of maniacal despair. Ah, what an army is this army of drug addicts, a million men and women. An army of the living dead marching through the golden fields of earth, but their dull eyes see only the distorted pictures drugs have painted in disordered brains.

We, sir, have been all along pursuing the wrong philosophy. We have relied on law and abandoned reason. We have come to believe in the logic of the lash, the persuasive power of force, and we have substituted handcuffs for moral precepts and chains for prayers. No longer do we hear the old appeal to reason and to right. No longer are there kindly words, gentle handclasps, and appeals to reason and to conscience. Rather the prison cell, the sound of shackles, the rattling of gyves, the death rattle in dungeons. Thus we seek to make men good. I affirm it to be true that in all the tides of time no law made by man ever made a good man or a good woman—not one. Law may have restrained the murderer's arm, but it did not remove the impulse of murder from his heart. It may have restrained the hand of the thief but it did not remove from his soul the desire to steal. It may have restrained the highwayman, but he still at heart was a robber. Law never made a man good. It may have protected the innocent from the wrongs of the wicked, it may have restrained the criminal, but it did not purge his heart or make white the blackness of his soul.

What is it then that we must look to? Ah, my friends, there are two realms of the law. First is the law passed by legislative bodies, the civil law. Its business is to protect life and property and restrain aggression and wrong. That is its realm. It is protective.

But there is another realm of law—the realm of the moral law. Its principles were written by Almighty God upon the hearts of men. They have been taught by the mother's gentle voice as in the ear of her daughter she whispered of rectitude and virtue, and by the father as he pointed his son the way of honor. That is the great law. It controls us in nearly all the acts of our lives.

What law of man has ever planted a noble impulse in the heart? Men will leap into the flood of rivers to rescue a stranger. They then obey not any man-made law; they answer the call of nature, the voice of conscience; they obey the impulse of nobility. Men will yield their lives to save a child. But no law of man commands the sacrifice. They respond to the mandate of the moral law.

On the great moral law we must at last rely. It alone makes men fit to live upon the earth. It alone will make them temperate, just, honest, and decent.

We have attempted to substitute for the persuasion of the moral law the force of the statute law. Senators, I warn you, the American people can not be forced to do anything. Nevertheless, "a man for the lion and a man for the tiger" is the cry of the day.

Mr. President, Montaigne has well said:

"It would be better for us to have no laws at all than to have them in so prodigious numbers as we have."

And Thomas Jefferson:

"The nation that is least governed is best governed."

I could quote the words of others of our mighty dead whose hands did "shape the anchors of our hope," but it would be useless to proceed further.

If you ask me, Mr. President, what remedy I would suggest, I answer, let us go back to the original principles upon which our Government was founded. Let us once more say that the States are capable of self-government. Let us repeal this obnoxious, this hideous amendment. Then let us say to the State of my friend from Utah [Mr. King], who is honoring me by his presence, "Let Utah handle this question as befits her people and as suits her purpose." To the State of my friend from Wyoming [Mr. Kendrick], let us give the same message, and so without going through the list of names, to all of the States let us say, "This is your business. It is a matter falling generally within police regulations. We trust you to apprehend the murderers, to put down crime, to suppress vice, to protect life and liberty and property, and we will trust you in this matter."

Then, sir, I am willing that the States shall be protected in the exercise of that right by the Federal Government providing, as it did provide under an amendment which years ago I offered to a bill of the Senator from Washington [Mr. Jones], that when a State prohibits the manufacture and sale of liquor within its borders liquor can not be sent into that State in interstate commerce without becoming immediately subject to those State laws. Let us then repeal this law. Let us then discharge the snoopers and the spies, the sneaks and the criminals who have been employed with our money to haunt our doors, to break open the windows of our habitations, and to murder our people upon the streets. Let us discharge them, and as they go let us say that in this country under this flag a system of spies and espionage is a foreign and an abominable thing, and that it shall be utterly wiped out in this Republic. Let us bring this business, wherever it is conducted or how it is conducted, into the open, where it can be carried on either by officers of the law or by men who are not criminals the moment they embark in it. Let us put it in the sunlight where it may be seen. Let us fix it so that the man who buys it buys it in the open and takes the responsibility before his neighbors and his friends. Let us go back to the old principles and old doctrines of the sovereignty of the States and the right of the American citizen to regulate his own life and control his own walk down the pathway of the years.

WILLIAM E. BORAH

THE LIQUOR PROBLEM

SPEECH IN THE UNITED STATES SENATE, FEBRUARY 18, 1929,
IN REPLY TO THE ADDRESS OF SENATOR JAMES A. REED

[Shortly after Senator Reed, on February 18, 1929, had concluded his speech in opposition to the Jones Act, Senator Borah made the following reply. It summarizes in a concise and effective way the arguments successfully used by him in his public debate with President Nicholas Murray Butler in Symphony Hall, Boston, on April 8, 1927.]

Mr. President, When I asked on Saturday last that the unanimous consent agreement might be vacated I did so not only because of my desire to hear the Senator from Missouri [Mr. Reed] in the full presentation of his views upon this important question, not only because I am always interested in any presentation he may choose to make upon a subject but for the further reason that I think it well to have full discussion of this subject from time to time. Indeed, I think the most unfortunate thing that could possibly happen to the present program of dealing with the liquor problem would be that of indifference or failure to call to the attention of the country the different phases which it from time to time presents for our consideration.

Mr. President, before I enter upon a discussion of this subject I take this occasion to say how sincerely our regret deepens as the time approaches when the Senator from Missouri is voluntarily to retire to private life. Those of us who have served with him during these long years—some of them tragic years— and have come to know of his great qualities, regard his retirement as not only a loss to this body but a loss to the country. It is the retirement of no ordinary man; it is the retirement of an extraordinary man, a man whose industry and courage and genius have placed him among the foremost men of his day. I regret that he is voluntarily to retire. I trust, however, Mr. President, that he will find time from the engagements of his profession, of which he is a distinct ornament, to consider and discuss public questions; that we may have the benefit, at least in that way, of those attributes of mind and qualities of character with which he is so richly and so rarely endowed. As these are the closing days of the session I felt I could not say less, and if I should entirely consult my feelings I would say much more.

Mr. President, with very many things which the Senator from Missouri has said I am in full accord. I think upon the fundamental question which is involved in this controversy I am in accord with the Senator. The Senator from Missouri referred to the fact that there are those who insist upon enacting such laws as this but who, nevertheless, live in violation of the law. He said that in his opinion such individuals were deserving of the severest condemnation. I am bound to say that with that statement I believe all right-thinking men and women will heartily agree. It ought to be an axiom of decent citizenship. If those who make the law live in violation of the law the axe has already been laid at the root of the tree of representative government. There is a peculiar and a heavier obligation resting upon those who make the law than upon those for whom the law is made, although, of course, it binds all. But, upon reflection, Mr. President, how are we to distinguish between those who make the law and those whose duty it is to execute the law. If there be included the latter with the former, then let the Senator from Missouri unleash his fine irony and his scathing invective; he has a subject worthy of his talents. I think one of the most serious conditions with which we have to deal not only with regard to this but with regard to other laws is that those of us who make the laws and those who execute the laws standing in places of trust and tremendous responsibility do not often enough think of the fact that, perhaps, more important than are laws is the example which we ourselves set to the citizen. I think that is a matter about which the entire country can well reflect; and the Senator has stated it in his own inimitable way.

The Senator said that prohibition was the crime of crimes which had been committed in the matter of legislation in the United States. With that I can not agree. It may have been a mistake, Mr. President; the people of the United States may have erred in their judgment; time and experience alone will demonstrate that fact; but it was not a crime. The people of the United States were in sincerity wrestling with that which was deemed to be one of the great evils of modern civilization. Everyone had been brought to realize that in some way, and in a more effective way, it was the duty of the people of this country to deal with this problem. The object was an exalted one; the purpose embodied something of the ideal, though possibly in the end it may prove impracticable. That, time, as I have said, will determine. But that which they would have accomplished was void of all intent to do injury to the people of the United States; it was to serve them. No; it was not a crime to undertake to control and bring under the direction of law and under the domination of civilization that which would undermine and destroy civilization. It was and is a great evil, and to struggle for its control or to be rid of it can in no way be regarded as a crime. We may not have found as yet the right remedy; I do not know. The fight against the liquor traffic is not for 10 days or 10 years; it is an eternal fight, and only from step to step and from progressive acts can we finally determine how we shall ultimately deal with it. But the question is whether or not it was an error, whether or not it was a mistake.

I am not committed, Mr. President, to all opposition against the modification or even the repeal of the Eighteenth Amendment; I am not committed against the modification or even the repeal of the Volstead Act; I am only committed against the change, the repeal either of the amendment or of the law, so long as nothing better and more effective has been or can be presented.

If there be a better way to control the evil of drink, a more effective way, more thorough, and with better results to those whom we would serve, let us have it. The object is to secure the best possible remedy, that experience and the human mind can give us upon this subject; and, while at the present time, in my judgment, no better plan has been proposed, no better scheme devised, and I stand for the program as it is, let it be understood at all times that we are open, as I presume all advocates of better regulation or better control are open, to consider any plan which may be presented and which will stand the test of reason. But it must be a better plan. It must give assurance that we are making progress. There is to be no retreat. Revolutions do not go backward.

I do not find fault with those who advocate the repeal of the Eighteenth Amendment. I may differ with them as to the arguments which they put forth, and as to the reasons with which they undertake to sustain their position; but the right to advocate the repeal is a sacred right—just as sacred as the right to put an amendment in the Constitution in the first place. The test of free government, the right of the people to write and unwrite laws, the test of good citizenship, is obedience to the law when written. We are not quarreling with our friends about their right to urge a repeal; and, far from quarreling about a better scheme, we invite them to present it, to present it with all their power and ability, and let the American people ultimately pass upon it.

But this much I venture to say in the beginning of my remarks: That the Eighteenth Amendment will stand in the Constitution of the United States until the moral forces of the United States decide that something better is presented to control the liquor problem. There will be no going backward upon the effort of the human family to control this evil which has been torturing and tormenting them for 3,000 years and more.

No one need argue with me, Mr. President, as to his right to urge the repeal; but, while not committed against a change, as I have stated, I am committed to the enforcement of the present provision in every reasonable, practical way so long as it is a part of the Constitution of the United States. That presents a question far superior, to my mind, to the question of "wet" or "dry," of liquor or no liquor, important and vital as it is. The question of enforcing prohibition while it stands, of massing and crystallizing and organizing the moral sentiment of the country and the legal forces of the country to maintain our Constitution, presents a question infinitely more important to me than the question of liquor or no liquor. That involves the existence of our Government, the preservation of the principles upon which we build, the hope of the future. The only things we can expect of the future are the liberties and the rights which a regard for the Constitution as the people have written it will give to us. When we are fighting for that principle we are fighting for free government—for the right of the people to rule. That transcends all other issues. That is the issue which holds me to this contest against all adversity, against all criticism; upon that issue I stand.

The Constitution says:

"The manufacture, sale, or transportation of intoxicating liquors within, the importation thereof into, or the exportation thereof from the United States and all territory subject to the jurisdiction thereof for beverage purposes is hereby prohibited."

There it is, the fundamental law of the land, adopted according to the method provided by the fathers; just as much a part of the law of the land as the fifth amendment to the Constitution of the United States; just as much a part of the law of the land as that which gives a man the right of trial by jury; just as much a part of the law of the land as that which protects his right under *habeas corpus;* just as much as that which protects the freedom of the press, or the right to worship God according to the dictates of one's own conscience; just as much as any other provision of the Constitution of the United States; and the obligation is upon us here, and elsewhere in the country, to support it, maintain it, and to enforce it so long as it is a part of the Constitution.

The Supreme Court has said that—

"The first section of the amendment"—the one embodying prohibition—"is operative throughout the entire territorial limits of the United States, binds all legislative bodies, courts, public officers, and individuals within those limits, and of its own force invalidates every legislative act—whether by Congress, by a State legislature, or by territorial assembly—which authorizes or sanctions what the section prohibits."

This was not only writing into the Constitution a specific provision of law; it was the adoption of a great national policy. The people had struggled with the liquor question in one way and another for many years. They had tried the license system, local option, State control, and different methods by which to control the saloon. They finally came to the conclusion that as a matter of national policy they would adopt the prohibition policy and write it into the Constitution of the United States. That presents to me the only problem that there is before us at the present time, and that is, "The Constitution being there, how shall we maintain our system of government?"

Upon that question the able Senator from Missouri and I are not in disagreement, as I understand. I understand that he takes the position which he has always taken: While he would repeal the Eighteenth Amendment, for reasons to which I shall refer later, while it is there, as I understand, and, knowing him as a great lawyer and a patriot, as I would expect him to be, he is for the enforcement of the Constitution of the United States.

Upon another occasion he said:

"When the Constitution was amended it became the paramount, the supreme law of the land. When the Volstead Act was passed it became the statute law, and Constitution and law became binding upon all citizens and all public officials."

An axiomatic proposition, yet too often forgotten in these days; a simple proposition upon which all free government rests, yet too often forgotten in these days. Written into the Constitution, the law adopted, they bind all citizens, and all citizens ought to recognize that fact.

Mr. President, the trouble in this situation lies deeper than the prohibition law itself, as I shall undertake to show later. I fear sometimes—although I am not a pessimist, I trust—that we have come to forget in this country just what a constitutional government means. It means this, and practically nothing more: That unless the people have that reverence for the Constitution which commands of them obedience and respect there is no such thing left as constitutional government. There may be many individuals who will violate the law or violate the Constitution; but the great mass of the American people must come again to realize—if they do not now realize—that when they themselves write the law, as they do when they adopt a constitution, they must be bound by and respect that law until they themselves rewrite it.

Again the Senator said:

"The Constitution and the statutes must stand and be obeyed

unless they are changed or repealed in the manner and form laid down by the Constitution. There should be no evasion; there should be no attempt to accomplish their destruction by indirection. In my opinion, the Eighteenth Amendment will stand until and unless the moral forces of the Nation become convinced that there is some better way to deal with the liquor problem."

Yes, until the moral forces conclude there is a better way.

As I understand the Senator's position and mine, they are identical upon this great, fundamental question that the Constitution is there, adopted by the people; the law is there, enacted by Congress; they should not be evaded; they should not be circumvented; all good citizens and all right-minded people should assist in maintaining them and enforcing them. With that question settled, Mr. President, we have nothing before us until we come to the consideration of some new scheme which involves a repeal or an entire change of the law. Let us have the new plan. Let us have the next forward step in the settlement of the liquor problem.

I shall not, of course, take issue with the Senator upon the question that there are violations of the law. I know that. I certainly shall not take issue with him upon the question that the law has led to corruption. I know that. I call his attention to the fact, however, that there never has been a law with reference to liquor placed upon the statute books of any civilized nation on the earth but that the liquor forces undertook to break it down, to violate it, to undermine it, and to corrupt the officials. It is the history of liquor legislation from the beginning until this hour. It is not within the ingenuity of the human mind to devise a liquor law that will be satisfactory to the liquor interests. They are seeking to do with this law what they sought to do with every law. I do not care where you go, when it was, or how you undertake to deal with it; we had the same condition of violation, of corruption, of deceit, of fraud that we have now in regard to this matter; and as I shall undertake to show in a few moments, every system of dealing with liquor at the present time is having to meet that exact problem.

Before I go on further, let me go back to early days of the Republic, when it was proposed to place a high tax upon the importation of liquor into the United States. If you will take up the debates which occurred upon that question, you will find just the same contention that is made now—that that kind of a law can not be enforced; that it will lead to smuggling, to bootlegging, to violations of the law. There must be no law. The evil wants a free rein.

Here is one paragraph from a noted Member of Congress at that time:

"But suppose we yield to the reasoning of my opponent and lay a high duty and check the importation of rum. What will happen? We shall defeat our purpose. The country will be just as immoral and much poorer than at present. Not a hogshead of the liquor will be seen on our wharves, not a shilling of revenue will be collected from it by our customhouse officers. Yet at all the inns and taverns in the land rum will be as plentiful and as cheap as ever. Does any man suppose for a moment that the thousands of artisans, and the mechanics, the tradesmen, and the fishermen, to whom liquor is as much a necessity of life"—blessed old thought, ancient and faded, how often it returns—"as meat and bread, will upon a sudden cease to drink it because it is taxed with a great tax? Will they not rather set on foot 10,000 schemes to evade the duty? And is there any ingenuity so marvelous as the ingenuity of men who seek to circumvent an unwise law? Lay such a tax and in a few months every creek, every secluded bay, every swamp along the whole coast from Maine to Georgia will be a nest of smugglers. There, in the dark of each moon and in the blackness of each stormy night, hogsheads of the forbidden liquor will be run ashore and buried in the marsh, or hidden in the cellar of some fisherman's hut, to be reshipped to the great seaports of the country. Then will spring up a mode of tax gathering odious to all. On the land, an army of customhouse officers, tide waiters, and gaugers. On the sea, a navy of ships, hailing every schooner, boarding every packet, giving chase to every shallop that comes in sight. And when the money collected with so much pains has been counted, the cost of ships and officers paid, and the books balanced, it will indeed be astonishing if a single shilling remains over in the Treasury."

The same tender regard for the Treasury of the United States, the appetities of the workmen, the possibility of evading the law, the application of smuggling and spying and treachery upon the part of the officers, all advanced from time to time, and every time that the United States has proposed in any way to deal with the liquor question. No new arguments under the sun.

I repeat, there is violation now, there is corruption now, there has always been violation, there will always be corruption whenever a liquor law is advanced and put upon the statute books and undertaken to be enforced. What the liquor interests crave is the right, uncontrolled and unhampered, to prey upon the human race to its full insatiable appetite.

Just a word, Mr. President, before I pass on to the different systems. I wish that violation of law and corruption of officials were confined to the liquor problem. What a fortunate country this would be. I wish, as we survey the situation, that we could feel that only with regard to prohibition or enforcement is there violation or crime. Unfortunately it is not so. What are the violations of the liquor law compared to the corruption—the saturnalia of corruption in this country in 1921, 1922, and 1923 of the highest officials, men most responsible in Government—with corruption permeating the entire country; apparently more money involved and more taken in one transaction than these pilfering thieves in the department of prohibition would take in a hundred years.

Perhaps this arises to some extent out of a condition that followed the war. Let us hope so. We find it in other countries. We find it remarkably strong in other countries. Let us hope that it is a condition which followed from the war.

Yet, when we make that allowance, we must refer to one thing more, that is, unfortunate as it is and humiliating as it is to admit it, the United States has not yet learned the science of enforcing its criminal laws. That is to-day the greatest and most profound domestic problem, in my opinion, in this country, the application and the enforcement of the criminal law, not alone with reference to prohibition—that is but one department

—but with reference to the entire scope of human activity undertaken to be covered by the law.

We have had in this country, on an average for the last 15 years, 8,700 murders a year. In 1918 there were 18 murders in the city of London. Fifteen of the murderers were apprehended and punished. In the same year there were 230 murders in the largest city in the United States. I have not the exact figures, but I am informed that only a small percentage were punished.

In the year 1922 there were 17 murders in London. In 1922 in the largest city in the United States there were 260 murders, and in the next largest city there were 137 murders.

In 1921 there were 121 robberies in all England and Wales combined. There were 1,445 robberies in one city in the United States and 2,400 in another.

Underlying this entire question is the fact that the American people must gird themselves for the supreme task in civilization, and the crucial test of a self-governing people; that is, whether or not they can enforce the laws which they themselves write. That is the test of a self-governing people, whether the people can enforce the rules which they lay down for themselves.

We have been so busy in conquering a continent, in clearing the forests and reclaiming the deserts, and getting ourselves ahead in the great struggle for dominancy of our natural wealth that perhaps we have not given to this other problem the consideration which older communities have given to it. But it is here; it confronts us. Let us not be misled by reference to prohibition alone. It is an underlying proposition with which the American people must deal; and just such speeches as that made by the able Senator from Missouri will, although devoted largely to one question, emphasize and call to the attention of the people the fact that they are facing the proposition of preserving the first principles of representative government.

In one sense I am not surprised that there should be this disregard of law throughout the United States. We have a class of individuals—fortunately there are none of them in the Senate, the people are too careful about that—we have a class of individuals in this country, learned gentlemen, who seem to regret that their ancestors ever came to this country, who are engaged constantly in attacking the first principles of free government, and now they would lay down the rule in this country that if an individual does not like the law he has a right to violate it, to disregard it, to join with others and nullify it. They have laid down the rule that if I do not like a particular provision of the Constitution I need not appeal to my fellow countrymen to repeal it, but I may violate it and disregard it.

In one of the leading magazines of the United States, an old magazine of high standing, I read an article in which I find this:

"He who obeys a law which is wrong contributes by that to the final debacle, the intensity of which is increased because delayed by that obedience."

"The man who obeys a law which he does not think is right." Who determines whether or not it is right? Who determines in this country whether a law is right or wrong, and how is it determined? Do individuals determine that question? Are there 117,000,000 individuals passing 117,000,000 judgments on a provision of the Constitution?

The fathers were too wise for that. They provided that the Constitution could be amended in a certain way, and when it is amended, that is a determination that what is contained in the amendment is right under our form of government, until the people in the same way revise their judgment and determine another course; and a man who teaches that an individual has the right to determine for himself is a traitor to the institutions framed by our fathers and maintained by our forebears. I do not care what his standing may be—lawyer or professor—or for whom he may presume to speak, he is disloyal to American institutions.

"If a large number of citizens are convinced that an act compels them to live lives of hypocrisy, cowardice, and servility, they will feel no moral obligation to observe the law. On the contrary, they will develop an esprit and morale in the breaking of it in the name of patriotism."

Are you surprised that the ordinary bootlegger, looking up to those of learning, perhaps able to read the literature of the day, finds that he is pursuing a course marked out by those who as-

sume to speak with authority? Are you surprised that the
young men or the young women, inclined, perhaps, to disregard
the precedents of their father and mother, find here in the literature of our country a statement that they may go counter to
and disregard the laws of the land?

Ah, Mr. President, the able Senator spoke of the moral law.
Let us appeal to it here. Let us invoke it here. The highest
evidence of morality in a republic or a democracy is to observe
the law which the majority have written. There is no morality
that can be governed by political principles if that is not true.

Then this author says, in concluding his atrocious article:

"The nullification of the fugitive slave law developed men
like Abraham Lincoln."

What a miserable slander, what a cowardly implication, telling the young people of this country that Abraham Lincoln
built his character and his career upon disregard for the Constitution of the United States.

Lincoln said upon one occasion—I quote from memory—"I
hate slavery"—using a word which seldom fell from the sacred
lips of the martyr. I never saw it except with reference to
slavery.

"I hate slavery; but it is in the Constitution of the United
States. It is protected by the provisions of the Constitution of
the United States. So long as it is, it must be protected. Therefore," said he, and I quote, I believe, almost his exact words,
"we are in duty bound to preserve that Constitution in letter and
in spirit."

When he came to be inaugurated President of the United
States out here in front of the Capitol, his last plea before the
dread carnage of the Civil War broke, and brother was arrayed
against brother, hero against hero—the last plea of the martyred
Lincoln was that the northern people respect the Constitution
of the United States, give the southern people their fugitive
slave law, and enforce it, as the Constitution of the United
States obligated them to do. Yet there is circulated here as a
part of the literature of the day the statement that the then President of the United States was an advocate of lawlessness, an
advocate of the violation of the Constitution of the United
States.

Let me read another statement. A lawyer of Connecticut—I understand him to be a member of the Connecticut bar in good standing—has written a book upon constitutional government and the duty of the citizen, particularly around the Volstead Act and the Constitution of the United States, particularly the Eighteenth Amendment. Let me read from this book, which is being circulated now by an organization which is engaged in trying to convince the people of the United States that the Eighteenth Amendment can not be enforced. This is what I find in that book:

"The Eighteenth Amendment is void in so far as it purports to give the United States authority over intrastate business. The decisions of the Supreme Court of the United States which purport to authorize the transfer of police power from the States to the United States under the Eighteenth Amendment are not binding upon the State or its people."

Mr. President, if I were going to reach out and get a man who ought to have this $10,000 fine and five years' imprisonment applied to him, he would be the first gentleman I would hunt for. I would punish, if I could, the man who teaches violence rather than the poor creature who listens to and practices such teachings. I believe in free speech, but I believe that, when a man preaches a doctrine disloyal to his government, he ought to take the responsibility for having abused free speech. He may urge repeal, he may urge change but defiance to law ought to bring shame if there be no way to punish.

Mr. President, we are not the only people in the world who are struggling with the prohibition question or with the liquor problem. They have it, for instance, now in Italy. Not many Americans agree with Mussolini as to his political philosophy or his methods, but we have to admit that he is getting results. Perhaps the particular environment amid which he works necessitates some methods and some principles with which we would not be in accord.

In surveying the situation in Italy, in trying to rehabilitate and reinvigorate the Italian people and to restore them to something of their ancient prestige, this marvelous man came up against the liquor problem and realized at once and without hesitation that it is one of the things with which Italy had to contend.

Upon a certain occasion in a public address he gave a number of figures and facts as to the deplorable condition in Italy, and stated unmistakably that the problem would have to be dealt with in a drastic way. He referred to the fact that the death rate through alcoholism was excessively high. He further referred to the fact that mortality and insanity and suicides due to the use of liquor were progressing at such a rate that the Italian people could no longer disregard the problem. Then he said:

"From these figures you will perceive that the picture is black and tragic and merits our deep attention."

The first thing he did, which is a more simple process in Italy, was to close 25,000 saloons overnight by an imperial decree, if I may be permitted to use the word "imperial" in connection with Mussolini. He closed 25,000 saloons and gave assurance that that was the first step in ridding his country of this evil which was at war with the moral and economic life of the Italian people.

We are not the only people who are struggling with it. It is a world-wide problem working its devastation and its ruin in all countries, and the problem is what are we to do with it? In England it is now one of the vital issues or problems. They discovered some time ago that in 1927 the liquor bill of England was $1,506,000,000, and that the profits made out of those who drank it was $120,000,000. England, with 1,500,000 unemployed, with her superhuman burden of taxation, struggling for her economic life, found that she was expending $1,500,000,-000 for liquor and paying somebody a profit of $120,000,000.

England has tried in every way to deal with this problem except that of absolute prohibition, which is now being discussed. They undertook in the first place to close the saloons earlier in the day. They found that the saloons or the liquor traffic paid no attention practically to the regulation. They then undertook to reduce the amount of alcoholic content. They found that that did not have the desired effect.

Then they went into a town of considerable size and purchased the entire liquor interests, purchased all the means and methods that they had of supplying it, and undertook to demonstrate in that way what they could do by Government ownership. What was the result? As usual, the liquor traffic began to break down the little experiment in that town alone. They bootlegged liquor in every possible way, and that experiment, of course, has failed to demonstrate, therefore, what Government ownership could do under proper circumstances.

But it is the same old law, the same old rule. It does not make any difference what you do or how you try or how small your efforts may be, wherever the liquor traffic can fasten its fangs upon progress, progress dies.

Let us take one more illustration. Over in Canada they had prohibition in a number of Provinces; I have forgotten just how many. Then along came the moderates, those who said that "man has to have some liquor. Get rid of the bootlegger. Get rid of corruption. Get rid of destroying our young men and our young women. Therefore let us adopt Government control."

The argument in Canada was that by this method they would be rid of those things which my able friend thinks we can be rid of in this country by going back to State rights. We will examine that in a few moments.

What happened under the Canadian liquor law? Let us go first to the official record. I have referred to this elsewhere. I have been accused of being misinformed. Mr. President, I am not misinformed. I was over in Canada last summer and the summer before. I am not misinformed.

The British Columbia liquor board reports:

"Since the opening of the beer parlors the sale of "hard liquors" has increased 50 per cent. As much liquor is sold by bootleggers as is sold in the Government stores."

That is the way Canada got rid of the bootlegger. It does not make any difference, I repeat, what we do; the lawbreaker is there.

The Quebec liquor commission said:

"Sale of hard spirits increased 32,275 gallons in one year. Drunkenness among women has increased 53 per cent."

These are official reports and not denied, except outside of Canada. The Saskatchewan liquor board said:

"The sale of hard liquor increased 33 per cent. in the last two years. Bootlegging increased in this Province 111 per cent. in the first year."

The Alberta liquor board said that 60,000 permits were issued the first year; two years later, 144,000 permits. The greatest problem is moonshine bootlegging. Four million gallons of liquor were sold in the second year without control.

During the first four months of Government control the Ontario board said that 220,440 permits were issued and people were buying liquor at the rate of $1,000,000 a week.

Mr. President, let us turn to a different source than the official record, and that is to the representatives of the church. I am not going to take members of some organization which has for its particular purposes the advocacy of prohibition or the liquor law, but call upon those who are interested from the standpoint of Christian ministers. Father Lavergne, speaking of government ownership in his paper said:

"With due respect to those at the head of our Government I must say that since they have become the advocates of beer and booze and have set the seal of the Government approval upon drinking, they have almost annihilated the work of the church through years of preaching temperance and sobriety."

An effort at true temperance!

Cardinal Begin said:

"You know what a vigorous battle we have fought for the virtue of temperance in our diocese, our beloved coadjutor and the group of ecclesiastical and lay apostles who have aided him in his efforts. After about 15 years' work they had almost conquered the enemy, and we were overjoyed in foreseeing the end of the destruction caused by the excesses of alcohol. But alas, there is now spreading everywhere the intolerable abuse which we denounce, and in particular the surreptitious fabrication of an alcohol more harmful than any other to the health of the body and the soul."

Let us turn to the newspapers. They are a source of information. The Vancouver *Sun* said:

"The people decided on a policy of restricting alcoholic consumption to the lowest possible degree. The government has made this piling up of revenue the chief purpose of the act.

HICKS' SP.A.S.—59

Moderation does not moderate. Government control does not control. The British Columbia liquor system has actually failed."

Sir Hugh McDonald, son of the famous John A. McDonald, said:

"There is just as much unlawful drinking under the government control act as there ever was under prohibition. The present law was in the very nature of things difficult of enforcement. It was far less difficult to secure convictions under prohibition than under government control."

The World, published at Vancouver, said:

"Rum runners, gunmen, thugs, and all the parasites which thrive on the miasma of the underworld of the Pacific coast are fostered by the policy now in force. Calculations show that bootleggers in this Province handle as much liquor as the government stores."

Hon. H. H. Stevens, a public official, said:

"Never in the history of this country was bootlegging comparable in magnitude and murderous results to what it is to-day."

Now, Mr. President, let us take a description of the liquor depot in Canada.

"The Montreal warehouse of the Quebec Liquor Commission contains nine acres of floor space and is full of vats, tuns, and hogsheads of alcoholic drinks from its topmost floor to the cold basement underground, where wines are kept. Two large rooms of this building are used for storing the seized wet goods and stills that are constantly being taken from Montreal bootleggers, smugglers, and proprietors of blind pigs."

There is not a problem involved in the situation in the United States that is not involved under the system of government control of liquor in Canada. They have the same bootlegger to contend with, the blind pig, the poisoning of liquor, and all the corrupting influences that we have in the United States.

Let me quote from another source. In the Montreal *Star* I find the following headlines:

"Innocent girls lured into dens."

And again:

"Dens of iniquity flourishing here must go."

These are places, so the report shows, where liquor is sold either legally or illegally.

Attorney General Craig recently said:

"Seventy-five per cent of the troubles of law enforcement are now due to the illicit sale of beer and most of that is due to the brewers that furnish the supplies and abuse the privileges granted to them under the government liquor control act."

Rev. Father Coyle, of St. Mary's Cathedral at Kingston, is quoted as saying:

"It is appalling the extent to which drinking is indulged in by young men, even boys of 'teen age. The drinking habit has reached an unbelievable stage."

There is no end to the story. They are having the same fight under government control that we are having under prohibition, and that is, to restrain those who never propose to be restrained by any law.

I said in the beginning that this is not a fight of ten days or ten years. Neither, in my judgment, are the evils which accompany our effort peculiar to the method which we have employed. It does not make any difference how we shall undertake to deal with it—we shall have the same evils to contend with.

The Senator from Missouri, with his usual candor, said that he was in favor of going back to State rights; that he was in favor of giving this question over to the control of the States. Of course, Mr. President, that means the saloon. I do not believe the Senator from Missouri believes in the saloon; I do not believe anybody any longer believes in the saloon.

Let me digress long enough to say that while we have for many years been disposed to jeer at the temperance reformers, at those who are advocating prohibition, I think they have accomplished one thing: They have gotten rid of the saloon. I do not think anyone wants to go back to the saloon. That is one monument to those who were spoken of for so long as cranks, as fanatics. They have convinced the American people that the saloon is intolerable; that it is a cancer upon the body politic; that it can not be tolerated; and no one, I presume, wants to go back to it. However, Mr. President, would the temperance reformers have ever closed the saloon by moral suasion? Good as they were, and noble as were their purposes, effective as they were in their appeal for needed reform, how long would it have taken the temperance reformer to have closed one saloon by moral suasion, by appeal to the moral law?

We had to invoke the law somewhere in order to incorporate and crystallize the effect of the work of these people for 75 years. The moral influence and the moral suasion and the preaching had their place, and let them never be abandoned; but there must be something more, and that is the law and the authority of the Government back of the law. That finally resulted in the destruction of the saloon, and, in my opinion, if we go back to the States we shall inevitably go back to the saloon in some of the States; when we go back to the saloon in some of the States the result will be that we will go back in all the States.

Mr. President, I live in a State which was bone dry according to law before the Eighteenth Amendment was adopted, but there was no way by which the people of Idaho could protect themselves from those States which were not dry. The people who are now urging their belief in State rights—I am not speaking now of individuals, but of the liquor interests—in no sense respected the right of Idaho to be dry. They shipped their wet goods into the State over the border, established their saloons within five feet of the border, and supplied the State in a way that the State was powerless to prevent. State rights was then not so sacred in the eyes of the liquor interests as it is to-day.

It is true that the able Senator from Missouri secured the adoption here of an amendment to a bill which provided that when liquor was shipped into a State it became subject to the control of the laws of the State. By a majority of the Supreme Court that provision of the law was upheld, but the court also held that while one could not ship liquor into the State there was no power to prevent one from shipping it across the State, and we discovered that when the liquor started it never got across. It was impossible to enforce the law with all the States whose people were engaged in the liquor business undertaking to break it down.

Suppose we should let it go back to the States, and suppose the State of Missouri adopted the old system, how should we protect the border States? We should have to have spies; we should have to have policemen; we should have to have the militia to protect the four borders of the States if we expected the law not to be violated by those who intended to have liquor cross the State line. There is no more reason to believe that they will respect the borders of the State of Idaho than that they will respect the Constitution of the United States.

Mr. President, do what we will and try as we may, we have these evils to contend with. They are a part of any effort to undertake to control or deal with the liquor problem, and I had rather undertake to deal with it by the Government of the United States having to protect only the borders of the United States than having 48 States undertake to control four times 48 boundary lines.

The Senator from Missouri referred to the awful condition with reference to the use of narcotics. He is quite right; it is one of the most alarming situations with which we have to deal; but has not the man who wants a narcotic the right to have it? If we have no right to deny a man the right to have liquor, what right have we to deny him the right to take narcotics? One may be more dangerous than the other, but the question of individual liberty, of individual right, to my mind, is precisely the same. But we do deny it, and we deny it upon the theory that when an individual indulges in a practice which is harmful to the community or to those who are dependent upon him, it becomes a subject for the consideration of the public, and the public has the right to determine what the rule shall be.

I noticed the other day that the Prince of Wales, almost on the point of becoming the ruler of his kingdom, though fortunately the exigency passed, concluded to go out and visit the poor of England. He was astounded at the condition which he found among his people; he was moved to pathos when he found 11 and 12 people, men, women, and children, boys and girls, huddled in one common room, sleeping together like so many swine, with all the finer things of life driven out. It shocked the Prince. I read in a newspaper that while he was on his visit there came home a father with 17 cents in his pocket. When asked where the other part of the 50 cents was which he had earned for the day, he stated that he had left it at the grog shop. Do you tell me, Mr. President, that government has no duty and no power to protect the hungry children who were waiting for the 50 cents to supply the food for which their pallid lips were pleading? In a republic whatever the community determines is essential to the public welfare binds you and binds me during that time. If we do not believe in that rule, we do not believe in a democracy.

The Senator from Missouri was of the opinion that the use of narcotics had increased since prohibition. I can not dispute that; I have not examined the figures. I only know that in England, where there is no control of the liquor traffic, the use of narcotics is sweeping forward the same as it is in this country. I only know that Canada has the same problem to deal with. I rather suspect that if the Senator will take into consideration population, the population of the United States of 120,-000,000 and the population of England and the population of Canada, he will find that the increase in the use of narcotics in those countries has kept pace with that in the United States. At any rate, it is going forward in those countries at such a rapid pace that it is alarming to all the people who take concern of the public welfare.

What shall we do about the liquor traffic? Possibly we can not prevent it entirely; possibly we can not ever prevent the use of alcoholic drinks altogether, but shall we continue the effort or shall we surrender in the fight? So far as I am concerned, Mr. President, so long as it is written in the Constitution of the United States that the sale of intoxicating liquors is injurious to the public welfare, and that declaration embodies the policy of the people, I propose in every way that is reasonable and fair to undertake to maintain that Constitution. Let us all combine in that effort. The Senator from Missouri will never see the day, I will never see the day, when the Eighteenth Amendment is out of the Constitution of the United States. In the meantime, using our influence, our moral leadership, and our public office as Senators and citizens, let us see to it that it is enforced in so far as it is possible for human ingenuity to enforce it. Let us maintain it and support it with the fervor and the devotion with which we would support and maintain the sacred principles upon which all free governments rest.

HARRY W. CHASE

THE SPIRIT OF WASHINGTON

ADDRESS DELIVERED AT GEORGIA PRESS INSTITUTE, UNIVERSITY OF GEORGIA, ATHENS, FEBRUARY 22, 1929

[Harry Woodburn Chase was born in Groveland, Massachusetts, on April 11, 1883. He was graduated from Dartmouth College in 1904, received his Doctorate in Philosophy from Clark University in 1910, and has had honorary degrees conferred upon him by four institutions. He was Director of the Clinic for Subnormal Children at Clark University from 1909 to 1910; and at the University of North Carolina has been successively Professor of the Philosophy of Education, Professor of Psychology, Acting Dean of the College of Liberal Arts, Chairman of the Faculty, and, since June, 1919, President of the University.]

It is two centuries, lacking three years, since George Washington was born. He lived through stirring times that brought stupendous changes. He must, in his old age, have looked back to his boyhood as to an era far distant and remote. And yet all the changes that he saw, vast as was their significance, left the ways of common men almost untouched. Springtime and harvest brought the same old round of duties. Transportation was still slow and difficult. Books were scarce and dear. Education was—well, read Coulter's charming story of the early days of this institution. Most of America was still untrodden wilderness. The very bases of an industrial civilization were still to be laid.

All this is commonplace, of course. We would all instantly agree that no political revolution, however significant, has ever changed the world one-tenth as much as has that great industrial revolution that began in England a century and a half ago, and that has, for better and for worse, built a new civilization. The men of Washington's day were, in many fundamental respects, far nearer to the Greek and Roman civilization than to our own. A Roman gentleman would have been very much at home in the Virginia of Washington's day. He might not altogether have agreed with it, but he would have understood it thoroughly. He would have been at home in its politics, its social life, its whole outlook. On the other hand, let us take this Roman gentleman and set before him the headlines in our morning paper. He reads of a man away down on the Southmost icebound rim of the world, thousands of miles from civilization, and yet we know day by day exactly what he has been doing and how his gallant adventure fares. The Roman reads of "wireless" and "radio"; he shakes his head and mutters of black magic and passes on. Then in the next column he reads of one city so rich that its wealth has increased $1,291,642,486 during the past twelve months. Increased! Why? And they try to explain to him what modern industry is, and what mass production means, and what the stock market is for, and how machines do things well that slaves used to do badly, and what modern transportation is, and how millions of people can live together to-day in a great city without being wiped out by the plague, and that space has been so annihilated that the other day a man flew across America in eighteen and one-half hours, and what movies are, and newspapers and magazines and automobiles. But that, I think, is the end of the lesson. For by that time our poor Roman has fled back beyond the Styx to the congenial company of his own type and kind of civilization.

Well! The sad truth is that Washington and Jefferson and Hamilton and the rest would fare almost as badly. The world they knew was so much simpler, so much more continuous with all that had gone before in human history, that it is almost different in kind as well as in degree from the world of to-day. The two centuries since Washington's birth have seen vast directive forces emerge in human history, which we understand badly and control even less well.

I have wanted to make this simple and obvious point because this fine impulse that we call hero worship is itself such a great force in human affairs. A great name comes to us out of the past, buttressed by such authority and prestige that we do not always stop to ask ourselves one very important question: Just what is it in the life of the hero that we ought to pattern after? Here, for example, is Washington. His figure towers among his contemporaries. He so impressed the men of his own generation that Jefferson, whose mind certainly worked very differently, found himself obliged to recognize the greatness of the man. "On the whole, his character was, in its mass, perfect, in nothing bad, in few points indifferent; and it may be truly said that never did nature and fortune combine more perfectly to make a man great, and to place him in the same constellation with whatever worthies have merited from man an everlasting remembrance. For his was the singular destiny and merit of leading the armies of his country successfully through an arduous war for the establishment of its independence; of conducting its councils through the birth of a government, new in its forms and principles, until it had settled down into a quiet and orderly train; and of scrupulously obeying the laws through the whole of his career, civil and military, of which the history of the world furnishes no other example."

What does such a figure as that mean to you and me? Perhaps it will be clearer if you will let me turn the question around and ask—what ought it not to mean? We may find its true significance more easily by such a process of elimination.

In the first place then, I do not think the real meaning of the lives of great men of the past lies for us in any literal acceptance of their ideas, their attitudes, or the formulae by which they acted. You recall that all through the middle ages the great authority on all questions of science was Aristotle. It made no difference what you thought you saw with your own eyes. They might deceive you. Look in the book and find what Aristotle said. A dead hand ruled the intellectual life of Europe, and it was because men so venerated that great hero of the intellectual life that they gave final authority to his pronouncements instead of setting out in his spirit to do what he did— to open their eyes and see for themselves. Consider Washington. He once warned America to beware of entangling alliances. We have all heard that statement advanced as an argument against our entry into the League of Nations—as though Washington's views about foreign affairs in his day and time could possibly be of the slightest importance in the new civilization of to-day that Graham Wallas has so aptly termed the Great Society. We might just as well suppose that we ought to pay attention to Washington's attitude toward prohibition. Perhaps attitude is too strong a word. I do not suppose that he ever considered its possibility for a moment, any more than any other Virginia gentleman of his own day. But, in a new age, with new problems, would anybody seriously argue against prohibition that Washington liked his dram? And yet that would be every bit as sensible as the formula which would seek to regulate our relations toward Europe by his farewell address. In just the same way Washington's theory of government was aristocratic, quite out of keeping with the whole drift toward democracy after his time; and again, his ideas about that have nothing in particular to do with the question whether that drift has been right or wrong.

What I am trying to say is that your hero is, after all, conditioned by the environment he lives in. He is a creature of his own age, and, for the most part, even the greatest of men do not get beyond the beliefs and the opinions of their fellows. His solutions of the problems that confront him are worked out in terms of the material that is available to him. We attach too much importance, it seems to me, to what, in the concrete, great men of the past actually believed about this or that particular thing. Even in the realm of science such beliefs have a disturbing habit of being upset by future generations. They may stand for hundreds of years, but, in the end, every Newton has his Einstein, and man's thought rises "on stepping stones of the dead self to higher things." But is Newton any lesser now because after centuries there arises another who supplements his thought? Not at all, I think. Take another illustration. Martin Luther was one of the great progressives of his time. Yet he failed altogether to grasp the new scientific movement that was going on about him. He referred contemptuously to Copernicus as an "upstart astrologer." To him, as to so many men of his time, Protestant and Catholic alike, the revolution in astronomy seemed to threaten the very foundations of religion and morals. But Martin Luther was a great man, and so were Washington, and Newton, and Jefferson, and the rest of the long historic roll. We can appreciate that fact to the full. But surely we can rise above a merely literal subservience to the particular conclusions they have reached in terms of their own knowledge in their own age, and surrounded by a particular sort of environment. The hero as a stimulus is one thing; the hero as a hindrance to independent mental and moral effort is another thing altogether; and, like Aristotle, he may so hold men's minds in thrall that he becomes a menace and a detriment to the advance of mankind. We must always be on the watch that we don't take our hero worship too literally.

A friend of mine told me the other day that there was no point whatever in preaching a doctrine like this to college students. He said that if there ever had been a generation in the world's history that had already dispensed with all respect and veneration for the past it was the generation that was growing up nowadays. He said that in his opinion they had no veneration for anybody or anything and what were we coming to anyhow when the great principles of Thomas Jefferson—You know all the rest, I am sure. Now I am convinced that were Thomas Jefferson alive and running for office, with the same platform that he used in his own campaigns, my friend wouldn't vote for him for dog catcher. I think he would probably call the police. But he thinks of himself as a great Jeffersonian. Well, he isn't. His whole outlook on life is totally different. Jefferson believed in man as a creature that ought to be largely let alone under conditions as free and as stimulating as you can possibly make them and that under such conditions he moves upward. My friend believes that man ought to be regulated and controlled, saved from himself at every turn, which is exactly what Jefferson did not believe. Now Jefferson may have been right or he may have been wrong. The point is simply that most of us, when we say that we are following the beliefs and opinions of the great men of the past, are really not doing so to anything like the extent we think. And this is inevitable. We are creatures of our own time. We are sensitive to the thought currents of our own age, as these men were to theirs. We cannot, even though we may try to do so, literally subject our minds to theirs.

I have been talking in negatives. I have been trying to say what it was that great men did not mean. Woodrow Wilson once summed up the whole matter, in his birthday address on Robert E. Lee. Here are his words: "We are not at liberty to walk with our eyes over our shoulders, recalling the things which were done in the past; we are bound in conscience to march with our eyes forward, with the accents of such men on our ears saying: 'We lived not as you must live. We lived for our generation; we tried to do its task. Turn your faces and your heads likewise to the tasks that you have to do.'"

These, to me, are words of keen insight. What is it to follow a great leader? It is not necessarily to do what he did; it is perhaps not even to believe what he believed. It is rather to go about our present task in the spirit and temper that distinguished him. We do not of necessity cherish our leaders best when we adhere blindly to each jot and tittle of whatever system of thought they may have laid down, or to the details of whatever cause of conduct they pursued. "The letter killeth, but the spirit maketh alive." It is the spirit of greatness with which we ought to be concerned.

There is this in common, I think, about the great of the earth whom men delight to honor. They lived with freshness and vigor in their own world. They had a keen sense of the particular problem that confronted them. They brought to bear on that problem keenness of insight and the best resources of the thought of their own day. They did not overlook the past. They had respect for its wisdom and its heritage. But, one and all, they went beyond the past; they saw their own present steadily and whole, and in that present they lived their lives. Look at the statesman's task that confronted Washington. Here was a new thing in earth's history; a nation whose charter begins with these tremendous words, "We, the people of the United States"—a nation "conceived in liberty, and dedicated to the proposition that all men are created equal." Into a nation it was his task to weld a group of feeble and divided states stretched along the edge of a vast and almost unknown wilderness; far from centers of culture and without great resources in learning, in finance or in prestige. It was a task for which the past simply held no precedent. It could have been accomplished only by a man who saw the problem, not in terms of archaic theories of government, not in terms of precedent and tradition, but in terms of its own real essence and nature as it then existed. They did their task. They would have been the first to say to us, "Now go do yours."

It is not only your rare genius who is creative. Every leader whose reputation endures, every great man who has led his followers a little further on the upward path, is creative. In some respect he goes beyond the old familiar ways of doing things. He has a keen sense of the world he is living in, and in this way or that way he moulds it and shapes it. It is *his* world, not the world of his predecessors, and it is different because he has lived in it.

You and I are living in an age and in a civilization that is new. Here in these Southern States a new order is coming into being. But it is not an order peculiar to the South. It is not even exclusively American. It is rather as broad as is the Western world. There is no isolation any more in this new world. Space and time and distance have shrunk almost to infinitesimals. The great structures of modern finance and commerce are bigger than any nation or any people. Science and art and literature are international. The very moving pictures that you see here this week may be flickering to-day on the screen in Paris and in Cape Town. We are in the grip, you and I, of these great planetary forces. We can not escape them if we would. We can, if we choose, stand passive until we are submerged by them.

Here is all this great rich heritage of the South, with all its splendid history and high romance, its ideals and its values. Here is the long line of Southern leaders that call to us out of the past—her Washingtons and Jeffersons and Lees and Gradys and Aycocks. What is our duty to them? I think that they would say to us: "The South we loved and fought for and labored to rebuild was *our* South. We did our duty to what she was. Try to do equally your duty to what she is and will be. Strive at your problem as we strove at ours. So, and only so, do you truly perpetuate our work."

There has never been a day, gentlemen, which sounded such a challenge to Southern youth. Here is a section caught up in this new thing that we call modern industrial civilization, thrown into competition with the best brains of the Western world. And, gentlemen, the way lies forward. It is not through dwelling on the glories of a stoical past, it is not through satisfaction with what has been done, or excuses for what is unaccomplished. The task of leadership in the South to-day is what the task of great leadership has always and everywhere been— it is in courageous, sustained, intelligent attack on the problems that exist here and now. It is in the creation of a social order that shall reflect for our own day the aspirations for justice and good will and happiness that, in terms of their own generation, Washington and his colleagues strove to make realities.

These may be, they will be, very different in detail from those of a century and a half ago—but the spirit of the task remains eternally the same. It is a spirit which bases on the old where it is possible, but which goes beyond it whenever that is necessary. It is a spirit which does not yield to the faint heart's shrinking from the difficulty of the task—did Washington yield at Valley Forge? The task is difficult. Southern brains, Southern capacity and energy and ability, must stand up with the world's best. We can not any more think of business or education or technical skill or art or science in terms of whether it is good enough for home consumption. We are part of a great national current, a great world current, and we sink or swim by the same laws that govern the balance of mankind. Our specific gravity is the same as that of the rest of the world.

It is in such a day, that sees the passing of what is isolated and local, that you are coming to maturity. It is a very different time from that of him whose birthday we are met to observe. But the spirit he worked in does not pass—that patient, fearless, and just attempt to make a better and a happier world. May that spirit be yours—so are you true followers of Washington.

GRACE H. BROSSEAU

DEFENSE OF HOME AND COUNTRY

ADDRESS OF THE PRESIDENT-GENERAL OF THE NATIONAL SOCIETY, DAUGHTERS OF THE AMERICAN REVOLUTION, AT THE OPENING SESSION OF THE THIRTY-EIGHTH CONTINENTAL CONGRESS, WASHINGTON, D. C., APRIL 15, 1929

[Mrs. Alfred J. Brosseau was born in Aledo, Illinois, on December 6, 1872. She attended public and private schools and took a business course in Davenport, Iowa. She has done much newspaper and magazine writing, especially in relation to the Daughters of the American Revolution. From 1916 to 1917, she was Secretary of the Michigan Daughters of the American Revolution, and she has held the following offices in the National Society: National Chairman of Transportation, 1921 to 1923; Treasurer-General, 1923 to 1926; President-General, 1926–1929. She is now Honorary President-General and Chairman of the Building Committee of Constitution Hall, which is being erected by the Society. She is a member of the following patriotic societies; Barons of Runnymede, Colonial Daughters of the Seventeenth Century, Daughters of the Colonial Wars, Daughters of Founders and Patriots, Mary Washington Memorial Association, Colonial Dames of America, Daughters of 1812, Patriotic Women of America, and Order of the Crown. She is an active worker in the American Red Cross and other philanthropic societies.]

In the Italian opera "Aïda," the stage settings present a scene of royal splendor such as befits the crowning of the conquering hero amid the plaudits of an idolatrous multitude. His dramatic entrance is heralded by a band of trumpeters who proudly sound the exultant note of the hour.

In coming before you this morning, I have a definite purpose and a happy task to perform. For you, Daughters of the American Revolution, I am but a trumpeter sounding the high, triumphant note ere you enter upon the scene to proclaim your great achievements. For you is reserved the privilege of demonstrating the need and worth of those objectives for which this Society stands accredited before the world. I can touch only the cloud tips but, from the potentialities that have been revealed to me during these few years of leadership, I do not

need to be endowed with the gift of prophecy to be able to forecast the developments of the future.

To-day there is an existing belief that woman has at last
come into her own. Whether this condition is due to her unrelenting effort of years to reach that strategic point or whether
the gradual easement of economic conditions is responsible, is
an interesting but irrelevant question in the face of the undeniable fact that woman has attained a definite place right in the
foreground of world affairs.

In a measure, women have always been opportunists. Molly
Stark is a glorious example, for she came promptly into her
own when she sprang unhesitatingly to the place of cannonier.
The pages of history are enriched by the valorous deeds and
the unselfish acts of the great women whom succeeding centuries have produced.

The statement has frequently been made of late—and no
doubt in all sincerity—that women's organizations have become
superfluous; that because of the greatly expanded individual
contacts, the many groups now cumber the field of action.

Undoubtedly some clever women leaders who are a decade
ahead of their time do find the confines of the strictly feminine
organization irksome, but to my mind the group has yet its
greatest function to perform. Scattered throughout this country, and particularly in the smaller centers, are countless millions of women who are finding themselves and becoming articulate through the medium of their favorite local society. They
constitute a tremendous power whose resources have scarcely
been tapped.

Upon organization leaders, therefore, does an immense responsibility devolve. Through them must be transmitted the
vital spark that galvanizes into action the latent energies of
this vast host of heart-hungry women who have all too long
been suppressed by their environment. From the vitalization
of this inertion, there will result untold benefits provided always there exists the proper co-ordination between the groups
and their leaders. The freshness and originality animating the
newly acquired viewpoint will convert it into a valuable asset
for the clearing house of experience. Wisdom when guided
by experience is the sustaining power of the world, for it seizes

the opportune—the golden moment—the vivid thought, and moulds all according to its own profound plan.

The Daughters of the American Revolution is a dynamic organization, solidified by highly patriotic motives and having as its objective the protection of home, the defense of country and the enlightenment of its people. To properly present, to thoroughly safeguard and to unitedly and wisely direct the great and varied activities is the inescapable duty of the leaders, National, State and Chapter. Leadership is not relative but absolute, and therein exist the same potency and the same responsibility whether the group represents the minority or the majority as to numbers.

"Of the whole sum of human life," said Gladstone, "no small part is that which consists of a man's relations to his country and his feelings concerning it."

That truism applies with equal force to the organized body; therefore the obvious duty of both leaders and members in their relation to their society is first to know it thoroughly. To such I say: study it in the intent of its founders; its traditional methods and firmly established custom of initiating policies; and the equally rigid mandates imposed upon the National Officers to obey the will of the majority as expressed by the acts of Continental Congress.

As the Federal Government has found no more satisfactory system than majority rule in the conduct of the nation's business, it is hardly possible that any single organization could improve upon that super-eminent method.

The fallacy as well as the impossibility, under this quite inflexible procedure, of first submitting the policies of the Society to the chapters for consideration before presentation to Continental Congress, need not be dwelt upon now.

The fundamental or governing laws are augmented or amended only after submission to the individual chapters; but the policies created within the scope of the law are brought to Congress literally in the pockets of the delegated body. Therein lies the great triumphant note of democracy in the organization of the Daughters of the American Revolution. If a member in North Dakota or Texas or China has a brilliant idea which might be developed into a constructive policy worthy of adoption by this Society, hers is the privilege of presenting it for consideration. Should it strike a responsive chord, be feasible and in conformity with the Constitution and By-Laws, that remote idea stands a chance of becoming a national policy. Furthermore, the woman who conceives it ought to have the exclusive control of her plan until its submission to the governing body. She should not be compelled to hawk about her precious brain product to be commented upon, criticized and ultimately annihilated by endless and puerile discussion before it has seen the real light of day. Policies that may prove to be unworkable or even highly unsatisfactory after a trial are liable to creep in through this method. But better that than lack of initiative, particularly so as Continental Congress has power, through abrogation, at any time to retrieve its own errors.

General Grant once said, "The best way to get rid of a bad law is to enforce it," and a few months spent in mistaken or futile effort count for nothing when compared with a century of great achievement.

The whole argument reverts back to original principles— which are, basically, information and understanding all along the line.

At the risk of seeming trite and reiterative, I again say that most necessary is the study and careful analyzation of resolutions adopted at Continental Congress. No time should be lost in making the chapter members thoroughly cognizant of these important measures. Chapter regents and delegates are in honor bound to give faithful and detailed reports upon all such vital matters. They are of far more consequence—though I do not minimize these essentials, being a woman—than descriptions of social affairs and the gowns of prominent women. If such information is given and the members attend the chapter meetings, or in other ways take the trouble to inform themselves, there need be no occasion for round robin letters devoted to useless discussion and unwarranted criticism of perfectly obvious and well established National policies and official duties.

Furthermore, it is your business, not only as Daughters of the American Revolution but as loyal American citizens as well, to be prepared at all times intelligently to state and loyally to defend the position of your organization in its relation to national and international issues.

There is not—and let this fact sink deep into your consciousness—there is not a crisis of any kind or condition threatening the Society of the Daughters of the American Revolution.

Grave issues are confronting our country, now as always since its foundation. Unequivocally committed to an ardent defense of home and country and loyalty to the institutions of Government, naturally we are bound to be sympathetically and actively involved in such issues. Therefore I say to you, Daughters, that if adherence to principles and to policies in which defense of our nation is in any way concerned means a crisis, then and then only, you stand facing it shoulder to shoulder with the Government of your own United States.

For that privilege you should never be ashamed or apologetic, but absolutely and eternally proud and thankful. The Daughters of the American Revolution have ever been deaf to the shameful call of retreat. In any future battles for the right, I do not believe they will ever be found with bullet wounds in their backs.

No one will question the right of individuals or the public at large to criticize the activities of this Society or to disagree with its policies. By the same token, there need be no limit placed upon the nature and the amount of defense voiced for it by both members and friends. Not that I would advocate going out of your way to confute every Shimei who sits by the roadside and vents his curses upon the passersby, but I would urge definite refutation when truth and self-respect make imperative demands. Only too well do I know that such defense takes courage and the marshaling of invincible facts, but in the battle for ideals one must stand or fall upon one's shield of truth.

Furthermore, the important fact should always be borne in mind that this Society is amply self sustaining; that it carries its own financial burdens in the furtherance of its work and that it asks no help from the public in general. Therefore it would seem that, as an independent institution, it might be pardoned if it did reserve the right to initiate its own policies and to enact them in such manner as is deemed fitting and proper.

Mine is not the right to enjoin upon you any line of action for the future, but it is within my province to commend you for the effectiveness with which you have carried on the work that your able and willing hands have found to do, and to urge you to keep the faith in the years to come. Whenever home and country are in jeopardy, instantly should you spring, as did brave Molly Stark, to the front line of defense.

Our work in Americanism has been expanded to meet the needs of an ever deepening and perplexing problem. The aliens who are admitted under our quota laws to this country, automatically become objects of concern and protection.

Thomas Jefferson once said: "We must Americanize the immigrant or the immigrant will foreignize us."

The aid that we, as an organization, can render our Government in Americanizing the immigrant is valuable and far reaching. From coast to coast we touch—through our chapters—ports of entry, industrial centers and farming communities.

The generous and free distribution of Manuals for Immigrants, of practical work for idle hands, the organization of day and evening schools and clubs, personal attendance at courts of naturalization—in fact, all avenues of aid and enlightenment should be continually broadened with the passing of time.

We have on our list of educational institutions four Americanization trade and art schools. They are entitled to our financial support so long as they continue to teach sound American doctrines. What these schools can do in the way of helping satisfactorily to establish the alien home seekers in the United States is of immeasurable value.

In return for benefits received, this country is quite privileged to demand that the immigrants whom it has welcomed should become a part of its citizenry with fealty to no other Government and loyalty to no other flag save the Stars and Stripes.

Men and women with revolutionary and ultra liberal social theories have no place in America. When they are proven guilty of an attempt to disseminate disruptive ideas and to propagandize the unwary, they should be summarily dealt with and promptly deported.

Economy in Government is most admirable and, as an exemplification of national good housekeeping, is most salutary for oncoming young America. But even with the best of intentions, curtailment can be carried so far that it reaches a vital spot and paralyzes action. Patriotic Americans should thoroughly inform themselves to what extent appropriations for this sort of protection have been reduced, and why. The effort of rounding up envoys of disruption and anarchy and the criminal element of Europe, are futile unless there are sufficient funds available with which to enforce a speedy exit of these unwelcome guests.

Furthermore, it would seem to be the privilege of the United States to determine the immigration quota of each foreign nation, and to do it with an intelligent and fine discrimination. Only by such procedure may we be assured that one hundred years from now our population will have the proper elements of homogeneity which are being sought in the restrictions of to-day.

Devotion to the present is the greatest possible guarantee that the future will be worthy of the past; and upon that principle do we proclaim our right at all times to defend our avowed policies.

The Thirty-Seventh Continental Congress endorsed the National Origins Provision and urged that it be made a part of the 1924 Immigration Law. Therefore, when that provision was placed in jeopardy during the last session of Congress by the introduction of a resolution calling for the postponement of its enactment, the Daughters in every state in the Union rallied to its defense.

The same active interest was displayed in the much discussed Cruiser Bill, which finally reached port after being buffeted about by the winds of opposition until its fate was regarded as dubious by even its most optimistic friends.

These two measures cannot be considered as other than strong arms of National Defense. It is indeed unfortunate that their espousal by individuals and organizations immediately places all such adherents under the classification of "militarists."

At that, the title is not so opprobrious since the dictionary defines militarism as "a spirit and temper that exalt the military virtues and ideals." Is it altogether discreditable to exalt the virtues and sustain the ideals of those who voluntarily risked life and limb in the defense of this country?

The most honorable method of discharging our debt to those brave spirits is to insure the protection of the land which they deemed worthy of the supreme sacrifice.

In answer to the accusation that defensivists are controlled by the so-called "interests" of the United States, it might be well to quote Abraham Lincoln who, when urged to correct a false report, said:

"If I were to try to read, much less to answer, all the attacks made upon me, this shop might as well be closed for any other business. * * * If the end brings me out all right, what is said against me won't amount to anything. If the end brings me out wrong, ten angels swearing I was right would make no difference."

However, if, individually or collectively, there were such a thing as "interest" control, it would much better come through the expenditure of honest American dollars than from funds emanating from dubious foreign sources.

Conforming to the precedent, long established, of supporting all efforts of our Government directed toward the greater good of the greatest number, the Daughters of the American Revolution were among the first of the organizations heartily and sincerely to endorse Secretary Kellogg's treaty making efforts for the renunciation of war as an instrument of national policy. We hoped then, as we hope now, for its ultimate and worldwide effectiveness, and rejoice that our country has twice within recent years led the way toward the goal of universal peace.

We would promptly challenge any accusation of inconsistency in this support of pacific measures. War, bloodshed, havoc and the useless sacrifice of young life constitute conditions revolting to the soul of woman. Better than anyone else does she know the price.

At the same time, this Society rigidly adheres to a position of caution and concern for all that this country holds dear; and while ardently yearning for peace, it is the belief that so long as other nations retain their sovereign rights of defense, America is justified in maintaining what George Washington quaintly described as a "respectable defensive posture."

Further, the support of the defensive measures just alluded to does not signify that the Daughters of the American Revolution is becoming seriously immersed in politics. It is a far cry from the support of legislative measures, having a direct bearing upon civic and national life, to alignment with partisan politics. For a patriotic organization, such a procedure would be unwise, unethical and in violation of the principles of neutrality of position as regards religious and political faiths.

There is much idle speculation about the fundamental purposes of the founders of this Society. The statement is frequently made that the original intent has been lost sight of in the welter of present day activities. It would seem that these astute women sighted the future with exceptional clarity when they charged the Daughters in the second article of the constitution to "cherish, maintain and extend the institutions of American freedom, to foster true patriotism and love of country and to aid in securing for mankind all the blessings of liberty."

Such injunctions not only rigidly impose an obligation but they leave unhampered those who, in carrying on after them, are compelled to meet the emergencies of the times.

Since the constitution of the Society was adopted a little over thirty-eight years ago, the women of America have attained a new status. Therefore, as individuals and as members, true Daughters cannot shirk the responsibilities that the exigencies of the moment have thrust upon them. Every Daughter of the American Revolution who has sworn to uphold her Constitution is thereby bound to do her utmost to help maintain the institutions of this Government and to be an absolutely loyal citizen. If that be politics, then politics is her duty.

The erection of monuments—to which some kindly souls have suggested we confine our efforts—is an excellent piece of work, but nowadays we must place substantial milestones along the highway of progress or be left to languish in the shadow of memorial monuments.

"Sitting still for five hundred years is one way of becoming an aristocrat," remarked W. L. George, the English novelist.

Obviously that is a theory quite contrary to the accepted method of development in a powerful and active organization of the type of the Daughters of the American Revolution.

Concern yourselves, I beg of you, with the sinister influences which are so palpably menacing the inner life of your America and mine. More particularly should safeguards be thrown about the youth of to-day.

National Defense does not connote material and physical protection alone. It means concerted effort to keep alive the spiritual flame, without which the idealism of any country cannot long be sustained.

Other things beside charity begin at home, and one does not have to reach out very far to encounter an alarming number of existing evils. Naturally, our first thought is for the public schools. Assure yourselves that the instructors in your communities are of the right calibre and are teaching sound Americanism instead of instilling pernicious doctrines into the minds of their pupils.

A nationwide movement is on foot to enact laws compelling professors in colleges and state universities and teachers in public schools to take the oath of allegiance. In some states, bills of this nature have already been passed by their legislatures. The critics of this law maintain that it hampers personal liberty and the right of free expression. In what way is one restricted by promising to uphold the Constitution of the United States? The Chief Executive of our land, the Judges of the Supreme Court, the members of Congress—in short, all who assume high offices of power and control, are required to take the oath of allegiance. Then why not those in whose hands virtually rests the future of this country?

We have an excellent public school system, supported by taxpayers of all classes, from the men who labor in mine or factory to the acknowledged captains of industry. The universities and colleges are maintained by American citizens. Therefore, why should not the producers have something to say about the manner in which their money is to be spent.

Flagrant cases of un-American tendencies have been brought to light and exposed. Exotic theories are promulgated in the name of science. Disdain for law and order, and contempt for our accepted form of Government are subtly injected into the teachings of history. Such practices are defended by the advancement of the decrepit theory that both sides of the question should be presented to permit the forming of unbiased opinions. This may be the proper system for the seasoned adult who presumably can, if he will, revoke his errors when faced with the consequences of an unwise choice. With the young, the chances are too great, for there a dangerous inequality exists. One does not place before a delicate child a cup of strong black coffee and a glass of milk; or a big cigar and a stick of barley candy; or a narcotic and an orange, and in the name of progress and freedom insist that both must be tested in order that the child be given the right of choice. Instead, one carefully supplies only what will make for the development of the young body and assure its normal growth. Why then apply the very opposite theory when dealing with the delicate and impressionable fabric of the mind?

Are you sure that in the public schools of your community there is not a well organized and flourishing group known as "The Young Pioneers"? And if so, are you aware that its object is to defeat the purposes of religion, of the Boy and Girl Scout movement and of the Reserve Officers' Training Corps and Citizens' Military Training Camps? That it preaches communism and the ultimate destruction of this Government?

Not long ago, the Principal of one of the public schools in New York City appealed to us here in Washington for help in combating such an organization. He stated that, single handed and alone, he had for two years fought its specious doctrines and the invasion of the red flag into his school, but felt the time had arrived when he must have the aid and support of patriotic citizens. It is needless to say that he received what he wanted from Headquarters; and the Daughters in New York City and Westchester County have further assisted him by visiting the school and talking to the pupils upon patriotic subjects.

A very definite drive is being launched against the establishment of the Reserve Officers' Training Corps in the schools and colleges of this country, as well as the elimination of those already organized and successfully functioning. Sad to relate, some of the leaders of the opposition are American citizens.

The theory is advanced—and to many it carries an appeal—that this bit of military training will tend to develop a war instinct in the heart of youth. That seems about as fallacious as the idea that instruction in athletics will breed a generation of prize fighters; or that lessons in aesthetic dancing will convert dainty little girls into cabaret performers.

As against this imaginary result should be balanced the definite and inestimable benefits to adolescent youth accruing from discipline, punctuality, orderly ways and synchronous training of mind and body.

The opponents of military training in the schools have appeared in strong protesting numbers at the various public hearings on the subject. I am happy to say that in many instances, Daughters of the American Revolution have arrayed themselves in support of this training as an important branch of our Government's plan for National Defense.

Wherever our educational system is under dispute by opposing forces as, for instance, in the case of the Reserve Officers' Training Corps, it is the duty of all loyal Daughters to uphold our avowed stand upon such issues. You who venture forth in the role of defenders may be dubbed "reactionaries" and "pregmatists," and you may be obliged to openly differ with your best friends. But be conscious of your own inherent rights as to free expression and have the courage to stand by your convictions.

The active opposition of this organization to atheism, which is being indoctrinated into our institutions of learning, and very generally into the group life of the young, is now so well known that comment seems hardly necessary. However, we must do more than spread resolutions upon our records, if we are to be an effective force in arresting the downward trend so apparent in the social and religious life of this country.

> God breathed His life into the dull contented sod;
> The sod looked up and said, "There is no God,"

One wonders by what right certain societies or cults elevate themselves to the post of advocates of a Godless universe. To attempt to uproot tradition and to destroy existing social conditions is a serious matter. Only one utterly lacking in social responsibility and reckless of consequences would dare make the attempt. Here again we find the small minority vociferous and working over time while the great majority dozes in its comfortable arm chair.

Out of the halls of learning walks the youth of America, serene and undismayed, and with ample justification, for it possesses both physical fitness and high mental development. But, alas, too often the spiritual is dwarfed or is totally lacking. Cold, hard scientific facts have captured the imagination and have displaced the old faiths, relegating them to the limbo of things archaic and outworn.

In estimating the strength of his organization, the secretary of a certain well established atheistic society, known to be committed to the absolute destruction of all forms of religion, said boastfully not long ago:

"The beauty of it is that we have so many atheists in the college faculties in America. But of course they can't say much about it, or they would be thrown out, and then where would their living come from? But they encourage the students all they can. As the movement grows, the professors will become more and more open in their private beliefs."

And there you have it. The average graduate holds the deep conviction that from out of the crucibles of his college experience will emerge the solution of all vexatious problems. When he comes to real grips with life he finds, to his dismay, that he must have something more than brittle scientific theories or the sounding brass of atheism as a sustaining force in the encounter.

One would not assume the right to trespass upon individual opinion were it not that in this situation the individual is the index to the generation—that generation now being the one upon which our eyes are focussed.

"Such as are the leading men of the state, such is the state," quoth Cicero, and it is upon the future of the whole great state that we must concentrate our efforts.

Atheism, false idealism and disruptive theories allure youth into alien paths. Will you not put up your hands, women of America, and signal danger? Recognition of the acute peril facing our established order is one of the most important functions of your work for National Defense.

Daughters of the American Revolution, this is my last message to you as your President-General. The endeavor has been made to address you from a practical viewpoint, and if I have been too matter-of-fact, it is only because I feel that the realities are pressing closely upon us and challenging our too evident inertia.

For those who have a vivid consciousness of the real, it is, after all, but a step over the borderland into the ideal. In order that we may realize our ideals, we must first have within us the capacity to idealize our reals.

In closing, I quote to you from the pen of an unknown author a clear-cut call to duty:

"I am of the opinion that my life belongs to the whole community, and as long as I live it is my privilege to do for it whatever I can. * * * The harder I work, the more I live. I rejoice in life for its own sake. Life is no brief candle for me. It is a sort of splendid torch which I have got hold of for a moment; and I want to make it burn as brightly as possible before handing it on to future generations."

These lofty sentiments and their visible application do I commend to you as honorable, God-fearing women, as devoted Daughters of the American Revolution and as loyal American citizens.

HERBERT HOOVER

OBEDIENCE TO LAW AND ITS ENFORCEMENT

ADDRESS DELIVERED AT THE ANNUAL LUNCHEON OF THE ASSOCIATED PRESS, NEW YORK CITY, APRIL 22, 1929

[In his inaugural address, delivered in Washington on March 4, 1929, President Hoover said: "I propose to appoint a national commission for a searching investigation of the whole structure of our Federal system of jurisprudence, to include the method of enforcement of the Eighteenth Amendment and the causes of abuse under it. Its purpose will be to make such recommendations for reorganization of the administration of Federal laws and court procedure as may be found desirable." In the speech printed below he elaborated his proposal, and on May 20, 1929, he created a National Law Enforcement Commission of twelve, under the Chairmanship of former Attorney General George W. Wickersham.]

Members and Friends of the Associated Press:

I have accepted this occasion for a frank statement of what I consider the dominant issue before the American people. Its solution is more vital to the preservation of our institutions than any other question before us. That is the enforcement and obedience to the laws of the United States, both Federal and State.

I ask only that you weigh this for yourselves, and if my position is right, that you support it—not to support me but to support something infinitely more precious—the one force that holds our civilization together—law. And I wish to discuss it as law, not as to the merits or demerits of a particular law but all law, Federal and State, for ours is a government of laws made by the people themselves.

A surprising number of our people, otherwise of responsibility in the community, have drifted into the extraordinary notion that laws are made for those who choose to obey them. And in addition, our law-enforcement machinery is suffering from many infirmities arising out of its technicalities, its circumlocutions, its involved procedures, and too often, I regret, from inefficient and delinquent officials.

We are reaping the harvest of these defects. More than 9,000 human beings are lawlessly killed every year in the United States. Little more than half as many arrests follow. Less than one-sixth of these slayers are convicted, and but a scandalously small percentage are adequately punished. Twenty times as many people in proportion to population are lawlessly killed in the United States as in Great Britain. In many of our great cities murder can apparently be committed with impunity. At least fifty times as many robberies in proportion to population are committed in the United States as in Great Britain, and three times as many burglaries.

Even in such premeditated crimes as embezzlement and forgery our record stands no comparison with stable nations. No part of the country, rural or urban, is immune. Life and property are relatively more unsafe than in any other civilized country in the world. In spite of all this we have reason to pride ourselves on our institutions and the high moral instincts of the great majority of our people. No one will assert that such crimes would be committed if we had even a normal respect for law and if the laws of our country were properly enforced.

In order to dispel certain illusions in the public mind on this subject, let me say at once that while violations of law have been increased by inclusion of crimes under the Eighteenth Amendment and by the vast sums that are poured into the hands of the criminal classes by the patronage of illicit liquor by otherwise responsible citizens, yet this is but one segment of our problem. I have purposely cited the extent of murder, burglary, robbery, forgery, and embezzlement, for but a small percentage of these can be attributed to the Eighteenth Amendment. In fact, of the total number of convictions for felony last year, less than 8 per cent came from that source. It is therefore but a sector of the invasion of lawlessness.

What we are facing to-day is something far larger and more fundamental—the possibility that respect for law as law is fading from the sensibilities of our people. Whatever the value of any law may be, the enforcement of that law written in plain terms upon our statute books is not, in my mind, a debatable question. Law should be observed and must be enforced until it is repealed by the proper processes of our democracy. The duty to enforce the laws rests upon every public official and the duty to obey it rests upon every citizen.

No individual has the right to determine what law shall be obeyed and what law shall not be enforced. If a law is wrong, its rigid enforcement is the surest guaranty of its repeal. If it is right, its enforcement is the quickest method of compelling respect for it. I have seen statements published within a few days encouraging citizens to defy a law because that particular journal did not approve of the law itself. I leave comment on such an attitude to any citizen with a sense of responsibility to his country.

In my position, with my obligations, there can be no argument on these points. There is no citizen who would approve of the President of the United States assuming any other attitude. It may be said by some that the larger responsibility for the enforcement of laws against crime rests with State and local authorities and it does not concern the Federal Government. But it does concern the President of the United States, both as a citizen and as the one upon whom rests the primary responsibility of leadership for the establishment of standards of law enforcement in this country. Respect for law and obedience to law does not distinguish between Federal and State laws— it is a common conscience.

After all, the processes of criminal-law enforcement are simply methods of instilling respect and fear into the minds of those who have not the intelligence and moral instinct to obey the law as a matter of conscience. The real problem is to awaken this consciousness, this moral sense, and if necessary to segregate such degenerate minds where they can do no future harm.

We have two immediate problems before us in government. To investigate our existing agencies of enforcement and to reorganize our system of enforcement in such manner as to eliminate its weaknesses. It is the purpose of the Federal administration systematically to strengthen its law-enforcement agencies week by week, month by month, year by year, not by dramatic displays and violent attacks in order to make headlines, not by violating the law itself through misuse of the law in its enforcement, but by steady pressure, steady weeding out of all incapable and negligent officials no matter what their status; by encour-

agement, promotion, and recognition for those who do their duty; and by the most rigid scrutiny of the records and attitudes
of all persons suggested for appointment to official posts in our
entire law-enforcement machinery. That is administration for
which my colleagues and I are fully responsible so far as the
human material which can be assembled for the task will permit. Furthermore, I wish to determine and, as far as possible,
remove the scores of inherent defects in our present system
that defeat the most devoted officials.

Every student of our law-enforcement mechanism knows full
well that it is in need of vigorous reorganization; that its procedure unduly favors the criminal; that our judiciary needs to
be strengthened; that the method of assembling our juries needs
revision; that justice must be more swift and sure. In our desire to be merciful the pendulum has swung in favor of the
prisoner and far away from the protection of society. The
sympathetic mind of the American people in its overconcern
about those who are in difficulties has swung too far from the
family of the murdered to the family of the murderer.

With a view to enlisting public understanding, public support, accurate determination of the facts, and constructive conclusions, I have proposed to establish a national commission to
study and report upon the whole of our problems involved in
criminal-law enforcement. That proposal has met with gratifying support, and I am sure it will have the co-operation of the
bar associations and crime commissions in our various States
in the widespread effort now being made by them. I do not propose to be hasty in the selection of this commission. I want
time and advice, in order that I may select high-minded men,
impartial in their judgment, skilled in the science of the law
and our judicial system, clear in their conception of our institutions. Such a commission can perform the greatest of service to our generation.

There is another and vastly wider field than the nature of
laws and the methods of their enforcement. This is the basic
question of the understanding, the ideals, the relationship of the
individual citizen to the law itself. It is in this field that the
press plays a dominant part. It is almost final in its potency to
arouse the interest and consciousness of our people. It can de-

stroy their finer sensibilities or it can invigorate them. I am well aware that the great majority of our important journals day by day give support to these high ideals.

I wonder, sometimes, however, if perhaps a little more support to our laws could not be given in one direction. If, instead of the glamor of romance and heroism, which our American imaginative minds too frequently throw around those who break the law, we would invest with a little romance and heroism those thousands of our officers who are endeavoring to enforce the law it would itself decrease crime. Praise and respect for those who properly enforce the laws and daily condemnation of those who defy the laws would help. Perhaps a little better proportioned balance of news concerning those criminals who are convicted and punished would serve to instill the fear of the law.

I need not repeat that absolute freedom of the press to discuss public questions is a foundation stone of American liberty. I put the question, however, to every individual conscience, whether flippance is a useful or even legitimate device in such discussions. I do not believe it is. Its effect is as misleading and as distorting of public conscience as deliberate misrepresentation. Not clarification, but confusion of issues arises from it.

Our people for many years have been intensely absorbed in business, in the astonishing upbuilding of a great country, and we have attempted to specialize in our occupations, to strive to achieve in our own specialties and to respect competency of others in theirs. Unconsciously, we have carried this psychology into our state of mind toward government. We tend to regard the making of laws and their administration as a function of a group of specialists in government whom we hired for this purpose and whom we call public servants. After hiring them it is our purpose casually to review their actions, to accept those which we approve, and to reject the rest.

This attitude of mind is destructive of self-government, for self-government is predicated upon the fact that every responsible citizen will take his part in the creation of law, the obedience to law, and the selection of officials and methods for its enforcement.

Hicks' Sp.A.S.—61

Finally, I wish to again reiterate that the problem of law enforcement is not alone a function or business of government. If law can be upheld only by enforcement officers, then our scheme of government is at an end. Every citizen has a personal duty in it—the duty to order his own actions, to so weigh the effect of his example, that his conduct shall be a positive force in his community with respect to the law.

I have no criticism to make of the American press. I greatly admire its independence and its courage. I sometimes feel that it could give more emphasis to one phase or another of our national problems, but I realize the difficulties under which it operates. I am wondering whether the time has not come, however, to realize that we are confronted with a national necessity of the first degree, that we are not suffering from an ephemeral crime wave but from a subsidence of our foundations.

Possibly the time is at hand for the press to systematically demand and support the reorganization of our law-enforcement machinery—Federal, State, and local—so that crime may be reduced, and on the other hand to demand that our citizens shall awake to the fundamental consciousness of democracy which is that the laws are theirs and that every responsible member of a democracy has the primary duty to obey the law.

It is unnecessary for me to argue the fact that the very essence of freedom is obedience to law; that liberty itself has but one foundation, and that is in the law.

And in conclusion let me recall an oft-repeated word from Abraham Lincoln, whose invisible presence lives hourly at the very desk and in the very halls which it is my honor to occupy:

Let every man remember that to violate the law is to trample on the blood of his father, and to tear the character of his own and his children's liberty. Let reverence for the laws be breathed by every American mother to the lisping babe that prattles on her lap. Let it be taught in the schools, in seminaries, in colleges. Let it be preached from the pulpit, proclaimed in the legislative halls, and enforced in courts of justice. And, in short, let it become the political religion of the Nation, and let the old and the young, the rich and the poor, the grave and the gay of all sexes and tongues and colors and conditions sacrifice unceasingly upon its altar.

INDEX

The figures refer to pages

Law, enforcement, 389, 529, 833, 900, 910, 957.

Administrative law, 471.

The higher, 1, 28.

International, 6, 18, 23, 479, 531, 686.

Natural, 6, 18, 23.

Sumptuary, 474.

Teachers of, 463–465.

Unconstitutional, 798.

Lawyers, 460, 461.

League of Nations, 420, 541, 546, 548, 562, 592, 623, 626, 627, 629, 631, 696, 698, 700, 719, 720, 731, 867, 871, 937.

League to Enforce Peace, 565, 613.

Lecompton constitution, 51.

Lee, Richard Henry, 745.

Lee, Robert E., 153, 365, 432, 433, 707, 939.

Legal education, 463–465.

Legislatures, 388.

Leisy v. Hardin, 225, 259.

Les Miserables, 552.

Level of prices, 632.

Lewis, James Hamilton, 548.

Lewis, Sir George, 57.

Lewis, William Draper, 411.

Liancourt, Duke de, 742.

Liberia, 16.

Liberty, 304, 385, 410, 411, 422, 459, 475, 654, 760.

Liberty Memorial, Kansas City, 762.

Lieber, Francis, 319.

Limitation of armaments, 444, 545, 576, 592, 694, 774.

Lincoln, Abraham, 1, 48, 103, 188, 195, 214, 220, 299, 300, 304, 305, 307, 309, 319, 336, 359, 429, 434, 498, 522, 652, 698, 703, 711, 727, 782, 801, 925, 950, 962.

Livingston, Robert R., 559, 746.

Lloyd-George, David, 505, 543, 646.

Loan Association v. Topeka, 394.

Local government, 473, 474.

Locarno, 421.

Lodge, Henry Cabot, 216, 548, 565, 568, 592.

Longfellow, Henry W., 139.

Louisiana, 94, 95, 191, 299, 559, 742, 747.

Lowell, James R., 427, 758, 759.

HICKS, SP.A.S.—62

Porter, Stephen, 908.

Porto Rico, 189, 192, 216, 219.

Presidential message, 478.

Press, 960.

Prisoners of war, 322.

Privateers, 480.

Private property, 385.

Privilege, 397, 406, 412, 458, 748, 781.

Procedure, 467.

Proctor, Redfield, 254, 262.

Progress and Poverty, Henry George, 121.

Progressive party, 384, 396, 398.

Prohibition, 887, 888, 914.

Property, 31, 44.

Prostitution, 383.

Protection, 184.

Protectorates, 190.

Proviso of Freedom, 20.

Public Opinion, 196, 203, 426, 582.

Public service by the bar, 458.

Public utilities, 813.

Pugh, George Ellis, 85.

Puritans, 337.

Pythagoras, 731.

Quarles, Joseph Very, 255, 279, 280.

Quebec Liquor Commission, 930.

Quigg, Lemuel E., 445, 451.

Race question, 138, 361, 626.

Radicalism, 412.

Radio activity, 670, 676.

Rahrer case, 226, 253, 257.

Railways, 804.

Rainbow Division, 763.

Randolph, Edmund, 67, 72.

Real estate, 129.

Rebellion, 81, 82.

Recall of public officers, 398.

    Of judges, 384, 396, 399.

    Of judicial decisions, 383, 390, 391.

Reciprocity, 192.

Reconcentrado camps, 309, 328, 339.

WEST PUBLISHING CO., PRINTERS, ST. PAUL, MINN.